RESURRECTION AND RENEWAL

The Making of the Babi Movement in Iran, 1844–1850

Iran in the nineteenth century

RESURRECTION AND RENEWAL

The Making of the Babi Movement in Iran, 1844–1850

ABBAS AMANAT

Cornell University Press

ITHACA AND LONDON

Publication of this book was assisted by a grant from the Division of Research Programs of the National Endowment for the Humanities, an independent federal agency.

The publication of this book has been partially supported by the Persian Heritage Foundation.

First published 1989 by Cornell University Press.

International Standard Book Number 0-8014-2098-9
Library of Congress Catalog Card Number 88-47716
Printed in the United States of America
Librarians: Library of Congress cataloging information appears on the last page of the book.

The paper in this book is acid-free and meets the guidelines for permanence and durability of the Committee on Production Guidelines for Book Longevity of the Council on Library Resources.

To Fereshteh

For the sake of our years of companionship,
recount a tale of those sweet ecstasies.
Rūmī, *Masnavī* I, 126

Contents

Tables

Preface

The challenge of writing about the Babi movement was to understand the making of a messianic mind, its dynamics, and its rationale set against the background of a changing world still dominated by religious norms and symbols. To construct a history of this nineteenth-century millenarian religion of Iran, the historian must follow a path with few signposts and many byways. In making sense of the events, personalities, and issues that shape the brief but vigorous course of early Babi history, he must consider not only aspects of Shiʿite doctrine, theology, mystical thought, and popular beliefs, but also political and economic changes, emerging social classes, as well as personal aspirations and motives. For a student of heterodoxies, diversity of approach is perhaps the only way to appreciate a movement in its totality.

In taking such an approach to the formative phase of the Babi movement, I hope to answer a deceivingly simple question: Do religious movements really matter? More specifically, was the shaping of Islamic history, particularly the Perso-Shiʿite history, influenced in any substantial way by what may be loosely defined as Shiʿite messianic dissent? The short answer to this general question is presumably positive, considering the pivotal role that sectarian Shiʿism has played all through Islamic history, and more assertively in the case of Iran since the fifteenth century. The detailed answer, however, requires a painstaking examination of two religious milieus, the mainstream and the sectarian, and of the historical circumstances that shaped them and were eventually affected by them. Only when this inquiry arrives at some convincing answers can we begin to seek the reasons for the continuity of heterodox currents and the peculiar characteristics associated with their emergence, development, and demise.

The Babi movement presents a unique case for it makes the relevance of religious doctrine to sociopolitical processes exceptionally lucid. It does so in part because it was the heir to a legacy of dissent perhaps older than Islam itself, and in part because it appeared at a crucial juncture in the evolution of Shiʿism as well as in the transformation of Persian society as a whole. Certainly, Babism was much more than a mere symptomatic upheaval, as it has sometimes been portrayed, and its defeat, at least in its immediate aims, calls for a thorough investigation. If it had the potential to become a major vehicle for change, and if it did demonstrate certain features that could ideally have transformed its environment (as similar movements of religious reform did in the Christian West), what then prevented it from overcoming the forces of opposition? Is it fair to suggest that Babism was an unfinished Reformation that perished in inception? If so, was it the weight of its own dramatic ethos that turned the proclaimed Babi Resurrection into an abortive enterprise? How far did the absence of a favorable climate, on the other hand, contribute to the suppression of its message of renewal?

Such questions set the stage, or at least served as stimuli, for some of the undertakings in this study. Of prime interest to me in Part One is the historical continuity that connects the Babi movement, in both its theoretical and its social genesis, to the antinomian Shiʿite currents of the distant and immediate past. In the Introduction I have attempted to explore some of the eschatological dilemmas of Shiʿism and demonstrate their relevance to several sociopolitical themes in Iran of the early nineteenth century. The following two chapters trace in greater depth different aspects of learned and popular religion in the same period and immediately prior to the rise of the Babi movement.

Part Two examines in some detail the circumstances that led to the formation of the movement as a distinct ideological and communal entity. It focuses on the personalities involved, above all the Bab and some of his important followers, as well as on the embryonic Babi doctrine and organization. The special priority given to the study of key individuals—their upbringings, outlooks, and expectations—may provide clues to their motives for rejecting the prevailing religious order and instead seeking a charismatic alternative in messianic religion.

Part Three investigates the dimensions of the Babi success and failure: the methods the Bab and his disciples employed to publicize the new call, their recruiting efforts among various social groups, and the nature of the criticism and opposition they encountered. In this effort, I concentrate on selective Babi figures and their missionary endeavors, their earliest attempts to reach the general public, and their systematic proselytizing among specific sectarian groups, most notably the Shaykhis. It is at this "grass roots" level that the seeds of the Babi activism bore some fruit. The conspicuous presence of converts from the lower ranks of the clerical hierarchy, of members of the mercantile and artisan classes, as well as of social outcasts of various sorts, demonstrates the movement's broad appeal to all forces of protest and discontent. Notwithstanding the limitations that the selective treatment of the Babi doctrine may entail, in this part some efforts have also been made to show the prevailing desire within the movement for doctrinal and communal independence. Culmination of this tendency among some radical Babis and the formulation of a new religious system by the Bab was concomitant with pressures from the religious and state authorities, pressures that eventually led to a fatal confrontation.

Babi studies have remained largely unexplored, and save for a few recent studies by contemporary scholars, most of the earlier works have not been truly historical in their orientation. Any critical work of historiography, including this one, is therefore likely to be controversial to some believers and nonbelievers alike, for the Babi religion has long attracted venomous accusation or uncritical praise. What has been recorded of the Babis presents them either as condemned heretics or as revered saints. But getting behind the screen of polemical diatribe and distorted hagiography involves more than deciphering a historical riddle. It often amounts to "demythologizing" personalities, events, and ideals without, I hope, undermining their historical relevance or losing touch with their aspirations and predicaments. If this work succeeds in transmitting some of that messianic spirit, I shall consider my effort worthwhile.

The original version of this study was submitted to the Faculty of Oriental Studies at the University of Oxford in 1981. Having benefited greatly from the intellectual guidance and scholarly advice of Albert Hourani and John Gurney, I here record my sincere gratitude for their encouragement, academic advice, and generous friendship. I also thank Marian Elligworth for her abundant help toward the production of the original version. I acknowledge the assistance I have received at various stages from Abolqasim Afnan, Ivo Banac, Amin Banani, Juan Cole, the late Hamid Enayat, Wilfred Madelung, Kayvan Mahjoor, Moojan Momen, and Foad Sanei. The Whitney Humanities Center of Yale University kindly provided me with a grant from the Frederick W. Hilles Publication Fund for the preparation of the final version of the manuscript.

To my father and my mother I am indebted for the moral support they have given me over the years.

A.A.

New Haven, Connecticut

Note on Transliteration

The system of transliteration adopted for Persian and Arabic is that used by the *International Journal of Middle East Studies,* with certain modifications. Words that occur frequently in the text are rendered without diacritical marks; therefore Bāb, Bābī, Shaykhī, Ṣufī, and ʿulamāʾ appear as Bab, Babi, Shaykhi, Sufi, and ʿulama. The Anglicized form Shiʿite has been chosen over Shīʿī. Well-known place names are written either in their common form (as in *The Oxford Atlas*) or without diacritical marks; therefore Tihrān, Iṣfahān, Shīrāz, and Tabrīz are written as Tehran, Isfahan, Shiraz, and Tabriz. Mashhad and Būshihr are used instead of Mashad and Bushir. Less familiar place names are fully transliterated. All names of people are transliterated—Persian names as pronounced in Persian, and Arabic names as in Arabic. Technical terms that exist in both Persian and Arabic are transliterated according to the original language; therefore *risāla* rather than *risālih*. The silent *h* in Persian is represented by *ih,* but in Arabic by *a*. The Arabic definite article *al-* is not assimilated to the noun; for example, *Nāsikh al-Tawārīkh* and not *Nāsikh at-Tawārīkh* or *Nāsikh ut-Tawārīkh*. One exception to this are the proper nouns ending with *allāh*, which are transliterated *ullāh*; for example, *Ḥabībullāh* and not *Ḥabīballāh*. Persian works with Arabic titles are transliterated in their Arabic forms: *Tadhkirat al-Wafāʾ* and not *Taẕkirat al-Vafā*. The letter *ʿayn* is represented by ʿ and *hamza,* regardless of its bearer, is ʾ.

Abbreviations

Ahmad Khan Bahadur, Agha Mirza Muhammad, trans. "Some New Notes on Babiism." *JRAS* n.v. [July 1927], 443–69. (Extracts translated into English from the unpublished history of Mīrzā Aḥmad ibn Abul-Ḥasan Sharīf Shīrāzī Dīvān-Bagī.)

Baghdādī Al-Baghdādī, Āqā Muḥammad Muṣṭafā ibn Shaykh Muḥammad Shibl. *Risāla*. Cairo, 1338/1919.

Bayān The Bab, Sayyid ʿAlī Muḥammad Shīrāzī. *Kitāb-i Bayān-i Fārsī*. Tehran, n.d.

Browne, JRAS Browne, Edward G. "The *Bābīs* of Persia: I. Sketch of Their History and Personal Experience amongst Them. II. Their Literature and Doctrines." *JRAS* 21 (1889), 458–526, 881–1009.

Browne Or. MSS E. G. Browne Oriental Manuscripts, Cambridge University Central Library.

al-Dharīʿa Ṭihrānī, Āghā Buzurg (Muḥammad Muḥsin). *al-Dharīʿa ilā Taṣānīf al-Shīʿa*. 25 vols. Najaf and Tehran, 1335–1398/1916–1978.

EI[1] *The Encyclopaedia of Islam*. 1st ed., 4 vols., London and Leiden, 1908–1936.

EI[2] *The Encyclopaedia of Islam*. 2d ed., Leiden, 1960.

EIr *Encyclopaedia Iranica*. Ed. E. Yarshater. London and Boston, 1982.

FN Fasāʾī, Ḥājjī Mīrzā Ḥasan. *Fārs Nāmih-yi Nāṣirī*. 2 vols. (in one). Tehran, 1312–1313/1894–1895.

Fihrist Ibrāhīmī Kirmānī, Abul-Qāsim ibn Zayn al-ʿĀbidīn [Sarkār Āqā]. *Fihrist-i Kutub-i Shaykh-i Ajall-i Auḥad Marḥūm-i Shaykh Aḥmad Aḥsāʾī va Sāʾir-i Mashāyikh-i ʿIẓām*. 2 vols. (in one). 3d ed. Kirman, n.d.

Fuʾādī Fuʾādī Bushrūʾī, Ḥasan. *Manāẓir-i Tārīkhī-yi Nihẓat-i Amr-i Bahāʾī dar Khurāsān*, being the first part of *Tārīkh-i Amrī-yi Khurāsān*. INBA Library.

INBA Iran National Bahāʾī Archive. Library and private photostat publications.

Kazem Beg Kazem-Beg, Mirza Alexandr. "Bab et les Babis, ou Le soulèvement politique et religieux en Perse, de 1845 à 1853." *Journal Asiatique* 7 (1866), 329–84, 457–522; 8 (1866), 196–252, 357–400, 473–507.

KD Āvārih, ʿAbd al-Ḥusayn Āyatī Taftī. *al-Kawākib al-Durrīya fī Maʾāthir al-Bahāʾīya*. 2 vols. Cairo, 1342/1923–1924.

MA Muʿallim Ḥabībābādī, Muḥammad ʿAlī. *Makārim al-Athār dar Aḥwāl-i Rijāl-i Daurih-yi Qājār.* 5 vols. Isfahan, 1377–1396/1958–1976.

MSBR Browne, Edward G. *Materials for the Study of the Bābī Religion.* Cambridge, 1918.

Muʿīn Muʿīn al-Saltana Tabrīzī, Ḥājjī Muḥammad ibn ʿAbd al-Bāqī. *Tārīkh-i Amr[-i Bahāʾī].* INBA Library MS A.

Nabil Nabīl Zarandī, Shaykh Muḥammad. *The Dawn-Breakers: Nabīl's Narrative of the Early Days of the Bahāʾī Revelation.* Trans. and ed. Shoghi Effendi. Wilmette, Ill., 1932.

NH Browne, Edward G., ed. and trans. *The Tārīkh-i-Jadīd or New History of Mīrzā ʿAlī Muḥammad the Bāb.* Cambridge, 1893.

NK Browne, Edward G., ed. *Nuqṭatu'l-Kāf [Nuqṭat al-Kāf] Compiled by Ḥājjī Mīrzā Jānī of Kāshān.* London and Leiden, 1910.

NT Sipihr, Mīrzā Muḥammad Taqī [Lisān al-Mulk]. *Nāsikh al-Tawārīkh: Qājārīya.* Ed. M. B. Bihbūdī. 4 vols. Tehran, 1385/1965.

QA The Bab, Sayyid ʿAlī Muḥammad Shīrāzī. *Qayyūm al-Asmāʾ* (commentary on *Sūrat Yūsuf*). Browne Or. MSS. no. F.11(9).

Qatīl al-Qatīl al-Karbalāʾī. *Risāla.* Published in Fāżil Māzandarānī *Ẓuhūr al-Ḥaqq,* III, appendix 2, 502–32.

Qazvīnī Qazvīnī, Mullā Jaʿfar. Historical account published in *Tārīkh-i Samandar va Mulḥaqqāt.* Ed. ʿA. ʿAlāʾī. Tehran, 131 Badīʿ/1975, 446–500.

QU Tunkābunī, Mīrzā Muḥammad ibn Sulaymān. *Qiṣaṣ al-ʿUlamāʾ.* Tehran, 1304/1886. 2d ed. Tehran, n.d.

RA Mudarris Tabrīzī Khiyābānī, Muḥammad ʿAlī. *Rayḥānat al-Adab.* Tehran and Tabriz, 1326-1333 Sh./1947–1954.

RJ Khvānsārī, Muḥammad Bāqir. *Rauḍāt al-Jannāt fī Aḥwāl al-ʿUlamāʾ wa al-Sādāt.* Tehran, 1307/1889.

RPAC Gobineau, Comte Joseph A. de. *Religions et philosophies dans l'Asie centrale.* Paris, 1865 (2d ed. 1900).

RS Hidāyat, Riżā Qulī Khān. *Rauḍat al-Ṣafāʾ-yi Nāṣirī.* 3d ed., viii–x. Tehran, 1338–1339 Sh./1959–1960.

Samandar Samandar Qazvīnī, Shaykh Kāẓim ibn Shaykh Muḥammad. *Tārīkh-i Samandar.* Published in *Tārīkh-i Samandar va Mulḥaqqāt.* Ed. ʿA. ʿAlāʾī. Tehran, 131 Badīʿ/1975.

SAMB Nicolas, A. L. M. *Seyyèd Ali Mohammad dit le Bâb.* Paris, 1905.

TAS Ṭihrānī, Āghā Buzurg [Muḥammad Muḥsin]. *Ṭabaqāt Aʿlām al-Shīʿa:* I (in 3 parts): *Nuqabāʾ al-Bashar fī al-Qarn al-Rābiʿ ʿAshar.* II (in 2 parts): *al-Kirām al-Barara fī al-Qarn al-Thālith baʿd al-ʿAshara.* Najaf, 1373–1388/1954–1968.

TH Shīrāzī, Muḥammad Maʿṣūm Nāʾib al-Ṣadr Maʿṣūm ʿAlī Shāh. *Ṭarāʾiq al-Ḥaqāʾiq.* 2d ed. Ed. M. J. Maḥjūb. 3 vols. Tehran, 1345 Sh./1966.

TN Browne, Edward G., ed. and trans. *A Traveller's Narrative Written to Illustrate the Episode of the Bab.* 2 vols. (text and translation). Cambridge, 1891.

ZH Fāżil Māzandarānī, Mīrzā Asadullāh. *Kitāb-i Ẓuhūr al-Ḥaqq.* Tehran, n.d. [1323 Sh./1944?] III.

RESURRECTION AND RENEWAL

The Making of the Babi Movement in Iran, 1844–1850

Introduction

Ever since the rise of the Penitents' movement of Mukhtār al-Thaqafī (66/685–686) and the subsequent disappearance, circa 700 A.D., of the declared Mahdi (the "rightly guided one"), Muḥammad al-Ḥanafīya, the heterodox milieu of the Islamic world has yearned for a savior whose return will restore true guidance to the community. For the Shiʿites, the Mahdi's return will correct the course of history, which they believe went tragically astray as early as 10/632, with the death of the Prophet when ʿAlī, the first Imam, was denied the leadership of the community.[1] At about the same time as the assumed disappearance of the first Islamic Mahdi, the earliest versions of a prophetic hadith were circulated. This prophecy reminded believers: "If there remains but one day for the world, God will prolong that day until a man from my progeny will rise and fill the earth with equity and justice, as it has been filled with oppression and tyranny."[2] This message

[1]Early Islamic Mahdism was a subject of some interest to both Muslim and Western scholars. Besides entries in the Islamic works of heresiography, hadith, and the Shiʿite books of Occultation, Ibn Khaldūn *The Muqaddimah* (trans. F. Rosenthal [New York, 1958] II, 156–200) provides a concise and skeptical treatment. Earliest among European scholars to pay attention to Islamic messianism, often as a side interest, were S. Hurgronje "Der Mahdi" in *Verspreide Geschriften* (Bonn, 1923) I, 147–81; J. Darmesteter *Le Mahdi depuis les origines de l'islam jusqu'à nos jours* (Paris, 1885); E. Blochet *Le Messianisme dans l'hétérodoxie musulman* (Paris, 1903); I. Friedländer "Die Messiasidee im Islam" in *Berliner Festschrift* (Frankfurt-am-Main, 1903) 116–30; D. S. Margoliouth "On Mahdi and Mahdism" in *Proceedings of the British Academy* (1915–1916) 213–33; and *EI*[1]:al-MAHDĪ (D. B. Macdonald). More recent works include E. Sarkisyanz *Russland und der Messianismus des Orients* (Tubingen, 1955); A. Sachedina *Islamic Messianism: The Idea of the Mahdi in Twelver Shiʿism* (Albany, 1981); J. Blichfeldt *Early Mahdism: Politics and Religion in the Formative Period of Islam* (Leiden, 1985); and *EI*[2]: al-MAHDĪ (W. Madelung).

[2]Apparently first recorded by Kūfan pro-Shīʿa traditionalists on the authority of Abu'l-Ṭufayl ʿĀmir (d. 100/718–719), a version of this famous hadith appears in all collections on the Mahdi (see *EI*[2]:al-MAHDĪ). On the identity of the Mahdi and the circumstances of his return see *The Muqaddimah* II, 156–64; Abu Muḥammad al-Farrā' al Baghāwī *Mishkāt al-Maṣābīḥ* trans. J. Robson (Lahore, 1975) II, 1137–42; and A. J. Wensinck *Handbook of Early Muhammadan Traditions* (Leiden, 1927) (under "Mahdi").

encouraged the Shiʿites of the ensuing centuries, especially from the time of Jaʿfar Ṣādiq, the Sixth Imam (d. 765), to identify the Mahdi with the Imams of the ʿAlīd lineage. The time of his return, however, came to be associated with the apocalyptic events of the Final Day. A lengthy hadith, related by Mufaḍḍal ibn ʿUmar, a disciple of Jaʿfar Ṣādiq, unequivocally sets the appearance of the Mahdi as a prelude to the events of the Day of Resurrection *(Yaum al-Qiyāma)*.[3]

The Dynamics of Shiʿite Eschatology

The crucial connection between the Advent *(Ẓuhūr)* of the Mahdi and the events of the Resurrection (*Qiyāma*) inspired the Muslim imagination with the same intensity that messianic prophecies had aroused in the followers of earlier religions. In the Perso-Mesopotamian melting pot of the formative Islamic age, the Mahdi of Muslim eschatology acquired many features of his Zoroastrian, Jewish, and Christian predecessors. In Zoroastrian-Mazdian eschatology the final rehabilitation of creation is to occur when the savior (*Saushyānt,* lit. "he who will bring good fortune") is born miraculously from the progeny of Zoroaster: "The dead shall rise again and the living shall be visited by immortality, and [all] existence shall be made most excellent in accordance with his will. . . . The material world will no more pass away . . . and the lie shall perish."[4] The prophecies of the Book of Daniel (second century B.C.) and the Book of Revelation also had their fair share in linking the Return *(Rajʿa)* of the Mahdi with the Judaic Day of the Lord *(Yum Idūnāy)* and the Christian Parousia.[5]

But if the messianic prophecies of this syncretic milieu provided the precedent and the raw material, the Qur'ān and the exegesis provided the context and the legitimacy. In a desperate search for an answer to the enigma of

[3]Later Shiʿite works on the Occultation of the Twelfth Imam heavily rely on this hadith to underline the preresurrectionary circumstances of the Imam's Advent. See, for instance, Muḥammad Bāqir Majlisī *Biḥār al-Anwār* 1st ed. (Tehran, 1301–1315/1883–97) XIII, chapter 23. Earlier Shiʿite works only briefly refer to Mufaḍḍal's account. Al-Ṭusī in his *Kitāb al-Ghayba* (Najaf, 1385/1965) on the signs of deliverance *(ʿalāmāt al-faraj)* only briefly alludes to the apocalyptic dimensions.

[4]*Yasht* 19 *(Zamyād Yasht)* cited in R. C. Zaehner "Zoroastrianism" *The Concise Encyclopedia of Living Faiths* (London, 1959) 214; cf. *The Zand-Avesta* trans. J. Darmesteter, *The Sacred Books of the East* XXIII (Oxford, 1884) xix, 306–7. For later elaboration of *frashkart* see "The Selection of Zātspram" (chap. 34) in R. C. Zaehner *Zurvan, a Zoroastrian Dilemma* (London, 1955) 348–54. Also see Zaehner *The Dawn and Twilight of Zoroastrianism* (London, 1961), 302–21.

[5]On mutual interaction between Islam and earlier monotheistic traditions on the themes of eschatology and messianic yearnings, see S. O. Goitein *Jews and Arabs* (New York, 1955) 46–61, 167–76; R. Bell *The Origins of Islam in Its Christian Environment* (London, 1926 [1968]) 103–7, 201–7; B. Lewis *The Jew of Islam* (Princeton, 1984) 68–106; and P. Crone and M. Cook *Hagarism: The Making of the Islamic World* (Cambridge, 1977). Also, *EI*²: ʿĪSĀ (G. C. Anawati) and the cited sources.

sacred leadership, and as an alternative to the yet uncanonized Caliphate, the early Islamic dissenters (perhaps as early as the time of the first Shiʿite Imam, ʿAlī ibn Abī Ṭālib) found in the Qur'ān, the "all-comprehensive Book," allusions to the Mahdi. The verse "Guide us *(ihdinā)* on the straight path"[6] was interpreted to mean "Give us a guide [*mahdī*] on the straight path."[7] Other verses gave a clearer direction to the eager seeker: "Whomsoever God guides, he is rightly guided *(al-muhtadā)*,"[8] an attribute that earlier might even have been conferred as an honorific on the Rightly Guided caliphs.[9]

As such, at least since Umayyad times the piety-minded Muslims had found enough reason to idealize the Mahdi as an apocalyptic deliverer with a divine mandate. Increasingly, the sectarian conflicts of the early Islamic centuries prompted the non-conformist to envisage the Advent of the Mahdi as the beginning of a utopian era, and every major political upheaval helped to embellish this image. In a scriptural world view dominated by the Qur'ān and the hadith, the moral dichotomy between good and evil made it inevitable that pious believers would hope for a redeemer to direct them to ultimate salvation.

The Mahdistic theme thus persisted throughout Islamic history, but the barrier between millennial thought (belief in the eventual Advent of the Mahdi), on the one hand, and actual attempts to fulfill messianic prophecies on the other remained firmly in place. Even in Shiʿism, where the yearning for the Advent of the Mahdi was linked with the chief doctrine of the Imamate and therefore, contrary to Sunni Islam, was deeply assimilated into Shiʿite dogma, any attempt to give substance to these yearnings, to deputize the Imam in person or to anticipate his imminent coming, met with great resistance from the representatives of the religious establishment. Although it can be convincingly argued that the whole of Shiʿism was bound with Mahdistic expectations, the task of materializing the messianic expectations almost exclusively fell within the domain of heterodoxy, if not heresy.[10]

[6]Qurʿān I, 5.

[7]L. Massignon *The Passion of al-Hallāj* trans. H. Mason (Princeton, 1982) I, 297–303; II, 96.

[8]Qurʿān XVII, 97. Also XXXIX, 23, and XVIII, 18, for other entries. For the Qurʿānic entries with messianic implications, see H. Hirschfeld *New Researches into the Composition and Exegesis of the Qurʿan* Asiatic Monographs III (London, 1902), 47–58.

[9]For nuances implied in both terms *Mahdī* and *Muhtadī*, see *EI*[1]: al-MAHDĪ (D. B. Macdonald).

[10]A general study of the Twelver Shiʿite messianic expectations appears in H. Corbin "Étude sur l'Imam caché et la rénovation de l'homme en théologie Shiʿite" *Eranos-Jahrbuch* XXVIII (Zurich, 1960). Also see Sachedina *Islamic Messianism;* W. M. Watt "The Muslim Yearning for a Saviour: Aspects of Early ʿAbbāsid Shiʿism" in *The Saviour God* ed. S. G. F. Brandon (Oxford, 1963); *EI*[2]: GHAYBA (D. B. Macdonald, M. G. S. Hodgson) and ḲĀ'IM ĀL MUḤAMMAD (W. Madelung); I. Friedländer "The Heterodoxies of the Shiʿites in the Presentation of Ibn Ḥazum" *Journal of the American Oriental Society* 28 (1907) 1–80 and 29 (1908) 1–183; M. G. S. Hodgson "How Did the Early Shīʿa Become Sectarian?" *Journal of the American Oriental Society* 75 (1955) 1–13; ʿA. Iqbāl *Khandān-i Naubakhtī* (Tehran, 1311

The contrast between theory and practice, however, did not deter many, Shiʿites in particular, from delving into the hazardous subject of messianic speculations. Millennial beliefs sometimes showed themselves in the moderate expectations and speculations of theologians and other orthodox thinkers as well as in the words of popular preachers and semilearned laymen. They also appeared in discreet forms in the discourses and divinations of those mystics whom the community esteemed for their intuitions, their piety, or their holy descent. More often, the belief in the continual presence of the Imam inspired claimants to assume on his behalf a role variously defined as deputyship *(niyāba)*, gateship *(bābīya)*, or guardianship *(wilāya)*.[11] Centered around a holy figure and often consisting of a nucleus of devoted followers, the currents of conviction based on these claims invariably conveyed a protomessianic message. The ideas adopted by these claimants were often popularized versions of the learned prophecies. Though these currents seldom passed beyond the boundaries of the accepted theology, it was in the interpretation of the prophecies and, still further, in the purpose for which these interpretations were made that they differed from those of the learned scholars.[12] In later stages of their development, these protomessianic currents often led to full-scale claims to Mahdihood, and the eschatological dilemmas within them were intensified in the process.[13]

To representatives of the established religion, these claimants posed no

Sh./1932); J. M. Hussain *The Occultations of the Twelfth Imam* (London, 1982); and M. Momen *Shiʿi Islam* (New Haven, 1985) 161–71.

[11]On the mystical and messianic connotations of the above terms, see *EI*[2]: KHILĀFA, iii (F. DeJong) and BĀB (B. Lewis). Also, Massignon *The Passion* I, 315–23; II, 18–21; H. Corbin *En Islam iranien* (Paris, 1971) I, 219–84; S. J. Sajjādī *Farhang-i Lughāt va Iṣṭilāḥāt va Taʿbīrāt-i ʿIrfānī* (Tehran, 1350 Sh./1971) 492–94; and A. Schimmel *Mystical Dimensions of Islam* (Chapel Hill, N.C. 1975) 199–213. For the implications of the vicegerency in orthodox Shiʿism, see S. A. Arjomand *The Shadow of God and the Hidden Imam* (Chicago, 1984) 141–44, 224–29.

[12]On the theoretical dimensions of religious leadership and organization, see M. Weber *The Sociology of Religion* trans. E. Fishchoff (London, 1965) chaps. 4 and 5 (46–94); and R. Bendix *Max Weber, an Intellectual Portrait* (Berkeley, 1977) 83–97. For two applications of the Weberian approach, see B. S. Turner *Weber and Islam* (London, 1974) and Arjomand *Shadow of God* 1–23. For general comparative studies of millenarian movements, see contributions by S. L. Thrupp, N. Cohn, G. Shepperson, M. Eliade, H. Kamisky and M. G. S. Hodgson in *Millennial Dreams in Action* ed. S. L. Thrupp (New York, 1970); and G. Lewy *Religion and Revolution* (New York, 1974) 237–74.

[13]Examples of this gradual unfolding of Mahdistic claims can be observed in the Sufi-messianic movements of eighteenth- and nineteenth-century North Africa. The Sanūsīya order of Muḥammad al-Sanūsī (d. 1859), itself an offshoot of the Idrīsīya reform movement, began with claims to the deputyship of the Mahdi and later augmented to full messianic claims during the leadership of Sayyid al-Mahdi, Muḥammad's son and successor. See N. Ziadeh *Sanūsīyah* (Leiden, 1958). A similar pattern occurs in the Mushaʿshaʿī movement of Khūzistān in the fifteenth century. While Sayyid Muḥammad Mushaʿshaʿ, the founder of the movement (d. circa 1461), barely exceeded a claim to deputyship, his son Maulā ʿAlī went beyond Mahdihood and claimed to be the reincarnation of the First Imam ʿAlī. Given the Nuṣayrī-Mandaean background of the movement, such claims, even of divinity, are not unusual. See A. Kasravī *Tārīkh-i Pānṣad-Sālih-yi Khūzistān* 2d ed. (Tehran, 1333 Sh./1954) 11–17.

great threat as long as they had no determined following or coherent doctrine. In contrast, the messianic revolts that appeared at the end of long periods of widespread speculation, in an atmosphere charged with anticipation, presented a real danger. Unlike the diffused forms of messianism, which were tolerated to an extent, these explicit realizations of the Mahdi were bound to be condemned as signs of deviation and blasphemy. They were denounced as heresies and their upholders were branded innovators, extremists, apostates, and atheists who incited sedition and strife.[14]

Diversity in messianic aspirations no doubt generated very different messianic responses. Not all Mahdi claimants sought to dislodge the established order, even if they were accused of doing so. Allowing for some degree of simplification, we can identify two types of claimants, each with a distinct mandate and objective: the Mahdi with the self-proclaimed mission of reestablishing the true Islamic dispensation (the *sharīʿa*), often on the basis of an idealized model of early Islam; and the eschatological Mahdi, whose aim of establishing the "pure religion" ultimately took him beyond the accepted norms of the Islamic sharīʿa. Although many Mahdi claimants demonstrated characteristics of both tendencies, the first type arose often within Sunni heterodoxy and the second within the Shiʿite environment.

In both tendencies there existed a desire to idealize the pristine Islam of prophetic and postprophetic times. But the Sunni Mahdi claimants tended to look back at the prophetic legacy as a model for the reassertion of the sharīʿa, and most notably as a call for "the enjoyment of the good and the prohibition of the evil." This vision of Mahdism corresponded to a world view in which Muḥammadan sharīʿa was regarded as complete and everlasting. The Mahdi, and the community of his believers, were thus perceived to be themselves divine instruments in the struggle against the internal and external forces of disbelief and injustice, an injunction that easily led to the notion of the holy war *(jihād)*. It is noteworthy that this interpretation of Mahdihood seldom concerned itself with the eschatological aspects of religion. The proclamation of the Mahdi did not announce the beginning of an apocalyptic era or guarantee ultimate salvation for converts. Instead, in a fashion similar to that of the Islamic orthodox renovators and reformers, this Mahdi advocated greater adherence to Islamic dogma while strongly disagreeing with the religious establishment over its implications.

Into this category fall many Mahdi movements of the later Middle Ages and early modern times—those of Ibn Tūmart of North Africa (d. 1130), Sayyid Muḥammad Jaunpūrī of India (d. 1504), Muḥammad ibn ʿAlī al-Sanūsī (d. 1859), and other North African claimants of the eighteenth and nineteenth centuries, and the Mahdi of the Sudan, Muḥammad ibn ʿAbdul-

[14]On fitna as heretical sedition see B. Lewis "The Significance of Heresy in Islam" and two other articles on revolution in his *Islam in History* (London, 1973) 217–63. Also *EI*²: FITNA (L. Gardet) and *EI*¹: ZINDĪK (L. Massignon) for early Islamic precedence.

lāh (d. 1885). Historically, these movements may be seen as popular variations on the theme of Ḥanbalite puritanism.[15]

Preoccupation with the "pure Islam" of the formative age is also evident in Shiʿite Mahdism and frequently plays a vital role in forming of the messianic scenario. But here the myth of the heroic past serves as a vehicle to transmit a whole spectrum of esoteric ideas that in strictest terms are not Islamic. The Shiʿite Mahdi is the *Qāʾim* (Riser), whose state of occultation will end suddenly when he makes his Advent prior to the day of Resurrection. His claim to Mahdihood tends to go beyond a mere assertion of the Islamic sharīʿa and its natural consequences: the *ḥisba* (assertion of Islamic law) and the jihād. His return to the prophetic age of Islam is a return to the age of religious creativity, a return to prophetic paradigm and the model of the Imams with the aim of constructing a new religious dispensation. Despite apparent resemblances to Sunni Mahdism, this eschatological Mahdi of Shiʿism should not be regarded, as an agent chosen only to restore a moribund sharīʿa. He is more likely to be the abrogator of the existing order and the initiator of a new one. Remarkably, the crucial link between his return and the advent of the Resurrection would thus provide the only possible channel through which such a formidable break can occur.

The Resurrection (Qiyāma), in Islam, maintains an organic connection with the two other fundamental articles of the faith: the Unity of God (*Tawḥīd*) and the Prophethood. Belief in the Day of Resurrection serves as a safeguard for devotion to God and his prophet. On the Day of Reckoning man will be rewarded for his loyalty to God and Islam, or punished for his lack of it. But the link between Tawḥīd and Qiyāma is more than a mere penal device. The other component of Islamic eschatology, the Return of the Dead (*Maʿād*) and the reunion of the body and the soul, ultimately requires a celestial encounter with God, which is a prerequisite for the Judgment. The Resurrection comes after a series of apocalyptic events that terminate historic time and put an end to the decaying terrestrial world, of which the Islamic sharīʿa is also a part. According to the prophetic tradition, what is lawful and unlawful in the Muḥammadan revelation is valid only until the Day of Judgment. Thus, Islamic sharīʿa ceases its purpose once the Qiyāma occurs. The purpose of religion, according to Islam, is to prepare the way in this world for man's ultimate salvation. After the Day of Judgment, the

[15]For Ibn Tūmart and the Almohad movement see *EI*²: IBN TŪMART (J. F. P. Hopkins) and cited sources. For Sayyid Muḥammad Jaunpūrī see S. M. Ikram *Muslim Civilization in India* (New York, 1964) 140–42; M. Mujeeb *The Indian Muslims* (London, 1966) 103–7. For Sanūsīya and other north African reformers see J. S. Trimingham *The Sufi Orders of Islam* (London, 1971) 105–32; Ziadeh *Sanūsīyah*; J. Abun-Nasr *The Tijaniyya* (London, 1965). On Mahdi of the Sudan see P. M. Holt *Mahdist State in the Sudan, 1881–1889* 2d ed. (Oxford, 1970) and *EI*²: al-MAHDIYYA (P. M. Holt). For a collection of primary readings on Mahdi movements in Islam, see J. A. Williams, ed. *Themes of Islamic Civilization* (Berkeley, 1971) 191–251. On *mujaddids*, see *EI*²: IṢLĀḤ (A. Merad and J. Voll) and J. Voll "Renewal and Reform in Islamic History: *Tajdid* and *Islah*" in J. Esposito, ed. *Voices of Resurgent Islam* (New York, 1983).

redeemed will live eternally in Paradise (a non-sharʿī world), and the sinner will be punished in Hell by means known only to God. Thus the sharīʿa, although it is the main criterion for salvation in the Day of Judgment, is not operative in Heaven or in Hell. The encounter with God, as the Traditions emphasize, will occur during the Reckoning and Judgment. After that (theoretically) man will remain in the proximity of God (if not in union with Him).[16]

In spite of some allusions in the Qur'ān and the prophetic Traditions, orthodox Islam as a whole shies away from the idea of a direct encounter with God. The Allāh of Islamic theology remains transcendental and therefore inaccessible. Such an inherent notion of God cannot be easily reconciled with the idea that man can witness God's countenance. In spite of some Traditions that render God an anthropomorphic image, He remains invisible and abstract and cannot directly encounter believers, even on the Plain of Gathering (*Maḥshar*). This orthodox concept places major theoretical obstacles in the way of conceptualizing the Qiyāma. The authority and functions of Allāh are not delegated to the Prophets, the angels, or other divinely appointed agents and without God's effective presence, the Maʿād is unachievable and Day of Judgment cannot take place.

The theological obstacles thus reduce the chances of the Qiyāma being perceived as an allegory by the seekers of Resurrection achievable in the material world. Accordingly, the obstacles to the occurrence of the Qiyāma also remove the contingency for a new prophetic revelation. The finality of Islam and its endurance are guaranteed until the Day of Judgment, and any attempt to initiate a new phase of prophecy must be considered illegitimate. As the Qur'ān itself points out, Islam is the final revelation and Muḥammad the "seal of the prophets." This claim, consistently upheld by Islamic orthodoxy, not only militates against the notion of prophetic continuity but also hinders any attempt at the renovation of doctrine. No intellectual current in the course of Islamic history—not even the Sufis' claim to intuitive inspirations or the philosophers' rational exposition of the fundamentals of the Islamic faith—has ever escaped this predicament. Claimants to Mahdihood who choose to break with the accepted orthodoxy, however, faced the additional charges of innovation and heresy. For Mahdis who aimed primarily at consolidating the sharīʿa, the question of renewal might not necessarily result in eschatological projections. But when a claimant went so far as to declare the abrogation of the accepted sharīʿa, he would be compelled

[16]For a Muslim theological exposition of the Qiyāma see Abū Ḥāmid al-Ghazālī *Kitāb al-Durra al-Fākhira fī Kashf ʿUlūm al-Ākhira* trans. J. I. Smith as *The Precious Pearl* (Missoula, Montana, 1979); ʿAbd al-Raḥīm al-Qāḍī *Daqāʾiq al-Akhbār fī dhikr al Janna wa al-Nār* trans. A. Abd al-Rahman as *The Islamic Book of the Dead* (Norwich, 1977). For a concise Shiʿite account see Muḥammad Bāqir Majlisī *Ḥaqq al-Yaqīn* (Tehran, n.d.). See also J. Macdonald's three articles on Islamic eschatology in *Islamic Studies* 4 (1965) 137–79, and 5 (1966) 129–97 and 331–83; J. I. Smith and Y. Y. Haddad *The Islamic Understanding of Death and Resurrection* (Albany, 1981) and *EI*[2]: ḲIYĀMA (L. Gardet).

to provide a symbolic interpretation for the occurrence, or the near occurrence, of the Qiyāma—without which the previous sharīʿa could not be nullified.

Given the theoretical obstacles in the way of any symbolic realization of Qiyāma, the eschatological Mahdi of Shiʿism faced a formidable challenge. The proximity of his emergence (Ẓuhūr) to the impending Qiyāma logically made his attempt to consolidate Islam obsolete, if not absurd. Most Shiʿite prophecies agree that after victory over the forces of evil, Mahdi's reign will be relatively short, ranging between seven and seventy years, before he dies of natural causes or is slain by the remnants of evil. Though he will establish a reign of justice and equity on earth, his endeavor will eventually be overwhelmed by the chaos of the preresurrectionary time. Indeed, most of his acts, and particularly his bloody revenge against the historical enemies of his house, will combine to undermine his throne. His efforts are destined to fail. His ultimate function, it seems, is to hasten the obliteration of the cosmos and thus facilitate the coming of the Qiyāma. Though he is primarily a precursor for the Resurrection to come, his reign is not devoid of apocalyptic scenes. The Return (Rajʿa) of the House of the Prophet (together with the prophets of the past and "the best of the people and the worst of the people"), which occurs immediately before the Qiyāma, is a prelude to the final Maʿād. Moreover, in the course of the Judgment the Mahdi acts as the intercessor for the believers and at times as the executor of the divine verdict. His destructive and vengeful task also has a constructive side. Unlike the Christ in the Second Coming, the Mahdi is not given the authority to judge. But in his capacity as redeemer, he has the potential to invoke powers that, strictly speaking, are beyond prophethood.

The extension of the Mahdi's action to the realm of Qiyāma has revolutionary consequences. The resurrection of man on the Plain of Gathering, where he undergoes Reckoning and Judgment, ultimately results in man's eternal abode in a timeless realm. Time stops at the doorstep of Paradise, and the End of Time is the termination of human history. But the conventional Islamic concept of the hereafter also asserts that human existence, after the reunion of Maʿād, continues beyond resurrection. The sense of evolutionary progression is not altogether absent in Islam since the Qurʾān and the hadith do not place man in a situation from which he cannot escape. Most sinners, once having endured their punishments, will be elevated to the lower levels of Heaven. As the Tradition assures the believers, there is even some limited promotion in the heavenly ranks as the human soul is gradually purified.

Yet for all the elaborations of Islamic theology, the nature of man's timeless existence beyond Qiyāma remains largely obscure. The conventional theology seldom concerns itself with the duration of the postresurrectionary period, and when it does, the perceived picture is one of a celestial dead end. The belief in the finality of the Muḥammadan revelation contributes to this break in historical continuity, for Islamic theology does not anticipate the start of a new time cycle. Instead, it simply encourages the believer to fear the everlasting fire of the inferno and to seek recompense in the timelessness of the heavenly garden. Its limited notion of celestial progression does not generate a sense of historical continuity in the hereafter that could be even mildly reminiscent of man's terrestrial existence.

The doctrines of Qiyāma and its corollary, the Mahdihood, received a distinctly allegorical treatment by the Bāṭinīs: those who sought an esoteric interpretation beyond the literal meaning of the Qur'ān and the prophetic Traditions. The belief in a cyclical flow of time, held by most Bāṭinīs from the early Islamic middle ages, reasserts an ancient Gnostic belief that probably has its origins in the Greek notion of the rotating heavens. For all its allegorical implications, this belief militates against the salvational concept of the termination of historical time, for when each cycle nears its end, time will be renewed by the symbolic occurrence of the Qiyāma. This process of renewal—explained as a revelatory dispensation initiated by prophets—implies an unfolding progression. But even in esoteric interpretations of the Bāṭinīs, this progression is not indefinite, and there are indications that a final cycle will ultimately bring an end to the process.[17]

Bāṭinī thought has consistently been preoccupied with the notion of cyclical time—from the early Kaysānīya of the eighth and ninth centuries to the Qarmaṭī-Ismā'īlīs of the tenth century to the articulated Ismāī'īlī-Bāṭinī writers, to the pro-Shi'ite Sufis of Ni'matullāhīya and Nūrbakhshīya, to the rustic Nuṣayrīya and Ahl-i Ḥaqq, and to the Ḥurūfī and Nuqṭavī movements of the fourteenth and fifteenth centuries. Throughout these centuries, Bāṭinī thought has tried to stretch the Islamic revelation by implicitly challenging the accepted doctrine of Islam's finality—and therefore its perfection. The entire body of the esoteric exegesis was employed to extract appropriate evidence from the Islamic scripture.

Actually, the Qur'ān does not wholly dismiss the concept of prophetic continuity. By insisting on the accomplishments of Islam, it nurtures the idea of successive prophetic phases. The People of the Book (believers in monotheistic religions, recognized by Islam) are recipients of divine guidance from a chain of "the messengers who possessed constancy."[18] But the chain ends with Muḥammad. The Qur'ān asserts: "Muḥammad is not the father of any of your men, but the messenger of God, and the Seal of the

[17]On the theory of cyclical time see *Rasā'il Ikhwān al-Ṣafā'* 12 vols. (Beirut, 1957) XI, no. 35: *fī al-adwār wa'l-akwār;* H. Corbin *Cyclical Time and Ismaili Gnosis* (London, 1983); W. Madelung "Aspects of Ismā'īlī Theology: The Prophetic Chain and the God beyond Being" in *Ismā'īlī Contributions to Islamic Culture* ed. S. H. Nasr (Tehran, 1977) 51–65; *EI*² (supplement): DAWR (H. Halm); *EI*²: DAHRIYYA (I. Goldziher [A. M. Goichon]); Y. Marquet "Imāmat, résurrection et hiérarchie selon les Ikhwān aṣ-ṣafā'" *Revue des Études Islamiques* 30 (1962) 49–142.

[18]Qur'ān XLVI, 34.

prophets; God has knowledge of everything."[19] Both Sunni and Shiʿite theology interpret that oft-quoted verse as the keystone for the doctrine of "special prophethood." Moreover, in Shiʿism, the doctrines of *naṣṣ* (designation of the Imam by the previous Imam) and "Muḥammadan light" promulgated by Jaʿfar Ṣādiq, ensure the legitimacy of the Imams by attributing to them a residual prophetic charisma. By virtue of their "gnosis" and their sacred lineage, they are the true interpreters of the scripture and the Traditions, and also, in effect, the perpetual receivers after Muḥammad of divine inspiration.[20]

As noted earlier, the doctrine of Occultation (*Ghayba:* belief in the disappearance of the Imam from the material world) gained some popularity among the proto-Shiʿites, as early as the late seventh century, but it took well over a century before it was fully incorporated into the Shiʿite-Imāmī belief system. The assumed Occultation of the Imams, most notably that of Muḥammad ibn Ḥasan al-ʿAskarī, the Twelfth Imam (who went into the Lesser Occultation in 260/873–74), was considered to be the inevitable outcome of the hostile circumstances of the time: the Abbasid persecution and the enmity of the caliphs toward the potential candidates for leadership. It was assumed that, at an appropriate moment in the future, the living Imam would come out of his Occultation and resume his lapsed mission to guide the believers. For the Shiʿite-Imāmīs, the "Lord of the Age" (*Ṣāḥib al-Zamān*) will rise to redress the past injustice that was inflicted to his house and to establish the just kingdom. The corollary of the Imam's Advent thus becomes an inseparable part of the Occultation both among the Ithnā ʿAsharī (Twelver) Shiʿites and among other Imāmīs, notably the Ismāʿīlīs.

The consecutive phases of Occultation and Advent, once they were infused into the gnostic themes of sacred knowledge and the prophetic light, were likely to promote a dynamic view of history, for the emergence of the Imam would begin a new age essentially different from the old. On the other hand, the fact that he was the same Imam now returning from the seclusion of occultation strongly implied the recurrence of an age modeled on the primordial paradigm of prophethood. And so, although the idea of Advent (Ẓuhūr) almost always remained within the realm of Islamic dispensation, it nevertheless preserved the rudiments of a spiral progression in time, which was essentially alien to orthodox Islam.

The Twelver Shiʿites of the formative Islamic centuries dealt with the issue of the Occultation in a distinctly ambivalent way. The Occultation of the Twelfth Imam might very well have been a temporary remedy to ensure the continuity in the line of Ḥasan al-ʿAskarī when the Abbasid pressure was particularly acute. It can be argued that his Occultation served the interests of the Shiʿite notables who were willing to make peace with the Abbasids,

[19]Ibid. XXXIII, 40.

[20]See Corbin *En Islam iranien* I, 39–85, 135–218; M. G. S. Hodgson *The Venture of Islam* (Chicago, 1974) I, 256–65, 372–81; Momen *Shiʿi Islam* 147–60.

for it ensured both the theoretical presence and the physical absence of the Imam—an ideal condition for the Shiʿite dignitaries, particularly when four successive representatives of the Hidden Imam (*al-Imām al-Ghāʾib*) were to be appointed from their own ranks. The prolonged absence of the Imam, it is argued, facilitated the formulation of Shiʿite theology and jurisprudence. In a process similar to that of the four Sunni denominations some generations earlier, Shiʿite scholarship was able to produce a systematic creed, a process that could not have been achieved when the source of inspiration was still physically present. Between the early tenth century and the mid-eleventh century, Shiʿite jurists and theologians from Abū Sahl Ismāʿīl Naubakhtī (d. 311/923–1034) to Shaykh Ṭusī (d. 460/1067–1068) consistently tried to disentangle the Shiʿite creed from the heterodoxies surrounding the image of the Imam. As they inclined toward the Muʿtazilite theology and Shāfiʿī jurisprudence, the prospect for the immediate Insurrection *(Khurūj)* of the Hidden Imam was safely relegated to a distant background.[21]

After the occurrence of the Greater Occultation circa 329/940 (when the Return of the Hidden Imam was indefinitely postponed), the Shiʿite scholars, in their endeavor to formulate a viable theory of occultation, employed a variety of current eschatological themes. But in contrast to the advocates of the impending Ẓuhūr, they tended to stress the apocalyptic preconditions essential to the release from suffering and the occurrence of the moment of deliverance. The Signs of the Hour came to occupy a large portion of the books of Occultation as more insurmountable requisites were placed in the way of Imam's return. Speculations on the time of the Advent of the Imam were repudiated, and various evidence was presented to prove the longevity of the Imam in his state of nonterrestrial existence.[22]

Of some importance in this process was the adaptation of the Christian-Gnostic prophecies concerning the Second Coming. Identification of the Islamic Mahdi with ʿĪsā (Jesus) presumably has its roots in the Qurʾān. The verse "It is knowledge of the Hour; doubt not concerning it"[23] was read by some commentators as an intentional reference to Jesus, and it led others to make a crucial link between the Mahdi and the Christ of the Final Hour. For Ḥusayn ibn Manṣūr al-Ḥallāj, the great Sufi martyr of the tenth century, for instance, the Advent of the Mahdi was tantamount to the return of Christ. His own theophanic claim advocated the renovation of the Imamate and did not exclude a claim to the position of deputyship of the Hidden Imam.[24] At another level, Sunni popular belief reiterated the early tradition of "no Mahdi but Jesus." As late as 484/1089, during the riots between the Sunnis

[21]For the circumstances leading to the occultation and the subsequent developments in early Imami Shiʿism see Iqbāl *Naubakhtī* 96–124, 212–38; Sachedina *Messianism* 78–149; Massignon *Ḥallāj* I, 307–37.

[22]See below, chaps. 2 and 4.

[23]Qurʾān XLIII, 61.

[24]Massignon *Ḥallāj* I, 323–25; II, 219–21.

and the Shiʿites of Baghdad, the Sunnis were shouting "victory to the Messiah" while the Shiʿites were supporting the Fāṭimid caliph.[25]

The credit for "Shiʿitization" of the Mahdi need not necessarily go to the early Shiʿite scholars; belief in the Mahdi's descent from the Prophet was in circulation long before the eleventh century. Yet Shiʿite scholarship, by employing prophecies similar to the Christian Second Coming, allowed the Shiʿite Mahdi to supersede Jesus, who was demoted to the position of the Mahdi's lieutenant. The confusion in later sources, and the contradictory traditions on the circumstances of the Ẓuhūr, only helped the Shiʿte popular mind to perceive this event as an overture to the Qiyāma. Learned Shiʿism, never totally divorced from the popular eschatology, tended to confirm this association.

After the tenth century, orthodox Shiʿism relinquished any desire to elaborate a cyclical view of the Imamate. Instead, the Ismāʿīlī Shiʿites and other less articulate "extremists" *(ghulāt)* became increasingly preoccupied with the cyclical model and developed sophisticated schemes. The presence of two complementary figures, the "speaker" and the "silent one," in every cycle, a standard feature of all such models, was designed to maintain the necessary equilibrium between realities of the "exterior" *(ẓāhir)* and ideals of the "interior" *(bāṭin)*. As in the Ismāʿīlī theory of prophethood, the binary of Muḥammad as the speaker and ʿAlī (the First Imam) as the silent one of the Islamic cycle corresponded to the exterior and the interior of Islam. Although the need for conformity with the exterior of the faith, the sharīʿa, was acknowledged, the underlying tendency was to substantiate the sharīʿa with the esoteric truth that emanated from the silent one. The same pattern was repeated to create similar cycles in the past and in the future. Thus the silent one of the final cycle, the seventh imam of the Ismāʿīlī line, would emerge out of concealment as a new speaker only when the age of the exterior had reached its Qiyāma. The new cycle of the inner truth would then prevail.[26]

In the long and turbulent history of Ismāʿīlīsm, chiliastic aspirations for renewal of the prophetic cycle more than once resulted in the declaration of the Resurrection. Perhaps the most explicit was the Qiyāma in Alamūt announced by the Ismāʿīlī leader of Alamūt Ḥasan ʿalā dhikrihī al-Salām in 559/1164 on behalf of the Hidden Imam (who was eventually identified as being Ḥasan himself). Yet even in the Alamūt, the age of inner truth and the abrogation of the exterior did not last long before the Islamic sharīʿa, this time Sunni, was reimposed.[27] Other Ismāʿīlīs, from Fāṭimids to Ṭayyibids

[25]Ibid. II, 99.

[26]For a general survey of the Ismāʿīlī-Bāṭinī doctrine see Corbin *Cyclical Time* 84–150; W. Ivanow *Ismaili Tradition Concerning the Rise of the Fatimids* (London, 1942); M. G. S. Hodgson *The Order of the Assassins* (The Hague, 1955); *EI*²: BĀṬINIYYA (M. G. S. Hodgson) and ISMĀʿĪLIYYA (W. Madelung).

[27]Hodgson, *Assassins* chaps. 7–8 and 10; J. J. Buckley "The Nizārī Ismāʿīlītes' Abolishment of the Sharīʿa during the 'Great Resurrection' of 1164 A.D./599 A.M." *Studia Islamica* 60 (1984) 137–65.

and even the later Nizārīs, however, tended to stretch the age of the exterior and repeatedly postpone the emergence of the Hidden Imam. Ṭayyibī doctrine emphasizes the succession of countless cycles of manifestation and concealment until the Great Resurrection (*Qiyāmat al-Qiyāmāt*) consummates the megacycle in the distant future.[28] Such a scheme theoretically barred the occurrence of the final Qiyāma, but in reality it did not prevent the frequent appearance in the later Middle Ages of men who claimed to be representatives and deputies of the Hidden Imam.

A whole range of crypto-Ismāʿīlī currents in the fourteenth and fifteenth centuries bears witness to the persistence of the theory of cycles. The presence of latent messianic aspirations in Shaykh Khalīfa (d. 1335) and Shaykh Ḥasan Jūrī (d. 1342), Shaykh Isḥāq Khutalānī (the founder of the Ightishāshīya, d. 1423), Sayyid Muḥammad Nūrbakhsh (d. 1465), and Shāh Nīʿmatullāh Walī (d. 1431) made the Sufi orders they represented a fertile ground for chiliastic speculation. Yet neither the Sufi Mahdis nor the claimants to the position of deputyship of the Imam went so far as to proclaim a new cycle of inner truth free from the exterior realities of the Islamic sharīʿa.[29]

With greater clarity and vehemence, the extremist movements of the fourteenth and fifteenth centuries revived the Bāṭinī legacy, often with the aim of combining religious and temporal authority. Fażlullāh Astarābādī, the founder of the Ḥurūfīya (d. 1394), Maḥmūd Pisīkhānī, the founder of the Nuqṭavīya (d. 1427), and Sayyid Muḥammad Mushaʿshaʿ, the founder of the Mushaʿshaʿīya (d. circa 1461), are the outstanding representatives of such movements. In spite of their popular Sufi guise, they were nascent religiopolitical trends essentially independent of Islam.[30] Perhaps the most remarkable echo of their desire to break away from the dominant religion is apparent in the Nuqṭavī urge to terminate the "Arab cycle" and restore a new "Persian cycle." Summarizing the beliefs of the Nuqṭavīs, Muḥsin Fānī, the author of the *Dabistān al-Madhāhib*, maintains: "When the Persian

[28]*EI*²: ISMĀʿĪLIYYA.

[29]On the Jurīya order and the Sarbidārī movement see I. P. Petrushevsky *Kishāvarzī va Munāsibāt-i Arżī dar Īrān-i ʿAhd-i Mughul* Persian trans. K. Kishāvarz, 2 vols. (Tehran, 1347 Sh./1968) II, 796–918; J. Aubin "Aux origines d'un mouvement populaire médieval: Le Cheykhisme de Bayhaq et de Nichâpour" *Studia Iranica* 5 (1976) 213–24. On Nūrbakhshīya see M. Molé "Les Kubrawiya entre Sunnisme et Shiisme aux huitième et neuvième siècles de l'Hégire" *Revue des Études Islamiques* 29 (1961) 61–142; Arjomand *Shadow of God* 74–76; *EI*¹: NŪRBAKHSHĪYA (D. S. Margoliouth). For Shāh Niʿmatullāh see E. G. Browne *The Literary History of Persia* 4 vols. (London and Cambridge, 1902–1924) III, 463–73; N. Pourjavady and P. L. Wilson *Kings of Love* (Tehran, 1978) 13–69; J. Aubin *Matériaux pour la biographie de Shāh Niʿmatullāh Walī Kermanī* (Tehran, 1956); J. Nurbakhsh *Zindigī va Āsār-i Shāh Niʿmatullāh Walī Kirmānī* (Tehran, 1337 Sh./1958). See also below chap. 2.

[30]On Ḥurūfīya see H. Ritter "Die Anfänge der Hurūfīsekte" *Oriens* 7 (1954) 1–54; C. Huart *Textes persans relatifs à la religion des Houroufis* (Leiden, 1909); E. G. Browne "Some Notes on the Literature and Doctrines of the Ḥurūfī Sect" *JRAS* 30 (1898) 61–89 and "Further Notes" *JRAS* 39 (1907) 533–81; *EI*²: ḤURŪFIYYA (A. Bausani). On Nuqṭavīya see Ṣ. Kīyā *Nuqṭavīyān yā Pisīkhānīyān, Īrān Kudih* (Tehran, 1320 Sh./1941) XIII and cited sources. On Mushaʿshaʿīya see *EI*¹ (supplement): MUSHAʿSHAʿ (V. Minorsky) and Kasravī *Khūzistān* 5–31.

cycle prevails, people will discover the truth and worship man and hold the human essence to be the truth. . . . Maḥmūd [Pisīkhānī] calls himself the unique person and the promised Mahdi whose Ẓuhūr was prophesied by the Prophet; he says that the religion of Muḥammad is abrogated; now the religion is that of Maḥmūd."[31]

The culmination of the fifteenth-century sectarian currents came with the Safavid revolution of 902/1501. Both in spirit and organization, the Sufi ghulāt movement under the leadership of the Ṣafavī order, the initial mystical order around which the Safavid movement was organized, benefited from the long-accumulated energies of the Persian heterodox milieu. It was the successful fusion of chiliastic aspirations of the time with the rustic extremism of the Turkoman nomads of Anatolia and northwestern Iran, the chief supporters of the movement, that gave the Safavids the potency most other movements lacked. Whatever claim was made by or on behalf of Ismāʿīl, the founder of the dynasty—whether it was a claim to divinity, Mahdihood, or the deputyship of the promised Imam—it marked the zenith of an epoch of intense though diffused messianic yearnings. The rise of the Safavids, it can be argued, had the potential to transform the heterodox aspirations of the fifteenth century into a religious revolution far broader in scope than the mere introduction of orthodox Twelver Shiʿism. The fact that, almost from the outset, the Safavids resorted to Ithnā ʿAsharī religion as an alternative to their own Sufi extremism demonstrates the volatile nature of these movements of protest and their inability to establish a solid ground for state functions. To produce a viable politicoreligious base that could resist not only pressure from the hostile Sunni neighbors, the Ottoman Empire and later the Uzbeks in the northeast, but also competition from rival messianic movements at home, the Safavids were bound to employ orthodox Twelver Shiʿism as an ideological buttress for their newly emerging state. This was an ironic turning point in the history of Shiʿite dissent, for the realization of a new Safavid state could be legitimized only when the notion of cyclical Qiyāma was abandoned in favor of stretching the Safavid duration of rule into the distant future, to that of the Qā'im. As the sword of Ismāʿīl and his successors imposed the Twelver creed over their empire, the heterodox trends gradually sank under the weight of institutionalized religion. By the end of the seventeenth century, Niʿmatullāhīs, Nuqṭavīs, Ḥurūfīs, and the Sufi ghulāt were systematically persecuted and removed from the political scene.[32]

The tension between the orthodox and heterodox religions persisted, however, though with less intensity than in pre-Safavid times. In spite of the

[31](Lucknow, 1228/1880–1881) 302 (trans. D. Shea and A. Troyer as *Oriental Literature or the Dabistan* [New York, 1937] 341–42).

[32]See J. Aubin "La politique religieuse des Safavides" in *Le shiʿism imamite. Colloque de Strasbourg 1968* (Paris, 1970) 235–44; N. Falsafī *Zindigānī-yi Shāh ʿAbbās Awwal* 5 vols. (Tehran, 1334–52 Sh./1955–1973) III, 31–53.

ʿulama's efforts to enshrine the residual authority of the Imam in the two complementary institutions of the monarchy and the religious establishment, the yearning for "deliverance" remained an integral part of Safavid and post-Safavid Shiʿism at all levels. In a peculiar way, learned Shiʿism even contributed to the survival of these redemptive aspirations. The Shiʿite establishment of late Safavid times was still dependent on the state for moral and financial support. Yet the decline in the influence of the office of *ṣadr*, the state official in charge of religious administration, made it possible for the Shiʿite scholars, the ʿulama, to try to fill the vacuum by extending their own independent control over the judiciary and the pious endowments. Claim to the collective deputyship of the Twelfth Imam, as it was implicitly made by the *mujtahids* (jurisconsults), trivialized the sacred authority of the Safavid monarch. As part of their endeavor to popularize their own brand of Shiʿite religion, the scholarship of Muḥammad Bāqir Majlisī (d. 1699) and his school helped to simplify, disseminate, and substantially enlarge the eschatological literature, thus asserting the authority of the mujtahids during the prolonged concealment of the Imam. The unintended result of this effort, often accomplished by the systematic compilation of the hadith materials in Persian with copious commentaries, was that the lay Shiʿite, more than ever before, came into direct contact with the sources of eschatological tradition.[33]

At a more sophisticated level, the works of the theologians and theosophists of the seventeenth century—from Bahāʾ al-Dīn ʿĀmilī (d. 1629) and Mīr-i Dāmād (d. 1631) to Ṣadr al-Dīn Shīrāzī (d. 1641), ʿAbd al-Razzāq Lāhījī (d. 1642), and Mullā Muḥsin Fayż Kāshānī (d. 1680)—encouraged philosophical inquiries with obvious eschatological concerns. The immortality of the soul, the nature of the life hereafter, and, most troubling of all, the doctrine of the corporal resurrection came to occupy a substantial part of the theosophists' discourse.[34] Though the audience for the theosophists remained relatively small, their esoteric approach was increasingly attacked by the mujtahids, who considered it dangerously close to free thinking.

The world of the theosophists, unlike the historically static world of the sharīʿa-minded ʿulama, entailed a dynamic view of history that was decidedly at odds with the conventional notion of ultimate salvation. The philosophical framework of Ṣadr al-Dīn Shīrāzī, better known as Mullā Ṣadrā, and his disciples essentially remained that of the Peripatetics of classical Islamic times. Yet their preoccupation with the problems of the beings' everlasting motion in time was decidedly a breakthrough from the old

[33]On the popularization of Shīʿism in the late Safavid period see Arjomand *Shadow of God* 160–78; Momen *Shiʿi Islam* 114–15. Among Majlisī's numerous Persian works, *Zād al-Maʿād* and *Ḥaqq al-Yaqīn* are particularly representative of the popular Shiʿite eschatology.

[34]For the school of Isfahan see S. H. Nasr "The School of Ispahan" in *A History of Muslim Philosophy* ed. M. M. Sharif (Wiesbaden, 1966) II, 904–32; S. H. Nasr *Ṣadr al-Dīn Shīrāzī and His Transcendent Theosophy* (Tehran, 1978); F. Rahman *The Philosophy of Mullā Ṣadrā* (Albany, 1975); Corbin *En Islam iranien* IV.

scheme of the recurring time cycles. The theosophists inherited through the Illuminationists of earlier Islamic centuries the idea of flowing time. "The whole world originates in time," writes Mullā Ṣadrā, "since everything in it is preceded in its being by nonexistence in time. And everything in it is essentially renewed, in the sense that there is absolutely no ipseity or individuality—be it celestial or elemental, simple or composite, substantial or accidental—but that its nonexistence precedes its being in time, and its being likewise precedes its nonexistence in time. In general, every body and every bodily thing whose being is in any way connected with matter is constantly renewed in its ipseity and is impermanent in its being and its individuality."[35] The "essential motion" (*ḥaraka jawharīya*) of being, therefore, "is the source of all motions in the accidents of place and position, and all changes of quantity and quality." The universe "is ceaselessly being renewed and passing away, originating and ending. There is no cause for its continual origination and renewal, since what is essential is something not caused by anything but its own essence. And the Maker, when He made [the essence of being] made it to be continually renewed. This continual renewal is not made or acted upon or influenced by anything."[36]

The dimensions of such a self-perpetuating force of renewal were immense, perhaps far greater than Mullā Ṣadrā himself was prepared to admit. He makes the point, however, that his theory of essential motion differs from that of the earlier philosophers because it defines time not as an independent entity but as a measure for the course of renewal. Unlike either the fixed rotary theory of certain Ismāʿīlī advocates or the almost ahistorical approach of the conventional theologians, the Ṣadrā'ī concept of transubstantiation seems to point in the direction of a linear, or at least a spiral, course of history. Man, as part of being, is constantly renewed in order to witness not the return of the same but a new creation. Though the notion of forward progress does not appear in Mullā Ṣadrā's philosophy, it is not hard to see it anticipated there. The Ṣadrā'īs hesitated to stretch the theory of transubstantiation so far that it would conflict with the doctrine of final salvation, yet they took care to emphasize the incompatability of conventional eschatology with the precepts of theosophical wisdom. This is particularly evident in the discourses on the subject of the corporal resurrection. In his discussion on the nature of the hereafter, Mullā Ṣadrā's leading student, ʿAbd al-Razzāq Lāhījī, emphasizes: "To prescribe the existence of another world that would be structurally identical with this world, it is not possible to employ the rules of reason and theosophical wisdom (*ḥikma*)."[37] Further on, he reiterates the philosopher's classical objection to corporal resurrection and concludes: "The confirmation of corporal resurrection is

[35]Ṣadr al-Dīn Shīrāzī *al-Ḥikmat al-ʿArshīya* trans. J. W. Morris as *The Wisdom of the Throne* (Princeton, 1981) 119–20.

[36]Ibid. 121–22.

[37]*Gauhar-i Murād* (Tehran, 1377/1957) 440.

only possible because of the assurances of the prophets; the verification of such resurrection upon the merits of reason is impossible."[38] Although Lāhījī, like Mullā Ṣadrā himself, accepts the corporal resurrection, his endorsement of the theory of transubstantiation and the renewal of being in new modalities paved the way for speculations that ultimately led to a theory of cyclical renewal.[39]

Even more clearly, the hesitation of Ṣadrā'ī theosophists to cross the frontiers of accepted theology can be observed in Lāhījī's treatment of the doctrine of the finality of the Muḥammadan revelation. Elaborating on the familiar neo-Platonic "cycle of the two arches," he argues that Muḥammad, being the most perfect of the prophets, would stand at the top of the ascending arch in the cycle of creation parallel to the First Intellect, which is on the top of the descending arch of the same cycle. The Prophet's existence is thus the ultimate stage in the transformation of the "primordial substance" to the state of Perfect Man. Both the First Intellect and the Seal of the Prophets, therefore, are unsurpassable and at the same time indistinguishable from the Primal Being: "Since being emanates from Him [the Primal Being], it would return to Him; and both the true beginning and return originate in the Primal Being. . . . Thus the existence of the Seal of the Prophets terminates the circle of the being where the beginning and the end, both tributary and essential, would meet and unify."[40] With little philosophical skepticism and almost total lack of interest in the theory of transubstantiation, Lāhījī terminates the ascending arch in the cycle of creation with the Seal of the Prophet. Though he briefly remarks on the idea of the "regeneration of nothingness," he does not venture to suggest that the new emanation of the Primal Being may initiate a new cycle of being.[41]

At its philosophical roots, learned Shiʿism remained fundamentally committed to the doctrine of Islam's perfection and consequent finality. The theosophists, in spite of their remarkably dynamic orientation toward the idea of regeneration and renewal, demonstrated little willingness to draw conclusions that might challenge the dominant sharīʿa view by implying a progressive line of continuity in the course of divine revelation. Given all the potentials that the theory of "essential motion" entailed, the notion of renewal in religion remained a mere possibility. For reasons of personal faith, if not fear of persecution, the theosophists, like the philosophers before them, chose to speculate on issues that were not directly related to the

[38]Ibid. 450–51.

[39]For further information on Mullā Ṣadrā's treatment of Shiʿite eschatology see *The Wisdom of the Throne* 76–85, 152–249. Also his *Kitāb al-Mabdaʾ wa al-Maʿād* ed. J. Āshtīyānī (Tehran, 1355 Sh./1976). For Ṣadrā's critical views on the conventional theory of corporal Maʿād see his *al-Ḥikmat al-Mutaʿālīya fī al-Asfār al-Arbaʿa al-ʿAqlīya* (Beirut, 1964) IX, 21–24, 148–58, 174–78. For an interesting reference to the Perfect Man see "Du nāmih-yi Fārsī az Ṣadr al-Dīn Shīrāzī" *Farhang-i Īrān Zamīn* 13 (1344 Sh./1965) 84–100.

[40]*Gauhar-i Murād* 262.

[41]Ibid. 440.

dogmas of religion. Ironically, their greatest conformity with accepted doctrine often appeared in their discourses on the subject of prophethood. As always, it remained the task of sectarians and messianists to apply theoretical possibilities to social realities.

Society and State in the Age of Decline

Bāṭinī thought held the potential to achieve a degree of actuality whenever historical circumstances allowed eschatological tensions to resurface. Most vital for such a realization is perhaps the very idea of change. For better or worse, dramatic social change has usually given man a sense of insecurity and disorder, and in premodern societies he expressed this sense almost exclusively in religious terms. It has often been noted that the teleological interpretation of history does not seek causality in historical events initiated by man or nature but in metaphysical forces—variously defined as God's will, destiny, the rotation of the universe, or the circular flow of time. Misfortunes and natural calamities always persuaded premodern man to ponder his lot, and the Muslims were no exception.

The man of the post-Safavid era had every reason to feel puzzled, if not skeptical, about the general turn of events. The seventy-five years between the Afghan invasion of 1722 and the succession of Fatḥ ʿAlī Shāh to the Qajar throne, in 1797, with the possible exception of an interlude during Karīm Khān's reign (1763–1779), were gloomy enough to aggravate the symptoms of decline already evident in the late Safavid period.[42] Even by the end of the eighteenth century, Iran was still suffering the aftershocks of the Safavid collapse. What is perhaps most conspicuous in the history of nineteenth-century Iran is the persistence of elements of stagnation and decay which, in spite of relative political stability and economic improvement, continued to undermine the structure of material life.[43]

The conventional picture of Qajar decadence would certainly not with-

[42]For remarkable reflections of this sense of despair and loss among the eighteenth-century writers see Shaykh Muḥammad ʿAlī Ḥazīn Lāhījī *The Life of Scheikh Mohammad Ali Hazin* ed. and trans. F. C. Belfour, 2 vols. (London, 1830–1831); Mīrzā Muḥammad Kalāntar *Rūznāmih* ed. ʿA. Iqbāl (Tehran, 1325 Sh./1946). Also A. K. S. Lambton "Some New Trends in Islamic Political Thought in Late 18th Century and Early 19th Century Persia" *Studia Islamica* 39 (1974) 95–128.

[43]On the general improvement of the socioeconomic conditions during the first decade of the nineteenth century found in many accounts by European observers see J. Malcolm *The History of Persia* 2 vols. (London, 1815) II, 203–426; idem. *The Melville Papers* (London, 1930); H. Jones Brydges *An Account of the Transactions of His Majesty's Mission to the Court of Persia* (London, 1834); cf. idem. *The Dynasty of the Kajars* (London, 1833) i-cxci. For a laudatory account of the rise of the Qajars, but one that was nevertheless critical of their policies, see Muḥammad Hāshim Āṣaf (Rustam al-Ḥukamāʾ) *Rustam al-Tawārīkh* ed. M. Mushīrī (Tehran, 1348 Sh./1969). Also see Mīrzā Ṣāliḥ Shīrāzī *Rūznāmih* (MS Ouseley 159, Bodleian Library, Oxford) for a favorable assessment of the economic conditions in 1812; and A. Amanat "Hamrāh-i Mīrzā Ṣāliḥ az Iṣfahān bi Ṭihrān" *Āyandih* 9 (1362 Sh./1983) no. 1, 36–49.

stand the test of objective historical scrutiny. Indeed, the record of the Qajar rule is more impressive than their popular reputation or the hasty judgment of contemporary observers would have it. Yet they simply lacked the means, and the incentive, for creating a climate conducive to long-term improvement. Despite their success in returning security and peace to the cities, and to a lesser extent to the countryside, they were unable to control the sources of tension and conflict sufficiently to make themselves the effective sovereigns of their realm. Nor were they able to resolve the host of economic problems that gradually exhausted their financial resources. The nature of their rule, a familar mixture of nomadic patriarchy and monarchical absolutism, obliged them to sustain a policy of perpetual coercion and punitive measures against all potential rivals. The survival of Qajar rule, in turn, depended on their ability to collect taxes, raise armies, and maintain a reasonably satisfied ruling elite by means of persuasion and consent. Their limited organizational or financial resources, however, required them to permit a degree of decentralization and uneasy compromise with other sources of power and influence. Most of Qajar history during the first half of the nineteenth century was characterized by bouts of conflict and reconciliation between the central authority and the peripheral powers. Occasionally highlighted by the heavyhanded policies of the central government, the interaction between the two often brought only marginal victory to the government and its local agents. Even when improved by the use of modern communications and weaponry, the government's control succeeded only in maintaining a delicate balance of power with potentially adverse forces—whether tribal khans, overambitious princes, or city folk.[44]

[44]Except for religious aspects, which have received a fair amount of attention in H. Algar *Religion and State in Iran, 1785–1906* (Berkeley, 1969), most other aspects of early-nineteenth-century Qajar history remain understudied. Among the few modern works on the political history and institutions we may refer to A. K. S. Lambton "Persian Society under the Qājārs" *Journal of the Royal Asiatic Society* (*Asian Affairs*) 48 (1961) 123–39; E. Abrahamian "Oriental Despotism: The Case of Qājār Iran" *International Journal of Middle East Studies* 5 (1974) 3–31; S. Bakhash "Center-Periphery Relations in Nineteenth Century Iran" *Iranian Studies* 14 (1981) 29–51; and N. R. Keddie "Class Structure and Political Power in Iran since 1796" *Iranian Studies* 11 (1978) 305–30; and other articles by her in *International Journal of Middle East Studies* 2 (1971) 3–20 and in *The Islamic Middle East 700–1900* ed. A. Udovitch (Princeton, 1981). On the administration see C. Meredith "Early Qajar Administration: An Analysis of Its Development and Functions" *Iranian Studies* 4 (1971) 59–84; S. Bakhash "The Evolution of Qajar Bureaucracy: 1779–1879" *Middle East Studies* 7 (1971) 139–68. For two case studies of provincial administration see G. Bournoutian *Eastern Armenia in the Last Decades of Persian Rule, 1807–1828* (Malibu, 1982) and M. D. Good "Social Hierarchy in Provincial Iran: The Case of Qajar Maragheh" *Iranian Studies* 10 (1977) 129–63. For various aspects of Qajar urban administration and social institutions see W. M. Floor's articles, especially "The Office of Kalantar in Qajar Persia" *Journal of the Economic and Social History of the Orient* 14 (1971) 253–263; "Market Police in Qajar Persia" *Die Welt des Islams* 14 (1972) 221–29; and "The Police in Qajar Persia" *Zeitschrift des Deutschen Morgenländischen Gessellschaft* 123 (1973) 293–315. For the biography of a minister in the early nineteenth century see *EIr*: AMĪN al-DAULA, ʿAbdullāh Khān (A. Amanat). On the rise of the Qajars to power see G. R. G. Hambly "Āqā Muḥammad Khān and the establishment of the Qājār Dynasty" *Royal Central Asian Journal* 50 (1963) 161–74. Also S. Nafīsī *Tārīkh-i Ijtimāʿī va Sīyāsī-yi Īrān dar Daurih-yi Muʿāṣir* 2 vols. (Tehran, 1344 Sh./1965) and *EI*²: ḲĀDJĀR (A. Lambton).

Resistance to the authority of the central government was further complicated by the inclusion of new elements in the political structure. Throughout the first decades of his rule, Fatḥ ʿAlī Shāh felt increasingly obliged to accommodate the rising influence of the urban notables, most significantly those of the clerical class. It became a crucial component of the shah's policy, endorsed and facilitated by the proclerical and urban-based bureaucracy, to enhance the already entrenched position of the ʿulama in the cities by dispensing patronage and shows of personal devotion. Support of the clerical establishment, inconsistent as it was, was deemed necessary to rally public support behind a still insecure monarchy. Religious dissent and popular discontent had to be met on their own terms, and the ʿulama, as long as they were not deprived of their privileges, were prepared to heed the authority of the temporal rulers. The threat posed by neighboring imperial powers only made the rulers more conscious of the need to accommodate the clerical class.[45]

During the reign of Muḥammad Shāh, the third Qajar monarch (1834–1848), the policy of clerical appeasement was partially modified as the state tried to use the backing of the Sufi Niʿmatullāhī order as an alternative to that of the ʿulama. At the same point, although the structure of the bureaucracy and military remained as before, their efficiency was further eroded. What Muḥammad Shāh inherited from his predecessor was a weaker provincial administration and a stronger local resistance, which could not easily be overcome by insecure and often incompetent officialdom.

The central administration under Ḥājjī Mīrzā Āqāsī, the premier between 1835 and 1848, showed signs of serious deterioration owing to mismanagement, factional rivalry, court intrigues, and nepotism. To cope with declining state revenue—caused partly by the long-term transfer of crown lands to private owners and partly by the government's inability to collect taxes regularly—the Qajars resorted to the practice of auctioning provincial posts. Except in provinces that remained the monopoly of powerful semi-autonomous governors (particularly Isfahan and Khurasan), governors often served no longer than one or two years, which seriously affected the performance of the provincial administration, itself divided by factional disputes. Profligacy and greed, the inevitable outcome of such policy, could only encourage corruption and oppression at all levels. Wronged by the governors' indiscriminate extortions and terrorized by the undisciplined and badly paid troops (who were themselves often in revolt against the provincial governors), the public frequently turned for protection to the city notables and religious dignitaries, who more often than not exploited the popular discontent for their own purposes. The reign of Muḥammad Shāh was particularly marred by urban violence and the frequent eruption of popular discontent.[46]

[45]See below, chaps. 1 and 2.

[46]For the deteriorating state of affairs under Muḥammad Shāh see particularly Āqā Mahdī Navvāb Ṭihrānī *Risāla-yi Dastūr al-Aʿqāb* cited in K. M. Sāsānī *Sīyāsatgarān-i Daurih-yi Qājār*

Events in Fars province offer a case in point. Between 1810 and 1835, under the governorship of Ḥusayn ʿAlī Mīrzā, Fatḥ ʿAlī Shāh's son, a revival in local trade and agricultural production made Fars the country's second most prosperous province (after Azarbaijan). But it was a fragile prosperity, seldom free of tribal incursions and urban conflicts. A series of riots and violent clashes in the provincial capital of Shiraz, as well as in other towns and villages of the province, reached a climax in the early 1840s, when open rebellions against an exceptionally ineffective governor brought Fars to the brink of chaos.[47] Commenting on the agitation that followed the appointment of a new governor, the British envoy to the Qajar court, Colonel Sheil, observed: "The province of Fars still remains in the same disturbed state. Mirza Nabee Khan [Māzandarānī], the Governor, being perfectly destitute of authority, is unable to levy the revenue."[48]

Mīrzā Nabī Khān, whose only qualification for the governorship was his top bid for the post, lacked not only the support of Premier Ḥājjī Mīrzā Āqāsī in the capital but also the consent of the local notables, who at times emerged as natural leaders and enjoyed the support of the public. One such influential figure was Ḥājjī Mīrzā Muḥammad Khān Qavām al-Mulk, the well-established chief magistrate of Fars, who combined land ownership with the tribal chieftainship of the Khamsa tribal confederacy and had effective control over a large section of the city. For him, the consolidation of the new governor's authority meant less control over the administration of Fars, as well as a loss of revenue. Correspondingly, for Muḥammad Khān, the chief of Qashqāʾī tribe, the establishment of a strong provincial government meant a restriction on the tribe's movements and the payment of the taxes due. While Qavām al-Mulk and his allies practically controlled the city quarters and the Qashqāʾī chief guaranteed the necessary force to check the government troops, the brigands (*lūṭīs*) of the rival city quarters were left free to incite violence. In mid-1844 a British agent in Shiraz reported to the Tehran mission that "in Fars there is not a village or district, not to speak of Shiraz, where fighting and disturbances do not occur."[49] Giving a vivid account of the Ḥaydarī-Niʿmatī factional clashes between rival brigands as well as simultaneous disturbances in other towns and

---

2 vols. (Tehran, 1346 Sh./1967) II, 70–101. Also, Comte de Sercey *Une ambassade extraordinaire: La Perse en 1839–40* (Paris, 1928); W. Stuart *Journal of a Residence in Northern Persia* (London, 1854); J. B. Fraser *A Winter's Journey (Tatar) from Constantinople to Tehran* 2 vols. (London, 1838) and *Travels in Koordistan, Mesopotamia, Etc.* (London, 1840); R. G. Watson *A History of Persia* (London, 1866). Also *EIr*: ĀQĀSĪ (A. Amanat) and the cited sources.

[47]On Fars in the early nineteenth century see E. S. Waring *A Tour to Sheeraz* (London, 1807) and *FN* I, 234–301 (trans. H. Busse as *History of Persia under Qajar Rule* [New York and London, 1972]). A systematic coverage of the events of Fars appears in a series of Foreign Office dispatches during the 1840s (see F.O. 60/104 to 113).

[48]F.O. 60/105, no. 87, 1 Aug. 1844, Sheil to Aberdeen. *FN* (I, 299) agrees that besides the offering *(pīshkish)*, Mīrzā Nabī had no real support in either the capital or in Fars.

[49]F.O. 60/105, no. 90, 19 Aug. 1844 supplement: translation of substance of a letter from the agent at Shiraz to Lieutenant Colonel Sheil.

villages of Fars, and also the disputes that broke out between the rival government troops over their lodging in Shiraz, the agent stated: "The majority of the houses and shops adjoining the scene of conflict were plundered and destroyed. During the two or three days that the [lastest round of] the fight lasted, four persons were killed and at least a hundred wounded."[50] Appealing to the British representative to intervene, the agent concluded: "The people here come to me and say that they are in despair, that their representatives to the Court are useless, and they beg me to inform you of the desperate state of affairs, with the hope that you may be prevailed upon to use your influence at Tehran for ameliorating their condition."[51]

The situation in Fars was typical of that in most other provinces. The government's failure to maintain law and order, as well as the shortcomings of administration and finance under Premier Āqāsī, brought the Qajars to the verge of collapse. At no time since their rise to power had they faced a crisis of such proportions.

Obviously the Qajar state under Muḥammad Shāh and Premier Āqāsī cannot be held responsible for all the problems troubling the country at the time. Nor should the degree of the administration's malfunction or the corruption of its officials be exaggerated. It can be argued with some justification that even if the government of Muḥammad Shāh had been more efficient and farsighted, the more serious problems could not have been avoided. Indeed, the domestic crisis of the 1830s and 1840s was dwarfed by the overall problems of economic stagnation, depopulation caused by epidemic diseases, and the challenge of imperial powers.

As early as the beginning of the nineteenth century, the European presence was felt primarily in the military and diplomatic spheres. The territorial ambitions of Tsarist Russia in the Caucasus and beyond were soon to confront the British concern for the security of India. Caught in the middle, nineteenth-century Iran was destined to remain a buffer state, whose precarious sovereignty, and course of foreign policy, were to be

[50]Ibid. In the dispatch cited above, with reference to urban factional conflicts, Sheil observes: "In all the principal towns of Persia, the inhabitants are divided into two parties, the Hydarees and the Neʿmetees, who engage in contests which are usually periodical and insignificant, but which increase in fierceness and frequency under a weak government." On the same subject see Lady M. Sheil *Glimpses of Life and Manners in Persia* (London, 1856) Note C: pp. 322–26 and *FN* II, 22. Also H. Mirjafari "The Haydari-Nimati Conflicts in Iran" *Iranian Studies* 12 (1979) 135–62. On Lūṭīs see *FN* I, 287; W. M. Floor "The Lutis, A Social Phenomenon in Qajar Persia" *Die Welt des Islams* 13 (1971) 103–20; and H. G. Migeod "Die Lūṭīs" in *Journal of the Economic and Social History of the Orient* 2 (1959) 82–91. On Qavām al-Mulk see *FN* I, 198; II, 47–53; and on Qashqā'ī khans *FN* I, 285, and II, 115–17.

[51]F.O. 60/105, no. 90, supplement. Sheil adds that in mid-August 1844, when Mīrzā Nabī attempted to publish in the principal mosque the *farmān* for commercial regulation regarding the recovery of debts due to English merchants, "the rabble and disaffected persons in Sheeraz assembled around, and would allow no one to approach the mosque. Their supposition was probably that the Ferman contained an order to replace [i.e., confirm] Mīrzā Nabee Khan in Government."

influenced profoundly by the dictates of the neighboring powers. The military might of these powers forced the Qajars to acknowledge their own inadequacies in the battlefield. The Russo-Persian wars of 1805–1813 and 1826–1828 had persuaded them that their safety was more likely to be secured by adhering to a policy of defensive appeasement than by relying on the promises of the other party or on lukewarm reforms of the military. The unsuccessful Herat campaign of 1838 and 1857, during Nāṣir al-Dīn Shāh's reign (1848–1896), only confirmed the conviction that preserving the heartlands required painful sacrifices on the periphery. For most of the time after 1828, the military threat from foreign powers was accompanied by diplomatic pressure, political blackmail, and humiliation. The Qajar monarchs could not fail to realize that their survival depended as much on their ability to preserve internal equilibrium as on their capacity to accommodate the conflicting interests of their neighbors.[52]

Maintenance of the policy of bilateral agreement became increasingly difficult as the moribund administration under Āqāsī was systematically undermined by outside intervention and blackmail. Writing in the early 1840s, Āqāsī expressed in a private note to Muḥammad Shāh the depth of his frustration with European powers: "If I may bring to the sublime attention of that glorious majesty the misery that these Farangīs [Europeans] have brought upon this humblest of creatures, your majesty would judge that this oppression is beyond human tolerance. This is not an [honorable] life. May God sustain the bounty of his [the shah's] shadow over the people of Islam."[53]

Complaints like this represented more than personal attempts to draw the sympathy of a monarch always susceptible to the emotional supplications of his premier. The misery was real. Toward the end of Muḥammad Shāh's reign, Britain and Russia entered an unprecedented contest for further diplomatic, commercial, and territorial gains. Weak and demoralized though it was, the Persian government still hoped to maintain at least a façade of integrity and steadfastness. For the Persian monarch and his minister, the European intrusion was at bottom the work of the infidels, and resistance to it was an Islamic duty. Even in the quixotic world of Āqāsī's despairing

[52]Compared to other aspects, the study of diplomatic relations and power politics has received more attention, though it has been based almost exclusively on Western materials. On Anglo-Persian relations in the first half of the nineteenth century see M. E. Yapp "The Control of the Persian Mission, 1822– 1838" *University of Birmingham Historical Journal* 8 (1959–1960) 162–79; E. Ingram *The Beginning of the Great Game in Asia 1828–1834* (Oxford, 1979); idem. *In Defence of British India* (London, 1984); R. Savory "British and French Diplomacy in Persia, 1800–1810" *Iran* 10 (1972) 31–44; S. F. Shadman "A Review of Anglo-Persian Relations 1798–1815" *Proceedings of the Iran Society* (1943) 23–39. On Russo-Persian relations see M. Atkin *Russia and Iran 1780–1828* (Minneapolis, 1980); F. Kazemzadeh "Russian Penetration of the Caucasus" in *Russian Imperialism from Ivan the Great to the Revolution* (New Brunswick, N.J., 1974) 239–63; A. Tājbakhsh *Tārīkh-i Ravābiṭ-i Īrān va Rūsīyih dar Nīmih-yi Awwal-i Qarn-i Nūzdahum* (Tabriz, 1338 Sh./1959).

[53]Ghanī Collection, Sterling Memorial Library, Yale University, Series I, no. 13.

fantasies, hope of salvation from the yoke of infidels was not lost. In another private note to the shah, written in Muḥarram 1260/February 1844 apparently in response to the shah's decree calling for new initiative against the excesses of the Russians in the north, Āqāsī wrote:

> On the night of *ʿĀshūrā* [the tenth of Muḥarram, the anniversary of Ḥasayn's death in Karbalāʾ] it occurred to me that one thousand and two hundred and sixty years have passed since the *Hijra* and one thousand and two hundred years since the martyrdom of the Lord of the Martyrs, may God's blessing be upon him. And now not a single Muslim is concerned with the strength of Islam and [the need for] victory over the enemies and the infidels. "There is no power and no strength save in God." The religion of Islam is now tarnished. That night in a dream I heard an invisible caller saying: Tomorrow it will become apparent. Now [the next day] that I read the imperial decree, to my amazement I read your majesty expressing concern with victory over the infidels. My hopes are revived. God's will, the strength of Islam will return through the initiative of your majesty, the vicegerent of God. That is certain. . . . May God sustain your rule till the end of the world and God's wrath and curse be upon those who are the opponents of His vicegerent, His shadow, the protector of Islam."[54]

The assurances of the premier and his hopes for the ultimate victory of Islam, however, could hardly boost the Muḥammad Shāh's morale. No less disheartened than his minister by the sinking power of his house, he increasingly relied on Āqāsī, his worldly minister as well as his spiritual guide, to protect his throne against the depredations of his European neighbors. In 1840, despite the protests of the Persian government, the Russians occupied the Caspian island of Āshūrādih in the Gulf of Astarābād. Seeing in this an ominous sign of further Russian encroachments, the shah wrote bitterly to Āqāsī of his humiliation and rage: "Ashur Ada [Āshūrādih] is my property (with its occupants); I am dissatisfied, I am dissatisfied, I am dissatisfied, and there is an end to the matter. . . . Now [the Russians] consider our destruction as easy as the death of an ant crushed under a horse's hoof, but it is not so, [and] please He ever, it will [not] so appear to the whole world; the curse of God on the man who is craven."[55] But the shah's curse seems to have doomed his own throne above all. When he died in 1848, his country was on the verge of civil war, financial bankruptcy, and a religious revolution.

Domestic unrest and foreign threat served in a peculiar way as a catalyst in shaping Iran's political identity. The loss of the territory on the fringes of the country, most notably in the northwest and the northeast but also along

[54]Ibid. no. 3.

[55]F.O. 60/113, no. 32, 27 March 1845, Sheil to Aberdeen, supplement: translation of a private letter from Muḥammad Shāh to Āqāsī.

the Perso-Ottoman frontiers and the southwestern provinces, helped to redefine Iran's geographical boundaries. By the mid-nineteenth century, the notion of the "Protected Domains" (*Mamālik-i Maḥrūsa*), which had been the basis of the Persian imperial system and a safeguard for regional autonomy, began to be replaced with a more cohesive notion of a central state. No doubt the inherent weaknesses of the Qajar government hindered the process of centralization and state building; regional autonomy, in one form or another, persisted well into the twentieth century. Yet paradoxically, external pressures and peripheral unrest were strong enough, almost by default, to accelerate a new political consolidation. Moreover, many of the Qajars' successful campaigns to quell tribal insubordination on the frontiers, particularly in the late eighteenth century and the first quarter of the nineteenth, contributed to this process.

The emerging Qajar state under Fatḥ ʿAlī Shāh and his successors was not wholly devoid of a national identity. To the extent that the Qajars were able to transform the Persian cultural heritage, the Shiʿite religion, and the old monarchical legacy into sources of legitimacy, they were successful in curbing, and occasionally eliminating, the threat of disintegration. In this respect the monarchy did function as a sovereign state vis-à-vis foreign powers and domestic challengers, and with varied fortune it maintained Iran's territorial integrity even while it was being circumscribed into a buffer state.

The emerging state, however, failed to generate among its citizens the sense of affinity and social cohesion needed to support a nation. It remained essentially distant from its subjects. It could not give substance to their ideals and aspirations, nor did it intend to redress their grievances in any serious way. For the majority of the people, the Qajar defeat in the war and their country's humiliation and disgrace at the hands of foreign powers hardly inspired a sense of affection toward the ruling dynasty. For some, no doubt, the weakening of the central government even came as an unexpected relief from the customary ill-treatment and extortion at the hands of government agents.

The victories of European intruders, the colonial arrogance of their envoys, and the might of their armies, however, were more likely to be viewed by ordinary people as a breach of Islam's dominance and an affirmation of its vulnerability. This was the first time in recent history that Persian society had encountered, on any sizable scale, the superior powers of non-Muslim nations. It was the material advantages of the people of Europe that were perceived by all but a small minority as the overpowering strength of Christianity. The European Christians with whom they now had to deal were markedly different from the protected religious minorities in the Islamic world. The obedient "people of the pact," as these minorities were called, hardly ever posed a challenge to the Muslims, and least of all to the Shiʿites, whose stringent rules of ritual purity and communal segregation not only had kept them at a safe distance from the Christian (notably Armenian) and Jewish communities among them, but also had assured them of their own religious proficiency.[56]

Emerging out of the turmoil of the eighteenth century, the Shiʿites of Iran could no longer cherish with confidence their earlier self-image as the "saved nation." Their complacent view of themselves had already begun to fade with the fall of the Safavids, when both temporal and religious symbols of Shiʿism were submerged under the weight of hostile forces. The mid-nineteenth-century European interventions only helped to exacerbate this protracted crisis of confidence.

The average Persian city dweller now had daily opportunities to witness the visible presence of Europeans—diplomats, soldiers, merchants, adventurers, and missionaries. The advances of the West in military, commercial, and material life became increasingly apparent. By the 1830s and 1840s, Persian markets were filled with European textiles. Manchester prints were becoming as popular as any domestic fabric, and imported European manufactures were beginning to replace local products. In the large commercial centers, the mercantile community learned to cope with and occasionally to suffer from the competition of the European merchants and their agents: the Hindus, Greeks, Armenians, Jews, and others. Many of these agents, by virtue of their European protection, were now enjoying the capitulatory rights extended to the most favored nations and interpolated in the treaties with Russia and Britain.[57] The Persian merchants in the ports of entry—Būshihr, Muḥammara, Bandar ʿAbbās, Anzalī, and Mashhadsar—could witness the arrival of British and Russian vessels. Occasionally, at times of high tension, they could even sense the power of their cannons, more accurate and deadly than any weapon they had ever seen, targeting their merchant houses and their merchandise.[58]

After the first round of wars with Russia, in an attempt to escape the disadvantages of an irregular tribal force, the New Army (Niẓām-i Jadīd) was formed.[59] Modeled on European armies and dressed in their fashion, soon after its creation it was reduced to a poorly drilled and equipped force

[56]For a selected bibliography of the Shiʿite legal treatises on the dhimmīs see H. Modarressi Tabātabāʾī "On Non-Muslims" *An Introduction to Shīʿi Law* (London, 1984) 169. On the treatment of the minorities in the nineteenth century see Malcolm *History* II 425–26, 521; Curzon *Persia* I, 510–11; II, 51–56, 240–42 (and the cited sources); E. G. Browne *A Year amongst the Persians* (London, 1950) 397–530; N. Malcolm *Five Years in a Persian Town* (London, 1905). See also W. J. Fischel "The Jews of Persia, 1795–1940" *Jewish Social Studies* 5 (1950) 119–60.

[57]For the adverse effects of foreign trade see C. Issawi *The Economic History of Iran 1800–1914* (Chicago, 1971) 70–151, 258–309; A. Amanat, ed. *Cities and Trade: Consul Abbott on the Economy and Society of Iran 1847–1866* (London, 1983). See also below, chap. 8.

[58]See for example J. B. Kelly *Britain and the Persian Gulf* ([Oxford, 1968] 306–20, 425–99) for the British occupation of Khārg and Būshihr (1838) and the naval attack on Muḥammara (1857). Also J. H. Standish "The Persian War of 1856–1857" *Middle Eastern Studies* 3 (1966) 18–45.

[59]On the New Army see Sheil *Glimpses* 380–85; Curzon *Persia* I, 576–81; A. de Gardane

that ultimately became a serious nuisance to villagers and city folk alike. If it was no match for Russian or British troops, it nonetheless proved effective against domestic insurgency. The Qajars were content to let its half-starving and badly paid troops plunder the already impoverished countryside, disturb the peace in the cities, raze the fortresses of the rebellious khans, and live off their booty.[60]

In the months prior to the second round of Russo-Persian wars, the people's attention was also drawn to the threat of foreign invasion. The ʿulama preached from the pulpit about the sufferings of the Caucasian Shiʿites at the hands of Russian invaders and warned their congregations of a similar fate. After the war, there were enough refugees from Īrvān to confirm their fears. On a smaller scale, particularly after the annexation of Sind in 1844, the news of the British and their expanding empire was received with a mixture of awe and bewilderment.[61]

Once the sphere of Western intrusion reached the mosque, it was no longer possible to overlook the flagrant abuse of diplomatic privileges by European envoys. The Griboyedov affair and the massacre of the Russian legation in Tehran in 1829, whatever its exact causes, clearly reflected the public's rage over the Europeans' interference in the social and religious customs and practices of the country. The mob's action, ugly as it was, was perhaps symbolic of a deeper problem.[62] Coming to terms with the triumphant Europeans, not only on the battlefields of the Caucasus and Herat but also in the bazaars of Tabriz, Shiraz, and Yazd, by any definition, was a torturous course of adjustment.

At another level, an urge for partial accommodation with Europe characterized the attitude of a minority within the ruling elite. From the crown prince, ʿAbbās Mīrzā (d. 1833), and his minister, Mīrzā Abul-Qāsim Qāʾim Maqām (d. 1835), to Muḥammad Shāh's premier, Āqāsī—and later to Nāṣir al-Dīn Shāh's celebrated premier, Mīrzā Taqī Khān Amīr Kabīr (d. 1851)—there is a recognizable line of reformers. They all promoted the idea of reform with varying perseverance. But with the important exception of Amīr Kabīr, their attempts never went beyond a few steps toward modernizing of the army and the state machinery. Even toward the end of the cen-

---

Mission du Général Gardane en Perse sous le Premier Empire (Paris, 1865); J. Qāʾim Maqāmī *Tārīkh-i Taḥavvulāt Sīyāsī-yi Niẓām-i Īrān* (Tehran, 1326 Sh./1947) 15–51.

[60]For ʿAbbās Mīrzā's mission in Khurasan and beyond between 1832 and 1833, and the campaigns of the Nīẓām Jadīd forces against the confederacy of the eastern tribes, see Fraser *A Winter's Journey* II, 195–286; H. Nāṭiq "ʿAbbās Mīrzā va Fatḥ-i Khurāsān" in *Az Māst ki bar Māst* (Tehran, 1354 Sh./1975) 43–91.

[61]On the developments leading to the second round of the wars with Russia see Algar *Religion and State* 82–102; Atkin *Russia* 145–61; P. Avery "An Enquiry into the Outbreak of the Second Russo-Persian War, 1826–28" *Iran and Islam* ed. C. E. Bosworth (Edinburgh, 1971) 26–40.

[62]On the Griboyedov incident see D. P. Costello "The Murder of Griboedov" *Oxford Slavic Papers* 8 (1958) 66–89; E. J. Harden "Griboyedov in Persia: December 1828" *Slavonic and East European Review* 57 (1979) 255–67; Algar *Religion and State* 94–99.

tury, the concept of reform almost never broadened enough to touch social and political issues, let alone religious questions. The reformers of early nineteenth-century Iran were lay statesmen who tended to regard the orthodox religion as a sanctified domain beyond their reach. If ever they addressed religious issues, their concern was not with religious doctrine, or even with the clerical establishment as such, but with the ʿulama's infringements into the realm of the government.[63]

The confrontational nature of Iran's early contacts with the West also led the ʿulama to respond negatively to reform. As they saw it, the forces of tradition and the obligations of the sharīʿa dictated at the least an uncomfortable tolerance of Europe and at the most an unceasing revulsion at its deceptive secular values. With few exceptions, the Shiʿite ʿulama of the nineteenth century never took upon themselves a serious inquiry about the West. Nor did they ever consider readjusting the doctrine of Islam to fit modern needs. Associating Europe with Christianity gave them a convenient reassurance of their own superior faith, a conviction that their occasional encounters with Christian missionaries only helped confirm.

The society's transition into a new era of exposure to the West was not smoothed by the failure of the state to reform. Instead, the state's stagnation helped exacerbate the polarity between the ruling elite and the subjects. Those sections of the populace that were most affected by the state's policies (merchants, artisans, petty traders, small landowners, middle peasantry, and lower-ranking state officials) were least represented in the political system. The widening gap between ruler and ruled was partially compensated for by upward mobility within the bureaucracy and by the fluid structure of the society as a whole. Yet the inner ethos of Persian society remained essentially untouched. With a remarkable continuity, traditional social values and norms, as well as traditional religious dilemmas and preoccupations, were passed on to later generations. The state's consolidation allowed the society to gain more cohesiveness and homogeneity than ever before, but it also permitted the emergence of a dynamism conducive to drastic social change. The dichotomy between state and society was further sharpened by the appearance of Europe on the political horizon. The lethargic existence of the Qajar state, its political desperation and economic bankruptcy, particularly in the latter part of Muḥammad Shāh's reign, sharply contrasted with the apparent vitality and prowess of the Europeans. The reassertion of social identity thus went hand in hand with a sense of doom

[63]On reform and modernization in early-nineteenth-century Iran see H. Farman Farmaian "The Forces of Modernization in Nineteenth Century Iran" in R. Polk and R. Chamber, ed. *The Beginnings of Modernization in the Middle East* (Chicago, 1968) 119–51; Ḥ. Maḥbūbī Ardakānī *Tārīkh-i Muʾassisāt-i Tamaddunī-yi Jadīd dar Īrān* 2 vols. (Tehran, 1354 Sh./1975) I, 49–317; F. Ādamīyat *Amīr Kabīr va Īrān* 3d ed. (Tehran, 1348 Sh./1969) 157–91; ʿAbbās Iqbāl *Mīrzā Taqī Khān Amīr Kabīr* (Tehran, 1340 Sh./1961) 141–62, 178–266; *EIr*: AMĪR KABĪR (H. Algar) and J. H. Lorentz "Iran's Greatest Reformer of the Nineteenth Century" *Iranian Studies* 4 (1971) 85–103. See also H. Pakdaman and W. Royce "Abbas Mirza's Will" *Iranian Studies* 6 (1973) 136–51.

and despair over the society's material destitution and inferiority. Endemic corruption and intransigence in the political system demonstrated the futility of modernization initiated from above. The failures of Amīr Kabīr's reforms illustrated this ineptitude and the unwillingness of the ruling elite to undertake measures that might jeopardize its vested interests.

So long as Shiʿism remained the chief component of Iran's religious identity, the infirmity of the community and the feebleness of the state would be taken as synonomous with Islam, for it was impossible to explain the perceived material and moral regression in any terms but religious ones. In earlier times, so long as the totality of Islam was not tarnished and its eschatological guarantees were not questioned, this explanation could be accepted, for worldly suffering and humiliation would be rewarded with salvation in the hereafter. It might have still been possible to hope for celestial recompense if earthly life was not circumstanced by an outlook increasingly conscious of the changing times. But Europe was now challenging Islam's totality, and also offering enticements that could not have been ignored even by the pious merchant of the bazaar or the God-fearing man of the madrasa. In such an age of crisis, steadfast adherence to the promises of the hereafter could only be endured if the problem of Islam's historic reversal could be satisfactorily answered.

The acute crises of faith increasingly persuaded later religious reformers, particularly in the Sunni world, to blame the Muslim community for deviating from the path of "true Islam." But for Shiʿites of Iran at a stage when the two processes of internal decay and external danger first coincided, the crisis tended to revive the inherent predicaments of their eschatology. In such a world view, religion could be rejuvenated by the savior Mahdi only when decadence and decrepitude had brought the community to its lowest ebb. Thus, if not for all, then at least for those who had more reasons to be discontented with the status quo, the prerequisite for the return of the Mahdi had already been fulfilled. Material regression and social injustice were viewed by some as signs of moral weakness and the prelude to impending doom. Shiʿite orthodoxy, when it concerned itself with the deteriorating affairs of the community, tended to attribute it to the rapacities of the state and the mischiefs of heretics, and accordingly to seek remedies in the assertion of the sharīʿa. Nonorthodox Shiʿite thought, however, began to lean back on its esoteric legacy: improvements in the affairs of the world were conceivable only when coupled with a charismatic renewal that could restore the pristine glory of the prophetic age. The Qiyāma could thus be envisaged not as a cataclysmic upheaval at an unpredictable moment of time but as a revolutionary change in this world—a change that required active human participation. Contrary to the advocates of the status quo, both religious and temporal, and unlike those few who heralded secular reforms, the purveyors of messianic doctrine sought the secret of renewal within the realm of religion.

PART I

HISTORICAL BACKGROUND

I

Orthodoxy and Heterodoxy: The Evolution of Learned Shiʿism

More than seventy-five years after the fall of the Safavids (1722), nineteenth-century Iran emerged from long periods of political unrest and social suffering with two complementary institutions: a new tribal dynasty, the Qajars (1785–1925), and a consolidated Shiʿite clerical class, the ʿulama. The development of religious authority and of secular power were in many ways complementary. The Qajars consolidated their position in the urban centers by means of a military and administrative presence, while the ʿulama strengthened their stand by exerting a religious authority that embraced a variety of judicial, educational, and executive functions.

The emergence of the ʿulama as an influential urban force during the final decades of the eighteenth century occurred partly because of the chronic and often prolonged absence of a dominant central power. But it was in the early nineteenth century that, benefiting from the relative security of the cities provided by the Qajars, the ʿulama flourished to become one of the most potent forces in the urban setting. Their relation with the Qajar state can be defined as one of guarded coexistence, if not implicit cooperation. Although frequently portrayed as militant champions of the urban masses in the fight against oppression, the ʿulama often found themselves obliged to compromise with the secular power whose legitimacy they seldom questioned, particularly when their own existence was endangered.

In their own sphere of influence in the cities, the ʿulama enjoyed a relative independence, particularly in their control over the nongovernmental judiciary as well as the educational institutions. By supervising most of the public endowments and by receiving alms, the "share of the Imam," and other religious dues, they maintained a considerable financial leverage outside the traditional zone of government intervention. Through the mosques, where they preached sermons and conducted public prayers, they were able to establish direct contact with the people. They often enjoyed the support of the public, who sought among them revered models of knowledge and piety and looked to them for justice and protection. In particular, they benefited from the backing of those groups of notables such as merchants or local officials who shared with them some common interests in the marketplace or in the citadel. This area of the ʿulama's influence was usually recognized by both central and provincial governments. Frictions and disputes with the state were either on ill-defined borderline issues or more often sprang up because of each side's determination to expand its area of control beyond the recognized boundaries. Though each party was ready to undermine the authority of the other, both were unwilling to risk any serious confrontation. The delicate equilibrium of the ʿulama and the government allowed little room for any other force to question the legitimacy of either. In moments of need, when the survival of both was at stake, the task of preserving this balance often brought them into a united front.

The Uṣūlī Establishment

The social and religious role of the ʿulama and its political implications cannot be examined in isolation, without some attention to earlier resurgence of theological and jurisprudential pursuits in Shiʿite scholarly circles. The triumph of the newly revived school of jurisprudence known as Uṣūlism (Uṣūlīya, from *uṣūl al-fiqh,* "principles of jurisprudence") was more than a scholastic exercise in methodology and approach. Uṣūlism, in its essence, facilitates the intervention of the religious authority in the affairs of the world, and hence provided a new outlook through which the ʿulama justified their increasingly noticeable presence in the society.

The revivified Uṣūli underwent a long evolution that occurred mostly outside the milieu of the Persian cities and against the background of other religious trends common in the ʿAtabāt (the Shiʿite shrine cities of southern Iraq) during the eighteenth century. The rival Akhbārī school of jurisprudence; the ascetic and even mystical tendencies of some of the ʿulama; and the Shaykhi school are three of the more significant landmarks in that development. The circumstances that led to the shaping of the Uṣūlī school and later interactions with the above-mentioned trends provided an intellectual precedent within the sphere of learned Shiʿism that was essential for the later emergence of messianic expectations.

The flight of the Persian ʿulama to Iraq throughout the eighteenth century brought about some distinctive changes in the religious climate of the ʿAtabāt. The doctrinal encounter between Akhbārīs and Uṣūlīs, which ended in the victory of the latter school, was the most prominent of those changes. The Uṣūlī school was first revived by those Persian ʿulama (or ʿulama of Persian descent) who had received their formal training in the religious colleges of the ʿAtabāt, the madrasas, and hence were barely influenced by earlier Traditionist school of Isfahan developed by Muḥammad Bāqir Majlisī and his disciples. Āqā Muḥammad Bāqir Bihbahānī (1118–1205/1706–1790), the recognized "founder" of the modern Uṣūlī school, is often regarded as the first to realize the need for a more critical approach to *fiqh* (jurisprudence). He was a young Iṣfahānī *ṭalaba* (seminarian) in his twenties when he arrived in the Shiʿite cities of Iraq. Though he received his early training from his father in Isfahan (himself with Uṣūlī leanings), it was during his first residence in the ʿAtabāt that he seriously undertook studies under such well-known scholars as Shaykh Yūsuf Baḥrānī, Sayyid Muḥammad Ṭabāṭabā'ī, and Sayyid Ṣadr al-Dīn Qumī.[1] These scholars are all considered Akhbārīs, since their main emphasis was on the theory that in addition to the Scripture, the entire body of *akhbār* (Traditions as transmitted from past generations[2]) provided the only other premise for juristic investigation. They were not totally unaware of the need for some reconsideration of the methods and means of such an investigation, however. Baḥrānī, for instance, who by origin and training came from the "Traditionist" school of Bahrain, is considered representative of the Akhbārī school in the ʿAtabāt, yet it was from his moderate views that the first signs of a new Uṣūlī outlook emerged.[3] A more critical approach is evident not only in his selective use of the Shiʿite akhbār but in his pragmatic treatment of fiqh. His endeavor in the field of *rijāl* (biographical study of the transmitters of the Traditions) and his criticism of Mullā Muḥsin Fayż and Mullā Muḥammad Amīn Astarābādī, the renowned advocates of Akhbārism,[4] further demon-

[1]For Āqā Muḥammad Bāqir, among other sources see A. Davānī *Vaḥīd-i Bihbahānī* (Qum, 1337 Sh./1958), which provides a full biographical account of Bihbahānī and his family. Also *RJ* 122–24; *QU* 199–204; *TAS* II/1, 171–74; *MA* I, 220–35. For his teachers see *Vaḥīd* 180–85 and *MA* I, 229–30. An important biographical source on Bihbahānī is the unpublished work of his grandson Aḥmad Ibn Muḥammad ʿAlī Bihbahānī *Mir'āt al-Aḥwāl Jahān-namā* (British Library, MS Add. 24052), which contains among other things an account of Majlisī's descendants up to Bihbahānī and beyond. See also J. Cole "Shi'i Clerics in Iraq and Iran, 1722–1780: The Akhbari-Usuli Conflict Reconsidered" *Iranian Studies* 28 (1985) 3–34.

[2]Barely distinct from *aḥādīth* (Traditions) in Shiʿism as it refers to a more comprehensive body of reports from the Prophet and the Imams. For a discussion on the definitions of *khabar* see M. A. al-Tahānawī *Kashshāf Iṣṭilāḥāt al-Funūn wa'l-ʿUlūm* ed. A. Sprenger et al., 2 vols. (Calcutta, 1854–1862) 281, 410–12.

[3]Baḥrānī's autobiography appears at the end of his well-known biographical dictionary *Lu'lu'at al-Baḥrayn* (Tehran, 1269/1852–1853). (See *al-Dharīʿa* XVIII, 379–80.) Also translated in *QU* pp. 271–75. *Vaḥīd* (187–95) provides some additional information. H. Algar in *Religion and State* (33–34)—not taking into account Baḥrānī's important contributions such as the above-mentioned *Lu'lu'* and the still better known *Ḥadā'iq al-Nāḍira (al-Dharīʿa* VI, 289–90) for which the author is known as Ṣāḥib-i Ḥadā'iq—states that Baḥrānī's *Kashkūl (al-Dharīʿa* XVIII, 81; cf. II, 465–66), which is a relatively unknown work, was the only work among later Akhbārīs that attained any fame.

[4]Study of rijāl (genealogical and biographical study of the chains of transmitters of hadith) was not enthusiastically pursued by the staunch Akhbārīs, who believed that the Traditions collected by the early scholars must be accepted in their entirety and without critical analysis. See Āqā Buzurg Ṭihrānī *Muṣaffī al-Maqāl fī Muṣannafi ʿIlm al-Rijāl,* ed. A. Munzavī (Tehran, 1378/1959) j-d; ʿAlī Kanī *Tawḍīḥ al-Maqāl fī ʿIlm al-Dirāyat wa'l-Rijāl (Tehran,* 1302/1884–

strate his gradual divergence from the Akhbārīs' literalism and their indiscriminate authentication of all Traditions. It was against this background that Bihbahānī and others developed Uṣūlism into a definite school with strong emphasis on a deductive methodology.

The conditions of the time had a bearing on the adoption of this new approach. Throughout the Afshārid and the Zand periods (1730–1780) the vacuum in the religious leadership of the smaller Persian cities had accelerated the immigration of many Akhbārī ʿulama of Bahrain and the coasts of the Persian Gulf, in flight from greater insecurities, and later the growing threat of the Wahhābīya as well as non-Shiʿite tribes, in their homelands. In Bihbahān, where during in the second quarter of the eighteenth century many Persian ʿulama had taken refuge after Afghan incursion, friction developed between the two groups of Persian and Arab ʿulama both in urban factions and in the form of theoretical dispute. The two main quarters of the city paid allegiance to the two main groups of Persian and Arab ʿulama. In his encounters with the Baḥrainī ʿulama in Bihbahān, where Bihbahānī spent twenty-five years of his life, this sectarianism gave him an immediate reason to oppose the Akhbārīs' predominance.[5]

Prior to his final settlement in the ʿAtabāt (1159/1746), then, Bihbahānī had already observed the Akhbārīs' inflexibility in the face of a new social climate. But it was in the ʿAtabāt that during the eighteenth century a serious intellectual confrontation took place between the representatives of the two tenets.[6] While the Akhbārīs, vulnerable to criticism through their failure to sort out the deficiencies of the Akhbārī theory, were losing ground to their opponents, Bihbahānī and his disciples, many of them Akhbārī converts, developed Uṣūlism into a methodological theory for the emerging body of the mujtahids trained in the ʿAtabāt madrasas. For Bihbahānī and his disciples, contrary to the Akhbārīs, the first priority was to use deductive reasoning to draw conclusions applicable to practical needs, based on premises inherent in the Qurʾān and the Shiʿite Traditions. The major political changes at the time and the crisis of legitimacy in post-Safavid times demanded such a logical approach in order to give the ʿulama the necessary means to play their part in the affairs of the temporal world.[7] Far from

1885). Tunkābunī admits (*QU* 274) that while being the head of the Akhbārīs in the ʿAtabāt, Baḥrānī often "undertook the path of *ijtihād*."

[5]For Bihbahānī's long residence in Bihbahān see *Vaḥīd* 128–30, 140–43. For some of the contemporary Akhbārīs in Bihbahān, see 134–40.

[6]Ibid. 143–56.

[7]Many sources list the theoretical points of difference between the Akhbārīs and Uṣūlīs. Among them, *RJ* 34 gives a list of thirty points of distinction between the two schools. See also Sayyid Kāẓim Rashtī "*Risāla* in reply to enquiries from Isfahan" in *Majmaʿ al-Rasāʾil* (Persian), 2 ed. (Kirman, n.d.) 276–359. Davānī in *Vaḥīd* (70–76) cites some of the differences, using, among other sources, *al-Ḥaqq al-Mubīn* by Shaykh Jaʿfar Kāshif al-Ghiṭāʾ. He also discusses Bihbahānī's refutations of the Akhbārīs (76–95) and cites some examples. The Akhbārī view on differences with Uṣūlīs appears in the works of Mīrzā Muḥammad Akhbārī, including *Ḥirz*

being an instantaneous victory of Bihbahānī over his rivals, as is usually assumed, the decline of the Akhbārīs during the eighteenth century was the outcome of a long process from the uncritical method of mere transmission of Traditions to a method of deductive reasoning.[8]

Bihbahānī's efforts resulted in consolidation of *ijtihād* (the process of arriving at independent legal judgment by employing limited deductive reasoning), both in theory and in practice. The precept of "acting in accordance with presumption," the maxim of the Uṣūlī doctrine, enabled mujtahids to go far beyond the former practice of jurisprudence both in gaining particular judgment and in formulating general principles. But Uṣūlism also made it clear that ijtihād, or more specifically the process of arriving at judgements in specific matters, was restricted to mujtahids who, because of their legal knowledge and training, acquired exclusive skills that enabled them to deduce facts and draw conclusions from the Qur'ān and Traditions (which themselves were the subject of great scrutiny), and to a lesser extent through consensus *(ijmāʿ)*.[9] Hence, by defining terms and conditions of ijtihād, and by recognizing the superior intellectual and moral advantages of mujtahids, the Uṣūlīs designated themselves a religious elite entitled to rights and priorities above others, and most of all to moral leadership of the community. This claim to exclusive guidance, almost unprecedented in the past history of Shiʿism, was of great importance to the course of modern Persian history. The theoretical ground for this approach is evident in the writings of Bihbahānī's colleagues and students. Its practical implications, however, are more discernible in the activities of the second generation of the Uṣūlīs.

The theoretical progress of the school owed much to these ʿulama who gathered in Bihbahānī's circle. By producing numerous specialized works on uṣūl al-fiqh, *furūʿ* (the actual body of law), and to a lesser extent the ḥadīth and its related fields and indoctrinating a new generation of students, the Uṣūlī nucleus reconstructed the backbone of Shiʿite orthodoxy for the whole of the nineteenth century. Famous scholars such as Shaykh Jaʿfar Najafī (1156–1228/1743–1813) and Sayyid Muḥammad Ṭabāṭabā'ī, later known as Mujāhid (d. 1242/1826) specialized in furūʿ, while others such as Sayyid ʿAlī Ṭabāṭabā'ī (d. 1231/1816) and Mīrzā Abul-Qāsim Qumī, known as Mīrzā-yi Qumī (d. 1231/1816) concentrated on uṣūl. Some like Sharīf al-ʿUlamā' Āmulī (d. 1246/1830) devoted their time to organizing a more

---

al-Ḥawāss; al-Mumṭir al-Fāṣil bayn al-Ḥaqq wa al-Bāṭil and his numerous refutations of the Uṣūlīs. See *MA* III, 935–40.

[8]See for example *QU* 201, which is the source for Algar *Religion and State* 33–36 and others. The Akhbārī-Uṣūlī controversy is also discussed in G. Scarcia "Intorno alle controversie tra Aḫbārī e Uṣūlī presso gli Imamiti di Persia" *Rivista degli Studi Orientali* 33 (1958), 211–50; and J. Cole "Shi'i Clerics" 13–23.

[9]The works of Bihbahānī and his followers in uṣūl al-fiqh argue at some length the merits of "rational proof" *(dalīl-i ʿaql)* and its superiority over mere "transmissions" *(naql)*. Bihbahānī in *al-Fawā'id al-Ḥā'irīya* [Tehran, 1270/1853] (see *al-Dharīʿa* XVI, 330–31) and *al-Ijtihād wa'l-*

systematic method of teaching, whereas Sayyid Muḥammad Mahdī Baḥr al-ʿUlūm (d. 1212/1797) and later Mullā Aḥmad Narāqī (d. 1244/1828) attempted to attain an overall knowledge in all fields.[10] Independent works such as *Kashf al-Ghiṭā'*, by Najafī,[11] and Qumī's *Qawānīn al-Uṣūl*[12] were to become the classic texts in Shiʿite curricula. Important commentaries on the works of earlier scholars such as *Rīyaḍ al-Masā'il*, by Sayyid ʿAlī Ṭabāṭabā'ī,[13] were written both to satisfy a need for a concise account of Shiʿite jurisprudence and to elaborate on the points essential for the justification of the Uṣūlī stand.

The second generation of students trained under Uṣūlī teachers extended the mujtahids' sphere of influence beyond academic circles and into the community. They consisted of three major groups. The first was that of sons and grandsons of some eminent teachers of the ʿAtabāt. Often in close family contact with each other, the Ṭabāṭabā'īs (Sayyid Muḥammad and his brother Sayyid Muḥammad Mahdī),[14] the Bihbahānīs (Āqā Muḥammad ʿAlī and the others),[15] the Najafīs (Shaykh Mūsā and his brothers Shaykh ʿAlī and Shaykh Ḥasan, known as Āl-i Kāshif al-Ghiṭā'),[16] and other ʿulama of high descent managed to maintain a form of monopoly, or at least control, over teaching circles. They continued their fathers' efforts to strengthen the Uṣūlī positions by encouraging their students to settle in various urban centers after completion of their studies and by traveling extensively in Iran, where they maintained a dialogue with the Qajar monarchs, the ruling princes, and the urban notables.

The second group of the ʿulama often came from humble origins in the towns and villages of central and northern Iran. They began to arrive in the ʿAtabāt in the late eighteenth century, usually after completing their preliminary studies in Isfahan, Qazvin, Qum, Mashhad, and other religious centers. Their long residence in the ʿAtabāt studying under eminent teachers and acquiring authorization *(ijāza)* to exercise ijtihād usually acquainted them with certain norms and values, and gave them a sense of group solidarity, characteristic of all the Uṣūlī ʿulama in the nineteenth century. A majority of them made the main provincial centers of Iran their permanent

---

Akhbār [Tehran, 1314/1897] (see *al-Dharīʿa* I, 269), while accepting logical reasoning in principle, favors more subtle methods of deduction.

[10] A full account of Bihbahānī's students appears in *Vaḥīd* 208–335 (cf. *QU* 125–98 and *MA* I, 231–33) which gives the biography of thirty-one individuals.

[11] *Al-Dharīʿa* 45. For the author see *EI*[2]: KĀSHIF al-GHIṬĀ' (W. Madelung); *QU* 183, 188–98; *TAS* II/1, 248–52; *Vaḥīd* 246–57.

[12] *Al-Dharīʿa* XVII, 202–3 and *TAS* II/1, 52–55. For the author see *QU* 180–83; *MA* III, 911–19; *Vaḥīd* 256–65.

[13] *QU* 175–80; *RJ* 414; *MA* III, 901–11; *Vaḥīd* 240–46.

[14] For their account see *QU* 124–29; *Vaḥīd* 342–56.

[15] For descendants of Bihbahānī see *Vaḥīd* 356–401.

[16] For their account see *QU* 183–88.

residence, only a few remaining to achieve high positions in the ʿAtabāt. Toward the middle of the century some reached the position of "headship" (*riyāsa*).[17] Both in Iraq and in Iran, these ʿulama trained a larger number of students and established a vast network of Uṣūlī mujtahids, who dominated the religious and educational activities in Persian cities.[18]

The third group of high-ranking ʿulama consisted of mujtahids who had studied in the ʿAtabāt under Uṣūlī teachers but also held hereditary offices such as *imām jumʿa* (leader of the Friday communal prayer) and *shaykh al-Islām* (chief religious judge) of large cities. They retained their traditional positions, some dating from the time of the Safavids, often carrying status, influence, and economic privileges. Throughout the nineteenth century these religious officials, usually in competition with other mujtahids, acted as the judges and even the executors of sharīʿa as well as the official representatives of the ʿulama class. No doubt the support given by the government assisted them in maintaining such authority, but cases of conflict with the state as well as with other prominent members of the ʿulama class were not rare. The Khātūnābādī imām jumʿas in Isfahan and later Tehran are one of the oldest families of the ʿulama in Iran, and other clerical families in all major cities enjoyed similar influence and esteem.[19]

These three groups formed the highest layers of a religious establishment that included other groups of middle- and lower-ranking clergy. The middle ranks, included the lesser-educated clergy in the smaller towns and large

[17]Sayyid Ibrāhīm Qazvīnī in Karbalā' and Shaykh Muḥammad Ḥasan Najafī (Iṣfahānī) in Najaf are two examples.

[18]In Isfahan, Sayyid Muḥammad Bāqir Shaftī, Ḥājjī Ibrāhīm Karbāsī, Muḥammad Taqī, and Muḥammad Ḥusayn Najafī; in Qazvin, Sayyid Muḥammad Bāqir Qazvīnī and the Baraghānī brothers (Mullā Muḥammad Ṣāliḥ, Mullā Muḥammad Taqī, and Mullā ʿAlī); in Kashan, the Narāqīs (Mullā Mahdī, his son Mullā Aḥmad, his grandson Mullā Muḥammad, and others); in Tabriz, Mīrzā Aḥmad Mujtahid, and Mullā Muḥammad Mamaqānī (a Shaykhī); in Shiraz, Ḥājjī Muḥammad Ḥasan Qazvīnī Shīrāzī, Ḥājjī Mīrzā Ibrāhīm Fasā'ī, Shaykh Ḥusayn Nāẓim al-Sharīʿa, Ḥājjī Shaykh Mahdī Kujūrī, and Mullā Muḥammad Maḥallātī; in Kirman, Sayyid Jawād Shīrāzī; in Kirmānshāh, Āqā Muḥammad ʿAlī Bihbahānī; in Zanjān, Mīrzā Muḥammad Zanjānī; in Bārfurūsh, Mīrzā Saʿīd Bārfurūshī; in Tehran, Mullā Āqā Darbandī and later Mullā ʿAlī Kanī; and, in Mashhad, Sayyid Muḥammad Qaṣīr Rażavī (and other Rażavīs) are only a few better-known Uṣūlī mujtahids of the time.

[19]For the imām jumʿas of Isfahan see *MA* II, 314–20 (and other individual entries). For relation to imām jumʿas of Tehran see *MA* II, 547–79. Also Muḥammad Ḥasan Khān Iʿtimād al-Salṭana *al-Ma'āthir wa'l-Āthār* (Tehran, 1306/1888) 141–42. For Shaykh al-Islāms of Isfahan see *MA* 820–28. For imām jumʿas of Shiraz see *FN* II, 61–62; *TAS* II/1, 28–29. For Shaykh al-Islām of Shiraz see *FN* II, 27–28. For Shaykh al-Islāms of Tabriz see Nādir Mīrzā *Tārīkh va Jughrāfī-yi Tabrīz* (Tehran, 1323/1905) 222–27; Muḥammad ʿAlī Qāżī *Khāndān-i ʿAbd al-Wahhāb; TAS* II/1, 57, 209; *MA* III, 701–3. For imām jumʿas of Tabriz see *TAS* II/1, 77, 168; *al-Ma'āthir wa'l-Āthār* 173–74. For imām jumʿas of Mashhad see *MA* II, 399–400; *al-Ma'āthir wa'l-Āthār* 156; Muḥammad Ḥasan Khān Iʿṭimād al-Salṭana *Maṭlaʿ al-Shams* 3 vols. (Tehran, 1300–1303/1882–1885) II, 397. For imām jumʿas of Zanjān see *al-Ma'āthir wa'l-Āthār* 149; *TAS* I/1, 61–62; *MA* III, 780–82; also Ibrāhīm Zanjānī Mūsawī *Tārīkh-i Zanjān, ʿUlamā' va Dānishmandān* (Tehran, n.d.) 175–86.

villages, the aides and entourage of prominent mujtahids, teachers at the intermediary level in the local madrasa, and secretaries of the religious courts. The lower ranks included the professional reciters of religious tragedies and martyrdoms of the Imams *(rawża khwāns)* and other "preachers of the pulpit," high- and low-level seminarians, teachers of the Qur'ānic schools and instructors of the elementary level, deacons, and low-level trustees of shrines, mosques, and madrasas, semiprofessional and rural mullas and *sayyids* (descendants of the House of the Prophet) with no fixed occupations. These middle- and lower-ranking clerics provided an important support for the mujtahids. Financially and hierarchically dependent on their superiors, they often functioned as a means of influence and if necessary instruments of propaganda and incitement in the community.

The lower ranks of this informal hierarchy did not always remain wholly loyal to the upper echelons, however. Many sparks of protest, dissidence, and revolt first flared among these very groups, sometimes reacting against the domination of the mujtahids. It took a long time, however, before these scattered signs of discontent developed into any significant movement of protest. The loosely formed hierarchy of the Shiʿite ʿulama, largely based on personal loyalties, allowed occasional upsurges of discontent but also prevented a durable and concerted reaction. Hence, up to the first quarter of the nineteenth century, the voice of the higher ʿulama expressed that of the greater part of the religious community.

Thanks to the Uṣūlī doctrine of active practice of the sharīʿa, the ʿulama successfully monopolized all rights to interpretation of the sources and body of the law. Moreover, they effectively controlled civil and commercial courts and even tried to expand to the sphere of criminal law, leaving limited room for the secular judicial system *(ʿurf)* administered by the government. They also enjoyed largely independent economic resources. These advantages gave them not only the necessary means to support their students, aides, and subordinates, but also a powerful leverage in their dealings with the government and other urban groups, most noticeably merchants and landlords. Eventually some of the ʿulama themselves entered the economic market. The absence of a centralized judicial authority, the chronic weaknesses of the state in controlling its own agencies, and the common misappropriation of endowment revenues, among other factors, provided powerful incentives for the ʿulama to venture into trade, agriculture, moneylending, and property, often commissioning the same merchants and small landowners as their agents.[20] Some mujtahids such as Sayyid Muḥammad Bāqir Shaftī, the Imām Jumʿas of Isfahan, the Baraghānīs of Qazvin, and the Shaykh al-Islāms of Tabriz owed their power and influence, more than

[20]See below, chap. 8, the case of the Nahrī brothers in Isfahan and their cooperation with both Muḥammad Bāqir Shaftī and Sayyid Muḥammad Imām Jumʿa.

anything else, to the very economic power that elevated them above other teachers and jurists.

The integration of this clerical body into a more coherent entity, in such a manner that it could guarantee the predominance of the mujtahids, necessitated the adoption of more systematic lines of authority. Above all, the recognition of a "head" *(raʾīs)* was intended to fulfill the need for a superior model who, by embodying both rational capacity and moral piety, could sanctify the righteousness of the entire hierarchy. In the late eighteenth century, perhaps with some attention to the great scholars of the past and in comparison with the Sunnī religious hierarchy, Āqā Muḥammad Bāqir Bihbahānī was acknowledged as the "master of all," the "unique," and the "promoter" of the modern Uṣūlī school.[21] Some scholars, most of them Bihbahānī's own students, regarded him as "the renewer of the beginning of the century," a concept more familiar in Sunnī than in Shiʿite thought.[22]

For several decades after Bihbahānī, however, the problem of recognition of a head remained unresolved. Some regarded Bihbahānī's prominent student Sayyid Mahdī Baḥr al-ʿUlūm as the most eminent of the teachers of the ʿAtabāt,[23] yet for almost four decades, from his early death (1212/1797) up to the mid-1840s, no Shiʿite divine emerged as the sole leader of the community. This was probably because few of Bihbahānī's students enjoyed an equal degree of academic respect and popular support.[24] Later, however, when almost all the students of the first generation had died, a few mujtahids of the second generation emerged simultaneously as leaders.[25] The collective leadership achieved in the mid-nineteenth century, however, did not, perhaps could not, claim superiority in jurisdiction and universal constituency over the entire community. Rather, clergy and lay followers alike regarded the collective leadership as a symbol of conciliation between worldly achievement and moral rectitude. In the second half of the century, however, Shaykh Murtażā Anṣārī (d. 1281/1864) and after him Mīrzā Ḥasan Shīrāzī (d. 1312/1895) emerged as the "source of emulation" *(marjaʿ-i taqlīd),* and their status was acknowledged by most ʿulama of both Arab and Persian origins.[26]

[21]*QU* 198–99; cf. *MA* I, 222–23, and *Vaḥīd* 152–62, which all give various titles quoted by the contemporary sources.

[22]Both Bihbahānī and his student and colleague Sayyid Muḥammad Mahdī Baḥr al-ʿUlūm quoted traditions (apparently from Sunnī sources) regarding the emergence of centennial *murawwij* during the period of the Greater Occultation, perhaps with some sense of self-attribution. See *Vaḥīd* 152–61.

[23]For his details see below, this chapter.

[24]Most notably Jaʿfar Najafī, Baḥr al-ʿUlūm, and Abul-Qāsim Qumī.

[25]During the 1820s and 1840s, Sayyid Muḥammad Ṭabāṭabāʾī, Sayyid Muḥammad Bāqir Shaftī (Ḥujjat al-Islām), Sayyid Ibrāhīm Qazvīnī, Shaykh Ḥasan Kāshif al-Ghiṭāʾ, and Shaykh Muḥammad Ḥasan Najafī were considered the chief religious authorities.

[26]For the evolution of *marjaʿīya* see A. Amanat "In Between the *Madrasa* and the Mar-

Beyond its legal and judicial implications, the emergence of the head reflected a profound need in the religious community for a spiritual model. Though the Uṣūlī doctrine equipped the high-ranking ʿulama with the weapon of ijtihād, its limited rationalism lacked the spiritual dimension necessary to uphold the mujtahids' prestige in the eyes of their followers. To compensate for this shortcoming, attributions of such unworldly qualities as piety, lack of temporal desire, devotion, and asceticism are frequently found in reference to prominent mujtahids. (Their exaggerated pietistic behavior and many of their devotional characteristics can be interpreted as attempts to compensate for excessive worldly attachments.)

Thus claims to the "general deputyship" of the Imam, as it was first adopted by Bihbahānī and his students (especially Shaykh Jaʿfar Najafī), relied not merely on the rationale of ijtihād. Nor were these claims introduced solely as means of justifying the practical benefits of leadership, namely the exclusive reception of the newly revived "share of the Imam." With all its emphasis on logical queries, Uṣūlism was still not free, at least in practice, from elements of nonrationality essential for legitimizing its superior stance. When, for instance, Bihbahānī announced in the shrine of Ḥusayn in Karbalāʾ that he was "the Proof of God" he did not mean to proclaim a messianic message.[27] What he implied was the superiority of his Uṣūlī approach over the Akhbārī creed. This is further evidenced when he continues by denouncing Baḥrānī, the chief of the Akhbārīs and his own teacher, and demanding a place in his pulpit and requiring Baḥrānī's students to attend his lectures.[28] Indeed, Bihbahānī's logical approach would not have allowed him to expect an obscure savior who was supposed to appear under the most unimaginable circumstances. Rather, his Uṣūlīsm would permit the spiritual guidance of the Imam to be manifested in general deputyship of the mujtahids.[29] But judgments were not only achieved by mere rational "effort," but also by an intuitive and illuminative perception from the word of the infallible Prophet and the Imams. This latter concept was an Akhbārī legacy that, having some precedent through past Shiʿite scholars from Bahāʾal-Dīn ʿĀmilī and Fayż Kāshānī to Muḥammad Taqī and Muḥammad Bāqir Majlisī, found some resonance among Uṣūlīs. From the 1770s onward, in spite of a general orientation of the ʿulama to consolidate the foundations of fiqh, examples of asceticism and mystical experience were

---

ketplace: The Designation of Clerical Leadership in Modern Shiʿism" in *Authority and Political Culture in Shiʿism* ed. S. A. Arjamand (Albany, 1988) 98-132.

27 Shaykh ʿAbdullāh Mamaqānī *Tanqīḥ al-Maqāl* cited in *Vaḥīd* 144–45.

28 Ibid.

29 In one of his sermons, Bihbahānī even implied the futility of awaiting the "Resurgence" (Khurūj) of the Imam, arguing that present circumstances would not tolerate the austerity and burden of his advent. This claim temporarily put him out of favor and even endangered his life. Shaykh ʿAlī Akbar Nahāvandī *Khazīnat al-Jawāhir*, quoted in *Vaḥīd* 166–68.

extant, often at peace with Shiʿite orthodoxy. Although at first glance these intuitive experiences seem to fall strictly within the lawful framework of sharīʿa, upon closer examination they reveal traces of gnostic and even protomessianic trends.

Signs of intuitive experiences, asceticism, ultraphysical visitations of the Imams, and holy dreams parallel to the preoccupation with fiqh first appear in Sayyid Mahdī Baḥr al-ʿUlūm, whose efforts to bring together intuition and reason make him an interesting case.[30] While his association with Bihbahānī qualified him as one of the pillars of the Uṣūlī school, his former tutelage under the Akhbārīs, plus his studies of theosophy and mysticism under Abul-Qāsim Khātūnābādī and Quṭb al-Dīn Nayrīzī, introduced him to less orthodox subjects.[31] It is not known to what extent the seclusion of his last years were due to ascetic motives, nor is it certain that his alleged interviews with Nūr ʿAlī Shāh,[32] an adept of the Niʿmatullāhī Sufi order, in Karbalāʾ converted him to Sufism. *Ṭarāʾiq al-Ḥaqāʾiq* reports that Nūr ʿAlī's popular preachings during his stay in the ʿAtabāt moved his opponents to seek the opinion of Baḥr al-ʿUlūm, who interviewed Nūr ʿAlī and was impressed by his character.[33] Baḥr al-ʿUlūm's sympathetic attitude toward the Niʿmatullāhīs should not be exaggerated, however. In a brief *fatwā* (legal opinion) directed to Āqā Muḥammad ʿAlī Bihbahānī son of Muḥammad Bāqir) on the question of the Niʿmatullāhīs' activities, he declared: "Beyond any doubt, the deviation of this condemned group from the path of rightfulness and true guidance, and their efforts to provoke discontent and to corrupt people of the cities, have become obvious and apparent."[34]

However, if his sympathetic attitude toward Sufis is in doubt, there is evidence supporting his preoccupation with mystical experiences. *Qiṣaṣ al-ʿUlamāʾ* refers to frequent retreats and excessive acts of devotion in the mosques of Sahla and Kūfa.[35] On a few occasions the author refers to "concealed secrets" and mystical encounters in the course of which he visited the Hidden Imam both in dreams and awake. During one such encoun-

[30]For Baḥr al-ʿUlūm see *RJ* 648–49; *QU* 168–74; *MA* II, 414–29; and *Vaḥīd* 212–36.

[31]*Vaḥīd* 224–32 cited a few anecdotes from various sources on his piety and mystical experiences. For the list of his works see *MA* II, 419–22. Among his works there is one commentary on *Sharḥ Risālat al-Sayr waʾl Sulūk* of Sayyid ibn Ṭāwūs in which Baḥr al-ʿUlūm has given his spiritual ancestry. For his alleged Sufi training see *TH* III, 217, 339.

[32]For details on Nūr ʿAlī Shāh see below, chap. 2.

[33]*TH* III, 199–200. In reply to Baḥr al-ʿUlūm's inquiry on the reason for his assuming the title *shāh,* Nūr ʿAlī replied that he has "sovereignty, domination, and power" over his own soul and that of the others.

[34]Abul-Fażl Burqaʿī *Haqīqat al-ʿIrfān* (Tehran, n.d.) 161. The problem of Baḥr al-ʿUlūm's Sufi affiliation became even more enigmatic when toward the end of the century a subbranch of Niʿmatullāhīs claimed a chain of spiritual descendancy through Baḥr al-ʿUlūm from Nūr ʿAlī Shāh. S. Parvīzī *Tadhkirat al-Awlīyāʾ* (Tabriz, 1333 Sh./1954) 88.

[35]*QU* 169, 171–74.

ter with the Hidden Imam, interestingly enough in reply to Baḥr al ʿUlum's enquiry on certain points of fiqh, he was instructed by the Imam "to follow the path of literal proofs in the affairs of religion."[36] These experiences, and other supernatural feats reported in biographical sources, served to sanctify use of intuitive method in the pursuit of jurisprudence; a method similar to that of some advocates of mystical knowledge. The fame achieved because of them, however, was effective to raise Baḥr al-ʿUlūm's status, and led some sources to suggest close association between him and the Imam of the Age.[37] A chronogram composed on his demise reads: "Mahdī of the Lord of the Age [the Hidden Imam] has passed away."[38]

Many students, including some of the most prominent mujtahids of the next generation, recognized Baḥr al-ʿUlūm as Bihbahānī's sole successor and considered him a model.[39] However, few of them seem to have ventured a serious intuitive approach. ʿAbd al-Ṣamad Hamadānī was later converted to the Niʿmatullāhī order,[40] whereas Mīrzā Muḥammad Akhbārī and Shaykh Aḥmad Aḥsāʾī, while remaining in the ranks of the ʿulama, maintained diverse esoteric interests.

In his unorthodox approach to the question of the cognition of the Imam, Mīrzā Muḥammad Nīshāpūrī, better known as Akhbārī (d. 1232/1817), a theologian and jurist of some caliber and chief advocate of later Akhbārīsm, went far beyond the mild asceticism of his teacher Baḥr al-ʿUlūm.[41] His strong reaction against the prevalence of Uṣūlism, and his efforts to re-introduce the declining Akhbārī school, made him a dangerous enemy of the religious establishment. To the mujtahids this was perhaps the most provoking challenge since the setback of the Niʿmatullāhīs about a decade earlier, at the turn of the nineteenth century.[42] In his writings, as in his frequent public debates with the prominent Usūlīs of his time, he sharply criticized the mujtahids' positions and their excessive use of logical devices.[43] He vehemently attacked three arch defenders of Uṣūlīsm. He criticized Mīrzā Abul-Qāsim Qumī and his disciples, for their domination of teaching circles. Sayyid ʿAlī Ṭabaṭabāʾī and his adherents, whom he called *Azāriqa*,[44] he

[36]Ibid. 173.

[37]Mīrzā Ḥusayn Ṭabarsī Nūrī *Dār al-Salām fīmā yuṭlaqu biʾl-ruʾyā waʾl-manām* 2 vols., (Tehran, 1306/1888) II, 391; cf. *RJ* 680.

[38]*MA* II, 427.

[39]For the list of his students see *MA* II, 423–25.

[40]*TH* III, 211–13 and *MA* II, 600–610. Ḥājjī Mīrzā Āqāsī was one of ʿAbd al-Ṣamad's disciples. See *EIr:* ĀQĀSĪ.

[41]For Akhbārī's account see *RJ* 653–54 (using Mīrzā Muḥammad's own biographical account in *Ṣaḥīfat al-Ṣafāʾ*) and *MA* III, 925–44.

[42]See below, chap. 2.

[43]*RJ* 518.

[44]This sarcastic epithet may have been given to Ṭabāṭabāʾī by allusion to the original Azāriqa, one of the main branches of Khārijites in the first century A. H., who believed that all other Muslims who hold beliefs opposed to theirs or all those who did not join their ranks were to be considered polytheists (ʿAbd al-Qāhir Baghdādī *al-Farq Bayn al-Firaq* Persian trans. M. J. Mashkūr *Tārīkh-i Maẕāhib-i Islām* [Tabriz, 1333 Sh.] 75–80; *EI*[2]: AZĀRIḲA [R. Rubinacci]).

attacked for their innovations in the field of fiqh and their deviations from the lawful framework of traditions. In his debates with Shaykh Jaʿfar Najafī, his skill in disputation many times silenced the old mujtahid.[45]

Although a traditional Akhbārī in his pursuit of law and doctrine, preoccupation with occult sciences gave Mīrzā Muḥammad Akhbārī the reputation of an eccentric with supernatural powers. During the Russo-Persian wars (1805–1813) he offered to bring Fatḥ ʿAlī Shāh the head of the Russian commander Tsitsianov by magic in exchange for eradication of the mujtahids' influence in Iran[46]—a bargain reminiscent of earlier attempts by Sufi figures to attract the secular power in the hope of defeating the ʿulama. He also produced a number of works on the subjects of the occult, of which *Anmūẕaj al-Murtāḍīn* (Manual for the Ascetics) is an example.[47] He was a prolific writer who, like his teacher Baḥr al-ʿUlūm and his contemporary Shaykh Aḥmad Aḥsāʾī, was known for his comprehensive knowledge *(jāmiʿīya)*.[48]

Akhbārī's views on the question of establishing contact with the Hidden Imam imply that contrary to the general deputyship of the Uṣūlīs, he considered the "gate of knowledge" *(bāb-i ʿilm)* open to those who can grasp the presence of the Imam by their intuitive experience.[49] An important passage in *Durr al-Thamīn* clearly underlines Akhbāri's views on the continuous existence of a "gate" or human mediator between the Hidden Imam and his followers.

> It should be realized that the pole of the progeny [of the Prophet] is the pole of poles who is also called the greatest aid. In his own time, he is the Riser [Qāʾim] and the Lord of the Age and the pole of the time and the heralder. Without his manifestation [Ẓuhūr], the Occultation of the Imām will not take place since according to rational norms it is obvious that if the conditions of the time necessitate the concealment of the Proof [*Ḥujja*], his gate [*bāb*] should inevitably be present in the community in order to settle the affairs of the people and resolve their doubts.[50]

Akhbārī's numerological prognostications also lay stress on expectations not unlike those of the contemporary Sufis or scholars like Shaykh Aḥmad

---

Hence Mīrzā Muḥammad condemns Ṭabāṭabāʾī and his adherents for their intolerance of non-Uṣūlīs.

45 *QU* 177–78.

46 The full account given by *NT* I, 143–45; cf. *QU* 179.

47 *RJ* 653; cf. *al-Dharīʿa* VIII, 267.

48 A list of fifty-eight works appears in *MA* III, 935–40. The term *jāmiʿīya* may more accurately be translated as comprehensive understanding of all the sciences of the age.

49 Discussed in his *Fatḥ al-Bāb ilā Ṭarīq al-Ḥaqq waʾl-Ṣawāb* (Baghdad, 1342/1923), and *Ḥadīqat al-Shuhūd*. See also *MA* 938 and *al-Dharīʿa* XVI, 105.

50 Cited in Ḥ. Farīd Gulpāygānī *Qānūn-i Asāsī-yi Islām* (Tehran, 1349 Sh./1970) 285. See also A. Munzavī *Fihrist-i Nuskhahā-yi Khaṭṭī-yi Fārsī* (Tehran, 1349 Sh./1970) II, 1, 941 for some details.

Aḥsā'ī and Sayyid Jaʿfar Dārābī (Kashfī).[51] In a cryptic poem, with reference to a tradition ascribed to ʿAlī, Akhbārī states: "In the year *ghars* [with the numerical value of 1260] the earth shall be illumined by His light, and in *gharasa* [1265] the world shall be suffused with His glory. If thou livest until the year *gharsī* [1270], thou shalt witness how the nations, the rulers, the people, and the faith of God shall all have been renewed."[52]

More than his speculations, it was his unreserved opposition to the mujtahids that put him in constant danger, and finally cost him his life. Charging him with heresy, blasphemy, and "constant abuse of the ʿulama," Shaykh Musā Najafī (son of Jaʿfar) issued a fatwā declaring that "his execution is a religious obligation, and whoever participates in the shedding of his blood, his entrance to Heaven will be guaranteed." The fatwā was signed by all the other prominent Uṣūlīs of the ʿAtabāt, and Mīrzā Muḥammad Akhbārī was killed by the mob in Kaẓimayn.[53]

The anti-Uṣūlī activism of Akhbārī was largely unprecedented, but his intuitive approach was not uncommon among distinguished divines of the period. A few decades earlier, Āqā Muḥammad Bīdābādī (d. 1197/1783), one of the last survivors of the old theosophical school of Isfahan, had shown an interest in mystical experiences. Though he had a conventional training, it was his interest in alchemy and other occult sciences (mainly derived from his family's mystical background) that made him popular, especially among the Sufis.[54] Though his alleged adherence to Quṭb al-Dīn Nayrīzī cannot be decisively proven,[55] his attachment to mysticism is apparent from his aphorisms and sermons.[56]

Another scholar, Sayyid Jaʿfar Dārābī (d. 1267/1851), known as Kashfī

[51]Zayn al-ʿAbīdīn Shīrvānī's *Bustān al-Sīyāḥa* ([Tehran, 1315/1897] 611) claims that Mīrzā Muḥammad Akhbārī was a friend and supporter of the Sufis and even alleges that he was himself affiliated to the Mahdīya order. Indeed, in *Nafthat al-Ṣudūr* Mīrzā Muḥammad devoted some parts to the refutation of the Sufis (*MA* III, 940).

[52]*Nabil* 49–50. Sayyid ʿAlī Muḥammad the Bab also seems to have been familiar with Akhbārī's speculations, as he wrote a commentary on his *al-Burhān fī al-Taklīf wa'l-Bayān* (Baghdad, 1341/1922) in which he criticized some of the author's views (*al-Dharīʿa* III, 92). To this criticism Mīrzā Muḥammad Bāqir Rashtī, one of Akhbārī's disciples, wrote a reply with the title *al-Kalimā al-Ḥaqqānīya*. In *Dalā'il-i Sabʿa*, the Bab refers to Akhbārī as one of those who forecast his imminent manifestation. He quotes him in a gathering in Kāẓimayn being asked about the Ẓuhūr of the Imam. Akhbārī pointed at one present, ʿAbd al-Ḥusayn Shūshtarī, assuring him, "You will witness the time of the Ẓuhūr" (Tehran(?), n.d., 59–60).

[53]Sayyid ʿAbdullāh Thiqat al-Islām *Lu'lu' al-Ṣadaf dar Tārīkh-i Najaf* (Isfahan, 1379/1959), 134–45. Shīrvānī in *Bustān al-Sīyāḥa* (610; cf. *NT* I, 83) states that he had even forecast his own death in a chronogram: "*ṣadūq ghuliba*" = 1232 (the truthful was overcome).

[54]For his biography see *MA* I, 66–70; *TH* III, 214–15; Rustam al-Ḥukamā' *Rustam al-Tawārīkh* 405–8; and ʿAbd al-Karīm Jazī *Rijāl-i Iṣfahān yā Tadhkirat al-Qubūr* ed. M. Mahdavī, 2 ed. (Isfahan [?] 1328 Sh./1949) 79–81.

[55]*TH* III, 215–19.

[56]*Tadhkirat al-Qubūr* 81.

(intuitionist),[57] claimed a similar intuitive knowledge. He was a grandson of Shaykh Ḥusayn Āl ʿUṣfūr, a well-known Akhbārī scholar who himself was the nephew of Shaykh Yūsuf Baḥrānī.[58] Shaykh Ḥusayn was a key figure in the diffusion of the Baḥrainī school both in the ʿAtabāt and in southern Iran, and it is not unlikely that his views influenced his grandson. When Kashfī for example declares that through a holy dream he has realized that the Friday communal prayer during the Greater Occultation is unlawful, he echoes an Akhbārī view.[59] The symbolic significance of this statement lies in the fact that it allows the exercise of religious authority only after the Advent of the Imam. Whoever conducts this prayer, Kashfī pointed out, "is ambitious for riyāsa [headship] and is a usurper of the right position of the venerable Imam."[60] Moreover, Kashfī questioned the veracity of the "seekers of riyāsa" neither by authority of traditions nor by exercise of logical deduction but by relying on dreams and intuition.

The attitude is shared by Mullā Asadullāh Burūjirdī Ḥujjat al-Islām (d. 1271/1854),[61] who appears to have had Uṣūlī ties. He claimed to be the most learned of all the ʿulama, mainly on the ground that "the door of the divine knowledge" was not closed to him. He was also known for his intuitions and his ascetic devotion. He claimed that these merits came to him as a result of a *tauqīʿ* (ordinance) from the Hidden Imam.[62]

In spite of occasional manifestations of an intuitive method, the remnants of Akhbārism or offshoots of this school, which employed intuition as an alternative to inquiry, largely lacked the necessary impulse to leave a permanent mark. The general current of Uṣūlī orthodoxy, then in full spate, was powerful enough to be unaffected by any outburst of dissent. In its evolution toward orthodoxy, Uṣūlism employed limited reasoning not to present a new alternative to the time-honored values of the past, but to reassert them. In the process mainstream Shiʿism rejected the primitive Traditionism, but it could not fully erradicate the influence of esoterism, ascetic practices, and intuitive aspirations. These survived and developed in learned circles parallel to the growth of Uṣūlī thought and institutions. As the two interpretations became increasingly distinct from each other, the intuitive approach, in its search for suprarational cognition, emphasized the need for continuity in divine guidance and called for charismatic leadership. These aspirations, deeply rooted in the mystical and theosophic traditions of the past, reemerged in the Shaykhi school.

[57]For Kashfī see below, chap. 4.

[58]For Shaykh Ḥusayn and his relationship with Shaykh Yūsuf and with Kashfī and for the Āl ʿUṣfūr see *FN* II, 236; *MA* II, 569–73 (and cited sources); and *TAS* II/1, 427–29.

[59]Sayyid Jaʿfar Kashfī *Kifāyat al-Itām fī Maʿārif al-Aḥkām,* cited in *MA* V, 1856.

[60]Ibid.

[61]For his account see *al-Maʾāthir waʾl-Āthār* 140, and *TAS* II/1, 128.

[62]*Al-Maʾāthir* 140.

The Shaykhi School

With Shaykh Aḥmad Aḥsā'ī (1166–1241/1756–1825) and his visionary theophany, Shiʿism generated a synthesis essential for the later formation of the Babi thought. The Babi movement derived both its theoretical formulation and its converts more from Shaykhism than from any other school. Such a continuity in esoteric thought can be best appreciated when Shaykhism in itself is considered as the final outcome of a fusion of three major trends in post-Safavid Shiʿism: (1) the Ṣadrā'ī theosophic school of Isfahan, which itself benefited from the theoretical Sufism of Ibn ʿArabī, as well as the illuminist theosophy of Suhravardī; (2) the Akhbārī Traditionist school of Bahrain, which traced its chain of transmission to the early narrators of ḥadīth and (3) the diffuse gnosticism that was strongly influenced by crypto-Ismāʿīlī ideas as well as other heterodoxies of southern and southwestern Iran. However, this syncretism, the zenith of late eighteenth-century Shiʿite universality, does not detract from the originality of Aḥsā'ī's thought. For a time he successfully incorporated the two diverse worlds of jurisconsults and the theosophists, the exoteric (ẓāhir) and the esoteric (bāṭin), into one comprehensive system that he believed could compensate for the weaknesses of both worlds. To achieve an overall cohesion[63] and arrive at what Aḥsā'ī himself refers to as the status of the Perfect Shiʿa *(al-Shīʿa al-Kāmil)* required as much philosophical skepticism as intuitive experience and knowledge of fiqh and Traditions. Such a goal had been pursued in Islamic intellectual history for centuries, from the Ismāʿīlī hermeneutics of Nāṣir Khusrau (d. circa 1072–1077) and others to the theosophy of Shihāb al-Dīn Suhravardī (d. 1191), the theology of Rajab Bursī (fourteenth century) and Ibn Abī Jumhūr Aḥsā'ī (early sixteenth century) and later in the Safavid period the theosophy of Mullā Ṣadrā. But Aḥsā'ī's thought, which called not only for reconciliation between theosophy (ḥikma) and sharīʿa but for application of his theological approach to fundamental issues of prophecy and resurrection ventured on new ground.

Aḥsā'ī's articulations in two major areas—the problem of spiritual legitimacy delegated by the Imam and the esoteric interpretation of Maʿād, the core of his eschatological theory—were in obvious contrast to Uṣūlī premises.[64] As with the early Niʿmatullāhīs and later with Mīrzā Muḥammad

[63]H. Corbin, *L'École Shaykhie en théologie Shīʿite* (extract from *L'Annuaire de l'Ecole Pratique des Hautes Etudes, Section des Sciences Religieuses* 1960–1961) (Tehran, 1967) 3.

[64]On the theoretical aspects of Shaykhism see H. Corbin *L'École Shaykhie*; idem. *Terre céleste et corps de résurrection* (Paris, 1960), 99–174 (trans. N. Pearson as *Spiritual Body and Celestial Earth* [Princeton, 1977] 51–105); idem. *En Islam iranien* IV, livre VI, 205–300. Also A. L. M. Nicolas *Essai sur le Chéïkhisme* III: *La doctrine* (extract from *Revue du Monde Musulman)* (Paris, 1911) and IV: *La science de Dieu* (Paris, 1911); *TN* II, 234–44; *NK* (Persian introduction, pp. *kāf-yā vāv,* English introduction, xx–xxiii). For the treatment of the Shaykhi doctrine by the later Shaykhi writers see the wide range of works catalogued in *Fibrist*

Akhbārī, attempts were made to isolate Shaykhism almost to the point of total denunciation. This was a formidable challenge, since Shaykhism was equally at home with Shiʿite hadith and jurisprudence as with ḥikma discourses. Aḥsāʾī's concept of transmission relied on the Akhbārī school, without being totally restrained by its limitations. Whereas the Akhbārīs based their conclusions on traditions, Aḥsāʾi asserted his propositions more on the basis of intuition.

During his elementary education, Aḥsāʾī may have been exposed to some local esoteric trends in his homeland, al-Aḥsāʾ.[65] Corbin tends to believe that he was a noninitiated mystic with no formal training except a "*suprasensible* [invisible] guide."[66] There is reason to believe that by way of self-education he benefited from available sources in his vicinity. Tunkābunī implies in *Qiṣaṣ al-ʿUlamāʾ* that Aḥsāʾī had access to the remnants of Ibn Abī Jumhūr Aḥsāʾī's library, and found many points in common with his forebear in delving into his books.[67] Indeed, considering the local scholars' care and attention in preserving their precious collections,[68] it is possible that some of the texts had survived to Shaykh Aḥmad's Aḥsāʾī's time. The fact that his views on many subjects resemble those of Ibn Abī Jumhūr also supports this premise.[69] Moreover, the continuous contacts of the Baḥraynī ʿulama with centers of learning in Iran throughout the seventeenth and eighteenth centuries made possible the diffusion of some theological trends

---

II, 360–653. Of these the most comprehensive are Ḥājjī Muḥammad Karīm Khān Kirmānī *Irshād al-ʿAwāmm* 5th ed., 4 vols. (Kirman, 1353–1355 Sh./1974–1976); idem. *Ṭarīq al-Najāt* 2d ed. (Kirman, 1355 Sh./1976); Ḥājjī Muḥammad Khān Kirmānī *Yanābīʿ al-Ḥikma* 3 vols. (Kirman, 1383–1396/1963–1976); Abul-Qāsim Khān Ibrāhīmī Kirmānī *Tanzīh al-Awlīyāʾ* (Kirman, 1367/1947). For a non-Shaykhi point of view see Ismāʿīl Ṭabarsī Nūrī *Kifāyat al-Muwaḥḥidīn* 3 vols. (Tehran, n.d.) I.

65Shaykh Aḥmad Aḥsāʾī's short autobiography (cited in *Fihrist* I, 132–43) is particularly interesting because of his account of dreams and spiritual experiences. Other biographies were also produced by Shaykhi writers. Shaykh ʿAbdullāh ibn Aḥmad Aḥsāʾī wrote an account of his father's life, *Risāla-yi Sharḥ-i Aḥvāl-i Shaykh Aḥmad ibn Zayn al-Dīn Aḥsāʾī* Persian trans. Muḥammad Ṭāhir Kirmānī 2d ed. (Kirman, 1387/1967). Also Āqā Sayyid Hādī Hindī *Tanbīh al-Ghāfilīn wa Surūr al-Nāẓirīn* and ʿAlī Naqī Qumī (Hindī) *Nūr al-Anwār*. More scattered references are to be found in Sayyid Kāẓim Rashtī *Dalīl al-Mutaḥayyirīn* (Kirman, n.d.) (Persian trans. Muḥammad Riżā in 1261/1845, [Tehran, n.d.]) and Muḥammad Karīm Khān Kirmānī *Hidāyat al-Ṭālibīn* 2d ed. (Kirman, 1380/1960). Of Shiʿite biographers, *RJ* (25–26, 285–86) and *TH* (III, 337–79) give the most impartial accounts, whereas *QU* (34–43) gives a distorted view. *TAS* II/1, 88–91 and *MA* (IV) cite new sources. In the Babi and Bahāʾī sources, *NK* (99–100), *Nabil* (1–18), and *Qazvīnī* (447–57) provide some additional information. *L'École Shaykhie* (9–24) and A. L. M. Nicolas *Essai sur le Chéïkisme* I: *Cheïkh Ahmed Lahçahi* (Paris, 1910) also give accounts of his life.

66*L'École Shaykhie* 12.

67*QU* 35.

68See, for example, the efforts of Shaykh Yūsuf Baḥrānī and his father to preserve their books at the time of insecurity and strife in Bahrain. *(Lu'lu't al-Baḥrayn* cited in *QU* 271).

69For Ibn Abī Jumhūr see W. Madelung "Ibn Abī Ǧumhūr al-Aḥsāʾī's Synthesis of *Kalām*, Philosophy and Sufism" in *Acts du 8me Congrès de l'Union Européenne des Arabisants et Islamisants* (Aix-en-Provence, 1978), 147–56 and the cited sources. Also *RJ* 595–98 and Mīrzā Ḥusayn Ṭabarsī Nūrī *Mustadrak al-Wasāʾil* 3 vols. (Tehran, 1321/1903) III 361–65.

and even the circulation of religious and philosophical texts, in a remote area like al-Aḥsā'. Aḥsā'ī's son, on the other hand, in a biographical account of his father, states that in al-Aḥsā' the majority of the Sunnī population had Sufi tendencies. The remaining Ithnā ʿAsharī Shiʿites were dominated by dogmatic literalists "who had nothing to do with theosophy, let alone with the secrets of creation." This attitude, he maintains, obliged Shaykh Aḥmad Aḥsā'ī to emigrate to Iraq "in the hope of finding someone who could sympathize with his views."[70]

In the ʿAtabāt, his attendance at the lectures of Uṣūlīs like Bihbahānī, ʿAlī Ṭabāṭabā'ī, and possibly Jaʿfar Najafī, and his acquiring further authorizations from Akhbārīs such as Ḥusayn Āl ʿUṣfūr, did not convert him to either of these two schools. The ascetic practices of Baḥr al-ʿUlūm,[71] however, might have had special appeal. Aḥsā'ī had earlier experienced revelatory dreams and visions in which he claimed to have contacted the holy Imams and even received instructions from them.[72] The symbolic interpretations of these dreams and his preoccupation with life hereafter provided a ground for the young man to posit the existence of an intermediary world beyond terrestrial life, and to lay the basis for future visionary experiences.

In his keen interest in occult sciences in general and alchemy in particular, Aḥsā'ī bore some resemblance to a few of his contemporaries, but his use of occult symbolism was more for the purpose of explaining his philosophical methodology. In his discussions of the transcendental evolution of the body and soul, he frequently draws analogies with the alchemical process,[73] attaining an intuitive perception of the complex states of man's existence through the metaphor of alchemy.

Aḥsā'ī employed holy dreams, asceticism, and occult sciences as symbolic devices in a complex eschatological system in which the nature of both the individual and collective resurrections are considered at great length. In his theory of the hereafter, in a cyclic process, a divine substance accompanies man's spirit in its descent from the realm of the eternal truth to earth, and after passing through earthly life, eventually reascends to its origin. In this journey, man's being also passes through an intermediary realm that belongs neither to elemental existence nor to the realm of eternal truth.

This celestial world of *Hūrqalyā*, a purifying stage of archetypal purga-

[70]*Sharḥ-i Aḥvāl* 17–18.

[71]For his list of *ijāzāt* see *TAS* II/1, 91; cf. *Fihrist* II, 162–63. Nearly all sources agree that Aḥsā'ī studied under Baḥr al-ʿUlūm.

[72]For his recollection of his dreams and experiences in childhood see his autobiography in *Fihrist* I, 136–42. See below, chap. 3, for comparison with the Bab's experiences in childhood.

[73]A comparison between the alchemical process and spiritual perfection appears, for example, in Aḥsā'ī's *Risālat al-Khāqānīya* in *Jawāmiʿ al-Kalim* (collection of his tracts and treatises) 2 vols. (Tabriz, 1273–1276/1856–1859), II, part 1, 122–24; and *Sharḥ Kitāb al-Ḥikmat al-ʿArshīya* (of Mullā Ṣadrā) Tabriz, 1278/1861) 165–66, 331–32. Also frequent references to the use of the occult sciences and science of letters (*ḥurūf*) in his works appear in *Fihrist* II, 227 (no. 18 and 19), 229 (no. 27), 255 (no. 100, *Risālat al-Tubilīya).*

tory (*barzakh*) through which all beings must pass before being finally judged on the Day of Resurrection, is of cardinal importance in Aḥsāʾī's scheme. It is the "earth" of the soul, "a world whose state is neither the absolutely subtle state of separate substances, nor the opaque density of the material things of our world."[74]

Corresponding to the two-dimensional existence conceived by Aḥsāʾī, man's being is comprised of a twofold accidental body and a twofold essential body.[75] The elemental corpse, which is a compound of physical elements, perishes after death, decomposes to its original elements, and will never return; the spiritual corpse, accompanied by the celestial body and the essential body, ascends to the world of Hūrqalyā. The threefold body remains in this celestial conservatory, till the Last Day when man will be resurrected to meet the final judgment and claim a new elemental existence. Then he will again be stripped of all bodily existence (except the essential body) in order to be reunited with the original essence.

> Thus when the spirit enters post mortem the world of barzakh [purgatory], it exists there in the archetypal body, to which a body originating in this barzakh provisionally adheres. In fact the latter is not a part of it, but is a temporary accident. On the Resurrection Day, man in his wholeness returns and leaves behind him that which was not part of him, which was not *himself*. Compare this: Break your seal; see how the form of it departs. Refashion it, now you see the first seal, returned to its original form, identical to itself. Nevertheless, the first form has not returned and never will. This is the esoteric meaning of the verse: "Each time their skin is consumed, we will replace it with another skin."[76]

To emphasize his point, Aḥsāʾī quotes a verse by Jaʿfar Ṣādiq: "It is the same and yet it is another."[77]

The theme of multifold existence was posited by earlier thinkers. A parallel is found in Platonic archetypal images as they are interpreted among neo-Platonists.[78] It can also be observed in Suhravardī, who uses the term *Hūrqalyā* to describe the location of his intuitive experience.[79] Aḥsāʾī acknowledged that he adopted the Syriac term *Hūrqalyā* from the Sabeans (Mandaeans) of Baṣra.[80] As Corbin points out, Aḥsāʾī's concept of Hūrqalyā

[74]Aḥsāʾī *Risāla*, in reply to Mullā Muḥammad Anārī in *Jawāmiʿ al-Kalim* I/3, 153–54 (trans. cited in *Terre Céleste* 297, English trans. 193).

[75]Extracts from Aḥsāʾī *Sharḥ al-Ziyāra al-Jāmʿia al-Kabīra* 2 vols. (Tabriz, 1276/1856); 4th ed. 4 vols. (Kirman, 1355 Sh./1976) cited in *Terre Céleste,* 146–64, 281–92, trans. 180–89.

[76]Qurʾān IV, 59.

[77]Reply to Anārī I/3, 154 (*Terre Céleste* 299, trans. 195).

[78]*Terre Céleste* 148–51, trans. 92–95.

[79]Ibid. (189–212; trans. 118–34) cites extracts from Suhravardī's works on the subject of Hūrqalyā.

[80]Reply to Anārī I/3, 153 (*Terre Céleste* 259, trans. 191–92).

corresponds to the world of doubles or celestial images in Mandaean cosmology.[81]

More significantly, the presence of mystical intuition *(kashf)* and the intermediary world of immortal images together with an esoteric interpretation of Shiʿite theology and Traditions, bears out the possibility of Ibn Abī Jumhūr Aḥsāʾī's influence on Shaykh Aḥmad Aḥsāʾī. Ibn Abī Jumhūr maintains that "the Imam's soul does not disintegrate at the time of death." Souls of other people, depending on the forms they have acquired through good and evil actions, will either enter the "world of images" in incorporal shape and enjoy its pleasures, or will be returned to the earth to endure punishment in the bodies of lowly animals.[82] The concept of transmigration, as it appears in Ibn Abī Jumhūr's work is foreign to Aḥsāʾī but on the point of the minor resurrection (the individual resurrection of man in the intermediary world), some resemblance can be discerned. In more modern times, Fayż Kāshānī describes purgatory as "a world through which bodies are spiritualized, and spirits embodied."[83]

Aḥsāʾi's definition of the celestial world pointed in a messianic direction. By introducing this intermediary stage, he tried to resolve some of the major obstacles in the way of Shiʿite eschatological thinking. First by esoteric interpretation of the Qurʾānic verses or the Shiʿite Traditions, Aḥsāʾī redefined the concept of resurrection contrary to the view held by the literalists. The survival of the spiritual being in the world of Hūrqalyā, removes the problem of corporal resurrection from the earthly grave. The bodily corpse perishes. The spiritual corpse, however, remains as a shapeless, luminous, and refined substance composed of elements of the world of Hūrqalyā, and will be resurrected and recast in a new, though identical, elemental corpse.

Aḥsāʾī describes the final resurrection of man as the last stage in the process of reunion between spirit and celestial body:

> When the divine will intends to renew creation and to cause the seeds from the preceding existence to germinate, Seraph is commanded to blow into the trumpet the breath of the great awakening. As opposed to the "blazing sound," this is a propulsive breath. Entering the sixth dwelling, it propels the intellect towards the *pneuma* [spirit] in the fifth dwelling; next it propels intellect and pneuma together toward the soul in the fourth dwelling; then it propels all three together, intellect, pneuma, and soul, toward the subtle consubstantial matter in the second dwelling; finally it propels all five toward the Image or archetypal form in the first dwelling. Then the "I" spirit finds again its composition and structure, its consciousness and capacity to feel.
>
> On the other hand, before the vibration of the breath of the great awakening,

[81] *Terre Céleste* 161–63, trans. 102–4.
[82] Madelung "Ibn Abī Ǧumhūr" 149.
[83] *Terre Céleste* 159, trans. 101.

> the water of the sea of Ṣād, situated below the Throne, comes down and rains over the surface of the earth. Then the spiritual body, made of the elements of Hūrqalyā, serves as a "vehicle" for the new form. . . . Its structure being completed, its "I" spirit enters it. This is what is meant when the "headstone of the tomb's bursting" is symbolically mentioned. For then the individual arises in his imperishable form, shaking the terrestrial dust from his head. "As you were made in the beginning, that you will again become," as it is said.[84]

The intermediary world provides a location for the visionary encounter with the Hidden Imam. The allegorical interpretation of the eschatological cities, which long preoccupied Shiʿite esoteric thinkers, provides a clue to the Imam's whereabouts. "When we speak of *Jābalqā* and *Jābarṣā,*" Aḥsāʾī writes, "we mean the lower regions of this intermediate world. Jābalqā is the city of the East, that is, in the direction of the beginning. Jābarṣā is the city of the West, that is, in the direction of the return and ending."[85] It is only in this visionary world of meditation that the existence of the Imam and his eternal presence can be experienced, and it is from this liminal world that the Imam will reappear. The placement of the Imam in this subtle, visionary state where he can be spiritually encountered rescues him from the obscure and inaccessible realm of the invisible and at the same time subjects his existence in the world of Hūrqalyā to limitations of time and space.

The tangle of confused Shiʿite Traditions and the orthodox eschatological literature produced on the subject of occultation had served to undermine the possibility of any tangible existence of the Imam, relegating him to the timeless oblivion of a never-coming future. The mainstream Shiʿite theology, discouraging a flesh-and-blood image of the Imam, replaced his authority with the general deputyship of the mujtahids. Aḥsāʾī's state of visionary existence, on the other hand, paved the way not only for contact with the Imam, but for his eventual reappearance into the world of elemental existence, by making it incumbent upon him to undertake an active responsibility toward the community.

The necessity for the Imam's direct guidance was never discussed beyond the point of metaphorical allusion, however. More clearly emphasized is the possibility of an encounter with the Imam in visions and holy dreams. Aḥsāʾī maintained that so long as the Imam remains in Occultation, while the world is still undergoing the process of final separation between good and evil, only presential knowledge can lead the seeking man to the Hidden Imam. Hūrqalyā is not only an intermediary world that one enters after physical death but is the very state of intuitive imagination accessible only by acquiring a transcendental consciousness. If thinking in a horizontal dimension enables man to grasp a static understanding of elemental cre-

[84]Ibid. 327, trans. 217–18. The verse referred to is from the Qurʾān VII, 28.
[85]Ibid. 295–96, trans. 192.

ation, the longitudinal dimension transcends him to the state of Hūrqalyā where he can attend the presence of the Imam.[86]

By introducing this longitudinal dimension in which the past is "under our feet" and not behind us, Aḥsā'ī proposes a historical consciousness shared by all those who are elevated to the state of presence but perfected only by one individual who can visualize this all-embracing state of consciousness in the person of the Hidden Imam. Such a concept was not without precedence in Islamic history. Both Ismāʿīlīsm and Sufism pondered the necessity of the perfect guide in the course of man's spiritual evolution. The Perfect Shiʿa or the Unique Speaker[87] in Shaykhism find counterparts in the Ismāʿīlī Speaker and the Sufi Perfect Man.[88] After the first three principles of the unity of God, prophethood, and recognition of the Imam, vicegerency (*wilāya*), which is defined as the position of the Perfect Shiʿa, becomes the Fourth Pillar of the Shaykhi doctrine. Henceforth the Perfect Shiʿa is the same gate or deputy who in the state of revelatory meditation comes into the presence of the Hidden Imam.[89]

These three aspects of Aḥsā'ī's thought—the redefinition of the resurrection of man, the location of the Imam in the intermediary world of Hūrqalyā, and the encounter between the Imam and the Perfect Shiʿa in the state of meditation—more than any other influenced the evolution of chiliastic

[86]*L'École Shaykhie* 15. Also see *Fihrist* II, 282–83, no. 124, and *Irshād al-Awāmm* II, 57–66.

[87]On *ṣāmit* (silent one) and *nāṭiq* see *Sharḥ al-Zīyāra* 4th ed., III 150–51, and two letters by Sayyid Kāẓim Rashtī, *Fihrist* I, 342–48.

[88]For comparison with the Sufi concept of *Insān-i Kāmil* see ʿAzīz al-Dīn Nasafī *Kitāb al-Insān al-Kāmil* ed. M. Molé (Tehran, 1962) 4–8 and EI^2: al-INSĀN al-KĀMIL (R. Arnaldez). For comparison with Suhravardī see *En Islam iranien* II, 67–80. After indicating different names and attributes of the Perfect Man by which he is identified in various trends and schools of thought, Nasafī maintains: "The Perfect Man is always [present] in the world and there is never more than one [at a time], inasmuch as all beings together are like one man, and the Perfect Man is the Heart of this man, and beings cannot live without a heart. . . .There are many wise men in the world but that which is the heart of the world may not be more than one. Others are at various stages, each at his own level. When that Unique One passes away, the next one reaches his level and seats himself in his place. Therefore the world [always] has its heart" *(al-Insān al-Kāmil* 4–5).

[89]Unlike the definition of *Shīʿa al-Kāmil,* the question of the Fourth Pillar always remained a controversial issue in the later Shaykhi school. Though there are occasional references in the works of Aḥsā'ī and Rashtī to *Arkān al-Arbaʿa* and *Rukn al-Rābiʿ* (e.g. *Sharḥ al-Zīyāra* 4th ed., I, 397–400; *Fihrist* I, 75–79) it is important to note that both writers in most of their general works (Aḥsā'ī *Ḥayāt al-Nafs* Wadham Collection, Oxford, MS no. 282, Persian trans. Sayyid Kāẓim Rashtī, 2d ed. [Kirman, n.d.]; and Sayyid Kāẓim Rashtī *Risāla-yi Fārsī dar Uṣūl-i ʿAqā'id* INBA. no. 4, I), complied with the categorization of the principles of religion *(uṣūl al-dīn).* Rashtī himself emphasizes *(Uṣūl-i ʿAqā'id* 41) that although divine justice *(ʿadl)* is one of the affirmative attributes and thus may not be considered as a principle, he nevertheless compiles his work with the traditional divisions. After the time of Rashtī, passing references to the Fourth Pillar appear in the early Babi works (*Qatīl* 513), but the main emphasis is in the works of Kirmānī Shaykhis. In *Fihrist* (79–112) Ibrāhīmī discusses the later Shaykhi opinion of the Fourth Pillar and nāṭiq. He noticeably tries to reconcile the Shaykhi positions with the conventional notion of leadership in Shiʿism. See Karīm Khān Kirmānī *Risāla-yi Rukn-i Rābiʿ* (Kirman, 1368/1948). See also below, chap. 4.

expectations within the Shaykhi school. Despite attempts made by Aḥsā'ī's successors to readjust the Shaykhi doctrine to the accepted theory of Occultation, the two remained largely incompatible, and were bound to come into collision.

The Shiʿite literature on the subject of Occultation, from the time of early scholars like Shaykh Ṭūsī and Shaykh Mufīd up to the nineteenth century,[90] focused chiefly on the possibility of the Imam's invisible existence by emphasizing that a prolonged biological life for the Imam was not impossible.[91] But since the Imam was in Occultation, and since after the completion of Lesser Occultation and the time of the Four Agents the chances of any regular contact with the Imam were remote, the mainstream learned Shiʿism insisted that the responsibility of guiding believers during this interregnum rested upon the ʿulama. However, this attitude did not dismiss repeated claims concerning mystical encounters. Part of the literature on Occultation was devoted to these experiences,[92] mainly to prove three points: to provide evidence for the abiding presence of the Imam throughout history; to sanctify the position of the ʿulama as the Imam's true representatives; and to allow mystical experiences within the body of Shiʿite orthodoxy.

But these experiences hardly ever went beyond a subsidiary support. The books of Occultation in no way encouraged any real expectation for the Advent of the Qā'im. On the contrary, they implied greatest obstacles to the materialization of any of the prophecies that were the very basis of the Ithnā ʿAsharī theory of the Return (Rajʿa) of the Imam. The prohibition on setting a date for the Revelation (Ẓuhūr) and chastisement of the "fixers of the Time," the prohibition on identifying any name for the Imam or on the possibility of declaring specific deputyship naturally made any attempt to fulfill the prophecies, or even any speculation on the subject, a matter of controversy, if not heresy.[93] The considerable number of treatises written to

[90] *al-Dharīʿa* lists forty works under *kitāb al-Ghayba* (book of Occultation) (XVI, 74–84) and under *kitāb al-Rajʿa* (book of Return) (X, 161–63). Also see Mīrzā Ḥusayn Ṭabarsī Nūrī *al-Najm al-Thāqib dar Aḥvāl-i Imām-i Ghā'ib* (Tehran, n.d.) and especially the list of forty Shiʿite works on the subject (4–5). Murtażā Mudarrisī Chahārdihī, in *Tārīkh-i Ravābiṭ-i Īrān va ʿIrāq* ([Tehran, 1351 Sh./1972] 334–37) also lists twenty-one works by Shiʿite scholars and sixteen by Sunnis on the subject of the Twelfth Imam. For Sunni sources on the Mahdī see bibliographical list in *Yādnāmih-yi ʿAllāma Amīnī* ed. S. J. Shahīdī and M. R. Ḥakīmī (Tehran, 1353 Sh./1974) I, 519–20; and H. Khurāsānī *Maktab-i Tashayyuʿ* (Tehran, 1341 Sh./1962) 183, n. 1. For a concise survey of the Ithnā ʿAsharī view on Occultation see Sachedina *Islamic Messianism* 78–108. Also *EI*²: GHAYBA (D. B. Macdonald and M. G. S. Hodgson) and cited sources; I. Goldziher *Introduction to Islamic Theology and Law* trans. R. Hamori (Princeton, 1981) 200, n. 95.

[91] See, for example, Muḥammad Bāqir Majlisī *Ḥaqq al-Yaqīn* (Tehran, n.d.) 185–212.

[92] For some of these experiences and encounters with the Imam, see Muḥammad Bāqir Majlisī *Biḥār al-Anwār* 25 vols. (Tehran, 1301–15/1883–1897) XIII/6, 17–24, Persian trans. (Tehran, 1397/1976) 74–84; *Ḥaqq al-Yaqīn* viii, 305–46; Nūrī *al-Najm al-Thāqib* iv-viii, 102–412. For Sunni visitation of the Mahdi see Goldziher *Introduction* 201, n. 98.

[93] For prohibitions on setting a date see *Biḥār al-Anwār* XIII, 3, Pers. 26–27, 406–23. Also Goldziher *Introduction* 195–96 and cited sources.

remove doubts about any single point of prohibition indicates the potential danger that the unconventional approach might have had for orthodoxy.[94]

In this context the position of Aḥsāʾī and his successor, Sayyid Kāẓim Rashtī, is somewhat complicated. In spite of his messianic orientation in the theory of the Perfect Shiʿa, in instances, at least on the surface, Aḥsāʾī agrees with the common interpretation of the prophecies. In *Sharḥ al-Ziyāra* he devotes a whole section to the question of Return of the Qāʾim, largely on the model of earlier Shiʿite scholars. Though providing a consistent account of the Shiʿite Traditions, and equally noteworthy for demonstrating their messianic content, he barely elaborates, as one might expect, on esoteric meanings.[95] In his more popular works like *Ḥayāt al-Nafs*,[96] or a treatise in response to the Qajar prince governor Muḥammad ʿAlī Mīrzā[97] dealing with the question of Resurrection Aḥsāʾī cites Traditions common to all books of Rajʿa, virtually ignoring the allegorical meaning of apocalyptic signs or the interrelation between the Mahdī and the Perfect Shiʿa. A short tract in which he denounces a claimant who declared himself to be the deputy of the Imam of the Age confirms his cautious outlook.[98]

The ostensible contradiction between Aḥsāʾī's theosophical assumptions and his doctrinal position is at least partly reconciled by his efforts to combine the internal and the external. The practice of dissimulation *(taqīya)* of true religious beliefs, confined the Shaykhi eschatology to philosophical arguments. Aḥsāʾī's frequent references to the necessity of taqīya owing to the limited capacity of the ordinary believer to grasp the true meaning of the secrets of religion indicates his hesitation to declare his more controversial views.[99] Moreover, his configuration of the Perfect Shiʿa did not necessarily affirm the immediate resurgence of the Hidden Imam. The Perfect Shiʿa was a protomessianic figure but his guidance, to the extent that it was recognized by the public, did not herald the Return of the Imam, at least in consistent theological language.

The same approach can be observed in the works of Aḥsāʾī's successor, Sayyid Kāẓim Rashtī.[100] Rashtī acknowledges these intellectual limits thus:

> Elaboration on the secrets of the subject of Maʿād, would lead us to raise various matters which are not appropriate to our time, since the people of this age cannot tolerate them, and this would accelerate their denial. As our lord [Jaʿfar] Ṣādiq, peace be upon him, has said: "Not all that is known is to be said,

[94]For example *Risāla* on prohibition of naming the Lord of the Age *(Ṣāḥib al-Zamān)* by Shaykh Sulaymān Baḥrānī cited in *QU* 277. Also Muḥammad Ibn Yaʿqūb Kulaynī *Uṣūl al-Kāfī* Persian trans. and commentary J. Muṣṭafavī (Tehran, n.d.) II, 126–27.

[95]4th ed., III, 54–121.

[96]Wadham Collection, Oxford, MS folio 30/a-40/a, Pers.85–120.

[97]*Al-ʿIṣma wa al-Rajʿa* in *Jawāmiʿ al-Kalim* (also cited in *Fihrist* II, 242).

[98]*Risāla al-Mūsawīya* in *Jawāmiʿ al-Kalim* I (also cited in *Fihrist* II, 244).

[99]For example in *Risāla al-Ḥamlīya,* in *Jawāmiʿ al-Kalim* (also in *Fihrist* II, 246).

[100]*Uṣūl-i ʿAqāʾid* 185–215; *Risāla* in reply to a few questions, Wadham Collection, Oxford, MS folio 113/a-21/b (also *Fihrist* II, 353, no. 295).

> and not the right time has come for all that is to be said, and not all appropriate sayings should be said to those who are incompetent of understanding." Therefore, owing to their complexity, references to these matters, without full explanation, are beyond public comprehension. This is the reason why the holy Imams and the adepts among Shiʿites constantly covered the delicate details of this subject under the cloak of outward expressions so that the secret gem would be safely protected from the encroachments of the ignorant.[101]

Prudence and secrecy inspired an allegorical language, a fairly common device in earlier protomillenarian trends. Signs of these metaphorical speculations can be detected in Aḥsāʾī's works, which on one occasion specify the dates of birth and of revelation of the Qāʾim in a codified message.[102] In another instance he quotes a Tradition in which, regarding the appearance of the Mahdi, Jaʿfar Ṣādiq is reported to have said, "His cause will appear and his name will arise in the year sixty."[103]

Some cryptic speculations are also evident in a brief letter written in response to Rashtī's complaints about persecutions inflicted upon Shaykhis in the ʿAtabāt, and perhaps with reference to his inquiries about the time when the appearance of the Imam would resolve the hostilities: "Regarding the possibilities [of Ẓuhūr?] mentioned [in Traditions], there is no other way but to wait. . . . There is no alteration in this cause, and for every call there is a deliverer but setting a precise date is not favorable. 'You will surely have news of it after a while.'"[104]

The allusion in the above Qurʾānic verse to "after a while" *(baʿda ḥīn)* encouraged Shaykhis, like many esoterics before them, to search for a definite date. Mullā Jaʿfar Kirmānshāhī, who met Aḥsāʾī in 1241/1825–1826, shortly before his death, related that when asked to indicate signs of deliverance, Aḥsāʾī replied, "sixty-eight." When pressed for an explanation, he replied with the same verse from the Qurʾān: "You will surely have news of it after a while." Then his questioner asked for further elaboration, to which he replied: "Is it not that the numerical value of *ḥīn* is equal to sixty-eight?"[105]

Such hints to the Advent of the Promised One *(Mauʿūd)* sometimes drew the attention of non-Shaykhi writers.[106] In *Qiṣaṣ al-ʿUlamāʾ*, Tunkābunī states that according to Aḥsāʾī the existence of the Imam in this world is an assumption that could not be reached by deductive reasoning. Aḥsāʾī's reliance on esoteric cognition, he declares, differs from the majority view,

[101]Risāla in reply to questions on Maʿād. INBA. no. 4, II, 216–63 (220–21).

[102]*Fāʾida* in request of Shaykh Mūsā Baḥrānī in *Jawāmiʿ al-Kalim* (*Fihrist* II, 242–43).

[103]*Qatīl* (513) cited a certain *Kitāb al-Rajʿa* by Aḥsāʾī, possibly the risāla, in reply to Sayyid Ḥusayn on the question of Rajʿa in *Jawāmiʿ al-Kalim* I; *Fihrist* II, 259.

[104]*Dalīl al-Mutaḥayyirīn* Pers. trans. 52. Also *Nabil* 17–18. The verse quoted in the passage is from the Qurʾan XXXVIII, 88.

[105]*Qatīl* 514.

[106]*QU* 46–54.

which usually substantiates the existence of the Imam with the rule of benevolence.[107] Tunkābunī also recalls Rashtī commenting on a verse by Aḥsā'ī: "The smoke you see will ascend after me, I am the ignitor of that flame." The author then remarks that this prophecy was fully realized. Not only did a great animosity develop between Rashtī and the jurists but two of his students, Ḥājjī Muḥammad Karīm Khān Kirmānī and Sayyid ʿAlī Muḥammad the Bāb, caused the greatest schism in the community. "The flames of that fire are still alive,"[108] Tunkābunī comments. The author, as a representative of the ʿulama establishment, notices a continuous line between the ideas of Aḥsā'ī and the Babi schism.

In spite of its pronounced messianic overtones, Shaykhism remained a theological school, close in many ways to orthodox Shiʿism though not in harmony with the interpretation of prominent jurists. Rashtī accepted the Uṣūlī approach to external matters, and went to great lengths to represent the Shaykhi point of view on fiqh and uṣūl in an academic manner.[109] This conformance to the orthodoxy increasingly pressured the Shaykhis during incessant waves of criticism and persecution at the end of Aḥsā'ī's life and throughout Rashtī's leadership. In response to charges of deviation and blasphemy, Rashtī tried to clarify, and even in some instances to readjust, the Shaykhi positions in accordance with mainstream Shiʿite principles.[110]

In his numerous works on the true meaning of Resurrection, the inner secrets of the Qur'ānic verse, and methods of achieving spiritual purification, Rashtī also addressed the dilemma concerning the return of the Hidden Imam.[111] In *Dalīl al-Mutaḥayyirīn,* as in his other works on the question of *walāya,* he maintains that contrary to the Sunni view (for adopting which he condemns the Shiʿite ʿulama), walāya of the Imam should not be defined only in terms of affection since according to the Shiʿite principles walāya must be regarded as active intervention of the Imam in the affairs of the world. In theory the Imam is the only rightful source of authority, whose function cannot be replaced by ijtihād.[112]

Rashtī's views on the nature of Ẓuhūr appear with greater lucidity in a commentary on *Qaṣida Lāmīya.*[113] Here, Rashtī introduces a cyclical concept of prophethood that highly resembles the Ismāʿīlī theory of cyclical

[107]Ibid. 88–89; cf. 93. For discussion on the rule of benevolence in Shiʿite theology see Sachedina *Islamic Messianism* 120–25.

[108]Ibid. 52.

[109]Risāla in reply to enquiries from Isfahan in *Majmaʿ al-Rasā'il* (Persian) 2d ed. (Kirman, n.d.) 305.

[110]*Dalīl al-Mutaḥayyirīn* 56, 81–82.

[111]For the list of fifty-six works by Rashtī on ḥikma and esoterics see *Fihrist* 288–309. The remaining 114 works cited in *Fihrist* (309–59), including commentaries, treatises on doctrinal and denominational issues, and answers to theological questions, frequently contain entries on eschatological and messianic issues.

[112]Ibid. 113–15. Also risāla in reply to Shaykh Muḥammad Qaṭīfī (cited in *Fihrist* II, 314).

[113]*Sharḥ Lāmīya (ʿan) ʿAbd al-Bāqī al-ʿAmrī* (Tabriz, 1270/1853), compiled by Rashtī in 1257/1841 toward the end of his life.

revelations. He maintains that at the end of the twelfth century, the first cycle of prophethood, which corresponded to the Prophet and eleven Imams, came to an end. This was the cycle of exteriors, designed to perfect the external capacities of the human soul. The cycle of interiors, or the cycle of unveiling secrets, is to perfect the capacities of the human spirit. As the first cycle was an embryonic phase for spiritual evolution, the second is the age of adolescence.

> Thus when the first solar cycle of the prophethood, which belongs to the perfection of exteriors and corresponds to the revelation of the name of Muḥammad, is completed, there begins the second solar cycle of prophethood for the perfection of the interiors, and exteriors in this cycle are subordinates as in the first cycle the interiors were subordinates. And in this second cycle the name of the messenger of God in Heaven is Aḥmad, and Aḥmad also is the name of the *murawwij* [promoter] and *ra'īs* [head] at the beginning of this century, and certainly he came from the best land and purest climate.[114]

Here, a new cycle is contemplated, which starts in the thirteenth century A.H. The divine sun manifests itself again in Aḥmad, who is the heavenly prototype of Muḥammad in the past cycle, and whose reflections on the earth illuminated the new cycle of interior (*bāṭin*). The initiator of the new cycle, is none other than Shaykh Aḥmad Aḥsā'ī. But if Shaykh Aḥmad is the initiator of the cycle of internal, where does the Twelfth Imam fit in this picture? Here, as far as the revelation of the Qā'im is concerned, Rashtī's enigmatic answer is open to interpretation. It is likely that he regarded Aḥsā'ī and possibly himself as precursors, gates, or even reflections of the Hidden Imam, whose celestial existence is to unravel the secrets of the interior. This is more understandable if Aḥsā'ī's theory of multifold bodies is considered. If the Imam, the internal name of the new revelation is still in the intermediary world of Hūrqalyā, the gate (bāb), who is the Perfect Shiʿa, will be the only physical representation of him in this world. Al-Qatīl al-Karbalā'ī, a student of Rashtī and later a Babi adherent, elaborates on the same theme. He states that in the course of the second cycle, from the beginning of the thirteenth century A.H. up to the end of Rashtī's life (1259/1844) was the age of bāṭin. The representatives of this age, Aḥsā'ī and Rashtī, were indeed like elemental corpses for the celestial body of the messenger, namely Sayyid ʿAlī Muḥammad the Bab, who is the Imam of the Age. In the year sixty, thus, the spiritual body, which is the "interior of the interior," appeared.[115] At this stage of the development of the Shaykhi

[114]Ibid. Also translated in A. L. M. Nicolas *Essai sur le Chéïkhisme* II: *Seyyed Kazem Rechti* (Paris, 1914) 37–44 (43). For Ismāʿīlī views see W. Madelung "Aspects of Ismā'īlī Theology: The Prophetic Chain and the God beyond Being" *Ismāʿīlī Contributions to Islamic Culture* 53–65.

[115]*Qatīl* 513.

thought under Rashtī, however, while the gate of the recognition of the Imam is regarded as being reopened by Aḥsā'ī, his corporal return is still awaited.

Further hints of the future appearance of the Imam can also be found in the oral accounts related from Rashtī. Considering the danger of any open speculation, it is not surprising that these oral references were confined to a small circle of devotees and were later related by students eager to witness the realization of their former master's prognostication in Babi revelation. The possibility of exaggeration by the Babis as to the extent to which Rashtī was preoccupied with a near messianic revelation cannot be ruled out. But even non-Babi accounts agree that toward the end of his life, Rashtī became increasingly interested in the Advent of the Promised One. Ḥājjī Muḥammad Karīm Khān Kirmānī, who because of his opposition to the Babis constantly tries to play down the messianic content of Rashtī's teachings, still agrees that when Rashtī was asked about his successor, he replied that "soon the cause of God would reach its maturity." On other occasions, in reply to the same question, he hinted, "Those who are destined to be destroyed will be destroyed by the proof and those who are destined to be resurrected will be resurrected by the proof."[116] It is also related that after twenty years, during which Rashtī had implicitly propounded the circumstances of the Advent of the Promised One, in Ramaḍān 1258/1842, just before the revolt of the Shi'ite population of Karbalā' and the massacre of its inhabitants by the Ottoman forces,[117] he openly publicized the imminence of the next Ẓuhūr: "After maintaining that he [the Promised One] is clear of any physical defect and imperfection, he [Rashtī] then specified his heavenly name, as the Prophet said my name in Heaven is Aḥmad and on the earth is Muḥammad. Sayyid Kāẓim ended that month in describing his virtues, perfections, and characteristics.[118]

It appears, however, that the increasing hostility of his opponents, and the allegations brought against him regarding his role in the events of Karbalā', discouraged Rashtī from further publicizing his views. Again Qatīl reports that when in Ramaḍān 1259/1843 Rashtī was asked by his students to disclose the secrets of the Perfect Shi'a, he replied: "Last year we paid greatest attention and fully discussed [this question], but we saw neither any enthusiastic response from the companions, nor any acceptance from our opponents, until what befell them from the sword in that horrific disaster [the massacre of Karbalā']. Now, if I want to begin explaining and repeating what I have already said, I do not see in you the right capacities and you are not capable of understanding; therefore, it is better to leave the matter and alter the style."[119]

[116]Ḥājjī Muḥammad Karīm Khān Kirmānī *Izhāq al-Bāṭil* (Kirmān, 1392) 14.
[117]See below, this chapter.
[118]*Qatīl* 507, quoting Mullā 'Alī Tabrīzī.
[119]Ibid. 508.

Despite his reluctance to speak in public, during the remaining three months of his life, from the beginning of Ramaḍān to 11 Dhu al-Ḥijja 1259/2 January 1844, Rashtī again emphasized to his close companions the possibility of the revelation of the cause of God soon after his death, which he implied would occur in the near future. Though he never made it clear to whom or to what position he referred, some of his students believed that this was a reference to the appearance of a messianic figure more significant than Aḥsā'ī or Rashtī themselves. Early Babi sources reported that in Dhu al-Ḥijja 1259, during annual pilgrimage to Kāẓimayn, when his students showed their grief and distress over his predicted death, Rashtī replied: "Would you not wish me to die so the cause of your Imam may be revealed?"[120] He warned his students not to fall out after his death over the question of succession, since "in thirty weeks the cause will be revealed to you."[121] At a gathering of his followers in Baghdad, he pointed to a sword and repeated three times: "Swear to God, the sword is closer than what you might imagine."[122] Many people misunderstood him, Qatīl adds, but when Mullā Muḥammad Taqī Harātī later asked him the real meaning of his allusion, he replied that "the cause of God would reach its maturity," and added: "But our cause is not the same as that of the Gates [*Abwāb:* the Four Agents of the Hidden Imam]."[123]

Rashtī's allusive remarks are not entirely clear, but regarding his overall influence on the Shaykhi school at least three conclusions can be reached. His first preoccupation is with messianic prophecies, the fulfillment of which he anticipated in the near future, when the evolution of the cycle would reach its maturity. However, it is unlikely that this was an anticipation of the emergence of the Twelfth Imam in its full traditional definition, as his own writings made such emergence conditional on the fulfillment of a series of complex eschatological processes.[124] But he attached far greater importance to the spiritual position of this Promised One and to the circumstances of his revelation than of any early agent of the Imam. The process that was started by Aḥsā'ī at the beginning of the century, he implied, was a preliminary phase that would reach its culmination during the next critical stage. Whether this Mauʿūd could be defined as the bāb, the Perfect Shiʿa, the deputy of the Imam, or the Imam himself remained a matter for his followers to speculate upon.

Second, the teaching of Aḥsā'ī and the esoteric interpretation alluded to by Rashtī motivated many of his students and followers to adopt a mes-

[120]*Qatīl* 508; cf. *Nabil* 45. *Qatīl* gives the list of fourteen of Rashtī's students who were present on that occasion. References to other speculations and allusions reported from Aḥsā'ī and Rashtī can be found in *NK* 99–104; *Nabil* 13–46; *Qazvīnī* 462–64; and other sources.

[121]*Qatīl* 508.

[122]Ibid.

[123]Ibid.

[124]*Uṣūl-i ʿAqā'id* 186–89 and risāla in reply to Muḥammad Riżā Mīrzā 220–63.

sianic outlook, often in contrast to the academic norms of their time. The crisis of succession that followed Rashtī's death and the widening difference between the conservative and radical factions in the Shaykhi school can best be explained in terms of the interpretation of messianic anticipations. While Ḥājjī Muḥammad Karīm Khān Kirmānī, Mullā Ḥasan Gauhar, and Mīrzā Muḥīṭ Kirmānī each justified his own claim to the leadership of the Shaykhī school in terms of academic and communal support, Mullā Ḥusayn Bushrū'ī, Mullā ʿAlī Basṭāmī, and many other future Babis regarded the age of Aḥsā'ī and Rashtī merely as a preparatory period for achieving "the interior of the interior" to which Rashtī was considered the "primary divine gate."[125]

Finally, Shaykhism under Rashtī evolved, both in theory and practice, from a pure theological school to a sectarian tendency with a defined doctrine, a growing following, and resolute leadership. Paralleling this process, the increasing polarization and sharper divisions with mainstream Shiʿism further tilted Shaykhism (the students more than Rashtī himself) toward radical theological and political positions. This trend was reflected in a protomessianic aspiration for a drastic breakthrough on religious as well as political grounds. Increasing involvement in the community and efforts to organize and expand the Shaykhi school did not reduce Rashtī's status as a scholar and interpreter of Aḥsā'ī. His overall vision of Ẓuhūr, however, distinctly differed from his teacher's in laying greater emphasis on the intervention of the Perfect Shiʿa in the affairs of the world.

The development of the theory of the messianic Advent in the theosophic system of Aḥsā'ī and Rashtī was only partly responsible for the reception, enthusiastic or hostile, that the Shaykhi school met during its forty years of advocacy in Iraq and in Iran. The Shaykhi leaders' pronounced piety and lack of material attachments, reinforced by the fact that for nearly twenty years (circa 1221–1240/1806–1824), Aḥsā'ī spent much of his life visiting the important cities in western, central, and eastern Iran, greatly assisted the formation of a community of followers throughout the country. Prominent mutjathids of the ʿAtabāt[126] commonly visited Kirman, Tehran, Mashhad, Yazd, Isfahan, Shiraz, Qazvin, and other cities, usually by invitation of the local ʿulama, notables, governors, and state officials who had a special devotion to them. Aḥsā'ī's visits attracted followers from the middle and lower ranks of ʿulama, local merchants, local officials, and some members of the Qajar family. The presence in cities like Yazd, Shiraz, and Kirman of ʿulama of Baḥraynī descent who had studied under Aḥsā'ī, were acquainted

[125]Early Babi sources such as *Qatīl* (502) and *NK* (99–100) occasionally referred to Aḥsā'ī and Rashtī with the titles *bāb* and *bāb-i Imām*. For the interfactional dispute within the Shaykhi school see below, chap. 4.

[126]See for example *QU* on Shaykh Jaʿfar Najafī (191–98), Sayyid Muḥammad Ṭabāṭabā'ī (125–29), and Sayyid Mahdī Ṭabāṭabā'ī (124–25).

with him, or venerated him as their head, facilitated these visits. These were mostly the middle-rank ʿulama, possibly with Akhbārī tendencies, who in the second half of the eighteenth century, chiefly because of the non-Shiʿite tribal incursions on the western coast of the Persian Gulf, immigrated to Iran.[127]

Toward the end of Aḥsāʾī's life, many of the Persian ʿulama who had studied under him in the ʿAtabāt or met him during his visits to Iran, began to set up teaching circles in their home towns and villages, drawing public attention to the Shaykhi cause. Shaykhi communities in Yazd, Azarbaijan, Mazandaran, and Kirman were the first to flourish as a result of the efforts of Aḥsāʾī's students.[128] Though Isfahan was firmly in the hand of Uṣūlīs, there were still eminent ʿulama like Ḥājjī Mullā Ibrāhīm Karbāsī (d. 1260/1844), who had studied under Aḥsāʾī and showed great respect for him.[129] The chief support, however, came from another quarter. Throughout his journeys, Aḥsāʾī was enthusiastically received, and on many occasions was invited by the Qajar princes, governors, and notables to reside in their cities. In some cases they even squabbled over his place of residence. Hospitality and devotion were exhibited by such powerful figures as prince governor Muḥammad ʿAlī Mīrzā Daulatshāh (d. 1237/1821), in Kirmānshāh;[130] Ibrāhīm Khān Ẓahīr al-Daula, the governor of Kirman (d. 1240/1824), who was Fatḥ ʿAlī Shāh's uncle and the father of Ḥājjī Muḥammad Karīm Khān Kirmānī, the future Shaykhi leader;[131] ʿAbdullāh Khān Amīn al-Daula,[132] in Yazd; and Fatḥ ʿAlī Shāh himself, in the capital. Their patronage included monetary gifts in the form of religious alms, payment of Aḥsāʾī's debts, and assignment of villages for his private use (*tuyūl*).[133] Such gestures of favor and devotion were not free from political incentives, although genuine re-

[127]Among them Ḥājjī Muḥammad Aḥsāʾī in Rafsanjān, Shaykh Niʿmatullāh Akhbārī, the imām jumʿa of Kirman, and Shaykh ʿAbd al-Ḥasan Jazāyirī in Kirman (Murtażā Mudarrisī Chāhārdihī *Shaykhīgarī va Bābīgarī* 2d ed. [Tehran, 1351 Sh./1972] citing Shaykh Yaḥyā Aḥmadī Kirmānī and Mīrzā Abul-Ḥasan Kalāntarī Kirmānī). Also Shaykh ʿAbdullāh ibn Mubārak Qaṭīfī in Shiraz (*TAS* II/2, 787–89), the Āl ʿUṣfūr family in Būshihr and the Baḥrānī family of Bihbahān. Both Shaykh Niʿmatullāh and Ḥājjī Sayyid Muḥammad were among Aḥsāʾī's admirers.

[128]Distinguished students of Aḥsāʾī like Ḥājjī Shaykh ʿAbd al-Wahhāb Qazvīnī in Qazvin, Mullā Muḥammad Ḥamza Sharīʿatmadār Māzandarānī in Bārfrūsh, Mullā ʿAbd al-Kāliq Yazdī in Yazd, and later in Shiraz and Mashhad, Mullā Muḥammad Mamaqānī in Tabriz, Mīrzā Sulaymān Yazdī and Mullā Ismāʿīl ʿAqdāʾī in Yazd helped the expansion of Shaykhism in various provinces.

[129]On Aḥsāʾī's reception in Iran see *Dalīl al-Mutaḥayyirīn* 21; *QU* 22–23 cf. 34; and *Sharḥ-i Aḥvāl* 22–40.

[130]For some indications of Muḥammad ʿAlī Mīrzā's respect for Aḥsāʾī see *QU* 35–36; *RJ* 25; *Sharḥ-i Aḥval* 34.

[131]On Ẓahīr al-Daula see M. Bāmdād *Sharḥ-i Ḥāl-i Rijāl-i Īrān* 6 vols. (Tehran, 1347–1351 Sh./1968–1972) I, 21; and Shaykh Yaḥyā Aḥmadī *Farmandihān-i Kirmān* ed. and ann. Bāstanī Pārīzī, 2d ed. (Tehran, 1354 Sh./1975) 50–55.

[132]For the above mentioned see *EIr*: AMIN AL-DAULA, ʿAbdullāh Khān and the cited sources.

[133]*Shaykhīgarī va Bābīgarī* 132–33.

ligious motives can be discerned. Muḥammad ʿAlī Mīrzā particularly raised him above the other ʿulama. Exploiting Aḥsāʾī's fame, the Qajar establishment promoted the peripatetic Arab theologian to provide an effective alternative to the rising influence of the domestic mujtahids. The Niʿmatullāhī Sufis and extremists like Mīrzā Muḥammad Akhbārī, through eccentricity or inconsistency, reduced their chances as reliable collaborators to the state. Aḥsāʾī, however, was too distant from his secular benefactors, and too uninterested in temporal power to pose any threat to them, and therefore seemed a credible ally to the state.

In practice, however, Aḥsāʾī's dealings with the Qajars rarely stretched to the political sphere. Unlike many contemporary mujtahids, who remained indecisive in their relation with the government, he declared his position openly. Maintaining in a letter to Fatḥ ʿAlī Shāh that "all kings and governors enforce their edicts and orders by means of oppression," he resigned to the fact that since there is no other immediate alternative, the affairs of religion and state should remain separate. "My intervention with the King can have only one of two results: either he will accept it, and thus his rule will be suspended; or he will reject it, and I will be humiliated."[134] Indeed contrary to what is sometimes implied, Aḥsāʾī's opinion on this issue complied better with a traditional noninterventionist Ithnā ʿAsharī view than that of the ʿulama of the period, whose negative interference in political affairs often bore no doctrinal justification.[135]

The sense of devotion and austerity that pervade all accounts of Aḥsāʾī's life, usually distorting its realities, corresponded to the public need for a saintly figure who exemplified the highly admired values of the Islamic ethos. In this sense Shaykhism responded to a public demand for a charismatic leadership that by its assumed purity and unworldliness could surpass any temporal or clerical authority. This need became even more tangible during the early 1800s, when the growing power of the Uṣūlīs gradually eliminated most of the nonconformist elements and weakened the rival influences of the Sufis in Iran.

By its very essence, and owing to its limited margin for any intuitive meditation, the Uṣūlī orthodoxy was only partly able to satisfy the public aspiration for holy men. References to excessive devotion and "lawful asceticism," which were attributed by Uṣūlī sources to eminent mujtahids, can be taken as signs of a general trend among the jurists to add spiritual virtues to their ijtihād qualities, so as to form a complete image of a perfect divine. In their biographical accounts, from Bihbahānī to Murtażā Anṣārī, though leadership was often justified in terms of superior qualities of ijtihād, some sense of exceptional moral values was also attached to their status.

[134]The text of the letter appears in *Dalīl al-Mutaḥayyirīn* 23–24 and a shorter version in *Sharḥ-i Aḥvāl* 22, which is translated in Algar *Religion and State* 67.

[135]See for example Algar *Religion and State* 66–69.

In spite of spiritual attributions, however, the concept of ijtihād was always predominant. One might suggest that the vacuum created between the public and the clerical body as a result of the mujtahids' elitist tendencies was filled by Shaykhism, when all other avenues were effectively barred by orthodoxy. This emphasis on moral values seems to have appealed especially to certain sections of society, most noticeably were merchants and the middle-rank mullas who traditionally looked to the high-ranking ʿulama for support. According to his son, Aḥsāʾī's long residence in Yazd was chiefly due to the devotion that the inhabitants showed for him, almost to the point of adulation.[136] The bulk of this favorable response came from the merchants *(tujjār)* of Yazd, arguably the most important trade center in the whole of southern Iran in the early 1800s.[137] Veneration was also expressed during Aḥsāʾī's visits to such other important trade centers as Isfahan, Qazvin, Shiraz, and Kirmānshāh.[138]

Sayyid Kāẓim Rashtī himself, son of a silk merchant from Gīlān,[139] was a symbol of the growing attraction of Shaykhism for the merchant class. After some ascetic retreat in local shrines,[140] Rashtī was attracted to Aḥsāʾī's discourses in Yazd, when he was still in his early twenties.[141] Such preoccupation was not unprecedented in the merchant families. Other examples of Shaykhi merchants or religious seminarians *(ṭullāb)* with mercantile background can be found among Rashtī's students. The network of Shaykhi sympathizers, developed under Rashtī, played an important role in the future progress of the Babi movement. Though at this stage the Shaykhi community consisted mainly of ʿulama and the religious students, it was also dependent on merchants, artisans, and the semiurban population of Persian towns. The points of distinction between Shaykhis and non-Shaykhis (known to Shaykhis as Bālāsarīs) were not entirely based on ritualistic or theological differences. Many of the Shaykhi sympathizers had a limited understanding of the theoretical subtleties that set Aḥsāʾī apart. The theological background of the merchants, small landowners, local state officials, and other educated and semieducated groups who, together with the middle- and lower-rank mullas, were attracted to Shaykhism was often too limited to permit them to follow any philosophical argument. What inter-

136 *Sharḥ-i Aḥvāl* 22–23, 28, 35.

137 See A. K. S. Lambton "Persian Trade under the Early Qajars" in *Islam and the Trade of Asia* ed. D. S. Richards (Oxford, 1970) 215–44 (218–19); Amanat *Cities and Trade* 79–80, 104–8, 131–36.

138 *Sharḥ-i Aḥvāl* 33–34; cf. *QU* 35–36.

139 *KD* I, 36; cf. *Fihrist* I, 115.

140 *Shaykhīgarī va Bābīgarī* (135–36) and *TN* (II, 238), maintaining that his retirement was in the shrine of Shaykh Ṣafī al-Dīn Ardabīlī in Ardabīl. However, Nūr al-Dīn Mudarrisī Chāhārdihī in *Khāksār va Ahl-i Ḥaqq* ([Tehran, 1358 Sh./1979] 4) refers to Masjid-i Ṣafī in Rasht to which, according to the author, Shaykh Ṣafī used to retire. The mosque is known for the mysterious well, Chāh-i Ṣāḥib al-Zamān. It is probable that Rashtī retired to this mosque rather than to the shrine in Ardabīl.

141 *TN* 238; *Nabil* 9–11.

ested them, like the multitudes of town dwellers and villagers who followed Shaykhi mullas in Friday prayers, was the moral and spiritual values they attributed to these leaders.

During Rashtī's leadership (1241–1259/1825–1844), Shaykhi circles were further expanded by the second generation of Shaykhi students, who had first been brought up in the local centers of learning in Iran, often under students of Aḥsā'ī, and then studied with Rashtī in the ʿAtabāt. They were more actively and firmly committed to Shaykhi teachings than their predecessors, whose attachment to Shaykhism rarely went beyond sympathy or personal admiration. They tended to turn Shaykhism into more of a sectarian school, with a relatively strong nucleus in Karbalā' and a growing network of students and followers in Iran, Iraq, and India. Though Shaykhism was still within the boundary of religious orthodoxy, by Rashtī's time it was increasingly defined as an independent school, if not a sect.[142] Local mullas and religious students often came from a humble background. The circles of the prominent Uṣūlīs were partly, though not entirely, formed of the students with clerical backgrounds, and more particularly of sons and relatives of high-ranking ʿulama of the ʿAtabāt and Iran. In contrast, the majority of the students in Rashtī's circle shared rural origins. Under Rashtī the sense of solidarity and common identity among his adherents was further strengthened by the critical circumstances in which he and his students found themselves almost immediately after his succession.

Rashtī was only twenty-nine when Aḥsā'ī appointed him to establish a teaching circle in Karbalā' (circa 1240/1824), and had barely experienced the conventional training that qualified most of his contemporaries to establish independent teaching circles.[143] However, he was a prolific and talented writer and a skillful theologian who tried with some success to continue the universality of his teacher, though he rarely claimed to have mystical experiences. This did not spare him repeated denunciations by hostile mujtahids. Ever since Aḥsā'ī's rise to prominence, the Shaykhis faced the threat of excommunication. From the very beginning of his leadership to the end of his life, Rashtī was under continuous attack by the Uṣūlī jurists. Hard-liner mujtahids of Iran and the ʿAtabāt saw Shaykhism as a threat more potent than Sufism or Akhbārism. And the esoteric teachings of the Shaykhi school provided ample evidence for charges of heresy. Some attempts were made by Muḥammad Taqī Baraghānī and his allies to issue denunciations *(takfīr)* of Aḥsā'ī on the ground of his theory of spiritual resurrection *(maʿād rūḥānī)*. The issue was heatedly debated from the time of Mullā Ṣadrā and

[142]*Dalīl al-Mutaḥayyirīn* (e.g. 10–11, 70–75, 138–40) gives clear indications of Rashtī's own notion of Shaykhism as an independent theological school.

[143]None of the available sources on the life of Rashtī specifies his study under any particular teacher besides Aḥsā'ī. However, he had authorizations (ijāzāt) for transmitting Traditions from Shaykh Mūsā Najafī, Sayyid ʿAbdullāh Shibr, and others, as is cited in Rashtī's own authorization for Āqā Muḥammad Sharīf Kirmānī cited in *Fihrist* I, 126–27.

was rejected by the mujtahids in favor of corporal resurrection.[144] Condemnations and harsh criticism damaged Aḥsāʾī's reputation, proving once again the effective control of the ʿulama over their constituencies. Though he was not branded as an outright heretic, in the eye of the public, he was reduced to a shady nonconformist. As anti-Shaykhi harassments were intensified, Rashtī was less able than his teacher to rely on his position and public respect. The same motives that encouraged the mujtahids to drive Aḥsāʾī out of Iran and then the ʿAtabāt prompted them to attack Rashtī as he gradually managed to solidify his base in Karbalāʾ by broadening the Shaykhi network, attracting more students, and involving himself in local politics.[145] Persecutions in the ʿAtabāt, however, only partially affected the spread of Shaykhism in Iran, especially the towns and villages of Khurasan, Azarbaijan, and Mazandaran. Indeed, this seems to have been a source of anxiety for many local ʿulama of Uṣūlī persuasion.

The jurists' response came primarily from the hereditary ʿulama families, amplified by other mujtahids who claimed rīyāsa in the ʿAtabāt. Unlike the Arab Shaykh Mūsā and Shaykh ʿAlī Najafī, sons of Shaykh Jaʿfar, who at the end of Aḥsāʾī's life, tried to patch up the differences between the two sides, the Persian Sayyid Muḥammad Mahdī Ṭabāṭabāʾī (son of Sayyid ʿAlī and grandson of Bihbahānī) was the archenemy of Shaykhis and the chief instigator of numerous takfīrs.[146] Though the Baḥraynī ʿulama generally remained silent, or occasionally sympathized with Rashtī, and though Muḥammad Bāqir Shaftī, the most influential of all the mujtahids in the 1830s and 1840s in Iran, refused to ratify the fatwā of denunciation,[147] the anti-Shaykhī propaganda was still effective. The dispute with the Bālāsarīs was occasionally renewed; and the Shaykhis were gradually forced into a defensive position. By the end of Rashtī's life the Shaykhis were largely isolated, at least in the ʿAtabāt.

The uprising of Karbalāʾ in 1258/1842, climaxing a period of riots and civil strife in the Shiʿite holy cities of Iraq after the restoration of the Ottoman central authority, temporarily strengthened the Shaykhis' hand from a political viewpoint, though it further damaged their relations with their adversaries.[148] The age-old Shiʿite-Sunni conflict inherent in southern Iraq was intensified by the Perso-Ottoman political disputes. Months of open

[144]Account of denunciation of Aḥsāʾī is given by various contemporary sources, among them *QU* 42–46 and *Dalīl al-Mutaḥayyirīn* 52–68. See also below, chap. 3.

[145]More details of the ʿulamas' opposition appear in *Dalīl al-Mutaḥayyirīn* 70–113; *QU* 55–56; *NK* 102–3; *Shaykhīgarī va Bābīgarī* 171–73 (quoting *Asrār al-Shahāda* by Mullā Muḥammad Ḥamza Sharīʿatmadār Māzandarānī).

[146]Others such as Shaykh Muḥammad Ḥasan Najafī, Shaykh Muḥammad Ḥusyn Najafī, and Sayyid Ibrāhīm Karbalāʾī in the ʿAtabāt, and Mullā Muḥammad Taqī Baraghānī, Mullā Muḥammad Jaʿfar Astarābādī, Mullā Āqā Darbandī, and Mullā Saʿīd Bārfurūshī among others in Iran assisted the ʿulama of the ʿAtabāt in their anti-Shaykhi campaign.

[147]See below, chap. 3.

[148]The best account on the siege of Karbalāʾ by Ottoman forces and the ensuing massacre appears in a long report from Farrant to Canning, F.O. 248/108, 15 May 1843 (partly cited in

defiance of the Turkish authorities eventually ended in a brutal massacre of thousands of inhabitants of Karbalā'. Throughout the period, Rashtī's role remained crucial, though somewhat enigmatic. His negotiation with Najīb Pasha, the governor general of Baghdad province, and the safe conduct he secured for his followers when the Ottomans sacked the city indicate a friendly relation, in contrast to the stance of other mujtahids like Sayyid Ibrāhīm Qazvīnī.[149] Yet Rashtī's policy cannot be seen as wholly pro-Ottoman, since he appears to have been connected with some of the leaders of the rebels in the city of Karbalā', such as Ibrāhīm Zaʿfarānī, a lūṭī (brigand) of Persian origin who was said to be instrumental in instigating the rebellion. Rashtī's preachings in Ramaḍān 1258/November 1842, shortly before the Karbalā' massacre, regarding the advent of the divine cause suggest that the popular movement first started with some messianic overtones and with Rashtī blessing but soon got out of hand and turned into a full-scale rebellion with disastrous consequences.[150]

By and large, however, involvement in politics remained a secondary issue for Shaykhis, compared with their main conflict with their Bālāsarī opponents. The hostility that the close students and followers of Rashtī increasingly encountered from their adversaries decisively turned them against the mainstream religion of the jurists and toward a messianic alternative. Rashtī's attempts to reduce the tension and to pursue a moderate, and on many occasions compromising, policy brought him even to the point of recantation. Yet for many members of the circle of the ʿAtabāt in the early 1840s, this pressure for conformity and assimilation had a reverse effect. The internal divisions in the Shaykhi ranks, even prior to Rashtī's death, basically resulted from the differing policies recommended by each of the two factions in response to the outside hostilities. One faction was more devoted to the messianism preached by the school and sought the answer to the Shaykhi prophecies to fulfill what the present bāb, namely Sayyid Kāẓim Rashtī, was unable to carry out. The other, evaded the messianic message embedded in Shaykhism and minimized points of difference with the dominant orthodoxy. The first trend eventually culminated in the Babi movement, the second in submission to orthodoxy (as with the Āẕarbaijānī

H. M. Balyuzi *The Bāb* [Oxford, 1974] App. I, 193–201). Also other reports by Sheil (F.O. 60/95, no. 96, Feb. 1843). Other accounts given by S. H. al-Ṭuʿma *Turāth Karbalā'* (Najaf, 1383/1964) 270–73; A. al-ʿAzzāwī *Tārīkh al-ʿIrāq bayn Iḥtilālayn* 8 vols. (Baghdad, 1373 Q.) VII, 64–69; A. al-Wardī *Lamaḥāt Ijtimāʿīya min Tārīkh al-ʿIrāq al-Ḥadīth* 3 vols. (Baghdad, 1971) II, 116–26; and *Nabil* 35–37 provide additional information. For full discussion see J. Cole and M. Momen's article "Mafia, Mob and Shiism in Iraq: The Rebellion of Ottoman Karbala, 1824–1843" *Past and Present* 112 (1986) 112–43.

149See below, chap. 5.

150In the years prior to the events of Karbalā', Rashtī maintained a limited but friendly relationship with the Persian government, especially after the death of Fatḥ ʿAlī Shāh with the Qajar princes exiled in the ʿAtabāt. But he also managed to develop intimate relations with the Ottoman provincial authorities. See *Shaykhīgarī va Bābīgarī* 238.

Shaykhis), or in the sectarianism of Kirmānī Shaykhis. A quietist minority followed Gauhar and Muḥīṭ Kirmānī. Although Corbin and others treated Babism as a deviation that "departed from" the mainstream of Shaykhi thought,[151] it should be emphasized that not only did Shaykhism offer the greatest contribution to the making of the Babi movement in theory and practice, but in fact the movement was the final outcome of almost half a century of Shaykhi speculation on the problem of Resurrection.

[151]*En Islam iranien* IV, 228, 283.

2

Prophets and Prophecies: Sufism and Popular Religion

The theoretical discussions put forward by Shaykhis and by individual scholars within the learned circles were part of a greater concern with the messianic themes in the Shiʿite environment. From the last quarter of the eighteenth century, the elements of messianism also reemerged in two other areas: the revived Sufi orders and the widespread popular prophecies. Though these trends seldom went beyond speculation and intuitive meditation, they were influential in a process that eventually brought about a heightened atmosphere of expectation for Ẓuhūr.

The revival of the Sufi orders in Iran was part of a greater resurgence of neo-Sufism in the Islamic world,[1] manifested both in the reorganization of the old Sufi orders and in the preaching of the wandering dervishes. While underlying causes for this renewed interest in Sufism have not been fully investigated,[2] it is possible that the vacuum in the intellectual climate of mid-eighteenth-century Iran was largely reponsible for its growth. After the Safavids, the weakening of the ʿulama's domination, demonstrated in the transfer of religious scholarship to the ʿAtabāt, was exacerbated by the unenthusiastic reception of the remnant of the Safavid ʿulama under Nādir and even Karīm Khān Zand. This to some extent temporarily reduced their

[1]For a general survey of early-nineteenth-century revivalism in North Africa, India, and Kurdistān, see J. S. Trimingham *The Sufi Orders in Islam* (Oxford, 1971) 105–32; F. Rahman *Islam* 2nd ed. (Chicago, 1979) 193–211.

[2]Besides primary sources dealing with Sufi orders in Iran in the nineteenth century and a number of Sufi biographical dictionaries written by the heads and followers of different orders, the only comprehensive study in a European language is R. Gramlich *Die Schiitischen Derwischorden Persiens* 2 vols., (Wiesbaden, 1975–1976), in which the author studied the history and developments in the Zahabī, Niʿmatullāhī, and Khāksār orders. N. Pourjavady and P. L. Wilson *Kings of Love: The Poetry and History of the Niʿmatullāhī Sufi Order* (Tehran, 1978) provides a brief and not always impartial account of Niʿmatullāhī history. J. Nurbakhsh *Masters of the Path: A History of the Masters of the Nimatullahi Sufi Order* (New York, 1980) is no more than a popularized chronicle of Niʿmatullāhī saints (chiefly based on *TH* III) aimed at Western converts to modern Niʿmatullāhī order.

influence, permitting revitalization and a wider diffusion of nonorthodox tendencies. In the cities, especially in central and southern Iran, leadership during the turbulent interregnum between the Zands and the Qajars (1779–1785) was provided by local figures, who often adopted Sufi affiliations to mobilize popular support. Relative prosperity under Karīm Khān in the regional economy of the south, the recovery of trade, and the improvement of communication among urban centers permitted the Sufi missionaries to seek new bases among the increasing population of Persian cities. One of the important signs of this revival was the diffusion of the Indian Sufism, which was reintroduced into Iran more than a century after the decline of orders in the Safavid era.

The Sufi Millenarians

The most outstanding example of this revival can be seen in the activities of Niʿmatullāhī emissaries, who by the second half of the eighteenth century had attracted a large audience in southern and central provinces. Despite a gradual decline in the Persian branch of the order during the seventeenth century, scattered groups of Niʿmatullāhīs survived in remote areas of eastern Iran. The Indian branch, however, thrived in Deccan, where it enjoyed favor and influence under Bahmanī and Niẓām Shāhī rulers. In the latter part of Riżā ʿAlī Shāh's life (d. circa 1214 /1799)—the last important *quṭb* (spiritual leader) of the order in India[3]—some of his disciples were dispatched to Iran for the purpose of providing guidance to the remnants of the order. Such attempts to explore new grounds appear to be not unconnected with the pressures imposed on the Riżā 'Alī after the death of his Daccani patron. As early as the 1760s a certain Shāh Ṭāhir Dakanī had visited Mashhad and Yazd, where he recruited new disciples and even dispatched a convert, the son of a Yazdī merchant, to his master.[4]

But it was some time later, when another well-known Niʿmatullāhī emissary, Mīr ʿAbd al-Ḥamīd Maʿṣūm ʿAlī Shāh, arrived in Shiraz in 1190 /1776, that these efforts yielded some results.[5] The Persian chronicler Riżā Qulī Khān Hidāyat states that Maʿṣūm ʿAlī's dispatch was the result of a demand by Persian followers for a delegation to preach the long-eclipsed Niʿm-

[3]On Riżā ʿAlī Shāh see *TH* III, 167–68; Z. Shīrvānī (Mast ʿAlī Shāh) *Ḥadāʾiq al-Sīyāḥa* ed. N. Tābandih (Tehran, 1348 Sh./1969) 197. On the brief account of the Indian branch of the order between the fifteenth and the eighteenth centuries see *TH* III, 84–104, 160–62. Also N. Pourjavady and P. L. Wilson "The Descendants of Shāh Niʿmatullāh Wali" *Islamic Culture* (Hyderabad, Jan. 1974); Gramlich *Derwischorden* I, 3; Pourjavady *Kings of Love* 86–88.

[4]*TH* III, 168–69. Not to be confused with the better-known Shāh Ṭāhir Qazvīnī Dakanī of the sixteenth century.

[5]On Maʿṣūm ʿAlī Shāh, besides entries in Shīrvānī's works, see *TH* III, 170–87; Nūr ʿAlī Shāh Iṣfahānī *Masnavī-yi Jannāt al-Wiṣāl* (completed by Raunaq ʿAlī Shāh Kirmānī and Niẓām ʿAlī Shāh Kirmānī), ed. J. Nūrbakhsh (Tehran, 1348 Sh./1969) 860–67. Also *MA* II, 405–6.

atullāhī cause.[6] During his two-and-a-half-year stay in the capital of Karīm Khān, he succeeded in organizing a small but active group of followers, recruited principally from the remaining survivors of the Niʿmatullāhī-Ismāʿīlī communities or other inactive orders of central and eastern Iran.[7]

One of Maʿsūm ʿAlī's earliest converts was Mīrzā ʿAbd al-Ḥusayn, known as Fayż ʿAlī Shāh, who was the hereditary imām jumʿa of Tūn, in Quhistān, before being converted to Sufism (possibly first to the Nūrbakhshī order). It is said that a mysterious message in his father's notes, advising him to "take knowledge from mouths of the adepts and make it a lamp for your path," made him abandon his position, don old clothing, sew patches on his robe as a sign of voluntary poverty, and travel to Isfahan, where he practiced numerical divination *(jafr)* and other occult sciences before finally reaching Shiraz.[8] This shift to voluntary poverty, the practice of occult sciences, and then adherence to an Indian wandering dervish like Maʿṣūm ʿAlī were typical signs of a renewed esoterism that had long persisted in communities with dormant heterodox tradition. The conversion of many other early disciples from towns and villages of eastern Iran, such as the famous Mushtāq ʿAlī Shāh, originally from Turbat Ḥaydarīya, and others from Sīrjān, Bam, Kirman, and Herat indicates the success of the Niʿmatullāhīs in recruiting from areas with long crypto-Ismāʿīlī tradition.[9]

What Maʿṣūm ʿAlī and other adepts preached on the surface was no more than the common Sufi guidance. They largely reconstructed the old pattern of hierarchy[10] but in spite of charges of blasphemy and disbelief, the Niʿmatullāhīs frequently advocated the necessity of sharīʿa.[11] Yet in its essence

[6]*Riyāḍ al-ʿĀrifīn* (Tehran, 1316 Sh./1927) 451; cf. *TH* III, 170–71.

[7]Some valuable points on the early phase of the Niʿmatullāhīs in Iran appear in the account given by Malcolm *History* II, 417–23. The details of the manuscript upon which Malcolm based his account of the Niʿmatullāhīs is not given, but internal evidence suggests that the source in the author's possession was the above-mentioned *Jannāt al-Wiṣāl*.

[8]On Fayż ʿAlī Shāh see *TH* III, 187–88; *Jannāt al-Wiṣāl* 864–67. Malcolm (*History*, 418) maintains that Fayż ʿAlī was a member of the Nūrbakhshī order in Quhistān before being initiated by Maʿṣūm ʿAlī Shāh. The long-lasting influence of the Nūrbakhshī order in Quhistān suggests that such a connection is not wholly unlikely.

[9]For the above Sufi converts and other possible Ismāʿīlī-Niʿmatullāhī connections in eastern and southeastern Iran see *TH* III, 188–211, 35–37, 268–95; Gramlich *Derwischorden* I, 32–33. For Ismāʿīlī connections in Maḥallāt see for example under ʿIzzat ʿAlī Shāh Maḥallātī in *TH* III, 263–64. For some suggestions on the nature of the relations between the two groups see N. Pourjavady and P. L. Wilson "Ismāʿīlīs and Niʿmatullāhīs" *Studia Islamica* 41 (1975) 113–35; W. Ivanow *Ismaili Literature: A Bibliographical Survey* (Tehran, 1963) 183–84.

[10]Many references to hierarchical titles and positions appear in *TH* III; *Bustān al-Sīyāḥa* and other sources. Nūr ʿAlī Shāh was promoted to the position of *Khalīfat al-Khulafāʾ wa al-Murshidīn* (*TH* III, 198) and Ḥusayn ʿAlī Shāh acquired an ijāza from Nūr ʿAlī (222, 231). See also Gramlich *Derwischorden* II, 39–251, for a study of of the Sufi hierarchy with references to Niʿmatullāhīs.

[11]See for example Maʿṣūm ʿAlī Shāh's tract *Sī va yik Kalama* (cited in *TH* III, 184–86) which among other moral advice and instructions for Sufi life emphasizes respect for sharīʿa. However, such a definition of sharīʿa differed widely from that of the contemporary mujtahids—a fact that led to charges of blasphemy and heresy. See also the seventeen Niʿmatullāhī principles cited in Malcolm *History* 418.

their message carried traits of messianic conviction. The large audience that was attracted to Maʿṣūm ʿAlī and his two young disciples, Nūr ʿAlī Shāh[12] and Mushtāq ʿAlī Shāh, first in Isfahan and then in Kirman, Herat, Mashhad, Shiraz, the ʿAtabāt and Kirmānshāh, saw in them saintly characters with exceptional detachment and poverty. Their outward eccentricity, their meditations, wanderings, and claims to divinely endowed gifts to prognosticate and influence the course of events, made them popular with the common people.

Maʿṣūm ʿAlī himself appears not to have claimed any specific spiritual mission beyond customary Sufi titles, though he maintained that his mission was the result of a dream in which his master had been instructed by the Eighth Imam to send his disciples to Iran.[13] The writings of his early followers, however, bear evidence of some claims with unmistakable protomessianic tone. The poetry of Nūr ʿAlī Shāh, perhaps the most gifted of all early Niʿmatullāhīs, makes frequent references to his claim to vicegerency (wilāya) on behalf of the Imam:

> I came again like Moses to reveal the Magic Hand
> Drown Pharaoh and his legions again in the Sea.
> I came again like Jesus to cut the throat of Antichrist.
> And by Mahdi's command resurrect the universe with a breath.[14]

In this passage, Nūr ʿAlī Shāh sees himself as the chief actor in the drama of resurrection, which is a reenactment of the prophecies of the past. His Mosaic miracles prevail over Pharaoh and his Christlike powers destroy the Antichrist (Dajjāl). This is a picture strongly reminiscent of the Shiʿite scenario of the Final Day. Yet he envisages himself only as the bearer of the Mahdi's command to rejuvenate the world. In another passage, filled with Qur'ānic references and allusions to hadith, he describes his intimate encounter with the Imam in a utopian Heaven not unlike Aḥsā'ī's Hurqalyā:

> I am the sun in the heaven of nowhere,
> beyond the realms of body and soul.
> I am the key to the mystery of the [hidden] treasure,[15]
> The whole [meaning] of the secret of "Be and it is."[16]
> In the sacred solitude of love,
> I am the intimate companion of the Lord of the Final Day.[17]

[12]Most of the materials on the early activities of Nūr ʿAlī Shāh came from his own account in a treatise called "Uṣūl wa al-Furūʿ" (cited in *Majmūʿa-ī az Āsār-i Nūr ʿAlī Shāh* ed. J. Nūrbakhsh [Tehran, 1350 Sh./1971] 56–60). For his short biography see *TH* III, 197–203, and cited sources. For the list of his works see Gramlich *Derwischorden* I, 34–35.

[13]*Riyaḍ al-ʿArifīn* 451.

[14]*Dīvān-i Nūr ʿAlī Shāh Iṣfahānī* ed. J. Nūrbakhsh (Tehran, 1349 Sh./1970) 105–6 (also translated in Pourjavady *Kings of Love* 201).

[15]Reference to a famous prophetic hadith.

[16]Qur'ān II, 111.

[17]*Dīvān-i Nūr ʿAlī Shāh* 196–97.

The same message comes through more vividly in the work of another Niʿmatullāhī poet, Muẓaffar ʿAlī, who in praise of his guide, Mushtāq ʿAlī, recites:

> I am the treasure of prophethood.
> I am the mirror of Iskandar.
> Swear to God, I am the eternal essence of this cycle.
> I am the seeker of Ḥaydarī wine.
> Swear to God, I am the minstrel in this cycle,
> the nightingale of the Jaʿfarī song.
> Swear to God that in this cycle,
> I am the deputy to the Mahdi of the ʿAskarī faith.
> I am the sun of Truth, I am the one,
> who was taught the art of fostering the inferiors.
> In the path of Walī [i.e., Shāh Niʿmatullāh] I am the teacher,
> like Salmān or Qanbar.
> On the spur of the moment, I remove from the King's head,
> the crown and headgear of sovereignty.
> Today, Mushtāq ʿAlī made it publicly manifest,
> the secret of the qalandar [wandering Sufi].[18]

These and many similar pieces reflected a new direction in the traditional Sufi interpretation of vicegerency. In assigning this status to their quṭb, the Niʿmatullāhī Sufis underlined the necessity for direct communication with the Imam. Such interpretation of wilāya was similar to the reassertion of an earlier Ismāʿīlī position, to which Niʿmatullāhīs were the closest heirs. Their notion of the Return of the Imam and Resurrection, however, hardly differed from that of Shaykhis, since it considered the coming of the Final Day as an extraordinary upheaval in unknown future. Though not as spectacular (and therefore as implausible) as in conventional accounts, there was little urgency attached to the necessity for the Advent of the Hidden Imam.[19] Nūr ʿAlī Shāh hints at a claim of deputyship in the return of the past manifestations. Muẓaffar ʿAlī's references to Ḥaydar (ʿAlī), Jaʿfar Ṣādiq, the Sixth Imam, and Ḥasan Askarī, the Eleventh Imam, are also important because they indicate a new orientation among the Niʿmatullāhīs, who in the past had largely remained uncommitted to Twelver Shiʿism.

Ambiguous references to deputyship, not uncommon in past Niʿmatullāhī

[18]Muẓaffar ʿAlī Shāh *Dīvān-i Mushtāqīya* (Tehran, 1347 Sh./1968) also cited in Abul-Fażl Burqaʿī *Ḥaqīqat al-ʿIrfān* (Tehran, n.d.) 165.

[19]See for example Nūr ʿAlī's description of Imāmat and Maʿād in his "Uṣūl wa al-Furūʿ" (*Majmuʿa* 45–47) and *Jannāt al-Wiṣāl* (21–23, 376, 754–55). He states: "And his [ʿAlī's] eleventh descendant is the Twelfth Imam who is the delegated deputy of the exalted the best of mankind [Muḥammad the Prophet]. He is the center of the circle of Being, the Lord of the Command and the Age and the Time [*Ṣāḥab al-Amr wa al-ʿAṣr wa al-Zamān*]. The order of the universe and the sustenance of mankind are blessed by his precious existence and by God's command he will manifest and remove oppression and injustice from the people of the world" (*Majmuʿa* 46).

history, were connected to their attraction to the holders of secular power. Assuming that the vicegerent of the time was assigned by the Hidden Imam to supervise and implement both secular and spiritual aspects of the Imam's authority, Niʿmatullāhīs were content to vest the secular power in the just ruler of the time. This delegation of power was a fifteenth-century legacy of Shāh Niʿmatullāh and his other contemporaries and was originally designed to reconcile the position of the quṭb with those rulers who showed favor and respect toward the Sufis. In the same fashion, dervishes of the late eighteenth century made several attempts to take sides with the "rightful" ruler, especially during the course of struggle between the Zands and the rising Qajars.[20] In Shiraz, secret contacts had been made as early as the late 1770s between Maʿṣūm ʿAlī and the founder of the Qajar dynasty, Āqā Muḥammad Khān, then still under detention in Karīm Khān's court, which suggest the Niʿmatullāhīs' search for an alternative secular support.[21] Indeed, Karīm Khān's suspicion of the newly arrived Sufis was not wholly unfounded.

The growing popularity of the Indian emissary, if Malcolm's figure can be believed, soon amounted to more than thirty thousand followers in the city of Shiraz.[22] The dervishes' possible alignment with the Qajars is hinted at in the charges of a certain pro-Zand dervish who accused Maʿṣūm ʿAlī and his disciples of plotting against Karīm Khān.[23] However, when the ʿulama's pressure forced the ruler to expel Sufis from Shiraz, they found temporary shelter in Isfahan. There they offered their support and assistance to ʿAlī Murād Khān, the Zand chief and governor of the city, in his bid for power against his numerous rivals just after Karīm Khān's death.[24] But when ʿAlī Murād temporarily withdrew from Isfahan, the Niʿmatullāhīs, together with other dervishes, shifted their allegiance to the victorious Āqā Muḥammad Khān Qājār. On the Zands' recapture of the city, the Niʿmatullāhīs were accused of having seditious ambitions similar to those of Safavid propagandists for bringing the Qajars to power. They were disgraced, mutilated, and expelled from the city. In their support of the Qajars, the Niʿmatullāhīs reflected the yearning of the inhabitants of Isfahan for peace and security that could only be achieved if the Zands' declining control over the cities of central and southern Iran were replaced by a more viable, and more enduring, power.

Ten years later, the Niʿmatullāhīs became involved in a new round of tense political conflict in the city of Kirman. Between 1205/1790 and 1207/1792, in alliance with the head of the Ismāʿīlī sect, Abul-Ḥasan Khān (the chief administrator of the province), they mobilized the people of Kirman to

[20]Nūr ʿAlī Shāh's view on the question of secular power is apparent in a tract called "Hidāyat Nāmih" cited in *Majmūʿa*.

[21]*Jannāt al-Wiṣāl* 108–9.

[22]Malcolm *History* II, 417.

[23]*Bustān al-Sīyāḥa* 254.

[24]R. Q. Hidāyat *Uṣūl al-Fuṣūl fī Ḥuṣūl al-Wuṣūl* (MS) cited in *Kings of Love* 114–15; cf. *TH* III, 187.

hold out against the Zands' last desperate attempts to recapture the city.[25] The age-old connections between the Ismāʿīlīs and Niʿmatullāhīs channeled popular support for Nūr ʿAlī and Mushtāq ʿAlī in favor of pro-Qajar Ismāʿīlī notables.[26] In response, Mullā ʿAbdullāh, the chief mujtahid of Kirman, encouraged his supporters to attack dervishes. At a public meeting in the Jāmiʿ mosque, an agitated mob stoned Mushtāq ʿAlī to death and injured other dervishes. Nūr ʿAlī Shāh fled from Kirman and the anti-Qajars achieved a brief victory. Shortly afterward, however, Kirman was captured by Āqā Muḥammad Khān and a brutal purge of the hostile elements began.[27]

The Niʿmatullāhīs' support of the Qajars never really paid off. As the Sufis began to realize with great dismay, once the Qajars were consolidated, whether out of political expediency or religious conviction, they preferred cooperation with the ʿulama to the blessings of the dervishes. In the following years, Niʿmatullāhī sphere of influence gradually moved westward, only to be restrained by the ʿulama, who themselves had returned to the cities of western and central Iran after the restoration of political stability. In the period between 1793 and 1795 Nūr ʿAlī Shāh moved to the ʿAtabāt and began to preach among pilgrims and students of the religious schools, followed by Maʿṣūm ʿAlī and his close disciples.[28] A few brief dialogues with the prominent ʿulama are reported, but the generally hostile reception pushed Niʿmatullāhīs back to the border towns of Kurdistān, where they seem to have enjoyed some popularity in the areas traditionally influenced by Ahl-i Ḥaqq.[29]

Despite their great though ephemeral popularity, the Sufis were losing ground to the ʿulama, who under Fatḥ ʿAlī Shāh (1797–1834) enjoyed even greater support. Fatḥ ʿAlī Shāh's attitude toward Sufis was one of reticence and suspicion, which no doubt contributed to the increasing hostility of the

[25]For this episode between the death of Karīm Khān Zand and the conquest of the city by the Qajars see *RS* IX, 254–61; Aḥmad ʿAlī Khān Vazīrī Kirmānī *Tārīkh-i Kirmān (Sālārīya)* ed. M. I. Bāstānī Pārīzī (Tehran, 1340 Sh./1961) 332–69; R. G. Watson *A History of Persia* (London, 1866) 72–75.

[26]For Niʿmatullāhī involvement see "Ismāʿīlīs and Niʿmatullāhīs" 118–24. For the later Ismāʿīlī resurgence see below, this chapter.

[27]For Mushtāq's life and death see *Tārīkh-i Kirmān*, 346–50; *TH* 188–94. The original account is usually taken from *Jannāt al-Wiṣāl* 161–64, and *Masnavī-yi Gharāʾib* by Raunaq ʿAlī Shāh (ed. J. Nūrbakhsh [Tehran, 1352 Sh./1973]) which is entirely devoted to Mushtāq.

[28]For the episode of Nūr ʿAlī Shāh's abode in the ʿAtabāt and Baghdad see *TH* III, 199–203; *QU* 199–200; *MA* II, 443–48. It was in Baghdad, under the protection of Aḥmad Pāshā, the vālī of the province, that he wrote his *Jannāt al-Wiṣāl*. For a study of the content of this work see M. de Miras *La Méthode spirituelle d'un maître du Soufisme iranien: Nur ʿAli-Shah* (Paris, 1974).

[29]For the distribution of Ahl-i Ḥaqq in Kurdistān and Azarbaijan see V. Minorsky "The Sect of Ahl-i Ḥakk" in his *Iranica* (Tehran, 1964) 306–16 (314). It is also from this period that many new disciples from western Iran who had joined the order as a result of Nūr ʿAlī's efforts, dispersed to northwest and central Iran and established permanent circles during the first two decades of the nineteenth century.

ʿulama and reflected in their numerous anti-Sufi refutations.[30] The best-known of these, *Khayrātīya* was written by Āqā Muḥammad ʿAlī Bihbahānī, son of Muḥammad Bāqir.[31] The author sharply attacks Maʿṣūm ʿAlī and his followers for their "corrupt beliefs" and more, for "misguiding" the public. He accuses them of "undermining the rules of the applied sharīʿa" and condemns among other things their tolerance of other religions.[32]

The ʿulama's hostility did not stop at verbal condemnation. The execution of Maʿṣūm ʿAlī, Muẓaffar ʿAlī, and several other Sufis by Āqā Muḥammad ʿAlī Bihbahānī, known as the Sufi Killer (Ṣūfī Kush), around 1212 /1798,[33] and the death of Nūr ʿAlī Shāh in Mosul under suspicious circumstances three years later,[34] showed the ʿulama's increasing intolerance of the Sufis' growing audience, now nearing sixty thousand.[35] The ʿulama's desire, and ability, to destroy their rivals even at the cost short-term public discontent persuaded the newly enthroned Fatḥ ʿAlī Shāh to succumb to their self-assumed authority in dealing with religious dissent. Bihbahānī bluntly declared: "The responsibility of such acts [punishment of the Sufis] falls only within the jurisdiction of the ʿulama and the executors of the holy law."[36]

The monarch complied with the ʿulama's wishes with little hesitation. In a letter to Bihbahānī, Fatḥ ʿAlī Shāh (presumably with the advice of his powerful minister Ḥājjī Ibrāhīm Khān Iʿtimād al-Daula, an ally of Bihbahānī and enemy of the Sufis) expresses concern about the "alarming" degree to which the Sufis "extended their belief." Since this is "contrary to the interests of true religion," he assures the mujtahid, he has "ordered that the sect be extirpated and put an end to in order that the true faith may flourish." Informing Bihbahānī that he has already arrested two more Niʿmatullāhī

[30]See C. Rieu, comp., *Catalogue of Persian MSS. in the British Museum* 3 vols. (London, 1879–1883) I, 33–34; also partly cited in *TH* III, 175–84, and widely discussed in *Vaḥīd* 398–430 and in Z. Maḥallātī *Kashf al-Ishtibāh* (Tehran, 1336 Sh./1957) 197–200.

[31]In a biased but still useful refutation, *Ḥaqīqat al-ʿIrfān*, Burqaʿī devotes a whole section (33–56) to a discussion of works by the nineteenth-century ʿulama such as Mīrzā Abul-Qāsim Qumī's *Jāmiʿ al-Shatāt;* Mullā Aḥmad Narāqī's *Miʿrāj al-Saʿāda;* Mīrzā Ḥusayn Ṭabarsī Nūrī's *Mustadrak al-Wasāʾil*; and Muḥammad Kāẓim Yazdī's *ʿUrwat al-Wuthqā,* which all contain refutations of Sufis.

[32]Bihbahānī's sharp attacks in *Khayrātīya* appear to be a reply to Nūr ʿAlī's implicit criticism of the ʿulama. In his poetry he frequently blames shaykhs and *zāhids* (piety-minded) for their false piety, narrow-mindedness, and cupidity. In a famous *ghazal* he warns: "Thou zāhid! What is the boast for?/Return to your quarter and die in silence!/Or else, I will unveil all your hidden secrets" (*Dīvān* 106). Also see *Jannāt al-Wiṣāl* (106–7) for Sufi's reproachful tone toward their harassers.

[33]The account of the execution of Sufis appears in *Vaḥīd* 392–95 and *TH* III, 174–75. On Muḥammad ʿAlī Bihbahānī see *Vaḥīd* 361–80, 96–450; *MA* II, 561–67.

[34]*TH* III, 201; cf. *MA* II, 448. A. Izadgushasb *Nūr al-Abṣār* (Isfahan, 1325 Sh./1946) contradicts Malcolm's account *(History* II, 421–22) of Nūr ʿAlī's death.

[35]Malcolm *History* II, 421.

[36]*TH* III, 177. *Ḥaqīqat al-ʿIrfān* (161–62) produces the text of four fatwās by contemporary mujtahids in the ʿAtabāt—Baḥr al-ʿUlūm, ʿAlī Ṭabāṭabāʾī, Muḥammad Mahdī Shahristānī, and Abul-Qāsim Qumī—in condemnation of Maʿṣūm ʿAlī and his disciples.

agents and dispatched them to Kirmānshāh, he states: "We send them . . . to be delivered over to you, whom we consider as wisest, the most learned, and most virtuous of all the oulāmāhs [ʿulama] of our kingdom. Put them to death, confine them, or punish them in the way you deem most proper and most consonant to the decrees of the holy religion."[37] The ensuing persecution of Niʿmatullāhīs was the first successful case of ʿulama's vigorous campaign to involve government in the task of eradicating religious dissent.[38]

Over the next few decades, persecution and hostility reduced the messianic zeal of the wandering Niʿmatullāhīs, giving way to the urbanized quietism of well-versed Sufis, no longer eccentric figures but revered heads of an organized order. A nucleus of devoted Sufis was able to recruit from merchants, notables, and occasionally the Qajar aristocracy. But the Sufi orders generally lacked the institutional basis and the religious legitimacy that gave strength to their clerical rivals and greatly facilitated their establishment. The influence of the ʿulama over the public and the way they successfully channeled this influence to political ends persuaded the Qajars, or at least the dominant faction within the ruling family, to come to terms with them. Yet it appears that in most cases the government became involved in harassing the Sufis only when necessary to appease the ʿulama.[39]

Ḥusayn ʿAlī Shāh, the next quṭb (after Nūr ʿAlī Shāh), who himself came from a clerical background, made conciliatory efforts to open a dialogue with the ʿulama of Isfahan. His overtures were in vain, only increasing the isolation of the order.[40] His two disciples, Majẕūb ʿAlī Shāh and Kauṣar ʿAlī Shāh,[41] made attempts to seek support from the pro-Sufi elements in the Qajar state. In the course of Muḥammad Shāh's accession to the throne (1250/1834), and subsequently during the events that led to the downfall of

[37]Malcolm *History* II, 422–23.

[38]An interesting caricature of the ʿulama and their hostility toward Sufis appears in J. Morier *The Adventures of Hajji Baba* (London, 1824; New York, 1947). Morier's description of Qum seems to be based on his personal observation. A wandering dervish describes to Hajji Baba the character of Mīrzā Abul-Qāsim Qumī, the chief mujtahid of the city: "Such is his influence that many believe he could even subvert the authority of the Shah himself . . . and, except stoning his Sufi and holding us wandering dervishes as the dirt under his feet, I know of no fault in him" (XLV, 280). Later Mīrzā Abul-Qāsim himself, amidst cursing Sufis, proclaims: "All who call themselves dervishes, be they the followers of Nūr Ali Shahi [*sic*], be they Zahabīes, be they Nakshbendies, or be they of that accursed race of Uweisīes; all are Kafirs, or heretics, all are worthy of death" (XLVI, 308). The real Mīrzā-yi Qumī of *Jāmiʿ al-Shatāt* is no less scornful than the fictional one.

[39]*TH* III, 177, 181, 205–36.

[40]Ibid. 223–34; Gramlich *Derwischorden* I, 40–41, and cited sources.

[41]On Majẕūb ʿAlī see *TH* III, 257–63; Gramlich *Derwischorden* I, 41–43 and on Kauṣar ʿAlī see *TH* III, 264–66; Gramlich I, 44–45; *al-Maʾāthir waʾl-Āthār* 164; *MA* IV, 1300–1; *TAS* II/2, 549. For their joint ijāza by Nūr ʿAlī see *Majmūʿa* 90–97. On the division within the Niʿmatullāhīs as a result of a dispute over the leadership see Tābandih's introduction to *Ḥadāʾiq al-Sīyāḥa* iii–iv.

Abul-Qāsim Qā'im Maqām and the appointment of Ḥājjī Mīrzā Āqāsī, Ni'matullāhīs played some part.[42]

Muḥammad Shāh's Sufi tendencies allowed many Sufis to hold prominent offices during his reign.[43] In many ways his reign was an era of renewed Sufi activities, which were only achieved by a substantial modification of earlier aspirations. Muḥammad Shāh's reverence for other Sufis, only if and when it did not interfere with Ḥājjī Mīrzā Āqāsī's personal brand of Sufism,[44] hardly resulted in any striking shift of influence from the 'ulama to the Sufis. Save for a few minor cases, largely alienated from its original claims and unable to recapture the public attention, the Ni'matullāhī order remained politically passive throughout the rest of the nineteenth century.[45]

The revival of the order was the most outstanding example of Sufi revivalism in Iran, but it was not the only one. Other orders, such as the Z̲ahabīya, Nūrbakhshīya, and Khāksār, after a long period of virtual eclipse, began to emerge from obscurity. In Fars, Quṭb al-Dīn Muḥammad Z̲ahabī Nayrīzī (d. 1173/1760) gave a new impetus to the Z̲ahabī order. A student of religious sciences,he traveled in various parts of Iran and after a long residence in Najaf settled in Shiraz, where he lived and taught for the rest of his life. Some important Sufis of the next generation studied under him.[46] During the next few decades his successors promoted the order in Shiraz and attracted some local notables. The trusteeship of the shrine of Shāh Chirāgh (Aḥmad ibn Mūsā, son of Mūsā Kāẓim), the third most important pilgrimage shrine inside Iran, greatly assisted their stand. In the mid-nineteenth

[42]This was primarily due to the earlier influence of Sufis such as Kausar 'Alī Shāh, Zayn al-'Ābidīn Shīravānī, Naṣrullāh Ṣadr al-Mamālik Ardabīlī, and Mullā 'Abbās Īrvānī (Ḥājjī Mīrzā Āqāsī) on the royal family and the officials and courtiers of 'Abbās Mīrzā in Azarbaijan. For the life and works of Shīrvānī besides his autobiography in *Bustān al-Sīyāḥa* (348–50) and other biographical dictionaries, see Gramlich *Derwischorden* I, 50–53 and E. G. Browne *A Literary History of Persia* 4 vols. (Cambridge, 1902–1924) IV, 450–52.

[43]For the Ni'matullāhī involvement in the politics of the period see *TH* III; *RS* X, 67–68, 86–87, 96, 163 (which provides revealing evidence on the Ni'matullāhīs' influence on the monarch). Also Algar *Religion and State* 105; H. Algar "The Revolt of Āghā Khān Maḥallātī and the transference of the Ismā'īlī Imamate to India" *Studia Islamica* 29 (1969), 55–81 (74) and cited sources. For later suborder of the Ni'matullahīya see M. Humāyūnī *Tārīkh-i Silsilahā-yi Ṭarīqa-yi Ni'matullāhīya dar Īrān* (Tehran, n.d.) and N. Mudarrisī Chahārdihī *Silsilahā-yi Ṣūfīya-yi Īrān* (Tehran, 1360 Sh./1981).

[44]For some indications of this influence see below chap. 4.

[45]The exception was Ḥājjī Mullā Sulṭān 'Alī Gunābādī (1251–1327/1835–1909), the head of the Gunābādī suborder, who reemphasized the position of the quṭb not only as the guide but as the representative and gate to the Imam of the Age. The concepts of gateship and oath of allegiance to possessor of wilāya was a variation on the older themes. For his life and works see N. Tābandih *Nābigha-yi 'Ilm va 'Irfān* (Tehran, 1374/1928); *TH* III, 540–42.

[46]S. Parvīzī *Tadhkirat al-Awlīyā'* 534–37; *TH* III, 216–19, 339; Gramlich *Derwischorden* I, 17–18. The claim of some later Z̲ahabī sources regarding the pupilage of some well-known 'ulama of the 'Atabāt such as Ja'far Najafī, Baḥr al-'Ulūm, and Mullā Mihrāb Gīlānī, and that they were instructed by Quṭb al-Dīn for spiritual guidance, should be viewed with reservations. His assumed connection with Aḥsā'ī while the former was residing in Aḥsā' seems almost impossible if we consider the chronological difference.

century, under ʿAbd al-Nabī and Abul-Qāsim Sharīfī (known as Mīrzā Bābā), the order enjoyed some significance both in social standing and in the field of mystical and literary works, but it in no way infringed the norms of an orthodox order by venturing any antinomical claim.[47]

In the same period, the remnants of a branch of the messianic Nūrbakhshī order, which had survived from the pre-Safavid times in Khurasan and then in Nā'īn, also underwent some revival. Ḥājjī ʿAbd al-Wahhāb Nā'īnī (d. 1212/1797) was the first modern quṭb of any significance. References to his *uwaysī* knowledge (spiritual proficiency attained without a visible guide) indicate an intuitive approach similar to that of the founder of the order, Sayyid Muḥammad Nūrbakhsh.[48] Other branches and offshoots of the Nūrbakhshī were also known, in Quhistān and ʿIrāq-i ʿAjam, but it was under ʿAbd al-Wahhāb and his disciples that some messianic prophecies of the Nūrbakhshī tradition were renewed.[49]

The impact of Sufism, whether that of wandering dervishes or settled orders, upon the population of Iran was undeniable. Writing before 1815, Malcolm reports that "the progress of Sooffeeism has been of late very rapid." Though "the orthodox hierarchy of Persia have from the first made an open and violent war upon this sect" and though the ʿulama successfully convinced the monarch that "the established religion was necessary to the support of the state,"[50] the Sufis' challenge was still not wholly defeated. Malcolm questions the accuracy of the figure given by his unnamed sources of 200,000 to 300,000 Sufi converts in Iran, but adds: "It is impossible that they [the sources] can have any means of forming such a calculation; and they probably include in this number not only those who believe in the visionary doctrine of this sect, but those whose faith in the efficiency of the forms and usage of the established religion has been shaken by the tenets of Sooffee teachers. The latter class are very numerous; and they have probably been increased by the violent means which have been taken to defend the established religion."[51] One might argue, with a good deal of evidence in later sources, that in spite of consolidation of orthodoxy in the ensuing decades and in spite of the state's support of the ʿulama, the number of

[47]For the development of the Z̲ahabī order in modern times see *TH* III, 219, 329, 456; Gramlich *Derwischorden* I, 18–23; Mudarrisī Chahārdihī *Ṣūfīya* 148–78. On his visit to Shiraz the Anglican missionary Henry Martyn observed the wealth and the annual income of Shāh Chirāgh and its trustee (*A Memoir of the Rev. Henry Martyn* ed. J. Sargent [London, 1843] 364–65).

[48]Yet both *TH* (III, 215–16) and J. Ṣadaqīyānlū (*Taḥqīq dar Aḥvāl va Ās̲ār-i Sayyid Muḥammad Nūrbakhsh* [Tehran, 1351 Sh./1972] 63–64) trace the spiritual chain of ʿAbd al-Wahhāb back to Sayyid Muḥammad Nūrbakhsh.

[49]One of his best-known disciples, Mīrzā Abul-Qāsim Shīrāzī, known as Sukūt, was influential among the Sufis of Shiraz. See *TH* III, 247–50; M. H. Ruknzādih Ādamīyat *Dānishmandān va Sukhansarāyān-i Fārs* 4 vols. (Tehran, 1337–1340 Sh.) III, 167–70; *Memoir of H. Martyn* 351–53.

[50]Malcolm *History* II, pp. 414–15.

[51]Ibid. 423.

skeptics, agnostics, and more significantly antinomians increased even after the eclipse of the Niʿmatullāhīs and their counterparts. As Malcolm observes, the chief influence of Sufism on a larger portion of the urban population was to foster skepticism and dissent against the established religion. If Sufism could not survive as a movement of mass protest with a socioreligious program to replace sharīʿa, it nonetheless brought to surface the depth of antiorthodox feelings engrained in Shiʿite dissent.

Between 1790 to 1850, the growth and establishment of three abovementioned orders turned Shiraz into one of the important centers of Sufism in central and southern Iran, allowing the emergence of a less orthodox intellectual climate hardly discernible in any other part. The gradual inclination over three generations from orthodoxy to Niʿmatullāhī Sufism of the family of Ḥājjī Muḥammad Ḥasan Shīrazī, himself a staunch Uṣūlī, is an example of the Sufis' success in Shiraz.[52] Despite chronic waves of persecution and violent attacks by the mob, the Sufis of Shiraz held out against the ʿulama and recruited new converts from both merchants and religious students.[53]

Besides the established orders, however, the city also hosted a number of wandering dervishes with Jalālī, ʿAjam, and other Khāksār affiliations who in their journeys to and from India, Anatolia, and central Asia took up their abode in the Sufi convents of Shiraz.[54] Their vast network extended from Chishtīs of Punjab and Deccan to central and southern Iran, among the communities of Naqshbandī and Ahl-i Ḥaqq in Kurdistān and Azarbaijan, and then further to Anatolia, Roumelia, and as far as Albania, where they were connected with Bektāshī, Naqshbandī, and Mevlevī centers. In the east, they were concentrated in central Khurasan in Turbat-i Ḥaydarīya (the shrine of the Sufi saint Quṭb-al-Dīn Ḥaydar), and from there they traveled up to Marv, Khiva, Samarkand, and Bukhara, to visit the shrine of Sulṭān Jalāl al-Dīn Ḥaydar and stay in Naqshbandī convents. On the way back they passed through Balkh, Herat, and Kandihar to end up again in northern India. Their itinerary also included frequent visits to holy cities of southern Iraq, the Ḥijāz, and southern Arabia.

These widespread travels and contacts with various orders, sects, and ideas were defined as "exploring horizons and souls" and were intended to

[52]For the biography of Ḥājjī Muḥammad Ḥasan and his family, later quṭbs of Niʿmatullāhī order, see *TH* III, 340–45, 353, 387–94; *FN* II, 123–24; *Memoirs of H. Martyn* 360–63.

[53]For examples of persecution of Sufis in Shiraz see Z. Shīrvānī *Rīyāḍ al-Sīyāḥa* (Tehran, 1339 Sh./1958) 53–55; *TH* III, 335–36, 389.

[54]For Khāksār see Gramlich I, 70–88; Mudarrisī Chahārdihī *Khāksār;* S. H. Amīn "Iṭṭilāʿāṭī dar bārih-yi darvīshān-i Khāksār" *Rāhnamā-yi Kitāb* 20 (1356 Sh.) 229–34 (which surveys sources on the order); A. Mudarrisī (Maʿṣūm ʿAlī Shāh) *Ganjīnih-yi Aulīyā' yā A'īnih-yi ʿUrafā* (Tehran, 1338 Sh./1959). For general information on wandering dervishes see Trimingham *The Sufi Orders* 264–69; *EI*[2]: DARWĪSH (D. B. Macdonald); J. P. Brown *The Darvishes, or Oriental Spiritualism* (London, 1868). On their gatherings in Shiraz in Haft Tan and Chihil Tanān see *TH* III, 490–91.

purify the seeker so as to give him a material detachment and moral insight. In practice, such experience exposed the wandering dervishes to an amalgamation of broad and diverse ideas and attitudes. While they lacked a firm hierarchical order and a well-defined doctrine, their function as intermediary agents among various Muslim communities and over a large geographical territory was highly significant. The itinerant dervishes were responsible for the reintroduction and diffusion in the Persian environment of popular beliefs and prognostications, ranging from cabbalistic gnosticism of the Bektashīs (a legacy of the Ḥurūfīs) to the extremism of Ahl-i Ḥaqq and Nuṣayris of western Iran (or others in central Asia), popular Indian pantheism, and remnants of pre-Islamic pagan beliefs of Arabia. Their behavior and modes of expression were often too eccentric and spectacular to be taken seriously. They rarely troubled religious or civil authorities, and if they did they were easily thrown out of towns. But their eccentricity gave them a unique chance to transmit popular beliefs as well as news of political change and upheaval from neighboring lands. Through entertainment, storytelling, singing, and poetry reciting, or by performing magical acts, they captured people's imagination as effectively as any available public media.

Most sources rarely go beyond describing the appearance and behavior of wandering dervishes.[55] Accounts of encounters with dervishes affiliated with Jalālī and Khāksār orders, however, shed some light on their attitudes. The way they saw and interpreted the superiority of the Europeans (or the Christians, as they identified them) is an example of the apprehension that by the second quarter of the century was beginning to develop among the ordinary people of Iran, largely in response to the imminent threat by neighboring imperial powers. The widely traveled dervishes were among the first to notice these changes. Identifying them with past calamities or with the familiar examples of messianic trends, the dervishes conveyed to their audiences a vivid message of doom aptly fitting the public's fears of Christian domination. Fascinated by their wild appearance and dramatic exclamations, the poorly informed people of the cities and villages listened eagerly as the dervishes spun a blend of fantasy and reality about Europeans who came to conquer the world and vanquish Islam. The self-sponsored propaganda of dervishes, linked to familiar themes of an imminent apocalyptic future, could not have been more effective.

Joseph Wolff, an eccentric English traveler and an attentive, though careless recorder of popular thought, describes an encounter with a party of

[55]References to wandering dervishes in mid-nineteenth-century travel accounts are numerous. Lady M. Sheil *Glimpses of Life and Manners in Persia* (London, 1856) 152, 192–96; C. J. Wills *In the Land of the Lion and the Sun* (London, 1891) 42–52; J. B. Fraser, *Travels in Kurdistan, Mesopotamia, etc.* 2 vols. (London, 1840) I, 289–316; A. H. Layard *Early Adventures in Persia, Susiana and Babylonia* (London, 1894) 175–76, 230–32; R. B. M. Binning *A Journal of Two Years' Travel in Persia etc.* 2 vols. (London, 1857) II, 72–73; E. G. Browne *A Year amongst the Persians* 56–61, 195–98, 312. For storytellers see J. Malcolm *Sketches of Persia* (London, 1845) 91–103.

dervishes on his way back from a mission to the khanate of Bukhara in 1844. "The time will come when there shall be no difference between rich and poor, between high and low, when property shall be in common—even wives and children," they warned him.[56] Later, in a gathering in Marv, a dervish who was relating the deeds of Timur suddenly broke off, and turning to Wolff, said: "The English people are now Timur, for they are descendants of Ghengis Khan. The Inglees will be the conquerors of the world. On my pilgrimage to Mecca, I came to Aden, where they keep a strong force, and from whence they may march to Mecca whenever they please; and march towards Mecca they shall."[57] When a Turkoman in the audience said, "The Russians shall be the conquerors of the world" and "All is over with Islam," another dervish agreed with him: "The great mullas of Samarcand assert that Russia is the Jaaj-Majooj [Gog and Magog], and this has been already predicted by Ameer Sultan, the great derveesh of Room."[58] Then a dervish from Patna told the gathering of "the deeds of the British nation in Hindustan, of General Lake and Lord Clive," and another dervish from Sinde confirmed that the British governor of the newly annexed Sinde province, Lord Napier, "is like lightning flame." The astonished audience predicted in earnest, "They [i.e., the British] certainly will come here; and if they come, we submit at once." A local notable, present in the gathering, agreed: "The English are a people of integrity, and therefore God rewards their integrity."[59]

The Ismaʿīlī Revival and Other Trends

The revival of Persian Ismāʿīlīsm in the nineteenth century illustrated the renewal of long-forgotten aspirations in an area of Iran that not only was influenced by Sufism but preserved some aspects of crypto-Ismāʿīlī heterodoxy.[60] Among the Nizārīs of eastern Iran, in the period under Abul-Ḥasan Khān, the Ismāʿīlī imam and the governor of Kirman (d. 1206/1791), the past connections between the Niʿmatullāhīs and Ismāʿīlīs were further

[56]Rev. Joseph Wolff *Narrative of a Mission to Bokhara* 5th ed. (London, 1848) 297–98.

[57]Ibid. 313.

[58]Ibid. 313–14.

[59]Ibid. 314–15. Not everyone agreed with the gentleman from Marv. Earlier on his route Wolff heard of an Afghānī sayyid, sarcastically sneering at his claim to be a dervish: "I know these Frankee derveeshes—I know these English derveeshes. They go into a country, spy out mountains and valleys, seas and rivers; find out a convenient adit [passage] and then go home, inform a gentleman there—a chief, who has the name of Company, who sends soldiers, and takes the country." This idea was repeated by other dervishes. Ibid. 296–97.

[60]These aspirations might also have been inspired by similar developments in the communities of Ismāʿīlīs in India. As early as 1175/1762, among the Dāʾūdīs of Gujarat, a certain Hibatullāh ibn Ismāʿīl had claimed that he was in direct contact with the Hidden Imam and had been appointed by him to the rank of *al-Ḥujjat al-Ilāhī*. Ismail Poonawala *Biobibliography of Ismāʿīlī Literature* (Malibu, Calif., 1977) 13.

strengthened.[61] The next imam, Shāh Khalīlullāh, son of Abul-Ḥasan Khān, together with his political ambitions that brought him close to the Qajars, appears to have entertained some spiritual claims. His effort to organize the Ismāʿīlī sympathizers in Yazd, Kirman, and Quhistān regions, however, came to an abrupt end in 1817 when he was murdered in Yazd by the mob, incited by a local mujtahid.[62] Not much is recorded about his claim or the extent of his support, but from what is known about the revolt (1843–1844) of his son, Ḥusayn ʿAlī Shāh Āqā Khān, one can suspect that at least in the early stages a proto-messianic *daʿwa* (public call) was the mobilizing force behind a movement that subsequently turned into a political revolt.[63]

Whatever the motives of Khalīlullāh and Āqā Khān, their actions must have planted hope in the hearts of some followers. Qatīl al-Karbalāʾī, the early Babi apologist, states that though the Ismāʿīlīs are a small, insignificant community who "are mostly illiterate and ignorant," nevertheless they also anticipate a manifestation among the descendants of Khalīlullāh.[64] He relates that once in 1258/1842, in Najaf, he and his friends met an Ismāʿīlī mystic and scholar of high caliber, who prophesied the coming downfall of the Qajars and the transference of the monarchy to Āqā Khān.[65]

But if the claims of Khalīlullāh hardly extended beyond the limits of the Ismāʿīlī community, there were others who put forward more widespread and at the same time less sophisticated claims. A good example of this kind of rustic claimant, which often appeared in the garb of rural sainthood, can be traced in the communities of Ahl-i Ḥaqq in Azarbaijan. As early as 1191/1777, a certain Qāsim Shabān, a shepherd from the village of Dih-khwāriqān near Tabriz, following some experience and holy dreams, claimed to be the deputy *(nāʾib)* of the Imam.[66] He immediately gained popularity among the villagers in the area, and after expelling the village's local mulla, became an unchallenged saint in the whole area. Pilgrims came to the village to pay tribute to Shaykh Qāsim Shabān, the new nā'ib who could cure the sick and give sight to the blind. His fame even gave Karīm Khān Zand cause for concern. The increasing number of Shaykh Qāsim's followers persuaded the governor of the province, Najaf Qulī Khān Dunbulī, to invite him to Tabriz. He was warmly received and was put up in the governor's private quarters. When he was opposed by the ʿulama of the city, who denied his

[61] Pourjavādī and Wilson "Ismāʿīlīs and Niʿmatullāhīs" 118–24 and cited sources.

[62] On Khalīlullāh see Muḥammad Jaʿfar Nāʾīnī *Jāmiʿ-i Jaʿfarī* ed. Īraj Afshār (Tehran, 1353 Sh./1974) 558; M. Rousseau "Mémoire sur les Ismaelis et les Nosairis de Syrie" *Annales des Voyages de la Géographie et de l'Histoire* 14 (1811) 279–80; *RS* X, 551–52; Āqā Khān Maḥallātī *ʿIbrat Afzā* (Bombay, 1278/1861) 5–6.

[63] H. Algar "The Revolt of Āghā Khān Maḥallātī" 55–81 and the cited sources.

[64] *Qatīl* 516.

[65] Ibid.

[66] ʿAbd al-Razzāq Dunbulī (Maftūn) *Tajribat al-Aḥrār wa Taslīyat al-Abrār* ed. H. Qāżī Ṭabāṭabāʾī, 2 vols. (Tabriz, 1350 Sh./1971) II, 196–97.

supernatural capacities, Shaykh Qāsim's followers, perhaps with the blessing of the Khan, attacked the chief mujtahid, and forced him to flee from Tabriz.[67]

The popularity of Shaykh Qāsim remained at its height for some time, particularly at a transitory period when conflict and uncertainty over the contested monarchy generated popular speculations. Because of a dream in which Shaykh Qāsim saw the Mahdi performing prayers in a certain mosque in Tabriz, Najaf Qulī Khān, now a firm believer in the shepherd shaykh, complied with public demand and erected Maqām-i Ṣāḥib al-Amr (the sanctuary for the Lord of the Command) in the ruins of the old mosque.[68] Yet after two years his fame and reputation faded away, presumably because his prophecies regarding the Advent of the Qā'im did not come true. Some years later, ʿAbd al-Razzāq Dunbulī met him in the streets of Tabriz, a wretched wanderer who had lost all his past glory.[69] Had it not been for his fervent supporters, Dunbulī points out, who gathered around him and publicized his claim among the ignorant public, Shaykh Qāsim might never have gained such a high position and would have remained a simple shepherd in his own village. When he reached such a high degree of popularity, ʿAbd al-Razzāq concludes, his failure to revolt against the authority of the state, which would have secured him the whole province of Azarbaijan, brought about his decline.[70]

The sanctuary of Ṣāḥib al-Amr, completed in 1208/1793, remained one of the sacred places in Tabriz, attracting pilgrims from all over Azarbaijan,[71] and subsequently was associated with the Shaykhi ʿulama of Tabriz. In 1264/1848, following an alleged miracle in which a cow broke out of the slaughterhouse and took refuge in the shrine, a riot broke out in the city in which Ḥājjī Mīrzā ʿAlī Aṣghar Shaykh al-Islām played the major part. Like many other urban incidents in Tabriz, this riot had an implicit sectarian undercurrent reflected in the division of quarters between Shaykhi and non-Shaykhi factions. Nādir Mīrzā, himself an eyewitness of the two-months' turmoil, relates that people celebrated the Imam's miracle and "congratulated each other for Tabriz now became the city of the Ṣāḥib al-Amr and hence was exempted from taxation and the control of the government. From now on the authority rests with the lord of the sanctuary."[72] With

[67]Ibid. 202–3.

[68]Nādir Mīrzā *Tārīkh va Jughrāfī-yi Tabrīz* (Tehran, 1323/1905) 109; Bāmdād *Rijāl* IV, 332–34.

[69]*Tajribat al-Aḥrār* 206.

[70]Ibid. Two decades before Shaykh Qāsim, Taqī Khān Darānī, another shepherd from the outskirts of Kirman, rebelled against the governor of the city and with the help of the inhabitants managed to defeat the Zand forces. He ruled Kirman for several years before being captured and executed in Shiraz (circa 1179/1765). See Vazīrī *Tārīkh-i Kirmān* 322–29.

[71]Nādir Mīrzā *(Tabrīz* 109) mistakenly computed the epigram of the sanctuary's completion as 1200 Q. rather than 1208 Q.

[72]Ibid. 109–11.

much difficulty, the central government finally managed to reassert its control over Tabriz, and exiled the Shaykh al-Islām to Tehran.[73]

A more tragic end than that of the shepherd-prophet of Tabriz awaited the Kurdish poet Tīmūr of Bānyārān, who preached in the early 1840s among the Ahl-i Ḥaqq villages of Kirmānshāh region. Tīmūr's prophecies aroused great excitement among communities perpetually anticipating the Savior.[74] Tīmūr spoke enigmatically of his vision of a "crystal tower" within which he saw his master, "the king of blessing," the "white-clad shah":

> He shall come, the true distinguisher,
> like a two edged blade.
> He will divide the sincere from the deceitful.

The growing popularity of Tīmūr, who by the late 1840s had around six thousand followers among the Ahl-i Ḥaqq, brought him into trouble with local government. He was arrested in Kirmānshāh and put in jail as a Babi, and at the height of the Babi persecution of early 1850s was executed, by order of the mujtahids of Kirmānshāh.[75]

Of much greater consequence is Mullā Ṣādiq of Urdūbād, a village on the northern bank of the river Aras in Azarbaijan (annexed by Russia in 1828). During the late 1830s Mullā Ṣādiq preached the impending Advent of the Savior, chiefly among rural Ahl-i Ḥaqq communities of Azarbaijan and the Caucasus, and gained widespread popularity as far north as villages and towns of Georgia (Gurjistān). With apparent inspiration from Shaykhis,[76] Mullā Ṣādiq's message had a special appeal in Caucasus, which was still experiencing the aftershocks of Russian conquest. The puritanic tone of his "pretentions," according to an English observer, was "very humble" and confined to a restoration of "the ancient purity," or opposition to "the vices of the people, and the unfaithfulness of the priests."[77] The twenty thousand armed men who reportedly gathered round him worried the Russians, who foresaw the impending insurrection of the Muslim population. "The corrup-

[73]F. Ādamīyat *Amīr Kabīr va Īrān* 422–25; cf. Sheil *Glimpses* 165–66. See below, chap. 9.

[74]For their doctrine of successive manifestations and eschatology see *EI*^{2}: AHL-i ḤAḲḲ (V. Minorsky) and cited sources. For invocations among Ahl-i Ḥaqq see *Surūdhā-yi Dīnī-yi Yārsān* ed. and trans. M. Sūrī (Tehran, 1344 Sh./1967). For a specimen of their beliefs see *Majmūʿa-yi Rasa'il va Ashʿār-i Ahl-i Ḥaqq* ed. W. Ivanow (Tehran, 1338 Sh./1960). Some later messianic prophecies appear in *Istidlalīya barāyi Ahl-i Ḥaqq* by the Bahā'ī writer Mīrzā ʿAbdullāh Ṣaḥīḥ Furūsh, written in 1314/1896, 2 ed. (Tehran, 123 Badīʿ/1967).

[75]Ṣaḥīḥ Furūsh *Istidlālīya* 38–43. Even as late as 1891, the revolt of a man of Kurdish origin, Sayyid Ḥusayn Kalārdashtī (ʿĀlamgīr), who claimed the deputyship of the Imam, was another example of repeated messianic occurrences among Ahl-i Ḥaqq, this time in their communities in Mazandaran province. For details see Nikki R. Keddie *Religion and Rebellion in Iran* (London, 1966) app. I, 136–40; *Khāksār va Ahl-i Ḥaqq* 153–54; E. G. Browne *The Persian Revolution* (Cambridge, 1910) 52.

[76]Ḥājjī Muḥammad Karīm Khān Kirmānī *Izhāq al-Bāṭil* (Kirman, 1392/1972) 106.

[77]H. Southgate *Narrative of a Tour through Armenia, Kurdistan, Persia, and Mesopotamia* 2 vols. (New York, 1840) I, 308, quoting an English friend who at the time was in Georgia.

tion which had fallen" on the religion (i.e., Islam), as preached by Mullā Ṣādiq, could have been a dangerous allusion to the Muslim subjection to Russian "infidels"; a humiliation that had already triggered the second round of Russo-Persian wars. In spite of the will of his "enraged followers," who were prepared to resist, he gave himself up and was escorted to Tiflis, where he appears to have spent some time in captivity.[78] As is characteristic of most other messianic trends, his claims were exaggerated by his eager believers. Though "he declared that he had no power to work miracles," the enthusiastic public in the neighboring Tabriz and Urūmīya not only ascribed to him various miracles and feats, but even received his Persian book, a combination of "hyperbole and moral disquisitions," as a sign that "he might after all be the expected Imam."[79] The ensuing disturbances, possibly as a result of the ʿulama's denunciation, prompted the Russian authorities to exile Mullā Ṣādiq to Warsaw where he soon died.[80] The essence of his prophecies was carried through by another preacher from Urdūbād, Sayyid ʿAbd al-Karīm, who seems to have been a disciple of Mullā Ṣādiq. In the early 1840s ʿAbd al-Karīm apparently spent some time in the ʿAtabāt, where he became acquainted with the Babis, and reportedly became a Babi himself.[81] He assumed the leadership of Mullā Ṣādiq's followers in Urdūbād and his preaching among villagers of Irvān region, as in other areas, rekindled hopes for imminent manifestation of the Promised One. Denunciations by the ʿulama, however, once more renewed sectarian conflict, and provided the pretext for Russians to exile ʿAbd al-Karīm to Smolensk. After more than a decade in exile he returned to Caucasus, but was specifically banned from return to his home village Urdūbād.[82]

Another current of protomessianic claims can be observed in seminomadic and nomadic regions of central and eastern Iran, often with less sophisticated message and usually on the periphery. One such claimant appeared in 1216/1801 in Kashan during the governorship of Ḥusayn Qulī Khān. Muḥammad Qāsim Bag, a dervish from the Bīrāvand tribe—whom the author of *Rauḍat al-Ṣafā* believes to be the same person who earlier appeared under the assumed name of Mullā Bārānī, and claimed to possess the secrets of alchemy and other occult sciences—in collaboration with an unknown sayyid from Kashan who claimed to be the deputy of the Imam,

[78]Ibid.

[79]Ibid. 307.

[80]K. Kazemzadeh "Two Incidents in the Life of the Bab" *World Order* 5 (Spring 1971) no. 3, 21–24 (22). See M. Momen *The Bābī and Bahāʾī Religions, 1844–1944: Some Contemporary Western Accounts* (Oxford, 1981) 13–14.

[81]Kazemzadeh "Two Incidents" 22 and cited sources; Momen *Religions* 14 (n.). For information on ʿAbd al-Karīm, I am indebted to Dr. Momen, who drew my attention to an account in Mīrzā Ḥaydar ʿAlī Uskūʾī's *Tārīkh-i Amrī-yi Āẕarbāījān* (INBA Lib. MS no. 3030/a) additional notes, pp. 13–14.

[82]Uskūʾī *Tārīkh* 13; cf. *Kazem Beg* VIII, 395, 399, 473–81.

encouraged Ḥusayn Qulī to rebel for the second time against his brother, Fatḥ ʿAlī Shāh.[83] A brief success in capturing Naṭanz and then Isfahan soon turned to defeat at the hand of the Qajar forces. Ḥusayn Qulī and Muḥammad Qāsim fled to Luristān, where they might have hoped to receive some support from Bīrāvand and other affiliated tribes. Later on, however, because of disagreement among the Lur chiefs, Ḥusayn Qulī fled to Qum and took refuge in the shrine, and Muḥammad Qāsim fled to Baghdad.[84]

Other popular claimants emerged among the Sunni communities of eastern Iran and led tribal resurgence against the Qajars' repeated attempts to secure their control over Khurasan. In 1222/1807, an outcast dervish known as Ṣūfī Islām gained a wide acceptance among the nomads of eastern Khurasan. It is claimed that he organized fifty thousand Afghan and Uymāqāt horsemen, and then joined forces with the rebel governor of Herat, Fīrūz al-Dīn Mīrzā, against the Qajar governor of Khurasan, Muḥammad Valī Mīrzā.[85] The rebelling forces suffered a heavy defeat and Ṣūfī Islām, who supervised his forces himself from a golden houda, guarded by 366 of his close companions, was killed.[86]

A few years later, Khwāja Yūsuf Kāshgharī, a descendant of a family of central Asian Sufi emirs who for three generations had control over Kāshghar, tried to unify the Turkoman nomads of the northeastern frontiers. After some years of wandering in Kurdistan, Egypt, Bombay, Basra, Shiraz, and Tehran (which seems to have sharpened his militant attitude) Khwāja Yūsuf went among the Turkomans in the Gurgān region and tried to organize various subbranches of Kūklān and Yamūt into a united fighting force.[87] Skirmishes with local government troops culminated in 1228/1813 in a full scale battle in which Khwāja Yūsuf was killed and the Turkoman forces of twenty thousand strong were defeated.[88]

Besides their Sufi affiliation (possibly with the Naqshbandī order), Khwāja Yūsuf and Ṣūfī Islām tried to exploit the potential of tribal mobility, as well as their personal charisma, to create an independent base in the existing vacuum between the Persian central government and the semiautonomous power centers on the eastern periphery. In both cases they failed. Their failure was not so much because of the superiority of the Qajar forces, since it was from this period (1810s) that the Qajars suffered their earliest set-

[83] *RS* IX, 371; ʿAbd al-Razzāq Dunbulī *Maʾāthir-i Sulṭānīya* (Tabriz, 1242/1826) trans. H. Jones Brydges, as *The Dynasty of the Kajars* (London, 1833) 135.

[84] *RS* IX, 372–74.

[85] Ibid. 433. The chronicler's figure seems to be a mere exaggeration designed to show the immensity of the enemy's forces.

[86] Ibid. 434–35. An account of Ṣūfī Islām and his supernatural feats appears in Rustam al-Ḥukamāʾ *Tadhkirat al-Mulūk* folio 149/a (for this MS see below, this chapter).

[87] Ibid. 488–89.

[88] Ibid. 494. Watson (*History* 173) also refers to a certain Ḥājjī Yūsuf, a rebellious Turkoman chief from Badakhshān, who was killed in skirmishes with Qajar forces in Astarābād.

backs in northeastern Iran, but perhaps more due to the fragile unity within the tribal ranks, which undermined enduring loyalty to a united leadership.

One might suggest that Ahl-i Ḥaqq's influence in western Iran, and to a lesser extent the Naqshbandīs' influence on the eastern borders, kept the spirit of messianism alive in the rural and peripheral communities, in much the same way as Niʿmatullāhīs and other Sufi-affiliated groups did in the cities. The resurgence of messianic themes in the first half of the nineteenth century in communities of Shiʿite Ghulāt known as ʿAlīullāhī, Nuṣayrī, Yārsān, and ʿAlawī—all variations of the Ahl-i Ḥaqq—was the predictable outcome of the doctrine of successive revelations. This receptivity toward new prophecy, crude and unsystematic as it was, was reminiscent of the old Ismāʿīlī principles. The widespread network, thinly covered by a layer of Twelver Shiʿism, stretched throughout the Persian countryside from northern Azarbaijan to Kurdistan to ʿIraq-i ʿAjam and even as far east as Khurasan, where it apparently merged into the remnants of Ismāʿīlī and crypto-Ismāʿīlī communities of northern Khurasan. This rustic Bāṭinī tradition, particularly when immersed in Shaykhism and redefined by it, contributed to the subsequent expansion of Babism in rural communities.

Speculations of Rustam al-Ḥukamāʾ

Theories and speculations that developed among dervishes and Sufis often served to awaken a wide range of dormant anticipations on a popular level, usually among individuals who straddled the border between fantasy and scholarship. The works of an eccentric but observant historian Muḥammad Hāshim Āṣaf, known as Rustam al-Ḥukamāʾ, provide a clear example.[89] He belongs to a generation of the urban dwellers who in their lifetime witnessed the upheavals their country went through during the sixty-year span between the fall of the Zands and the end of Muḥammad Shāh's reign.[90] His simple, concise style, sometimes deliberately pompous and sar-

[89]Rustam al-Ḥukamāʾ was a prolific writer, although the full text of only one of his works, *Rustam al-Tawārīkh* (ed. M. Mushīrī [Tehran, 1348 Sh./1969]), is published. German trans. *Persische Geschichte 1694–1835 erlebt, erinnert und erfunden. Des Rustam aṭ-Ṭawārīḫ in deutscher Bearbeitung* trans. B. Hoffman, 2 vols. (Bamberg, 1986). Some extracts of his *Jung-i Aḥkām va Ashʿār,* written in 1244/1828, appear in H. Nāṭiq "Qatl-i Grībāyduf dar aḥkām va ashʿār-i Rustam al-Ḥukamāʾ" *Muṣībat-i Vabā va Balā-yi Ḥukūmat* (Tehran, 1358 Sh./1979) 155–75. Toward the end of his life, Rustam al-Ḥukamāʾ himself carefully compiled a list of his works *(Fihrist-i Munshaʾāt va Rasāʾil)* at the end of his *Naṣīḥat Nāmih* (MS no. 1270, Mīnāsīān Collection, UCLA Research Library).

[90]For the analysis of Rustam al-Ḥukamāʾ's views on political theory, economics, and history expressed in *Rustam al-Tawārīkh,* see B. Hoffman *Persische Geschichte* and A. K. S. Lambton "Some New Trends in Islamic Political Thought in Late 18th and Early 19th Century Persia" *Studia Islamica* 39 (1974) 95–128 (97–113). For his biography see *Rustam al-Tawārīkh* 55–56. In an epilogue to the above-mentioned *Naṣīḥat Nāmih* (71–73) he also gives some information on his own background.

castic, his imaginary characters, titles, positions, and events, and his constant shifts between reality and fiction are reminiscent of the oral style of the narrators of epics and other professional storytellers. Rustam al-Ḥukamā''s interpretations of historical facts and political realities are often mixed with fantastic, at times apocalyptic fiction, evident in his linking of the circumstances of the imminent Ẓuhūr of the Mahdi to the political upheavals of the time. Like the Sufis and the wandering dervishes, Rustam al-Ḥukamā' is in search of a deputy of the Mahdi, and like them he tries to explain political changes in terms of millenarian events.

An example of these speculations appears as early as 1244/1828–1829 in his collection of poetry and prose *(Jung-i Aḥkām va Āsh'ār-i Rustam al-Ḥukamā')*, where he predicts that the reign of Fatḥ 'Alī Shāh will end in 1250/1834–1835 and that 'Abbās Mīrzā will succeed him on the throne.[91] In this volume, compiled just after the completion of the second round of the Russo-Persian wars (1826–1828), he expresses his apprehension of the advances of the foreign powers. He bitterly criticizes the Qajars for their political and military failures and warns that now the "domestic enemy" is plotting again to plunge Iran into war and ruin the country.[92] Soon, he adds, at the end of 1250 and the beginning of 1251/1835 a catastrophe will occur that will make the seven kingdoms of the world mourn the fate of Iran, and this is the proof of the forthcoming Ẓuhūr of the Qā'im. When the warmonger prince 'Abbās Mīrzā comes to the throne, he will bring Iran into another disastrous war with Russia. "The ill-fated Russians will conquer and dominate Iran. Even if Iran and Rūm [the Ottoman Empire] and five other countries come to alliance, they will not be able to resist the Russians. In the year 1250 they [i.e., the Russians] will rise and conquer Iran in a ferocious war."[93]

He then forecasts that in the year 1260/1844–1845 a handsome, brave youth whose name is Amīr Mahdi will appear among the Arab tribes of Kufa, Karbalā', and Najaf. "He is wearing a cloak ['*abā*] and those wearing cloaks [the clergy] would join him, and they would wage such a great war with those ill-fated ones [Russians] that from time immemorial no one has ever heard or seen anything like it."[94] In a *qaṣīda* (panegyric) evidently composed in imitation of Shāh Ni'matullāh's famous prognostic poem,[95] he again asserts that the shortcomings and failures of the Muslims will inevitably result in a disastrous defeat by the Russians. But the pressure of the oppressors would not last long:

[91]Nāṭiq *Muṣībat* 173.
[92]Ibid. 170–73.
[93]Ibid. For his equally strong anti-British feelings see *Rustam al-Tawārīkh* 383–84.
[94]Ibid.
[95]For this qaṣīda, which has long drawn attention for its alleged messianic prophecies, see Browne *Literary History* III, 465–70; *Kings of Love* 200; *Kullīyāt-i Ash'ār-i Shāh Ni'matullāh-i Walī* ed. Jawād Nūrbakhsh (Tehran, 1347 Sh./1968) 716–19.

The Qā'im of the house of Muṣṭafā [Muḥammad] would appear
I see in him the glory,
He is the guide to all the misled in the world
I see the celebrated Mahdi.[96]

Six years later, another example of these speculations appears, in his *Rustam al-Tawārīkh*. In an additional introductory passage, probably written prior to the final draft,[97] Rustam al-Ḥukamā' hints at the Advent of the Mahdi: "By God's will in the year 1251 [1835–1836] in Iran, one of the sons of Fatḥ ʿAlī Shāh would ascend the throne as a deputy [nā'ib] of the Excellency [the Twelfth Imam], and would follow the path of justice and equity. But in the year 1262 [1846–1847] after unbelief has been victorious over Islam, the Imam himself would appear from Arż-i Gharrā' [Madina], overthrow unbelief and polytheism, and destroy oppression and darkness and conquer the world."[98] With the assistance of his minister, an old man from Fars who would be perfect in all virtues, embellished with honesty and faithfulness and skilled in all sciences, the Qā'im would rule with justice. "But the people of the world would never be content with justice and equity, and therefore when he is away to conquer the distant countries of the world, the people of Isfahan would rebel against him and would claim that he is a Sufyānī ruler." Then from the notables of Isfahan the Antichrist (Dajjāl) would appear, a one-eyed strong man who is shrewd, atheistic, ambitious, rich, and generous. He starts his rebellion from the province of Luristān riding a huge donkey. His minister and assistant is a wizardly, hemp-addicted dervish. Dajjāl's fame will extend to the seven regions of the world and whoever sees his face will become his disciple. He is an eloquent speaker and he is kind to all people. "He will battle with the Qā'im for ten to twelve years when he finally would be killed by the staff of Moses in the hand of Jesus."[99]

Adaptations of the Shiʿite prophecies are exceptionally interesting because

[96]Nāṭiq *Muṣībat* 174–75.

[97]*Rustam al-Tawārīkh* 475. The date of completion should be read Muḥarram 1251/1835 and not 1215 (see Lambton, "Some New Trends" 104). The confusion occurs because of Rustam al-Ḥukamā''s strange habit of deliberately changing the dates by transposing the last two digits. He also did the same at the end of *Naṣīḥat Nāmih* (76) dating it 1206, while in the text he makes it quite clear that he is writing in 1260/1844. This riddlelike dating is not unprecedented, especially when the author is making somewhat dangerous speculations.

[98]*Rustam al-Tawārīkh* 32. Summary translation in Lambton, "Some New Trends" 103–4. Part of this paragraph, from line 5 to line 14 in the original text, is deliberately omitted by the editor in later reprints of the text. Similarly, other passages and sentences in the text (such as lines 8–14 of p. 475) that contained speculations on the appearance of the Qā'im in 1260–1262/1844–1846 are absent. This is probably because of the embarrassing coincidence with the date of the Bab's declaration.

[99]*Rustam al-Tawārīkh* 32–33. It is possible that in here describing the qualities of the minister of the Imam, Rustam al-Ḥukamā' only refers to himself. He was born in Shiraz and was a resident of Isfahan.

of the suggested dates. In the year 1251/1835 Muḥammad Shāh had just ascended the throne, though he had not yet established his full authority throughout the country; and one might argue that Rustam al-Ḥukamā' chooses those dates for the deputy of the Mahdi with hindsight, in order to sanctify the questioned legitimacy of the Qajars. Indeed, recognition of possessors of secular power as rightful heirs of the Imam is an underlying theme of Rustam al-Ḥukamā''s works. A few years later, in 1255/1839, in another work of general history called *Tadhkirat al-Mulūk,* he praises Āqā Muḥammad Khān as "the mujtahid of the Kings," not only for his justice, competence, and ferocity (which the author believes rescued Iran from chaos) but for triumph in his disputations with the ʿulama. Recognizing him as the true "deputy of the excellency the Lord of the Command," he states:

> His helper is the Hidden Mahdi,
> Surely he is the agent of the king of the faith.[100]

The notion of a monarchical nā'ib, a restatement of the early Safavid assumption, is foreign to the mainstream nineteenth century mind and could perhaps have originated only in the mind of an eccentric "Aristotle of the age" (as Rustam al-Ḥukamā' was fond of calling himself) with a uniquely secular outlook. All the more remarkable is Rustam al-Ḥukamā''s preference for the Qajars, with all their shortcomings and their failures, over the eminent mujtahids as the bearers of the Imam's mandate. Rustam al-Ḥukamā''s concern over the ʿulama's excesses is clear in his sarcastic remarks.[101] As time goes on, however, he becomes increasingly disappointed with the Qajars, and references to their deputyship of the Imam gradually disappear from his works.

In an epilogue to the collection of his *Naṣīḥat Nāmih*, which was written in 1260–1261/1844–1845 when he was almost eighty years old, he lays emphasis more on the Mahdi and less on the nā'ib. It is difficult to know if his lack of interest was because of the poor performance of Muḥammad Shāh, who could hardly match the glorious deputy of the Mahdī of Rustam al-Ḥukamā', or because of a change in his attitude toward the "ill-fated Christians" whom he so gravely feared.[102] The idea of the Advent of the

[100] *Tadhkirat al-Mulūk*, written in Rabīʿ al-Thānī 1255/July 1839, "six years prior to the *Ẓuhūr* of the Lord of the Command" (original MS copy, School of Oriental and African Studies, Pers. MSS 35511/EW. folio 67). Among many other panegyrics in honor of the Qajar rulers, he also composed two *Bishārat Nāmih* in honor of Āqā Muḥammad Khān's "revolt."

[101] In *Rustam al-Tawārīkh* (98), for instance, he blames the ʿulama of the late Safavid period as the "fanatic fools and pious minded idiots devoid of sagacity." He is wisely, but sarcastically, reverential about the ʿulama of his own time.

[102] In a short passage written in 1262/1846 he admires the people of Rūm, Turkistān, India, Russia, and "the seven kingdoms of Europe": "In those places, there is justice, equity, and order, and in every matter law and order is prevalent in its highest degree, whereas in Iran, contrary to these places, the people are only capable of understanding traditional knowledge and are susceptible to fables" *(Naṣīḥat Nāmih* 106–7).

Mahdi persists, however. In spite of his earlier disappointments about the time of the Ẓuhūr and repeated postponements of the "great calamity," in December 1844 he confirms that in fifteen months' time, that is Rabīʿ al-Awwal 1262/April 1846, the Qāʾim will finally appear.[103] In another qaṣīda in which he describes the circumstances of the Ẓuhūr, Rustam al-Ḥukamāʾ praises the Qāʾim with the highest titles, and confirms that he will appear in the year *rabb-i ghanī* (the benevolent lord), which is numerologically equal to 1261 Q.[104] But he warns his reader to be on guard against impostors:

> Whoever makes such claims is either insane or melancholic or else under the influence of hemp and other drugs. He may also be possessed by the jinn and devils in which case he may even perform many supernatural feats which would fascinate the laymen and the ignorants. This seeker of truth [i.e., himself] has witnessed in the past many stories of this nature, and all the claimants were eventually either killed or stoned to death. Therefore let it be known to those with reason that those just kings who take refuge in Islam in their reigns, are the deputies of the Excellency [the Qāʾim], and those just and fair ʿulama in the sphere of sharīʿa are also the deputies of the Excellency.[105]

In spite of his long-lasting messianic anticipations, Rustam al-Ḥukamāʾ finally recognizes the "just king" and the "just divine," each in his own sphere, as the true holders of a divine mandate. His expectations thus eventually rested upon a partnership between secular and religious authorities within the existing system. The condemnation of the impostors, on the other hand, is perhaps an indirect reference to the Babis, who had at the time just begun to propagate the advent of a new bab.[106] Rustam al-Ḥukamāʾ quailed at the idea of a mass movement, which could only increase chaos and agitate "the laymen and the ignorants." Witnessing the rapid rise and the violent loss of many political fortunes in his own lifetime, he never wholly abandoned the collaboration of state and religion as the solution for the achievement of peace and stability as well as for the problem of deputyship. Correspondingly, his image of the expected Mahdi vacillated between that of the "King of Kings," whose minister is Jesus himself,[107] and that of the brave Arab youth from the ʿAtabāt and his cloak-wearing companions.

Popular Yearnings

Rustam al-Ḥukamāʾ was not the only one preoccupied with the time and the circumstances of the Mahdi's Advent. Premessianic speculations are

[103]Ibid. 75–76.

[104]Ibid. 86. He calls one of his qaṣīdas "Bishārat Nāmih-yi Fīrūzī, dar ʿalāmāt-i Ẓuhūr-i Ṣāḥib al-Zamān va tārīkh-i ẓuhūrash." Also *Tadhkirat al-Mulūk* folios 179/a, 195/b.

[105]*Naṣīḥat Nāmih* 94–95.

[106]See below, chap. 6, for the beginning of the Babi activities in Isfahan.

[107]*Tadhkirat al-Mulūk* folio 179/a.

particularly intense around the 1830s, and 1840s, especially among individual seekers of Ẓuhūr who were later converts to the Bab. Hence the messianic themes particularly caught the attention of the Babi-Bahā'ī sources, who often took care to record them, in order to emphasize the veracity of the new manifestation. Sayyid ʿAlī Muḥammad the Bab himself refers to the "coincidences" and the circumstantial signs and prophecies that he believed to have pointed emphatically toward his revelation, while maintaining that in spite of their sincerity and true inspiration, they could be taken only as secondary proofs of his claim.[108] Accounts of the earlier prophecies may well have been assembled retrospectively. Nevertheless the fact that the early Babis, as well as the writings of the Bab himself, frequently note such themes suggests that they were not only in circulation but were also influential in conversions.

The Bab occasionally refers to an unnamed Indian *jaffār* (an expert in numerological divinations) who prognosticated his name and computed the date of his revelation:

> The Lord will return to you amid the two initiations,
> To revitalize the religion after *rā* and *ghayn* [i.e., *rā* : 200 + *ghayn* : 1000 = 1200]
> Thus multiply the essence of *huwa* [i.e. *hā* : 5 + *wāw* : 6 = 11 : *huwa]* by the number of its letters [i.e. 2 x 11 = 22]
> And that is the name of the pole of the two worlds.[109]

Other sources also acknowledged the Indian jaffār in Karbalā' who heralded the emergence of the Bab, though not surprisingly, their interpretations differ. Qatīl al-Karbalā'ī maintained that the jaffār's mathematical calculations confirmed the authenticity of the Bab.[110] Tunkābunī, on the other hand, states that when Sayyid ʿAlī Muḥammad the Bab visited Karbalā' prior to 1260/1844, an ascetic (*murtāẑ*, usually Indian) forecast the evils that would soon arise from his claim.[111] More significantly, Sayyid Jawād Karbalā'ī, a follower of Rashtī and one of the early believers in the Bab,[112] relates that speculations of the Indian ascetic in Karbalā' assisted him in his search for the Promised One. The ascetic wrote a short message,

[108]Letter to Muḥammad Shāh, INBA no. 64 103–26 (124–25); cf. Sayyid ʿAlī Muḥammad the Bab *Dalā'il-i Sabʿa* (Tehran, n.d.) 60–62.

[109]INBA no. 64, 124; cf. *Dalā'il* 60–62; and also his *Shu'ūnāt-i Fārsī* (written in 1264/1848) INBA no. 64, 78–95 (78). From this enigmatic calculation the Bab extracted the numerical value of his own name, ʿAlī Muḥammad. The poetry referred to by the Indian jaffār originally belongs to Sayyid Muḥammad Akhlāṭī, whose works on numerology (*jafr*) were known to the Bab (*Dalā'il* 62).

[110]*Qatīl* 516, quoting Mīrzā Muḥammad ʿAlī and Mīrzā Hādī Nahrī.

[111]*QU* 59.

[112]For his details see below, chaps. 3 and 5.

containing a series of mysterious figures. When Sayyid Jawād deciphered it, each figure contained a message:

10 4 5 40 *yā dāl hā mīm* *mhdī : Mahdī*	4 6 3 6 40 *dāl vāv jīm vāv mīm* *mujud : maujūd* (exists)
2 200 *bā rā* *rb : rab[b]* (Lord)	4 40 8 40 10 30 70 *dāl mīm ḥā mīm yā lām ʿayn* *ʿlī mḥmmd : ʿAlī Muḥammad*[113]

Sayyid Baṣīr Hindī, a blind dervish from a family of Sufis of India whose search for the spiritual guide led him to Rashtī and then the Bab,[114] was first motivated by a report from a forebear prophesying the appearance of the "perfect soul" in the land of Iran.[115] The prophecies of another Indian aroused the curiosity of Muḥammad ʿAlī and Hādī Nahrī, two Babi brothers from Isfahan. In Karbalāʾ the brothers met a pilgrim from a remote part of India who told them that according to reports circulating in his homeland, the revelation of the Qāʾim would occur in the thirteenth century A.H.[116] Other allusions led the seekers to search for evidence of the Advent. Years before the appearance of the Bab, Shaykh ʿAlī Khurāsānī, another Babi convert, heard some poetry from a pilgrim in Mecca that alluded to the date of the Ẓuhūr.[117] ʿAbd al-Wahhāb Khurāsānī, who also was a Babi, met a jaffār who extracted the name of the Mahdi by numerological calculations.[118] The Bab himself refers to one of his followers who twenty years prior to the Bab's arrival in Azarbaijan in 1263/1847 saw in his dreams two men who read an Arabic quatrain:

> Sixty and two renewed,
> The cause which was unprecedented,
> He is a guardian [*walī*] or an assigned messenger,
> Who descended from two pure branches.[119]

Indeed, Azarbaijan was a breeding ground for speculations, not unrelated to the rich popular mysticism in the towns and villages of the province, that

[113]Account given by Sayyid Jawād Karbalāʾī to Mīrza Abul-Fażl Gulpāyigānī in *Kashf al-Ghiṭāʾ* (Tāshkand, n.d.) 76–77. Also noted in *Dalāʾil* 60.

[114]For his details see below, chap. 9.

[115]*NK* 255–56.

[116]*Qatīl* 516.

[117]*Dalāʾil* 60.

[118]Ibid. 60–61.

[119]Letter to Muḥammad Shāh, INBA no. 64, 124 and *Dalāʾil* 61–62 (on the authority of Mullā Yūsuf Ardabīlī relating from a certain Mīrzā Masʿūd). The identity of the original compiler of this quatrain is not known.

survived up to the nineteenth century. Ḥājjī Muʿīn al-Salṭana, himself a native of Tabriz, in a section of his history of the Babi movement devoted to the "Heralds of the Revelation," cites a number of individuals who were influenced by these messianic ideas. Among them was a humble old Tabrīzī who sometime prior to 1260/1844 used to decorate walls and gates of mosques and houses in Tabriz with a codified inscription: *Ẓ 1260*. When he was questioned by one of the ʿulama of the city about the meaning of his strange practice, he replied that it was an allusion to the forthcoming Ẓuhūr of the Proof of God, and that he was performing a duty for which he had no logical explanation.[120]

In spite of an evident contradiction with the Traditions about setting a date for the Advent of the Imam, emphasis on the significance of 1260 is found in abundance. The widespread circulation of Traditions concerning the death of the Eleventh Imam and the Occultation of the Twelfth Imam in 260/873–874 was a source of inspiration for messianic prophecies regarding the occurrence of the Ẓuhūr after the lapse of a millenium. The chronogram *Yā Ẓuhūr al-Ḥaqq* which equals in numerical value to 1261, was much favored by early Babi sources.[121] Qatīl al-Karbalāʾī points out that Christians, Europeans, Mandaeans (Sabaeans), Zoroastrians, and Jews as well as Niʿmatullāhīs, Ismāʿīlīs, and Zaydīs all acknowledged the importance of the year sixty-one.[122] He believes the Jews were expecting the coming of the messenger in the month of Rabīʿ al-Awwal of that year.[123] He gives some examples in Sufi writings, including poetry of Shāh Niʿmatullāh Walī and Muḥyī al-Dīn Ibn ʿArabī, who he claims both prophesied the occurrence of the Ẓuhūr in the year sixty-one.[124] Like most other Babi sources, Qatīl tends to emphasize that in spite of their clear implications, which he believed were directed solely toward the Bab's revelation, these prophecies had been misinterpreted by the commentators and followers of the above writers.

Some mystics with an Uwaysī approach also expressed interest in the mysteries of Ẓuhūr. The Babi chronicler Shaykh Muḥammad Nabīl Zarandī

[120]*Muʿīn* 6–7. Even up to the time of Muʿīn al-Salṭana in the late nineteenth century, some remnants of his cryptic inscriptions had survived on the wall of the Jāmaʿ mosque in Tabriz.

[121]See for example *NK* 93. Also the title of Mīrzā Asadullāh Fāżil Māzandarānī's *Ẓuhūr al-Ḥaqq* seems to have been inspired by the same epigram.

[122]*Qatīl* 515–16.

[123]Ibid. References to the Jewish prophecies and expectation of the Messiah *(Māshīa: ha-milikh)* in nineteenth-century Iran can be found in some accounts of the Christian missionaries, among them H. A. Stern *Dawning of the Light in the East* (London, 1854) 254–60 and H. Southgate *Narrative* 102–3. Stern (254–55) refers to his visit to Ḥakīm Hārūn, a well-known Jewish physician in Kashan, who professed that "Christian salvation was in perfect harmony with the Scriptures, and far superior to the fanciful system of Rabbinism." Hārūn assured Stern, so we are told, that many of the Jews in Kashan "will as intently love Christ and his Gospel, as they formerly rejected the one and despised the other."

[124]*Qatīl* (516) points out that twenty-five years previously (1238/1822) he had heard from Niʿmatullāhīs that manifestation would take place in the year sixty-one, as prophesied by the Imams.

quotes an aged Babi, Mīrzā Muḥammad Qamṣarī, who had himself visited the quṭb of Nūrbakhshīya Ḥājjī Muḥammad Ḥasan Nā'īnī. In his youth, in Kashan, Mīrzā Muḥammad heard of "a certain man in Nā'īn who had arisen to announce the tiding of a new Revelation, and under whose spell fell all who heard him, whether scholars, officials of the government, or the uneducated among the people."[125] In search of the truth of this claim, Mīrzā Muḥammad proceeded to Nā'īn, where he himself heard the mystic declare "Ere long will the earth be turned into a paradise. Ere long will Persia be made the Shrine around which will circle the people of the earth." On another occasion, Ḥājjī Muḥammad Ḥasan during his mystical recitation (*zikr*) informed Mīrzā Muḥammad, "That which I have been announcing to you is now revealed. At this very hour the light of the Promised One has broken and is shedding illumination upon the world."[126] This kind of intuitive prognostication is echoed by another ascetic, Mullā Ḥasan Ārandī Nā'īnī, one of Muḥammad Ḥasan's disciples. *Al-Ma'āthir wa'l-Āthār* states that Mullā Ḥasan's "intuitive knowledge was such that, as has been often mentioned, [he had] forecast the harm which would come to the sharīʿa from the Bab's appearance."[127]

Some astrologers were also credited with predicting the date or confirming the magnitude of a new revelation. Mīrzā Āqā Munajjim Iṣfahānī, who was an astrologer to Manūchihr Khān Muʿtamad al-Daula in Isfahan, predicted that the year 1260 would witness "incredible events."[128] Another astrologer, Mīrzā Jaʿfar Tabrīzī, believed that his astrological tables made it certain that the cause of the young Sayyid ʿAlī Muḥammad, then at the beginning of his mission, would expand in the world and would last for a millennium.[129]

Disasters and human miseries were also taken as signs preceding apocalyptic upheavals. Frequent outbreaks of cholera generated particular speculation. Mullā Muḥammad Ḥamza Sharīʿatmadār (d. 1281/1864), a student of Shaykh Aḥmad Aḥsā'ī, believed that the outbreaks of cholera and plague in the ʿAtabāt in the 1830s—which he reckons wiped out nine-tenths of the population—were a divine punishment for the ʿulama's negligence and hostility toward the true message of Shaykhism. He maintains that they

[125] *Nabil* 8. Zarandī also relates that as a result of his acquaintance with Aḥasā'ī, Ḥājjī ʿAbd al-Wahhāb Nā'īnī was "awakened by the message" as a result of which he retired from society and came to be regarded as a Sufi. However, such acquaintance between Nā'īnī and Aḥsā'ī is highly improbable. ʿAbd al-Wahhāb spent most of his later life in Nā'īn and died there in 1212/1797 (*TH* III, 215), when he was ninety-five years old, whereas Aḥsā'ī arrived for the first time in Yazd in 1221/1806 at the age of fifty-five (ʿAbdullāh Aḥsā'ī *Sharḥ-i Aḥvāl* 27). It is possible that Nabīl Zarandī confused ʿAbd al-Wahhāb and Ḥājjī Muḥammad Ḥasan Nā'īnī; the latter fits better with the description of "a modest and illiterate" man, and most probably he was still in Yazd at the time of Aḥsā'ī's frequent visits between 1221/1806 and 1234/1818).

[126] *Nabil* 8.

[127] Iʿtimād al-Salṭana 169.

[128] Aḥmad Suhrāb *al-Risāla al-Tisʿ ʿAshrīya, fī Tārīkh Ḥaḍrat al-Aʿlā* (Cairo, 1338/1919) 26.

[129] *Muʿīn* 17.

were a preparatory measure for the emergence of the Qā'im.[130] So does another Shaykhi, Mullā Jaʿfar Qazvīnī, who relates that while Aḥsā'ī was staying in Kirmānshāh, he warned the public of the imminent outbreak of cholera and plague as a sign of revelation.[131] The Bab himself implies that the cholera was a punishment for negligence toward his mission: "From the beginning of the Revelation [1260/1844], see the multitudes who lost their lives because of cholera. This is one of the signs of the Ẓuhūr which people tend to neglect. In four years, probably more than one hundred thousand souls from among the Shiʿites alone perished, and no one is aware of its [hidden] meaning."[132]

Cholera was only one of many "signs" of the emergence of a comprehensive "revolution" (*fitna*) at the End of Time mentioned in the Shiʿite apocalyptic Traditions. Babi writers like the author of *Nuqṭat al-Kāf* often speak of fitna and *imtiḥān* (torment) in describing the violent events that were to take place at the time of the Qā'im's manifestation.[133] The speculations of the astrologers, the poetry of the mystics, and other evidences, he declares, only confirm the proofs of reason, the Qur'ānic verses, and the Imam's sayings in establishing the occurrence of an inevitable fitna sometime after the year sixty. Though "common people may assume that the emergence of the Qā'im, may peace be upon him, will be immediately followed by a mass conversion," he points out, in reality it is almost impossible for him to prevail without being engaged in a violent struggle with his enemies. Basing his arguments on the Traditions, he emphasizes that the trial is so severe that even among the Qā'im's companions *(nuqabā')*, only a small group would be able to maintain their allegiance up to the very end.[134]

For the author of *Nuqṭat al-Kāf* the signs of the manifestation and the upheavals of the Final Day were not confined to the lands of Islam, but extended to European lands.[135] In his view, in the "Traditions" of the

[130] Muḥammad Ḥamza' Sharīʿatmadār *Asrār al-Shahāda* MS cited in ʿAbd al-Karīm Sharīʿatmadārīyān *Sharḥ-i Zindigī-yi Mullā Muḥammad Ḥamza' Sharīʿatmadār* MS. INBA Lib. 1009 D, 13–14.

[131] *Qazvīnī* 452.

[132] *Dalā'il* 63–64.

[133] *NK* 92–99. For references to fitna in Shiʿite Traditions see *Safīnat al-Biḥār* compiled by Shaykh ʿAbbās Qumī, 2 vols. (Najaf, 1355/1936) II, 345. For further details see also below, chap. 4.

[134] *NK* 93–94.

[135] Describing the events following the execution of the Bab in Tabriz in 1266/1850, the author refers to the inquiry made by the Russian and the Ottoman envoys regarding the Bab and the Babis. He believed that this was because they also had "oppressed subjects" *(żuʿafā-yi raʿīyat)* in their own countries, but treated them better and tried to understand their problems (266–67). Such inquiries on the doctrine of the Bab and the state of the Babis were carried out by foreign envoys in Iran. Prince D. Dolgorukov's dispatches to the Russian Foreign Ministry, written between 1848 and 1852 (excerpts published in M. S. Ivanov *Babidskie vosstaniya v Irane (1848–1852)* [Moscow, 1939] app. I, 141–59, and partly translated into English by F. Kazemzadeh in *World Order* [Fall, 1966] 17–24, and into Persian in *Shaykhīgarī va Bābīgarī* 269–89) and J. Sheil's special report to Palmerston, F.O. 60/152, no. 72, 21 June 1850 (with two enclosures) are two examples. Kazem Beg used reports prepared by the Russian consul in

Europeans, the Promised One would draw the sign of the Cross, which he believes is identical with the Bab's cabalistic inscriptions in the shape of the human body (*haykal*). One of the signs that has already been fulfilled, he states, is that the monarchy of France has collapsed and a republican state has been established in its stead.[136] The connection between the "suffering subjects," the fall of the monarchy, and the establishment of a republican state in Europe and the signs of a messianic fitna is particularly remarkable. Aside from the official chronicles, this is perhaps one of the earliest commentaries on the political developments in Europe.

A more realistic image of the Advent of the Imam emerged among some middle- and lower-rank mullas. Ḥājjī Mullā Iskandar, a preacher in Khuy known for his supernatural gifts, drew the attention of his audience to the plausible circumstances of the forthcoming Ẓuhūr and the utterance of the "Greatest Name," which he believed to be found in the prayers of Ramaḍān. His preaching created some excitement and his adherents eagerly anticipated imminent upheavals.[137] Ḥājjī Mullā ʿAlī Akbar, the shaykh al-Islām of Marāghih, also nurtured such expectations. Muʿīn al-Salṭana relates that some of the Babis from Marāghih such as Mullā Aḥmad Abdāl (a later member of the Babi nucleus known as *Ḥurūf-i Ḥayy*),[138] were influenced by ʿAlī Akbar.[139]

The origins of these preachings rested in the rural asceticism of Azarbaijan. In this context, the teachings of Ḥājjī Asadullāh Saysānī had a recognizable character. Originally a peasant from Saysān, a village near Tabriz with possible Ahl-i Ḥaqq population,[140] Asadullāh spent two years in the company of the other local ascetics on Mount Sahand, in religious retreat and mystical mortifications.[141] In his wanderings afterward he came across Aḥsā'ī, possibly in Kirmānshāh, and was deeply influenced by him. On his return to Saysān, his sermons, mostly composed of messianic admonitions, gained him popularity and respect.[142] Decidedly affected by the Shaykhi

---

Tabriz (*Kazem Beg* I, 332 n. 2, which is also confirmed by *NK* 267), whereas Nicolas used French reports filed in the French embassy in Tehran (Archive de la Légation de France à Téhéran et celles du Ministère des Affaires étrangères à Paris, *SAMB* 53).

[136] *NK* 267.

[137] *TMS* 17–21.

[138] See below, chap. 4.

[139] *Muʿīn* 21–22. See also *Nabil* 431–33 and *ZH* 59–60.

[140] In Azarbaijan the Turkish-speaking Ahl-i Ḥaqq are mainly concentrated in the region of Tabriz-Maraghih (around Mount Sahand) and in Mākū (V. Minorsky "The Ahl-i Ḥakk" in *Iranica* 306–16 [314] and cited sources).

[141] *Muʿīn* 22–29. Both Mount Sahand and Mount Savalān (Sabalān), because of the legends attached to them, were locally regarded as sacred places and visited by the pilgrims. Lady Sheil (*Glimpses* 102) and Edward Burgess (*Letters from Persia, 1828–1855* ed. B. Schwartz [New York, 1942] 44) give accounts regarding the legends of a prophet believed to be buried at the summit of Savalān. "The age in which this prophet lived is not known, nor his name but the Persians claim for him greater antiquity than the Christian era" (Burgess, 44). This may be connected with the legends regarding the retreat of Zoroaster in the Azarbaijan mountains.

[142] *Muʿīn* 23–24.

picture, Asadullāh presented a more plausible and human image of the Imam and the events of the Final Day. The Promised One, he said, would come to this world not by ascending from the eighth climate or the cities of Jābulqā and Jābarsā, but by natural birth, and would live a life like any other human being. He would inevitably endure suffering, hardship, and even subjugation at the hands of his enemies and the opposition of the ʿulama would be the best proof of his righteousness.[143] After Asadullāh's death in circa 1258/1842, in the early stages of the Babi conversion, almost the entire village of Saysān embraced the new religion, and in time the village became one of the Babi-Bahā'ī centers in Azarbaijan.[144]

The function of preachers like Asadullāh, one can argue, was to popularize the speculative eschatological theories of high culture for ordinary men of towns and villages. Many prominent future Babis who were responsible for mobilizing larger urban communities under the banners of the new movement performed the same intermediary function with even greater potency, and effect. Like Asadullāh, they were skillful orators known for their anticlerical and occasionally antigovernmental feelings, and above all for their nonorthodox beliefs. They often had in common great popularity in the communities of adherents, which was reinforced by bonds of family and clan loyalties.

The above-mentioned Mullā Muḥammad Ḥamza Sharīʿatmadār who durng his tutelage, on Ahsā'ī's advice, retired for forty days in the mosque of Kufa, was known to the people of Bārfurūsh for his prognostications.[145] He often dressed like the local shepherds and was admired for his unceremonious and humble manners. He spoke and preached in the local dialect of Mazandaran, exciting his audience by stressing the speculative themes common among the Shaykhis[146] and bitterly criticizing his chief rival, Mullā Saʿīd Bārfurūshī (later known as Saʿīd al-ʿUlamā').[147] Sharīʿatmadār was seldom on good terms with the governors and local state officials.[148] Predictably, the ideologically charged climate was translated into the existing social divisions. The prolonged urban conflicts in Bārfurūsh between Niʿmatī and Ḥaydarī quarters was largely expressed in Shaykhi-Uṣūlī dispute between Sharīʿatmadār and Saʿīd al-ʿUlamā'. By the time of Mullā Muḥammad ʿAlī Bārfurūshī (Quddūs)—a young student of Rashtī and later one of

[143]Ibid.

[144]Ibid. 26.

[145]*Sharḥ-i Zindigī; ZH* 134–45; *Shaykhīgarī va Bābīgarī* 140–75. All these accounts used various parts of Sharīʿatmadār's *Asrār al-Shahāda.*

[146]*Sharḥ-i Zindigī* 14, 18; cf *ZH* 437–41 (n.), which discusses his interpretation of the position of bābīya as it is applied to Sayyid ʿAlī Muḥammad the Bab, and later to Quddūs and Mullā Ḥusayn Bushrū'ī. For further details see below, chap. 4.

[147]Details concerning this zealous enemy of the Shaykhis, and in later times Babis, can be found among other sources in *ZH* 430–33 and *TAS* II/2, 599.

[148]*Sharḥ-i Zindigī* 23, 27–33 and *ZH* 442–43.

the prominent figures in the Babi movement, who himself at one stage was a student of Sharīʿatmadār—this conflict developed into full-scale confrontation.[149]

The same pattern of premessianic militancy is evident in the ideas and activities of Mullā Muḥammad ʿAlī Ḥujjat al-Islām Zanjānī (known in Babi sources as Ḥujjat),[150] who unlike the above men was influenced by Akhbārism.[151] Born in circa 1227/1812, he was the son of a local Zanjānī mulla, who was known for his supernatural feats. For some years Muḥammad ʿAlī was educated in the ʿAtabāt before moving to Hamadān, which in the early nineteenth century was one of the last Akhbārī strongholds in Iran. On his return to Zanjān after his father's death, Ḥujjat enjoyed immense popularity in the quarters of the city that had previously been loyal to his father. The introduction of a series of severe juristic prohibitions, inspired by Ḥujjat's Akhbārī views, provided the pretext for a clash with the rival ʿulama in the city. In his religious disputation with the chief Uṣūlī mujtahid of the city Ḥujjat openly asserted that "the prophets and their vicegerents [hence the Imams] in their corporal appearance are similar to other human beings but superior in the realm of morality and spirit." The ʿulama denounced Ḥujjat for the heretical opinion that the expected Imam might be conceived and born like any other human being.[152] The extension of the conflict between Ḥujjat and mujtahids of Zanjān in the late 1830s resulted in the intervention of first the local, then the central government. In accordance with Ḥājjī Mīrzā Āqāsī's religious policy, Ḥujjat was summoned to the capital and kept there in exile.[153] Once, during an audience with Muḥammad Shāh, Ḥujjat objected to Āqāsī's awarding of a pension to a mujtahid from Kashan. He argued that the practice was a legacy from Umayyad times to make the clergy corrupt and dependent and would be abolished by the Lord of the Time. Such objection to the state's sponsoring of the ʿulama was at odds with the Qajar policy of appeasement toward the clergy and thus could not have been endorsed by the shah and his premier.[154] After spending some time in Tehran, his triumphal return to Zanjān increased Ḥujjat's popu-

[149]Besides various sources on the situation in Bārfurūsh on the eve of Ṭabarsī, *ZH* (405–419) provides an extensive account of the earlier disputes between 1258/1842 and 1261/1845.

[150]Besides better-known Babi-Bahāʾī sources, accounts of Ḥujjat's life also appear in many narratives of the Zanjān episode, among them "Personal Reminiscences of the Bābī Insurrection at Zanjān in 1850" by Āqā ʿAbd al-Aḥad Zanjānī (Browne Or. MSS no. F.25(9) no. 6) translated in *JRAS* (1897) 761–827; "Narrative of Āqā Mīrzā Ḥusayn Zanjānī" INBA. Lib. MS no. 3037/a; "Narrative of ʿAbd al-Wahhāb Zāhid al-Zamān" INBA. Lib. MS 3037/b; "Narrative of Hāshim Fatḥī Muqaddam Khalkhālī" INBA. Lib. MS 3037/c.

[151]Most sources agree on his Akhbārī persuasion. See *Ahmad* 451; *NK* 125; and *Nabil* 178, 531–34. However, *KD* (I, 68–69) states that he also spent some time in Burūjird, which may suggest some influence from Sayyid Jaʿfar Kashfī.

[152]*ZH* 178–79.

[153]For other examples of exiled ʿulama under Ḥājjī Mīrzā Āqāsī, see below, chap. 8.

[154]Ibid.

larity, even to the extent of zealous devotion, at the expense of both Uṣūlī ʿulama and the local government.[155]

Ḥujjat became increasingly convinced in the following years that divine revelation would manifest itself in the form of a human being with no physical or supernatural imparity. His views on the appearance of the Promised One did not comply with the teachings of the Akhbārīs, who took the Traditions at face value, but were closer to those of Shaykhis. The realistic prospects for a Ẓuhūr increased the intensity of the expectations. The unreserved support offered by Ḥujjat following the Bab's proclamation indicates the enthusiasm and vigor with which he anticipated a messianic manifestation.[156]

Other individuals in communities in Fars, Yazd, and Khurasan were inspired by similar messianic prophecies. Their teachings, similar to those of the Shaykhi school, went beyond mere anticipation to prophetic utterances. Their appeal, especially in the proximity of learned leaders, remained limited and unnoticed. An interesting case is that of an ascetic in Karbalā', mentioned by Ḥājjī Muḥammad Karīm Khān Kirmānī as an example of a similar "impostor" prior to the Bab.[157] He was a recluse among Rashtī's students who seems to have enjoyed some popularity in the circle. Kirmānī describes him as a knowledgeable scholar who could resolve other students' problems. His reputation for piety was such that he led the Shaykhis in their prayers. But because of his unusual mortifications and isolation, he "had been possessed by the devil," and put forward "blasphemous claims" that were "beyond human capacity." As a result, Rashtī publicly expelled him from his circle.[158] Kirmānī also refers to two other claimants who seem to have appeared during Rashtī's last years. One used to send Rashtī "tablets" of incomprehensible words, presumably calling upon him to recognize his claims.[159]

In the half-century between the death of Karīm Khān Zand and the end of Fatḥ ʿAlī Shāh's reign, post-Safavid Shiʿism underwent a noticeable change. In its attempt to create an orthodox religious institution less reliant on the

[155] *Narrative of Āqā Muḥammad Ḥusayn Zanjānī* folios 2–3; cf. E. G. Browne trans. "Personal Reminiscences" *JRAS* 770–71.

[156] The circumstances of his conversion are described in *Narrative of Āqā Muḥammad Ḥusayn* folios 4–6; in "Personal Reminiscences" *JRAS* 771–75; and in *Nabil* 531–34.

[157] *Izhāq al-Bāṭil* (Kirman, 1392 Q.) 105.

[158] Ibid. No other source mentions the above person. Even Kirmānī seems to be deliberately vague about his identity. Similar examples of excessive piety and strong yearning for the Ẓuhūr, though in milder forms, can also be found among other students of Rashtī, who all later converted to the Babi movement. See below, chap. 4.

[159] Ibid. 106. To these claimants, showing Shaykhi influence, can also be added Mullā Muḥammad Ṭāhir Ḥakkāk Khurāsānī, who toward the end of the nineteenth century claimed to have a divine mission for reforming the world and unifying divided mankind in one universal community. It is said that in his youth he was a student of Sayyid Kāẓim Rashtī, but it was in the closing years of the century that he expounded his ideas in his work *Naṣīḥat al-ʿĀlam* which was a combination of morals and Sufi popular beliefs. Ḥusayn Qulī Jadīd al-Islām *Minhāj al-Ṭālibīn* (Bombay, 1320/1902) 200–1.

patronage of the state, Shiʿism established a clerical body that legitimized its authority by reemphasizing the general deputyship of the ʿulama. The emerging network of the religious divines consolidated its theoretical ground by redefining the doctrine of ijtihād on the basis of Uṣūlī methodology. Widespread application of Uṣūlī jurisprudence broadened their judicial constituency and paved the way for a wider participation of the ʿulama in sociopolitical affairs.

Reassertion of Uṣūlism and the elitist attitude of the mujtahids, who saw themselves as the sole interpreters of sharīʿa, brought them into repeated confrontations with rival trends both within and outside of learned Shiʿism. With little trouble the remnants of the Akhbārī school were defeated in the ʿAtabāt and their counterparts in Iran were reduced to a declining minority. Similarly, the philosophical heritage of the Ṣadrāʾī school and others was either subdued to the domination of fiqh or relegated to the realm of undesirable pursuits.

Simultaneous with and as a response to the growth of jurisprudence and the related sciences, Shaykhism emerged as the chief defender of theosophy and esoteric knowledge. Entrusting the spiritual authority to the Perfect Shiʿa, Aḥsāʾī and his successors, unlike the jurists, considered direct intuitive experience of the Imam the only source of legitimacy. Having its roots in the theosophy and the esoteric traditions of the past, both learned and popular, as well as in Shiʿite hadith, Shaykhism was able to fuse widespread currents of heterodoxy into a more consistent theology. As Shaykhism spread beyond teaching circles, the jurists' initial hesitation regarding Aḥsāʾī's visionary system hardened into forceful opposition. The ʿulama's denunciation pushed Shaykhism further toward the periphery of the Shiʿite scholastic world and closer to the world of antinomians and nonconformists. Perhaps for its founders this was a mixed blessing, as sectarian isolation and persecution transformed Shaykhism into a force of dissent and its adherents into vigorous seekers of an apocalyptic bāb. The Shaykhis' learned esoterism found a nonclerical equivalent in the contemporary Sufism and its affiliated trends. Similar to Shaykhis (and in spite of Aḥsāʾī's denunciation of the Sufis), the dervishes also regarded their walī as the sole proof of the Imam. They too benefited from the reservoir of the esoteric thought. While Shaykhism initially recruited among religious students and their affiliates, the Sufis appealed to the laity. But charges of heresy were more easily applicable to the Sufis than to the Shaykhis. Like Akhbārīs and others before them, the Sufis failed to secure the support of the state and therefore suffered sorely under the ʿulama's pressure.

By the early nineteenth century the reluctant state, convinced of the unrevertible reality of the ʿulama's sociopolitical power, relinquished further privileges to them. Greatly assisted in their self-assigned task of chastising the skeptic and eliminating the heretic, the ʿulama were able to successfully oppose the consolidation and expansion of any movement of dissent before the point of eruption. But in spite of their success in defeating Sufism and isolating Shaykhism, the predominance of the orthodoxy was not yet complete. The yearning for charismatic deputyship on behalf of the Imam was not fully extinguished. Numerous claimants with a mission to deputize the Imam continued to challenge the orthodox establishment. In the city and in the countryside, heterodoxy survived, fueled by the skepticism of agnostics as well as by the piety of ascetics and visionaries. The bulk of unshaped dissent was thus constantly recast in new molds.

Clearly, the predicament of legitimate authority in the nineteenth century was not merely confined to the division, and the potential tension, between the state and representatives of orthodox religion. Of equal significance to the question of righteous authority is the battle that was fought between dogmatic religion, defended by the ʿulama, and the alternative religion of the nonconformists: that is, the conflict between two notions of deputyship of the Imam, general and specific. This conflict remained unresolved and resurfaced in the confrontation between the forces of establishment and dissent during the Babi episode. In essence, it was a battle fought by those who sanctified and rationalized the status quo against those whose vision of the Imam reflected a nascent desire for renovation and change. Inevitably, these millenarians also tend to express a voice of protest and public discontent against secular authority.

But perhaps more than any other aspect, the contribution of these yearnings was to allow the emergence of a more realistic and humane vision of the invisible Imam. The Shaykhi school provided more favorable circumstances for the emergence of the Qāʾim, not only by rescuing him from the web of Shiʿite Traditions, which prevented his presence in any historical circumstances, but also by depicting a tangible, human leader whose extraordinary qualities lay in his moral and spiritual merits rather than in his supraphysical capabilities. In the Shaykhi view, the revelation of the Imam would be the inevitable consequence of the maturing of man's intellectual evolution in the course of history, rather than an apocalyptic punishment inflicted upon mankind. His appearance would not bring an immediate victory over the forces of falsehood, but only begin a long and painful torment, in the course of which many of his opponents as well as his supporters would be destroyed. This realistic concept of Resurrection and Return was essential in providing a coherent sense of expectation among the close followers of the Shaykhi leaders, as among other individuals or communities with similar views.

Development of esoteric thought thus reached a new momentum when it occurred to the advocates of specific deputyship that the mission of the deputy ought to be followed by the impending return of the Mahdi himself. Such a view became even more compelling for the adept, who looked upon the Traditions of the Ẓuhūr as allegorical descriptions of plausible events. The basic components of the Imam's character, his conduct, and his future acts began to be conceived in a more realistic light. The progression from premessianic expectations to their fulfillment became more apparent as Shaykhism gradually moved away from the ideals of learned messianism towards realizations of prophecies. The shift was accompanied, not accidentally, by a social reorientation and formation of stronger bonds of loyalty between the Shaykhi clergy and the Shaykhi laity. Claims of a charismatic self-educated laity with the asceticism highly esteemed by Shaykhi ethics were not entirely unpredictable. Sayyid ʿAlī Muḥammad the Bab was only the realization of what was already conceived in theory.

PART II

THE FORMATION OF THE MOVEMENT

3

The Merchant-Saint of Shiraz

In the summer of 1848, the provincial government of Azarbaijan instructed Dr. William Cormick, the crown prince's personal physician, to interview the Shīrāzī claimant Sayyid ʿAlī Muḥammad the Bab, then in detention in Tabriz, in order to determine "whether he was of sane mind or merely a mad man." Cormick recalled later: "Nothing of any importance transpired in the interview. To all enquiries he merely regarded us with a mild look, chanting in a low melodious voice some hymns, I suppose. . . . He was a very mild and delicate-looking man, rather small in stature and very fair for a Persian, with a melodious soft voice, which struck me much. . . . In fact his whole look and deportment went far to dispose one in his favor."[1]

In the four years prior to this interview, the young sayyid of Shiraz attracted a large following, and his prophetic claims gave rise to a movement that caused a good deal of excitement and anxiety. Yet the Bab's personality and background were to some degree overshadowed by the intensity of the events that followed his proclamation in May 1844. This chapter examines various aspects of his background, his upbringing, his material life, and his intellectual experiences that contributed to the development of his complex personality; first as a merchant, then as an ascetic, and finally as prophet who claimed to be chosen for the delivery of a long-awaited mission. What particularly interests us at this stage is to uncover the special merits that caused Sayyid ʿAlī Muḥammad Shīrāzī to put forward prophetic claims and, more important, to be accepted by a large group of followers.

[1] "Dr. Cormick's accounts of his personal impressions of Mīrzā ʿAlī Muḥammad the Bāb, extracted from letters written by him to the Rev. Benjamin Labaree, D. D.," *MSBR* 260–62. For Cormick see Momen *Religions* 497, and cited sources.

Childhood and Upbringing

Sayyid ʿAlī Muḥammad was born on 1 Muḥarram 1235/20 October 1819 in Shiraz.[2] He was the only child of Sayyid Muḥammad Riżā,[3] a small merchant in the Shiraz bazaar. His family had lived in the city for generations. Though Mīrzā Aḥmad Shīrāzī Īshīk-Āqāsī, who himself was acquainted with the Bab's family, believes that the Bab's forefathers were sayyids of Herat, and maintains that Sayyid Muḥammad Riżā himself emigrated from Herat and settled in Shiraz, the accuracy of this observation, which is not helped by the ambiguous style of the text, is open to question.[4]

As far as the genealogy of the Bab can be traced, it appears that up to the sixth generation his paternal ancestors were all sayyids from Shiraz. His great-grandfather in the sixth generation was Mīr Muḥammad Muʾmin Ḥusaynī Najafī Shīrāzī.[5] His mother, Fāṭima Baygum, who had a strong influence on the Bab's early life also came from a relatively well-known family of Shiraz sayyids. Her brothers and most of her paternal relatives, one of whose daughters later married Sayyid ʿAlī Muḥammad, were engaged in long-distance trade. The author of *Fārs Nāmih* notes that they were counted among the old and reputable merchants of Shiraz.[6] Though the status of *siyāda* (descendancy from the House of the Prophet) did not indicate any specific material advantage over other families, it contributed to the high esteem that its members enjoyed in Shiraz. The claim to siyāda later assisted the Bab and his followers as a major justification of his claims.

Some later sources imply that Sayyid ʿAlī Muḥammad's family on his father's side were also involved in large-scale trade, but it appears that Sayyid Muḥammad Riżā was more of a local trader than a big merchant like

[2]In *Ṣaḥīfa bayn al-Ḥaramayn* the Bab specifies the date of his birth (Browne Or. MSS F. 7(9)).

[3]Born circa 1195/1780. What Kazem Beg, on the basis of the unknown account of Shaykh ʿAjam (Cheikh-oul-Adjam), says about the name and the origin of the Bab's father (VII, 334, n. 3)—that his name was Salib and he was born in Tchaharchenbeh-pich—is a misreading of Ṣāliḥ, which was the name of the father of Mīrzā ʿAlī Muḥammad Bārfurūshī (Quddūs). The confusion between the Bab and Quddūs seems to have arisen because in the later years of the movement, the title of *Ḥażrat-i Aʿlā,* originally assumed by the Bab, was given by him to his loyal follower Quddūs.

[4]*Ahmad* 446; It is true that Mīrzā Aḥmad and his family "maintained an intimate relation" with the family of the Bab, and it is also true that the title *mīr,* which is used by some sources instead of *sayyid* for the Bab and his forebears, sometimes refers to Shiʿite sayyids of Heratī origin, and that in the early nineteenth century they not infrequently immigrated to towns and cities of Iran. Still, the Heratī origin of the Bab is not confirmed by any other source.

[5]See table of genealogy, produced from information supplied in *Ṣaḥīfa bayn al-Ḥaramayn;* Mīrzā Ḥabībullāh Afnān *Tārīkh-i Amrī-yi Shīrāz* (INBA, Lib. MS no. 1227 D); M. A. Fayżī *Khāndān-i Afnān* (Tehran, 127 Badīʿ/1971); *TAS* I, 443 (under Mīrzā Ḥasan Shīrāzī) and *FN* II. *Muʿīn* (28) speaks of a genealogy preserved in the Afnān family in which the Bab's ancestry is traced back to Ḥusayn ibn ʿAlī. No sign of this genealogy has been found. Considering the Bab's own reference, the order of ascendancy in Mīrzā Ḥabībullāh *Tārīkh* (1) and *Nabil* (ix, "Genealogy of the Bab") are both slightly confused.

[6]FN II, 45; cf. 131.

his brothers-in-law. Khadīja Khānum, the Bab's wife, remarks that her father-in-law was "engaged in retail trade."[7] Others state that the Bab's father "carried on a clothier's business in the bazaar of Shiraz."[8] While Sayyid Muḥammad Riżā was not an exceptionally prosperous trader, he did inherit a small fortune including a house[9] and a shop in a trading house at the Bāzār-i Vakīl.[10] He married into a family of big merchants (*tujjār*) and left enough savings to support his wife and son when he died at the age of forty-nine, possibly during one of the cholera outbreaks in Fars (circa 1243/1826).[11]

Such a union between retail traders with strong religious ties and an established merchant family often made it possible for members of the lower stratum to ascend the social ladder. The Bab's childhood, his education, and his later engagement in trade exemplify the norms and values of both traditions.

The Bab's family residence was in Bāzār-i Murgh quarter, one of five Ḥaydarī wards of Shiraz, probably the most important economic and religious quarter in the city. It housed most of the commercial premises and the dwellings of the merchants and their associates.[12] The city was divided into two rival blocs of Ḥaydarī and Niʿmatī, each controlling five quarters. Located at the center of the city, Bāzār-i Murgh frequently became a battleground of rival lūṭī gangs who fought for the supremacy of their local masters. The merchants and traders remained uncommitted bystanders, or at most reluctant partisans. In the prevailing climate of turmoil and uncertainty, life, property, and merchandise were too precious to be gambled in risky power games between nomadic chiefs and ambitious city dignitaries. The group solidarity and strong professional bonds among the merchants of Shiraz, as well as their traditional ties with the clerical community, arose in part from their efforts to preserve their vested interest through a policy of deliberate dissociation and distancing from sources of political power. Such mercantile and family loyalties and hatred of the unruly mob are evident in the Bab's later attitudes, which perhaps reflect his childhood experiences.

Apart from anecdotes that aimed directly to illustrate the extraordinary

[7]Account recorded by Munīra Khānum, cited in *Khāndān-i Afnān* 162.

[8]*Ahmad* 446; cf. *NT* III, 39. Also *Kazem Beg* VII, 334, and Mīrzā Abul-Fażl Gulpāyigānī *Tārīkh-i Ẓuhūr-i Dīyānat-i Ḥażrat-i Bāb va Ḥażrat-i Bahāʾullāh* INBA, no. 9, p. 3.

[9]Mīrzā Ḥabībullāh *Tārīkh;* cf. *Khāndān-i Afnān* 204–210.

[10]The shop contained a family business that could be traced back to the Zand period and beyond. Abul-Qāsim Afnān (son of Mīrzā Ḥabībullāh Afnān), unpublished notes on the history of Afnān family.

[11]The age of Sayyid Muḥammad Riżā could be worked out from Mullā Fatḥullāh Khādim's account cited in Mīrzā Ḥabibullāh *Tārīkh* 4, 9. What *Muʿīn* (30) and Gulpāyigānī (*Tārīkh-i Ẓuhūr,* 3) say about his death at an earlier time is incorrect. The Bab himself does not refer in his writings to his father's death. For the outbreak of cholera in the 1820s and 1830s in southern Iran see J. G. Lorimer *Gazetteer of the Persian Gulf, Oman and Central Arabia* 2 vols. (Calcutta, 1905) I, part 2, app. M, 2517–2662 and H. Nāṭiq *Muṣībat-i Vabā* 12–16.

[12]See *FN* II, 27–47 for Bāzār-i Murgh.

Genealogy of the Bab

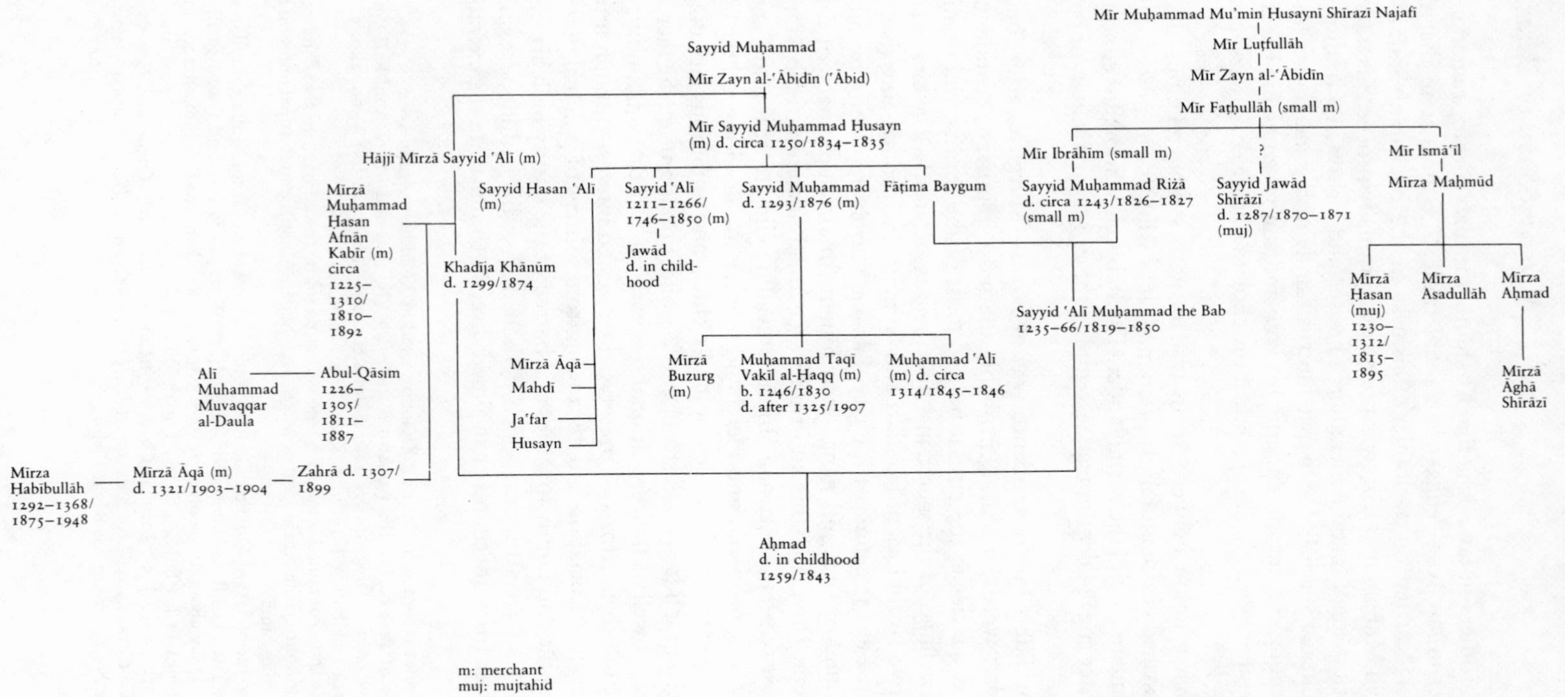

aspects of his character, little is known about the Bab's childhood. Like most children of the urban middle-class, Sayyid ʿAlī Muḥammad was sent to the nearby Qurʾānic school *(maktab)* of a certain Shaykh Zayn al-ʿĀbidīn (Shaykh ʿĀbid),[13] where he received some elementary education. According to Mullā Fatḥullāh Khādim, who was in the same maktab as the Bab, this school was for the children of "the tujjār, notables, and dignitaries," since Shaykh ʿĀbid "never admitted anybody's child, especially those of shop-keepers of bazaar."[14] The Bab's family was certainly not prosperous enough to provide private tuition. Binning, an English traveler who visited Shiraz in 1850, states that elementary schools were "very numerous" but only "the children of the wealthy" were educated at home.[15]

His teacher, Shaykh ʿĀbid, appears to have been no more than a simple schoolmaster. Being a mulla of middle status, he taught religious texts both to pupils at lower levels and to young elementary-level seminarians.[16] His acquaintance with Sayyid ʿAlī Muḥammad's father and with Ḥājjī Mīrzā Sayyid ʿAlī, his uncle, was not only due to their residence in the same quarter, or the occasional recitation of the Qurʾān in the house of the Bab's uncles, but also because Shaykh ʿĀbid was a follower of the Shaykhi school,[17] and thus in accord with relatives of the Bab, who also seem to have been followers of Shaykh Aḥmad Aḥsāʾī.[18] Though none of the sources directly mention their commitment, many indications suggest that they had sympathy toward the Shaykhi leaders and maintained contact with the Shaykhi followers.[19] Shaykh ʿĀbid's maktab was held in a dervish convent and, like many other Sufi gathering places in the city, was originally the tomb of a Sufi saint.[20]

The Bab's formal education, during both childhood and adolescence, forms a point of disagreement between his opponents and apologists, part of a greater controversy over one of his essential claims; namely, his "un-

[13]Known as Shaykh ʿĀbid, Shaykh-i Anām, and Shaykh-i Muʿallim.

[14]Mīrzā Ḥabībullāh *Tārīkh* 4.

[15]R. B. M. Binning *A Journal of Two Years' Travel in Persia etc.* 2 vols. (London, 1857) I, 283. An example of this private tutoring is Mīrzā Ḥasan Shīrāzī (b. 1230/1815), a distant cousin of the Bab and future clerical leader of the late nineteenth century, who first started his elementary schooling at the age of four at home (*TAS* I, 437).

[16]Account by the Bab's schoolmate Āqā Muḥammad Ibrāhīm Tājir cited in Mīrzā Ḥabībullāh *Tārīkh*.

[17]Ibid. 4.

[18]Years later when the claims of the Bab were publicized in Shiraz, Shaykh ʿĀbid first disclaimed his former pupil. But later, after an interview with Sayyid [Jawād] Karbalāʾī, he modified his attitude (Gulpāyigānī *Kashf al-Ghiṭāʾ* 82). It is also said that there is a manuscript of a tract by Shaykh ʿĀbid in which he states his recollections of the Bab's school days (A. Afnān *Notes;* cf. H. M. Balyuzi *The Bāb* [Oxford, 1973] 231). See also M. A. Fayżī *Ḥażrat-i Nuqṭa-yi Ūlā* (Tehran, 132 Badīʿ/1973) 178–79 (n.) for further details. Shaykh ʿĀbid died in 1263/1847.

[19]See below.

[20]See M. N. Furṣat al-Daula Shīrāzī *Āthār al-ʿAjam* (Bombay, 1314/1896) 465. Also Fayżī *Nuqṭa-yi Ūlā* 74–75.

learned knowledge." It is fairly clear that during his years in the maktab, between ages five and ten, he hardly received a solid and regular education, even in comparison with the standard of his own classmates. However, the existing sources also imply that he enjoyed an unusual level of intelligence and perception. Sipihr's remark that in his early years the Bab studied subjects in Persian and some elementary Arabic[21] gives some indication of his training, and samples of his handwriting, plus his exceptional enthusiasm for calligraphy, reveal some of his early artistic talents.[22] On the other hand, his irregular presence in the school and complaints by his teacher of his preoccupation with his own imaginary world suggest his difficulty in coping with a school system that is often described by himself and others as archaic, monotonous, and cruel. In the Arabic *Bayān* he calls upon his previous teacher not to flog his students with more than a limited number of lashes,[23] and in the Persian *Bayān* he specifies the limit: "It is forbidden to all to discipline children, even verbally, or cause any grief to them before the age of five, and [even] after reaching that age, punishment should not exceed more than five light lashes and not even on bare flesh."[24] Such instructions no doubt reflect the Bab's experience of the rough treatment that was an inseparable part of the traditional school system.

Like many children of his age and background, when he was only eight or nine, he began to spend part of his time in his father's shop.[25] "On his father's death," states Mīrzā Aḥmad, "his maternal uncles undertook his education, especially Hājjī Mīrzā Sayyid ʿAlī, who was reputed to be the most sympathetic of the brothers."[26] Sayyid ʿAlī's care and attention were not confined to the Bab's education or investing in trade the capital left by his brother-in-law to support him,[27] but revealed a deep sympathy toward his somewhat unusual nephew. Later he was to play a significant role in the development of the Bab's early claims and to take an important part in the events of the first two years of the Bab's residence in Shiraz after his declaration.

With his father's death, the hours spent in the bazaar occupied most of Sayyid ʿAlī Muḥammad's time as he continued his practical training in the office of his uncles.[28] Whether this was because of his own disinclination to continue school, lack of financial support, or more probably the concern of

[21] *NT* III, 39.
[22] For a sample of his calligraphy, see Balyuzi *The Bāb* 48. Sayyid Jawād Karbalā'ī once saw some remarkable samples of his writing in Shiraz when Sayyid ʿAlī Muḥammad was a young child. (*Kashf al-Ghiṭā'* 56). Later in his life, the Bab developed a skill in *shikastih,* which he himself especially favored and even recommended in *Bayān* as the best style of calligraphy (IX/2, 313).
[23] Cited in *Muʿīn* 34.
[24] VI/11, 216.
[25] *Ahmad* 447.
[26] Ibid.; cf. Mīrzā Ḥabībullāh *Tārīkh* 9.
[27] A. Afnān *Notes.*
[28] Fayżī *Nuqṭa-yi Ūlā* 82.

his uncles to train him as a merchant rather than anything else, the question of future studies was gradually set aside. One account states that Sayyid ʿAlī Muḥammad's own lack of enthusiasm for formal schoollearning finally forced Shaykh ʿĀbid to send him back to his mother complaining of his strange remarks which were, he thought, beyond the capacity of an ordinary child.[29] A conflicting account insists that when Sayyid ʿAlī Muḥammad was taken out of school in order to work full time in the bazaar, Shaykh ʿĀbid remarked that "if the father of this child were alive, he would never have let his son be deprived of learning, and instead be engaged in trade."[30]

Other reports on the early life of Sayyid ʿAlī Muḥammad support his portrayal as an unconventional child. It is related that once in his early days at the maktab, when his teacher instructed him to memorize the Qurʾānic verse "He is the Deliverer, the All-Knowing,"[31] he insisted first on understanding the meaning, enraging Shaykh ʿĀbid.[32] In another instance he replied to a fellow classmate who asked him about his reluctance to follow the other students in their reading exercises with a couplet from Ḥāfiẓ: "Hearest thou not the whistle's call, this snare should now thy prison be."[33] Mīrzā Muḥammad Ṣaḥḥāf, one of his school friends, remembered that while other students were playing games, Sayyid ʿAlī Muḥammad spent his time in prayers.[34] Sayyid Jawād Karbalāʾī, who was a friend of his uncles and a frequent visitor to their house, also related that the Bab was deeply devoted to his daily prayers when he was a child of about ten. One day, when Sayyid ʿAlī Muḥammad had come late to school and was questioned by the schoolmaster, he replied that he had been in the house of his ancestor, presumably referring to the Prophet. To his teacher's remonstration that as a child daily prayer was not demanded of him, he answered, "I wish to be like my ancestor."[35] Again on a day trip to the shrine of Sabzpūshān in the neighborhood of Shiraz, his uncle Sayyid ʿAlī was deeply impressed when he found his young nephew in a small cave in the nearby mountain reading his prayers in the middle of the night.[36]

Sayyid ʿAlī Muḥammad's inconsistent and disrupted education was not only due to his father's early death or his uncles' intentions, but also to the fact that the existing educational system was not designed to nurture an imaginative mind in a direction different from the accepted norms and

[29] A. Afnān *Notes.*

[30] *Muʿīn* 35.

[31] Qurʾān XXXIV, 25.

[32] Account given by Mullā Fatḥullāh cited in Mīrzā Ḥabībullāh *Tārīkh,* 6–7.

[33] Account given by Āqā Ibrāhim Tājir cited in Mīrzā Ḥabībullāh *Tārīkh* 7–8. Couplet translated by A. J. Arberry *Ḥāfiẓ* (Cambridge, 1962) 89.

[34] Cited in *Kashf al-Ghiṭāʾ* 84.

[35] Ibid. 83–84.

[36] Mīrzā Ḥabībullāh *Tārīkh* 10–11. Recollections of the same nature about childhood devotion, seclusion, and reluctance to associate with other children have also been narrated of both Aḥsāʾī (*Sharḥ-i Aḥvāl* 5–9 and his autobiography in *Fihrist* I, 132–35) and Rashtī (*Qazvīnī* 455, quoting Mīrzā ʿAlī Aṣghar Samīʿ Rashtī, a childhood friend of Rashtī).

standards. The Bab's profound dislike for conventional education seems to have persisted during his adolescence, when he was encouraged to resume formal religious studies. This lack of interest was no doubt an important element in his inclination toward unconventional fields of esoteric knowledge and spiritual experience.

Mullā ʿAbd al-Raḥīm Qazvīnī reports that when Sayyid ʿAlī Muḥammad was about fifteen years old (circa 1250/1834), his uncle arranged for him to resume his studies under Mullā ʿAbd al-Khāliq Yazdī.

> In Mashad, I visited Ākhūnd Mullā ʿAbd al-Khāliq Yazdī who was one of the eminent ʿulama and a follower of Shaykh [Aḥmad Aḥsa'i]. On one occasion, when a remark was made about his holiness [the Bab], he said, "I am bewildered of such great claims. I was a leader of prayer in Shiraz and held teaching lectures there. Once the uncle of this reverent man [i.e., the Bab] brought him to me saying that "this is a soul who is adorned with piety and austerity, but lacks learning, and I beg you to pay him some attention." After I had admitted him, I left him in the custody of my younger son. A few days later my son came back to me complaining that "the person you have left me to teach has not accomplished any of the elementaries. He first must learn *Amthila*,[37] and teaching *Amthila* is not suitable to my position." After that they sent him to Būshihr for the purpose of trade. Now I see such magnificent writings and unequalled verses as to make me astonished."[38]

The same indication is also given by Mullā Muḥammad Ḥamza Sharīʿatmadār Bārfurūshī, who states that the Bab did not study the rudimentary texts *(muqaddimāt)* beyond *Suyūṭī* and the *Ḥāshiya* of Mullā ʿAbdullāh.[39] Attempts to return to madrasa and to complicated texts of medieval logic and Arabic grammar further frustrated Sayyid ʿAlī Muḥammad and failed to turn him into a serious student of religious sciences. In later years, he expressed his reluctance for scholastic education and even discouraged his believers from excessive engagement in Arabic grammar.[40]

The Bab's distaste for formal education is understandable if the general level of scholarship in the madrasa system is taken into account. Binning observes that in the early 1850s the ten madrasas of Shiraz, either because of lack of funds or because of "the general decline in the standard of scholar-

[37] A bilingual Persian-Arabic elementary text on Arabic grammar by Sayyid Sharīf Jurjānī (d. 816/1413), part of the madrasa curriculum (first published in Tehran in 1268/1852).

[38] *ZH* 172 (n.). The Bab himself alluded to his pupilage under Mullā ʿAbd al-Khāliq.

[39] Sharīʿatmadārīyān *Sharḥ-i Zindigī* (MS p. 15) quoting *Asrār al-Shahāda.* Also *ZH* 437. The above-mentioned Suyūṭī is a shortened title for the well-known work *al-Bahjat al-Marḍīya fī Sharḥ al-Alfīya* by Jalāl al-Dīn Suyūṭī (d. 1505). This is a widely read commentary on the famous *Alfīya* of Ibn Mālik on Arabic grammar and syntax. The *Ḥāshīya* is a reference to the marginal gloss by Mullā ʿAbdullāh Yazdī (d. 1573) on the famous work in logic *Tahdhīb al-Manṭiq (wa'l-Kalām)* by Saʿd al-Dīn Taftāzānī (d. 1389). Both works were part of the elementary Shiʿite scholastic curriculum in the nineteenth century.

[40] *Bayān* IV, 10, and VIII, 2.

ship[,] were sunk into the condition of mere schools where little is taught, except simple elementary instructions."[41] He goes on:

> The usual studies in Persian colleges are the Persian and Arabic languages, the Koran and commentaries upon it, theology, law, moral philosophy, and logic. Of natural philosophy, geography, and general history, nothing is taught or known. Mathematics are but little studied, though they possess Euclid's Elements. The dry study of Arabic language is in general held more in estimation and repute than any other pursuit. The grammar of Arabic is complicated and difficult, and their grammarians have endeavored with all their might to make it more so. Volumes have been written on philological trifles and subtleties, which are calculated to perplex and confuse, rather than to assist and enlighten the student.[42]

It is precisely this "dry study of the Arabic language" that repelled the Bab. Years later, when his claims were published, his critics constantly attacked his weakness in Arabic and other rudiments.[43] His poor educational background, regarded by his critics as a great handicap to his claims, was considered by him as a divine merit demonstrating his intuitive knowledge: "The fact that on some occasions words were altered or words uttered contrary to the rules of the people of doubt is because people would be able to make certain that the claimant of this position [himself] received these verses and this knowledge not by the way of learning, but because his heart is illuminated with the divine knowledge. [Therefore] he justifies [lit. refers] these innovative alterations and what is contrary to rules, with the divine rules, as the same matter frequently occurred in the Book of God [the Qur'ān]."[44]

The same theme was expressed in another of his Arabic letters addressed to a divine, this time with more emphasis on his lack of school education: "I swear on my own soul that I did not read a word of the conventional [lit. apparent] sciences, and in the past there were no books of sciences with me whose words I have memorized, and there is no reason for this divine gift but God's generosity and His benevolence. Today if someone asks me of various scholarly matters cited in books, I swear to God that I do not know the answer, and I do not even know the grammar and syntax, and I am proud of it, since God in the Day of Resurrection will prove to all that I was assisted by His generosity."[45] The strains of Bāṭinī thought and the old

[41] *Journal* I, 282–83.

[42] Ibid.

[43] For questions raised during the Tabriz trial regarding the Bab's weakness in Arabic and other basics, and the Bab's response to these criticisms, among other sources see *RS* X, 423–28. Also see below, chap. 6, for Mullā Ḥusayn Bushrū'ī's reply to Mullā Muḥammad Narāqī on the Babi's view regarding Arabic grammar. Also Ḥājjī Muḥammad Karīm Khān Kirmānī *Izhāq al-Bāṭil* (83–104) for the earliest criticism by his Shaykhi opponents.

[44] *Ṣaḥīfa-yi ʿAdlīya* (Persian), INBA, no. 82, p. 155.

[45] *Tafsīr al-Hā'*, INBA, no. 67, pp. 1–84 (56–57).

distinction between "acquired knowledge" and "presential knowledge" are clearly visible. In all sincerity, the Bab attributes his lack of formal education and ignorance of conventional sciences to a divine mandate. Without dismissing the merits of formal knowledge, he considers his own writings the result of a different intuitive experience. His gradual awareness of a sheer ability to "reveal verses" increasingly convinced him as to the validity of his mission. That conviction functioned as a strong impulse, for himself and his future followers, to interpret nonconformity in content and peculiarity in style as proofs of his miracle.

In the earlier stages of his intellectual development, however, his thirst for learning seems to have been satisfied by a growing interest in esoterics and occult sciences as well as other, less-studied fields such as mathematics and astrology.[46] Particularly in post-Safavid times such subjects were relegated from the realms of scholastic learning to the sphere of mystics and eccentrics. The study of fiqh and uṣūl prevailed and esoteric themes, such as survived in the works of Shaykhis, Sufis, and their counterparts, presented an amalgam of theosophy, mysticism, occult and exact sciences, and even popular beliefs. Binning maintains that the study of astronomy has "gradually merged in the absurdities of astrology" and chemistry is "degenerated to alchemy."[47] To a Western traveler, lack of interest in experimental sciences meant decline and degeneration, but to the eager mind of a self-educated layman it meant a way to secrets of intuition. This intellectual incentive encouraged the Bab to escape the tedious rudiments, and to explore the more amusing, and certainly more mysterious, fields of esoterics instead.

To some extent, this interest in unconventional knowledge seems to reflect interest in religious scholarship in the merchant community. The Bab's family on the paternal side produced a number of clerical figures who, contrary to Sayyid ʿAlī Muḥammad's antipathy to the madrasa, proved their talent for scholastic discourses. One example is Ḥājjī Sayyid Jawād Shīrāzī (later known as Kirmānī), a distant cousin of the Bab.[48] After obtaining his ijāza (authorization) in the ʿAtabāt and then spending some time in the religious circles of Mecca and Medina, he returned to Shiraz in the mid-1820s and began giving lectures on theology and mysticism. Later (circa 1248/1832), he was invited to Kirman, where he assumed the office of imām jumʿa till the end of his life (1287/1870). He was a moderately orthodox mujtahid with mystical tendencies, whose lectures on the mystical masterpiece *Masnavī* of the thirteenth century poet Rūmī, an unusual subject for a Shiʿite mujtahid, attracted students from other places to Kirman, including the celebrated philosopher Ḥājjī Mullā Hādī Sabzivārī.[49]

[46] *Ahmad* 447.
[47] Binning *Journal* 283.
[48] See table of genealogy.
[49] Shaykh Yaḥyā Kirmānī *Farmāndihān-i Kirmān* ed. Bāstānī Pārīzī (Tehran, 1344 Sh./1965) 26, 50; M. H. Iʿtimād al-Salṭana *al-Maʾāthir waʾl-Āthār* 153 and *TAS* I/1, 317. For his later reaction toward the Shaykhis and the Babis see *Nabil* 181–87 and *Samandar* 167.

A later and much better-known example of the relatives of the Bab who pursued conventional religious studies is Ḥājjī Sayyid Muḥammad Ḥasan Shīrāzī, also known as Mīrzā-yi Shīrāzī, the *marja'-i taqlīd* (supreme exemplar) of the late nineteenth century. His father, Mīrzā Muḥammad Ḥusayn Shīrāzī, a cousin of the Bab's father,[50] was a distinguished calligrapher, who in spite of his mercantile background and some participation in trade and landowning was himself a tutor in Shiraz.[51] Mīrzā-yi Shīrāzī was born in 1230/1815, five years earlier than Sayyid 'Alī Muḥammad, and was brought up in Shiraz where he completed his elementary studies in Persian, Arabic, and religious law. In Isfahan as a young student he acquired his ijāza from Ḥājjī Mullā Ibrāhīm Karbāsī.[52] Later he moved to the 'Atabāt in the mid-1840s and there, after a long period of study under Shaykh Muḥammad Ḥasan Najafī[53] and then the celebrated Shaykh Murtażā Anṣārī, he eventually emerged as one of the most prominent jurists of his time. His crucial role in the tobacco protest of 1891–1892 brought him unprecedented respect and recognition.[54] Maintaining close contacts with merchants of his birthplace, Mīrzā-yi Shīrāzī never failed to emphasize, both in theory and in practice, the vital importance of reciprocal loyalty between the tujjār and the 'ulama.

These two examples reflect a drift toward religious studies at their most conventional. But some other relatives of the Bab, although they had enjoyed the same educational background in its early stages, showed less enthusiasm for madrasa studies. Sayyid Ḥasan Shīrāzī (son of Sayyid 'Alī Tājir, later known as Afnān-i Kabīr), a brother-in-law of the Bab born in circa 1225/1810, was basically a merchant, with an interest in sciences and theology. He was an amateur scholar who had spent part of his early life as a religious student in Shiraz and then in Isfahan in the company of the above-mentioned Mīrzā-yi Shīrāzī.[55] Throughout his later life he maintained his interest for "complex problems of theology," but he was also "skilful in material sciences such as mathematics, geometry, and geogra-

[50]See table of genealogy.

[51]*FN* II, 54, and A. Afnān *Notes*.

[52]For his details see references in chap. 6.

[53]For his details see chap. 5.

[54]For his details see *TAS* I, 436–41; Algar *Religion and State* 210–11 and cited sources; N. R. Keddie *Religion and Rebellion in Iran* (London, 1966) 66–117. His brother Mīrza Asadullāh Ṭabīb to whom *Fārs Nāmih* (II, 54) gives the religious title of Ḥujjat al-Islām, and his nephew Āghā Sayyid Mīrzā Shīrāzī were both resident in the 'Atabāt (*TAS* I, 172). An interesting interview between Mīrzā Ḥasan and Āqā Sayyid Muḥammad (Nūr al-Dīn) Afnān in Sāmirrā (cited in Mīrzā Ḥabībullāh *Tārīkh* 179–93) suggests that Mīrzā Ḥasan, like his predecessor and his teacher, Shaykh Murtażā Anṣārī, showed a tolerant and, in the case of the former, a fairminded view of the Bab and his cause. This is also confirmed by his general policy toward the Babis and Bahā'īs throughout the late nineteenth century. According to this account this sympathy first began when, during his residence in Isfahan, he was impressed by the Bab's replies to the inquiries of the 'ulama in the house of the governor Manūchihr Khān Mu'tamad al-Daula (*Tārīkh*, 189–90).

[55]'Abbās 'Abd al-Bahā' *Tadhkirat al-Wafā'* (Haifa, 1342/1924) 39–40, and *Khāndān-i Afnān*, 246–55.

phy."[56] His enthusiasm for astrology later led him to the study of Western astronomy, and he even built a private observatory in his home in Yazd for nocturnal observations.[57]

Perhaps it is not a coincidence that both Sayyid Ḥasan and the Bab developed an interest in secular subjects.[58] One could speculate that at some stage the Bab must have become interested in these trends. In the Bab's later work, allusions to secular sciences and even Western advances in technology are not infrequent. In Persian *Bayān* he states that "outside the Shiʿite world there are scientists in every branch,"[59] and further comments that the people of Jesus (*ummat-i ʿĪsā,* a synonym for Europeans in the Bab's terminology), in spite of their inner blindness to Muḥammad's revelation, have an apparent "sharp-sightedness by which through telescopes they can observe realms above earth and survey the moon."[60] Whatever the source of this information, the Bab's side interest in the exact sciences is in contrast to his disgust both in his works and in his correspondence for scholastic pursuits. While still a newly authorized mujtahid in Isfahan working on a treatise on uṣūl al-fiqh, Sayyid Ḥasan received a letter from the Bab pointing out the futility of uṣūl and urging him to abandon these useless speculations.[61] Sayyid Ḥasan seems to have complied, as he later abandoned ijtihād and became a merchant.

Another brother-in-law, Ḥājjī Muḥammad Mahdī Ḥijāb Shīrāzī (born 1224/1809), showed a similar disjunction from madrasa.[62] Coming from the same mercantile background, he also benefited from a similar education in literature, Arabic, logic, and ḥikma and later developed some interest in poetry and mysticism. After finishing his elementary studies, "he moved to India for commercial purposes and resided for a long time in Bombay, where he managed to accumulate some capital. Then returning to his homeland, he abandoned his trade and became acquainted with the followers of perfection and masters of ecstasy."[63] His Sufi affiliation, his poetical talent, and his excellent calligraphy made him a well-known figure in Shiraz in his own time.[64]

The above examples demonstrate noticeable diversity in Sayyid ʿAlī Muḥammad's family. While it allowed humble seminarians like Mīrzā-yi Shīrāzī or Sayyid Jawād Shīrāzī, both from nonclerical backgrounds, to

[56] *Tadhkirat al-Wafā*ʾ 39–40.

[57] A. Afnān *Notes.*

[58] Earlier contacts between the two families occurred even before the Bab's marriage. After the death of Sayyid Ḥasan's father, the guardianship of his family was entrusted to the Bab's eldest uncle (A. Afnān *Notes*).

[59] *Bayān* VI/13, 224.

[60] Ibid. 225.

[61] A. Afnān *Notes.*

[62] Maternal half-brother of Khadīja Khānum, the Bab's wife, and also brother-in-law of Sayyid ʿAlī, the Bab's uncle (see table of genealogy).

[63] *TH* III, 471–72; cf. *FN* II, 44.

[64] A. Afnān *Notes.*

reach high religious ranks, it diverted others to secular fields. Remaining on the borderline between the two, the Bab seems to have been drawn closer toward the latter group. Self-education and exploration of unconventional themes remained an incentive for him. But the closeknit network of merchant families of Shiraz provided few alternatives to madrasa. His disillusion with school, combined with a need "for earning his livelihood,"[65] left him no choice but to become an assistant to his uncles in their trade in Būshihr. As he himself points out, interestingly enough in his "letter to the ʿulamā": "When this youth reached the age of compulsory learning, in the tradition of the Prophet of God in the past, he arrived in *Jazīrat al-Baḥr* [lit. the island of the sea; i.e., Būshihr]. He did not study your scientific methods with any of you [i.e., with the ʿulama] and thus in the preserved tablet of the divine order, he is an uneducated *[ummī]* ʿAjamī [non-Arab, Persian] and descendant of the Prophet of God.[66]

Becoming a Merchant

Throughout his five years in Būshihr (1250–1256/1835–1840), sometimes in the company of one of his uncles but mostly in their absence, Sayyid ʿAlī Muḥammad participated in the family business mainly as a commercial agent. However, as time passed it appears that he became a partner, and even carried on some independent business.[67]

The commercial activities of the Bab's uncles throughout the mid-nineteenth century followed the general pattern of southern trade.[68] Based in Shiraz and Yazd, they traded between Būshihr and Bandar ʿAbbās and the Indian ports of Bombay, Madras, and Calcutta, plus other ports of the Persian Gulf and Arabian Sea such as Muscat and Bahrain, and as far away as Zanzibar and Java. The southern trade consisted of imports of European (mainly English) and Indian cotton and woolen manufactures, sugar, tea, pepper and other spices, coffee, indigo, luxury wares, and semiprocessed metals. The exports consisted largely of raw and semiprocessed products:

[65]*Aḥmad* 447.

[66]INBA, no. 91, XXII, 75–76; cf. Browne Or. MSS no. F. 21(9), letter no. 32, 224–35, Arabic, written about 1262/1846.

[67]*Muʿīn* (MS B) 23. This source believes that when he was about twenty years of age he abandoned his uncle's business and set up an independent trade. This is confirmed by A. Afnān (*Notes*), who maintains that along with his participation with his uncles, the Bab had invested in trade the remaining capital inherited from his father.

[68]On the trade of southern Iran in general, and on the trade of Būshihr in particular, references in A. K. S. Lambton "Persian Trade under the Early Qajars" in *Islam and the Trade of Asia* (Oxford, 1970) 215–44; and G. Hambly "An Introduction to the Economic Organization of Early Qajar Iran" *Iran* 2 (1964) 69–81 provide some general analysis. The reports of K. E. Abbott in the British Public Record Office are particularly useful. See K. E. Abbott *Cities and Trade* 80–92 and 112–16 for some details on the trade of Būshihr in this period. Also *The Economic History of Iran, 1800–1914* ed. C. Issawi (Chicago, 1971), 82–91 and the information supplied by Lorimer *Gazetteer* I, 2. For some further discussions on this trade see below, chap. 7.

grains, dried fruits, and other foodstuffs, vegetable dyes and natural gums, seeds and spices, raw silk, cotton, wool, tobacco, carpets, and livestock.[69] By the 1830s and 1840s, the trade of the south, because of competition from the newly opened northern route, was beginning to slow down. The exports of raw materials and cash crops barely compensated for the imports of European fabrics and the burden of trade deficit was becoming excessive.

Simultaneous with the Bab's years of residence in Būshihr, the city underwent a phase of turmoil that was the outcome of British retaliatory action against the Persian government and the occupation of Khārg Island between 1838 and 1842.[70] From the early nineteenth century, the British Residency in Būshihr implemented a dual policy, expanding the Persian trade with India and Europe while safeguarding the political interests of Britain in the Persian Gulf region. Following Muḥammad Shāh's attempt to reassert Persian control over Herat, in May 1837 the people of Būshihr witnessed the arrival of the British Indian navy.[71] In the ensuing months a series of urban riots with strong anti-British overtones disturbed the normal course of trade. The British, though anxious not to alienate the merchant community in the city, were not willing to give up what amounted to a clear example of their gunboat policy.

The confrontation between the two countries reached a new momentum when in March 1839 the inhabitants of Būshihr, encouraged by the Akhbārī leader Shaykh Ḥusayn Āl ʿUṣfūr and backed by the governor, Asadullāh Mīrzā, and his troops tried to prevent the landing of Rear Admiral Sir Frederick Maitland and his troops in the Būshihr Residency. The incident compelled the British to evacuate Būshihr and retreat to Khārg. The merchants of Būshihr, dreading the effects of the removal of the Residency on the trade of the port, tried in vain to mediate between the British and the local governor. They even sent a deputation to the British flagship to apologize for the behavior of the townspeople and to promise a written apology from the governor.[72] The apology was never submitted, but the Residency returned to Būshihr three years later.

The entire episode illustrates the mixed response of the local population to imperial aggression which in turn demonstrates the degree to which the Persian trade of the south was dependent on British good-will. By the late 1830s, the merchants of Fars found themselves in an undesirable situation where a large portion of their trade with India, and with it their financial

[69]*Cities and Trade* 106–9, 113–14.

[70]For a full account of this episode of British involvement in the south see among other sources J. B. Kelley *Britain and the Persian Gulf, 1795–1880* (Oxford, 1968) 290–301, 306–11, 343–53; Lorimer *Gazetteer* I, part 1, 222–25; part 2, 1962–66, 1970–95; *FN* I, 294–95 (trans. H. Busse as *History of Persia under Qājār Rule* [New York and London, 1972] 256–61). For Būshihr during the early nineteenth century see Kelly *Britain* 42–45; Lorimer *Gazetteer* II, A, 339–49; W. Heude, *A Voyage up the Persian Gulf,* (London, 1819) 41–44.

[71]Kelly *Britain* 294–95.

[72]Ibid. 309.

viability, were to be ransomed to a political conflict far beyond their control. It is not hard to detect the sources of merchants' moderation and their self-assumed mediatory role. The restraints of international market had already demanded from them an independent course of action. In the short term, one can assume that the commerical disruption between 1838 and 1842 must have contributed to the general stagnation of the southern trade prior to the introduction of new cash crops in the late 1850s.

Sayyid ʿAlī Muḥammad's trade accounts between 1250/1835 and 1256/1840[73] show that the family trade reached the main markets of southern and central Iran. References to transactions with the local merchants in Isfahan, Kashan, and Tehran mainly concern agricultural and food exports in exchange for imports of fabrics, tea, sugar, and spices. These documents confirm that the Bab had acquired the necessary skill for keeping accounts and handling commercial orders, and illustrate his acquaintance with the merchant network of the south in general and Būshihr in particular. The commercial background on both sides of the Bab's family doubtless helped him in finding his way in the mercantile community of Būshihr. Mīr Ismāʿīl, his paternal grandfather, lived there sometime during the Bab's childhood and had trade links with his uncles.[74] The extent of the family business sometimes stretched even to members who were not directly involved in trade: the above-mentioned Sayyid Jawād Shīrāzī, while on his way to the Ḥijāz for further studies, sold his father's merchandise in the Muscat market.[75]

The large-scale trade in the family really flourished at the time of his elder uncle, Ḥājjī Sayyid Muḥammad, whose marriage to one of the oldest tujjār families, the ʿAbd al-Ḥusaynīs, must have contributed to his success.[76] In spite of chronic waves of political insecurity and risks of economic failure, the ʿAbd al-Ḥusaynīs managed to establish a trade in Būshihr that according to *Fārs Nāmih* "extended from the remotest parts of India to the farthest corners of Farangistān,"[77] and survived for generations. Ḥājjī Sayyid Muḥammad, his brothers Ḥājjī Sayyid ʿAlī and Ḥājjī Sayyid Ḥasan ʿAlī, and their relatives and descendants, later known as Afnāns,[78] operated large-scale trade from Shiraz, Yazd, Būshihr, and Bandar ʿAbbās inside Iran, and Bombay, Hong Kong, Ashkhabad (ʿIshqābād), and Beirut outside Iran throughout the nineteenth century and into the twentieth. Muḥammad ʿAlī Afnān, one of the three sons of Ḥājjī Sayyid Muḥammad and a maternal cousin of the Bab, starting from Shiraz in the 1830s, moved to Bombay and

[73]INBA Collection of Documents, file no. 32.
[74]A. Afnān *Notes*.
[75]Ibid.
[76]*Khāndān-i Afnān* 46; cf. *FN* II, 76–77.
[77]*FN* II, 76–77.
[78]The title *Afnān* (lit. branches; i.e., of the Bab's family) was later conferred upon them by Bahāʾullāh.

then to Hong Kong where, together with his sons, his brothers, and his brothers-in-law, he managed to control "a large portion of the opium exports from Isfahan, Yazd, and Fars."[79] Another son, Ḥājjī Muḥammad Taqī (later Vakīl al-Ḥaqq), who succeeded the Bab in the Būshihr office in the 1840s, later moved to Yazd and then to Ashkhabad.[80] The Bab's younger uncle, Ḥājjī Sayyid Ḥasan ʿAlī, was based in Yazd. He married into another reputable merchant family of Shiraz, and in collaboration with his brothers handled their trade in the eastern markets of Kirman, Mashhad, and Ṭabas.[81]

The Bab's father-in-law, Ḥājjī Mīrzā ʿAlī Shīrāzī, was a descendant of another old merchant family, a branch of the Bab's maternal family. He and one of his sons, Mīrzā Abul-Qāsim (born 1226/1811), also participated in the Būshihr trade. *Fārs Nāmih* confirms that Mīrzā Abul-Qāsim's trade was substantial: "As he embarked on his forefathers' trade, he commissioned commercial agents in every corner."[82] When Sayyid ʿAlī Muḥammad returned to Shiraz for a brief period in the early 1840s he conducted some commercial ventures in collaboration with Mīrzā Abul-Qāsim. His office in Sarā-yi Gumruk in the Shiraz bazaar neighbored that of his brother-in-law.[83]

The intermarital links among tujjār families, of which the marriages of the Bab, and his relatives are examples, formed the base of a more comprehensive interrelation binding together the merchants of Shiraz. The prosperity of the community, though frequently threatened by political upheaval, urban disorder, and economic hazards, owed its survival chiefly to these family ties. This in turn allowed the formation of a close community with a cohesive and homogeneous identity distinguished by a collective response to outside threats, professional cooperation, economic flexibility, strong religious sentiments, and moral values.

First reflected in his personal piety and professional trustworthiness, then in vigorous asceticism and unorthodox interests, this communal ethic was a predominant theme in the Bab's business career. Connected to this ethos were the economic resources that enabled the merchants to afford education

[79]*FN* II, 45 under Mīrzā Āqā family; *Khāndān-i Afnān* 81–100.

[80]See *Khāndān-i Afnān* 100–31 for details of him and his descendants, who were merchants and landowners in Yazd. Ḥājjī Sayyid Muḥammad's five grandsons were all engaged in land and trade (ibid. 40–81). *Fārs Nāmih* (II, 45) states: "In the past few years, since trade had declined and commercial transactions were abandoned," the descendants of Ḥājjī Sayyid Muḥammad "invested part of their capital in land and property in various districts of Fars, and the other part in the opium trade which has flourished in the past ten years."

[81]*Khāndān-i Afnān* 140–58. *Nabil* 126 refers to the partners of the Bab's uncles in Yazd and Ṭabas.

[82]*FN* II, 131. Afterward, Mīrzā Abul-Qāsim left his trade in the hands of his four sons (ibid.). Also *Khāndān-i Afnān* 256–85.

[83]*Ahmad* 449 and Mīrzā Ḥabībullāh *Tārīkh* 256. In the events of 1262/1846, when the Bab managed to free himself from detention in the house of the chief magistrate *(dārūgha)* of Shiraz and move to Isfahan, Mīrzā Abul-Qāsim was held responsible by the governor and forced to give a guarantee to return his partner in a fortnight's time.

and other intellectual pursuits. The links with religious, and to a lesser extent Sufi, figures were also important. But such moral characteristics were further strengthened by the weight that was given to mercantile honesty and piety in a religious context. These were embellished by the Traditions and deeds of the Prophet and Imams and served as a theoretical framework for the emergence of a role model; Traditions that praised honesty and godliness in trade and cautioned evildoers.[84] The fact that trade was the profession of the Prophet, Muḥammad al-Amīn (the trustworthy), also had a special meaning. The Prophet guaranteed that "the trustworthy, just and believing merchant shall stand at the Day of Judgment among the witnesses of blood,"[85] and reminded them that "the merchants will be raised up on the Day of Resurrection as evildoers, except those who fear God, are honest, and speak the truth."[86] ʿAlī, the First Imam, walking in the streets of Kūfa, admonished them: "Ye, the merchants! Make your priority the seeking of good and bless yourselves with ease [in your dealings] and come close to the customers and ornate your souls with patience and avoid falsehood and perjury. Distance yourself from oppression and do justice to the oppressed and do not come close to usury or tamper with weights and scale and do not contaminate people with your goods and do not fill the earth with the corrupt."[87]But if the admonitions were severe, the incentive for integrity was equally great. Jaʿfar Ṣādiq, the Sixth Imam, promised them: "Three [groups] will enter God's paradise free of [final] reckoning: the just religious judge, the honest merchant, and the ascetic who spends his life in worship."[88]

A question remains as to what extent these moral values, emphasized in Traditions or in the legal code for transactions and trade, were observed in practice. No doubt a need for cooperation and mutual trust encouraged merchants to seek some practical application in their economic activity and even more in their personal conduct. Numerous references to the trustworthiness of merchants in Persian sources may not seem exaggerated when compared to those of contemporary Europeans. Gobineau gives an interesting account of the common characteristics of Persian merchants: "In Persia merchants are perhaps the most respectable part of the population. They are

[84]For Traditions regarding trade and merchants see *Concordance et indices de la tradition musulmane* ed. A. J. Wensinck et al., 7 vols. (Leiden, 1936–69) I, 264–66 and cited sources. Also *EI*[1]: TIDJĀRA (Heffening) and *EI*[2]: BAYʿ (Schacht) and cited sources. For the Shiʿite point of view, see *Biḥār al-Anwār* XXIII and sections under *makāsib* and *muʿāmalāt* in nineteenth-century works such as Muḥammad Ḥasan Najafī's *Jawāhir al-Kalām* (Isfahan, 1271/1854) and Mīrzā Muḥammad Ḥusayn Nūrī Ṭabarsī's work on Shiʿite ḥadīth titled *Mustadrak al-Wasāʾil* (Tehran, 1321/1903)II.

[85]Ḥadith quoted from the Prophet in Ibn Māja *Sunan* (Cairo, 1313/1895) Tijārāt, I, 1.

[86]Ibid. Other similar traditions quoted in Ibn al-Farrāʾ, Abū Muḥammad al-Baghāwī *Mishkāt al-Maṣābīḥ* English trans. J. Robson, 2d ed., 2 vols. (Lahore, 1975) I, book XII, 599.

[87]*Biḥār al-Anwār* XXIII/19, 25 related by Muḥammad Bāqir, the Fifth Imam, and cited in Shaykh Ṣaddūq's *al-Amālī*.

[88]Ibid. XIV/95, 683.

regarded as being very honest. Since they do not take unnecessary risks, and as merchants are more often than not sons of merchants who have inherited a more or less substantial fortune which they will transmit to their sons, they are devoid of worldly ambition and above many forms of intrigue. They need public esteem and carefully cultivate it."[89]

Although "the Persian merchant is almost always strictly honest" and "holds most of the capital in Persia," he points out, in some practices, such as delay in payment of bills of exchange, they do not measure up to their reputation. But "from the point of view of morality," he maintains, "it would perhaps be wrong to judge this mode of behavior with the vigor of our commercial principles. This kind of easygoing behavior does not stop Persian merchants from acting in good faith in their business dealings."[90]

Four decades earlier, almost the same characteristics were also detected by Malcolm, who on his second visit (circa 1810) met merchants in Būshihr, Shiraz, and Isfahan and everywhere "found their general characters nearly the same."[91] He also observes that security of their capital dictated certain modes of behavior upon the merchant: "The plunder of a merchant, without some pretext, would shake all confidence, and be fatal to that commerce from which a great proportion of the public revenue is derived; the most tyrannical monarchs, therefore, have seldom committed so impolitic an act of injustice. But this class have suffered so severely in the late revolutions of the country that they continue to act with great caution. . . . Some few make a display of their wealth; but in general their habits are not merely frugal, but penurious."[92]

Other sources attributed similar characteristics. Waring writes that "the merchants of Persia are a shrewd, sensible, and thrifty class of people, willing to undergo any hardship if they have a prospect of making money."[93] Edward Burgess, himself a merchant in Tabriz between 1828 and 1855, praises the honesty and thoroughness of Tabrīzī merchants, who were "so regular in their payments" that upon most occasions he did not even have to send a servant for the collection of the dues.[94] C. J. Wills, a medical officer in Iran in the late 1860s and early 1870s, believed on the other hand that the "merchant class are generally the most bigoted and penurious of the Persian race. Only on retiring from business do they dare to launch out into

[89]Joseph A. de Gobineau *Trois ans en Asie* (Paris, 1859) 392–93; also translated in Issawi *Economic History* 36.

[90]Ibid.

[91]Sir John Malcolm *Sketches of Persia* one-volume ed. (London, 1845) 132.

[92]Ibid. 132–33.

[93]Edward Scott Waring *A Tour to Sheeraz* (London, 1807) 77.

[94]Charles and Edward Burgess *Letters from Persia* ed. B. Schwartz (New York, 1942) 34. Edward Burgess, whose brother Charles's adventures and dishonest dealings caused great financial loss to the Persian merchants in Tabriz, was for years in debt to the merchants of this city due to his brother's bankruptcy, yet he never complains of any mistreatment or pressure on him by the local tujjār.

ostentation; for the mere suspicion of wealth in Persia exposed them to the exaction of those in power." Wills makes this comment in the context of Isfahan merchants, since he believes that "honesty cannot be expected in Ispahani or Teherani, but the Shirazi may be pretty fairly relied upon."[95]

Binning also observed: "In this country, no merchant can afford to be what we should consider an honest man. If he keeps his word, pays his debts, honors bills when due, and restores money entrusted to him, he is sure to be marked as a rich man, which is tantamount to being a criminal, and he will, as surely, be liable to be persecuted, fleeced and screwed without mercy. However good his intentions may be, he must affect to put off his engagements, or to meet them with greatest difficulty; otherwise his rapacious rulers will mark him for the prey."[96]

Regardless of the bias of some of the above reporters, due perhaps to a change of attitude of European travelers in the second half of the nineteenth century, one may also suspect changes in the habits and practices of the Persian merchants. In response to external threats, insecurity, governmental pressure, and changes in the economic climate, certain tactical and defensive methods were bound to emerge to enable the merchant community to preserve the principles vital for the survival of mutual trust and professional cooperation. Interfamily and intercommunity bonds among the big merchants—or among the various groups within the merchant community, or among merchants in different cities—provided a network within which the process of commercial and financial transactions was possible. Moreover, such ties helped to create a set of universal norms that were eventually engrained into the communities' standard ethical and ultimately intellectual ethos.

Trustworthiness and honesty in commercial activities are often reported in the members of the Bab's family. *Fārs Nāmih*'s remark that the uncles of the Bab "for generations . . . were engaged in trade and. . . known for their honesty"[97] goes beyond a casual compliment when a closer source, Mīrzā Aḥmad, states that "all of them [uncles of the Bab] are trustworthy merchants and reputed to be noble Sayyids."[98] The same qualities have also been attributed to the Bab himself in a number of anecdotes from his Būshihr days, when his strict standards for a thorough and honest trade contrasted with the "easygoing" behavior of some of his colleagues.

On one occasion, Ḥājjī Mīrzā Abul-Ḥasan Yazdī, a merchant in Būshihr on his way to the pilgrimage of Ḥajj, entrusted the Bab with some merchandise to be sold during his absence. The price of the merchandise fell and it was sold at a price cheaper than was expected. However, on his return to

[95]Wills *In The Land of the Lion and the Sun* 188.
[96]Binning *Journal* II, 34.
[97]*FN* II, 131.
[98]*Ahmad* 446. According to A. Afnān's *Notes* the maternal family of the Bab was always regarded as trustworthy in Shiraz.

Būshihr, Sayyid ʿAlī Muḥammad (contrary to the general practice of the time, which only obliged him to pay back the value of the sold merchandise), included 175 tūmāns extra, the difference between the original value and the price fetched, insisting that failing to pay the original price was contrary to the code of trustworthiness.[99] This was a vigorous interpretation of a legal injunction concerning custodianship of depositions in trust. Most Shiʿite jurists agree that if for reasons beyond the custodian's control a deposited item perishes or loses its value, the custodian should not be held responsible for the loss. Others argued that if the price is in dispute, it is the owner's word that counts, if accompanied by an oath. In this case, the Bab seems to have volunteered the payment of a compensation without the owner's solicitation.[100]

On another occasion, the sale of a cargo of indigo was agreed upon between Sayyid ʿAlī Muḥammad and some merchants in Būshihr. After the delivery of the goods, at the time of the payment, the purchasers came back to Sayyid ʿAlī Muḥammad and asked for a discount; a customary method of after-sale bargaining known as *dabba.*[101] When the Bab refused to consider the reduction the purchasers objected that such discount is a "national custom" and should be observed by everyone. Insisting that "soon many unlawful customs will be abolished," Sayyid ʿAlī Muḥammad took back the merchandise and made the contract void. The merchants who regarded the cancelation of the deal and the return of the merchandise harmful to their commercial credit, wrote complaints to Ḥājjī Sayyid Muḥammad, who blamed his nephew for not "acting in accordance with people's wishes and neglecting accepted customs and practices."[102] What the Bab seems to have been reacting against was the questionable justification for a common practice unclarified by the Shiʿite fiqh. The jurists consider it reprehensible for the purchaser to ask for a reduction in price after the exchange of contract, while it is commendable for the seller to agree on the cancellation of the contract if demanded by the buyer.[103] The ambiguity arising from the jurists' compromise was one example of interference of ethical obligations

[99]*Muʿīn* (78), without specifying his source, only saying that this has been reported by the opponents of the Bab. *Nabil* (79) quotes Sayyid Jawād Karbalāʾī relating a similar account. The above-mentioned merchant is probably the father of Aḥmad ibn Abul-Ḥasan Sharīf Shīrāzī (later Īshīk Āqāsī), who was a merchant and originally from Yazd and in close contact with the Bab's family.

[100]See among others Najafī's *Jawāhir,* book of *wadīʿa*; cf. Muḥaqqiq (Jaʿfar) Ḥillī *Sharāʾiʿ al-Islām* (Cairo, 1376/1956) XII (book of *wadīʿa),* Persian trans. A. Yazdī, ed. M. T. Dānishpazūh, 3 vols. (Tehran, 1349–1358 Sh./1970–1979) I, 285–91.

[101]C. J. Wills gives a description of the "peculiar custom" of *dabba*, which he reckons is "possibly legal by the religious law." He adds: "This is frequently done either to lower the price a little or, when the article is a fluctuating one, such as opium, to take advantage of a rise or fall in the market. For this reason it is that all contracts have to be in writing, and generally something is paid on account to bind the slippery Isphahani" (*In the Land of the Lion and the Sun* 188). In the case of the Bab a contract had been issued and deposits had been exchanged.

[102]Mīrzā Ḥabībullāh *Tārīkh* 12–14 citing an account by ʿAbd al-Bahāʾ; cf. *NK* 109.

[103]Ḥillī *Sharāʾiʿ*, the book of *tijāra* (trans. 152).

with market transactions. Such inconsistencies, not uncommon in legal discussions on contracts and rights of withdrawal, made strict conformity with the word of the law a formidable task, and not infrequently opened the way for evasion, fraud, and other dishonest practices.

This moralistic attitude was not devoid of pragmatism, however. The Bab's later instructions do not resonate the bookishness of madrasa jurists, nor do they lend themselves, at least as far as the trade was concerned, to a puritanical enthusiasm. Contrary to the restricted regulations set up by the sharīʿa, but in compliance with common practice, he allows a lawful interest on the borrowed money "as it is now practiced among the merchants," or allows agreement on the extension or delay of the repayment of exchange bills. He regards the mutual satisfaction of both parties as the essential condition for the lawfulness of any contract, whether they are "under age, adults, slaves, or free men."[104] On the subject of foreigners, he emphasizes that only those Christian merchants who follow useful trades and professions are permitted to dwell in the countries of believers.[105] On another occasion, he refers to changes in the monetary system and acknowledges that depreciation of currency, both gold and silver, brings losses to the tujjār. He hopes that in the future these fluctuations will settle.[106] He strictly forbids trade of opium, intoxicating drugs, and liquors for believers, but allows their use for medical purposes under certain conditions.[107]

Although the author of *Nuqṭāt al-Kāf,* himself a merchant, believes that the Bab was successful in his Būshihr business "to the extent that the chiefs of tujjār took notice of his holiness' mastery in commercial matters,"[108] he also maintains that the Bab became known to people because of "spending all his capital," either by giving away money to the poor, or by making substantial losses in the market through overabsorption in his prayers and devotions.[109] One can assume that it was this attitude that made the continuation of the partnership with his uncles undesirable. As Muʿīn al-Salṭana points out, "considering the existing necessities of the time," the Bab finally separated from his uncles and set up his own independent trade.[110]

For young Sayyid ʿAlī Muḥammad engagement in trade served not only as a means of earning his livelihood, but more significantly as a way to emphasize moral standards that he felt were declining, standards that were for him idealized in the words and deeds of the Prophet and Imams. In a letter written some years later, presumably to some merchants among his followers, he highlights these true qualities: "Say! What God formerly autho-

[104] *Bayān* V/18, 181.
[105] Ibid. VII/16, 263.
[106] Ibid. V/19, 183.
[107] Ibid. IX/8, 323–24.
[108] *NK* 109.
[109] Ibid.
[110] *Muʿīn* 78.

rized for Muḥammad, and then for ʿAlī Muḥammad [himself], was trade, of which you have also prospered and esteemed. Praise your Lord for sending down the blessing of the Heaven and Earth and in between, to those who are engaged in trade. O God! raise those who are fair in their dealings, and love those inferior to them as they love their own souls and give them respect and prosperity. You are the Omnipotent! Say! Whoever trades for the sake of God, and is honest in his business, God will guarantee him against fraud. Thereby, those of you who established your trade on the path of God, and thus [are partners] with the manifestation of God, are truthful in your trade."[111]

The sense of solidarity with the merchants is unmistakable. So is the Qur'ānic metaphor of trade with God and His manifestation. Only those who trade "for the sake of God" observe the high moral qualities of fairness and affection toward inferiors and only they will receive blessing, respect, and prosperity. The model for such thoroughness, as the Bab implies, is none other than God's messenger. This comparison between the Bab and the Prophet is also drawn in the writings of the followers of the Bab. *Nuqṭat al-Kāf* states that Sayyid ʿAlī Muḥammad's engagement in trade "was designed to accomplish the proof to the people, so they would not be able to claim that he lacked the capacity of dealing with people. Thus the same mysterious considerations behind the engagement of his venerated ancestor [the Prophet] in trade, could also be applied to him. So, in every sense he could be a sign of that original light even in his orphanhood."[112]

Compared to other professions, in most of his works, the Bab paid greater attention to the respectability of an honest and fair trade. Nonetheless, the extent of this attention should not be exaggerated. In fact the bulk of the Bab's writings in the years after his proclamation was focused on mystical, moral, devotional, and ritualistic themes, which in effect left little room for the formulation of a consistent social framework. This implies that the effect of professional background in the personality and teachings of the Bab is more subtle than a direct reflection of the material wishes of the merchant class.[113] This material life and the struggle for livelihood could only be valued when looked upon as an instrument for a more important moral struggle. For the Bab, as he himself writes, trade was an act of worship and veneration. He swears to God that during his days of trade, he never bent to put a hallmark on a bale of merchandise without remembering and venerating the greatness of God.[114] This is the outlook that underlay

[111] Arabic letter cited in *Muʿīn* 28.

[112] *NK* 110.

[113] An example of this kind of generalization on the theme of the Bab's teachings as the voice of "the rising bourgeoisie" is found in Ivanov *Babidskie vosstaniya v Iran* 135–37.

[114] A. Afnān *Notes*.

the Bab's approach to material life, and the one that gradually brought him closer to an ascetic life-style with strong mystical strains.

Asceticism and Ethics

The two aspects of professional honesty and lack of proper schooling in hagiographical accounts of the young Bab were supplemented by other extraordinary features. Asceticism, devotion, revealing dreams, and prophetic remarks helped to create a picture of innocence and holiness, which more than any intellectual faculty led his followers to believe that the Bab's mission was of a divine nature. They depict him as an exceptionally pure soul designated from the very beginning to receive inspiration.[115] Dreams in particular seem to have played a significant role in the Bab's own assumption of his spiritual faculties. It is widely related that in his childhood he had a dream of a huge balance suspended between heaven and earth. On one scale he saw Jaʿfar Ṣādiq, the Sixth Imam, who in Shiʿite Islam is renowned for his esoteric wisdom and comprehensive knowledge; then an unseen hand put the Bab on the other scale and his side proved heavier, and tended toward the earth.[116] He himself pointed to the influence of dreams on his ability to reveal verses: "Remember! The emanation of all these verses and prayers and all these unlearned sciences is because of a dream which I once had of the holy head of the Lord of Martyrs [Sayyid al-Shuhadā', i.e., Ḥusayn ibn ʿAlī], upon him be peace, detached from his holy body, together with the heads of other companions. I drank seven handfuls of his holy blood with greatest joy, and it is now the blessing of that blood which illuminated my heart with such verses and prayers."[117]

In 1262/1846 he dreamed that at the hour of the spring equinox (the Persian new year), some books were sent down to him. When he opened one of them he noticed that its pages were covered with the dust of Ḥusayn's tomb. He looked more closely and saw a tablet in an excellent *shikastih* style bearing an astral seal at the bottom with the epigram "I entrusted my cause to God," signed "Mahdi." The contents of the tablet, written in red ink, confirmed this claim.[118] References to dreams and the way they im-

[115]Elements of religious devotion could be traced in the Bab's family background. The Bab's maternal grandfather, Ḥājjī Sayyid Muḥammad Ḥusayn, himself a merchant, "was known to the people of Būshihr not only for his piety and godliness, but also for certain supernatural gifts which are reported of him" (*Khāndān-i Afnān* 105; brief biographical notes by Ḥājjī Muḥammad Taqī Afnān).

[116]Mīrza Ḥabībullāh *Tārīkh; Muʿīn* 29–30; and *KD* I, 33.

[117]*Saḥifa-yi ʿAdlīya,* INBA no. 82, 134–205 (160). In the Tabriz trial of 1264/1848, some of the ʿulama present in the gathering made sarcastic remarks about this very dream. See *Shaykhīgarī va Bābīgarī* 313, citing a manuscript written by Mullā Muḥammad Taqī ibn Mullā Muḥammad Mamaqānī.

[118]Commentary on verse 35 of *Sūrat al-Nūr* (Qur'ān XXIV), INBA no. 98, 55–63 (57–59). After describing his dream, the Bab interprets all its details, with strong emphasis on numerology and the science of letters. See chap. 4 for his dream at the time of Rashtī's death.

plicitly demonstrate certain spiritual faculties should be seen in the light of a continuous tradition of revelatory dreams of the Prophet and the Imams, particularly the Twelfth Imam.[119] The Bab's holy dreams, like those related by Shaykh Aḥmad Aḥsā'ī, disclose the secret of the Book, clarify obscure points of akhbār, and explain various theological and mystical problems by means of direct encounter with the Prophet or Imam.[120] These strong prophetic allusions, which could not have been delivered in a state of wakefulness, are a prelude to his later inspirations. The mystery of the holy dreams (and his unconventional words and deeds) can be only partly explained by the myth that later encompassed his image as a holy and infallible man. For the greater part, it was his own unconscious effort to express himself in symbolism of dreams in a language previously employed by other Sufi and Shaykhi adepts.

His years in Būshihr were also marked by devotion and austerity, developing as time passed into some mystical tendencies that were not far removed from the self-mortification and seclusion practiced by ascetics of his time. His devotion, self-denial, "extreme courtesy and the serene expression on his face," and "humility and lowliness" left a favorable effect on his friends, relatives, and colleagues. Ḥājjī Sayyid Jawād Karbalā'ī, who once dwelt for six months in the Bab's house in Būshihr, recounts: "I often heard those who were closely associated with him testify to the purity of his character, to the charm of his manner, to his self-effacement, to his high integrity, and to his extreme devotion to God."[121] The high praise of this follower of the Bab is confirmed in essence by Mīrzā Aḥmad, who reports: "I have gathered, as a result of my inquiries, that he was very quiet, modest and shy during his childhood, and that he showed signs of piety on reaching the age of maturity."[122] A more interesting account comes from Ḥājjī Muḥammad Ḥusayn, a colleague of the Bab in Būshihr: "Since the Bab was a native of Shiraz, and had not yet assumed any claims, I, in the company of other Shīrāzī merchants, used to go to Sarāy-i Maymandī to visit him, and we became intimate with him. But he was very taciturn, and would never utter a word unless it was necessary. He did not even answer our questions. He was constantly absorbed in his own thoughts, and was preoccupied with

[119]For the religious significance of dreams in Islam see *The Dream and Human Societies* ed. G. E. von Grunebaum and R. Caillois (Berkeley and Los Angeles, 1966), articles by von Grunebaum, H. Corbin, T. Fahd, J. Lecerf and F. Rahman. In Shi'ite literature on visitation of the Imams, and particularly the Hidden Imam, dreams were often recognized as an important medium. See for example Mīrzā Ḥusayn Nūrī Ṭabarsī's *al-Najm al-Thāqib* (Tehran, 1347 Sh./1968) chap. 7, 207–412), where the author cites one hundred cases of reported encounters with the Hidden Imam, many of them in dreams.

[120]For dreams of Aḥsā'ī see autobiographical treatise cited in *Fihrist* I, 136–43; *L'École Shaykhie* 11–12; *Risāla-yi Sharḥ-i Aḥvāl-i Shaykh Aḥmad Aḥsā'ī*, 9–17. Also compare with dreams reported by teacher, Muḥammad Mahdī Baḥr al-'Ulūm, cited in *QU* 171–74. *QU* (206) and *Shaykhīgarī va Bābīgarī* (83) give some interpretation of the authenticity of dreams.

[121]Cited in *Nabil* 79.

[122]*Ahmad* 446–47.

repetition of his prayers and verses. He was a handsome man with a thin beard, dressed in clean clothes, wearing a green shawl and a black turban."[123]

Signs of excessive devotion are also evident in a much-quoted reference to his ascetic exercises in Būshihr. Later these mortifications were criticized by his opponents as deviation from the path of true religion. The court chronicler, Sipihr, for instance, states: "When evil temptations and selfish ambition encouraged him, in spite of [the ordinance of] the holy sharīʿa, he yielded to arduous purifications, and tended to reach the high [spiritual] stages. As I have heard, once in Būshihr, where hot winds are as burning as the breath of a furnace, at the peak of the heat, he ascended up to the roofs and stood in the sun bare-headed, reciting his incantations."[124] Another chronicler adds that the purpose of these ascetic exercises was to "dominate the sun."[125] However implausible these reports may appear, they are in line with Mīrzā Aḥmad's reference to the Bab's intention of "mastering the science of planets, particularly the sun."[126] Nabīl Zarandī, too, confirms that each Friday in the oppressive heat of Būshihr, the Bab devoted several hours to continuous worship on the roof of his house, exposed to the fierce rays of the noontide sun.[127] Although "the heedless and ignorant around him thought him to be enamoured with the sun itself," in fact, "from early dawn till sunshine, and from midday till late in the afternoon, he dedicated his time to meditation and pious worship."[128]

In statements laden with sarcasm and interlaced with words chosen solely to rhyme, the Qajar chronicles attack the Bab's asceticism as the symptom of "evil temptations, which finally caused him to exhaust his body so relentlessly that his mind became defective and his brain was disturbed."[129] Hidāyat even suggests that "the effect of the sun's heat totally evaporated the moisture of his brain and led him to sun worship."[130] Yet the Bab's own liturgical instructions in his later works contain striking strains of ancient veneration for the sun as a symbol of God's glory. In *Bayān,* he instructs the believers to recite every Friday, the day of sabbath and purification, a verse in glory of God while standing vigil before the sun "taking it witness" to the uniqueness of God and faith in the point of revelation [i.e., the Bab].[131]

There is ample evidence that preoccupation with asceticism and devotion, which earlier were taken as the positive sign of Bab's holiness and sanctity,

[123]M. H. Ruknzādih Ādamīyat *Dānishmandān va Sukhansarāyān-i Fārs* 4 vols. (Tehran, 1337–1340 Sh./1958–1961) I, 387–88, citing his grandfather's uncle.

[124]*NT* III, 39.

[125]*RS* X, 310.

[126]*Ahmad* 447.

[127]*Nabil* 77–78.

[128]Ibid.

[129]*NT* III, 39.

[130]*RS* X, 310.

[131]*Bayān* VII/14, 263–64. For other remnants of Zoroastrian influences on the teaching and theology of the Bab see below.

were interpreted after his prophetic proclamation as evil. But in fact such ascetic practices further motivated an unorthodox quest for purity not only through austerity but by pursuing esoteric ideas. These tendencies perhaps prompted his contemporary Alexandr Kazem Beg to suggest that "in public he [the Bab] enjoyed the company of the learned and listened to the account of travelers who frequented this commercial town [Shiraz]; he also took pleasure to line up with the followers of *tarikat* [*ṭarīqa:* the Sufi path] who were highly respected among the people."[132]

The Bab's direct association with Sufi orders, or with guidance from a Sufi master, are denied by other sources. The author of *Nuqṭat al-Kāf*, however, himself a merchant with mystical inclinations, does not rule out a self-acquired mysticism in the Bab: "What has been circulated about the Holiness's practice of mortification, or that he benefited from an elder or a spiritual guide is nothing but mere accusation and absolute fabrication, since in appearance that point of perfection under no circumstances was in need of anyone, but nevertheless in reality he was a seeker (*faqīr*) of the Beloved."[133] This remark, originally given in support of the Bab's unlearned knowledge, is reminiscent of the definition of the Uwaysī mystics, who often were the least conformist in their conduct and most outspoken in their claims.

The effect of the environment on the shaping of the Bab's mystical outlook cannot be overlooked. Būshihr was one of the strongholds of Akhbārī ʿulama of Bahrain[134] among whom similar austerity and interest in occult sciences were not unknown. Moreover, long-established contacts between Aḥsāʾī and his successor, Rashtī, with the Akhbārī ʿulama of Bahrain and the Āl ʿUṣfūr family in Būshihr, of whom the Bab speaks with respect, may also have influenced the young Sayyid ʿAlī Muḥammad. Sayyid Jaʿfar Kashfī, a close member of Uṣfūr clan, also attracted the Bab's attention as a model of intuitive accomplishment.[135] None of the existing evidence, however, can lead us to any definitive conclusion.

The Bab remained largely silent on the subject of his past intellectual experiences, yet an interesting passage in *Ṣaḥīfa-yi ʿAdlīyā* suggests that, at least in his later years, he regarded all important currents in contemporary Shiʿism as deviant and misdirected—an attitude not wholly unexpected from a self-trained ascetic:

> Today, disagreements in the Ithnā ʿAsharī camp have reached their height. Some are known as Uṣūlīs who unanimously act according to their own presumption and believe that truth is with them, and some known as Akhbārīs who believe in

[132]*Kazem Beg* VII, 335.
[133]*NK* 109–10. For mystical tendencies of Ḥājjī Mīrzā Jānī, the author of *Nuqṭat al-Kāf*, see below, chap. 8.
[134]See above, chap. 2.
[135]For his details see above, chap. 1.

> the authority of the non-rational illumination, and think the truth is with them, and some consider themselves as followers of the late Shaykh Aḥmad ibn Zayn al-Dīn [Aḥsā'ī], may God sanctify the soil of his grave, and believe that the pure absolute truth is with them, and yet they did not even grasp the surface of his words, and some are known as Sufis who think that the inner truth (bāṭin) is in their hand, and yet they have remained far and isolated from both outward and inward, and instead have adopted the path of darkness and polytheism without ever knowing it. Amongst the followers of the four schools there is no illusion about their extreme differences, to the extent that some even denounce others of infidelity. Besides these four well known schools there are some who consider themselves superior to others such as followers of Mullā Ṣadrā and the like, and each one takes himself as the [embodiment of] pure truth and the rest as absolute falsehood. How appropriately sings the Arab poet, "They all claim that they seek Laylā's union, and at night they are restless in lamentation. But when tears flow from cheeks, then it will be known who weeps and who pretends weeping."[136]

The Bab's disapproval of the differences of opinion among various schools may have surfaced later at the time of greater intellectual maturity. The genesis of his disillusionment, however, may go back earlier, when he sought to express unconventional views in conventional molds. His interest in the Shaykhi schools first appears to have been aroused by Sayyid Jawād Karbalā'ī in Būshihr.[137] This seems to have coincided with the production of some of his earliest writings. Nicolas, the French historian of the Babi movement, refers to a certain *Risāla Fiqhīya* (treatise in jurisprudence) written in Būshihr, in which the Bab showed "real piety and Islamic effusion which seemed to have anticipated a brilliant future in the path of Shiʿite orthodoxy."[138] Apparently it is these early experiences (written toward the end of Būshihr period, around 1257/1841) that worried his uncle Ḥājjī Sayyid Muḥammad, and obliged him to ask Ḥājjī Sayyid Jawād for assistance by advising his nephew "not to write or to speak about certain matters, and not to reveal certain things which might arouse people's jealousy, because they cannot see how a young uneducated merchant would be able to reveal such learned words."[139]

Esoteric ideas and ascetic practices gradually led Sayyid ʿAlī Muḥammad to abandon his business and leave Būshihr for the Holy Cities of Iraq. Such a decision was partly due to his longing to visit the shrine of the Imams to pray and meditate. It was also due to his enthusiasm for attending teaching circles, in particular that of Rashtī, for whom he felt a special affection. His

[136]INBA no. 82, 156–57.
[137]*KD* I, 34; cf. *Kashf al-Ghiṭā'* 56–57 and *Nabil* 79.
[138]*SAMB* 190.
[139]Mīrzā Ḥabībullāh (*Tārīkh* 11–12), citing Sayyid Jawād Karbalā'ī. Presumably, some fragments of these writings were given to Sayyid Jawād before 1260/1841. A few years later, when the first news of the appearance of a new Bab reached Karbalā', these writings led Sayyid Jawād to identify Sayyid ʿAlī Muḥammad (see below, chap. 5).

decision met with the disapproval of his family, but Sayyid ʿAlī Muḥammad, determined in his plans, settled all the commercial accounts and left for the ʿAtabāt sometime in 1256–1257/1840–1841 after more than five years in Būshihr. The Bab's action apparently enraged his elder uncle, who, besides other concerns, worried about his own commercial reputation.[140]

Departure from Būshihr was not the end of Sayyid ʿAlī Muḥammad's commercial career, but it signaled a noticeable change in his life; a victory of religious emotions over material concern and hence the disruption of the balance between moral and material accomplishments so greatly praised among the tujjār.

In the Holy Cities

Although the Bab's abode in the Holy Cities lasted only eleven months[141] of which he spent eight in Karbalā' and three in various other places,[142] even this short stay was enough to draw the attention of observers, most of them students and followers of Rashtī, to the unusual character of the young Sayyid from Shiraz. The same behavior that had given him a halo of innocence in Būshihr appeared even more emphatically here in his ritualism on his frequent visits to the shrine of Imam Ḥusayn.

The Shaykhi Mullā Ṣadiq Khurāsānī, better known as Muqaddas, first saw the Bab in the shrine of Ḥusayn, where the young sayyid's lamentations and humbleness had a great effect on him. He was even more impressed when Sayyid ʿAlī Muḥammad, who at first had refused to reply to his greetings in the courtyard, on his exit from the shrine apologized courteously and explained that the "mosque is the place where attention should not be paid to anybody or any direction except to God."[143] A few years later, in *Ziyārat Nāmih,* the Bab instructs the pilgrims to "enter [the shrine], without uttering a single word, and walk with gravity until thou reachest [a distance of] seven paces below the foot [of the tomb]."[144]

Referring to the circumstances of the Bab's visit, *Nuqṭat al-Kāf* states: "At the time of his holiness' visit to the shrine of his holy ancestors, some strange and wonderful expositions, such as the manner of entering or visiting the

[140]Mīrzā Ḥabībullāh *Tārīkh* 15.

[141]Cited in an ordinance (*tauqīʿ*) written in Chihrīq (1265/1849) cited in *Shaykhīgarī va Bābīgarī,* 305–07. In this letter the Bab gave a brief chronological description of his early life, in which he confirms that after five years in Būshihr, he spent a year in the ʿAtabāt.

[142]*Qatīl* 529; cf. *NK* 110, and other sources believe that he spent only three months in Karbalā'.

[143]*SAMB* 191–92 and M. A. Malik Khusravī *Tārīkh-i Shuhadā-yi Amr* 3 vols. (Tehran, 130 Badīʿ/1972) II, 50, both quoting from the biography of Muqaddas written by his son, Ibn Aṣdaq. For Muqaddas see below, chap. 6. Mīrzā Ḥabībullāh (*Tārīkh* 16–17) relates a similar account about Mullā Ḥusayn Bushrū'ī, but no other source confirms this, although the possibility of a visit between the Bab and Mullā Ḥusayn during this period is not ruled out.

[144]Translation cited in Browne *JRAS* (1889) 900.

shrine, and the state of presence in which he was seen, astonished a great number of people."[145] To this Ḥājjī Rasūl, a Shaykhi merchant from Qazvīn, adds that he never saw any other person "whether from divines, mystics, spiritual guides, nobles, and merchants" who could match "the humility, devotion, or magnificence" in his visits.[146] Even the unsympathetic Mīrzā Muḥammad Tunkābunī, who at the time was a student, noticed the Bab's unusual method of visiting the shrine:

> One day I was sitting with a certain holy and pious man (*muqaddas-i ṣāliḥ*) above the head of his Holiness' holy tomb [Imam Ḥusayn] when we saw this Sayyid [the Bab] enter the Shrine. He stood in the doorway, read his visitation, and left without entering the Shrine. I asked Muqaddas, "Who was this man?" Muqaddas replied, "He was Mīr ʿAlī Muḥammad Shīrāzī, and he is a student of Sayyid Kāẓim." I asked, "Why did he visit the Shrine in this manner?" "Because he considers this as the most respectful way," he answered. I said, "This is wrong, since visiting is one of the devotions and therefore we should follow the way we were told and taught by our Imams, and they commanded us to approach the holy tomb and embrace it. Keeping a distance from the tomb is like failing to perform non-obligatory prayers on the grounds that we are not worthy to stand in the threshold of our Lord."[147]

The Bab's manner of visiting the shrine underscores his Shaykhi leanings. The ritual of visitation was one of the distinctive characteristics of the Shaykhis. In the symbolic worldview of Shaykhism, with its strong emphasis on personal recognition of the Imam, the visiting of shrines was equated with a visit of the Imam himself, with almost the same status as intuition and revelatory dreams. The followers of Aḥsāʾī when visiting shrines performed carefully observed rites to pay their full homage to the Imam.[148] In some of his early writings the Bab went to great lengths to describe the rites of visitation and the esoteric secret of every movement. In *Ṣaḥīfa bayn al-Ḥaramayn,* written at the beginning of 1261/1845, he gives minute in-

[145]*NK* 110.

[146]*Qazvīnī* 464; cf. *ZH* 379 and *Samandar* 17. Other Shaykhis—the Nahrī brothers, two young merchants from Isfahan attending Rashtī's lectures in Karbalāʾ, and Ḥājjī Mīrzā Javāhirī Iṣfahānī, also a merchant (*ZH* 101), and Shaykh Ḥasan Zunūzī *(Nabil* 30)—all related similar impressions.

[147]*QU* 59. Also translated by Browne in *JRAS* (1889) 894–95. The identity of Ṣāliḥ is unknown. However, there is a possibility that he refers to the above-mentioned Mullā Ṣādiq Muqaddas, whom he inaccurately called Ṣāliḥ. Browne translates Muqaddas as "holy and just person."

[148]Hence they spoke of non-Shaykhis, perhaps with a sense of disapproval, as *Bālāsarīs,* or those who approach the head of the Imam's tomb. See *Shaykhīgarī va Bābīgarī* 237; *RJ* 287 and *Fihrist* II, 642, which refers to *Risāla-yi Wādī-al-Salām* by Mīrzā Abul-Qāsim Khān on the manners of visiting the innocent Imams, especially II, 2, on visiting the shrine of Ḥusayn. This attention to the act of visiting and self-humiliation was not confined to the Shaykhis. Āqā Muḥammad Bāqir Bihbahāni visited the shrine of Ḥusayn in a spirit of submission and grief that is not far different from the practice of the Shaykhis or of Sayyid ʿAlī Muḥammad the Bab *(QU* 202).

structions for various acts of ritual ablution, entrance to the shrine, and recitation of the appropriate verses and prayers, while emphasizing the numerical and alphabetical significance of every stage.[149] Here again in his instructions,[150] the Bab adopted Shaykhi rituals and their symbolic interpretation.[151] Nevertheless, the tone of his devotional expressions and the nature of his longing for the Imam reveals a departure from Shaykhism. Indeed, signs of a new approach appear in one of his earlier works, *Ziyārat Nāmih-yi Āl Allāh,* perhaps written during or immediately after his pilgrimage to the ʿAtabāt. E. G. Browne rightly believes this work is of "the utmost interest and importance in tracing the gradual formation of the Bab's ideas," and is so far "the sole record of this early period of his life, before he put forward any claim to divine inspiration."[152] A clear longing for the Advent of the Imam are heard, perhaps for the first time, in its pages: "Where are the days of your empire, that I may struggle for you? and where are the days of your glory, that I may obtain the blessing of [beholding] your visage? and where are the days of your Kingdom, that I may take revenge for you on your enemies? and where are the days of your manifestation, that I may be independent of all except you? and where are the days of the appearance of the signs of your lordship, that by your permission I may say to whatsoever I will 'Be!' and it shall become existent before you? and where are the days which God hath promised unto His servants for your return?"[153]

One might suspect that such bold expressions of yearning for the Imam from a strange young ascetic who believed he was "admitted to the presence of the Lord"[154] had greatest appeal to those watchful Shaykhis who for some time had known persecution and harassment at the hands of the "enemies" of the Imam.

By the invitation of Mullā Ṣādiq Muqaddas, the Bab attended a Friday public gathering where he was introduced to Rashtī and reportedly received his sympathetic attention. At the same gathering, the Bab was said to have been deeply touched when Mullā Ḥusayn Bushrūʾī, his future "First Believ-

[149]Browne Or. MSS no. F.7(9), 101–22.

[150]Ibid. 112.

[151]Among many other Shiʿite writers who produced a vast literature on the esoteric meaning of the acts of worship, Sayyid Kāẓim Rashtī deals with the "secrets" *(asrār)* of various devotional prayers in a few of his works. See *al-Dharīʿa* II, nos. 169, 188, 208 and *Fihrist* II/2, 288–359. Also Arabic *risāla* in reply to four questions by Sayyid Kāẓim (MS no. 382, Wadham Collection, Oxford). Also mentioned in *Fihrist* II/2, 353 (no. 295), n.d., folio 126, copied in 1268/1852. In section two, where he deals with the secrets of prayers and other religious duties, he gives a similar symbolic treatment.

[152]Browne *JRAS* (1899) II, 881–1088 (on *Zīyārat Nāmih* pp. 896–902). In spite of a lengthy discussion on the identity of this work, Browne confuses it with *Saḥīfa bayn al-Ḥaramayn* and yet another *Zīyārat Nāmih* written in 1260/1844 for the shrine of ʿAlī and given to Mullā ʿAlī Basṭāmī (see below chap. 5).

[153]Browne Or. MSS no. F.22(5), trans. Browne *JRAS* (1899) II, 901. See also H. Roemer *Die Bābī-Behāʾī* (Potsdam, 1912) 1–11.

[154]*Ṣaḥīfa* 113.

er" recited some of the poetry of Shaykh Aḥmad Aḥsā'ī.[155] The gathering was probably the Dīwān al-Rashtī, a literary circle set up by Rashtī for ritual mourning for the Imams as well as poetical, literary, and theological exchange, which met in his library.[156] A spirit of patronage was augmented by Rashtī's desire to broaden his sphere of intellectual and political influence. Mostly at the expense of his rivals, it provided for substantial support not only from Persian religious students, but from a large and heterogeneous body of merchants, ʿulama, and literary and poetical figures.

In light of Rashtī's general enthusiasm for attracting new followers and supporters, it is not surprising that Sayyid ʿAlī Muḥammad, who came from a merchant family with Shaykhi connections, received attention in the circle. But it is hard to know to what extent this was a deliberate attempt by the Shaykhi leader to single out the Bab as exceptional. The account of Shaykh Ḥasan Zunūzī, an intimate disciple of Rashtī and a later follower of the Bab,[157] seems to have been affected by hindsight, if not his zeal. He accompanied his teacher to the abode of the Bab to pay back a visit by "a highly esteemed and distinguished person," and was bewildered by Rashtī's humble behavior before the young Shīrāzī merchant: "I could not explain the motive which could have induced the Sayyid [Rashtī] to manifest such profound reverence in the presence of that youth—a reverence which even the sight of the shrine of the Sayyidu'sh-Shuhadā' [i.e., Husayn] had failed to excite."[158] Other sources shed very little light on Rashtī's attitude toward the Bab. In one rare reference in the *Bayān*[159] to his personal acquaintance with Rashtī during "the days of the ʿAtabāt," the Bab does not imply any particular affiliation to the Shaykhi leader, at least in the sense of being his disciple, though he venerates him as "the tree of purity." This same reference to an interview with Rashtī—perhaps the same visit described by Zunūzī—is also indicative of the degree of hostility Rashtī experienced from Bālāsarī opponents in Karbalā'. Upon Rashtī's departure the unnamed owner of the guest house where the Bab was staying ritually purified the threshold where Rashtī had touched it.

Much has been said about the Bab's pupilage in the ʿAtabāt. Muslim sources, with the objective of discrediting the Bab's claim of unlearned knowledge, insist that he was a student of Rashtī. Sipihr, for example, maintains that "he attended the teaching circle of Sayyid Kāẓim Rashtī . . . and benefited from his words, and followed the path of Shaykh Aḥmad."[160]

[155]*SAMB*, 192–94 quotes Ibn Aṣdaq cf. Mīrzā Ḥabībullāh *Tārīkh* 17–19.

[156]Salmān H. al-Ṭuʿma *Turāth Karbalā'* (Najaf, 1964) 224–29, 238–39. Dīwān Āl-Rashtī survived a century after the death of its founder, up to 1360/1941, when Rashtī's grandson, Sayyid Qāsim Rashtī, died in Karbalā'. The library, which at one time housed more than ten thousand books, after suffering chronic waves of looting and arson was finally dispersed.

[157]Possibly the same Mīrzā Ḥasan Zunūzī mentioned in *TMS* I, 36.

[158]*Nabil* 25–27.

[159]V/4, 176–77.

[160]*NT* III, 39. Chronicler Hidāyat even suggests that the Bab "was encircled in the teaching circles of the ʿulama of the time, especially that of Sayyid Kāẓim Rashtī" (*RS* X, 310).

Tunkābunī, who claims to have attended Rashtī's lectures, writes: "Mīr ʿAlī Muḥammad also used to come to his lectures, and had with him pen and ink-stand, and whatever Sayyid Kāẓim said, of moist and dry, he used to write down in the same lecture."[161] Ḥājjī Muḥammad Karīm Khān Kirmānī, however, as early as 1845 in *Izhāq al-Bāṭil* (which is representative of the later Shaykhi attitude), points out "For a while he remained in the service of Sayyid [Rashtī], but due to the immense glory and loftiness of our center of faith and the protector of the splendid sharīʿa, he was not then able to reveal what he had in his heart."[162] He adds: "As it is reported, he possessed [qualities] of peacefulness, gravity, and dignity, but in his heart he possessed presumption and arrogance."[163]

Pro-Babi sources, on the other hand, insist that Sayyid ʿAlī Muḥammad's attendance in the circle of Karbalāʾ was short and infrequent. *Nuqṭat al-Kāf* in particular takes care to state that "what has been said about the presence of his holiness in the lectures of the late Sayyid is not correct, but his holiness every now and then attended the preachings of the late Sayyid."[164] It was at one of these gatherings that Zunūzī again noticed the presence of the Shīrāzī youth. As soon as Rashtī's eye fell upon the Bab, recalls Zunūzī, he discontinued his address: "Whereupon one of his disciples begged him to resume the argument which he had left unfinished. 'What more shall I say?' replied Sayyid Kāẓim, as he turned his face towards the Bab. 'Lo, the Truth is more manifest than the ray of light that has fallen upon that lap.' "[165] To what extent Zunūzī's account can be taken as a sign of Rashtī's approval of the Bab, or to what degree the master "benefited from the inner light"[166] of the youth, can be measured by the devotion of those Babi narrators who sought at least some convincing evidence for establishing a background for the Bab's later claims.

The real answer may lie with the better-informed Qatīl Karbalāʾī, one of the earliest Babi writers and himself a student under Rashtī for ten years. When in reply to Kirmānī's attacks he described his recollections of the Bab's abode in Karbalāʾ, he was more anxious to prove the Bab's unlearned knowledge and his command in various sciences than to underscore any sign of approval by Rashtī. He says: "It might possibly occur to some people that he [the Bab] might have received [his knowledge] from Sayyid the Primal Divine Gate [*Bābullāh al-Muqaddam,* i.e., Rashtī] and learned all these sciences from him. To them I say that the great remembrance [*al-dhikr al-akbar,* i.e., the Bab] God bless him and may my soul be a sacrifice for him . . . during his residence in Karbalāʾ attended his lectures only twice or three

[161]*QU* 59 translated in Browne *JRAS* (1889) 894.
[162]P. 104.
[163]Ibid. 105–6.
[164]*NK* 110.
[165]*Nabil* 27–28.
[166]*NK* 110.

times; once at the beginning, once in the middle, and once towards the end of his stay, and during this period I did not hear al-Sayyid al-Bāb [i.e., Rashtī] speak of any of the above-mentioned sciences."[167] What Qatīl implies is borne out by Mīrzā Aḥmad, who believes that once or twice the Bab heard "Traditions expounded by Sayyid Kāẓim Rashtī" while he was still studying "elementary subjects" with some members of the Shaykhi circle, which in due course led him to become "an adherent of the Shaykhi cause."[168] Mullā Ṣādiq Muqaddas himself confirms that once in Karbalā' he was asked to teach Sayyid ʿAlī Muḥammad, and that he was also determined to convert him to Shaykhism.[169]

An answer to the question whether the Bab studied under Rashtī is important, not only because it helps to clarify the Bab's familiarity with madrasa curriculum, but also to define the extent of his affiliation with the Shaykhi school. In any event he did not stay long enough in Karbalā' to fully grasp the essence of Rashtīs teachings; and if he attended only three of his lectures, as seems almost certain, his debt to Aḥsā'ī or to Rashtī is limited at most. His own writings indicate that he had at least enough knowledge of Shaykhi ideas to justify his later claims, or even argue Aḥsā'ī's or Rashtī's points. His small collection of books may have included a few well-known Shaykhi texts, such as Aḥsā'ī's *Sharḥ al-Ziyāra* and Rashtī's *Sharḥ al-Qaṣīda*.[170] It is doubtless with acknowledgment of benefit from their writings, and of the fact that they were his spiritual predecessors, that he refers to Rashtī as "the revered scholar and my intimate teacher."[171] The statement should be taken as a symbolic acknowledgment of their spiritual affinity and not as literal fact.

Self-Education

The debate surrounding the Bab's education and his own assertions about his intuitive abilities lead to a broader question concerning his level of acquaintance with the general knowledge of his time. The internal evidence in this writings answers the question only partially. The six years of captivity and isolation after his proclamation (1260–1266/1844–1850), spent in writing and meditation, occasionally provided time for study, but the greater part of his knowledge about conventional fields must have been acquired earlier. He seems to have had a fairly intimate knowledge of his Qur'ān, which remained his main source of inspiration, guide for literary

[167] *Qatīl* 529. This seems also to conform with Mullā Jaʿfar Qazvīnī (*Qazvīnī* 465), who states that he himself visited the Bab three times in Rashtī's lectures.

[168] *Ahmad* 447.

[169] *SAMB* 194–95.

[170] A. Afnān *Notes*.

[171] Commentary on *Sūrat al-Baqara;* cf. *Shaykhīgarī va Bābīgarī* 319.

style, and reference. It is the Qur'ān that provides him with parables as well as examples for comparison with his own prophetic mission. All through his works he frequently quotes Qur'ānic verses.

His commentaries on various *sūras* (chapters) of the Qur'ān, however, have little apparent connection to the text and are often employed to accentuate mystico-cabalistic views; sometimes as a means of expounding his mission, sometimes to relate personal sufferings, frequently as liturgies.[172] The apparent absence of references in his works to classical Qur'ānic commentaries is not surprising in light of the lack of enthusiasm for *tafsīr* (exegesis) in Shiʿite orthodox circles. Among the Bab's contemporaries, only the Sufis, and particularly the Niʿmatullāhīs, were compiling tafsīrs in classical Sufi tradition, though perhaps with a heavier Shiʿite veneer.[173] The Bab's notion of tafsīr is influenced far less by this Sufi tradition and more, one can assume, by the commentaries of heterodox writers of the past. In the study of *kalām* (theology) and ḥikma, he remotely follows Aḥsā'ī. The Bab's implicit criticism of the Sufi and Ṣadrā'ī theosophists seem to reflect Aḥsā'ī's thought, but he is not particularly hostile toward either group. Indeed the entire terminology of his theosophical discourse in the *Bayān* and other works is a constant reminder of the literature of both schools though his reasoning and approach are distinct from any philosopher, whether Shaykhi, Ṣadrā'ī, or Peripatetic.

There is enough evidence that even in the early stages, prior to his proclamation, the Bab had access to recent translations of the New Testament, though probably not the Old Testament.[174] Constant references in the *Bayān*, and in his earlier works to Jesus and to the "letters of the Gospel" (i.e., Christians) and their faith, leave little doubt as to his direct knowledge of the Gospel.[175]

To assess the Bab's degree of acquaintance with other conventional Shiʿite subjects is more difficult. References to Shiʿite ḥadīth appear repeatedly in

172The most significant of his commentaries on the Qur'ān includes seven independent exegeses on sūras: I (*al-Fātiḥa*); II (*al-Baqara*); XII (*Yūsuf*) entitled *Qayyūm al-Asmā'*; XXIV (*al-Nūr*); XCVII (*al-Qadr*); CIII (*al-ʿAṣr*) and CVIII (*al-Kawthar)*. In addition, he wrote a large number of commentaries on specific verses with eschatological or messianic connotations. See note on sources and bibliography.

173Among them Nūr ʿAlī Shāh's poetical work *Tafsīr-i Sūra-yi Baqara;* Muẓaffar ʿAlī Shāh's *Tafsīr al-Sabʿ al-Mathānī* and Mullā Riżā Hamadānī Kauṡar ʿAlī Shāh's *Durar al-Naẓīm* (*al-Dharīʿa* VIII, 83).

174First modern Persian translation of the New Testament by Rev. Henry Martyn, *Kitāb-i Paymān-i Jadīd-i Khudādvand va Rahānandih-yi Mā ʿIsā Masīḥ,* was published in St. Petersburg in 1815. Successive editions of the same translation were published in Calcutta (1816) and London (1827 and 1837) and distributed in Iran by Protestant missionaries. A translation of Psalms by Martyn, *Zabūr-i Dāvūd,* was also published in Calcutta (1816), but the modern Persian translation of the entire Old Testament by Thomas Robinson, *Kitāb-i Muqaddas wa huwa Kitāb-i ʿAhd al-ʿAtīq* (London, 1839), was not as widely circulated. Earlier translations of parts of both Old and New Testaments did exist in manuscript but were rarely accessible to the ordinary Muslim reader.

175See below, chap. 4, for some traces of the New Testament in the Bab's early ideas. Also *Dalā'il-i Sabʿa* 52–53 for references to the Gospel.

his works, almost always in the context of Mahdistic prophecies and circumstances of Ẓuhūr. The main sources of his knowledge seem to be the works of Aḥsāʾī, Rashtī, and possibly Mīrzā Muḥammad Akhbārī, for whom he shows some respect, and he must also have read selections on Occultation and related subjects compiled by Muḥammad Bāqir Majlisī, Jaʿfar Ṭusī, and other classical Shiʿite writers.[176] On the treatment of the ḥadīth, he does not seem to prefer the general Akhbārī approach over the Uṣūlī, but his method of *taʾwīl* (hermeneutics) is usually an elaboration of Shaykhi intuitive approach. He occasionally shows a surprising knowledge of details of fiqh, either by the way of criticism of the ʿulama or, later, by outlining his own Bayānī doctrine. He repeatedly condemns the excessive study of jurisprudence, both the theoretical uṣūl al-fiqh and the practical aspects *(furūʿ)*. In the *Bayān,* he clearly sums up his misgivings about all current scholastic pursuits: "It is prohibited to compose what is worthless and futile such as uṣūl [al-fiqh], logic, rules of fiqh and ḥikma and the science of obscure words and such like. As for what comes under grammar and syntax, it is only sufficient for learners to understand the subject and the object and other similar matters and beyond this God shall not forgive those who engage themselves in it."[177]

Of the other, less-specialized and peripheral fields, the Bab shows special attachment to the semihistorical narratives on the life of the Prophet and the Imams, particularly Muḥammad, ʿAlī, Ḥusayn, and occasionally Jaʿfar Ṣādiq, but seldom others. His predictable reverence for Muḥammad appears to be based on the books of *sīra* (biographies of the Prophet), as rendered by Shiʿite sources, and for Ḥusayn the books of *maṣāʾib* (sufferings) of the Imams. In several instances, the Bab expresses his deep emotions upon hearing *rawża*, the mournful recital of the tragedies of Karbalāʾ. Reportedly, the recitation of passages from the widely circulated *Muḥriq al-Qulūb*, by Mullā Mahdī Narāqī (d. 1209/1794),[178] provoked "intense emotion in the heart of the Bab."[179] By contrast, he makes very few references to nonreligious figures or events of the past, and those he does make are always in religious context. This is to be expected from a man so deeply immersed in the intensity of his own religious experience. Looking to Muḥammad as a model for initiation of a prophetic cycle, ʿAlī as the emanating source of divine authority, Ḥusayn as the symbol of suffering and sacrifice, and Jaʿfar Ṣādiq as the locus of celestial wisdom, the visionary pantheon of the Bab denied sanctity to secular idols.

Modern Western scientific scholarship remains largely unnoticed by the

[176]See for instance a citation from *Biḥār al-Anwār* in *Dalāʾil-i al-Sabʿa* 51. A collection of commentaries on hadith (INBA, Lib. 3032–C), possibly compiled by the Bab, cites Traditions on Occultation and circumstances of Ẓuhūr from books of *Ghayba* by Ṭūsī, Naʿmānī, and others.

[177]*Bayān* IV/10 130.

[178]*Al-Dharīʿa* XX, 149.

[179]*Nabīl* 252.

Bab. He alludes to astronomy, roads, postal communication, printing, and steamers, advances that he must have seen or heard of in his own surroundings. Commercial dealings with India may have provided him with fragmentary specimens of European geographical and historical works in Persian rendering. Any further dispersion of the exact sciences or works of European literature and philosophy through India, however, is highly unlikely, as the British inhibited their publication in their colonies. The Bab's awareness of European material superiority, however, is duly reflected in a religious context. Traces of "the people of the Gospel" are everywhere and the dilemma of their salvation is prevalent.[180]

With all his disenchantment with grammar and syntax, language remains a major source of inspiration for the Bab. He seems to have had no handicap in reading classical Arabic. He takes pride in writing in Arabic the rhythmic style of the Qur'ān and occasionally quotes passages of poetry and prose as well as Qur'ānic verses and Arabic hadith. Besides the Qur'ān, his vocabulary and terminology are heavily influenced by the Shiʿite books of liturgies. His style is not free from grammatical peculiarities (if not errors), however, as he himself admits. At times, he seems to deliberately ignore grammatical rules of gender, tenses, and pronouns.

His style in Persian suffers, even more seriously, from solecism, imprecision, and neology. Yet compared to the average literary style of his time, the Bab displays great skill in dramatic expression of his emotions. In this context language is only a vehicle for the delivery of concepts irrespective of form and style. At another level, however, it is the tongue: letters, words, and verses that dominate the thought; perhaps reminiscent of the Sufis' *shaṭḥīyāt* (theophanic locutions). The frequent eruption of this inspirational spontaneity, sometimes to the extent of incomprehensibility, turns the Bab's writing into a "stream of consciounsess" and himself into a prolific, almost compulsive, writer. The significance of such preoccupation with "revealing verses" cannot be exaggerated. Perhaps nowhere is the spirit of change and desire for independence more transparent than in the verses and the manner in which they were uttered; what he considered his miracle.[181]

Equally intriguing for the Bab is the mysterious world of letters, numbers, diagrams, and tables. Codified chronograms, cabalistic interpretations, talismanic figures, astrological tables, and numerological calculations are abundant in his writings, which in this respect bear a striking resemblance to the Bāṭinī heritage. The Ismāʿīlī and later Ahl-i Ḥaqq doctrine of prophetic cycles, the Ḥurūfī and Nuqṭavī cabalistic symbolism, even the remnants of Zoroastrian and other pre-Islamic ideas and practices, from veneration of the sun to the purification rites of the Mandaeans to the adaption of ancient

[180]See for instance *Bayān* III/15, 99; V/7, 162; VI/1, 186–87; VI/5, 198; VI/9, 214; VI/13, 225, 227.

[181]See below, chaps. 4 and 9.

Iranian calendar, all find a perplexing resonance in the esoteric domain of Sayyid ʿAlī Muḥammad the Bab.

A portion of these themes was no doubt transmitted through Shaykhi channels. But in all probability, the Bab must have also studied independent works on the occult sciences. Some of the instructions in the *Bayān* concerning the configuration of talismans suggest a belief in thaumaturgical properties of divine names, which are always qualified with allusions to their symbolic meanings. Through these works, and those of Aḥsāʾī and Rashtī, the Bab seems to have become sufficiently acquainted with numerology (*jafr al-jāmiʿa* and *ḥisāb al-jummal*). In the past, these branches of the occult sciences always denoted an implicit messianic theme, as they were meant to divulge to the adept, by means of complex calculations, the secrets of an apocalyptic future. They contained "the knowledge of what was and what is to come until the Day of Resurrection,"[182] though "only the Mahdi, expected at the end of the Time, could be capable of understanding its true significance."[183] The messianic connotations are obvious, but what made the study of jafr even more intriguing was an ecumenical concept of prophethood beyond the boundaries of Islamic revelation. The foundation of the jafr "pneumatic" interpretations, as they appear in books of numerology, rested upon a saying attributed to Jesus: "We the Prophets bring ye the revelation; its interpretation the Paraclete [*Fāriqlīṭ:* a Johannine epithet of the Holy Spirit], who shall come after me, will bring ye."[184] This prophetic interpretation was thought to clarify not only the ambiguities of the Qurʾān, but those of the Psalms, the Torah (especially the Book of Daniel), the Gospels, and the Book of Abraham.[185]

Quite possibly, the Bab had some access to lesser-known works of past occult writers. By the mid-nineteenth century, enough heterodox texts were still available, ranging from Ḥurūfī-Nuqṭavī to Ahl-i Ḥaqq and even Mushaʿshaʿī-Ṣābiʾī, to permit the transmission of various ancient themes to the young merchant of Shiraz. In addition, the works of many jafr experts, including Abul-ʿAbbās Aḥmad al-Būnī's (d. 622/1225) *Shams al-Maʿārif,*[186] were still popular in esoteric circles;[187] not to mention the impact of Shaykh Aḥmad Aḥsāʾī, who himself was influenced by writers such as Ibn Abī Jamhūr Aḥsāʾī, a crypto-Ismāʿīlī in Ithnā ʿAsharī disguise. The Bab could not have remained wholly unaware of the Sufi ideas and speculations of his own time. Some acquaintance with Ẕahabīs, the most influential order in Shiraz, is documented, and contact with other orders is not unlikely.[188]

182 *Al-Dharīʿa* V, 118 (n.) citing Bahāʾ al-Dīn ʿĀmilī's *Sharḥ al-Arbaʿīn.*

183 *EI*²: DJAFR (T. Fahd) citing Kātib Čelebi's (Ḥājjī Khalīfa) *Kashf al-Ẓunūn* II, 603.

184 Ibid.; cf. John XIV, 26.

185 *Al-Dharīʿa* V, 119 (n.) quoting a hadith by Ṣādiq cited in Kulaynī's *al-Kāfī.*

186 (Cairo, 1322–1324/1903–1906); cf. *al-Dharīʿa* XIV, 226–27.

187 See *al-Dharīʿa* under *Jafr* (V, 118–22) for some entries.

188 The details of later contact with the head of the Ẕahabī order, Mīrzā Sayyid Abul-Qāsim Rāz Shīrāzī (known as Mīrzā Bābā) (see *TH* III, 456), is recorded in a risāla by his son, Jalāl al-

Direct acknowledgment of the above strains appears in the Bab's writings. One can assume that in a gradual move toward a prophetic claim, the Bab must have absorbed and internalized some portions of this diffused esoteric body of knowledge. What a modern observer might describe as an effort to reconstruct and synthesize the knowledge learned by personal inquiry and unsystematic exposure to a complex intellectual milieu the Bab himself called "unlearned knowledge." The weaknesses of presentation and the handicaps of a still maturing mind are often detectable. But taking into account the brief time span in which he had the random opportunity to study, memorize, and contemplate, his accomplishments are impressive. Though he remained on the periphery of the learned world and was never fully assimilated into any scholastic or nonorthodox trend of thought, his inquisitive mind, his talent for hermeneutical interpretation, and the stamp of ascetic individualism so aptly printed into his personality made him an ideal "locus for inspiration."

Intuitive Experiences

One year in the ʿAatabāt was sufficient to acquaint Sayyid ʿAlī Muḥammad with the Shaykhis, but hardly to imbue in him a deep sense of affiliation to the Shaykhi school. The anxieties of his family, aggravated by his sudden departure from Būshihr, soon put an end to his spiritual quest in the holy land. His uncle Sayyid ʿAlī journeyed to Karbalā' especially to encourage his unwilling nephew to return. It appears that some of the students of Rashtī contributed to the Bab's reluctance. Muqaddas made some effort to convince Sayyid ʿAlī to allow his nephew to stay for further studies. But Sayyid ʿAlī, while admitting that Sayyid ʿAlī Muḥammad possessed remarkable moral qualities, pointed out that his nephew was interested neither in the family business nor in serious religious studies. Therefore, he was determined to remove the youth from the ʿAtabāt.[189]

It is said that the Bab's resistance finally obliged Sayyid ʿAlī to seek the advice of Rashtī. The Shaykhi leader at first declined to give any personal opinion, leaving the decision in the hands of the Bab himself; but upon Sayyid ʿAlī's insistence he reluctantly gave his consent for the Bab to leave Karbalā' and return to Shiraz.[190]

The Bab's return to Shiraz, in the beginning of 1258/1842, was soon followed by his marriage, at the age of twenty-three,[191] probably arranged

Dīn Muḥammad Majd al-Ashrāf, entitled *Mir'āt al-Mulk* and cited in S. Parvīzī's *Risāla-yi Nūrīya* (Tabriz, 1347 Sh./1968) 18–27. The Bab's *Risāla al-Zahabīyīn* in reply to Mīrzā Bābā appears in INBA, no. 80, III, pp. 70–98. For further details see below.

[189] Quoting Muqaddas himself.

[190] Mīrzā Ḥabībullāh *Tārīkh* 19–20.

[191] *Khāndān-i Afnān* 160–62. (Notes recorded by Munīra Khānum.)

to dissuade him from returning to the ʿAtabāt.[192] He settled with his wife, Khadīja Khānum, and mother in his own house and resumed his trade, this time with greater independence.[193]

During the next two years, in spite of the frequent recurrence of riots and civil disturbances in Shiraz,[194] Sayyid ʿAlī Muḥammad seems to have enjoyed a tranquil and relatively prosperous life. Some years later, during his imprisonment in Mākū (1847) he recalled those "happy days" with some nostalgia.[195] The new circumstances discouraged him from returning to Iraq, but his business life allowed him enough time to meditate and to concentrate on his newly discovered passion for writing verses. He gradually "eased off his commercial dealings and his business transactions."[196] Every morning, before dawn, he would spend some time in prayers and meditation before leaving for his office. Upon his return, an hour after sunset, he performed his evening prayers, and after supper "as it was customary among merchants, he asked for his account books."[197] But as his wife recollected, "I noticed that those [notes] did not resemble commercial accounts. Whenever I asked him what those papers were, he smilingly replied, 'This is the people's account book,' and if someone unexpectedly called upon him, he would cover the papers with a cloth."[198] Most probably the Bab's allusion was to the Day of Reading Accounts, when according to the Qurʾān every man will receive a book in which his actions are inscribed, and God "is prompt in demanding an account."[199] Very little is known about the Bab's writing of this period, but such references suggest that prior to his proclamation, he was preoccupied with redemptive and even messianic themes.[200] He once gave a cousin, Muḥammad Taqī Vakīl al-Ḥaqq, a piece that "resembled the prayers of *al-Ṣaḥīfa al-Sajjādīya*."[201]

At the time, however, it was his austerity that won him local recognition in the character of an evocative mystic. "As the fame of his devotion and piety grew," Sayyid ʿAlī Muḥammad "became known as *Sayyid-i Ẕikr*."[202] If Kazem Beg's reference can be relied on, even during his stay in K̄arbalāʾ, owing to his "singularity" and his "austerity" he acquired the epithet

[192]Mīrzā Ḥabībullāh *Tārīkh* 20–21.

[193]Ibid. and *Ahmad* 448 (n.).

[194]See above, introduction.

[195]*Bayān* VI/11, 218.

[196]*NK* 10.

[197]Mīrzā Ḥabībullāh *Tārīkh* 22–23 citing an account by Khadīja.

[198]Related by Khadīja to Munīra Khānum and cited in *Khāndān-i Afnān* 163.

[199]Qurʾāna II, 200. For full details see *EI*[2]: ḤISĀB and cited sources. For a Shiʿite point of view see *Biḥār al-Anwār* III/45, 264 and M. B. Majlisī *Ḥaqq al-Yaqīn* (Tehran, 1374/1954) V, VI.

[200]For the commentary on *Sūrat al-Baqara*, written on the eve of his proclamation, see below, chap. 4.

[201]Notes cited in *Khāndān-i Afnān* 111. *Al-Ṣaḥīfat al-Sajjādīya* is a collection of fifty-four prayers that is said to be written by ʿAlī b. Ḥusayn Zayn al-ʿĀbidīn (Sajjād), the Fourth Imam.

[202]*KD* I, 34. The epithet may roughly be rendered as "the praying Sayyid" or "Sayyid of evocations," which may suggest a magical mediatory connotation.

majzub (ecstatic).[203] Even before [the Bab's] departure from the holy land [the ʿAtabāt], where devotion attracts Muslims from all over Iran, everybody talked about him as an extraordinary young man. People thought of him as possessing a mystical consciousness. When it came to his peculiarity and his incomprehensible utterances, they attributed them to his profound wisdom. It was especially through the Shīrāzī pilgrims, the ordinary people who returned from Karbalāʾ, that his fame spread in his homeland."[204] The chief reason for his growing reputation, Kazem Beg adds, was that "on the threshold [of the shrine] of Ḥusayn, he acquired the name of the God elect." His name was on everyone's lips. "He is no longer like us sinners," said Shīrāzīs to each other. "He has become famous . . . and can perform miracles." Kazem Beg even believes that the family of the Bab were congratulated for such an auspicious development.[205]

Kazem Beg does not reveal his source, but regardless of his euphemistic language and sometimes inaccurate details it is hard to imagine that his account has no basis in fact. Other sources also hint that even before 1844 Sayyid ʿAlī Muḥammad must have aroused more excitement than is usually suggested. It is not difficult to believe that while in Karbalāʾ the Bab was singled out by Shaykhi admirers, and perhaps by Rashtī himself, as one blessed with the Imam's grace. The magical connotations of the assumed gracefulness caused some people in Shiraz to look upon him almost as a living saint. He might have been known for his intuitions or his austerity, but he was still only a young merchant with exemplary ethics. Mīrzā Aḥmad remarks: "He still retained his popularity by reason of his piety and honesty. No one suspected in him any ulterior or evil motives."[206] The Bab himself referred to these blessed virtues by drawing a comparison between his own mission and that of the Prophet: "Prior to the descent of the divine command, [people] testified to the godliness, nobility, and excellence of the Prophet of God. But see what they said about him, after the revelation of *Furqān* [i.e., the Qurʾān]. Even the pen is ashamed of mentioning it. In the same manner look at the Point of Bayān; prior to his revelation his merits were obvious to all those who knew him."[207]

Throughout 1258–1260/1842–1844, Sayyid ʿAlī Muḥammad came

[203]*Kazem Beg* VII, 339. The term *mazūb* is usually conferred on an unorthodox mystic who, according to ʿAbd al-Razzāq Kāshānī, "is designated by God, and purified by the water of sanctity, and thus without suffering or striving or hardship could reach the highest spiritual positions" (*Iṣṭilāḥāt-i Ṣūfīya* in the margin of *Manāzil al-Sāʾirīn* [Tehran, 1315 Sh./1936] 122). Shams al-Dīn Muḥammad Lāhījī defines *majzūb-i muṭlaq* as the one who, after the stage of annihilation, "totally shuns reason and remains in the state of intoxication and unconsciousness . . . and there is no obligation for them since obligation applies to reason and they are divine insanes. And one cannot deny these people nor follow them" (*Mafātīḥ al-Iʿjāz fī Sharḥ-i Gulshan-i Rāz* [Tehran, 1337 Sh./1958] 285).

[204]*Kazem Beg* VII, 339.

[205]Ibid.

[206]*Ahmad* 447.

[207]*Bayān* VI/11, 218.

closer to spontaneous intuition. If this was partly the outcome of the Shaykhi ontological approach to attain presential knowledge, it was also the result of his own preoccupation with inspirations that he thought were leading him toward an inescapable destiny. The example of the martyrdom of Ḥusayn, the esoteric tradition elaborated by Aḥsā'ī and Rashtī, and his interest in secrets of occult sciences increasingly drew his attention to eschatological themes.[208] He was beginning to believe that he must have been chosen for a divine mission, one that would bring him into direct contact not only with the Hidden Imam, as was common in the visions of mystics or prophesiers, but with a divine source as yet undivulged.

The nature of this mission and his own spiritual status remained unclear to him for some time. But earliest indications came shortly before 1260/1844, when he revealed his sincere inner beliefs to his family. According to one source, prior to that year he asserted that he was chosen to accomplish God's ordinance, hence implying that he was a deputy of the Imam, or even the Lord of the Command (*Ṣāḥib al-Amr*) himself. To substantiate his sincerity to his uncle Sayyid ʿAlī and his mother, the Bab relied on his own religious devotion and personal integrity, stressing that he only reflected what had been revealed to him.[209] His wife, Khadīja, who with great astonishment and perhaps even fear witnessed a strange development in her husband's character, relates that for the members of the family "who saw him being preoccupied most of the time with prayers and worship, it was only clear that his holiness was a superior person."[210] Other members of his family, however, "greatly horrified and distressed by such words, sharply blamed him and strongly advised him to repent from his blasphemy and return to God and never again utter any such words."[211] But in spite of strong protests, the Bab was able to win over his uncle Sayyid ʿAlī. Convincing him of the righteousness of his mission, the Bab cautioned that his claim must remain a secret, since "the will of God has not yet rested upon disclosure and publication."[212]

Reports of his uncle's recognition of the Bab, as an example of lay believers, would seem rather unconvincing, even simplistic, if two facts were not taken into account. First, at the time, the position the Bab claimed had broad and rather vague implications, and could still be fitted within the acceptable framework of popular sainthood, taking into account the Bab's character and background. As already noted, Shaykhi ideas as well as other manifestations of messianism advocated a sense of expectation for Ẓuhūr

[208]For the background on the eschatological and teleological aspects of the Shaykhis and other trends of the time, see above, chap. 1. Mīrzā Ḥabībullāh makes a few passing references to the Bab's interest in numerology, talismans, and other popular cults.

[209]*Muʿ* 79, citing from the yet-untraced narrative of Mullā Muḥammad Taqī Hashtrūdī.

[210]*Khāndān-i Afnān* 163.

[211]*Muʿīn* 77–79, citing the same narrative.

[212]Ibid.

without any direct or distinct indication of the exact nature, identity, or position of the Promised One. Second, Sayyid ʿAlī himself had been influenced by these expectations. His Shaykhi contacts made him especially vigilant. Muḥammad Taqī Vakīl al-Ḥaqq makes it clear that Sayyid ʿAlī "four years prior to the year sixty [1260 Q.] abandoned his trade and withdrew from the public, and was expectant [of Ẓuhūr]. At the time of the Ẓuhūr, when the cause [of the Bab] was declared, he immediately recognized it."[213] The seclusion, abandonment of material pursuits, and vigilant expectations provide some clues to the state of mind of many people like Ḥājjī Mīrzā Sayyid ʿAlī. On one occasion, when his younger brother, Ḥasan ʿAlī, disputed the righteousness of the Bab while complaining of the ill effects of his claims on the family, Sayyid ʿAlī replied that all the signs of piety and uniqueness that he had witnessed in the past in his nephew "convinced him beyond any doubt" of the rectitude of the new cause.[214]

Prior to the Bab's proclamation, and in the early days of the movement, Sayyid ʿAlī was no doubt a source of encouragement for his nephew. "It was he who surrounded him, while under his care, with unfailing solicitude, who served him with such devotion, and who acted as intermediary between him and the host of his followers who flocked to Shiraz to see him."[215] This intermediary role gave him an outstanding position in the early diffusion of the movement.[216]

Evidence scattered in the sources suggests that the news of the Bab's claim did not remain unnoticed in circles close to him and his relatives. In 1259/1843, writing from Būshihr, the Bab instructs Sayyid ʿAlī to inform an anonymous group of religious seminarians (ṭullāb) that "the cause [of God] is still not ripened, and the time has not matured. Therefore, if anyone attributes anything to me but submission to Islamic laws and beliefs, I and my holy ancestors will be discontented with him both in this world and in the next."[217]

[213]Notes cited in *Khāndān-i Afnān* 110. What Muḥammad Taqī states about Sayyid ʿAlī's abandonment of his trade has probably not been remembered accurately because of the amount of time that elapsed before he recorded his memoirs. (He was writing in 1905, at the age of seventy-nine. He himself remarks: "No memory has remained and it is impossible to be accurate.") It appears that up to 1261/1845 Sayyid ʿAlī did not completely abandon his trade. In his letters to his brother Ḥājjī Sayyid Muḥammad there are references to commercial transactions. It is possible that he gradually withdrew from trade about 1260/1844.

[214]Mīrzā Ḥabībullāh (*Tārikh* 7–9), quoting an account by Zahrā Baygum.

[215]*Nabil* 446.

[216]The scene recorded by Mīrzā Aḥmad clearly depicts Sayyid ʿAlī's attitude toward the Bab. When after the Bab's return from Ḥijāz, Mīrzā Aḥmad inquired about him from his uncle, saying, "In what condition is Ḥājjī Mīrzā ʿAlī Muḥammad?" Sayyid ʿAlī "blamed me for mentioning his name and ordered me to be respectful; whereupon I inquired jokingly whether he [the Bab] had attained to the position of a saint or prophet. He said, "He is more exalted than thou wottest of." I asked whether I could meet him. He said, "You can if he permits, otherwise no" *(Ahmad,* 451–52).

[217]*KD* I, 35–36. Unfortunately the author failed to produce the full text of the letter, which could have other important references.

The origin of this partly quoted letter is not clearly known, and it is only fair to make general speculations. This would mean that by the year 1259/1843, when Rashtī was still alive, the Bab's name was known to some people, or to groups, to the extent that there were some students who regarded him as the embodiment of some form of Ẓuhūr, and attributed to him certain virtues that were beyond the recognized limits of common religious beliefs. More significant, it appears that Sayyid ʿAlī Muḥammad assumed a certain position, and contemplated a new doctrine, but believed that the time of its publication had still not arrived. The above letter may also explain, to some degree, the arrival of Mullā Ḥusayn Bushrūʾī and his companions from Karbalāʾ in Būshihr and then Shiraz in 1260/1844.[218] Perhaps it is not unrealistic to assume that some of these unknown ṭullāb, even if they were not the same as those who came from Karbalāʾ, were at least in contact with the Shaykhis in the ʿAtabāt. Muqaddas, who at the time was traveling between Isfahan, Shiraz, and Khurasan, may have been a vital link. These speculations, however, can be extended only as far as a possible link between the Bab, probably through his uncle, and the Shaykhis in the ʿAtabāt—a link that is vital for the understanding of the otherwise inexplicable conversion of a large number of Shaykhi students to the Babi cause.

What prompted Sayyid ʿAlī Muḥammad Shīrāzī to believe that he was a divinely inspired figure and his claims an inevitable answer to the prophetic yearnings of his time? First, he was a self-educated layman who never truly benefited from the scholastic knowledge of the time. Second, he possessed a degree of devotion and sanctity that was considered exceptional. Third, in his intellectual and mystical pursuits, he demonstrated a singular passion for intuitive approach.

These characteristics developed mainly as a result of an interplay between two major themes in his early life; the mercantile ethic and esoteric beliefs. As a merchant brought up in a traditional urban family, he inherited the personal and social practices of the merchant class. However, these moral values were not confined to the sphere of personal and professional life. For him, departure from the practical ethic took a moralistic turn. His lack of sufficient schooling, whether voluntary or the outcome of his failure to cope with madrasa system; his strivings to reach the truth by way of asceticism; his self-comparisons with the Prophet and the Imams; and his attention to the secrets of gnostic knowledge were all features of the same moral drive. His contacts with Shaykhism helped him to see his claim in the perspective of Shaykhi theophany without being formally committed to it. This detachment enabled him to adopt a self-styled approach that ultimately led him to eschatological and millenarian themes. Such an approach echoed the values of heterodox Shiʿism, which in spite of the inroads of established religion

[218]See below, chap. 4.

were still preserved in the subterranean currents of Persian esotericism. Yet at the same time it heralded a new departure from the well-trodden path of popular prophecies and desires for deputizing the Imam. This was the unavoidable outcome of a merger between learned thought and popular yearnings for the Ẓuhūr.

4

Seeking the Secret Gate: The Emergence of the Movement

"I was alone in my own abode and nobody was aware of my status," recalls the Bab in a prayer. "Then You brought out some humble people from their dwellings and sent them to me. Afterwards, You made Your command to the [new] call (daʿwa) my intent and when Your command reached maturity, I acquired Your covenant from the heart of those who were aware of Your cause, and they submitted to Your cause in such a way that not one from that party denied me."[1] Sayyid ʿAlī Muḥammad Shīrāzī's prayer sums up the circumstances that led to the birth of the Babi movement. For him, the proclamation of Jumādā al-Ūlā 1260/May 1844 was part of a providential plan that made him aware of God's command and rewarded him with His proofs. But "the command of God," as the Bab indicates, may not have matured without the covenant of those who first recognized him in Shiraz. If a predestined will was in action, so was human initiative.

Mullā Ḥusayn Bushrūʾī, the First Believer

The death of Sayyid Kāẓim Rashtī, on 11 Dhū al-Ḥijja 1259/2 January 1844,[2] marked the end of the second stage in the development of the Shaykhi school. Even before his death, the problem of his succession and internecine struggle among conflicting factions had caused frictions. Rashtī's reluctance to acknowledge any of his disciples as his permanent successor can be attributed in part to his emphasis on the impending revelation. His frustration in the tense environment of the ʿAtabāt was further

[1] *ZH* 269, Arabic prayer written circa 1845–1846.

[2] *Qatīl* (509) cf. *Fihrist* I, 159, and *Nabil* 45. Chronograms commemorating his death are: *ghāba nūrun* (the light become occulted) and *ghāba badr al-hudā* (the full moon of guidance eclipsed). See *MA* I, 220.

augmented by internal conflict in the school.[3] Rashtī's followers were unwilling to subordinate themselves to the authority of a new leader unless he displayed the right signs and qualities, which they believed he had described meticulously. Rashtī's emphasis on the imminence of the Ẓuhūr, and his hints of critical events to occur in the near future, encouraged some radical disciples to search for the unknown leader, against the wishes of the moderate faction.

In the final years of his life, Rashtī tried to preserve unity within the school. Advising his students to guard their "unity and integrity" in the event of his death, he appointed Mullā Ḥasan Gauhar as temporary caretaker head, at the same time affirming that the Advent of the Promised One was at hand.[4] There is little reason to doubt the veracity of Qazvīnī's account of a conversation between Rashtī and his followers: "Then someone asked, 'After you, with whom should we take refuge?' He [Sayyid Kāẓim] replied, 'With none, for it is not permitted. Stay for a few days around Mullā Ḥasan Gauhar, God shall not leave you in darkness. The truth is bound to appear.' Then he confirmed that Mullā Ḥasan's leadership would not exceed forty-five days, and at the end of that period he [the Promised One] would appear to enlighten the world with the eternal beauty of his light."[5]

But Rashtī's strong caution against personal rivalries and sectarianism notwithstanding, disagreement over the future of the school was bound to occur. As Mullā Ḥasan Gauhar was assumed to be the executor of Rashtī's will, Mīrza Muḥīṭ Kirmānī, another leading student, claimed to be the supervisor and the guardian of Rashtī's family; claims that in those uncertain times encouraged the two men to seek leadership.[6] Since neither was capable by personal character or scholarly aptitude of satisfying the students who sought a spiritual guide rather than a scholar, they both failed to attract any serious following. Qatīl relates that after a few weeks, when they were reminded of Rashtī's promises of the nearness of Ẓuhūr, Gauhar denied any previous references to it in Rashtī's words, while Muḥīṭ replied: "I remember something, but he [Rashtī] did not say that he would appear immediately. Therefore, it is your duty not to be dispersed from Karbalā', and make it known among people that many claimants are not justified in their claims, since our master said that 'the cause will appear a year after me.'"[7] Though for a few months these promises persuaded the students to

[3]*Dalīl al-Mutaḥayyirīn*, 51 ff.; cf. *NK* 100–103; *Nabil* 36–40.
[4]*Qazvīnī* 463 and *Qatīl* 508–10.
[5]*Qazvīnī* 463.
[6]*Qatīl* 510. For Mullā Ḥasan Qarachihdāghī (Gauhar) see *TMS* I/2, 341, and *Dalīl al-Mutaḥayyirīn* 98. For his claim of succession *TH* III, 338, 345, and I'tiżād al-Salṭana *Mutanabbi'īn*, ed. G. Navā'ī as *Fitna-yi Bāb*, 2d ed. [Tehran, 1350 Sh./1971] margin of the original MS by Ḥishmat al-Salṭana, p. 232). Also remark cited by Muḥammad Taqī Hashtrūdī in *Abwāb al-Hudā* cited in *Mu'īn* 54–56. On Muḥīṭ Kirmānī see below, chap. 5.
[7]*Qatīl* 510.

remain in Karbalāʾ, many soon became disillusioned with both Muḥīṭ and Gauhar, and dispersed.[8]

By their conformism Muḥīṭ and Gauhar tried to minimize their differences with the mainstream Uṣūlīs of the ʿAtabāt, and thus presented Shaykhism as above all a scholastic discipline. Similarly, another candidate for leadership, Ḥājjī Muḥammad Karīm Khān Kirmānī, also tried to create an independent center away from the conflicts in Iraq. His family wealth and influence in Kirman—plus his talent and perseverence, especially in remolding Shaykhism as a systematic creed accessible to a larger audience—helped Kirmānī establish himself as a respectable head of a sect. He drew heavily on the authority of Aḥsāʾī and Rashtī to justify his own claims and to elaborate a theological system with all trace of militant messianism carefully weeded out. In Kirman he was also satisfying a need for religious leadership of one of many factions in a city that had long been torn by sectarianism.[9] This did not prevent him, however, from claiming a broader leadership over the whole Shaykhi community, including students in the ʿAtabāt. The propaganda of Sayyid ʿAlī Kirmānī, Rashtī's secretary, who Qatīl claims forged a tract in Rashtī's name to justify Kirmānī's succession, at least temporarily drew the attention of some followers in Karbalāʾ.[10]

Like Muḥīṭ and Gauhar, Kirmānī failed to attract the bulk of Shaykhi students. Not only was he away in far-distant Kirman, but his conservative attitude and his Qajar lineage hardly qualified him as the ideal bāb and spiritual guide. Indeed, the reluctance of any of the three to embrace or even acknowledge the messianic dimension left those who were expecting the Ẓuhūr with only one other alternative—Mullā Ḥusayn Bushrūʾī, another leading disciple of Rashtī's. No matter what the real intentions of Rashtī's allusions to Ẓuhūr were, for Mullā Ḥusayn and those who followed him these enigmatic statements were positive signs to seek for an unconventional figure outside the available choices of Rashtī's ex-students. When Mullā Ḥusayn arrived in Karbalāʾ from Khurasan, soon after Rashtī's death and after a year of absence from the ʿAtabāt, he soon found himself the main spokesman for the nonconformists. As Nabīl Zarandī relates, in discussion with Gauhar and Muḥīṭ, Mullā Ḥusayn reminded his fellow classmates of the allusive warnings of their teacher and reaffirmed his commitment to Rashtī's promises, but the intentions of the two moderate Shaykhis were far less ambitious. Fearful of the number and strength of the enemies of the Shaykhis, they had resolved to stay in Karbalāʾ, and eventually to occupy

[8]Ibid. In the later years, as Muḥīṭ tended more toward Ḥājjī Muḥammad Karīm Khān in Kirman, Gauhar instead developed a mild pro-orthodox attitude. *TH* remarks (III, 338) that according to Gauhar neither the Babis nor the Kirmānī Shaykhis had any real understanding of the Shaykhi teachings and only used them to justify their own claims.

[9]See below, chap. 6.

[10]*Qatīl* 518.

Rashtī's place.[11] They could "guard the vacant seat"[12] of Rashtī, they declared. Mulla Ḥusayn, however, determined to fulfill a far different goal away from academic endeavors.

No figure embodies the prevailing spirit of Shaykhi yearnings better than Mullā Ḥusayn. Few individuals in the course of the Babi history match his status, his influence and contribution—not only for his dedication and resoluteness in pursuing Babi ideals, but even more because of his determination to break away from the norms of the scholastic world to which he belonged. He is a key figure in the shaping of the Babi movement, and the chief architect of its expansion. The background and character of "the Gate of the Gate" [Bāb al-Bāb], as the Bab later named Mullā Ḥusayn, exemplifies the making of a millenarian.

Mullā Muḥammad Ḥusayn, the elder son of a small landowner and cloth dyer, was born in the hamlet of Zīrak near Bushrūyih, a small agricultural town on the edge of the Khurasan desert, around 1229/1814. Zīrak, and indeed the entire Bushrūyih region in northeastern Quhistān, remained among the few surviving Ismāʿīlī communities in eastern Iran.[13] The Ismāʿīlī affiliation of Mullā Ḥusayn's family cannot be verified, but it is safe to assume that he, like a large number of early Babis from the same region, belonged to an environment with some indigenous Ismāʿīlī components. The days of Nizārī activism were long gone by. Yet the diffused presence of Ismāʿīlism, as it was precariously preserved in local communities of Khurasan and Kirman, might have fostered a sense of sectarian awareness that perhaps was even boosted by Ismāʿīlī and Niʿmatullāhī activities earlier in the century.

Mullā Ḥusayn's father, Ḥājjī Mullā ʿAbdullāh Ṣabbāgh, originally came from Yasār, outside Bushrūyih, and "owned land and property."[14] A relatively affluent man, he owned a number of shops in which he employed some of his relatives.[15] The designation *ṣabbāgh* (cloth dyer) suggests that this was his main profession, while *mullā* indicates a religious status, possibly a parttime engagement as leader of prayers in a local mosque. Mullā Ḥusayn received his early education in the local religious madrasa.[16] His mother, who was "a knowledgeable poet" of some talent and enjoyed "respect among people,"[17] was a source of encouragement to him and took a personal interest in his education.

[11] *Nabil* 48.

[12] Ibid.

[13] W. Ivanow, the reknowned student of Ismāʿīlism, in his tour of central Khurasan, registers Zīrak among the villages with Ismāʿīlī inhabitants *(Ismaili Literature: A Bibliographical Survey* [Tehran, 1963]).

[14] Narrative of Shaykh Muḥammad Nabīl Zarandī, cited in *ZH* 112.

[15] *Fuʾādī* 23, based on oral accounts.

[16] Ibid. On the authority of Karbalāʾī Mīrzā ʿAlī, the attendant of the madrasa of Bushrūyih.

[17] Ibid.

In 1241/1826, as a child of twelve,[18] he was sent to Mashhad to study in the madrasa of Mīrzā Jaʿfar,[19] probably to fulfil his parents' ambitions. Like many other Khurāsānī ṭullāb, he studied under Sayyid Muḥammad Qaṣīr Rażavī, a student of Bihbahānī and Baḥr al-ʿUlūm and a well-known Uṣūlī.[20] Qatīl al-Karbalāʾī tells us that, attracted by the boy's talent and enthusiasm, Qaṣīr authorized him to issue minor religious judgments in the mujtahid's court.[21] Later, Mulla Ḥusayn moved to Isfahan and studied with Uṣūlī jurists Muḥammad Bāqir Shaftī, Muḥammad Taqī Najafī, and possibly Ibrāhīm Karbāsī.[22] Since there is little indication of any Shaykhi attachment in his family background, it was possibly in Mashhad that he first became acquainted with the teachings of Aḥsāʾī and Rashtī.[23] He may have decided to study in the ʿAtabāt not only in pursuit of higher studies, but also with the specific purpose of attending Rashtī's discourses. But before setting out for the ʿAtabāt, he returned to Bushrūyih, around 1248/1832. He was enthusiastically received by the local governor, who urged him to stay in town, presumably to occupy a religious position. After some hesitation, he declined, and eventually headed for the ʿAtabāt about 1251/1835.[24]

Even in his early youth Mullā Ḥusayn apparently had some curious dreams of the Prophet,[25] followed later by "strange spiritual behavior."[26] When still in Isfahan, it was apparently his striving to acquire true knowledge and pass through the "stages of mysticism" that drew him to Shaykhism.[27] In Karbalāʾ, he seems to have studied exclusively with Rashtī; at least, there is no evidence to suggest his pupilage under any other teacher. He distinguished himself among the Shaykhi students by demonstrating mastery of the Shaykhi texts, and soon was entrusted with the task of supervising the junior students and handling some of Rashtī's correspondence.[28] Qatīl points out that his position among the students was superior both in

[18]Ibid. 25, referring to a few verses on the wall of Mullā Ḥusayn's house in Bushrūyih signed "*Ḥarrara aqall al-ṭullāb Muḥammad Ḥusayn,*" dated 1241/1826. For a photograph of the house see *Nabil* 49.

[19]Ibid. 23. For madrasa of Mīrzā Jaʿfar see *Maṭlaʿ al-Shams,* II, 247–50.

[20]*Qatīl* 521. For Qaṣīr see *MA* V, 1487–88; *Fihrist-i Kitābkhānih-yi Āstān-i Quds-i Rażavī,* ed. Uktāʾī, 7 vols. (Mashhad, 1305–1346 Sh./1926–1967) V, 460; *Vaḥīd-i Bihbahānī* 323–25 and Mīrzā ʿAbd al-Raḥmān Mudarris Shīrāzī, *Tārīkh-i ʿUlamā-yi Khurāsān* ed. M. B. Sāʿīdī Khurāsānī (Mashhad, 1341 Sh./1962) 80–83.

[21]*Qatīl* 521.

[22]Ibid.

[23]Ibid.; cf. Nabīl Zarandī in *ZH* 113.

[24]*Qatīl* 521. In Tehran, he heard of his father's death, returned to Bushrūyih, sold some of his father's possessions, and then set out for the ʿAtabāt (Nabīl Zarandī in *ZH* 113).

[25]*Fuʾādī* 24; cf. *ZH* 113.

[26]"*Aṭvār-i ruḥīya-yi gharība,*" *ZH* 113.

[27]*Qatīl* 521.

[28]*Qatīl* (521) particularly refers to *Lawāmiʿ al-Ḥusaynīya*, by Rashtī (Tabriz, 1271/1854), a philosophical work on the subject of triple beings. See *Fihrist* II, 302, and *al-Dharīʿa* XVIII, 366.

knowledge and steadfastness, and gives as witness the names of a number of Shaykhis who either studied various texts with him or regarded him as a trustworthy and dedicated student.[29] Among them were many Khurāsānīs and Shiʿites of Iraq who were later converted to the Babi movement.[30]

While in the ʿAtabāt, Mullā Ḥusayn compiled two long works and a number of treatises.[31] *Sharḥ Surat al-Kawthar*, a commentary in Shaykhi style, won Rashtī's commendation. His praises of the young scholar from the pulpit led many Shaykhis to think that Mullā Ḥusayn might be an appropriate candidate as his successor. Such speculations compelled Mullā Ḥusayn to openly deny any particular claim.[32] Among his surviving writings, however, is an Arabic commentary concerning the Occultation and Return of the Imam, compiled in Qazvin circa 1263/1847. It examines (mostly on the basis of such Shiʿite works as *Kitāb al-ʿAwālim* of Nūrullāh Baḥrāni[33] and *Kitāb al-Ghayba* of Ṭūsī) the authenticity of those Traditions which emphasize the role of the Persians, and particularly Khurāsānīs, in assisting the Qā'im in his Insurrection (Khurūj).[34] This work was written on the eve of the Babi uprising of Ṭabarsī, perhaps to highlight the Bab's public call for the gathering of his followers in Khurasan. Another work attributed to Mullā Ḥusayn is highly reminiscent of popular anagogic writings of the time, both in content and style.[35] The main focus of the surviving portion of this risāla, a hybrid of theosophy and liturgy, is on allusive verses of the Qur'ān. For enthusiasts like Mullā Ḥusayn these verses were especially appealing, since they were thought to envelop secrets impenetrable by the conventional mind.

In Karbalā', Mullā Ḥusayn lived the humble life of a devoted ṭalaba. Mullā Ḥusayn Dakhīl Marāghihī, an intimate friend, recalls that for their living expenses they were dependent on copying Aḥsā'ī's works.[36] For seven months, while in Isfahan, Mullā Ḥusayn lived entirely by his own personal labor. "He was working one day a week as a hired laborer while he was living contentedly and mostly fasting."[37] Apparently no customary pension was allocated to Mullā Ḥusayn, even for missions undertaken on Rashtī's

[29] *Qatīl* (521–22) names eleven.

[30] According to *Qatīl* (522), Mullā Muḥammad Taqī Haravī studied *Sharḥ al-Fawā'id* of Aḥsā'ī (*Fihrist* II, 227) with Mullā Ḥusayn.

[31] *Qatīl* 522.

[32] Ibid.; cf. *Nabil* 48. Both sources again lay stress on Mullā Ḥusayn's popularity among Shaykhi students.

[33] *Al-Dharīʿa* XV, 356. This above-mentioned work is a largely unknown encyclopedic work written by a student of Majlisī in the style of *Biḥār al-Anwār* (partly published in 1318/1900). Vols. XLI to LIV deal with *Ghayba* and the description of *Ḥujja*.

[34] INBA, no. 80, II, 198–211.

[35] *ZH* 136–39 cites part of this Arabic treatise. The same source indicates that other works of Mullā Ḥusayn have survived.

[36] *ZH* 54–55. Dakhīl himself is a well-known elegist of Shiʿite tragedies. His Āẕarī *Dīvān* has been published in Tabriz (*al-Dharīʿa*, IX, i, 320). His biography appears in M. H. Mīlānī *Tārīkh-i Amrī-yi Āẕarbāījān*, INBA Lib. no. 3030/a, folios 11–12.

[37] *ZH* 114.

instruction. This is significant when it is noted that unlike Rashtī, some mujtahids having various endowments and bequests under their control were in a position to attract many students to their circle.

Personal labor was not unknown to Mullā Ḥusayn; yet most sources are explicit about his physical incapacities. Qatīl indicates that when he first arrived in Karbalā', he suffered from bad health.[38] Another source remarks upon his trembling hands and even epilepsy, which had to be treated with tincture of gold.[39] Others mention heart palpitations,[40] anxiety, and restlessness,[41] although apparently he was partly relieved from his sufferings in later years. Mullā Muḥammad Furūghī rejects the idea put forward in *Rauḍat al-Ṣafā* that Mullā Ḥusayn had "in his early youth been instructed in the art of swordsmanship" and "acquired his proficiency only after a considerable period of training,"[42] declaring: "This is a sheer fabrication. I have known him as a classmate and friend for a long time. I have never known him to be possessed of such strength and power. . . . His hand trembled as he wrote, and he often expressed his inability to write as fully and frequently as he wished. He was greatly handicapped in this respect, and he continued to suffer from its effects until his journey to Mazandaran."[43]

While in Karbalā', Mullā Ḥusayn witnessed the gradual intensification of factional harassment and anti-Shaykhi allegations. Particularly toward the end of Rashtī's life, as he became more isolated among the high-ranking ʿulama, his reliance on the support of his students and followers increased.[44] Toward the beginning of the 1840s, one of the leading mujtahids of the ʿAtabāt, Sayyid Ibrāhīm Qazvīnī,[45] in collaboration with Sayyid Muḥammad Mahdī Ṭabāṭabā'ī, Shaykh Muḥammad Ḥasan Najafī, and others, called for a unanimous denunciation of the Shaykhis.[46] Their fatwā received a considerable response from Uṣūlīs all around Iran and Iraq.[47] To be more effective, however, it required the approval of the influential mujtahid of Iran, Mullā Muḥammad Bāqir Shaftī.[48] Shaftī, who may have seen the grave consequences of a schism, was ambivalent about the wisdom of endorsing the fatwā. As a conciliatory move, he postponed ratification. He first dis-

[38]*Qatīl* 521.
[39]*NK* 156.
[40]*NH* 34.
[41]*Fu'ādī* 25–26.
[42]*RS* X, 432, and not *NT* as it is referred to in *Nabil* 333.
[43]*Nabil* 333–34.
[44]*Qatīl* 511; *NK* 102; *Nabil* 34; Sharīʿatmadār Māzandarānī *Asrār al-Shahāda* (Tehran, 1315/1897); *Fihrist* I, 148; and *Dalīl al-Mutaḥayyirīn* 51ff. give various accounts of the persecution of Shaykhis in the ʿAtabāt during Rashtī's time.
[45]For his details see below, chap. 5.
[46]The accounts of this new wave of Bālāsarī opposition are fully pictured in *Dalīl al-Mutaḥayyirīn* 70 ff.
[47]*QU* (42–44) gives the list of the most important mujtahids who approved the Shaykhi denunciation.
[48]*Qatīl* 522; cf. *Nabil* 20–24 and *Nicolas* 251–54.

patched a letter to Rashtī inviting him to Isfahan to defend Shaykhism.[49] Rashtī was encouraged to approach Shaftī with the intention of securing his support and good-will, rightly thinking that Shaftī's friendship might well protect him against his opponents in the ʿAtabāt.

Rashtī designated Mullā Ḥusayn to represent him in Isfahan. In passing over both Gauhar, who had once been nominated to present the Shaykhi case to the jurists of Najaf,[50] and Muḥīṭ, who actually volunteered for the mission,[51] he perhaps considered the delicacy of the undertaking, as well as Mullā Ḥusayn's acquaintance with Shaftī. No source confirms whether Mullā Ḥusayn had even acquired the usual authorization from Rashtī, yet we can assume that having spent more than nine years in the ʿAtabāt,[52] he had completed his studies and was himself willing to return to his homeland.

Mullā Ḥusayn appeared at Shaftī's lecture in Isfahan "clad in mean attire, and laden with the dust of travel."[53] The "ragged-robe ṭalaba"[54] of Karbalāʾ was something of a novelty amid the noisy student crowd. For three days he conversed with Shaftī on the "heretical beliefs" that were alleged in the proposed fatwā.[55] He argued the Shaykhi viewpoints on "the eternal presence and the unceasing vigilance of the Imam" and challenged the authors of the fatwā on their charges of Shaykhi extremist views, particularly on the doctrine of the Fourth Pillar.[56] His argument must have been convincing enough to oblige Shaftī to withhold his backing of the denunciation.[57] Tearing up the fatwā, he asked Mullā Ḥusayn to address the public on the subject of the Shaykhi beliefs.[58] In a conciliatory letter to Rashtī he even praised Aḥsāʾī, calling him "chief of the ʿulama."[59] He then invited Mullā Ḥusayn to clarify the Shaykhis' position from the pulpit by reading from Rashtī's *Dalīl al-Mutaḥayyirīn* and to discuss the views of his mentor. It is reported that he himself applauded Mullā Ḥusayn for his courage and dedication.[60] Following his custom to give financial assistance to "seekers and possessors of knowledge,"[61] he also offered the young scholar one hundred tumāns, which Mullā Ḥusayn reportedly sent back with the retort:

[49] *ZH* 114.
[50] *Dalīl al-Mutaḥayyirīn* 98.
[51] *Nabil* 20.
[52] *ZH* 135 on the authority of Nabīl Zarandī.
[53] *Nabil* 20.
[54] "*Yik ṭalaba-yi pīrhan chāk.*" That is how the Bab describes him in *Dalāʾil-i Sabʿa.*
[55] *Qatīl* 522.
[56] *ZH* 115.
[57] *Nabil* 21–22 and *Qatīl* 522.
[58] *Qatīl* 522.
[59] *ZH* 114 n.
[60] *Nabil* 22.
[61] *TAS* II/1, 194.

"We nourish your soul for the sake of God; we seek from you neither recompense nor thanks."[62]

No doubt other factors influenced Shaftī's decision. He may have thought that approval of the fatwā could be interpreted as a sign of his full support for the ʿulama of the ʿAtabāt, and hence establish their supremacy in the ongoing secret struggle for leadership. He may have needed Rashtī's friendship, because in the later years of his life his waning authority was in danger of being overshadowed by Sayyid Ibrāhīm Qazvīnī and Shaykh Muḥammad Ḥasan Najafī. Moreover, his close relation with Shaykhi merchants, such as the Nahrīs in Isfahan, may have prevented him from allowing any drastic rejection of the Shaykhi school.[63]

Shaftī's cooperation was an important victory for the Shaykhis. In *Dalāʾil-i Sabʿa* the Bab indicates the admiration Mullā Ḥusayn won as a result of this mission: "You yourself know the First Believer [Mullā Ḥusayn] whose knowledge and virtue is acknowledged by Shaykhi and Sayyidī ʿulama [i.e., the followers of Rashtī] as well as by the others. When I arrived at Isfahan, even the children were saying that a ragged-robe ṭalaba came on behalf of the Sayyid [Rashtī] and with reasoning and proofs, vanquished a certain Muḥammad Bāqir who was the greatest divine in that land."[64]

The same commendation was expressed by Rashtī himself in a letter addressed to Mullā Ḥusayn in Mashhad, presumably in reply to his report. Clearly delighted with his student's performance, Rashtī states:

> You have revealed the truth and rooted out the forces of falsehood. This is greater for you than all the devotions and prayers since all these are subsidiary to this essential cause. Praise be to God, it was with the blessings of our Lord the Imam of the Age, may God hasten his emergence, that you received this support and confirmation. Do not fear, the firmly committed are not fearful, and thus God is the defender of those who believe in Truth. Though his friends are few in number, they are not afraid of this faithless and evil people. . . . Your return to Isfahan is much recommended. Concerning the matters you raised, you should act with the utmost piety and circumspection, guarding the tongue from whatever may provoke suspicion and cause disorder. I entrust you to God.[65]

The reassurance and advice in this letter and the recommendation for return to Isfahan, possibly in response to Shaftī's request, indicate the degree of attention Rashtī paid to this mission. Mullā Ḥusayn's interview with Mīrzā-yi

[62]Qur'ān LXXXVI, 9. Indicated by both *Nabil* 23 and *Qatīl* 522. The latter reports that when Mullā Ḥusayn left Isfahan for Khurasan without notice, Shaftī sent after him and invited him to return to Isfahan.

[63]For the Nahrīs see below, chap. 8.

[64]Pp. 54–55. Also translated by A. L. M. Nicolas *Le livre des sept preuves* (Paris, 1902) 54.

[65]The full text of the letter appears in *ZH* 114–15. It is also partly cited in *Qatīl* 523 and in *Risāla* by Qurrat al-ʿAyn in reply to Mullā Jawād Valīyānī (*ZH*, app. I, 499).

ʿAskarī, the influential imām jumʿa of Mashhad, was indeed in compliance with the same explanatory mission.[66]

In the last days of 1259/1843, after spending some time in Khurasan, Mullā Ḥusayn set out for the ʿAtabāt. On the road, shortly before arriving in Karbalā', he learned of Rashtī's death.[67] Counting himself among the master's senior students, he felt committed to participate in the debate concerning the future of the Shaykhi school. Frequent allusions in Rashtī's discourses to the nearness of the Advent no doubt made the issue far more crucial than that of a conventional succession in an academic circle or even a Sufi order. Mullā Ḥusayn was a resolute man with the dedication of a warrior and zeal of a millenarian, a good orator and an astute student of Shaykhism. He hardly ever wished to assume any independent position or authority for himself; not so much out of modesty or lack of self-confidence but probably more because he did not believe that either he or any of the others around him possessed the qualities of the ideal man set forth in the teachings of Rashtī. His intention was not to occupy Rashtī's place. Neither was he prepared to yield to the seniority of any other of the students. He had lived long enough in Karbalā' to know the shortcomings of his former schoolmates and was equally aware of his own. The very essence of prophetic yearnings no doubt perpetuated his "high expectations."[68] For him, as for those who later joined him, the idealized image of the spiritual guide was still not fully developed, but they were certain that he was not to be found in the madrasas of the ʿAtabāt.

Amid the confusion and disagreement that prevailed after Rashtī's death, Mullā Ḥusayn advocated to his students a guideline that he believed originated with their late teacher—"to quit their homes, scatter far and wide, purge their hearts from every ideal desire, and dedicate themselves to the quest of Him."[69] This idea appealed to some students, who pledged him "their loyalty and obedience."[70] But among other senior students Mullā Ḥusayn seems to have encountered the apathy, if not hostility, which became apparent to him during his two-month stay in Karbalā' (Muḥarram and Ṣafar 1260/January and February 1844), when he witnessed the quarrels, allegations, and petty conflicts among rival factions.[71] His decision to

[66] *Nabil* 24.

[67] Qurrat al-ʿAyn *Risāla* 499, cf. *Qatīl* 524. *Nabil* 47 believes that he arrived in Karbalā' on 1 Muḥarram 1260/22 Jan. 1844.

[68] *RŚ* X, 432, is alluding to these expectations when it states that "in his head Mullā Ḥusayn nurtured high hopes" *(havāhā-yi buland dar sar dāsht).*

[69] *Nabil* 47.

[70] Ibid. and *Ahmad* 448 n.

[71] Some details of these early conflicts appear in two early accounts; *Qatīl* provides invaluable information on the disputes among Muḥīṭ, Gauhar, and Karīm Khān Kirmānī (517 ff.) while a risāla by Shaykh Sulṭān Karbalā'ī *(ZH* 245–59) gives some references to the involvement of Mullā Aḥmad Ḥiṣārī in the dispute.

leave Karbalāʾ and retire to the mosque of Kūfa, partly a gesture to register his frustration, was also a sincere effort in accordance with Rashtī's instructions, to try to explore the identity of the future leader.[72]

Accompanied by his brother, Mullā Ḥasan Bushrūʾī, he started his retreat *(iʿtikāf)* with prayers and contemplation.[73] Soon he was joined by other Shaykhi students. Some came to Kūfa individually, and some in the company of other senior students like Mullā ʿAlī Basṭāmī and Mullā Yūsuf Ardabīlī.[74] The identities and the exact number of the participants are unclear, but certainly between fifteen to twenty Shaykhis joined his iʿtikāf.[75] This was a modest victory for Mullā Ḥusayn over other claimants at a time when the Shaykhis, "disillusioned and discontented," were "scattered to the wind in the deserts and wastelands and took refuge in the shrines and mosques."[76]

The practice of iʿtikāf was not unprecedented for Shaykhis. It was regarded as a means for exploring the truth by abstinence from all desires and destruction of falsehood.[77] In practice iʿtikāf meant seclusion in a mosque for prayer and meditation usually for a period of forty days. Such periods of devotion, nightly vigilance, and fasting were widely practiced by all ascetics, including both Aḥsāʾī and Rashtī. Tunkābunī reports on the authority of Rashtī that Aḥsāʾī retired for days in order to attain a high spiritual state.[78] On his first visit to the ʿAtabāt, Mullā Jaʿfar Qazvīnī observed an earlier iʿtikāf by Mullā Ḥusayn, in Kūfa.[79]

One of the conditions for iʿtikāf was that it be held in one of the four holy mosques: Masjid al-Ḥarām, in Mecca; the mosque of the Prophet, in Madina; or the mosques of Kūfa or Baṣra.[80] The exceptional sanctity of the

[72]*Qatīl* 510; cf. *Nabil* 50 and *NK* 105.

[73]His maternal cousin Mullā Muḥammad Bāqir "attended to their daily needs" (*Nabil* 50).

[74]*Nabil* 50, and *Qatīl* 510; cf. *Kazem Beg* VII, 464.

[75]None of the sources give any detailed list, but on the basis of those who were later converted in Shiraz, it is possible to identify more than sixteen. *ZH* and *TN* also add new names. *Muʿīn* (possibly on the basis of Hashtrūdī) raises the number to more than forty, adding women, such as Qurrat al-ʿAyn. The author of *NT* (III, 39–40) and after him many other accounts such as *RPAC* (146) and *Kazem Beg* (VII, 388) wrongly note that the Bab was also present in Kūfa, even identify him the leader of the group. This confusion perhaps occurred as the result of Mullā Ḥusayn's later title of *Bāb*. The author of *NT* conflates the two similar titles and assumes that Sayyid ʿAlī Muḥammad was in Kūfa. The Shiʿite Tradition on the Qāʾim's appearance in the mosque of Kūfa, which the Bab intended to fulfil must have also contributed to this muddle.

[76]*Qatīl* 510.

[77]*Muʿtaqad al-Imāmīyā* ed. M.T. Dānishpazhūh (Tehran, 1339 Sh./1961) 294–96. See also S. J. Sajjādī *Farhang-i Maʿārif-i Islām* (Tehran, 1357 Sh./1978) I, 238–40; *Farhang-i Lughāt va Iṣṭilāḥāt va Taʿbīrāt-i ʿIrfānī* (Tehran, 1350 Sh./1971) 50; *Shorter EI*: RAMAḌĀN and *EI*[2]: KHALWA.

[78]*QU* 37–41. Aḥsāʾī's teacher, Baḥr al-ʿUlūm, is reported to have had visions of the Qāʾim in his retreat in the mosque of Sahla in Kūfa and sometimes even to have conversed with him about problems in jurisprudence.

[79]*Qazvīnī* 448.

[80]Sajjādī *Farrhang-i Maʿārif* 238–40.

ruined mosque of Kūfa, where in 39/656 ʿAlī was struck down with a poisoned sword, made it a specially sacred place for retreat, with a direct relation to apocalyptic events at the time of the Imam's Advent.[81] The Shiʿite prophecies declared it to be the capital of the Mahdī whence he would begin his historic vengeance.[82] Aḥsāʾī, on the subject of the "return of the believers' souls to their bodies" on the Day of Resurrection, states in his popular work *Ḥayāt al-Nafs*: "And then [the believers] will arrive at the Wādī al-Salām behind Kūfa and will remain there till the end of the Day [. . . and those who died in this world will return to be killed anew, and thus God will raise Muḥammad and his descendants from the earth and revive mankind for forty days."[83] Not surprisingly, many holy dreams and visitations of the Imam in the Kūfa mosque are recorded in Shiʿite literature. In this meeting place a visit from the Qāʾim might take place, in dream or in vision, or at least some indication of his presence could be sensed. For Shaykhis like Mullā Ḥusayn and his companions the presence of the Imam was an indisputable fact, and his contact with those who were seriously searching for him was an ever-present possiblity.

The days of retirement in Kūfa are shrouded in ambiguity, but there are enough indications to speculate on the motives that finally resulted in the departure of Mullā Ḥusayn and his followers for Iran in early Rabīʿ al-Thānī 1260/April 1844. Most Babi sources either simply give no explanation or attribute their departure to some supernatural inspiration. Qatīl states that Mullā Ḥusayn remained in retirement in Kūfa till he lost patience "and then after visiting the Shrine in Karbalāʾ, set out toward his destination."[84] Qurrat al-ʿAyn implies that his departure came after an intuitive awareness that he acquired in his prayers and asceticism.[85] Mīrzā Aḥmad, on the other hand, on the authority of an unnamed Shaykhi who claimed to have been present in Kūfa, believes that Mullā Ḥusayn's decision to depart for Iran was related to Rashtī's earlier instructions: "We were a large body who accompanied Mullā Ḥusayn everywhere and it was our belief that after the death of Ḥājjī Sayyid Kāẓim the leadership of the Shaykhi sect would be vested in Mullā Ḥusayn, because we did not know anyone in our group more pious than he."[86] In the course of the Kūfa iʿtikāf, we are told, Mullā

[81]For the religious significance of the mosque of Kūfa see *EI*[2]: KŪFA.

[82]See for instance Majlisī *Ḥaqq al-Yaqīn* 376.

[83]Wadham MS, folio 37a (trans. 92). "The Qāʾim will establish himself in Kūfa. His residence will be in the mosque of Sahla and he will execute his judgments from the mosque of Kūfa" (trans. 120–21).

[84]*Qatīl* 510.

[85]*Risāla* 500.

[86]*Aḥmad* 448 n. (confirmed by *NK* 105). Though Mīrzā Aḥmad does not disclose the name of the Shaykhi student, perhaps for reasons of security, we can assume that he is none other than Mullā Ḥasan Bajistānī, one of the early believers in Shiraz. He was the only one present in Kūfa (Brown misread him [*NH* 33] as Mullā Ḥasan of Najistān), in Shiraz in May 1844, and later at the beginning of Ṭabarsī upheaval prior to the fatal fighting. He later resided in Khurasan. This background corresponds fairly well with Mirza Aḥmad's unrevealed source.

Ḥusayn received a letter, presumably written by Rashtī. "We felt certain," recalls the anonymous reporter, "that the Sayyid had constituted him as his successor and leader of the sect." However, the content of the letter apparently instructed otherwise.

> On reading it Mullā Ḥusayn decided to leave, despite the fact that the purpose for which he had stayed there had not been completed. We asked him the reason for his departure, and he said: "I am ordered to undertake a journey and to go to the service of a great personage." We said: "We presumed that this is your turn to be leader." He burst into tears, saying: "How far from me! Where am I and where are these positions?" He thereupon prepared to go to Shiraz, and . . . [told] me, en route: "It has not been determined where I am to go, but I believe that I may go to Kirman and see Ḥājjī Muḥammad Karīm Khān, as it may be that the Sayyid meant that I should enter the service of the Imam through him."[87]

Although this source disagees with others on the time and duration of the iʿtikāf, other details indicate that the narrator was present at Kūfa. A few lines below, the same account makes it clear that Mullā Ḥusayn was ordered to travel not to Kirman but to Fars: "And since I did not anticipate seeing anyone in Fars," says Mullā Ḥusayn to his followers, "I presumed that my destination was Kirman."[88] One might still suppose that his apparent intention to visit Kirman was a purely tactical move. It is hard to believe—as indeed almost all the available evidence suggests the opposite—that Mullā Ḥusayn was prepared to accept Kirmānī's authority, as he had already rejected the claims of the other senior students in the ʿAtabāt. Mullā Muḥammad Taqī Hashtrūdī takes particular care to point out that Kirman was only "the apparent destination" of Mullā Ḥusayn.[89] There are other tantalizing indications that might be taken as signs of a vague intention to seek out Sayyid ʿAlī Muḥammad in Shiraz. If not Mullā Ḥusayn himself, at least some of his friends and ex-classmates had already become acquainted with the Bab, and reportedly were impressed by him at the time of his

---

Furthermore, the tone of the account in *Ahmad* suggests that the narrator was no longer a Babi, which again corresponds to Bajistānī, who later abandoned his Babi beliefs.

[87]Ibid.

[88]Ibid.

[89]*Muʿīn* 56, citing *Abwāb al-Hudā*. Similarly, *Qatīl*'s emphasis on the lack of support for Kirmānī among the Shaykhi students suggests that Mullā Ḥusayn was not particularly keen to visit Kirman. See also *Nabil* 39–40, citing Shaykh Abū Turāb Ishtihārdī. However, the matter seems even more enigmatic when another passage in *Qatīl* describes the activities of Mullā ʿAlī Kirmānī. Because of his hostility to Gauhar over the execution of Rashtī's will, he canvassed the succession of Karīm Khān with the help of a tract that he reputedly forged in the name and the style of Rashtī. In this tract Karīm Khān was praised in highest terms. He was described as the one who is aware of the "Point of Knowledge" and admired as the "most deserving of the students" through whom the others must seek guidance. Mullā ʿAlī later admitted to this forgery and because of it was forced to flee to Mecca, but at the time its publication created some excitement among the Shaykhis and "was one of the reasons for some to go to Shiraz with the intention of traveling to Kirman."

pilgrimage to the ʿAtabāt. The Bab's letter of late 1259/1843, which hinted at a connection between him and some unknown ṭullāb and the possibility of a proclamation in the near future, may have been addressed to Mullā Ḥusayn's party.[90] However, the significance of this probable contact should not be exaggerated, since Mullā Ḥusayn's later behavior in Shiraz showed that if indeed there had been a previous acquaintance, or even an intention to visit the Bab, it certainly was not with any clear idea of his acclaimed position.

The Proclamation of Shiraz

On his return to Iran, Mullā Ḥusayn apparently was ahead of other Shaykhis, who seemed to be still engaged in the forty-days retreat.[91] Accompanied by his brother and his cousin, he arrived in Būshihr via Baṣra.[92] After a short stay there, he reached Shiraz sometime in late Rabīʿ al-Thānī or early Jumādā al-Ūlā 1260/mid-May 1844. The others followed him shortly afterward on the same route. In Shiraz they met Sayyid ʿAlī Muḥammad and, after recognizing his claim as the Promised One formed the first group of his disciples (later known as Ḥurūf-i Ḥayy). The symbolic significance of this proclamation (*iẓhār-i amr*: lit. uttering the command) in the Babi movement cannot be overstressed. Although the nature of the Bab's claims, and probably even the purpose of it, was not yet quite clear, it is from this moment that the birth of a new revelatory cycle is celebrated by both the claimant and his believers.

Despite the numerous accounts of this germane episode, and its significance in the formation of the early Babi nucleus, the manner in which Mullā Ḥusayn and his companions first became acquainted with Sayyid ʿAlī Muḥammad is still not fully clear. The Shaykhi student quoted by Mīrzā Aḥmad relates that when the whole party reached the outskirts of Shiraz, they were received by the Abyssinian servant of Sayyid ʿAlī Muḥammad at Dukkān Rīva, a stage two miles from Shiraz, who enquired about Mullā Ḥusayn:

> We pointed him out, and the Abyssinian servant approached Mullā Ḥusayn and stopped him, whispering certain words in his ears while he remained on his horse. We saw Mullā Ḥusayn dismount, his attitude greatly changed. He made the servant walk ahead of him and he followed in his wake. We asked what we should do, and the servant told us to go to the Gumruk caravanserai. We followed. On reaching the caravanserai, the same servant guided us to a room.

[90]See above, chap. 3.
[91]*Qatīl* 511.
[92]Ibid.; cf. *Nabil* 51.

> We went in, and there we saw Mullā Ḥusayn sitting most reverently opposite a sayyid. They were engaged in a discussion. A little later both got up and went to the sayyid's house, [while] guiding us to another residence.[93]

In all probability the Bab had prior knowledge of the arrival of Mullā Ḥusayn's party, possibly through his uncle or a relative in Būshihr. This reinforces the possibility of an earlier acquaintance between the two. Ḥājjī Mīrzā Jānī, relating from Mullā Ḥusayn, declares that since Mullā Ḥusayn was previously acquainted with Sayyid ʿAlī Muḥammad in the ʿAtabāt, he "at once on reaching Shiraz sought out his abode" and was received with hospitality.[94] Hashtrūdī, on the other hand, relates that, having formed a brief acquaintance in Karbalā', they met again at the lectures of a religious teacher in Shiraz. There Sayyid ʿAlī Muḥammad gradually introduced Mullā Ḥusayn to his claims.[95] Mullā Jalīl Urūmī, who was himself present in Shiraz, informs us that the teacher was none other than Mullā Ḥusayn himself, now holding his teaching sessions on Aḥsā'ī's *Sharḥ al-Ziyāra* in the Vakīl mosque. In the course of these lectures, Sayyid ʿAlī Muḥammad asked Mullā Ḥusayn, "If someone expounded better than you, what would you say?" Mullā Ḥusayn answered, "I will obey and listen." Then Sayyid ʿAlī Muḥammad asked what his reaction would be if someone expounded better than Rashtī and even Aḥsā'ī, to which Mullā Ḥusayn gave the same reply. Then Sayyid ʿAlī Muḥammad presented him with some of his writings. "Immediately after reading them," recalls Urūmī, "he was overwhelmed and deeply moved. But the Bab advised him to conceal his emotions."[96]

Taking into account all the confusions, it is still possible to render a relatively plausible version of the process that eventually resulted in the formation of the movement. Even if Mullā Ḥusayn had a vague impression of Sayyid ʿAlī Muḥammad as a holy man, it is almost certain that he had no previous idea of finding in him the Promised One he was seeking. Their

[93] *Ahmad* 448 n. For the Gumruk caravanserai see *Fārs Nāmih* II, 146, and Binning I, 285. They were presumably directed to Sayyid ʿAlī Muḥammad's office.

[94] *NH* 34.

[95] *Muʿīn* 56–57.

[96] *Qazvīnī* 472. There is a certain degree of discrepancy in the sources over the proclamation of the Bab, thanks at least partly to the secrecy throughout the early stages. Some later sources give a supernatural sense to their accounts to make it more comparable to the traditional concept of prophetical revelation. *Nabil* (52), for instance, maintains that Mullā Ḥusayn met the Bab only accidentally outside the city gates on the afternoon of 5 Jumādā al-Ūlā/22 May, implying that an element of providential will was involved.

Nearly all the available materials on the Shiraz proclamation are based on seven primary sources: (1) Mullā Ḥusayn → ʿAbd al-Wahhāb Khurāsānī → Ḥājjī Mīrzā Jānī → *NH* (but not in *NK*); (2) Mullā Ḥusayn → Mīrzā Aḥmad Qazvīnī → *Nabil;* (3) Mullā Ḥusayn (?) → Mullā Muḥammad Taqī Hashtrūdī → *Muʿīn;* (4) Mullā Ḥasan Bajistānī → *Ahmad;* (5) Mullā Jalīl Urūmī → *Qazvīnī;* (6) *Qatīl;* (7) the writings of the Bab. While (1) and (2) quote directly from Mullā Ḥusayn; (3), (4), (5), and (6) are partly based on his account; (7) provides only scattered references.

encounter was not accidental, and it seems likely that Sayyid ʿAlī Muḥammad had the intention of proclaiming his "mission," though not especially to Mullā Ḥusayn Bushrūʾī.

Prior to this encounter and following his earlier dreams, Sayyid ʿAlī Muḥammad became more and more convinced that he was divinely inspired and that after Rashtī he was to become the "locus of inspiration." He states: "Nineteen days before the commencement of the revelation, he [i.e., Rashtī] joined the Heavenly Host and the beginning of 1260 was the time when the secret (bāṭin) was first revealed."[97] Sometime after, he became fully aware of these revelations. "In truth, the first day that the spirit descended in the heart of this slave, was the fifteenth of the month of Rabīʿ al-Awwal [4 April 1844]."[98] His image of the mission that he believed was entrusted to him is illustrated in a sermonal exordium on the commentary on *Surat al-Baqara,* one of his earliest works: "O My Lord! You instructed me on the day when I started composing this book. Verily I saw, on that night in a dream, the Holy Land [*Arḍ al-Muqaddas,* i.e., the ʿAtabāt] fallen in pieces and lifted in the air till it stopped in front of my house. Then afterward, news came of my teacher's death, the great, kind scholar, may God have mercy upon him."[99] This symbolic dream not only alludes to the new claims of the Bab by the announcement of the Rashtī's death, but also hints at the termination of the ʿAtabāt era, which in the Bab's view is concurrent with the commencement of the new dispensation.

First with allegorical remarks, then with greater clarity the Bab announced his claim to Mullā Ḥusayn. His manner, words, and writings during their conversations conveyed an inner conviction especially appealing to the Shaykhi scholar. The spirit of messianic anticipation that prevailed over the claimant as well as the prospective convert became explicit when Mullā Ḥusayn conversed at length with Sayyid ʿAlī Muḥammad in his house. First the Bab asked him: "Do not you Shaykhis believe that someone must take the place occupied by the late Sayyid Kāẓim? Five months have now elapsed since his death. Whom do you now recognize as your Master [of the Command (*Ṣāḥib-i Amr*)]?" "As yet," Mullā Ḥusayn replied, "we have recognized no one." "What manner of man," asked he, "must the Master be?" Thereupon Mullā Ḥusayn enumerated some requisite qualifi-

[97]Letter addressed to his family while in captivity in Mākū. INBA, no. 58, 160–62, also partly cited in *ZH* 223–35 and facsimile in 264. A tauqīʿ (ordinance) by the Bab with a similar content is cited in Ḥājjī Ḥusayn Qulī Jadīd al-Islām, *Minhāj al-Ṭālibīn fī al-Radd ʿalā al-Firqa al-Hālika al-Bābīya* (Bombay, 1320/1902) 101–4, which contains some extra passages. The author wrongly believes that this is part of the *Bayān.*

[98]*Kitāb al-Ḥaramayn,* cited in *SAMB* 206. This is written in Jumādā al-Thānī 1261/June 1845, later than *Ṣaḥīfat bayn al-Ḥaramayn.* The Persian translation of *SAMB* (Musīyu Nīkulā, *Mazāhib-i Milal-i Mutimaddina; Tārīkh-i Sayyid ʿAlī Muḥammad maʿrūf bi-Bāb* (Tehran, 1322 Sh./1943) trans. *ʿayn.mīm.fā.* (ʿAlī Muḥammad Farahvashī), 210 n., quotes the original passage in Arabic.

[99]INBA no. 98, IV, 23–27 (27), also cited in *Qazvīnī* 471. This was written in Muḥarram 1260/Jan.-Feb. 1844).

cations and characteristics. "Do you observe these in me?" the Bab asked bluntly. Mullā Ḥusayn gave a negative reply: "I see in you none of these qualities." Later in the same meeting, Mullā Ḥusayn observed a commentary of *Sūrat al-Baqara* on the shelf. When he inquired about the author, Sayyid ʿAlī Muḥammad said merely, "A mere youthful beginner who nevertheless lays claim to a high degree of knowledge and greatness."[100]

This exchange set up an inner struggle in Mullā Ḥusayn that lasted for several days. He was fascinated by his host; but he saw before him "a youthful merchant" whose theological training did not measure up to his claim that he had written a commentary on *Sūrat al-Baqara,* in which he expounded "the inmost of the inmost."[101] Obviously, in no way could an instant conversion have taken place, as some sources suggest. Mullā Ḥusayn later attributed his inner crisis to the persistence of scholastic values, confessing that his insistence on the traditional conditions set by the Shiʿite prophecies led him to dispute with the Bab. His friend Āqā Sayyid Mu'min Khurāsānī relates:

> One day in the presence of the Bāb al-Bāb [Mullā Ḥusayn's later title] in Khurasan [probably Mashhad], we were passing a madrasa. He looked at the school and recited this verse: "Not one warm-hearted man [*ahl-i dil*] has ever come out of a madrasa. Down with these schools which are houses of ignorance." I said, "By the Grace of God, eminent individuals like yourself have come out of these schools, why are you condemning them?" He replied, "Do not say that, Sayyid Mu'min, all that I ever learned in these wretched places was to make me argue with and oppose the Proof of God for forty days. I realized the meaning of the saying 'knowledge is the greatest veil' through the fruits of this ruined place. I wish I had no education."[102]

Contempt for scholastic values and denial of the years he believed he had wasted in madrasas demonstrate Mullā Ḥusayn's revolutionary spirit at its best. The same madrasa values had tormented him over the question of Sayyid ʿAlī Muḥammad's claims, though the duration of his argument with the Bab may be exaggerated. In the course of the Ṭabarsī upheaval (1264–1265/1848–1849), Mullā Ḥusayn stated: "I wish my steps had never reached the madrasa, so I would never have bothered the Proof of God for three days and nights."[103]

His inner conflict over the Bab's legitimacy gradually resolved itself to full conversion. One of his companions recalled: "We could see that there was

[100]*NH* 35.

[101]Ibid. 35–37. For the use of this term in Shaykhi doctrine see Aḥsā'ī *Sharḥ al-Zīyāra* III, 258–59.

[102]*Muʿīn* 62–63.

[103]Account given by Waraqat al-Firdaus, Mullā Ḥusayn's sister, relating it from Āqā (Mullā) Muḥammad Ḥasan Bushrū'ī, one of the survivors *(Baqīyat al-Sayf:* the Remnants of the Sword) in Ṭabarsī, cited in *Fu'ādī* 28.

some difference between the Sayyid [the Bab] and Mullā Ḥusayn; but at every subsequent meeting Mullā Ḥusayn showed more respect and loyalty [to the Sayyid] than on the previous occasion."[104] After his first few meetings with the Bab, Mullā Ḥusayn reported to his friends: "I have not satisfied my mind completely. We must hold several other conversations; and I must obtain full discernment, for the matter of religion is a difficult one."[105] Mullā Jalīl Urūmī adds that Mullā Ḥusayn "could not sleep the whole night for his inner struggle and mental occupation."[106]

After overcoming these uncertainties, perhaps as soon as three days later, Mullā Ḥusayn finally recognized the Bab and became his First Believer. All the sources agree with the Bab that it was on the night of 5 Jumādā al-Ūlā 1260/22 May 1844 that Mullā Ḥusayn fully accepted Sayyid ʿAlī Muḥammad's claim.[107] Perhaps nowhere in the course of their history is the collective nature of the Babis' messianic undertaking better highlighted than in this very recognition. It is not the moment of the Bab's first inspiration but his covenant with the First Believer that registers the birth of a new dispensation.

What led Mullā Ḥusayn, and later other Shaykhis, to acclaim the Bab as the ultimate goal of their search? What exactly were the claims set forth by the Bab and how were they perceived by the early believers? As we have seen, earlier teachings and practices psychologically prepared Mullā Ḥusayn and his followers for the mysterious Promised One to be revealed in someone who might not fulfill all those extraordinary and often impossible conditions that had long been regarded as signs of the expected Imam. Instead he could materialize the more plausible conditions set by the late Shaykhi teachers. All through Qazvīnī's account, Mullā Ḥusayn's "unrelaxing vigilance" and "singleness of mind" in searching for and identifying the Promised One are emphasized. When Mullā Ḥusayn first entered Sayyid ʿAlī Muḥammad's house, he thought: "Might not my visit to this house enable me to draw nearer to the object of my quest? Might it not hasten the period of intense longing, of strenuous search, of increasing anxiety, which such a quest involves?"[108] Again, when he stood beside the Bab for prayers, he prayed: "I have striven with all my soul, O my God, and until now have failed to find thy promised messenger. I testify that thy word fails not, and that thy promise is sure."[109] Although the tone of the recollections reveals Qazvīnī's or even more probably Nabīl Zarandī's style, still such enthusiasm is not uncharacteristic for a man engaged in a lifelong search for an

[104] *Aḥmad* 448–49 n.
[105] Ibid.
[106] *Qazvīnī* 472.
[107] *Bayān* II, 7 30.
[108] *Nabil* 54.
[109] Ibid. 56.

ideal guide: first in Sayyid Kāẓim Rashtī, then in Sayyid ʿAlī Muḥammad the Bab, and finally during the days of Ṭabarsī in Mullā Muḥammad ʿAlī Māzandarānī (Quddūs).

Moreover, for a ṭalaba like Mullā Ḥusayn, who had spent all his life in the isolation of the madrasas and retirement of the mosques, Sayyid ʿAlī Muḥammad's unusual intellectual orientation had a special appeal. He represented a different cultural background and upbringing, yet the two had enough in common to permit a dialogue. Sayyid ʿAlī Muḥammad was a man of austerity who despised madrasa education and considered it a barrier to the attainment of true knowledge. For the same reason he also held Aḥsāʾī and Rashtī and their ideas in high regard. Mullā Ḥusayn and other Shaykhi companions, on the other hand, saw in the Shīrāzī merchant unusual refinements. His appearance, his manner, and his hospitality were all appealing elements. Mullā Ḥusayn was "profoundly impressed by the gentle yet compelling manner in which that strange youth" spoke to him.[110] "The music of his voice . . . the radiance of the countenance . . . the expression of affection,"[111] and his posture in "sitting in a most dignified and majestic attitude"[112] all fascinated him and drew him to the point of conversion. In a traditional climate in which delicate manner, public appearance, and physical features were distinctive parts of one's character, such elements could arouse sympathy and loyalty. The description given of the Qāʾim in the Shiʿite prophecies not only idealized the holy lineage and the personal virtues of the Imam, but featured him as the ideal of handsomeness, mannerism, and deportment.

Equally instrumental in Mullā Ḥusayn conversion were the proofs that Sayyid ʿAlī Muḥammad offered in support of his claims. They basically stressed two points. First, he emphasized the prophecies of Rashtī, and hence laid claim to a position that throughout his early encounters with Mullā Ḥasayn was described as that of the Master and the Promised One.[113] Sayyid ʿAlī Muḥammad did not consider himself merely Rashtī's successor or even the Perfect Shiʿa, but assumed a position much closer to a prophetic status. It is with this consideration that titles like *Bāb, Z̲ikr* (lit. remembrance), and *Nuqṭa* (point) were adopted, with a sense of deputyship delegated to him not merely from the Twelfth Imam but from a divine authority.[114] As has already been noted, in some Shaykhi-Babi texts Rashtī had been referred to as "Primary Divine Gate" (Bābullāh al-Muqaddam).[115] But it is in regard to Sayyid ʿAlī Muḥammad that the title directly points to an open messianic manifestation. One can suppose that the title Bābullāh al-

[110]Ibid. 53.
[111]Ibid. 52–62.
[112]*NH* 37.
[113]*Nabil* 57, cf. *NH* 35, calling himself *Ṣāḥib-i Amr* and *Aḥmad* 449 n., "the True One."
[114]See below.
[115]See above, chap 1.

Muqaddam was in use in a small circle of Shaykhis, with some implications of the status of the Perfect Shiʿa. As became more apparent to the Shaykhi converts over the next few years, Sayyid ʿAlī Muḥammad's goal in assuming the gateship (bābīya) was different from the aims of past Shaykhi leaders. It is not unlikely that the adjective *muqaddam* (primary) in Rashtī's title was applied with a sense of continuous progression. As Rashtī was believed to be higher in his position of bābīya than the classical Four Deputies so he himself was a preliminary gate to the next bāb who would make his stand public.[116] The same consideration, it appears, was Sayyid ʿAlī Muḥammad's concern in conferring the title of Bāb al-Bāb (the Gate of the Gate) on his First Believer. Hence, Mullā Ḥusayn would also be the preliminary gate for access to the Bab.[117]

The second proof put forward by the Bab was his writing, especially his skill and efficiency in producing and compiling numerous works. This was the most positive proof, which he consistently presented as his incontrovertible miracle. No doubt this was postulated in direct reference to the saying in the Qur'ān that the Book that is "sent down" to the Prophet is the "sign" from God.[118] First instances of the Bab's unusual speed in uttering verses occurred in reply to some questions raised in a short tract that Mullā Ḥusayn had written on some Shaykhi topics. Then he wrote in reply *Qayyūm al-Asmā'*, a commentary on *Sūrat Yūsuf,* unquestionably his most important work of the early period. On the night of the 5 Jumādā al-Ūlā'/22 May he composed the first few chapters, and in the following days he compiled the rest.[119] The speed with which he "revealed verses" particularly impressed Mullā Ḥusayn, who recalled: "Not for one moment did he interrupt the flow of the verses that streamed from his pen."[120] On another occasion Mullā Ḥusayn observed with "amazement" the commentary that the Bab wrote on the well-known ḥadīth al-Jāriya, recalling that Rashtī used to attribute the compilation of the commentary on this ḥadīth to the Lord of the Command.[121]

As far as can be verified, up to this time the Bab had not produced any work of significance, and it was only during his encounters with his early

[116]Qurrat al-ʿAyn *Risāla* in *ZH* 493.

[117]*Nabil* 63. This must have been after the assumption of the position of Qā'imīya by the Bab. In most works of the Bab prior to 1264/1848 he is referred to as the Letter *Sīn (Ṣaḥīfa-yi ʿAdlīya,* INBA no. 82, 139); *al-Awwal man Āman; Awwal Mu'min* (*Dalā'il-i Sabʿa* 54) or *aḥabb al-khalq* (the dearest of all people) (letter to Mullā ʿAbd al-Khāliq Yazdī, INBA no. 91, 94–102).

[118]XXIX, 50–51. Also see *Shorter EI*: ḲUR'ĀN 273–74.

[119]In a letter to Mullā Ibrāhīm Shīrāzī, INBA no. 36, 170–80 (174) written in 1261/1845 the Bab specifies that he had finished this work in forty days. For details of this work see Browne *JRAS* (1889) 904–9, and "Catalogue and Description" *Journal of the Royal Asiatic Society* 24 (1892) 261–68, 699–701.

[120]*Nabil* 61.

[121]*NK* 106; *Muʿīn* 60. The text of this commentary appears in INBA no. 67, 157–60. The hadith related from ʿAlī by Jārīya ibn Qudāma appears in *Biḥār al-Anwār* VIII, chap. 64, 671–77.

believers that he became fully aware of his talent for producing Qur'anic commentaries. To Mullā Ḥusayn and the other early Babis, these works of the Bab were valued not as examples of conventional exegesis but because of their novelty, their admonitory style, and their messianic content. Again the preconceived attributes of the prophecies, which required the Qā'im to reveal a commentary on the "best of the stories" *(aḥsan al-qiṣaṣ;* i.e., *Sūrat Yūsuf),* convinced the Bab as much as his believers that his writings possessed extraordinary prophetic qualities. In *Qayyūm al-Asmā'* the Bab first lays claim to the unrivaled nature of his writings. Closely emulating the Qurʿān both in style and tone, he declares: "If capable, let them bring similar to this book which is witness from God, the Truth, by the Truth, for the Truth. . . . If the human beings and the jinn gather [in order] to bring similar to this book, by Truth, they are incapable even if [all] the people of the earth, and alike, came to their support. Swear to your Lord, the Truth, they are incapable of bringing even some of its letters and of its interpretations of the mysteries, none."[122] To a modern reader, such claims for what after all was a repetition of admonitory phrases in the style of the Qur'ān, would appear quite irrational. To a millenarian frame of mind, however, they were miraculous. The sheer unconventionality of the language was effective enough to be regarded as a proof of veracity. The revolutionary ideas set forth in *Qayyūm al-Asmā'* were even more penetrating when uttered aloud in the pounding rhythm adopted throughout the text.

The experience of Mullā Ḥusayn exemplifies many ensuing conversions to the movement. At least at this early stage, recognition was less a commitment to a set of ideas and beliefs than devotion to the person of the Bab as a charismatic saint. The obligation to seek and support the Proof of God required believers to search for the Qā'im and his companions and helpers and to recognize them once any indication of them appeared. Conversion therefore was a religious obligation, as was the cognition of the truthfulness of any claimant.

Some opponents of the Bab as early as the time of Qatīl insist that it was Mullā Ḥusayn who instigated and even induced Sayyid ʿAlī Muḥammad to claim bābīya, and that he was the author of the writings attributed to the Bab.[123] To assume that Sayyid ʿAlī Muḥammad was no more than an instrument in the hand of Mullā Ḥusayn, or that indeed Mullā Ḥusayn had the intention of manipulating the alleged "simplicity" of the Bab for his own purposes, is too simplistic. The events of the next four years provide enough historical proof to establish the baselessness of such an assertion. Yet it is equally unrealistic to think, as the Babi writers usually imply, that Sayyid ʿAlī Muḥammad was purely independent and free of any outside influence in the course of his proclamation.

[122] *QA* IX, folio 13b.
[123] *Qatīl* 524.

Such committed views, from either side, should not prevent us from recognizing that in the charged circumstances of the time, the encounter between the two figures, one with a strong desire to discern the messianic signs and the other with a sincere belief in his own inspiration, would result in a claim in which both parties played an active role. One can suggest, then, that if Mullā Ḥusayn at that particular moment had not met him in Shiraz, the course of Sayyid ʿAlī Muḥammad's spiritual development might have taken a very different direction. The role performed by Mullā Ḥusayn and other early believers, who directed this undefined and still unintelligible inspirations of the Bab into the preconceived framework of Shaykhi prophecies, was far greater than is usually attributed to them. The ideas contained in the Bab's writings soon created a theoretical system different from that of Shaykhi or in some instances Shiʿite thought. Yet in practice the early believers elaborated on these ideas, mostly with the benefit of their own Shaykhi outlook.

The position of the early believers in the writings of the Bab is highly exalted, partly in order to stress this very contribution. Qatīl's enigmatic remark that the Shaykhi ṭullāb first entered Shiraz without Sayyid ʿAlī Muḥammad's consent and "submitted themselves to his claim" can be taken as another evidence of their crucial role.[124] Shaykh Sulṭān Karbalāʾī only confirms this: If the early believers had not entered "the land of safety [*balad al-amn*: i.e., Shiraz], the cause of God would never have emerged. When God's will rested upon that, then they were sent toward the Imam [i.e., the Bab], may peace be upon him."[125]

The Early Disciples

In the days following his meeting with the Bab, Mullā Ḥusayn gave lectures and public sermons in the mosque of Īlkhānī, in the neighborhood of Sayyid ʿAlī Muḥammad's house, where he also took up his residence, and soon managed to attract a number of Shaykhis. Besides Mīrzā Aḥmad Shīrāzī, who attended these meetings, Sayyid ʿAlī Muḥammad himself invited other merchants of the bazaar.[126] These sessions served the purpose of acquainting the Bab with other companions of Mullā Ḥusayn, who mostly stayed in the same mosque. It is likely that after the conversion of Mullā Ḥusayn, the Bab instructed him that prior to the time of his public proclamation, in the near future, the matter must remain secret to all but a few.[127] It is for this reason that Mīrzā Aḥmad noted: "Mīrzā ʿAlī Muḥammad used to attend the assemblage, and each of them [the Bab and Mullā Ḥusayn]

[124]Ibid. 520.
[125]*ZH* 249.
[126]*NH* 36; *Nabil* 65.
[127]*Nabil* 66–67.

evinced the utmost respect for the other. On leaving the public gathering, they used to retire to a small mosque near Ḥājjī Mīrzā ʿAlī Muḥammad's house, and there they busied themselves in composing and writing correspondence. No one at the time knew what they were doing, except one or two men who enjoyed their full confidence."[128]

Mullā Ḥusayn could have hardly concealed from his companions his dramatic change of attitude toward the Bab. When he was questioned by the rest of the party for the reasons of their prolonged stay in Shiraz, he replied: "I am stranded here." Referring to Rashtī's instruction, he added: "I was ordered not to Kirman but to Fars. . . I am inclined to think that this is the man whom the Sayyid [Rashtī] mentioned to me in his prediction about the appearance of the True One."[129] These revelations caused some commotion among the students, generally obedient to Mullā Ḥusayn. Mullā Ḥusayn was obliged, Hashtrūdī states, to direct his fellow travelers to the house of the Bab. "We had faith in you," said one of the students to Mullā Ḥusayn. He replied, "Here is he whom we had been seeking."[130] Hashtrūdī continues: "Then those ʿulama who supported his [the Bab's] claim argued with those who denied it, until each with a measure in hand to examine the initiator of the manifestation, some with prophecies and others with difficult [theological] problems, came into his presence. In his presence whether by written verses or orally, each received his answer [even] before raising his prepared question, and the dilemma of each of them was resolved until they all recognized him. Then Mullā Ḥusayn called upon Mullā ʿAlī [presumably Basṭāmī]: 'This is the one about whom you blamed me.'"[131]

Other sources also attribute the conversion of the rest of the group to guiding dreams, telepathy, and unmediated perceptions. Yet there is little doubt that gatherings in the Īlkhānī mosque and discussions with Mullā Ḥusayn were instrumental in assuring them that the Bab "in truth was the very man whose advent was promised." This was a slow process. The Bab himself states in the *Bayān*: "For forty days none except first the letter *sīn* [cipher name for Mullā Ḥusayn] believed in the *bā* [i.e., the Bab] and then gradually the other letters of *bismillāh* ["*Bismillāh al-raḥmān al-raḥīm*"] adorned the cloak of recognition, till the first unit (*vāḥid*) was completed."[132]

Regardless of the metaphors implied in this passage,[133] the above remarks make it certain that between 5 Jumādā al-Ūlāʾ and 15 Jumādā al-Thānī/22 May and 2 July eighteen individuals were initiated. The second believer, after Mullā Ḥusayn, was Mullā ʿAlī Basṭāmī, who recognized him

[128]*Ahmad* 448–49.
[129]Ibid. 449 n.
[130]*Muʿīn* 65.
[131]Ibid.
[132]*Bayān* VIII/15, 300.
[133]See below, this chap.

"by hearing a single verse without any other proof."[134] Basṭāmī's rapid conversion is of little surprise. Like many after him, he detected in the Bab an ideal location for a preconceived image. It conveniently fit Sayyid ʿAlī Muḥammad because it was already liberated from the restraints of orthodox religion without being isolated from its Shiʿite setting. In allegorical language the Bab identified Mullā ʿAlī Basṭāmī as ʿAlī, the First Imam, who "returned to earth with all those who believed in him, and he is the second who believed in the Point after the letter *sīn*." The Bab himself is the Point in the letter *bā* of "*Bismillāh al-raḥmān al-raḥīm*,"[135] so Mullā Ḥusayn is the *sīn* and Mullā ʿAlī and "all those who believed in him" the remaining seventeen letters of the original Arabic verse.[136]

But who were these other believers? Only two sources, Qatīl and, much later, Nabīl Zarandī, provide us with anything close to a comprehensive list. Although no clear chronological order can be established, it is evident from Qatīl that in addition to Mullā Muḥammad Ḥasan and Mullā Muḥammad Bāqir Bushrū'ī, who were counted among the believers after Mullā Ḥusayn, the six remaining members of a seven-man group headed by Basṭāmī were also converted.[137] In an order that apparently corresponds to their conversion they are named as follows: Mullā ʿAbd al-Jalīl Urūmī (Urdūbādī), Mullā Muḥammad ʿAlī Qazvīnī, Mullā Ḥasan Bajistānī, Mullā Muḥammad Mayāma'ī, Mullā Aḥmad Abdāl Marāghihī, and Mullā Maḥmūd Khu'ī. Following them came four others: Sayyid Ḥusayn Yazdī, Mullā Muḥammad (Rawża-Khwān) Yazdī, Mullā Muḥammad Bāqir Tabrīzī, and Mullā Muḥammad ʿAlī Bārfurūshī (later known as Quddūs).[138] Altogether Qatīl names fourteen individuals. But this list in some points contradicts Nabīl Zarandī, who believes that Basṭāmī's group numbered thirteen and seventeen individuals were in Shiraz in all.[139] Although Qatīl is the oldest of all the sources his list is not the most comprehensive; for instance, it omits Mullā Yūsuf Ardabīlī, who reportedly was present in Kūfa and Shiraz. Indeed, if we accept that the Bab's reference in 1263/1847 to a nineteen-man unit that actually existed in 1260/1844, then it is necessary to add the extra three individuals on Nabīl's list: Mullā Yūsuf Ardabīlī, Mullā Khudābakhsh Qūchānī, and Mullā Saʿīd Hindī. The eighteenth was the celebrated Babi heroine Zarrīn Tāj Baraghānī (Qurrat al-ʿAyn and later Ṭāhira, sister-in-law of Qazvīnī) whose name was included among the believers in her absence.[140]

[134]*Nabil* 69.

[135]"In the name of God, the merciful, the compassionate," this Qur'ānic rubric in the opening of all sūras received special attention from hermeneutists as having incapsulated the entire content of the Qur'ān.

[136]*Bayān* I/3, 8.

[137]*Qatīl* 510; cf. 520.

[138]Ibid. 520.

[139]*Nabil* 66; cf. 80–81.

[140]*Qatīl* 526. Nabīl also added to his list Mullā Hādī Qazvīnī (son of ʿAbd al-Wahhāb and brother of Mullā Muḥammad ʿAlī) instead of Mullā Muḥammad Mayāma'ī, but in light of

The discrepancies in the identity and number of believers are due in part to the secrecy that covered all the activities of the early days. The Bab's later attempts to put his early believers into a hierarchical order and the difference of opinion that arose over this distinction may have contributed to these inaccuracies. What is clear, however, is that from fourteen to seventeen people recognized the Bab.[141] Nevertheless, ideological disagreements persisted within the Shaykhi group. There are indications that not all those in the party recognized the Bab. He warned Mullā Ḥusayn that "certain ones among them will be counted, in the sight of God, as His chosen and favored disciples. Like the others they will tread the middle way. The fate of the rest will remain undeclared until the hour when all that is hidden shall be made manifest."[142] This is further clarified by Shaykh Sulṭān Karbalā'ī:

> All those who set out [from Kūfa] and went on the quest to achieve the faith were among the forerunners [*sābiqīn*] but yet there were two persons from Kirman who were not amongst those who reached this cause and when [the Bab] revealed himself and the cause was delivered to them, they did not accept it and said that "we did not intend to recognize anyone but Ḥājjī Muḥammad Karīm Khān in succession to the Sayyid [Rashtī]." Hence they left the forerunners and distanced themselves from them. [The Bab] said to his First Believer, "Tell those two souls who are traveling to the land of malice that they are searching in vain."[143]

Ḥājjī Muḥammad Karīm Khān Kirmānī no doubt posed a serious challenge to the Bab. But even in the early days, Sayyid ʿAlī Muḥammad's appeal seems to have gone beyond the Kūfa group. Some of the early converts might indeed have been informed directly of the proclamation of the Bab, or at least of its possibility. All the sources agree that Mullā Muḥammad ʿAlī Bārfurūshī (Quddūs), who was the last to be counted among the early believers and was later entitled by the Bab as the Last Letter in the Name of

---

what Qatīl says about the former (that in spite of his brother's vigor, "he was in darkness") and of the fact that in the later years he never showed any serious interest in the movement (*ZH* 306), we can assume that he was not among the early believers. The preachings of Mullā Muḥammad Mayāma'ī in his home town Mayāmay, on the other hand, increases the probability of his being in this group. Strangely enough, of other persons in Nabīl's list besides Mullā Hādī, Mullā Saʿīd Hindī and Mullā Khudābakhsh Qūchānī either remained inactive or, in the case of the former, completely obscure. For the circumstances of Qurrat al-ʿAyn's conversion see below, chaps. 5 and 7.

[141]The facsimiles of the nineteen "tablets" that appear in the beginning of the English edition of *Nabil* and are described as the Bab's "autograph tablets addressed to the Letters of the Living" (xxi) do not bear the names or the identities of the Letters and appear to have been written by the Bab toward the end of his life. "The nineteenth Letter of the Living" which is described as "the Bab himself," could not logically exist, as *ḥayy* is numerologically equal to 18. It seems that in this "tablet" he refers to himself as *haykal*. Besides the largely undiscovered information given in *Qatīl*, up to very recently before the publication of *Nabil*, even the identity of most of the Letters was not known. See, for example, Azal's reply to Browne (*NH* 417) and *RPAC* 277–79.

[142]*Nabil* 66.

[143]Maktūb in *ZH* 249.

God (*Ismallāh al-Ākhir*) and the Other Point (*Nuqṭat al-Ukhrā*), came to Shiraz not in the company of Mullā Ḥusayn or Basṭāmī but directly from Mazandaran.[144] He was a student of Rashtī who, after spending some time in the ʿAtabāt, had returned to Bārfurūsh prior to his teacher's death. His arrival in Shiraz toward the end of Jumādā al-Ūlā/June may not have been accidental. It has been said that while passing through Shiraz on his way to the Mecca pilgrimage, Quddūs owing to his previous acquaintance with other Shaykhis, became aware of the Bab's claim and eventually recognized him.[145] However, it is unreasonable to think that Quddūs had started his journey to Mecca seven months prior to the actual time of the pilgrimage without taking into consideration the possibility of his having some previous knowlege of Sayyid ʿAlī Muḥammad and perhaps intending to join the others.[146]

Qatīl's reference to three other individuals, Sayyid Ḥusayn Yazdī, Mullā Muḥammad Yazdī, and Mullā Muḥammad Bāqir Tabrīzī, who joined after the "seven-man group," may also indicate their independent decisions.[147] Āqā Mīrzā Ḥaydar ʿAlī Uskūʾī reports that Mullā Aḥmad Abdāl Marāghihī, another of the early believers, "before the proclamation [of the Bab] took up his staff and set out from Marāghih to Shiraz where he was honored [by visiting the Bab]."[148] This too may reflect some advance knowledge of the Bab's. Finally, the circumstances of Qurrat al-ʿAyn's conversion suggest that she had been informed by other Shaykhi students of the search for the Promised One when she first arrived in the ʿAtabāt sometime in late 1259/1843–1844. As she herself hints, she had a vague idea of the possibility of the revelation in Shiraz.[149] The letter that she gave to Mullā Muḥammad ʿAlī Qazvīnī, her brother-in-law, to be delivered to the Promised One can also be seen as a sign of this previous awareness.[150]

The actual part played by the early disciples differed from one individual to another and to some extent was inconsistent with the theoretical hierarchy set up by the Bab. The sources provide only limited information on the early believers' geographical distribution, social background, and past religious affiliations, but some general observations are possible. Of the eighteen, seven were from Khurasan, five from Azarbaijan, two from Qazvin, two from Yazd, one from Mazandaran, and one from India. Shaykhis enjoyed a high degree of popularity and following in both Khurasan and Azarbaijan provinces. In Qazvin, Yazd, and Mazandaran (in the city of Bārfurūsh in particular), Aḥsāʾī's students were active. The seven

144 *Nabil* 59; *Muʿīn* 63–64.

145 *Muʿīn* 63–64.

146 Moreover, it is unlikely that a humble mulla like him could have afforded the high cost of pilgrimage to Mecca.

147 *Qatīl* 520.

148 *Tārīkh-i Amrī-yi Azarbāījān* 2.

149 *Nabil* 314.

150 *ZH* 494.

Khurāsānīs and three of the Āzarbāījānīs originated in large villages or semirural towns; the remaining seven were from commercial and provincial centers.[151]

With the exception of two, all the disciples were from humble or relatively modest backgrounds, mostly from families similar to Mullā Ḥusayn's. Quddūs was the son of a poor rice cultivator on the outskirts of Bārfurūsh.[152] Sayyid Ḥusayn Yazdī was the son of a low-ranking Shaykhi mulla.[153] Basṭāmī may have come from a small landowning family.[154] Mullā Muḥammad Rawża Khwān Yazdī, as his name suggests, was a professional reciter of the Shiʿite tragedies. Mullā Muḥammad ʿAlī Qazvīnī and Qurrat al-ʿAyn were the only exceptions coming from families of high-ranking mujtahids.[155] Their relatively homogeneous background no doubt had some bearing on the early disciples' social coherence, and in due course influenced the pattern of conversion in the early Babi community.

In the course of the first four years, up to the time of the Badasht gathering (Rajab-Shaʿbān 1264/June 1848) and the events that led to the upheaval of Ṭabarsī, the early disciples hardly had the opportunity to act collectively or indeed to implement a common policy. Their efforts and activities were largely guided by their own individual initiatives. According to their actual contribution to the progress of the movement, they can be divided into four groups. First are those who played leading parts, both by converting new individuals and by expounding the Babi doctrine: Mullā Ḥusayn, Mullā ʿAlī Basṭāmī, Qurrat al-ʿAyn, and Quddūs. Second are those who played a major part in the expansion of the movement but could not be defined as leaders: Jalīl Urūmī, Muḥammad ʿAlī Qazvīnī, Aḥmad Abdāl Marāghihī, Muḥammad Bāqir Tabrīzī, Yūsuf Ardabīlī, Muḥammad Mayāma'ī, and Sayyid Ḥusayn Yazdī. Ḥasan Bushrū'ī, Muḥammad Bāqir Bushrū'ī, and Maḥmūd Khu'ī, who made up the third group, did not play an important part in the course of the events, but remained dedicated Babis. Fourth are those who remained totally inactive or obscure, or else defected from the Babi ranks: Muḥammad Rawża Khwān Yazdī, Khudābakhsh Qūchānī, Saʿīd Hindī, and Ḥasan Bajistānī.

With the exception of the limited success of the Bab in converting new individuals to the movement, the main burden of advocating the new creed rested on the shoulders of the first group. In cooperation with the members

[151]There is no indication of the origins of Saʿīd Hindī. Being from Shiʿites of northern India, he may have originated in Lucknow, where the Shaykhis enjoyed some following.

[152]*NK* 199.

[153]*ZH* 459.

[154]*Qatīl* 524.

[155]He was the son of Mullā ʿAbd al-Wahhāb Qazvīnī. (See below, chap. 6.) *Qatīl* (526) points out that he was not typical of the sons of eminent ʿulama and did not show their usual ambition to inherit their fathers' positions. He compares Mullā Muḥammad ʿAlī with sons of other important mujtahids of the time, whom he accuses of being ambitious and preoccupied with worldly affairs.

of the second group, as well as other important figures who later joined the movement, they created a network that, though small, was active enough to expand the movement even beyond the community of the Shaykhis.[156]

The two elements of geographical distribution and social background are complementary to the religious bonds of the early disciples. Though there are various references both in Babi and non-Babi sources to the theological knowledge and steadfastness of senior students, there is no clear indication to confirm their ijtihād. However, it is likely that a few of the leading believers, who had already returned home after years of study, acquired their authorizations. A few of them may also be classified as senior students near completing their studies.

Except for Sayyid Ḥusayn Yazdī, Mullā Muḥammad Qazvīnī, and Qurrat al-ʿAyn, the past religious affiliation of the early disciples' families is not clearly known. In most cases they themselves were converted to Shaykhism either when they were still in their home towns or in the early stages of their studies in such provincial centers as Isfahan, Mashhad, or Tabriz. In almost all cases their earlier interest in Shaykhism was followed by study under Rashtī—an indication of the importance of the local ʿulama in recruiting students for the Shaykhi circle in the ʿAtabāt.

Strong chiliastic aspirations among early Babis may correspond to preexisting sectarian elements. It is not unrealistic to assume that Mullā Jalīl Urdūbādī (Urūmī), who came from an Ahl-i Ḥaqq community in Azarbaijan, had at one stage been exposed to the teachings of a messianic preacher like Mullā Ṣādiq Urdūbādī.[157] Some of his disciples might have joined Rashtī's circle in Karbalāʾ, and Mullā Jalīl could have been one of them. His longing for the Ẓuhūr apparently inspired a risāla by Rashtī, in reply to his questions.[158] His enthusiasm was shared by other Āzarbāījānī students. A yearning to be in the presence of the Qāʾim combined with scrupulous observation is evident in Mullā Yūsuf Ardabīlī, for instance. As *Nuqṭat al-Kāf* relates, for three years, on the basis of a treatise that Rashtī wrote in reply to his queries on the identity of the bāb of the Imam, Mullā Yūsuf examined all the possible candidates before finally recognizing Sayyid ʿAlī Muḥammad in Shiraz.[159] Even at the time of Rashtī, Mullā Yūsuf freely preached ideas that were considered extremist (*ghulūw*). This free advocacy, particularly attributing the status of the Promised One to Rashtī himself, caused many to accuse him of being a *ghālī* (extremist) and even a heretic. Following some students' protests, Rashtī was forced to intervene and denounce Mullā Yūsuf. Later he warned him against revealing "secrets" that

[156]Of the fourteen individuals mentioned in the first three groups above—with the exception of Mullā ʿAlī Basṭāmī, who died in captivity (see below, chap. 5) and Mullā Muḥammad Bāqir Tabrīzī, who died a natural death—all were either killed in Ṭabarsī or executed in 1268 in Tehran.

[157]See above, chap. 2.

[158]*ZH* 47.

[159]*NK* 104.

are only granted to adepts, by referring to a ḥadīth by Jaʿfar Ṣādiq: "Whoever reveals our secrets, suffers the agony of the sword."[160] Mullā Mahdī Khu'ī, brother of Mullā Maḥmūd, another of the early believers, who was also accused of ghulūw, was strongly condemned by Rashtī and even threatened with expulsion from the Shaykhi circle.[161]

In Khurasan, we have already noted Mullā Ḥusayn's possible Ismāʿīlī connection which may also be applicable to Mullā ʿAlī of Bajistān, a small town in Quhistān close to Bushrūyih. The paucity of details on this often most hidden aspect of Babi history, plus our insufficient knowledge on the pattern of sectarian diffusion throughout Iran, denies us any firm conclusions. But even the above examples, in the appropriate context, suggest a realignment of the old millenarian aspirations in the new body of the Babi movement. With little hesitation we can suggest that behind most leading Babi figures, if not all the Babi converts, lay a latent heterodox affiliation in one form or another.

Mullā Muḥammad ʿAlī Bārfurūshī, Quddūs

The life of Mullā Muḥammad ʿAlī Bārfurūshī provides an excellent example of the evolution from latent expectation imbedded in socioreligious sectarianism to manifest messianic action. He was born in circa 1235/1819–1820[162] to a humble family of rice cultivators from Āq-rūd, a small hamlet on the outskirts of the thriving commercial Caspian town of Bārfurūsh. His father, Āqā Ṣāliḥ, and his relatives were "poor and devoid of wealth."[163] Residing in the Niʿmatī section of Bārfurūsh, a city sharply divided along sectarian lines, his family paid allegiance to the popular

[160] *Muʿīn* 43–44.

[161] *Nabil* 25. To this group of believers from sectarian backgrounds we may add Mullā Aḥmad Abdāl Marāghihī, whose curious middle name Abdāl may suggest a Sufi-Ahl-i Ḥaqq connection. For hierarchical connotations of this term see *EI*²: ABDĀL (by H. J. Kissling) and Tahānavī *Kashshāf* I, 146–48.

[162] Different dates are given for his birth: 1231/1815 (*ZH* 406); to 1238/1822 (*Nabil* 72). *NK* (208) specifies that at the time of his execution in 1265/1849 Quddūs was thirty years old, which makes 1235/1819 the most plausible date since it corresponds to the internal evidence in Muḥammad ʿAlī's own writings (*ZH* 413).

[163] *ZH* 413, citing Quddus' second letter to Saʿīd al-ʿUlamā', Persian, written circa 1260/1844. *KD* (42) is certainly in error to identify an "affluent and noble" Ḥājji Mullā Mahdī Bārfurūshī as Muḥammad ʿAlī's father. *Kazem Beg* VII, 334, n. 3, confuses Mullā Muḥammad ʿAlī's father with Sayyid ʿAlī Muḥammad's father (see above, chap. 3 n. 3). No trace of the account of Shaykh ʿAjam (a narrative of the event of Ṭabarsī and some biographical details on Quddūs in Māzandarānī dialect), used by Kazem Beg, can be found except for references in Bernard Dorn's "Nachträge zu dem Verzeichniss der von der Kaiserlichen öffentlichen Bibliothek erworbenen Chanykou'schen Handschriften" in *Bulletin de l'Académie Impériale des Sciences de St. Petersburg* IX (1865) 202–31. For full discussion see Momen, *Religions* 15–16, 535. Āq-rūd was located on the extreme eastern end of Bārfurūsh. *Kazem Beg* (VII, 334, n. 3) gives the quarter of Chahārshanbih-pīsh as Quddūs' birthplace. For some details of the above locations see P. Ḥusaynzādih *Shahr-i Bābul* (Tehran, 1343 Sh./1964) 72, 103–4. This monograph contains some useful details on the geographical history of Bārfurūsh.

Shaykhi leader Muḥammad Ḥamza Sharīʿatmadār Bārfurūshī.[164] Young Muḥammad ʿAlī seems to have spent part of his childhood as a house servant in the service of Sharīʿatmadār.[165] Presumably with the latter's encouragement, the bright youngster, when about twelve, was sent to a madrasa in the nearby town of Sārī.[166] Sometime in the mid-1830s, he joined a small group of students in Mashhad, which among other future Babis also included Mullā Ḥusayn Bushrūʾī.[167]

At the age of eighteen Muḥammad ʿAlī left for Karbalāʾ, where for four years he was an affiliated student to Rashtī's circle. He "used to sit at the last row and at the end of lectures rise up and leave before others."[168] Like other Shaykhis, he observed hermetical retreats in the mosque of Kūfa. Most of his adolescence was spent in the ʿAtabāt, where he developed a curious sense of affinity to the shrines of the Imams. "I was brought up in the holy land," he later remarked, "and grew up on that pure soil and reached what was bestowed upon me by my Lord on that sublime threshold."[169] After nearly thirteen years of study, Muḥammad ʿAlī returned to his home town, in 1259/1843.

As became more apparent over the following months, his return was more than a simple homecoming. Soon Muḥammad ʿAlī found himself as a chief target in a secret war waged between his previous mentor, Sharīʿatmadār, and his rival, the Uṣūlī mujtahid Mullā Saʿīd Bārfurūshī, better known as Saʿīd al-ʿUlamāʾ.[170] The existing Ḥaydarī-Niʿmatī division had

[164]The old center of Bārfurūsh appears to have been originally surrounded by a cluster of agricultural districts, which were gradually integrated into the city. Altogether, Bārfurūsh was a conglomerate of more than sixty quarters. Ḥusaynzādeh *Bābul* 104–5 gives the list and rough location of the major quarters. Neither the affiliation of the quarters nor the Ḥaydarī-Niʿmatī dividing line is clear. However, if the Bāzār avenue, as in many other Persian cities, is the dividing line between the two factions, then the mosque of Kāẓim Bag (*Bābul*, 58–59), the headquarters of Sharīʿatmadār (*ZH* 435), and the quarters east of this mosque would be Niʿmatīs. That includes Chahārshanbih-pīsh and Āq-rūd. Accordingly, the mosque of Saʿīd al-ʿUlamāʾ in the center (adjacent to Jāmiʿ mosque) (*Babūl* 51), and the quarters in the west of Bāzār avenue would be Ḥaydarīs.

[165]*NT* III, 238. Muḥammad ʿAlī received some elementary education in Bārfurūsh, possibly by some members of Sharīʿatmadār's retinue.

[166]*ZH* 413.

[167]*Fuʾādī* 74. According to this source, in the madrasa of Mīrzā Jaʿfar, Muḥammad ʿAlī swore an oath of fraternity with his classmate Āqā ʿAlī Riżā Shīrāzī, later a Babi merchant in Mashhad.

[168]*ZH* 406. Sharīʿatmadār maintains that Muḥammad ʿAlī never studied conventional sciences beyond basics but after many years of study in the madrasa it is hard to believe that he was not acquainted with advanced Shiʿite curriculum. His own writings show some grammatical errors but he is well versed in the Qurʾān and the hadith.

[169]Ibid. 408, first letter to Saʿīd al-ʿUlamā, Arabic, written circa 1259/1843.

[170]Though not a first-rank faqīh by scholastic standards, Saʿīd al-ʿUlamāʾ (d. 1270/1853) exercised extensive power in his home province, Mazandaran. His unrelenting hostility toward the Babis earned him his title from Nāṣir al-Dīn Shāh and recognition from Shaykh Murtażā Anṣārī, who in 1268/1851 acknowledged him as the ablest mujtahid in Iran and reportedly mentioned him for leadership of the Shiʿite community (see M. Anṣārī *Zindigānī va Shakhṣī-*

already acquired a new dimension in the Shaykhi-Uṣūlī polarity as each of the two rival leaders came to present the interests of his constituency. The support for Sharīʿatmadār, and later for Quddūs, in Niʿmatī quarters was broad, but perhaps not exclusive. It was based on personal loyalty rather than ideological conviction, although some heterodox affiliation cannot be ruled out.[171]

The significance of these urban tensions becomes more obvious when it is noted that in the mid-nineteenth century, Bārfurūsh was the main trade emporium in the Caspian region, with a growing volume of import-export trade with Russia. With nearly four hundred shops and four caravanserais, the busy market of Bārfurūsh housed a considerable body of merchants, petty traders, and shopkeepers. The chief agricultural product of the region was rice. Its production steadily increased as merchants of Bārfurūsh found this cash crop a lucrative export item in exchange for precious metals from Russia.[172] The hazy picture of an escalating social polarity in Bārfurūsh looms parallel to the rising fortune of the entrepreneurial merchant-landowners of the region.[173] It is only fair to assume that Sharīʿatmadār was the representative of the indigenous population of peasants and small landowners with seminomadic kinship ties, while Saʿīd al-ʿUlamāʾ and his clerical allies aligned themselves with the more affluent groups.[174] The growing tension in the city and its surroundings can thus to an extent be attributed to the efforts of the merchant-landowners to take fuller control of the economic market by exploiting sectarian loyalties.

The presence of a charismatic mulla like Muḥammad ʿAlī, with his "affability, combined with dignity and bearing," and meticulous observance of religious rites, could hardly remain unnoticed. "Whoever was intimately associated with him was seized with an insatiable admiration for the charm

yat-i Shaykh-i Anṣārī [n.p., 1339 Sh./1950] 74; cf. *TAS* II, 599, and *RA* 201–2). Most sources on the Ṭabarsī upheaval provide additional information, among them *ZH* 430–33 and *NK* 174–75, 201.

[171] Beside Shaykhi-Uṣulī division, the pattern of religious affiliation in Bārfurūsh is unclear. H. L. Rabino's reports in the 1900s (see A. T. Wilson *A Bibliography of Persia* [Oxford, 1930] 181–82, for the full list) speak of ʿAlīullāhīs (i.e., Ahl-i Ḥaqq). See Ḥusaynzādih, *Bābul* 93, and cited sources. We can assume that even by the mid-nineteenth century some Ḥurūfī texts in Māzandarānī dialect were still in circulation and were accessible to Mullā Muḥammad ʿAlī and other Babis of the province.

[172] For the trade and economy of Bārfurūsh during the mid-nineteenth century see M. L. Entner *Russo-Persian Commercial Relations, 1828–1914* (Gainesville, Fla. 1965); K. E. Abbott in *Cities and Trade* especially 11–12; C. MacKenzie *Safarnāmih-yi Shumāl,* ed. and trans. M. Ittiḥādīya (Tehran, 1359 Sh./1980) 80–113. The most extensive report during the 1840s is that of K. E. Abbott, "Narrative of a Journey from Tabreez along the Shores of the Caspian Sea to Tehran, 1844" F.O. 60/108, Abbott to Aberdeen, 23 August 1844, Tehran, no. 8.

[173] Abbott to Aberdeen, 26 July 1844, Rasht "Disturbances in Barfurush and in Eastern Caucasus."

[174] For Sharīʿatmadār's biography see *ZH,* 434–47; Ḥusaynzādih *Bābul* 139–42, and cited sources. For some evidence of Saʿīd al-ʿUlamāʾ's cooperation with the local and central governments see *NK* 154 ff., and *ZH* 430–33.

of the youth."[175] In his appeal to the public, as in many other respects, Muḥammad ʿAlī of Bārfurūsh was a redoubtable echo of ʿAlī Muḥammad of Shiraz. Though from a different social background and with bonds of loyalty to a community fundamentally different from Shiraz, he embodied many features apparent in the early Bab. Here too, the veneration of the Imam, the Lord of the Time, and a longing for his speedy Advent, exudes an aura of sanctitude. It is not surprising that the Bab, the Primal Point, should observe in Muḥammad ʿAlī, the Quddūs (lit.: the most holy), a reflection of himself; a companion *(ḥabīb)* and the Last Divine Name.[176] Neither is it unlikely that in his search for the true representative of the Imam Mullā Muḥammad ʿAlī should have acquired some vague knowledge of the sayyid of Shiraz even before his instant recognition of the Bab upon his arrival in that city.

After 1261/1845, when Muḥammad ʿAlī returned from Ḥajj, his reputation of sanctity had already earned him some popularity in Bārfurūsh. The support in the Niʿmatī constituency seems to have worried Saʿīd al-ʿUlamā' and other minor clerics in the surrounding quarters almost from the start. Quddūs' moral criticism of the mischievous ʿulama and his controversial theology soon betrayed his messianic yearnings. The open advocation of these views, expressed in a series of disputations between him and Saʿīd al-ʿUlamā', culminated in denunciation of Quddūs by the Uṣūlī jurist.[177]

What is known about these early controversies is largely drawn from a few surviving tracts by Quddūs in reply to Saʿīd al-ʿUlamā''s inquisitorial criticism.[178] With some clarity and skill Quddūs argues the continuity of divine emanation. "It is imperative that a deputy from God of the universe, may his name be exalted, should always be apparent among people. Otherwise, the ministry [of the prophets] and revelations of their scriptures would be futile. And this is a necessity for God and not for his people."[179] This explanation is given in the context of Imamate, but its tone clearly denotes a permanent implication. It is only by the renewal of this divine covenant, he argues, that "the problem of decay and infiltration of the corrupt and the tyrant into [the affairs of] religion" can be avoided.[180] During the Occultation of the Imam, the time of "the heaviest burden," the people are left with "the Book, the Traditions, and those who would understand them, those who embody the word of the Imam, peace be upon him, and what has been

[175] *Nabil* 183, citing Mīrzā Mūsā Nūrī, who in 1262/1846 met Quddūs in Tehran.

[176] Both titles were conferred upon him by the Bab. The latter appears in a visitation prayer composed for Quddūs and other martyrs of Ṭabarsī, INBA no. 64, 1–53.

[177] *ZH* (407) refers to one gathering in which Saʿīd al-ʿUlamā' was enraged by the attention the "little studied" Muḥammad ʿAlī received from the audience.

[178] All three letters by Quddūs, one Arabic and two Persian, cited in *ZH* 407–18, must have been written sometime in late 1263 and early 1264/1847 and 1848, over the course of few months. Some idea of Saʿīd al-ʿUlamā''s criticism can be sensed from allusions in these letters.

[179] *ZH* 409–10, second letter to Saʿīd al-ʿUlamā'.

[180] Ibid.

related from him. They are appointed by him as his proof as he himself stated, 'They are my proofs to you and I am the proof of God'; their command is his command and denial of them is denial of him and denial of him is denial of God."[181] Quddūs views the recognition of this divine proof as man's principal task:

> It is imperative for every person to examine, before himself and his God, all matters to which he commits himself, and above all in matters of religion, with all fairness of mind and firmness of reason. . . . If anyone puts forth a claim and presents proofs from the precise verses of the Book of God and also from akhbār, he then is rightful [in his claim] and his [claim] is justified amongst the wise and people of the faith. If on the other hand someone claims a position for which, may God forbid, he does not have a firm proof from the Book of God and from the reliable ḥadīth, to the above-mentioned groups his [claim] is weak and void.[182]

In the mind of Quddūs, the necessity for divine guidance and a sense of urgency for the coming of the Imam are firmly linked to the seeker's rational inquiry. This clearly exemplifies the outlook of that generation of Shaykhis who saw the recognition of the Bab as the outcome of a personal quest assisted by divine guidance. Both the seeker, and to some extent the claimant, are subject to this guided search. Such a position contradicts the Uṣūlī theory of *taqlīd* (emulation), as it denies the mujtahids' prerogative of "general deputyship" and their claim to exclusive religious guidance. Quddūs shares with the Akhbārīs their emphasis on the normative value of the Book and akhbār but distances himself from them as he underlines guided inquiry and human initiative. This search for certitude, Quddūs emphasizes, "could be fruitful if only it is benefited from the blessing of the Imam, may God hasten his glad Advent."[183]

Where did Quddūs himself stand in this search? He repeatedly insisted that he was no more than a "detached soul" who took refuge with "the clan of God." He condemned the mischief-makers who accused him of bad faith and frivolous fabrications. They are the "scum of the people" who because he refused to heed their base demands are now trying to defame him. The pleas of the persecuted seeker who questioned conventional wisdom of his time become louder when he declares:

> For what worldly desires are you harassing this adherent to God's clan? Though I enjoy no high status, in the eye of my forefathers, may peace be upon them, I

[181]Ibid.
[182]Ibid. 411.
[183]Ibid. In his third letter, in response to Mullā Saʿīd's further allegation concerning his unorthodox denial of "the proof of reason" and "action according to presumption," Quddūs argues that he approves the employment of the reason in matters of religion only to the extent that is permitted by Islam and all the people of the Book (415).

> am no less than the dispersed people of Israel. . . . I am a youth detached [from this world and oriented towards] the clan of God. . . . I do not know of any other refuge and retreat but to the Lord of the Time, may God hasten his Advent. . . . Neither have I claimed any cause, nor have I interfered in or disposed over anything. I have taken the path of Sayyid-i Sajjād [ʿAlī Ibn Ḥusayn, the Fourth Imam] peace be upon him, and it is going to be like this till God will reveal His command. . . . Leave me alone and let me retire in the solitude of my abode and engage in what is the tradition of my forefathers.[184]

The nature of these "baseless accusations" is not quite clear. Nor is the identity of the mischief makers and their "evil designs." No doubt other mullas—including Mullā Qāsim, the imām jumʿa of Āq-rūd—were instrumental in manipulating the public, and particularly the lūṭīs (brigands), against Quddūs. From the second day of his arrival in Bārfurūsh, he remarks, he was the subject of allegations and mistreatment. He acted with "utmost modesty" and had no desire to benefit from "what they possess of worldly luxuries," but nevertheless he was the target of "shameless slanders."[185] In spite of his appeals for opening a dialogue with the mujtahids, the growing concern over Quddūs' popularity must have encouraged the gradual formation of a coalition against him—a coalition that most probably took advantage of urban rivalries and recruited from the lūṭīs as well as the ṭullāb of Bārfurūsh's seven madrasas. Hence, even prior to 1264/1848, the seeds of the far broader conflict of Ṭabarsī had been sown. The chief actors—the nonconformist millenarian, the forces of established ʿulama supported by the state, the factional urban divisions, the conflicting economic interests—are all present.

It is difficult to doubt the sincerity of Quddūs' pleas for reconciliation and seclusion. Yet his growing impatience with the harassment and intolerance he was experiencing seems to have led him to a vision of a turbulent messianic revolution. A combination of suffering, nonconformity, and asceticism made him envisage himself as an active participant in the Ẓuhūr. Over the next few years, his role in the Babi messianic scenario became more explicit. Like the Bab, his position gradually evolved over the course of four years, between 1844 and 1848—first as one of the early disciples and member of the first Vāḥid; then in the days prior to Ṭabarsī as the bāb to Sayyid ʿAlī Muḥammad, who then claimed the status of Qā'imīya; and finally, in Ṭabarsī, as the Qā'im of Gilan.[186] Throughout most of this mes-

184Ibid. 413–14. "Forefathers" is undoubtedly a reference to the House of the Prophet. *Nabil* (71) states that Muḥammad ʿAlī's mother was "a direct descendant of the Imam Ḥasan [the Second Imam]."

185Ibid.

186Most sources on the Ṭabarsī episode refer intermittently to the above titles. Sharīʿatmadār's *Asrār al-Shahāda* (cited in *ZH* 438) refers to Quddūs as the second bāb, next to Sayyid ʿAlī Muḥammad Shīrāzī. *NK* (152–53), like most narratives of Ṭabarsī, gives him an exalted status equal to that of the Bab himself. The author of *ZH* (424) believes that during Ṭabarsī, Quddūs was identified as the Ḥasanī, the Nafs-i Zakīya (the pure soul) of the Shiʿite apocalyptic prophecies.

sianic evolution, Quddūs saw himself as the chief lieutenant of the Bab, and later a reflection of him—a role that in the Shiʿite prophecies is often assigned to Jesus.[187]

In his earlier years, perhaps even before becoming a Babi, Quddūs appears to have been fascinated with the personality of Jesus as portrayed in the Qur'ān, Islamic apocryphal stories, and perhaps even translations of the Gospel. Like the Bab, he too was inspired by Christ's apocalyptic role. He saw in the story of Jesus parallels to his own asceticism, suffering, and yearning for martyrdom.[188] In the days preceding Ṭabarsī he was recognized by the Babis as "the Spirit of the Messiah" who soon would descend in the "Green Island" and destroy the forces of the Antichrist (Dajjāl).[189]

Identification with Jesus also appears to have been deliberately emphasized by Quddūs in order to refute the "slanderous allegations" concerning his illegitimate birth.[190] Curiously enough, though, during Ṭabarsī days, he himself disowned his father. *Nuqṭat al-Kāf* relates that when Mahdī Qulī Mīrzā, the military governor of Mazandaran, sent Āqā Ṣāliḥ to the fortress of Ṭabarsī to plea with his son for cessation of hostilities, Muḥammad ʿAlī warned him: "Beware, I am not your son! Your son on that day when you sent him to collect fire-wood, lost his way and now is in such and such a town. I am Christ and I have appeared in the guise of your son and only chose you as my father out of expediency."[191] In all probability, Quddūs made up his own version of a familiar folk tale, fantastical as it sounds, to relieve his captive father from persecution in the Qajar military camp. Nevertheless, the assumption of being the return of Jesus is not inconceivable, even though the naïveté of the narrator's tone might have given it a popular color.

In Quddūs' mind this allegorical identification is interconnected with a nascent current of social concern. For him, God's new call is primarily addressed to the authorities and more particularly to the ʿulama. His behavior in Ṭabarsī illustrates the depth of his feelings toward the clerical establishment. His reply to Mahdī Qulī Mīrzā's inquiry about the nature of

[187]See Majlisī *Biḥār* XIII, chaps. 6, 11, and 12; *Ḥaqq al-Yaqīn* II, chap. 9; *EI*[2]: ʿĪSĀ (G. C. Anawatī) XII–XIII, and cited sources.

[188]There even seems to be a connection between his title "Quddūs" and the prophetic role model he chose for himself. This title is said to have been conferred upon him by the Bab. In his early writings, Muḥammad ʿAlī makes frequent references to *quddūsīya* as a divine attribute granted to the prophets and the Imams (compare with *NK* 152). The same concept is likely to be the origin of the Babi war cry during Ṭabarsī: "Praiseworthy and the most sacred is our Lord, the Lord of the angels and the spirit" *(sabbūḥun quddūs rabbanā wa rabb al-malāʾakat wa al-rūḥ)*. One can see in this an allusion to *rūḥ al-quds,* as the Holy Ghost is translated in Islamic sources.

[189]*ZH* 420–21, citing Nabīl Zarandī. This passage, directly quoted from his original Persian narrative, is one of many that in the English translation of *Nabīl's Narrative* are either summarized or omitted altogether.

[190]*NK* 199. It is likely that the charge of illegitimacy is one of the unlisted allegations in Muḥammad ʿAlī's writings. It is also possible that Quddūs' claims were deliberately misinterpreted by his opponents to tarnish his image.

[191]Ibid. 199–200.

the Babis' claims aptly summarizes his objectives: "Our dispute concerns religion. First the ʿulama must converse with us and understand our legitimacy and submit to it. Then the sultan of Muslims should obey and support the truthful religion and the subjects also should acknowledge [it]."[192] In spite of the Babis' constant efforts to open a dialogue with the ʿulama and their appeals to them "to understand the true cause" and "guide the people toward it," Quddūs goes on to say, "some of them paid no attention, some ridiculed, some chastised or harassed us, some incited people against us and made the king vengeful."[193] The tone of this letter, like many other of his writings, reflects his bitterness and impatience with the ʿulama. In an amuletic prayer composed for his Ṭabarsī companions, he declares: "My Lord! curse them with all the curse you sent down to the 'father of evils' and with all the curses with which you damned Pharaoh and his party."[194] In a similar prayer he makes his intention more explicit. "O Lord! make dominant over them your slave whom you have preserved [in order] to take revenge upon them."[195] This strong urge for vengeance on "enemies of God" and "those who foster oppression" sharpened over the four years after 1844, as persecutions, house arrest, and physical threats increased, culminating in banishment from his home town. He and many Babis of his time came to realize with great bitterness and disappointment that the only alternative to forced recantation was self-defense. When on 20 October 1848 he finally set foot in the fortress of Ṭabarsī, he was a long way from the conciliatory path of Sayyid-i Sajjād to which he earlier subscribed. He fought in self-defense with the conviction of a millenarian par excellence who saw himself waging the fitna of the Final Day against the forces of Dajjāl. Seven months later on 16 May 1849, he died in the public square of Bārfurūsh with no less conviction of a crucified messiah.[196] The verse on his signet ring read: "If thou seest me, [that] I am less than thou in wealth and children."[197]

Early Doctrine and Organization

The crucial role played by Quddūs and some other leading Babi figures can partly be explained in terms of the theoretical provisions embedded in

[192]The entire text of the letter paraphrased in *NK* 163–66.

[193]Ibid.

[194]*ZH* 429.

[195]Ibid.

[196]In a sermon entitled *al-shahādat al-azalīya* (the eternal martyrdom), written sometime in 1264/1848, Quddūs alludes to the suffering and death that await him and other fellow Babis: "and I will bury my soul with my own hand" (*NK* 198), perhaps a remote echo of Jesus forecasting his imminent death (John 12:7). No trace of this important sermon, which was addressed to Mullā Ḥusayn Bushrū'ī, has yet been found.

[197]Qur'ān XVIII, 39, cited in *ZH* 426. The full passage (verses 39–40) reads: "If thou seest me, that I am less than those in wealth and children, yet it may be that my Lord will give me

the new doctrine. To appreciate the way the idea of Ẓuhūr was conceived by the Bab and his early disciples, the formation of the Babi nucleus should be understood. Each and every member of the group, often regardless of his real identity, was assigned a theoretical function in the Bab's ideal order. The gradual evolution of this order had a direct bearing on the movement's expansion and to some extent was responsible for the problem of leadership, or indeed the lack of it. One of the Bab's earliest known references to the formation of the group is in a letter written in mid-1845: "After the death of the late Sayyid [Rashtī] someone like him must exist in their sect [Shaykhis] in every age. Nevertheless no one left the darkness except those humble men who emigrated from the Holy Land. They are recorded in the book of the True Imam as the most virtuous people, although outwardly no one pays attention to them."[198]

Here, the early believers are only described as the "virtuous people," without any other hierarchical distinction, yet the Bab acknowledged their importance as the main support for the expansion of his movement. Over the course of the next three years, as restrictions from outside and tensions from within the movement increased, the Bab's unpredicted isolation weighed further in favor of the early believers, a handful of the more active ones in particular. His writings and correspondence increasingly exalted his disciples with distinctive titles. Moreover, he entrusted his cause to the "guardians of the earth,"[199] an allusion which may indicate his intention to leave the practical aspects of his cause to his chief disciples.

In *Ṣaḥīfa-yi ʿAdlīya*, written in 1846 at "the height of grief and isolation" under house arrest in Shiraz,[200] the Bab elaborated his eschatological hierarchy on the model of the Shiʿite prophecies. Below the position of the Imam, he makes it essential for the believers to have the "cognition" of the two other successive groups, the leaders (*nuqabāʾ*) and the nobles (*nujabāʾ*). The nuqabāʾ are the closest to the Imam. "They are among the people and are intimate with them, but their identities are not known to people except to some of the nujabāʾ who know some of them."[201] They are the "bearers of the emanation" and responsible for the appointment of the nujabāʾ.[202] The conduct of "worldly affairs" is bestowed upon them. The nujabāʾ, on the other hand, are known to the people, but their real status is unclear.

---

better than thy garden, and loose on yours a thunderbolt out of heaven, so that it will be a slope of dust." The entire parable (33–43) is a warning for those who doubt the coming of the Hour.

[198]Letter in reply to Mullā Ibrāhīm Shīrāzī, INBA no. 91, XXXVI, 170–80. Also cited in *ZH* 283–86. The person to whom this letter is addressed is one of the group of three who later questioned the superiority of Mullā Ḥusayn and in due course defected from the movement (*Nabil* 161–62). Even from the very early days, the authority entrusted to Mullā Ḥusayn and the influence he exerted upon the rest of the members doubtless disenchanted some who perhaps knew the Bab prior to the party from the ʿAtabāt.

[199]Letter in reply to Sayyid Jaʿfar Shibr sometime in 1262/1846, INBA no. 91, 165–66.

[200]INBA no. 82, 139.

[201]Ibid. 188–89.

[202]Ibid. 189.

Their number is not certain but a few of them whose number is equal to "the soul of *hā'* [numerically equal to 7] are the closest to the sublime sight." They are hidden from the public, but the identities of some of them are divulged because of the hostility of some "devils in human guise."[203]

These enigmatic references indicate the necessity for creating a systematic order by borrowing from the existing terminology. The Bab tries to protect the movement from hostile forces by covering his own acclaimed position as well as that of his disciples. But he makes an important concession by entrusting "worldly affairs" to the hands of the nuqabā'. This graded scheme allowed representation of the Imam on a broader scale. More important, it made possible the sharing of responsibility, at least in practical terms, between the Bab and his leading disciples. In elaborating this system, the Bab may have been inspired by the role assigned to the nuqabā' in Shi'ite prophecies, or even by that of the disciples in the Gospel. Nevertheless, it was a new departure from the spiritual absolutism that was traditionally attached to the doctrine of Imamate and even deputyship.

These attempts in the Bab's writings encouraged speculations among the Babis over the identity of the nujabā' and the forerunners (sābiqīn).[204] The criticism directed against Mullā Ḥusayn and other believers of Shiraz subsequently made it necessary for the Babi writers to provide some interpretation of the Bab's allusions.[205] In response to mounting tension, the Bab himself made some attempts to clarify the position and the number of his early disciples. In a letter written around 1846–1847, he reasserts the status of his early disciples as the symbolic return of the holy men of the past. Borrowing the favorite allegory of Yūsuf (Joseph), "the best of the stories" in the Qur'ān, he maintains: "At the time of the revelation, the first who swore allegiance to [the Bab] was Muḥammad and then the Amīr al-Mu'minīn [The Commander of the Faithful, i.e. 'Alī] and then the Imams, on whom be peace. This is the secret of the verse, 'When Joseph said to his father: "Father, I saw eleven stars, and the sun and the moon; I saw them bowing down before me."'[206] The number of Yūsuf [i.e., the numerical value] is 156 which is [equal] to the number of *qayyūm* [everlasting]. This refers to the Qā'im of the House of Muḥammad and he who is *ḥayy al-qayyūm* [everlastingly living]."[207] The numerological connection between

[203]Ibid. 191–92.

[204]Also *sābiqūn*. The term is Qur'ānic (LVI, 10), also translated as "outstrippers" (see A. J. Arberry *The Koran Interpreted* [London, 1964] 560). The messianic connotation of these and other supporters of the Mahdī—nuqabā', nujabā', and *ṣulaḥā'* (the virtuous)—is highlighted in the Shi'ite prophecies. See for example the famous hadith of Mufaḍḍal cited in Majlisī *Biḥār*, XXIII/32. *Sābiqīn* occurs in some of the Bab's early writings such as the letter to Mullā Ḥusayn, Muḥarram 1261/January 1845, INBA no. 91, 14.

[205]Indications of disputes over the identity, status, and authority of some of the early believers are particularly visible in the 'Atabāt. Qurrat al-'Ayn's *Risāla* (*ZH*, 500), *Qatīl* 527–29, and the letter of Shaykh Sulṭān Karbalā'ī (*ZH* 249) all tried to provide answers. The criticism came from the Babis as well as the rival Shaykhis.

[206]Qur'ān XII, 4.

[207]INBA no. 58, 160–62.

the words *Yūsuf* and *qayyūm* was considered a Qur'ānic secret code for the Qā'im. Moreover the term *ḥayy* (living) in the Qur'ānic verse: "And faces shall be humbled unto the Living, the Eternal"[208] was interpreted as an allusion to those who were reanimated by the qayyūm and revered the Qā'im as the stars, the sun, and the moon worshiped Joseph.

In 1263/1847 he referred for the first time to the Ḥurūf-i Ḥayy (the Letters of the Living) as the members of the first Vāḥid of nineteen headed by himself. The significance of this new classification was twofold: in his theory the first Vāḥid was the basis of the All-Beings *(Kullu-Shay')*; and second, the Bab shared with the Letters of the Living the formation of this unit, hence sharing with them the gradual formulation of the new Babi religious order. In the *Bayān* he reveals the metaphorical identity of the Letters: "And for the Best Names, God specified in this cycle the names of the Letters of the Living, because there were fourteen sacred, hidden, and secure souls [which] together with the four gates or lights of the throne or bearers of creation, livelihood, death, and life total the number of ḥayy. These are the most proximate Names of God and the rest of the names will follow their guidance."[209] The numerological value of the word *ḥayy* is 18 and the word *ḥurūf* indicates the relation of each letter in alphabetical system with the position of each member of the group.[210] The word *ḥayy*, on the other hand, means not only living and alive but also clan or tribe. Thus, a sense of group loyalty as well as regeneration or rebirth is attached to the word.[211] The number 18 therefore represents the fourteen Infallibles—the Prophet Muḥammad, the twelve Imams, and Fāṭima—plus the four Archangels. The equivalence of these two values, namely the early disciples and the Shi'ite Infallibles, is not accidental. Representatives of the past revelation now are regenerated in the Letters of Ḥayy to witness the resurrection where each letter represents the corporal existence of a name. The whole of the first unit of *Bayān* deals with the Return of the Imams and

[208]Qur'ān XX, 110.

[209]*Bayān* II/2, 7.

[210]In the Babi doctrine *jafr* (numerology) plays an important role. The transposition of one letter in a word by another, representation of a secret name or a concept by one letter, and substitution of words with equal numerical values throw some light on certain problems in the Babi writings. In most cases these techniques were used to create cryptic codes for names and concepts that should have remained secret within the community of believers. Numerous references to *jafr* exist in the writings of Shaykhis including *al-Risāla al-Rashtīya* by Aḥsā'ī *(Fihrist* II, 260–62).

[211]*EI*[2]: ḤAYY (by J. Lecerf). In ancient Arab tradition the *ḥayy* alliance is cemented by magico-religious rites. It has a common Semitic origin (Genesis 3:20) and in the Qur'ānic context the term usually denotes life and living, as in XXI, 34: ". . . and of water fashioned every living thing" *(. . .wa-ja'alnā min al-mā'i kulla shay'in ḥayyin)*. In the seventeenth-century crypto-Jewish sect of the Dönmeh (the followers of Sabbatai Ṣevi) we find the use of the same term and its sacred numerological value. "In the nineteenth century," writes G. Scholem, "the Dönmeh assumed eighteen such reincarnations of the soul of Adam and the Messiah. The Eighteen Commands, the basis of the Dönmeh conduct, correspond to the Eighteen Benedictions which are the basic prayers of the daily Jewish liturgy; eighteen also possesses the numerical value of the Hebrew word "*hai*" (living)" *(The Messianic Ideas in Judaism* [New York, 1971] 146–48).

the Four Deputies in the Babi revelation. Each chapter refers to one Letter of Living as the return of one character, which also includes the return of those who were accompanying him.[212] In a letter written in 1266/1850 the Bab declares that his first two disciples were the return of the Prophet and ʿAlī to the earth: "The first who returned to the world was God's Messenger, who was the first messenger from the Qā'im, and then [came] the Commander of the Faithful, who carried out the mission to Būshihr, and he came to you and you did not recognize him."[213]

But this first unit (*vāḥid:* 19) is not complete without the Bab who is now manifested not only as the the Point of Bayān but as the essence of the seven letters. Both titles are indications of a new dispensation. Therefore the number 19 indicates the formation of the first unit and as the "Explanatory Unit" (*Vāḥid-i Mubīn),* it originates "All-Beings" (Kullu-Shay'): "In this revelation the result is the multiplication of the first unit, until the heavens, the earth, and that which is in between is completed . . . and all these units in their degrees end in the first unit. If you divide the whole universe into units, each one is supported by one above it, till it reaches the last one. This is the first unit which everybody is bound to recognize . . . It is evident that the secret of the unit flows through the Kullu-Shay."[214] The numerical value of Kullu-Shay' is 361, which is also equal to nineteen units of the value of 19. The Kullu-Shay' = 361 could only be constituted if the Explanatory Vāḥid = 19 is multiplied by its own value. But the first Vāḥid can be generated when ḥayy = 18 is completed by the Point (Nuqṭa). On the other hand, the Kullu-Shay' is associated with God's face, as in the Qur'ānic verse "All things [Kullu-Shay'] perish, except His face [*vajhahū*]."[215] The Bab, like the Sufis and Ḥurūfīs in the past, interpreted the "face of God" *(vajhahū* = 19) as the secret of All-Beings. Thus the secret of all things is concealed in the first Vāḥid and the secret of the Vāḥid is in the Point of Bayān which is the point of bā of the nineteen-lettered "*Bismillāh al-raḥmān al-raḥīm.*"

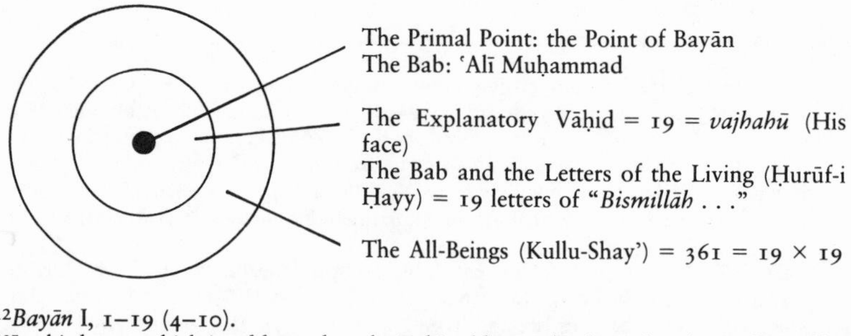

[212] *Bayān* I, 1–19 (4–10).

[213] In this letter, which is addressed to the Bab's elder uncle, the Bab refers to himself as the Qā'im, who has instructed his disciples, the reincarnations of Muḥammad and ʿAlī, to deliver his mission (*ZH* 224). *Ahmad* (451) confirms that at the time of the Bab's first proclamation it was said "that those who first believed in him were Muḥammad and ʿAlī" (cf. *NT* III, 40–41, and *Nabil,* 87–88).

[214] *Bayān* VII/8, 248.

[215] Qur'ān XXVIII, 88.

This theoretical framework served as a metaphor for what the Bab intended to create in reality. In the formation of the first Vāḥid he implied a collective responsibility shared by other Letters: "God the one and only provided for his own manifestation [i.e., the Bab's] eighteen souls who had been created before Kullu-Shay' for his soul [i.e., the Bab's] and established the sign of their recognition within the existence of all things."[216] The first Vāḥid and the eighteen successive units that follow in the process of the formation of Kullu-Shay' are the basis of the whole Babi organization. In this emanatory scheme, the Bab is the initiator of the first unit. However, it is the first unit that reflects the "face of God." The presence of a neo-Platonistic monism is unmistakable, but the Bab's system has some unique features. Unlike similar schemes among the Sufis, and closer to classical Bāṭinī currents of the past, the vāḥid system not only provides theological explanation but attempts to reconstruct the world, the All-Beings. It has an ambiguous but still recognizable worldly orientation. The organization of Kullu-Shay' on the basis of units was to create an administrative body upon which the future Babi community was to be built. The order of 19 therefore is to flow through all things: "The first unit multiplies until the heaven and the earth and in between are permeated. . . . Divide the world into units and put the support of one beneath from the one above until it arrives to that unit which is the first unit."[217]

Although this sacred order never materialized beyond the first Vāḥid, it created a justification for a collective leadership. The monistic tendency engrained in this outlook promoted the believer beyond the level of an ordinary convert. Thus, claims by some members of the first Vāḥid to the status of gateship (bābīya) and later even Qā'imīya during and after the Bab's time should be regarded as attempts to occupy the appropriate grades in this all-embracing order.[218]

Fulfilling the Prophecies

To justify the new Ẓuhūr, the Bab and his followers relied on past prophecies. On a few occasions, particularly in his later works, the Bab tried to minimize the significance of the Shiʿite prophecies in substantiating his claim. Nevertheless, neither he nor his followers escaped their overwhelming influence. In *Dalā'il-i Sabʿa* the Bab points out: "Since your orientation is still toward the past words of the "People of the House" [*Ahl-i Bayt,* i.e., the Prophet and the Imams], thus you search in the prophecies to find justifications. However, it is not right to establish the [truthfulness] of the possessor

[216] *Bayān* Exordium 2.
[217] *Bayān* VII/9, 248.
[218] For later attempts to create more units see *KD* II, 227; *RPAC* 277–78; and Shaykh Aḥmad Rūḥī Kirmānī (?) *Hasht Bihisht* (Tehran, n.d.) 284–85.

of the proofs and signs [i.e., the Bab himself] by means of the past Traditions since the return of the authors of these Traditions would be brought about by his words."[219] Yet in the same work, as in many others, he refers to Traditions related by Mufaḍḍal, Abū Lubayd Makhzūnī, Ibn ʿAbbās, to *al-Khuṭba al-Tuṭunjīya*, attributed to ʿAlī; to the Tradition of the tablet of Fāṭima; and to the prophecies about Azarbaijan and the prayers of *Nudba* (seeking repentance) and (the holy month of) Ramaḍān to make the same justification.[220] In his letter to Muḥammad Shāh he concludes: "And all the torments reported in the akhbār, which are cited on innumerable occasions, are now fulfilled."[221] These Traditions, whether in their original form or in more hermeneutical context suggested by Aḥsāʾī and Rashtī,[222] remained at the center of the early Babi propagation. In this adoption of the past prophecies, the Babis approached a more symbolic presentation of the Resurrection, yet the idealistic aspect of their interpretation was dominant enough to formulate the basic scenario for what they tried to fulfill.

Setting aside the discrepancies in the Shiʿite messianic Traditions, one can discern a distinction between the Day of Return and the Day of Resurrection. Majlisī argues that there is no clear evidence regarding the exact time of Rajʿa, yet it is most probable that it will take place just before Resurrection.[223] For the Babis, the Day of Return was the period when the Bab and his disciples, as the symbolic reincarnations of the past holy figures, fulfill certain tasks that were to be accomplished prior to the Resurrection. As the Traditions say, in the period of Rajʿa simultaneously with the appearance of the Qāʾim, "some of the best of the people and the worst of the evil will return to the earth."[224] The Prophet, ʿAlī, the other Imams, the saints, and the prophets of the past will return to accompany the Mahdi in his Insurrection (Khurūj). As most of the sources imply, this Return "is not applicable to all creatures—only those who are perfect in their beliefs or those who sunk in sheer blasphemy."[225] Thus, in this period prior to Qiyāma only the special Return (as opposed to general Return) would occur to allow the Mahdi and his companions to prepare themselves against the forces of evil.[226]

219P. 44.

220Ibid. 34–50.

221INBA no. 64, 103–26 (111).

222Examples of this approach appear in *Sharḥ al-Zīyāra* under the titles "About *Rajʿa* and *Ẓuhūr*" (III, 54–87) and "About the meaning of the time of *Rajʿa*" (III, 357).

223*Ḥaqq al-Yaqīn* 210–12, cf. 224. In a hadith related from ʿAlī, in reply to the question "whether the dead will rise before *Qiyāma* and die after it," he replied: "Yes, I swear to God that the blasphemy which will take place at the time of *Rajʿa* is far greater than anything which happened before" Majlisī (*Biḥār* XIII, 33; Persian translation 693). A Tradition related from Jaʿfar Ṣādiq interprets a Qurʾānic verse (XXVII, 85) and puts a clear distinction between the two events.

224Ibid. 212.

225*Biḥār* XIII, 33, Pers. 675.

226Ibid. Pers. 675–84; *Ḥaqq al-Yaqīn* 213–22. For a general outline of the circumstances leading to the Day of Judgment see Smith and Haddad *Islamic Resurrection*, 63–97 and cited

The well-known ḥadīth related by al-Mufaḍḍal ibn ʿUmar from Jaʿfar Ṣādiq[227] further clarifies the circumstances of the special Return. After the occurrence of the signs of the Hour, the Qāʾim will first appear in Mecca at the time of the annual pilgrimage. "He will stand between the *Rukn* [Pillar] and the *Maqām* [place (of Ibrāhīm)] and call loudly: 'O! My noble men and my companions and those whom God spared for the purpose of my assistance prior to the day of my appearance on the face of the earth, now come to me.'"[228] Thereupon God makes His call to be heard by His companions, wherever they may be throughout the world. Then, after declaring his manifestation to the people of Mecca and preaching "with truthfulness and wisdom," the Qāʾim will call his companions to come to his assistance. In response 313 Shiʿite noblemen (nuqabāʾ) will join him and swear to him the oath of allegiance. On his arrival in Madīna, he will put the inhabitants to a test, to examine their faithfulness to the House of ʿAlī. He then will severely punish the sinful and reward the faithful, who will all join him in his holy Insurrection. Then he will set out for Kūfa where, "on the land between Najaf and Kūfa," he will be received by his great ancestors. The Prophet, ʿAlī, his son Ḥusayn, and all other Imams, prophets, and saints, companions and firm believers, will be resurrected to join the Imam of the Age. From the outskirts of Kūfa, he will start his Khurūj against the forces of evil in order to revenge the wrong and oppression suffered by the House of ʿAlī and their supporters throughout time. From Kūfa, which will be his headquarters, the Qāʾim will lead his forces to the four corners of the earth. He will wage war against the Dajjāl and the Sufyānīs (i.e., the house of Abū Sufyān, the Umayyads), which are the symbols of evil, with the help of such other messianic figures as the Ḥasanī Youth *(al-Fatā al-Ḥasanī),* the Pure Soul *(al-Nafs al-Zakīya)*, and the warriors of Ṭāliqān, Khurasan, Yemen, and Arabia. After fierce battles, he will finally crush all the forces of his enemies, slay the Dajjāl, and conquer the world. Thus, "when the earth is filled with oppression and tyranny, he will rise to fill it with justice and equity."[229]

This schematic account of the events of the Final Day in the Mufaḍḍal Tradition differs in some details from numerous other Traditions on the overall picture of this eschatological event. No attempt has been made here

---

sources. Full discussion on the circumstances of the Mahdī's Return and relevant Traditions appears in Sachedina *Islamic Messianism* 150–79 (particularly 161–66 for the hadith of Mufaḍḍal). Also see *EI*²: ḲAʾIM (W. Madelung). A concise description of the Shiʿite prophecies on Return and Resurrection appears in Muḥammad Shafīʿ ibn Muḥammad Ṣāliḥ *Majmaʿ al-Maʿārif fī al-ʿAqabāt al-Khamsīn Yaum al-Qiyāma*, appendix to M. B. Majlisī *Ḥulyat al-Muttaqīn* (Tehran, n.d.) 2–164. This Persian account, possibly by a nineteenth-century writer (see *al-Dharīʿa* XX, 45), is an attempt to reach a logical order for the sequence of eschatological events as they appear in Shiʿite Traditions.

227 *Biḥār* XIII/32, 200–209; Pers. 640–75. Partly translated in *Ḥaqq al-Yaqīn* 225–33. Also Sachedina *Islamic Messianism* 74–76.

228 *Biḥār* XIII/32, 202; Pers. 645.

229 Ibid. XIII/1, 2; Pers. 5 citing Abī Ghanām al-Khādim who is relating from Imām Ḥasan ʿAskarī. Also related from the Prophet (ibid. XIII/6a; Pers. 64–65).

to unravel the complexities of this drama or to give an explanation for its discrepancies. What is intended, however, is to show the general impact of these Traditions on the thoughts and actions of the early Babis. It is clear from the account of Mufaḍḍal that some time prior to the Qiyāma the Mahdi commences his mission in Mecca, then marches to Medina and on to the Shiʿite Holy Land, where he begins his Insurrection. Throughout his campaign, whether in Kūfa, Najaf, or Karbalāʾ, he and his companions are engaged in a holy war (jihād). The Qāʾim, the one who shall rise with the sword, therefore, fulfill the historic vengeance that was postponed by the Imams to a proper moment in the future. With ruthlessness and severity peculiar to these prophecies, the Imam takes revenge upon the old enemies of his house. In Medina, he digs up the corpses of two Rightly Guided caliphs, Abū Bakr and ʿUmar, brings them back to life, and puts them on trial before hanging them and directing his supporters to set their bodies on fire. He then kills most of the inhabitants of Mecca and Medina, since "not even one in a thousand" would have believed in him.[230]

These events could not take place without the participation of the same holy persons who were involved in the original events. Hence the Prophet, ʿAlī, and, perhaps most important of all, Ḥusayn ibn ʿAlī are bound to return to the same scenes to witness, mostly passively, the ultimate redressing of historical wrongs. But in spite of all the fighting, the conquest of the world, and punishment of the oppressors, the final fate of the Qāʾim and the other holy figures in his company is not wholly clear. Though some Traditions envisage his long reign over the world and the total annihilation of all the evil forces, others foretell the Qāʾim's death in battle or at the hands of the evil-doers only a few years after his appearance.[231] Perhaps the essence of the Qāʾim, the Riser, lies not so much in the ultimate triumph of the truth over evil and justice over oppression as in his very act of rising.

In a symbolic reenactment, the Bab and his followers were to perform this eschatological drama. The Bab himself was convinced that though externally he was the Gate to the Imam, internally he was the long-awaited Imam himself.[232] So each of his followers was to fulfill the return of the Imams and the saints. The Traditions provided the general context, whereas the Shaykhi theory of nonmaterial Maʿād[233] permitted symbolic identification with past heroes. For instance, the Bab argues that the essence of the cognition of the Imams is the belief in their Return. *Baqīyatullāh* (the Remnant of God), who is the Imam of the Age, would lead the Return of the other Imams. "Belief in the Occultation is equal to the belief in the Return and the

[230]Muḥammad Shafīʿ *Majmaʿ al-Maʿārif* 49–53.

[231]*Biḥār* XIII/6; Pers. 66–67; *Ḥaqq al-Yaqīn* 185–86; *Sharḥ al-Zīyāra* III, 57–61; and *NK* 201. All the above sources supply different Traditions regarding the fate of the Qāʾim and his companions.

[232]See below, chap. 9.

[233]See above, chap. 1.

greatest sign of the Return is the emergence of the Commander of the Faithful [ʿAlī] whose body is wrapped in the cloak of light. Though he is evident, people are in darkness."[234]

The way the doctrine of Return was understood by the Bab and his followers, exemplifies the general tendency to arrive at a pragmatic framework. Seeking allegorical representation, the Babis tried to rationalize the course of action prescribed in the prophecies while ignoring their less unachievable and fantastic aspects. The Traditions drew the principal lines for the future plans of the movement: the disciples would disperse all through the Shiʿite lands to mobilize support for the Ẓuhūr; the Bab himself would travel to Mecca to declare the Advent of the Imam and the imminence of the Insurrection, though not necessarily revealing himself as the Mahdi; then he and his disciples, accompanied by other supporters, would gather in the ʿAtabāt to fulfill the next stage of the prophecies.[235]

In practice this meant the accomplishment of three main tasks: to inform those elements who because of a similar outlook were likely to recognize the Bab; to prepare the public for the general declaration; and to address the religious and secular authorities. These objectives were to be achieved by mobilizing the Shaykhis in the ʿAtabāt and inside Iran, preaching in public, admonishing the eminent mujtahids, and addressing the monarch and the state dignitaries. These measures were to be carried out simultaneously with the Bab's journey to Mecca and then to the ʿAtabāt, where he would declare the coming of the Mahdi and if prudent, divulge his real identity. Though this was never clearly pronounced, the ensuing assembly of the Bab and his followers in the ʿAtabāt was to be regarded as the commencement of the Khurūj proper.

The Shiʿite Traditions were doubtless the main impetus for the Bab and his followers, yet acquaintance with *Biḥār al-Anwār* of Majlisī[236] and with the Shaykhi treatment of these Traditions were not the only sources of inspiration. The speech the Bab delivered to his disciples in the summer of 1260/1844, just before departure to their assigned missions, also shows traces of Christian influence. He even drew a direct comparison with Christ and his disciples.[237] After expressing his hopes for the progress of the movement and emphasizing the moral strength and sacrifice needed for fulfilling their mission, the Bab cautions his followers to shun any hesitation or weakness that might lead them to retreat and silence. He then directly refers to the words of Jesus: "Ye are even as the fire which in the darkness of the night has been kindled upon the mountain-top. Let your light shine before the eyes of men. . . . You are the salt of the earth, but if the salt have lost its

[234]*Saḥīfa-yi ʿAdlīya* 183–86.

[235]Both the non-Babi sources, such as *Izhāq al-Bāṭil*, and the early Babi sources, such as *NK* 111 and Hashtrūdī (cited in *Muʿīn* 70), confirm this plan.

[236]*Dalāʾil-i Sabʿa* 50.

[237]*Nabil* 92–94.

savor, wherewith shall it be salted? . . . The Heavenly Father is ever with you and keeps watch over you. . . and will exalt you above all the rulers and kings of the world."[238] These and other remarks appear to be free references to the Gospel,[239] chosen particularly to underscore the approach of the millennium. "Scatter throughout the length and breadth of this land. . . .[240] I am preparing you for the advent of a mighty Day."[241]

This preoccupation with Christ was beyond the common Muslim knowledge of the time, which was mainly confined to the Qur'ān and other Islamic sources. He must have taken his references directly from the Gospel,[242] the study of which had given him an understanding of revelation and divinity somewhat different from that of the Qur'ān. No doubt the Bab found the personality of Christ appealing and his message of affection and self-sacrifice in conformity with his own. Traces of Christian doctrines of Trinity and Atonement is apparent even in his earliest works.[243] The idea of Second Coming, once blended with the apocalyptic role assigned to Jesus in Shiʿism, had become a very compelling model for a notion of a savior considerably different from the destructive and vengeful Mahdi of the Shiʿite prophecies. The Christlike Mahdi of the Bab saw salvation in suffering rather than in violent revanchism. It was this preoccupation with theophany that led some of his opponents to accuse him "of believing in Christianity and preaching the Trinity."[244]

Whatever the effect of Christianity on his ideas, the Bab was still firmly tied to Shiʿism. As has already been pointed out, the claims of bābīya and zikrīya were given a vague relationship to the ideas propounded by the past Shaykhi teachers. But it was apparent even from the early days that he postulated a position beyond what was usually intended by the Perfect Shiʿa. In his early works he tends to explain his status by attaching it to the sacred genealogy of the house of the Prophet. In the opening of the commentary on the *Sūrat Yūsuf,* he describes his relation to the holy chain of the Imams: "God ordained the revelation of this book as a commentary to *aḥsan al-qiṣaṣ* [the best of the stories] from the presence of Muḥammad, son of Ḥasan, son of ʿAlī, son of Muḥammad, son of ʿAlī, son of Mūsā, son of Jaʿfar, son of Muḥammad, son of ʿAlī, son of Ḥusayn, son of ʿAlī ibn Abī Ṭālib, to his servant. This is a perfect divine proof from Dhikr [Zikr] to the world.[245] This perhaps is the most direct reference the Bab made in his early

[238]Ibid. 92–93.
[239]Compare to Matthew V, 14–16 (cf. X, 27); XI, 27; V, 13; X, 11–14, 20 (also Luke IX, 5) respectively. *Nabil* makes no specific reference to any of the Gospels.
[240]*Nabil* 94, cf. Matthew XI, 3.
[241]*Nabil* 93, cf. Matthew X, 7, 23.
[242]See above, chap. 3.
[243]For instance in his commentary on *Sūra al-Baqara,* INBA no. 69, 298 and a letter in reply to questions by Mīrzā Muḥammad Saʿīd Ardistānī, INBA no. 69, 424.
[244]*Saḥīfa fī Sharḥ Duʿāʾihī fī Zamān al-Ghayba,* INBA no. 98, 87–94.
[245]*QA* (Browne Or. MSS.) folio 1/a; cf. Commentary on *Surat al-Baqara,* INBA no. 69, 294.

works to his relation to Muḥammad ibn Ḥasan the hidden Twelfth Imam. But still the authority that is entrusted to this Imam is purely hypothetical.

References to the Hidden Imam in the Bab's works, even in the early stages, allude to the status that inwardly he claimed for himself. When for instance in *Ṣaḥīfa-yi ʿAdlīya* he maintains: "The Hidden Imam, may God hasten his appearance, designated one of his servants among the Persians (*Aʿjām*) and nobles of the House [of the Prophet] to protect the religion";[246] or in a letter in 1261/1845 he places the position of babīya below the positions of prophets and guardians,[247] these statements are only intended to conceal his real claims. In his address to Muḥammad Shāh he emphasizes: "In the year *sittīn* [1260 Q.] God filled my heart with firm evidence and positive knowledge of Ḥujjat [the Twelfth Imam],"[248] yet shortly after, in 1263/1847, in an important passage in *Dalāʾil-i Sabʿa,* he explains his reasons for gradual publication of his claims: "See how the manifestation of God revealed himself [first] in the position of the bābīya of the Qāʾim and even reaffirmed in his first book the validity of the Qurʾān in order to prevent people from being agitated by the coming of the new book and the new cause and to persuade them to recognize and identify it with themselves and not to remain in the darkness or ignorance of what has been provided for them."[249]

Less than a year later, during the Tabriz trial of 1264/1848, after four years of hesitation and ambivalence, the Bab finally made his claim of Qāʾimīya public.[250] Gradual publication was designed to acquaint the public with the movement in successive stages and to protect the Bab and his followers from unnecessary criticism and opposition. Thus, for people outside the early Babi nucleus, in the early stages up to 1264/1848 Sayyid ʿAlī Muḥammad only professed to be the bāb to of the Twelfth Imam. Even his personal identity was supposed to remain a closely guarded secret until the time of open declaration.

The Babi disciples also tried to adopt this gradual tactic in their attempts to win over new converts by laying down four conditions for the veracity of a revelation[251] and then applying them to the claims of the Bab at various stages.[252] During the interrogation of Mīrzā Muḥammad ʿAlī Zunūzī (known as Anīs) in 1266/1850 in Tabriz, he confirmed that the gradual manifestation of the Bab from bābīya to ẕikrīya and then to Qāʾimīya and finally *Maẓharīya* (divine manifestation) was for "the gradual promotion of

[246]P. 158; cf. 146–50.
[247]Letter addressed to the Nahrī brothers, INBA no. 91, 137.
[248]INBA no. 64, 113.
[249]P. 29.
[250]*Nabil* 313. The text of the "tablet" on which he finally disclosed his claim to Qāʾimīya appears in *ZH* 164–66 and *NK* 209. See also *SAMB* 218–28 (219) and below, chap. 9.
[251]*NK* 106–7.
[252]Ibid. 111, 208.

the people's spiritual status."[253] No doubt it was in pursuit of the same policy and in response to differences of opinion over the Bab's exact claim that in 1845 in Isfahan Mullā Ḥusayn argued the necessity for the appearance of the Promised One in familiar Shaykhi terms.[254] In addition to the term *bāb,* he uses the term *ḥāmil,* which is often used by the Shaykhis to indicate the spiritual position of Aḥsā'ī and Rashtī as bearers of the knowledge or bearers of the pillar.[255]

The uncertainties as to the real status of Sayyid ʿAlī Muḥammad created a great deal of confusion. What Qatīl reported of the instructions of the Bab to his followers in Shiraz is typical of what most of the early Babis outside the close circle of the early disciples knew of the claims of the "deputy" the term by which he refers to the Bab.[256] He quotes a Babi as saying: "I have been ordered to explain only up to a point and neither to specify the person nor reveal the name . . . until the promised person appears in Karbalā' . . . and refuse to recognize him without proofs and arguments and without his claim being substantiated by Traditions of the Qā'im and the firm proof of the Qur'ān. Thus intensify your search and multiply your enquiry."[257] This indeed was the impression that the Bab and his disciples wished to transmit to the public and even to believers, prior to the assembly of the ʿAtabāt; a sense of anticipation for the appearance of an unidentified promised person.

Qatīl also maintains that at the time the Bab was practicing a policy of dissimulation.[258] Many indications in the early writings of the Bab bear out Qatīl's view. In Muḥarram 1261/December 1844, for example, he strongly advises Mullā Ḥusayn not to reveal his identity indiscreetly. "Do not reveal the word of your Lord to those who would deny it. . . . Observe the practice of dissimulation [*taqīya*] in order to avoid persecution and imprisonment."[259] In *Dalā'il-i Sabʿa* he declares: "Since I was aware of the limits of the public, I ordered the concealment of my name."[260] Similarly, in other early correspondence with his disciples he strongly forbade them to divulge his identity.[261]

The emphasis on prudence for protection and safety was often justified by stressing the precedents for it in the Shiʿite Traditions.[262] On a few occa-

[253] *ZH* 31–32.
[254] *Samandar* 163–64.
[255] Kirmānī *Izhāq al-Bāṭil.*
[256] *Qatīl* 510.
[257] Ibid. 511.
[258] Ibid.
[259] INBA no. 91, IV, 10–14 (13).
[260] P. 59.
[261] For instance in his letters to Mullā Muḥammad Ibrāhīm Shīrāzī, INBA no. 91, XXXVI, 170–80 (176) and to Salmān from Masqaṭ (Muscat), INBA no. 91, XVI, 52–56 (55). Both letters were written in mid-1216/1845.
[262] For references to taqīya in *Biḥār al-Anwār* see Shaykh ʿAbbās Qumī *Safīnat al-Biḥār,* 2 vols. (Najaf, 1355/1936) II, 468–70 under *kitmān* and 679–82 under *taqīya.* Also *Shorter EI:* TAḲĪYA.

sions the Bab quoted well-known Traditions on the necessity of concealment: "Taqīya is my faith and the faith of my forefathers. Anyone who does not practice taqīya has no faith."[263] With this advice in mind, the Bab stated in a prayer: "By your refined wisdom, my Lord, you made taqīya your command, thus people practiced it from the beginning of the Occultation up to now and that practice was the testimony to [people's] eagerness to come to your presence."[264]

Even with these justifications, the ambiguity of the position claimed by the Bab makes it hard to believe that he was fully confident of his own success from the outset. His reluctance to hold a consistent stand in the face of criticism and his constant reminder to his disciples to act with the utmost caution were major obstacles in the way of the movement. Until circumstances forced the Bab to abandon his previous hesitation and declare his claim of Qā'imīya in the trial of Tabriz, the concept of taqīya was not wholly absent from his words and actions.[265] The issue of dissimilation remained an unspoken point of difference in policy between the Bab and his followers. While he intended to introduce his mission in a gradual and rather secretive way, his radical disciples were willing to take the risk of opposition. This duality in method was the source of a twofold process in the history of the movement. As the Bab resigned himself further to an isolation that was forced upon him, his disciples resorted to an open appeal to the public, which eventually led them to confrontation with secular and religious authorities.

Notwithstanding the setbacks of the policy of concealment, the initial plan to introduce the claim of the movement in successive stages still seems to have been a sound device for drawing attention without causing agitation and distress. One might even speculate that if the dissemination of the movement had taken place in this manner, the Bab would have been able to save himself and the movement from persecution and ultimate destruction. In reality, however, the Bab's message, no matter how skillfully hidden in a labyrinth of metaphors, was, in its essence, in opposition to the whole Shiʿite concept of expectation.

Qayyūm al-Asmā': A Babi Manifesto

In the early stages of his revelation, the Bab regarded the commentary on the *Sūrat Yūsuf* as the major "Distinguisher" (*Furqān*):[266] "At the beginning

[263]Tradition related from Jaʿfar Ṣādiq cited in a letter in reply to the believers of Qazvīn written circa 1263/1847, INBA no. 91, XL, 192–94 (193). In the case of the Hidden Imam in particular, a series of Traditions strongly prohibit even mentioning his name (Majlisī, *Biḥār,* XIII/3, 7–8; Pers. 26–28).

[264]Letter to Sayyid Jaʿfar Shibr, INBA no. 91, XXXIV, 165–66.

[265]See below, chap. 9.

[266]*QA* III, folio 5/a.

of his appearance," writes the Bab, "he [i.e., himself] interpreted the sūra of his own name and entitled each chapter [of this commentary] with one verse from the Qur'ān, so that it be the indication that he is the Point of Furqān in the *bā* of '*Bismillāh*. . . .' "[267] The Bab saw "the best of the stories"[268] as the allegorical account of his own prophecy, not only because he found in himself a resemblance to Joseph[269] or because the story of Joseph contained the secret of taqīya, but also because he considered it "a lesson to men possessed of minds" and "an explanation of All–Beings [Kullu-Shay']."[270] In this long and complex commentary,[271] the Bab adopted a similar classification to the Qur'ān and attempted to open the gate of the "divine inspiration" and resolve the unintelligible problem of the Book. According to certain Traditions the secret of the Qiyāma is embedded in this sūra. The story of Joseph, "the true one" is a "sign for those who ask questions" because it warns that the Hour shall come upon those who doubt, "suddenly when they are unaware."[272]

Qayyūm al-Asmā' presents a concise outline of the Bab's claims as it was conceived in the early days. He is the "great remembrance,"[273] the "true guardian" and the "measure for cognition." Though he is only a youth of twenty-five,[274] God "has sent down light" to him so "he would be a direct line [between] the two worlds."[275] He is only a "slave of God" who "brought proofs from the Remnant of God, the Imam whom you are expecting."[276] His book is the "explanatory book" and the "new truth" and the "preserved tablet," which encompasses all the scriptures of the past[277] and is free from ambiguities. God taught him "the knowledge of the Furqān [i.e., the Qur'ān] and the Gospel and the Torah and the Psalms and other scriptures" and near his Lord he is "the Point of the secret *bā*."[278] It contains the "pure knowledge" that is the essence of Islam.[279]

[267] *ZH* 244.

[268] Qur'ān XII, 3.

[269] *Bayān* IV/4 (116). Traditions indicating some points of resemblance between the Qā'im and Joseph appear in *Biḥār* (citing Shaykh Ṣadīq in *Kamāl al-Dīn)* XIII/6, 11 Pers. 101–3.

[270] Qur'ān XII, 111. See also *Shorter EI²*: YŪSUF b. YA'ḲŪB.

[271] In a letter from Mākū concerning the date of this commentary the Bab writes: "This humble servant [of God] accomplished the Yūsuf commentary in forty days; each day composing a part of it, till it was completed. Whenever I intended to write something, the Holy Spirit [*Rūḥullāh*] was a support" *(ZH* 285).

[272] Qur'ān XII, 45, 7, 107.

[273] *QA* I, folio 26. This meaning of the *dhikr* (Zikr) as the word of the messenger of God originates in the Qur'ān (VII, 61, 67): "What, do you wonder that a reminder [dhikr] from your Lord should come to you by the lips of a man from among you?" Interestingly enough, the Bab refers to himself as the dhikr and not the person who would utter the dhikr. Aḥsā'ī recognizes Muḥammad, the Prophet, as the dhikr and 'Alī, the First Imam as the *dhikr al-akbar*. For full discussion on the Shi'ite background of this Qur'ānic term see his *Sharḥ al-Zīyāra* I, 258–60. For mystical nuances see *EI²*: DHIKR (L. Gardet).

[274] *QA* IX, folio 13b.

[275] Ibid. II, folio 4a.

[276] Ibid. IX, folio 13b.

[277] Ibid. X, folio 15a.

[278] Ibid. III, folio 6a.

[279] Ibid. II, folio 3b.

A significant aspect of this commentary is the attention paid in the first two chapters to the two sources of authority, the state and the ʿulama, demonstrating the importance attached to them as leaders responsible for the community. In the opening chapter, entitled "*al-Malik*" (The King), the Bab declares: "O! assembly of the rulers of the earth and descendants of rulers. Resign yourselves, every one of you, to the Kingdom of God for the sake of truth to the Truth. O! ruler of Muslims, support the book of the greatest Z̲ikr with truth, for God already ordained for you and for the circle around you in the Day of Resurrection standing on the final path responsible to the truth. Beware, O King, I swear by God that if you turn not towards the Z̲ikr, God will judge you on the Day of Resurrection among the rulers with fire, and you will not find on that Day any support except God the Sublime, for the truth by the Truth."[280] In this forceful address the "veracious guardian" assumes for himself the initial possession of "sovereignty" *(mulk)* but he will entrust it to the king only on the condition that he will be "content with the ordinance of God." The Bab thus confirms the legitimacy of the secular power on the condition that the soul and the sword of the king will be in his service to "subdue the countries" and "purify the Sacred Land from the people of denial." The Bab's view on the question of political power is clear. He does not claim the throne or consider the rulers illegitimate usurpers of power, so long as they are implementing the policies initiated or rectified by the new "Distinguisher." In such delegation of power one can see an unconscious reconciliation; a pragmatic concern for distinction between political and spiritual authorities. The impending Resurrection makes it incumbent upon the rulers to recognize the way to Paradise and avoid being relegated to the "circle of fire."

In reference to the "descendants of the kings," and the "circles around" them, there is a greater reflection of the political realities of the time. The admonitory warnings in the passage below may well refer to the Qajars in general and Muḥammad Shāh in particular.

> O King! purify the Sacred Land of the people who are rejecting the Book before that Day when the Z̲ikr will arrive all of a sudden and relentlessly, by the leave of God the Sublime, for a potent cause. Verily, God has prescribed for you that you should submit to the Z̲ikr and His cause and subdue the countries with the Truth and by His leave, for in this world you have been mercifully granted dominion and in the next you will dwell among the people of the Paradise of His approval around the seat of holiness. Let not sovereignty blind you for verily "All souls will taste death," for this is written by the order of God the Truth, for sovereignty, as it is recorded in the Mother of the Books by the hand of God, is the prerogative of the Z̲ikr. Assist the cause of God with your souls and your swords vigorously in the shadow of the greatest Z̲ikr on behalf of the pure religion *(al-dīn al-khāliṣ)*.[281]

[280]Ibid. I, folio 2a–2b.
[281]Ibid. folio 3b.

Besides a general call for conversion, the main demands on the king are to assist the Z̲ikr and purify the Sacred Land. In this invitation to worldly conquest one can see not only a hint to the Bab's plan to solicit the shah's support for his final Insurrection from the ʿAtabāt but a reflection of the public demand for action in response to persecution of the Shiʿites in the ʿAtabāt.[282] The agitation that was aroused among the Persian public following the massacre of Karbalāʾ by the Ottomans, in 1258/1842, put the Qajar monarch and his minister, Ḥājjī Mīrzā Āqāsī, in an embarrassing position. Āqāsī recognized that to retaliate against the Ottomans would invite another military disaster and possibly intervention of the European powers. As on many other occasions, the policy of inaction was perhaps the only avenue open to the minister, but understandably, he could expect little sympathy from the public, and least of all from the doubly persecuted Shaykhis. It is not therefore surprising that the Bab's sharp edge of criticism is directed against the prime minister: "O minister of the King! be fearful of God, for there is no God except He who is the Truth, the Just. Withdraw your soul from the King. Verily, I am the one who has inherited the earth, and whatsoever is upon it by the leave of God the Wise."[283] Needless to say, the Bab recognizes Āqāsī as the chief animator behind the throne and blames him for his sinister influence over the monarch. He further warns the shah: "By God, your sovereignty is futile [so long as] worldly possession is placed in the hand of the idolators";[284] a reference to Āqāsī and his supporters, whose eccentric Sufi beliefs were widely despised.[285]

In the Bab's view, the sphere of his "new cause" should not be confined to his home country or the Shiʿite world, but should extend to the land beyond. He calls on the "assembly of rulers": "Swiftly deliver my signs [or verses] to [the land of] the Turks and the land of Hind [India] and from there to the East and the West."[286] The Bab's broad appeal to the non-Shiʿite and non-Muslim world is not inconsistent with the Mahdi's global triumph. It nonetheless highlights the traditional Islamic distinction between the abode of Islam and the abode of war. A few chapters later the Bab, goes so far as to admit the People of the Book into his Paradise, but this inclusion of the Christians does not specify the European nations.[287]

[282]See above, chap. 1.

[283]*QA* I, folio 3a.

[284]Ibid.

[285]Āqāsī's influence on Muḥammad Shāh is described by many sources. (See for example Jahāngīr Mīrzā *Tārīkh-i Nau* ed. ʿA. Iqbāl [Tehran, 1327 Sh./1948] 90–92 and Muḥammad Ḥasan Khān Iʿtimād al-Salṭana *Ṣadr al-Tawārīkh* ed. M̲. Mushīrī [Tehran, 1349 Sh./1970] 184–85). The private correspondence of Ḥājjī Mīrzā Āqāsī also throws some light on the nature of this relationship. On many occasions Āqāsī humbly and piously denies any official authority and confesses his "total dependence" on the shah. Yet he constantly applies pressure to compel the shah to ratify his policies (Archives of Iran Ministry of Foreign Affairs, Tehran, file no. 18, original documents). *TH* (III, 304–14) cites an interesting treatise by Āqāsī called *S̲h̲iyam-i Fakhrī*, in which he alludes to his spiritual authority over the shah. See also *EIr*: ĀQĀSĪ and cited sources.

[286]*QA* I, folio 3a.

[287]Ibid. VII, folio 11b.

The Bab's more immediate concern, however, is with the responsibility of religious authority. He identifies the ʿulama as a strong force in the society and urges them to ponder the truthfulness of his claims and to announce the glad tidings of his appearance. He then warns them:

> O! assembly of the ʿulama, fear God in your verdicts from this day for the Z̲ikr is among you from our presence and truly he is the witness and the judge. S̲hun all that you are receiving from other than the Book of God, the Truth. For on the day of Resurrection you will stand on the path and will be answerable to the Truth. God has verily placed doubts in every tablet which is sinful, and haply God may forgive you for whatever you acquired for yourself before the Day, and God is merciful and forgiving to those who repent. Verily God has made unlawful to you any but the pure knowledge from this book, and any ruling and ijtihād but the truth.[288]

In the same admonitory tone, as he addressed the king the Bab calls upon the ʿulama not to be conceited about their knowledge and to submit to the authority of his divinely inspired book. Though he does not appear to reject the notion of ijtihād, he asserts that any judgment independent of his superior authority is void and unlawful. Those who go against him and doubt his truthfulness will find their abode in fire.

Throughout *Qayyūm al-Asmāʾ*, the distinction between the believers and "the people of denial" is sharply drawn. The measure for distinction is the recognition of the Z̲ikr and support for his cause prior to the impending Resurrection. The "people of the Bāb," and prior to them all "the forerunners [sābiqīn] among the believers,"[289] are the only group who will be saved in the "day of gloom."[290] Their number may still be small but they are created from the life-giving water of Paradise. The essence of the nonbelievers, on the other hand, is of salty waters, which has its origins in Hell. Some room is allowed for the undecided and even for skeptics, so long as they do not actively oppose the Z̲ikr. People are warned of the graveness of the Day and cautioned "not to place for themselves another authority except the Bab."[291]

What perhaps comes through most vividly in this document of the early Babi aspirations is a conscious attempt by the Bab to initiate a new prophetic system modeled on Islamic religion but deliberately independent from it. His vision of a prophetic mission and utopian preoccupation with the forthcoming Resurrection is profoundly influenced by the Qurʾān but the same idealism allows little room for pragmatic undertakings of any substance. General criticism of both political and religious authentics is scarcely developed into a practical program of reform and admonitory warning to them hardly goes beyond a vague outline. The presence of the divine will still

[288]Ibid. II, folio 3a.
[289]Ibid. III, folio 5b.
[290]Ibid. II, folio 3a.
[291]Ibid. IV, folio 7b.

prevail over human initiative. Nonetheless, the allegorical choice between the fire and Paradise is left to man.

Calls for purification and for return to the Book exist in the past "puritanistic" currents in Islam. From the traditionalism of Ibn Ḥanbal to Ibn Taymīya and the "unitarianism" of Muḥammad Ibn ʿAbd al-Wahhāb, the Sunni Islam frequently entertained a strict adherence to the apparent text of the Qurʾān and the Traditions of the Prophet.[292] Akhbārī Shiʿism, on the other hand, preached sole, largely uncritical, reliance on the Traditions of the Prophet and the Imams, rejecting the use of rational criteria. The early Babi doctrine shared with both currents their rejection of the existing orthodoxy but drastically differed from them because of its unequivocal emphasis on the need for continual divine guidance. It also rejected in strong terms the rigidity of the "literalist" approach. By insisting on the irreplaceable function of the divine agent, the Babi theory remained faithful to the general precepts of the Bāṭinī Shiʿism, which also advocated "pure religion" but sought it in the guidance of the speaking Imam.[293]

But to consider Babi thought as merely a recurrence of the heterodoxies of the past does not do justice to its novelties. The openness of the Babi message were far removed from the secrecy of esoteric thought. Even compared to Shaykhism, the Babi movement was not content with the prospect of preserving esoteric knowledge among the elect. It had neither the means nor the intention of producing a scholastic discipline for the learned. Whatever continuity does exist between Shaykhism and Babism, it is wrong to believe that Sayyid ʿAlī Muḥammad Shīrāzī only popularized Shaykhi theophany. From the very outset the potential of the Babi notion of prophethood dictated a course of action different from Shaykhism. In due course such orientation was bound to result in a conscious break from Islam.

The Bab saw his "ecumenical" mission to include Muslims as well as others, and his book as the celestial key to the Qurʾān and other scriptures of the past. The Bab's preoccupation with creating a new religion advocated a substantial, later a revolutionary, change that was to extend beyond the boundaries of Islam. In the later years of the movement, this gave rise to a theory of progressive revelation more advanced than past Bātinīs had con-

[292]For the development of the Ḥanbalite school and rigorous adherence to *sunna* in Sunni Islam see H. Laoust *Les schismes dans l'Islām: Introduction à une étude de la religion musulmane* (Paris, 1965). Also *EI*²: AḤMAD IBN ḤANBAL.

[293]The Qurʾānic term *al-dīn al-khāliṣ* (pure or sincere religion) (XXXIX, 3) came to denote in the heterodox thought, among other things, a rejection of "those who take guardians apart from Him." See, for example, *Vajh al-Dīn*, attributed to Nāṣir Khusraw Qubādīyānī, ed. T. Irānī (Berlin, 1343/1924) 100–3. The similarities between this work, still in circulation in Ismāʿīlī communities in the nineteenth century, and *Qayyūm al-Asmāʾ* are most revealing. Similarity of such themes as the preoccupation with hermeneutics and numerology, the meaning of *dhikr* and *ḥujja,* the common origin of the divine scriptures, the cosmic hierarchy, the cabalistic interpretation of the nineteen letters of *Bismallāh al-raḥmān al-raḥīm*, and above all the imperative presence of the Imam of the Age suggest a more direct acquaintance with Ismāʿīlī themes.

templated. The unfolding course of Islamic revelation, the Bab believed, was to reach its culmination with the commencement of the Qiyāma. As such the Babi effort was not to reform or rationalize Islam to the new needs of the time. It was a search for renewal of the divine covenant, which could be achieved only if the existing religious order was replaced and loyalties to religious and secular institutions were shaken.

What happened in the earliest days of the Bab's proclamation was seen by the Bab and his disciples as the prototype of the new mission. The wandering Shaykhis who came to recognize Sayyid ʿAlī Muḥammad were sectarians already on the verge of defection from the dominant orthodoxy. The careers of Mullā Ḥusayn Bushruʾī and Mullā Muḥammad ʿAlī Bārfurūshī (Quddūs) prior to their conversions exemplify such gradual distancing from norms of the religious community. The real break, however, was materialized when new bonds of loyalty were struck between this group of low-ranking clerics and ʿAlī Muḥammad of Shiraz. It is all the more remarkable that they paid their allegiance not to a learned divine but to a visionary merchant, outside the scholastic world. From both ideological and social points of view, this covenant was the cornerstone of a new "circle of Paradise" that they hoped to construct by infusing the "water of living (ḥayy)" into the plain of "All-Beings." The formation of the new unit in its entirety was thus regarded as the source of rejuvenation of the cycle of time and instrumental for bringing vitality to the world.

The birth of the Babi movement should thus be seen as a spontaneous process that engaged claimant and converts alike in a messianic enterprise. The fulfillment of such an enterprise may seem like an irrational indulgence in fantasies by a handful of remote individuals isolated from the realities of their time. Yet owing to its very formation, the Babi movement was an attempt to employ the sanctified ideals of the past—almost a mythological rather than historical past—to interpret a changing age. The Bab and his disciples were unaware of the intricacies and even sometimes the symptoms of this change, but in their own ways they had a consciousness of the inadequacies of the existing order. They were too preoccupied with their utopian ideals to plan a sensible and effective course of action and, as we will see, too inconsistent to execute it. Yet they had a dynamism in their outlook and a will to put their message across that most of their contemporaries lacked.

PART III

EXPANSION AND OPPOSITION

5

Facing the World: Declarations of Iraq and Ḥijāz

The formation of the Vāḥid was the first step toward the publication of the new claims. The Bab and his disciples felt an urgency to make their call public, but the prevailing urge for the symbolic reenactment of the prophecies and trust in God's ultimate support obviated the need for systematic planning by human agents. *Qayyūm al-Asmā'* broadly defined the message that was to be preached, and identified its audience—the rulers, the ʿulama, and the public, presumably all at once. All the disciples had the general assignment of attracting favorable elements, and some were entrusted with specific tasks. It was conceived that a gathering of potential followers in the ʿAtabāt in anticipation of the Bab's public declaration would engender mass support. The Bab's pilgrimage to Mecca, as prophesied, was the start of the Ẓuhūr proper, to be culminated in the holy shrines of Iraq.

Mullā Ḥusayn was assigned to undertake the mission inside Iran, traveling to Isfahan, Tehran, and Khurasan. He would then lead the Babi supporters to the ʿAtabāt. He was also instructed to deliver *Qayyūm al-Asmā'*, and possibly some other works of the Bab, to the shah and his minister. Another disciple, Mullā Yūsuf Ardabīlī, was instructed to return to his homeland, Azarbaijan, perhaps with the same intention of gathering new converts to accompany him to Iraq. A few others also returned to their home towns. The Bab himself, accompanied by Mullā Muḥammad ʿAlī Bārfurūshī (Quddūs), was to travel to the Ḥijāz later in the same year. The largest group of disciples, including Mullā ʿAlī Basṭāmī, Mullā Jalīl Urūmī, Mullā Muḥammad ʿAlī Qazvīnī, and possibly others, was assigned to Iraq.

Basṭāmī, Emissary to the Holy Land

Basṭāmī's mission to the Holy Land was a critical test for the future success of the movement. The dual objective of winning over the Shaykhis and addressing leading mujtahids made the ʿAtabāt the principal focus of Babi attention, since the Holy Cities were to be the arena of the Khurūj. The task of preparation rested on Bastāmī's shoulders.

Mullā ʿAlī Basṭāmī, the *thānī man āman* (second who believed), was ranked third in importance after the Bab and Mullā Ḥusayn.[1] He was born in the vicinity of the small agricultural town of Basṭām on the northwestern border of Khurasan. He first studied rudimentaries in his home town before moving to Mashhad where under the influence of Mullā Jaʿfar Kirmānshāhī, himself a student of Aḥsāʾī,[2] he gradually turned away "from superficial knowledge . . . toward the higher plain of contemplation."[3] Later, in the ʿAtabāt, he studied under Rashtī for seven years. His knowledge of Shaykhi literature and his reported "piety and lack of worldly interests" apparently made him one of the senior students and a close companion of Rashtī. Sometime in the 1840s he returned to Basṭām, but stayed in his home village only two years before returning to Iraq. Commitment to wife and family and the prospect of becoming a local mulla were apparently not persuasive enough to keep him in Basṭām.[4] Like many of his former classmates, he remained distanced from the unexciting life of the village, preferring the company of his teacher and his peers. He accompanied Rashtī on his last annual pilgrimage to Najaf in 1259/1843, shortly before the latter's death. Qatīl names Basṭāmī among those who understood Rashtī's allusions to the imminence of Ẓuhūr.[5]

After his conversion in Shiraz, Basṭāmī set out for Iraq. He passed on his way through Būshihr, where according to his instructions he visited the Bab's uncle, Ḥājjī Sayyid Muḥammad Shīrāzī, and gave the news of the Bab's proclamation.[6] From Būshihr, via Baṣra, Bastāmī arrived at the ʿAtabāt in Rajab-Shaʿbān 1260/August–September 1844. Some of the early disciples who had first accompanied him to Shiraz also left for Iraq.[7] The

[1]*Qatīl* 524. Qatīl al-Karbalāʾī, a fellow classmate, provides us with the only known account of Basṭāmī's early life (524–26).

[2]*Qatīl* 525. No further details are available on the above person, but he should not be confused with Shaykh Muḥammad Jaʿfar Kirmānshāhī, son of Muḥammad ʿAlī and grandson of Muḥammad Bāqir Bihbahānī, cited in *TAS* II/1, 263–64.

[3]*Qatīl* 525.

[4]Ibid.

[5]Ibid.

[6]As appears from later evidence, Ḥājjī Sayyid Muḥammad did not accept the Bab's call. (Letter by the Bab, *ZH* 223–25, and also letters by his brother Sayyid ʿAlī to his family cited in *Khāndān-i Afnān* 25–31.) It was long after 1260/1844, during Sayyid Muḥammad's pilgrimage to the ʿAtabāt in 1277/1860–61 (accompanied by his youngest brother, Ḥasan ʿAlī) and following his visit to Bahāʾullāh, that he finally recognized the Bab. Some recent accounts, such as *Khāndān-i Afnāṇ* (25, 30–31) and subsequently A. Taherzadeh (*The Revelation of Bahāʾullāh* [Oxford, 1974] I, 153–54), which hint at the partial conversion of Sayyid Muḥammad in 1260–1261/1844–1845, seem to contradict the Bab's own reference to his uncle's early refusal.

[7]As far as can be traced, five— Mullā Jalīl Urūmī, Mullā Muḥammad ʿAlī Qazvīnī, Mullā Maḥmūd Khuʾī, Mullā Khudābakhsh Qūchānī, and Mullā Bāqir Tabrīzī—were present in Karbalāʾ. There is some confusion over their departure date. *Nabil* (87) has Basṭāmi precede the

arrival of these "messengers," nearly seven months after Rashtī's death, intensified the leadership crisis within the Shaykhi camp. Shaykh Sulṭān Karbalā'ī, himself an early convert of the ʿAtabāt, vividly depicts the conflicts that brought the entire Shaykhi camp to the verge of collapse.[8] In the tense climate of bitter rivalry, accusations, and despair that prevailed, Basṭāmī, the "messenger from Shiraz," came as an unexpected relief to those who found the utterances of *Qayyūm al-Asmā'* a perfect match for Rashtī's forecast, plus a way out of the perplexing deadlock. Āqā Muḥammad Muṣṭafā al-Baghdādī, whose father was a well-known Shaykhi, records that before the appearance of the Bab "all the [Shaykhi] adherents in Baghdad and its outskirts were mournful at the departure of the late sayyid, but in the meantime they remained vigilant and watchful for the appearance of the Promised One till they came to the honor of his presence."[9]

Qatīl reveals a like shift from confusion to certainty in describing his own state of mind shortly after Rashtī's death: "I could not decide whether I should lead my way toward . . . determinists or toward fatalists or toward Bālāsarīs [Uṣūlīs]. . . . Then when the time elapsed, after four months and a few days, the herald called from Heaven the name of Qā'im from the land of Fars."[10] This suggests that in early Jumādā al-Ūlā 1260/April 1844, the claims of Sayyid ʿAlī Muḥammad were already known in the ʿAtabāt. Qatīl also informs us about the first public announcement by the unknown Babi disciples, on 26 Rajab/11 August 1844 in Najaf. It took place with the utmost caution, when the Shiʿite public were gathered from Baghdad, Ḥilla, Karbalā', and other places in Najaf to celebrate the day of the Prophet's designation.[11] During what appears to be the earliest encounter between the Babis and the Shiʿite community, the Babis announced: "to the seekers what knowledge they had in their possession and what they were allowed to utter, but concealed what they saw of their new master; emanation and the mysteries they witnessed, fearing that the best of the people might not tolerate them and the worst of them might cause agitation and strife. [Therefore] obeying the orders of the virtuous Imams, they did not speak of what might have directed [public] opinion toward denial."[12]

The general tone of the Babi missionaries was to prepare the public for the forthcoming arrival of the Bab. Mullā ʿAbd al-Jalīl Urūmī in particular

---

others in his journey; *Qatīl* (503, 511–12) remembers his arrival in the ʿAtabāt shortly after them. It is almost certain that he traveled by himself.

8Shaykh Sulṭān Karbalā'ī, apologia written in circa 1263/1847 in the ʿAtabāt, INBA no. 80, 310, 332, also cited in *ZH*, 245, 254.

9*Baghdādī* 105.

10*Qatīl* (502). The author's references to theological and philosophical schools are made in a metaphorical sense.

11Ibid. 511.

12Ibid. In the same passage, Qatīl refers to one of pseudojurisprudents *(al-mutafaqqihīn)*, which suggests that perhaps one of the ʿulama, who for an unknown reason had some knowledge of the new message, provoked the public.

emphasized the events that were due to take place at the time of the Advent of the Imam. He made no specific reference to the name of the Promised One, and although he referred to him as the bāb of the Imam, and even in some places as Rashtī's successor, at the same time he attributed to him qualities that were traditionally expected of the Qā'im.[13] After Rajab 1260/ August 1844, as Qatīl confirms, "the cause of the Imam, peace be upon him, became so well known that no one from the committed people of that region [the ʿAtabāt] remained who had not heard or did not understand . . . and all those who had seen the Bab previously said that if the claimant is the one we know of, then we will be among his followers. There were even some believers among the Bālāsarīs and those people of Kāẓimayn who were weak in their Shiʿite beliefs, and also the attendants of the Holy Shrines and all those who in the past frequently had the honor of his presence."[14]

By late summer 1844, news of the Bab had already begun to capture people's attention. As Qatīl points out, one of the most persuasive factors in this early enthusiasm was previous acquaintance with Sayyid ʿAlī Muḥammad. But the recognition of claims by self-educated merchant to babīya was still a formidable problem, even for the most vigilant Shaykhis. Sayyid Jawād Karbalā'ī confesses his uncertainty when he was informed of the appearance of the Bab:[15]

> [Basṭāmī] was only content to reveal the title of his excellency and absolutely refused to mention his name. He said: "The Bab has appeared and we had the honor of his presence but he forbade us to mention his venerated name or origin. Soon his call will be fully revealed and his identity and his origin will become apparent to all." The issue of the appearance of the Bab was discussed in every circle and caused great excitement in Iraq. Everybody had an opinion and every soul predicted a particular person to be the Bab. But the person that no one ever expected was the Primal Point, glory be to his name, since because of his excellency's youth and his involvement in trade, nobody had any thought about him. They unanimously anticipated and were even firmly confident that the gate of the divine knowledge would come from a house of knowledge and learning and not from the ranks of the guilds and trades. A majority, particularly among Shaykhis, presumed that he would surely be one of the senior students of the Sayyid [Rashtī], may God elevate his status.[16]

The Babi community that formed around the nucleus of early believers was made up primarily of Shaykhis, although some sources allude to a number of other sympathizers. The British consul general in Baghdad, Hen-

[13]Ibid.

[14]*Qatīl* 512. By the "people of Kāẓimayn" Qatīl apparently refers to some Arab adherents of Rashtī, mainly from the Bushr clan. "Weak in their Shiʿite beliefs" may be a reference to those who were attracted to Rashtī's circle (al-Ṭuʿma *Turāth Karbalā'* 224–29).

[15]*Kashf al-Ghiṭā'* 70–77, recorded by Mīrzā Abul-Fażl Gulpāyigānī during his frequent visits to Sayyid Jawād between 1293 and 1299/1876 and 1881 in Tehran.

[16]Ibid. 71.

ry Rawlinson, who kept a close watch over the rapid spread of the new "schism," confirms that "a considerable section of the Sheeahs [Shiʿites] of Najaf" supported Mullā ʿAlī Basṭāmī.[17] Muḥammad Muṣṭafā al-Baghdādī mentions various groups of students who, following their mujtahids, were attracted to the new movement,[18] and Qatīl confirms the overwhelming support of the Shaykhis prior to the first signs of strong Bālāsarī opposition.[19] Of the more than one hundred committed converts in the ʿAtabāt, nearly half were either Persian or of Persian origin. Of the remaining half, more than two-thirds were natives of Iraq who resided in Karbalā', Najaf, and Baghdad and its environs.[20] The Arab group included some mujtahids of relative importance, such as Shaykh Bashīr Najafī, an old mujtahid with Shaykhi leanings;[21] Shaykh Muḥammad Shibl al-Baghdādī, an early student of Rashtī and his representative in Baghdad;[22] Shaykh Sulṭān Karbalā'ī, a young mujtahid among the later generation of Shaykhis;[23] and Sayyid Jawād Karbalā'ī, a grandson of Baḥr al-ʿUlūm.[24] Of other Arab converts from the ranks of the ʿulama, Shaykh Ṣāliḥ Karīmāwī,[25] Sayyid Muḥsin Kāẓimaynī, and Sayyid ʿAlī Bushr are the best known. Over the next two years several nonclerical Arabs also joined. Saʿīd Jabāwī later became a devoted follower of Qurrat al-ʿAyn.[26] Ḥājjī Muḥammad Karrādī, an aged moneylender and former officer in the Ottoman army before settling in Baghdad and joining Rashtī's circle, composed panegyrics in praise of Rashtī.[27] Ḥājjī Sayyid Khalīl Madā'inī, a local Arab chief, had studied for some time with Rashtī and is even said to have participated in the Kūfa retreat.[28]

The Persian converts, though more numerous, were less prominent in clerical rank. They included Shaykh Ḥasan Zunūzī, who had met the Bab in Karbalā', Mullā Ibrāhīm Maḥallātī,[29] Sayyid Muḥammad Gulpāyigānī,[30]

[17]F.O. 248/114, no. 1, 8 Jan. 1845, Rawlinson to Sheil.

[18]*Baghdādī* 106.

[19]*Qatīl* 512.

[20]This rough estimate of the number of Babis in the ʿAtabāt was made on the basis of information in *Baghdādī, Qatīl, Qazvīnī, Samandar, Nabil, Fu'ādī, Muʿīn, Kashf al-Ghiṭā'*, and biographies of some early believers in *ZH*.

[21]*Baghdādī* 106.

[22]Ibid. 105.

[23]*Nabil* 190, 270–71; *ZH* 107, 244–45. His above-mentioned apologia also supplies some details about himself and other Babis of Iraq.

[24]Sayyid Jawād's acquaintance with the Bab's family was no doubt effective in his conversion. His full biography appears in *Kashf al-Ghiṭā'* 55–90 and in *ZH* 238–44.

[25]A companion of Qurrat al-ʿAyn, Shaykh Ṣālih was the first Babi to be executed, in 1263/1847 in Tehran.

[26]He was one of the participants of Ṭabarsī killed in battle.

[27]*Nabil* 426; *Baghdādī* 120–22; and *ZH* 261–62; cf. *Turāth Karbalā'* 225–28. Karrādī was a *bīnbashī* (head of a thousand) in the army that fought against Ibrāhīm Pāshā of Egypt. in his retirement became a moneylender. He was killed in Ṭabarsī at the age of about eighty.

[28]*ZH* 262–63.

[29]One of the companions of Qurrat al-ʿAyn, he was executed in Qazvīn in 1263/1847. Earlier he was involved in the events of Shiraz in 1845–1846. (INBA no. 91, XXVIII, 139–45.) His biography appears in *ZH* 389–91.

[30]A reference to him appears in *Baghdādī* 108 and *Qazvīnī* 494.

Sayyid Aḥmad Yazdī,[31] Shaykh Abū Turāb Ishtihārdī,[32] and Mullā Aḥmad Muʿallim Ḥiṣārī.[33] A few Persian merchants with Shaykhi tendencies also joined, among them the Nahrīs, who later were active in Isfahan,[34] and Ḥājjī ʿAbd al-Muṭṭalib, a resident of Kāẓimayn, who in 1264/1848 provided the means for fifty Babis to participate in the Babi crusade to Mazandaran.[35] During the ensuing months groups of Shaykhis from Qazvin, Isfahan, and Mashhad hastened to Karbalāʾ to participate in the public declaration of the Bab at the beginning of 1261/1845. Of these, the Qazvin group, headed by Mullā Jawād Valīyānī, included some of the Qazvīnī converts who later, after the cancellation of the ʿAtabāt plan, returned to Shiraz and met the Bab.

While the preaching of Mullā ʿAlī Basṭāmī was the main impetus for new converts, over the next few years it was the influential personality of Qurrat al-ʿAyn that secured solidarity in the Babi ranks. References by contemporary writers to Qurratīya, her followers, indicate her significance.[36]

By the end of Ramaḍān 1260/October 1844, the Babi propagation reached a new momentum. On 23 of Ramaḍān/6 October, Basṭāmī officially presented the people of Karbalāʾ with *Qayyūm al-Asmāʾ*.[37] A week later, at the celebration of Fiṭr (1 Shawwāl 1260/14 October 1844),[38] he announced the "approaching advent" to the people of Najaf, "bearing a copy of the Koran which he stated to have been delivered to him by the forerunner of Imam Mahdī."[39] It is not a coincidence that on both occasions

[31]Father of Sayyid Ḥusayn and Sayyid Ḥasan Yazdī. Sayyid Ḥusayn later became a close companion of the Bab. *Baghdādī* 108 and *KD* 63.

[32]*Samandar* 114; *Nabil* 39; *ZH* 233–34.

[33]*Fuʾādī* 276–97.

[34]See below, chap. 8.

[35]*Baghdādī* 122–23.

[36]See below for his role in the ʿAtabāt.

[37]*Qatīl* 512. In Qurʾānic tradition, the term *Furqān* has a broad and rather complicated meaning. It occurs in various connections in the Qurʾān and in most cases corresponds to the concepts of deliverance, redemption, and salvation from judgment. In a broader sense the word indicates the holy scripture in each revelation and particularly in Islam as a sign that confirms the prophethood. Furqān also represents the separation of an accepted religious community from the unbelievers (see *EI*²: FURḲĀN [R. Paret]). However, in the Babi literature, the term is used not only for the past scriptures but also to stress the point of unity and conformity between past and present revelations (*QA* III, 5a). In reply to Muḥammad Karīm Khān Kirmānī's attack on the Bab's "falsely compiled *Furqān*" (*Izhāq al-Bāṭil* 14–15), Qatīl argues that the new *Furqān* is the inner truth of Muḥammad's Qurʾān fundamentally reinterpreted and reappearing in its complete version. On this basis, Qatīl sugests that the Bab's Furqān is a new version of the Qurʾān that contains revelations according to the necessities of its time. Qatīl also cites a tradition by Jaʿfar Ṣādiq: "The Book [*al-Kitāb*, i.e., the Qurʾān] is the brief version and the Furqān is the comprehensive one, which appears according to the [need of the] time" (530–31).

[38]*Qatīl* 530–31.

[39]F.O. 248/114, no. 1, Rawlinson to Sheil. According to *Baghdādī* 106, Bastāmī first appeared in Kūfa, but no doubt in this matter *Qatīl* is a more reliable source. Lady Sheil, on the other hand, when writing about the Babis, confused Basṭāmī with the Bab, and seems to have Basṭāmī's journey in mind when she states: "After some changes he settled in Kazemein [Kāẓimayn] near Baghdad, where he first divulged his pretensions to the character of a prophet" (*Life and Manners* 177).

Islamic celebrations were chosen.[40] The Qur'ān of the Bab, as *Qayyūm al-Asmā'* came to be known,[41] aroused a great deal of excitement. The experiences of the past few years—the threat of another Turkish onslaught like the massacre of 1843, Shaykhi-Bālāsarī hostility, and the crisis of leadership in the Shaykhi camp—made the climate particularly receptive to *Qayyūm al-Asmā'*'s admonitory message of deliverance.

The sharp edge of these messianic promulgations, however, was directed toward the prominent Uṣūlī ʿulama: Shaykh Muḥammad Ḥasan Najafī in Najaf and Sayyid Ibrāhīm Qazvīnī in Karbalā'. The intensification of sectarian hatred no doubt prompted the Bab and his disciples to address their warning to them. As a beginning, Bastāmī presented Shaykh Muḥammad Ḥasan Najafī, the chief jurist (*shaykh al-fuqahā'*)[42] and one of the leaders of the Bālāsarīs, with the Bab's writings.[43]

Shaykh Muḥammad Ḥasan Najafī, the author of *Jawāhir al-Kalām*,[44] was one of the most celebrated jurists of the whole nineteenth century. Toward the end of his life, he was recognized as the head[45] and "the leadership of the Imamis . . . among Arab and ʿAjam, devolved on him."[46] Even by 1260/1844, while both Ibrāhīm Qazvīnī and Muḥammad Bāqir Shaftī were still alive, Shaykh Muḥammad Ḥasan enjoyed a prominent position, particularly in Najaf. Although he even received an ijāza from Aḥsā'ī,[47] he did not hesitate to denounce the Shaykhis. His condemnation of the Shaykhis was aimed particularly at their criticism of jurists, but also at their treatment of ḥadīth.[48] Rashtī alludes to his direct involvement in persecutions after Aḥsā'ī's death. In a new initiative, together with two other established mujtahids of Iraq, Shaykh Muḥammad Ḥasan denounced the new Shaykhi leader.[49] In Rashtī's view, the chief reason for the whole opposi-

[40]The night of 23 Ramaḍān is, according to some traditions, regarded as *laylat al-qadr*, the night that is "better than a thousand months." It was on this night that the first sūras of the Qur'ān were revealed to Muḥammad: "Behold, we sent it down on the Night of Qadr," Qur'ān XCII, 3. See *Shorter EI:* IʿTIKĀF, and RAMAḌĀN.

[41]*QU* 60, 185–86.

[42]*RA* II, 420. Also mentioned by his title *Shaykh-i Kabīr* in Rashtī's *Dalīl al-Mutaḥayyirīn*, 96.

[43]*Nabil* 90; cf. F.O. 60/114, no. 1, Rawlinson to Sheil.

[44]One of the most comprehensive works in Shiʿite jurisprudence. Shaykh Muḥammad Ḥasan spent more than thirty years compiling this twenty-five-volume work, which was finally completed in 1257/1841. Published in 1271/1853–1854, it remained a major work of reference up to the present day (*al-Dharīʿa* V, 275–77).

[45]*QU* 103; Iʿtimād al-Salṭana *al-Ma'āthir wa'l-Āthār* 135–36.

[46]*RJ* 182. The earliest references to the position of *marjaʿ al-taqlīd* (source of emulation) appeared toward the end of Muḥammad Ḥasan's life when he designated one of his students, Shaykh Murtażā Anṣārī, as his successor. Tunkābunī (*QU* 10, 103), who was primarily an adherent of Sayyid Ibrāhīm Qazvīnī, places Muḥammad Ḥasan's leadership chronologically later than Muḥammad Bāqir Shaftī and Sayyid Ibrāhīm Qazvīnī. Others hint at his prominence: "He took the burdens of deputyship and obligations of leadership" (*TAS* II/1, 311).

[47]The text of this ijāza is cited in the appendix of the third volume of *Jawāhir al-Kalām* (*al-Dharīʿa* 275–77).

[48]*QU* 54–58 and *Dalīl al-Mutaḥayyirīn* 72–73.

[49]*Dalīl al-Mutaḥayyirīn* 88–102. The content of the fatwā issued by the mujtahids of Najaf

tional drive, which extended even to India, was the increasing popularity of Shaykhism, causing eminent mujtahids to fear that "the public may abandon their obedience."[50] Tunkābunī, in contrast to other sources,[51] does not venerate Muḥammad Ḥasan as he does other prominent mujtahids. He gives some evidence of his wealth and hints that even his laxity and lack of clear discipline in bestowing authorizations on his students were due not only to his weak judgment, but to his desire to strengthen his clerical support.[52]

Basṭāmī must have been fully aware of Muḥammad Ḥasan's reputation when he approached him in Najaf to inform him of "the immediate manifestation of the Imam."[53] Addressing him in the presence of students and followers, Basṭāmī proclaimed the appearance of the Proof[54] and maintained that "in the year 1261, the mystery will be revealed and the victorious cause [of God] will dominate."[55] He also supplied Muḥammad Ḥasan with the Bab's works including a special ordinance addressed to the jurist.[56] Basṭāmī reminded him that as the head of the Shiʿite community, he is bound to respond to a message that calls for reevaluation of the ʿulama's position.[57] The Bab unequivocally warned the ʿulama: "God has forbidden after [the coming of] this book the teaching of anything other than it. Teach the people the laws of the book and turn them away from error, the baseless books among you."[58] On the same ground Basṭāmī claimed that by demonstrating an unequal ability to reveal the word of God, "the unschooled Hashimite youth of Persia" was the only righteous authority on earth.[59]

If these utterances were not bold enough to enrage the old Shaykh, the claims of divine inspiration and allusions to possess a prophetic status equal to that of the Prophet were. In a harsh and unequivocal response, the chief mujtahid not only rejected the contents of the Bab's message as "a blasphemous production" but also "denounced Mullā ʿAlī [Basṭāmī] as a heretic" and expelled him from the assembly.[60] Not surprisingly, Muḥammad Ḥasan only performed a religious obligation "to prohibit the evil." The fact that he was a leading mujtahid made it all the more imperative to set an example for his emulators. In the climate of confrontation, when to deviate

---

appears on p. 90. Rashtī refers to the triangle of the ʿAtabāt mujtahids who, with the help of their supporters, activated hostility and disturbance.

[50]Ibid. 90. Shaykh Muḥammad Ḥasan did not confine his opposition to the Shaykhis. *Qiṣaṣ al-ʿUlamāʾ* (105) quotes him as saying, "It was to abolish *ḥikmat* that God chose Muḥammad ibn ʿAbdullāh."

[51]*al-Maʾāthir waʾl-Āthār* 135–36 and *TMS* II/1, 314.

[52]*QU* 10, 104.

[53]F.O. 248/114, no. 1.

[54]*Nabil* 90; cf. *Qatīl* 512.

[55]*Qatīl* 512.

[56]*Samandar* (347) particularly refers to the tauqīʿ delivered by Basṭāmī.

[57]*QA* II, folio 5 (v. 13–15).

[58]Ibid. XXVII, folio 32 (v. 14).

[59]*Nabil* 90; cf. *QA* II (v. 7–8) and III (v. 2–3).

[60]F.O. 248/114, no. 1; cf. *Nabil* 90.

even slightly from the norm was to be branded as disbelief, claims as extraordinary as those of the Bab were bound to arouse vehement reactions.

Surely Basṭāmī must have foreseen, from the experiences of his madrasa days, the grave consequences of his pronouncement. One might have expected him to adopt a more prudent tactic and to confine his proselytism within the Shaykhi community. For Basṭāmī and other early Babis, however, a potentially-dangerous confrontation with a hostile mujtahid was part of an apocalyptic scenario in which both announcer and denier played predestined parts. In his rejection of the new revelation, Muḥammad Ḥasan was to be counted among the people of the fire, as *Qayyūm al-Asmā'* had predicted. The polarization of fire and Paradise was an inseparable part of Insurrection. There was little room for prudence and conciliation even if his followers had tried to comply with the Bab's recommended policy of prudence.

Perhaps less predictable were the extent and gravity of the measures adopted in response to Basṭāmī's address. An unexpected alliance of the ʿulama of Najaf and Karbalā', under the influence of Shaykh Muḥammad Ḥasan, also denounced the new movement.[61] More significantly, a number of the Shaykhis also took part in the action.[62] The widespread Babi preaching alarmed some individuals like Mullā Ḥasan Gauhar who, in spite of their earlier acquaintance with Basṭāmī, were anxious to register their opposition. "Even the Shaykhis who already testified to Mullā ʿAlī's [Basṭāmī's] piety, sincerity, and learning" joined hands with the supporters of Muḥammad Ḥasan, their original adversaries,[63] to warn Basṭāmī "of the danger which he incurred in giving currency" to the Babi claims.[64]

A large number of the Shaykhis of the ʿAtabāt appear to have continued to support Basṭāmi, however. They were "in avowed expectation of the speedy advent of the Imam," writes Rawlinson, "and declared themselves ready to join the Precursor, as soon as he should appear amongst them."[65]

The public support for the new claimant encouraged the opposition to seek assistance from a different quarter. Toward the middle of Shawwāl 1260/end of October 1844, Basṭāmī's opponents were finally able to draw the attention of Turkish authorities to the danger of the new heresy. The widespread distribution of the new Qur'ān provided concrete evidence to accuse the Babis of "local dissuasions."[66] The supporters of Shaykh Muḥammad Ḥasan took the initiative and even went as far as to arrest Basṭāmī, put him in chains, and deliver him to the local Turkish officials.[67]

[61]F.O. 248/114, no. 1.
[62]*Nabil* 90–91.
[63]Ibid. 91.
[64]F.O. 248/114, no. 1.
[65]Ibid. Rawlinson's remark verifies reports regarding the messianic expectations in the ʿAtabāt.
[66]Ibid.
[67]*Nabil* 91.

It is clear that his arrest was with the cooperation of the Shaykhi elements, who seem to have been sufficiently disturbed to bring the Ottoman's onto the scene. Basṭāmī was held on charges of blasphemy, dissemination of heretical literature, and disturbing the public peace, and sent to Baghdad to await further interrogation.[68]

The Baghdad Trial

The arrest of Mullā ʿAlī Basṭāmī by the Ottoman authorities added a new dimension to what had begun as an internal Shiʿite dispute. In due course, political circumstances in Iraq turned Basṭāmī's arrest and ensuing trial into an overwhelming issue in Shiʿite-Sunni relations. The question of a new prophetic revelation affected a wide range of political and religious interests and eventually led to a confrontation that to some extent overshadowed the primary issue of the Babi claims. The Ottoman governor of Baghdad, representatives of the Persian and British governments, and Sunni religious authorities of different attitudes as well became involved in the case. The new heresy had the effect of bringing to the surface the long-standing tensions between the government-supported Sunni ʿulama and the persecuted Shiʿite public. "Instead in fact of a mere dispute between two rival schools in the town of Najef [Najaf], the question has now become one of virulent contest between the Soonee [Sunni] and Sheah [Shiʿite] sects, or which is the same thing in this part of the Ottoman Empire, between Turkish and Persian population."[69]

In the renewal of these sectarian tensions, the events of the preceeding years—particularly the massacre of Karbalā' the year before by order of Najīb Pāshā, the governor of the province—had some bearing. The swift arrest of Basṭāmī was intended to deprive the Ottoman authorities of any pretext to cause further trouble. The appointment of Najīb Pāshā in 1842 as the governor *(vālī)* of Iraq in place of the more lenient Muḥammad Rizā Pāshā sharply increased the fears of the Shiʿite ʿulama who, particularly after the reassertion of the Turkish authority in Karbalā', were more conscious than before of the Ottomans.[70]

The change in the political climate of the province was further boosted by the attempt to impose more powerful and centralized government.[71] Najīb Pāshā, an exceptionally forceful governor, combined shrewdness with anti-

[68]Rawlinson sets 8 Jan. 1845 (28 Dhū al-Ḥijja 1260) as the beginning of Basṭāmī's public declaration, which led to his arrest about the beginning of Shawwāl 1260/October 1844. This roughly corresponds to Qatīl's date. Rawlinson's report of 30 April 1845 (F.O. 195/237) states that "the priest of Shiraz was sent to Constantinople a few days before." This gives us the date of his arrest as the end of October 1844, nearly a fortnight after his first public declaration.

[69]F.O. 248/114, no. 1.

[70]A. al-Azzāwī *Tārīkh al-ʿIrāq bayn Iḥtilālayn,* 8 vols. (Baghdad, VII, 1375/1955) VII, 58–63.

[71]S.T. Longrigg *Four Centuries of Modern Iraq* (Oxford, 1925) 278, 281–83.

Shiʿite convictions.[72] His appointment to the troublesome and relatively backward *pāshālīq* of Baghdad was partly due to the intention of the Tanẓīmāt reformers to introduce some reform into the province. The harsh suppression of the Karbalā' was justified as an attempt to achieve greater centralization, which was Najīb's mandate. Indeed, his governorship was distinguished by some degree of success and efficiency.[73] But it was marred by a combination of repressive measures, heavy taxation, and markedly discriminatory policies.[74]

Najīb's measures were regarded particularly unfavorably by the traditionally pro-Iranian Shiʿites, who saw the efforts of the vālī being directed toward the elimination of traditional liberties. Resistance to the Ottoman legal system in the Holy Cities, the persistence of the mujtahids in maintaining some form of autonomy,[75] dissatisfaction of the Persian merchant community in Baghdad with the newly imposed levies,[76] and grievance caused by the imposition of passport restrictions for Persian pilgrims created more discontent. This situation was further complicated by incessant tribal clashes on the eastern frontiers and unending border disputes with the Persian government over the Kurdish boundaries and the control of the port of Muḥammara.[77]

In dealing with the religious resistance, Najīb tolerated no challenge to the Ottoman jurisdiction. On a few occasions he strongly condemned the chief mujtahid of Karbalā', Sayyid Ibrāhīm Qazvīnī, for exercising Shiʿite jurisprudence instead of referring legal cases to Ottoman Ḥanafī courts. He writes to him: "The object of the present address to you is to warn you that there is no legal tribunal recognized in the Ottoman domination but that which is presided over by the Kadhi [Qāḍī] or his deputy—and the naib [deputy] of Karbela is thus the only constituted authority who can decide upon questions of civil law in the district which you inhabit."[78] In some instances he did not hesitate to act with more severity against those who openly challenged Ḥanafī law.[79] Such mujtahids as Shaykh Ḥasan Najafī

[72]F.O. 248/114, no. 1. Najīb Pāshā descended from a noble family of Istanbul that enjoyed close contact with the Ottoman court. Longrigg *Four Centuries* 283 and al-Azzāwī *Tārīkh* 64.

[73]Najīb Pāshā's measures to improve the affairs of the province to some extent helped the development of a new judicial and administrative system. A whole body of Ottoman officials, who gradually took over, limited the power of the local notables (Longrigg 281–82).

[74]F.O. 248/114, no. 12, 3 April 1845, Rawlinson to Sheil.

[75]F.O. 248/114, no. 12, and 195/237, no. 23, 23 June 1845, Rawlinson to Canning.

[76]In his dispatches to Canning, the Baghdad consul reports that the recent 4 percent tax that Najīb Pāshā levied on the exports of Persian merchants (F.O. 195/237, no. 22, 15 May 1844) caused "agitation amongst the mercantile community" of Baghdad (F.O. 195/237, no. 25, 29 May 1844).

[77]A large number of dispatches written by the British Consul General in Baghdad (F.O. 195/237, Rawlinson to Canning 1843–1846, and F.O. 248/114, Rawlinson to Sheil 1843–1846) are devoted primarily to the tribal and frontier disputes between Iran and the Ottoman Empire.

[78]Translation enclosed in F.O. 248/114, no. 12, 3 April 1845, Rawlinson to Sheil.

[79]al-ʿAzzāwī *Tārīkh* VII, 64 cites the case of Sulaymān al-Ghannām in 1258/1842, who was executed by Najīb Pāshā's order.

Kāshif al-Ghiṭā' and Sayyid Ibrāhīm Qazvīnī, who feared for their personal safety,[80] and Sayyid Kāẓim Rashtī, in order to be protected against his opponents, reconciled themselves with him. On the Najīb's return from his assault on Karbalā', for example, Ḥasan Kāshif al-Ghiṭā'—whose maternal uncle had already been executed under the previous vālī for contempt to Sunni law provided every hospitality for the vālī and his retinue, in hopes of forestalling similar reprisals on the Shi'ites of Najaf.[81]

The case of Mullā 'Alī Basṭāmī thus became the focal point for a community that was seeking an outlet for its resentments. It particularly attracted the sympathy of the low-ranking ṭullāb, Persian merchants, and all those who detested the mujtahids' compromise with the Turks. When Basṭāmī was brought to Baghdad, Najīb, treating the case as a religious one, referred it to the official Sunni court. Being aware of the general Shi'ite discontent, he was unlikely to disturb the uneasy peace that had been achieved in the past few months. Rawlinson reports: "The affair created no great sensation at the time and from the moderate language which Nejib Pasha held in conversing on the subject, I thought it likely that the obnoxious book[82] would be destroyed and that the bearer of it would merely be banished from the Turkish dominion—such indeed was the extreme punishment contemplated by the Sheeas of Nejaf."[83]

But the 'ulama of Baghdad seem not to have shared the same views. In the initial gathering of religious judges and officials in the Government House, the Sunni 'ulama were ready to demonstrate their full legal power.[84] In the brief cross-examination that followed the enumeration of Basṭāmī's charges, the 'ulama upheld the charge of blasphemy and recommended the maximum penalty of death for the Persian infidel.[85] To Rawlinson's disappointment, contrary to his earlier reassuring platitudes, the pasha, too, expressed approval of the verdict of the tribunal. "Nejib Pasha, whose sectarian prejudices are excitable, has, I regret to say, allowed himself to adapt to their full extent, the views of the Soonee [Sunni] officers and I foresee that a determined effort will be made to obtain the condemnation and the execution of the unfortunate Shirazee (Shīrāzī)."[86]

[80]*QU* 13–14.

[81]*TMS* II/1, 318 citing Shaykh 'Abbās Kāshif al-Ghiṭā' *Nabdhat al-Gharrā' fī Aḥwāl al-Ḥasan al-Ja'farī.* Also M. A. Amīn *A'yān al-Shī'a* (Damascus, 1946) XXI, 133–36. See *QU* (106), for Najīb's visit to Muḥammad Ḥasan Najafī and his sarcastic remark in the shrine of 'Alī.

[82]Referring to *Qayyūm 'al-Asmā'*.

[83]F.O. 248/114, no. 1, Rawlinson to Sheil.

[84]*Nabil* 91. *QU* (185) refers to "Sunni *qaḍīs, muftīs,* and *effendīs*" who were present in the first trial; the English edition of *Nabil's Narrative* calls them "notables and Government officials of that city." *Nabil,* quoting Ḥājjī Hāshim 'Aṭṭār, states that in this session the celebrated chief muftī of Baghdad, Shaykh Maḥmūd Ālūsī (see below), was also present, but on account of some disagreement he hastily left the gathering.

[85]F.O. 248/114, no. 1; *Nabil* 91; *QU* 185.

[86]F.O. 248/114, no. 1. By the name "Shīrāzī" Rawlinson refers to Basṭāmī, who throughout remains unnamed. Babis are only alluded to as the followers of the "new heresy." Rawlinson presumably uses the name Shīrāzī because of insufficient information on Basṭāmī's identity. However, the name was either adopted by Basṭāmī himself or was given to him by the public, who associated him with the Shīrāzī Bab.

The sentence passed by the Sunni court, which had "taken up the case in rancorous spirit of bigotry,"[87] was not acceptable to the Shiʿites. Regardless of the merits of the case, they saw the approval of the sentence as subordination to Sunni jurisdiction.[88] From their point of view, compliance with such a verdict would be tantamount to submission to other restrictions. In response to these apprehensions Najīb Pāshā, who feared that the "sympathies of the entire Sheeah [Shiʿite] sect"[89] might be provoked, in spite of his earlier approval, decided to postpone ratification of the court's verdict pending further investigation. A combination of factions interested in the outcome of the trial demanded a more cautious trial by a group of jurists who would represent the main parties involved.

After the long and bitter conflicts between the Persian and Ottoman governments over the preceding years, the response of the Persian authorities to Najīb's intentions was one of caution and mistrust. The consequences of the trial were bound to affect not only the Shiʿite community in Iraq but jeopardize the already shaky equilibrium in the Erzeroum conference, then under way.[90] As Rawlinson indicates: "In the present state of irritable feeling which exists between the governments of Persia and Turkey, I cannot doubt but that the capital punishment of the Shirazee [i.e., Basṭāmī] or the persecution of the Transcendentalists of Nejef will be viewed with much exasperation by the court of Tehran."[91]

Muḥibb ʿAlī Khān Mākū'ī, the governor of Kirmānshāh, probably acting with Ḥājjī Mīrza Āqāsī's approval, had already protested the improper arrest and imprisonment of a Persian subject on "mere accusation."[92] In a friendly letter to the British consul in Baghdad,[93] regarding the long deten-

[87]Ibid.

[88]Ibid.

[89]Ibid.

[90]At this time the Erzeroum (Arz-i Rūm) conference was being held. It was originally convened at the instigation of the British and Russian governments to settle various border disputes between the two countries as well as the traffic of pilgrims and the status of Persian citizens in the Holy Cities. These issues were directly connected to Najīb Pāshā and the Persian government could not afford another disaster like the Karbalā' massacre. For the Erzeroum conference see, among other sources: F. Ādamīyat *Amīr Kabīr va Irān* 3d ed. (Tehran, 1348/1969) 64–153; and R. Curzon *Armenia: A Year at Erzeroum, and on the Frontiers of Russia, Turkey, and Persia* (London, 1854).

[91]F.O. 248/114, no. 1. Rawlinson, in spite of his interest and involvement in the case, is still unfamiliar with the Shiʿite denominations. He wrongly identifies Shaykhis and Uṣūlīs and translates Ūṣūlī as "transcendentalists," which approximates the other title of Shaykhis, *Kashfīya* (Illuminists).

[92]Muḥibb ʿAlī Khān was governor of Kirmānshāh during the latter part of Muḥammad Shāh's reign. He was among the large number of Mākū'ī officials who came to power and almost monopolized local and provincial offices mainly because of their connection with Ḥājjī Mīrzā Āqāsī. Muḥibb ʿAlī Khān, who was promoted toward the end of his career to the rank of *mīr panj,* was finally disgraced and lost his office as a result of local disturbances and riots following the death of Muḥammad Shāh in 1264/1848. *NT* III, 166; cf. M. J. Khūrmūjī *Ḥaqā'iq al-Akhbār-i Nāṣirī* 2d ed. (Tehran, 1344 Sh./1965) 44. See also Momen *Religions* 85–86 n.

[93]Muḥibb ʿAlī Khān's friendship with the British consul in Baghdad was apparently established during Rawlinson's journey to Kirmānshāh in the previous year (F.O. 248/114, 1844). Translation of his letter enclosed in dispatch F.O. 248/114, no. 1.

tion of the "inferior priest of Shiraz,"[94] Muḥibb ʿAlī Khān insisted that even if he were guilty of the charges, "he ought not to be subjected to arrest—if his crime were proved, his punishment should be that of banishment from the Turkish territory." He then asked Rawlinson, "as a well-wisher for the preservation of friendship between the two governments," to intervene and to suggest to Najīb that "if the guilt of the Persian be fully substantiated, he may be sent to Kermanshah, in order that I may transfer him to Tehran for punishment, and if on the other hand, the accusation against him proves to be malicious and without foundation, he may be at once released and set at liberty."[95]

In acting in support of Basṭāmī the Persian authorities were not motivated by humanitarian or even sympathetic feelings. "The Persian Government has itself on several occasions sustained inconvenience from impostors professing to be the forerunners of the Imam Mahdi."[96] Rawlinson, who himself believed in "the necessity of crushing at the outset any popular movement connected with such a matter,"[97] nonetheless recommended to Stratford Canning, the British ambassador in Istanbul, to interpose "pleas both of humanity and policy in favor of the condemned parties."[98] He hoped to encourage Canning to take measures to reverse the Baghdad verdict. In other recent cases British intervention had saved the lives of religious offenders convicted by Sunni tribunals. A few months earlier, Rawlinson, in the case of a Christian who recanted after a forced conversion, reported to Canning: "There has been a good deal of discussion among the priesthood of this city on the subject of the concession which your Excellency has thus happily succeeded in obtaining from the Turkish Government and I have understood that they express themselves with much fanatical rancor, but both is the Government too strong and the populace too little under the influence of the Ulama, to give any reasonable cause for apprehending danger from their bigotry or disappointment."[99] Furthermore, he acknowledged that "Nejib Pasha had already received instructions from his Government to refer to Constantinople, wherever a case occurred in this Pashalic of a Christian who had embraced Islamism returning to his former faith."[100]

It seems, however, that in this case stubborn Najīb Pāshā resisted any intervention or mediation by a foreign representative. "His Excellency is not disposed to listen to any foreign mediation or interference," writes Rawlinson. "In reply to my own communication he has observed that Persian

[94]In the governor's letter, which relies on "accounts which have reached [him] from Baghdad," Basṭāmī was also referred to as "Shīrāzī."

[95]Ibid.

[96]F.O. 248/114, no. 1.

[97]Ibid.

[98]Ibid.

[99]F.O. 195/237, no. 20, 1 May 1844, Rawlinson to Canning. The execution of a Christian on charges of apostasy created great excitement in Europe. An account of the event appears in *Parliamentary Papers* 1844, vol. LI, 153–96, "Correspondence relating to the Executions in Turkey for Apostacy from Islamism."

[100]Ibid.

subjects residing in Turkey are in civil, criminal, and religious matters, entirely subject to Ottoman law, and that neither the Persian government, nor the Consuls of that power, nor the High Priests of the Sheeah [Shiʿite] sect have any further protective privilege than that of seeing justice duly administrated according to the forms and usages of Soonee tribunals."[101] To tackle so sensitive a problem, the pasha, perhaps on the advice of the central government, decided to stage an all-parties tribunal. "Nejib Pāshā at the same time, to give all due formality to his proceedings, and to divest the affair of the appearance of mere sectarian prosecution, has brought in the chief Priests from Najef and Karbela, to hold a solemn Court of Inquisition in conjunction with the heads of the Soonee religion in Baghdad."[102] Whatever the outcome of this tribunal, Najīb thought, it would be possible for him to overrule the verdict and refer the case to Istanbul. He assured Rawlinson that "he will not attempt to carry such sentence into execution either here or at Najef, pending reference to Constantinople."[103] As subsequent events showed, the fate of the Babi messenger was to be decided by the Sublime Porte. Yet the official gathering of twenty prominent Sunni ʿulama and twelve of their Shiʿite counterparts was in itself an unprecedented event.

The most eminent of the Sunni ʿulama who participated in the trial was Shaykh Abū al-Thanāʾ Shihāb al-Dīn Maḥmūd Ālūsī, the chief muftī of Baghdad and the author of a number of well-known theological works.[104] As one of the most prominent religious figures in the Ottoman empire, he had not hesitated in the past to take part in the political debates of the province.[105] With rare exceptions, Ālūsī was as a whole on the side of the Ottoman establishment. His view in relation to Shiʿism, however, seems to have undergone some change over the years. In 1249/1833 he devoted a whole chapter of his *al-Tibyān fī Sharḥ al-Burhān* to the subject of Imamate, strongly criticizing the Shiʿite doctrine and particularly attacking views on the expected Imam.[106] But Ālūsī's opposition seems to have been modified

[101]F.O. 248/114, no. 1.
[102]Ibid.
[103]Ibid.
[104]Most important of all is his comprehensive commentary on the Qurʾān, entitled *Rūḥ al-Maʿānī fī Tafsīr al-Qurʾān al-ʿAẓīm waʾl-Sabʿ al-Mathānī* (written circa 1254–1267/1838–1850), (Būlāq, 1301–1310/1883–1892; also Cairo, 1345/1926). A comprehensive list of Ālūsī's works appeared in M. ʿAbd al-Hamīd *Ālūsī Mufassiran* (Baghdad, 1969) and there is a shorter version in *EI*²: ĀLŪSĪ (2).
[105]During the Baghdad siege of 1831, Ālūsī collaborated with the Mamlūk vālī, Dāūd Pāshā, against the Ottoman supremacy in Iraq (see ʿAlī al-Wardī *Lamaḥāt Ijtimāʿīya min Tārīkh al-ʿIrāq al-Ḥadīth,* 3 vols. (Baghdad 1971) II, 101). He was promoted to the office of chief muftī when he was still in his late thirties (A. al-ʿAzzāwī *Dhikrā Abī al-Thanāʾ al-Ālūsī* [Baghdad, n.d.] 50–52). His support for Ottoman sovereignty during the critical years of the 1830s came at the time when the Ottomans was in dire need of local support against Muḥammad ʿAlī's threat to Iraq. In his *al-Tibyān fī Sharḥ al-Burhān* (*Ālūsī Mufassiran* 109–11) he glorified the Ottoman sultan and emphasized the necessity of obeying his sovereignty according to the Islamic sharīʿa.
[106]*Ālūsī Mufassiran* 109–11. Also in *al-Nafaḥāt al-Qudsīya fī al-Radd ʿalā al-Imāmīya,*

toward the end of his life. In his last work, *Nahj al-Salāma ilā Mabāḥith al-Imāma*[107] (1278/1861), where he deals with such contemporaries as Shaykhīs and Babis, he tries to maintain his impartiality.[108] Ālūsī's treatment of Shiʿism suggests a coexistence with Shiʿism so long as it does not pose a threat to the superiority of the Sunni law.[109]

The two major Shiʿite mujtahids, Sayyid Ibrāhīm Qazvīnī and Shaykh Ḥasan Kāshif al-Ghiṭā', were "most unwilling" to attend the Baghdad trial.[110] Their reluctance was presumably the result of their skeptical attitude toward a case that attracted so much publicity. To adopt an independent position from that of the Sunni authorities would have meant to defend a heretic whose Shaykhi background and present stand made him wholly unacceptable to the ʿulama. (Perhaps this very consideration prevented Shaykh Muḥammad Ḥasan Najafī from participating in the trial, since he was almost certainly invited to the gathering.) These disadvantages were balanced by the fact that for the first time a formal recognition of the position of the Shiʿite jurists was implied. Participation in the trial, so long as it did not result in the ratification of a severe anti-Shiʿite verdict, might even elevate the mujtahids in the Shiʿite clerical hierarchy.

Sayyid Ibrāhīm Qazvīnī in particular had the reputation of being "very prudent." Indeed, "no one ever heard him saying a word of condemnation or criticism in a gathering or in public."[111] The chief mujtahid of Karbalā',[112] he is mostly known because of his work *Ḍawābiṭ al-Uṣūl*.[113] A zealous jurist, he spent most of his life studying uṣūl al-fiqh.[114] His prolonged struggle with Rashtī was not limited to theoretical differences but extended to political rivalry.[115] Rapid expansion of Shaykhism, in particular, alarmed Qazvīnī.[116] Nevertheless, his dislike for Shaykhis seldom came to an open confrontation. In response to a request by the Shiʿites of India to give his opinion on the condemnation of the Shaykhis, for instance, he answered with a few equivocal quotations from the Qur'ān and ḥadīth.[117] We are told that later he even tried to prevent one of his adherents, Shaykh Mahdī Kujūrī, from publishing a refutation of Rashtī's *Dalīl al-Mutaḥa-*

---

written in 1269/1853–1854 (MS cited in *Ālūsī Mufassiran* 122), he attacks the Shiʿite theory of Imamate.

[107]Unfinished MS (Awqāf Library, Baghdad, no. B 4/678) listed in *Ālūsī Mufassiran*, 125.

[108]Ibid.

[109]Claims that Ālūsī's support for the Ottoman sultan and his opposition to Shiʿism were because of the practicing taqīya are highly improbable. (*QU* 186–87; cf. *Lamaḥāt Ijtimāʿīya*, 105–6).

[110]F.O. 248/114, no. 1.

[111]*QU* 55–56; cf. 14.

[112]Ibid. 10.

[113]First published in 1271/1854 (*al-Dharīʿa* XV, 119). A detailed account of Ibrāhīm Qazvīnī's numerous works appears in *RJ* 12–13, and *TAS* II/7, 10–11.

[114]Ibid. 17–18.

[115]Ibid. 7.

[116]*Dalīl al-Mutaḥayyirīn* 90.

[117]Ibid. 4–10; cf. *QU* 55–56.

yyirīn.[118] Qazvīnī was also for a long time the receiver and distributor of the Oudh Bequest and other endowments in Karbalā'.[119] This task, which in itself contributed to his high status in Iraq, incurred perpetual rivalry from other quarters in the Shi'ite community.[120] Qazvīnī's relations with the Turkish authorities were occasionally troubled by this and other issues such as the validity of his juristic authority, but thanks to his customary prudence he was able to maintain his influence in local politics.[121] On several occasions, his intervention saved Shi'ite lives in Sunni official courts.[122]

Shaykh Ḥasan Kāshif al-Ghiṭā', son of Shaykh Ja'far Najafī, mainly represented the Arab Shi'ites of Iraq.[123] A member of an outstanding jurist family, he enjoyed popularity and influence no less than his Persian contemporaries.[124] Some sources hold him above Shaykh Muḥammad Ḥasan Najafī in his mastery of jurisprudence.[125] His leadership gained him respect from Shi'ites and Sunnis alike.[126] Thanks to the friendly relations between Kāshif al-Ghiṭā''s family and Aḥsā'ī, it seems that his attitude toward the Shaykhis was moderate compared to other Uṣūlīs.[127] During the frequent waves of condemnation his two elder brothers tried to abate the Bālāsarī enmity and even to bring about a reconciliation between the two parties.

The composition of the 'ulama who attended the Baghdad trial reflects the governor's intention that all different factions be represented.[128] The thir-

[118]*QU* 56. Allegations concerning Rashtī's reproach of Ibrāhīm Qazvīnī contradicts *Dalīl*'s (6–7) deliberate avoidance of any personal attack on him.

[119]*QU* 7–10. The Shi'ite ruler of Oudh and Lucknow Sulṭān Ghāzī al-Dīn Ḥaydar had established an endowment of a hundred *lakhs* of rupees, the proceeds of which were to be divided among two mujtahids, one in Najaf and one in Karbalā', for distribution among ṭullāb and other deserving people (M. Maḥmūd *Tārīkh-i Ravābiṭ-i Sīyasī-yi Īrān va Inglīs dar Qarn-i Nūzdahum-i Mīlādī*, 8 vols. [Tehran, 1328 Sh./1949] VI, 1742).

[120]On a number of occasions it was not only eminent mujtahids like Shaykh Muḥammad Ḥasan Najafī who used all at their disposal to receive the lion's share (*QU* 10). Some ṭullāb (*Qatīl* 519) and even the head of the Yarmāzīya (brigandage) in Karbalā' virtually blackmailed Qazvīnī in order to get part of the annual benefits (*QU* 12).

[121]*QU* 13–15.

[122]Ibid.

[123]*RJ* 182.

[124]*RA* III, 343; *TAS* II/1, 316–20. Also for Kāshif al-Ghiṭā''s family see *EI*²: KĀSHĪF AL-GHIṬĀ' (W. Madelung). *QU* (186) states that "the whole family, whether male or female, were faqīhs."

[125]*QU* 185. Shaykh 'Alī Āl Kāshif al-Ghiṭā' confirms that "he was an Uṣūlī mujtahid with insight into akhbār and Arabic philology. He was also a writer and poet" *(al-Ḥuṣūn al-Manī'a*, cited in *TAS* II/1, 318).

[126]*RJ* 182. *RA* (III, 343) believes that Kāshif al-Ghiṭā' had a joint riyāsa with Shaykh Muḥammad Ḥasan Najafī over the Shi'ite community. *TAS* (II/1, 317), quoting Sayyid Muḥammad al-Hindī's *Naẓm al-Li'āl*, also refers to his joint leadership.

[127]*Dalīl al-Mutaḥayyirīn* refers to Aḥsā'ī's occasional visits to Shaykh Ja'far Najafī, father of Ḥasan Kāshif al-Ghiṭā', and quotes part of his ijāza praising Aḥsā'ī's scholarly treatise (33–34, 103–6).

[128]For the 'ulama present in the trial see M. Momen, "The Trial of Mullā 'Alī Basṭāmī: A Combined Sunnī-Shī'ī Fatwā against the Bāb," *Iran* 20 (1982), 113–43 (130–40). Besides the signers of the fatwā other Shi'ites seem to have attended the tribunal. *Baghdādī* (107), for instance, names two mujtahids from Kāẓimayn: Shaykh Ḥasan ibn Asadullāh, a student of Kāshif al-Ghiṭā', and Shaykh Muḥammad Ḥasan Yāsīnī, the chief mujtahid of Kāẓimayn.

teen known Shiʿite ʿulama who were invited represented almost all the different tendencies on the Shiʿite side. In addition to mujtahids from Karbalāʾ, Najaf and Kāẓimayn, the Shaykhis were also represented by Mullā Ḥasan Gauhar.[129] His presence side by side with the Uṣūlīs confirms his willingness to see his own ex-classmate condemned. In fact Gauhar's stand tilted so much in the opposite direction that Āghā Buzurg Ṭihrānī even states that "it is not possible to say that he was an absolute Shaykhi just because he studied under the above mentioned [Aḥsāʾī and Rashtī]. He should therefore be regarded as being of the orthodox camp."[130] His anti-Babi attitude is also noted by Nāʾib al-Ṣadr, who points out that although "he was one of the close adherents of the late Sayyid, he rejected both factions" of Bābī and Ruknī (followers of Kirmānī).[131] At a time when he was still regarded by some as the temporary successor of Rashtī, this inclination toward non-Shaykhis further weakened Gauhar's position.[132] Another Shaykhi dignitary, Shaykh Muḥammad Shibl al-Baghdādī, was also invited, presumably to represent the Arab followers of Rashtī. But being already a supporter of Basṭāmī, he decided not to participate. "He left Baghdad in haste since he reckoned that the vālī intended to obtain approval for the refutation of the cause of God."[133]

On the Sunni side it seems that the entire delegation fell under the influence of Ālūsī. Muḥammad Amīn al-Wāʿiẓ, a public orator and the head of the Qādirī order in Baghdad, was a former pupil of Ālūsī and maintained friendly relations with him.[134] The previous muftī of Baghdad, Muḥammad Saʿīd Afandī, who had earlier been dismissed by Muḥammad Riżā Pāshā, was also a Naqshbandī Sufi.[135] Ālūsī speaks of the other two Sunni participants with reverence and respect.[136] The Sufi attachment is also common among most other Sunni participants. Altogether the Sunni delegation consisted of five muftīs, nine teachers of the Baghdad madrasas, the *naqīb al-*

[129]Shaykh ʿAbbās ibn Shaykh Ḥasan Kāshif al-Ghiṭāʾ *Nabdhat al-Gharrā*ʾ MS cited in *TAS* II/1, 318. As a biography of the author's father, it contains some valuable information about the Baghdad gathering, including a list of some of the Shiʿite ʿulama.

[130]*TAS* II/1, 341–42, under al-Shaykh Mullā Ḥasan al-Qarachihdāghī.

[131]*TH* III, 338.

[132]*Qatīl* (508) refers to two Shaykhi ʿulama, Shaykh Aḥmad Mashkūr al-Najafī and Shaykh Raḍī Qaṣīr, who accepted Gauhar's leadership. Yet later, when writing a "treatise to establish Karīm Khān's delusion" *(TAS* II/1, 342), it looks as though Gauhar is fighting an already lost battle with his rivals.

[133]*Baghdādī* 107.

[134]ʿAlī ʿAlā al-Dīn Ālūsī *al-Durr al-Muntathar fī Rijāl al-Qarn al-Thāniya ʿAshar waʾl-Thālitha ʿAshar,* ed. J. Ālūsī and A. al-Jabūrī (Baghdad, 1976) 28; cf. 92 citing Maḥmūd Ālūsī's reference to him in *Tafsīr Rūḥ al-Maʿānī,* I. He is the author of a number of works on Ḥanafī fiqh.

[135]*TH* III, 560. His dismissal, according to most sources, was principally caused by the muftī's disregard for the previous vālī's Shiʿite sentiments (*Dhikrā Abī al-Thanā*ʾ *Ālūsī* 51–52; *al-Durr al-Muntathar* 170).

[136]*TH* III, 560–61, citing Ālūsī's *Nashwat al-Shumūl.*

ashrāf (chief of the notables), the nāʾib of Baghdad, two shaykhs of the Sunni Sufi orders, and a public orator *(khaṭīb)*.[137]

The Shiʿite-Sunni encounter was striking enough to capture the attention of the public. It is likely that Najīb Pāshā's attempt to hold the Baghdad trial was a primary experiment with the introduction of a provincial council (*majlis*) recommended by the Tanẓīmāt. Some Shiʿites regarded the tribunal as a step forward in gaining equal rights. The prospects of such a gathering were encouraging to Shiʿite notables. The Āl Kubba, an influential Shiʿite family of Baghdad, were anxious to provide all necessities, including a new robe for Shaykh Ḥasan Kāshif al-Ghiṭāʾ, in order to dignify the appearance of the Shiʿite ʿulama.[138]

Remote from the excitement and publicity that surrounded his case, Basṭāmī was spending his third month in the Baghdad jail. Al-Baghdādī reports that for three months his father, Shaykh Muḥammad, visited the "messenger" and heard from him the "word of God." Shaykh Muḥammad then "delivered whatever he had heard [from Basṭāmī] to the believers. During this brief period, a great number of people were converted."[139] Rawlinson, on the other hand, reports that Basṭāmī "pleaded on his first arrest that he was a mere messenger not responsible for the contents of the volume entrusted to his charge, and such a defense would probably have availed him in a Court of law, but whilst in confinement he has been unfortunately seduced in the presence of witnesses, suborned for the purpose of the Soonee mufti, into declaring his belief in the inspiration of the perverted passages, and I am apprehensive, therefore, that according to Muhammedan law, whether expounded by Sheeas or Soonees, he will be convicted of blasphemy."[140] This suggests that at the time of his arrest Basṭāmī probably tried not to reveal any direct connection between his own beliefs and the text of *Qayyūm al-Asmāʾ*. Later, however, during his confinement in Baghdad, either by his own wish or else under pressure, it seems that he confessed in the presence of witnesses to his belief that the author of *Qayyūm al-Asmāʾ* was divinely inspired. The growing popularity of the new daʿwa even during Basṭāmī's captivity no doubt hastened the date for the trial. "When the Government saw that the following of the cause is increasing day by day, the vālī, Najīb Pāshā, ordered the ʿulama to be present in

[137]For further details see Momen "Trial" 130–36. For the office of the muftī in the Ottoman system, among other sources see H. A. R. Gibb and H. Bowen *Islamic Society and the West* (London and New York, 1950–1957) I, part 2, 133–38; S. J. Shaw *History of the Ottoman Empire and Modern Turkey*, 2 vols. (London and New York, 1976) I, 137–38.

[138]*Lamaḥāt Ijtimāʿīya* II, 139–40. Recollections of an old Baghdādī from an unnamed source.

[139]*Baghdādī* 106.

[140]F.O. 248/114, no. 1.

Baghdad."[141] On 4 Muḥarram 1261/13 January 1845, when the court finally assembled,[142] it was less than a week to 10 Muḥarram (ʿĀshūrā': the day of Ḥusayn's martyrdom),[143] when the unknown Bab was supposed to appear in the holy land. This timing suggests that Najīb, anxious about the Shiʿite mournings and possible resurgence of anti-Ottoman sentiments, decided to hold the trial and gain the necessary fatwā before the due date.

With Najīb presiding the trial started. The first issue concerning the court was the nature of the prophecies contained in the new book. There was a unanimous belief that the book was "a blasphemous production."[144] The tribunal also agreed that "parties avowing a belief in the readings which it contained were to be liable to the punishment of death."[145] Though the Babis were not specifically mentioned by name, this is the first instance where belief in the new daʿwa required the death penalty.

The contents of the fatwā of the Baghdad trial, signed by thirty of the participants, illustrates the unanimity of opinion on the blasphemous nature of *Qayyūm al-Asmā'*.[146] In compliance with the common practice in the Ottoman legal proceedings, the first part defines the charges and elaborates on details, charging that *Qayyūm al-Asmā'* resembles the Qur'ān in format and takes liberties with the text of the Holy Book. It makes note of the author's claim to be divinely inspired and to be the Z̲ikr and the Bab; brings the charges of extremism (ghulūw), "mockery of religion," and "making light of the Sharīʿa;" and finally points out that the author inserted "a proscription against the ʿulama" teaching anything other than the new book.[147] After these charges, it asks the tribunal: "And so is he an unbeliever by virtue of all that we have mentioned or not? And is the one who has believed in him and has lent him credence in this matter and has assisted him in spreading and propagating it and has preached it to the people an unbeliever or not?"[148] To substantiate these charges, numerous passages are quoted from seventeen sūras of *Qayyūm al-Asmā'* in which the writer of the fatwā highlights the points in question.[149] The document does not refer to

[141] *Baghdādī* 106–7.

[142] F.O. 248/114 (also 195/237), no. 2, 16 Jan. 1845, Rawlinson to Sheil. The trial was held in the Government House (Dār al-Imāra) in Baghdad. (Shaykh Ḥusayn Nūrī *Mustadrak al-Wasā'il*, epilogue, cited in *TAS* II/1, 319).

[143] For its significance in Shiʿite Traditions see *EI*²: ʿĀSHŪRĀ'; *EIr:* ʿĀŠŪRĀ' and *Shorter EI:* MUḤARRAM. According to Shiʿite accounts, on this day the Qā'im would enter Karbalā' to avenge the martyrdom of Ḥusayn.

[144] F.O. 248/114, no. 2.

[145] Ibid.

[146] This important document, together with the accompanying reports of Najīb Pāshā, were found recently among miscellaneous files from Baghdad in the Ottoman Archive in Istanbul by Sami Doktoroglu. The entire text of the fatwā, consisting of the questions and the respective answers, has been translated and analyzed by M. Momen in "Trial" 118–40.

[147] Momen "Trial" 118–20.

[148] Ibid. 119.

[149] Ibid. 120–30. The cited passages of *QA* in the fatwā provide a good specimen of some of the Bab's earlier claims and his views on the ʿulama. Momen demonstrates the close re-

any names, since a fatwā was supposed to clarify general legal points rather than passing a verdicts on any specific case.[150] While its main emphasis is on the initiator of the heresy and his spurious book, by implication it also targets the disseminator.

In his answer to the proposed questions, the first signatory of the fatwā, Ālūsī, declares scornfully that the producer of the book "has brought kinds of disbelief against which the believer is angered," and that "the matter on account of its simpleness has no need of argumentation." He recommends that "the prudent thing [to do] is to join this unbeliever to his two brothers, [Musaylima] the Liar and [al-Aswad] the Lord of the Ass, and make an exemplary punishment upon whoever has assisted in the spreading of his cause by word or deed."[151] The nineteen Sunni signatories were quick to translate Ālūsī's historical allusion into plain Arabic. "They all deserve death according to the sharīʿa," wrote Muḥammad Saʿīd Afandī, and the others all agreed.[152] Besides Ālūsī, who asked for unspecified "exemplary punishment" for whoever publicizes the claim, five other Sunni ʿulama specifically extended the death sentence to the Bab's followers and disseminators.

Ḥasan Kāshif al-Ghiṭā', Sayyid Ibrāhīm Qazvīnī, Mullā Ḥasan Gauhar and seven other Shiʿite signatories agreed with their Sunni counterparts as to the claimant's blasphemy. Kāshif al-Ghiṭā' found that anyone who claims such "falsehoods" and concocted such "corrupt words" and whoever believes in them is "an outright unbeliever."[153] Qazvīnī was confident that whoever followed this "unbelief" has "followed Satan and is worthy of the anger of the All-Merciful."[154] Unlike the Sunnis, however, none of the Shiʿite mujtahids specified what punishment beside the "anger of the All-Merciful" the author of the book and his supporters deserved.

The Shiʿites' omission of specific punishment seems to have been deliberate. The fact that the Shiʿite ʿulama avoided ratifying an outright death sentence did not put an end to the proceedings, however. After reaching its conclusion on the blasphemous nature of the new heresy, the court proceeded to a second issue, Basṭāmī's personal belief. Here it seems that the court decision was meant not only to affect Basṭāmī but to set an example for other Babi activists. The Shiʿite and Sunni points of view, however,

semblance between verses of *QA* and those of the Qur'ān. One of the objectives of the composer of the fatwā was to illustrate the Bab's deliberate imitation of the Qur'ānic style and format. This was a forbidden undertaking, which by itself deserved denunciation.

[150]See *EI*²: FATWĀ, ii, Ottoman Empire (J. R. Walsh).

[151]Momen "Trial" 130–31. It is interesting that Ālūsī, in order to come up with a historical precedence for the Bab's blasphemy, resorted to so-called false prophets of early Islam. For Musaylima, the well-known rival prophet to Muḥammad, see W. M. Watt, *Muḥammad at Medina* (Oxford, 1956) 134–36, and *Shorter EI:* MUSAILIMA. For al-Aswad ibn Kaʿb (ʿAns), another contemporary rival of Muḥammad, see Watt *Medina* 118–20.

[152]Momen "Trial" 131.

[153]Ibid. 137.

[154]Ibid.

diverged. *Qiṣaṣ al-ʿUlamāʾ* maintains that the Sunnis who represented the dominating Ḥanafī law on the basis of earlier conclusions argued that since "this book is an innovation, its bearer is also an innovator and among the 'corruptors of the earth,'[155] and therefore liable to death."[156] Kāshif al-Ghiṭāʾ, expressing the Shiʿite consensus, put forward a delicate technical objection. After a long argument in support of his view, he concluded that in this circumstance "the book by itself could not be regarded as a piece of firm evidence"[157] and so long as its bearer was unaware of its contents and did not believe in its claims, it was impossible to pass a sentence of death.[158]

Mullā ʿAlī Basṭāmī was closely cross-examined. Nearly all sources agree that his belief in the contents of the *Furqān* was scrutinized by the court, but differ as to his reply. In response to the court's question about the identity of the Lord of the Command (Ṣāḥib al-Amr), Basṭāmī maintained that "he is the righteous expected soul. He appeared and he is the one who was anticipated by the Holy Books."[159] Al-Baghdādī even goes as far as to state that Basṭāmī "glorified the Cause" by reciting some of the verses and prayers of the Bab to the jury and invited them to recognize the Bab's call.[160] Rawlinson, on the other hand, reports that Basṭāmī "himself distinctly repudiated the charge."[161] *Qiṣaṣ al-ʿUlamāʾ*, too, holds that the accused maintained that he had no knowledge or insight into the contents of the book and his belief was the belief of all Muslims.[162] With such contradictory reports, a firm conclusion regarding Basṭāmī's response is impossible.[163] It seems probable that Basṭāmī, bearing in mind the Bab's recommendation for prudence, avoided any direct commitment to *Qayyūm al-Asmāʾ*.

Here the chief muftī, trying to substantiate the charge against the Shiʿite objection, presented his witnesses to the court.[164] But it seems that he was able to produce scarcely firm evidence against the accused. "Although witnesses were brought forward, who stated that he had in their presence

155 *Mufsidīn fī al-arḍ,* from the Qurʾān II, 11.

156 *QU* 186.

157 Ibid.

158 Ibid. Throughout his account of the trial, Tunkābunī's refers to two preachers or "the most reliable believers of the Bab" who were charged and then tried in Baghdad, but he fails to give any further details. It is highly implausible that another Babi besides Basṭāmī was on trial.

159 *Baghdādī* 107.

160 Ibid.

161 F.O. 248/114, no. 2.

162 *QU* 186.

163 Al-Baghdādī, a devout Babi, perhaps on this occasion only relates the recollections of his father, who in turn was absent from the trial. His sympathy toward Basṭāmī perhaps prevented him or his father from saying anything that in their minds could damage Bastāmī's image. Rawlinson, on the other hand, who was probably informed of the proceedings of the trial through Mullā ʿAbd al-ʿAzīz, the Persian agent in Baghdad, though he tried to be precise, still gives a second-hand account. *Qiṣaṣ al-ʿUlamāʾ*, which does not provide any source, should also be treated with caution.

164 One can assume that they were the same people who were instigated to interview Basṭāmī in jail.

declared his adoption of the spurious text, of which he was the bearer," reports Rawlinson, "yet as there was reason to suspect the fidelity of their evidence, the Shiʿite divines were disposed to give him the benefit of his present disavowal."[165] The author of *Nabdhat al-Gharrā'* also indicates that it was Kāshif al-Ghiṭā' who, in spite of the muftī's persistence, once again made an objection and referring to Bastāmī's own statement, maintained that "since he repented, according to Sharīʿa, I accept his penitence."[166] Following these remarks, according to Shiʿite sources, Kāshif al-Ghiṭā' finally established his point,[167] but in the end, in spite of a long legal discussion, the two sides could reach no agreement. As Rawlinson had predicted, "after much discussion the Soonee law officers adjudged the culprit to be convicted of blasphemy and passed sentence of death on him accordingly, while the Sheeahs returned a verdict, that he was only guilty of dissemination of blasphemy and liable in consequence to no heavier punishment than imprisonment or banishment."[168]

The Shiʿite defense of Basṭāmī illustrates the way in which the penal Islamic code was adopted in the case of heresy. *Qiṣaṣ al-ʿUlamā'* implies that the ground for the prosecution of Basṭāmī was *bidʿa* (unlawful innovation),[169] *Nabdhat al-Gharrā'* suggests that the charge brought against him was apostasy (*irtidād*), which is punishable both according to Shiʿite and Ḥanafī law by death, particularly in the case of an apostate who was born Muslim.[170] Thus it is very likely that the two sides disagreed principally on the right of the accused to repent and return to Islam, since the views of Shiʿite and Sunni differ.

A third issue was raised in the trial concerning "the other parties implicated in the affair." Rawlinson tells us, certainly referring to the pro-Basṭāmī Shaykhis, that "the same difference of opinion was found to prevail between the Sheeah and Soonee divines." While the Shiʿites were in favor of forcible removal of all "parties openly avowing a belief in the expected immediate advent of the Imam" from the Holy Cities, the Sunnis called for "punishment of death."[171]

Whatever the opinion of the two sides and however eager each was to have its verdict prevail, it was fairly clear to all involved that neither of the sentences passed was going to be put into effect before reference was made

[165]F.O. 248/114, no. 2.

[166]*Nabdhat al-Gharrā'* 318–19.

[167]Ibid.; also *QU* 186.

[168]F.O. 248/114, no. 2.

[169]For the definition of *bidʿa* in Islam and its various categories see *EI*²: BIDʿA (J. Robson). Also I. Goldziher *Muslim Studies* trans. S. M. Stern, 2 vols. (London, 1967–1971) II, 22–27; al-Tahānawī *Kashshāf* 131 ff., 1251–52. For a comparison with similar terms see B. Lewis "The Significance of Heresy in the History of Islam" in *Islam in History* (London 1973) 217–36.

[170]For *irtidād* see *Shorter EI:* MURTADD; cf. *EI*²: KĀFIR; Zwemer *The Law of Apostasy in Islam* (London, 1924).

[171]F.O. 248/114, no. 2.

to the Sublime Porte. As Rawlinson states: "The different opinions have been duly recorded and attested and a reference on the subject will be immediately made to Constantinople by H[is] E[xcellency] Najīb Pāshā."[172] This understanding among the ʿulama supports the view that the quarrel over the case was largely for the sake of legal and religious standing in relation to the Ottoman central government.

Basṭāmī remained in jail for another three months before any instruction from Istanbul concerning his case reached Baghdad.[173] As the date of the Bab's arrival approached, excitement reached its peak. A "considerable uneasiness is beginning to display itself at Karbilā and Najef in regard to the expected manifestation of the Imam," reports Rawlinson, "and I am apprehensive that the measures now in progress will rather increase than allay excitement."[174]

But as the critical period of mid-Muḥarram passed without incident, the delay and finally the cancellation of the Bab's journey caused bitter disillusion and resentment among those who believed his manifestation would end the hardship and persecution forced upon his messenger.[175] In spite of the presence, at least for a time, of a noticeable number of early disciples in the Holy Cities (who are surprisingly absent from all accounts of the trial), no fresh attempt was made either to organize the sympathizers or to challenge the governor's decision to keep Basṭāmī in custody. Even after the emergence of Qurrat al-ʿAyn as leader, the early Babi community in Iraq continued to suffer from the consequences of Basṭāmī's arrest and trial and the Bab's failure to visit the ʿAtabāt.

The efforts during the following months by the Persian and British governments to settle Basṭāmī's case through diplomatic channels produced no definite result. Toward early Ṣafar 1261/mid-February 1845, Ḥājjī Mīrzā Āqāsī, informed of the result of the Baghdad trial, instructed the Persian agent in Baghdad "to demand the delivery into his own hand of the priest of Shiraz imprisoned for blasphemy, with a view to his deportation to Persia."[176]

Why was Āqāsī so anxious about the fate of an "inferior priest of Persia"? If Bastāmī had preached his mission in Iran and been tried under Shiʿite jurisdiction, he would hardly have received any better treatment from the authorities; witness the persecution shortly afterward of many of the Bab's supporters. The answer lies in the Persian policy toward the Ottoman government. Āqāsī was obliged to take action on a case that had the potential of

[172]Ibid. This certainly is a reference to the joint fatwā.
[173]*Baghdādī* 107; also F.O. 248/114, no. 19, 30 April, 1845 Rawlinson to Canning.
[174]F.O. 248/114, no. 2.
[175]For the events that led the Bab's change of plans, see below.
[176]F.O. 248/114, no. 10, 3 April 1845, Rawlinson to Sheil. Same as F.O. 195/237, no. 14, 2 April 1845, Rawlinson to Canning.

endangering the security of Persian subjects in Iraq. As is evident from a dispatch sent by Rawlinson to Colonel Justin Sheil, the British representative in Tehran, the fears and apprehensions of the Persian population of Iraq had not fully diminished: "The condemnation to death of a Persian Moolla at Baghdad for heresy has not caused here the sensation or irritation which might be anticipated, arising chiefly, I conjecture, from a disbelief that the sentence will be carried into execution. I trust so extreme a penalty will not be inflicted, for with whatever indifference this government may regard his fate, as this preacher belongs to the priesthood, that fanatic and influential class might be able to raise an inconvenient excitement among the Persian population."[177]

A few days later, as a result of Rawlinson's report and perhaps also because of the Persian demand, the British ambassador in Istanbul in concert with the Russian minister, impressed upon the Porte "the expediency of issuing instruction to the Governor of Baghdad to abstain from putting the individual in question to death, inflicting on him the mildest punishment consistent with the public tranquility."[178] The joint action of the European envoys was to prevent any further deterioration in the Turko-Persian relations. The British consul general in Baghdad seems to have been conscious of the fact that Turkish persistence in carrying out any tough measures would result in further sectarian conflict: "The more in fact these Mujtahids are degraded by the Turkish government, the more complete, I think, will be their ascendancy over the minds of their disciples and the only results, therefore, which are likely to attend the proscription of their public duties, are the more complete isolation of the Persian community of this province, and an increase of the rancorous feeling with which the dominant Soonee party is regarded."[179]

Finally, on 24 Rabīʿ al-Awwal 1261/14 April 1845, Najīb Pāshā received instructions from Istanbul to transfer Basṭāmī to the capital.[180] On 30 April Rawlinson reports that with the last Baghdad post, "the Persian priest of Shiraz so long detained in confinement at this place, was sent to Constantinople."[181] The subsequent fate of Mullā ʿAlī Basṭāmī remains a mystery to Babi-Bahāʾī sources. Nabīl Zarandī notes: "A few believed that on his way to Constantinople he had fallen ill and died. Others maintained that he had suffered martyrdom."[182] According to Mīrzā Yaḥyā Ṣubḥ-i Azal, Basṭāmī was arrested in Baghdad on his way to Rūm (Istanbul),[183] and "near

[177]F.O. 60/113, no. 24, Rawlinson to Canning, 26 Feb. 1845 enclosed in dispatch of 1 March 1845, Sheil to Aberdeen.

[178]F.O. 248/114, no. 10.

[179]F.O. 195/237, no. 16, 15 April 1845, Rawlinson to Canning.

[180]Ibid.

[181]Ibid., no. 19, 30 April 1845, Rawlinson to Canning.

[182]*Nabil* 91.

[183]This remark by Ṣubḥ-i Azal, which is partly supported by the Bab's own comments, suggests that there were to have been further stages in Basṭāmī's mission.

Baghdad in a place known as Badrāʾī he was poisoned and suffered martyrdom."[184]

The most significant account is a brief report written by the Persian representative in Istanbul in reply to some inquiries in connection with the Basṭāmī affair, possibly from Tehran.[185] According to this report, about the facts of which the writer claims to have made personal inquiries, "a certain Mullā ʿAlī," on his way to the capital, "was held for a while in Būlī,[186] before being moved to the capital.[187] . . . [The Ottoman authorities in Istanbul] summoned him to a gathering and inquired about certain matters, and he, without practicing any taqīya, made certain verbal confessions. Therefore according to the declaration of the ʿulama of Baghdad and in view of his own confession, for a while he was sent for forced labor *(kürek)*."[188] The above remarks throw some light on the final stages of the Basṭāmī's life in Istanbul. It is clear that he did not hesitate to admit his faith. His confession in the Istanbul court no doubt confirmed the charges brought against him in Baghdad. However, there seems to have been some hesitation as to the appropriate punishment. An undated letter from the Sublime Porte to the Ottoman sultan, ʿAbd al-Majīd I, states (possibly on the basis of the findings of Baghdad and Istanbul courts and the previous suggestion by the governor of Bolu) that "if Mullā ʿAlī were to be exiled to one of the islands[189] it would be difficult to control his activities and prevent him spreading his false ideas. Therefore he should be put to hard labor imprison-

[184]*A Succinct Account of the Babi Movement Written by Mīrzā Yaḥyā Ṣubḥ-i Ezel,* English trans. *NH*, Appendix III, 401. Strangely enough, the author claims that Mullā ʿAlī Basṭāmī, who was reputed for his piety, was also known as Muqaddas Khurāsanī. No other source supports this title for Basṭāmī, since it is usually identified with Mullā Ṣādiq Khurāsānī (Muqaddas).

[185]This report is an official dispatch from a member of the Persian mission to Istanbul to another official in Tehran. (The title and style of the letter confirm this conjecture.) The facsimile of the report appeared on p. 109 (supplement) of *ZH* though the author neither paid much attention to its contents nor gave any information on its origin or writer. The report bears a seal *"sharʿ-i Muḥammad-i payāmbar 1262"* (the Law of Muḥammad the messenger), which suggests that the author's name might be Muḥammad. Probably the report was written by Mīrzā Muḥammad Khān Maṣlaḥat-Guzār, the Persian chargé d'affaires in Istanbul throughout the 1840s and fifties (see ʿA. Iqbāl *Mīrzā Taqī Khān Amīr Kabīr* ed. Ī. Afshār [Tehran, 1340 Sh./1961] 33, 159, 300; Ādamīyat *Amīr Kabīr va Īrān* 568; Bāmdād *Rijāl* III, 289). The dispatch was written in reply to a letter of 10 Dhu al-Qaʿda 1262/29 Oct. 1846, which reached Istanbul a month later. The date of the dispatch is 14 Dhu al-Ḥijja 1262/3 Dec. 1846. The addressee is perhaps Mīrzā Masʿūd Khān Garmrūdī Anṣārī, the Persian foreign minister under Āqāsī.

[186]Arabic name for Bolu, 260 km. east of Istanbul.

[187]*ZH* 109 (supp.)

[188]Denis MacEoin, in his note "The Fate of Mullā ʿAlī Basṭāmī" *Bahāʾī Studies Bulletin* 2 (June 1983) no. 1, 77, identified the enigmatic word *kürek* as the Turkish term for forced labor.

[189]The term *jazīra* (Turkish *cezīra:* island) could be a reference to Cyprus, Crete, Rhodes, or even islands of Marmara, but not Algeria (al-Jazira), since by 1846 the French conquest of Algeria (1830–1847) was nearly complete.

ment in His Majesty's naval yard."[190] After the sultan's confirmation, he was sent to the imperial dockyard.[191]

One month after Basṭāmī's new confinement the Persian representative sent an official to the Porte to protest against his imprisonment. Since the prisoner was a Persian subject, he maintains, he must be extradited to his own country, and "if he is found guilty of any charges, he will be punished by the exalted Persian government."[192] In response, the Ottoman authorities "first denied that he was a Persian subject by claiming that he had been a citizen of Baghdad, but after long persistence they gave way."[193] In spite of all these efforts, the close of Basṭāmī's brief mission was tragic. "When they sent orders to lift his chains and release him from forced labor, he had already passed away a few days earlier and come to the mercy of God."[194] The cause of his death is not clear. It is possible that he died because of hardship or through some illness. Had he survived, however, he could hardly have escaped a similar fate in his own country.

The early Babi propaganda in the ʿAtabāt and the subsequent Basṭāmī affair in many ways exemplify later actions and responses. The entire episode proved the prime appeal of the new daʿwa to the Shaykhi community. As a minority within a minority, the persecuted Shaykhis had already reached the point of radical schism prerequisite of chiliastic conversion. Threatened by the belligerent Ottoman local government, the volatile pilgrim community of the Holy Cities was given to messages of religious radicalism and messianic deliverance. The new daʿwa only scratched the surface of this incendiary enthusiasm.

The spirit of impending Qiyāma preached by the Babi emissaries alarmed the Shiʿite establishment to the extent of allowing solicitation from Turkish authorities. Fears of recurring unrest and the ominous prospects of a shifting loyalty among the Shiʿite rank and file were grave enough to push the reluctant mujtahids onto the bosom of the shrewd pasha. The Ottoman governor, employing a two-edged policy of coercion and cooption, used the occasion to convene an ecumenical assembly in the hope of isolating the chances of an anti-Turkish popular resurgence.

Despite all the traditional enmities and irreconcilable doctrinal divisions between the Sunnis and the Shiʿites, condemnation of a new heresy was one issue upon which a consensus was conceivable and necessary. The conclud-

[190]Momen *Religions* 90; cf. "Trial" 140 citing the documents inclusive in Najīb Pāshā's report dated 15 Muḥarram 1261/24 Jan. 1845, which accompanied the Baghdad fatwā.

[191]Momen *Religions* 90. The imperial dockyard *(Tersane-i Amire)* was located at Qāsimpāshā on the Golden Horn.

[192]*ZH* 109 (supp.).

[193]Ibid.

[194]Ibid.

ing fatwā condemning the new daʿwa in the strongest terms, marked a turning point in the troubled history of the Shiʿite-Sunni relations. It demonstrated that doctrinal conflicts, acute as they were even in the nineteenth century, could be temporarily bridged when the threat of a new schism loomed large.

The joint fatwā to a considerable degree reduced the already dim prospects of a Babi mass success in the ʿAtabāt and characterized the hostile reactions that they could expect in future. If there was any need for a demonstration, the ʿAtabāt experience proved the futility of the Babi expectations in opening a dialogue with the religious establishment. The message of the Bab, however prudently it was preached, was fundamentally opposed to the tenets of orthodox Islam, and was bound to clash with its representatives. In the religion of the learned divines, Sunni and Shiʿite alike, there was room neither for a new revelation nor for the fulfillment of the Qiyāma.

Of more immediate concern was the future of the Babi plan. The joint fatwā of the Baghdad tribunal, which confirmed the heresy of the Bab and by the verdict of the Sunni majority called for his execution, made the realization of the Insurrection an even more dangerous undertaking. As will be seen, the news of the Baghdad trial awoke the Babis from their naïve messianic dream to the unforeseen horrors of a hostile reality. Coming to terms with this reality was a tormenting experience for the Bab, as for his disciples. The pitiful death of the Shiraz emissary in the imperial dockyard of Istanbul was its first ominous sign.

The Bab's Pilgrimage to Mecca

Some two months after the departure of the early disciples from Shiraz, the Bab himself, "according to the previous arrangements,"[195] set out for Ḥijāz, where in the course of Ḥajj he intended to proclaim his mission. The Shiʿite prophecies required the declaration of the Mahdi before the Kaʿba, prior to the final Insurrection in the land of Kūfa. Reasserting the inevitable fulfilment of the prophecies, the Bab himself underlines the significance of the Mecca declaration: "Thus in that month [Dhū al-Ḥijja] whatever is promised by your God to every young and old, will happen. Soon he will appear in the Holy Land with the word that will "split asunder" whatever is in the heavens and earth. Behold his word; the righteous Qāʾim who is the just Qāʾim will arise in Mecca according to what has been uttered: 'When the Qāʾim appears, give him your support together with all those who will come to his assistance from distant corners.' When [his opponents] 'have corrupted the earth,' then he will commence the new cause in the hinterland

[195] *NT* III, 42.

of Kūfa."[196] The Bab attributed the fulfillment of these prophecies to a divine force beyond his control, which first assigned him to this mission to "set out for pilgrimage to the Holy Sanctuary of Mecca," promoted the cause "to reach the East and the West and in between," and "expanded the [intellectual] capacity of the people" to enable them to grasp "the cause of the inner heart," before "returning him" from Mecca "to his homeland."[197]

Predestined as it was for the Bab, the pilgrimage was affected by a host of other considerations that must have accelerated his hasty departure from Shiraz on 26 Shaʿbān 1260/10 September 1844.[198] In an early prayer, the Bab makes a brief but important allusion to the critical situation in which he left his home town: "I had warned those who know me not to reveal my name. But I set out for pilgrimage to Your House when I became terrified of the accomplices of the devil who were the corrupt people."[199] The same anxiety over the publication of his identity is expressed in another letter, in which the Bab complains bitterly of the carelessness of some of his followers: "When I left this city [Shiraz] for the destination of the Holy Sanctuary, if after my departure no one had divulged my name, no one would have been tormented. But my believers are responsible toward God. Now there happened what ought to have happened."[200] These complaints over the disclosure of his identity, even before his departure, are the first signs of the Bab's displeasure with the activities of some of his followers.[201] He feared that the untimely exposure of what should have remained a closely guarded secret would bring with it unnecessary harassment and persecution.

The source of the Bab's apprehension lay in the fact that in the disturbed conditions of Shiraz, widespread rumors that stimulated people's curiosity to learn about the new claimant could create agitation and trouble. Mīrzā Muḥammad Taqī, the Bab's maternal cousin, who at the time was residing in the city, recalls that "in the year 1260 in Shiraz, a rumor broke out that a noble sayyid claimed to be the deputy of the Qāʾim, but his sacred name was

[196]*ZH* 235, Arabic tauqīʿ. The word that "split asunder" probably refers to the Qurʾān XIX, 92, which in Shiʿite prophecies is interpreted as the sign of Revelation. "When the Qāʾim appears" is presumably a reference to a hadith related from Jaʿfar Ṣādiq (Majlisī *Biḥār* XIII/31 trans. 573).

[197]*ZH* 269, Arabic prayer.

[198]*Khuṭbat al-Jidda* (Arabic), INBA no. 91, XIX, 60–73 (66). In this important khuṭba, the Bab, in his enigmatic style, has recorded all the departure and arrival dates as well as the length of his stay in various places throughout his journey to the Ḥijāz.

[199]Arabic tauqīʿ to Mullā ʿAbd al-Khāliq Yazdī, INBA no. 91, 94–102 (96), written after his return from Ḥajj.

[200]Nicolas (*SAMB* 61–69), who translated the letter from a certain MS identified as AG, failed to realize the recipient's name. However, the letter's content points at Shaykh ʿAlī Qāʾinī, son of ʿAbd al-Khāliq. Both letters to father and son indicate a possible inquiry from ʿAbd al-Khāliq's quarter over the Bab's change of plans.

[201]It is difficult to identify any individual or group responsible for this disclosure. Certainly Mullā Ḥusayn (see below, chap. 6), and Basṭāmī were reluctant to reveal the name of the promised Bab and observed the secrecy.

not mentioned."[202] In the course of one of his visits to the Bab in the month of Shaʿbān, about a week before the Bab's departure, Muḥammad Taqī saw the Bab sitting on the terrace of his house writing prayers and verses. When he inquired about the rumor that the new deputy of the Imam prohibited the smoking of the water pipe, the Bab confirmed it without any further comment.[203]

This unwanted publicity is also reported by Kazem-Beg, who on the basis of an unspecified source confirms the Bab's secret departure from Shiraz. "At this time, the fame of the new master had already spread in the neighboring provinces; everywhere one would meet people who were ready to follow his doctrine and people were already discussing him in Mazandaran and Khurasan. In the absence of the master, who had left almost as a fugitive, his disciples actively engaged themselves in sustaining his name and spreading his fame."[204]

The deteriorating state of affairs in Shiraz and a series of riots in other towns and villages of Fars continued throughout 1844. During the next two years, inner-city clashes and open rebellions against unpopular governors reduced the province to near chaos. Under such circumstances, the publication of the Bab's claim would have been an invitation for trouble. The Bab recognized the dangers that the disclosure of his identity might cause, and chose to leave the city in haste.[205]

His decision to leave Shiraz should also be seen as a temporary remedy to a deeper struggle—a struggle between his self-assumed duty to declare his mission publicly and his more discreet inclination to confine it to his close circle of followers. The inner tension that had already started in Shiraz reached its height during Ḥajj. Later events during 1261–1262/1845–1846, brought this conflict more to the surface, and revealed the Bab's preoccupation with the nature of his mission.

After leaving Shiraz, the Bab arrived at the port of Būshihr on 6 Ramaḍān/20 September, where he stayed for two weeks before boarding the sailing vessel that took the pilgrims to Jidda. From Būshihr *(jazīrat al-baḥr)*,[206] he wrote a letter to his wife in which he speaks of his grief and his deep affection for her.[207] Here again he refers to considerations that prompted him to leave, and the destiny by which he was assigned to this mission: "God is my witness that since the time of our separation, such

[202]Memoirs of Mīrza Muḥammad Taqī cited in Fayżī *Khāndān-i Afnān* 104–17 (ii, 110–11).

[203]Ibid.

[204]*Kazem Beg* VII, 344–45.

[205]The same disturbed state of Shiraz that compelled the Bab to leave was to endanger him when he returned from Ḥajj. See below.

[206]The name by which Būshihr is referred to in the writings of the Bab *(Khuṭbat al-Jidda,* 66).

[207]He addresses his wife as "my sweetheart." Such expressions of affection for his wife, his mother, and other close relatives, scattered throughout his writings, illustrate his attachment to family and reveal human emotions too delicate for the stereotyped manly conduct of his time.

griefs encircled me as are beyond description. But since destiny is so all-powerful, it is due to a fitting purpose that this [separation] occurred in this way. May God, in the name of Five Holy Souls,[208] provide the means of my return as may be best. It is two days since I entered Būshihr. The weather is intensely hot, but God will protect [me]. At any rate, it appears that in the very month the ship will sail. Gracious God shall protect us."[209]

Beside his Abyssinian servant Mubārak, only Mullā Muḥammad ʿAlī Bārfurūshī (Quddūs) accompanied the Bab, on this journey[210] as his secretary. The Bab's affection for his young disciple seems to have dictated the choice.[211] Later, in Mecca, the two apparently even took the oath of fraternity.[212] It appears that Quddūs did not play any major part throughout the journey, however.

The sea journey took seventy-one days. As far as can be reckoned from various letters and addresses written en route, between the Persian Gulf and the Indian Ocean and then the Red Sea, the vessel stopped in Kangān,[213] Muscat, and Mocha before finally arriving at Jidda.[214] They reached Mecca on 1 Dhū al-Ḥijja 1260/22 December 1844. The excessively humid hot weather, the rough sea, and the inconvenience of the sailing vessel, added to the other hardships of a slow and tiresome voyage, had an unpleasant effect on the Bab, who had never before experienced the sea.[215] The behavior of some fellow pilgrims on board made matters worse: "On my journey to Mecca, I personally witnessed someone regarded as a respected figure in the vessel who undertook luxurious expenses, but deprived his fellow friend and roommate of even a glass of water."[216]

The agony of pilgrimage was such that later in *Bayān* he exempts from Ḥajj, among others, those who must undertake a sea voyage. Even for the

208A reference to the Prophet, ʿAlī, Fāṭima, Ḥasan, and Ḥusayn.

209*Khāndān-i Afnān* 166–67. The letter is written in a most excellent *shikastih* style facsimilied in Balyuzi *The Bab,* and partly translated on p. 57.

210*Bayān* IV/18, 146; *Nabil* 129; and Mīrzā Ḥabībullāh *Tārīkh* 37. Nicolas *(SAMB* 206) wrongly believes that Mullā Ḥusayn Bushrū'ī and Mīrzā Sayyid ʿAlī Shīrāzī, uncle of the Bab, also accompanied him. *Muʿīn* (73) believes that Mīrzā Sayyid ʿAlī Shīrāzī and Sayyid Kāẓim Zanjānī were present. Both sources seem to have wrongly identified Sayyid ʿAlī Kirmānī, mentioned in *Ṣaḥīfa bayn al-Ḥaramayn* with Sayyid ʿAlī Shīrāzī. As regards the other two, all the evidence confirms the opposite.

211*Muʿīn* 63 and *ZH* 418; cf. *NT* III, 238 and *Kazem Beg* VII, 344 n., 47/8 n. The two latter sources believe that Quddūs in fact first met the Bab in the course of Ḥajj, but the claim is not substantiated by any other sources.

212*Muʿīn* 81.

213A small port halfway between Būshihr and Bandar ʿAbbās, on the Persian coast. Lorimer *Gazetteer* II, A. Kangān.

214*ZH* 288, *Khuṭba fī Kangān* (partly cited in Fayżī *Nuqṭa-yi Ūlā* 134); INBA no. 91, 51–56, "Letters from Muscat"; ibid. 56–60, "Letter from Mocha." Besides the inland caravan routes to the Ḥijāz, the other transport available to Persian pilgrims was the sailing carriers that operated between the Persian Gulf and the Red Sea. The ships on this route, in addition to their cargo, carried passengers for the Ḥijāz at the pilgrimage season.

215*Bayān* highly recommended traveling by land and advised believers to avoid a sea voyage whenever possible (IV/16, 144).

216*Bayān* IV/16, 143.

affluent, he prescribes a pilgrimage only if "on the way there would be no grief for the traveler, since on the sea there is nothing but grief."[217] Indeed, contrary to the traditional view, which sometimes even extols the sufferings of the pilgrims as a necessary purifying process, the Bab looks forward to the improvement of roads and communications in the Islamic lands. He praises Europe's rapid and secure road and communication system and regrets that even the postal service in Iran is monopolized by the "possessors of authority" and is not available to the deprived and the poor.[218]

On the whole, the Bab's impression of his fellow pilgrims throughout Ḥajj, blended resentment and pity: "On the way to Mecca one matter that was most disgraceful toward God, and indeed diminishing to their [original] intention, was the pilgrims' quarrels with each other, since such behavior was prohibited, and remains so. Tradition for believers is nothing but forebearance, patience, decency, and moderation. The House [of God] repudiates such people."[219] In addition to the general discrimination and ill-treatment that all Persians experienced during Ḥajj, the Bab also suffered from provocation by his fellow pilgrims. References to "quarrels" between pilgrims and the "ignorance" of passengers should be seen in the light of criticism that was leveled at him. Among the passengers he encountered only one believer in the Book, "since the rest of the pilgrims were a bunch of useless and ignorant people."[220]

One incident illustrates the source of the Bab's grievance. His constant composition of *khuṭba*s (sermons) and letters prompted a troublesome fellow citizen, Shaykh Abū Hāshim Shīrāzī,[221] to ridicule and insult the young sayyid with "extraordinary and strange behavior."[222] But as his attacks became increasingly intolerable, the captain, probably fearing a full-scale fight aboard his overcrowded vessel, apparently ordered Abū Hāshim to be seized and thrown into the sea. However, the Bab stepped forward to intercede for him. Mīrzā Abul-Ḥasan, a merchant on board and a later convert, recounts that "the captain, who was impressed by the Bab's innocence and his attempt at mediation, finally yielded." Yet Abū Hāshim lost no time in creating more trouble for the Bab by reporting his activity to the ʿulama even before he returned to Shiraz.[223]

[217]Ibid. 144.

[218]Ibid. 144–45.

[219]Ibid. On this point the Bab seems to refer to the Qur'ān II, 194. "Whoso undertake the duty of pilgrimage in them shall not go to his womenfolk, nor indulge in ungodliness and disputing in the Pilgrimage." George August Wallin, the Finnish traveler who ventured through Ḥijāz in 1845, remarks that Persian pilgrims "are extremely awkward and tiresome on a desert journey." ("Narrative of a Journey from Cairo to Medina and Mecca etc." *JRGS* 24 (1854) 115–207 [206]).

[220]"Letter to the ʿUlama," INBA no. 91, 81–94 (93); also Browne Or. MSS. no. F21 (9), letter no. 32, 224–32.

[221]Son of Shaykh Muḥammad and younger brother of Shaykh Abū Turāb, imām jumʿa of Shiraz (*Fārs Nāmih* II, 61–62).

[222]*Muʿīn* 73.

[223]Mīrzā Ḥabībullāh *Tārīkh* 38–39.

At Muscat, the Bab delivered "the message of God" to the imam jumʿa of the city. Though at first sight he was impressed by his writings and "was counted among the rightly guided," later he "followed his own worldly desires, and thus the Book judged him among assailants."[224]

After arriving in Mecca the Bab performed the Ḥajj rituals. On the day of sacrifice he slew nineteen lambs in Minā; "nine in his own name, seven in the name of Quddūs, and three in the name of his Ethiopian servant."[225] He remained in Mecca for three weeks before moving to Madina, where he visited the shrine of the Prophet. After twenty-seven days in Medina, (until 6 February 1845), he returned to Jidda. After receiving the news of Basṭāmī's troubles, he decided that under the circumstances his initial plan for travel to Iraq was unrealistic. After a brief halt in Jidda he boarded the same vessel for Būshihr, and arrived there sometime in June 1845, after nearly seven months' travel.[226] The general insecurity of the Ḥijāz affected the Bab on the road.[227] After he departed from Medina, in spite of the constant vigilance of his companions, a roving Bedouin appeared and, snatching up the saddlebag that had been lying on the ground beside the Bab, "which contained his writings and papers," vanished into the desert.[228] Though this robbery was an act "decreed by God," and he had "read it in the Book of his soul" beforehand, the loss of various treatises, sermons, and commentaries augmented the troubles of the journey and encouraged the Bab to take the route to the "city of safety," Shiraz.[229]

Mubāhala and *Badā*ʾ

The Bab's pilgrimage to Mecca was intended primarily as the first stage of his public declaration. But the available accounts, whether of eyewitnesses or the Bab himself, are inconclusive as to the way this task was carried out. Mīrzā Abul-Ḥasan Shīrāzī alone clearly states that at the end of Ḥajj rites, when the floor and the roof of Masjid al-Ḥarām were entirely filled with pilgrims, the Bab stood against the wall, holding the ring knob of the Kaʿba door, and three times in "the most eloquent and exquisite voice" an-

[224]"Letter to the ʿUlamāʾ" 39. The identity of the imām jumʿa of Muscat is not clear. However, allusions in the Bab's writings points out Shaykh Sulaymān al-Qaṭīfī (d. 1266/1850) who was at the time the chief Shiʿite mujtahid of Muscat. He was a student of Baḥr al-ʿUlūm and a prolific writer (*TAS* II/2, 606–7). For his correspondence with Rashtī see *Fihrist* II, 336.

[225]*Nabil* 132–33.

[226]On his return from Medina, it appears that the Bab reached Jidda by way of Yanbūʿ and Rābigh, since he gives no indication of passing through Mecca for a second time.

[227]Around this time, the whole region was in a state of disturbance and revolt. Ibn Rūmī, the shaykh of the Ḥarb tribe, had revolted against Ottoman pasha (G. de Gaury *Rulers of Mecca* [New York, n.d.] 245–47).

[228]*Nabil* (132); cf. *Khuṭbat al-Jidda* (69).

[229]List of the stolen works appears in INBA no. 91, 57 "Letter to Khāl"; also *ZH* 289–90; cf. *Khuṭbat al-Jidda* 69.

nounced, "I am the Qā'im whom you were expecting."[230] Abul-Ḥasan continues: "It was extraordinary, that in spite of the noise, immediately the crowd became so silent that even the flapping of the wings of a passing sparrow was audible." All the pilgrims heard the Bab's call, he maintains, and interpreted it for one another. They discussed it, and reported the new proclamation in letters to the people in their homelands.[231] Although Abul-Ḥasan was an eyewitness, it seems likely that he allowed his imagination to color his account. He must have exaggerated not only the general reception of the Bab's call, but indeed the manner and the extent to which the Bab disclosed his claim. The Bab's enigmatic and multifaceted claim undoubtedly affected the clarity of vision of a believer who, at the distance of some years, could no longer distinguish the puzzling stages of his revelation.

The Bab's own account makes clear that his declaration did not meet wide response, favorable or unfavorable. However, it does not clarify to what extent he actually conveyed his message to the public, or, considering the practical obstacles, was inclined to do so. The Bab acknowledges the pilgrims' general lack of insight in recognizing his true position: "One thousand two hundred and seventy years from the [Prophet's] Designation have passed and each year innumerable people have circumambulated the House. In the final year, the founder of the House [the Bab] himself went for Ḥajj and saw that by God's grace, people from all creeds had come to Ḥajj. No one recognized him, but he recognized all. And the only one who recognized him was the one who accompanied him in his pilgrimage, and he is the one whose [name] is equal to eight vāḥid, and God is proud of him."[232] On another occasion he asserts that of all pilgrims only three managed to perform a correct Ḥajj, which again implies his disenchantment with the lack of public attention.[233]

Given the general circumstances of Ḥajj, when religious emotions were at their height, even if a public declaration was made it could hardly have had an effect on the audience, if it did not in fact provoke suspicion and anger. Becoming increasingly aware of this, the Bab decided to approach some known individuals in whom he invested some hope. His interview with

[230]Mīrzā Ḥabībullāh *Tārīkh* 40–41. *Mu'īn* 37 quotes the same verse with minor differences. The verses that the Qā'im is supposed to read at the time of declaration vary from source to source. Qur'ānic verses XXVI, 20 and XLVII, 9 are often quoted (see Majlisī *Biḥār* XIII, chaps. 30 and 32). The account of Mīrzā Abul-Ḥasan is influenced by the prophecies that anticipate Gabriels' announcement in eloquent Arabic of the appearance of the Mahdi *(Biḥār* XIII/32).

[231]Mīrzā Ḥabībullāh *Tārīkh* 40–41. The same account is also related by *Mu'īn* 73 and *KD I*, 43.

[232]*Bayān* IV/18, 148. In his writing, the Bab often computes from the year of *Ba'tha,* the beginning of the Islamic revelation, instead of the year of *Hijra,* which is the beginning of the Islamic calendar. *Quddūs* has the numerical value of 152, which is equal to 8 x 19.

[233]INBA no. 91, 172, "Letter to Mīrzā Muḥammad Ibrāhīm" (Maḥallātī), written in Būshihr in early 1261/1845.

Mullā Muḥammad Ḥusayn Muḥīṭ Kirmānī, to which he paid special attention, shows his disillusionment with the prospects for winning over the Shaykhi figures.

A well-known member of the circle in Karbalā', Muḥīṭ was regarded as one of the contenders for leadership. His presence in Mecca in the same year as the Bab could be in connection with the news that had reached him of the conversion of his ex-associates. Presumably it was their preachings that made Muḥīṭ decide to travel to Mecca and meet the new claimant for himself. Nonetheless, the Bab seems to have taken him by surprise when he approached him in the middle of the crowd. Urging him to clarify his attitude, the Bab demanded that Muḥīṭ either submit himself unreservedly to his cause or repudiate it entirely.[234] In the "peremptory challenge" the Bab acknowledged Muḥīṭ as heir of "those twin great lights,"[235] while pronouncing his own claim. "Verily I declare, none beside me in this day, whether in the East or in the West, can claim to be the Gate that leads men to the knowledge of God."[236]

Muḥīṭ was clearly faced with a claim that had gone well beyond the bounds of the Perfect Shiʿa. Like any good student of madrasa, he required theological evidence. His demand for satisfactory proofs was met by the Bab not by conventional reasoning, but by direct appeal to irrevocable divine arbitration (*mubāhala*). This approach was consciously inspired by, and no doubt strongly reminiscent of, the Prophet's mubāhala with the disavowing Christians of Najrān, which took place at roughly the same date, around 23 Dhū al-Ḥijja, on the outskirts of Madina.[237] Mubāhala was not an unfamiliar practice in later times, often as a last resort for settling doctrinal disputes between two unyielding parties with opposite views.[238] One significant case was Rashtī's call for mubāhala to Shaykh Muḥammad Ḥasan Najafī, to which he made no reply.[239]

The Bab, too, regarded mubāhala as the ultimate means for distinguishing truth from falsehood. "I accomplished the proof of mubāhala in Masjid

[234]*Nabil* 134, quoting Mīrzā Abul-Ḥasan Shīrāzī.

[235]A clear reference to Shaykh Aḥmad Aḥsā'ī and Sayyid Kāẓim Rashtī.

[236]*Nabil* 134.

[237]*Mubāhala* or mutual execration by means of humble and sincere prayer (*bahala:* to curse and *ibtihāl:* lamentation and prayer), in the hope of divine arbitration between good and evil. *Yaum al-mubāhala* refers to the day when Muḥammad, in the last year of his life, (10A.H./632), invited the Christians of Najrān to a challenge. Verses 60–65 and particularly 61 of *Sūrat Āl ʿImrān* (III) in the Qur'ān refer to the same occasion. Various classic accounts discuss *yaum al-mubāhala* (e.g. Ibn al-Athīr *al-Kāmil fī al-Tārīkh* [Leiden, 1868] II, 141–43). Qur'ānic commentaries such as al-Maybudī *Kashf al-Asrār*, 10 vols. (Tehran, 1338/1959) II, 145–50, and Ṭabarsī *Majmaʿ al-Bayān fī Tafsīr al-Qur'ān* (Tehran, 1371/1951) II, 451–53 also explain the significance of mubāhala. See also L. Massignon "La Mubahala de Médine et l'hyperdulie de Fatima" in *Opera Minora,* 3 vols. (Beirut 1963) I, 550–72, and R. Ustādī "Dar Bārih-yi Mubāhala va Manābiʿ-i ān etc," *Āyandeh* I–III, 1358 Sh./1979, p. 33.

[238]See for example *QU* (178) for proposed mubāhala between Jaʿfar Najafī and Muḥammad Akhbārī.

[239]*Dalīl al-Mutaḥayyirīn* 96–99.

al-Ḥarām in the presence of eyewitnesses, and the one who was addressed . . . was Muḥīṭ."[240] In *Ṣaḥīfat bayn al-Ḥaramayn,* his most important work of the Ḥajj period, the Bab implies that by following the example of the Prophet, he has evoked the divine verdict and thereby fulfilled the requirements of the prophecies: "My God! I take you as witness to what I said in Masjid al-Ḥarām, beside the Kaʿba of Bayt al-Ḥarām to the inquirer of these verses [Muḥīṭ], of what has been revealed in the past to your beloved friend Muḥammad in the Qur'ān, "And whoso dispute with thee, say, Come now, let us call our sons and your sons, our wives and your wives, ourselves and yourselves, then let us humbly pray and so lay God's curse upon the one who lies."[241]

Complaining of Muḥīṭ's refusal to accept the challenge of mubāhala, the Bab then addresses the skeptical Shaykhi: "O Muḥīṭ, the inquirer! Did I not call you in Masjid al-Ḥarām . . . to accept my summons and stand up for mubāhala with me beside the Pillar in front of the Black Stone, so that you will stand on behalf of all the people of the earth who renounce my covenant? Thus God will arbitrate between us with truth, and God has perfect knowledge of what has been said."[242] Twice more the Bab repeated his invitation for divine arbitration, but to no avail. He ends his dramatic call on Muḥīṭ with a typical admonitory note: "If you are not conscious of the cause of God, God is witness to what I said and to what I am revealing to you in this book; there is no pilgrimage for you without the command of the House. Whatever you have performed . . . has been erased from the Book, and God is the dearest and most wise."[243]

For the Bab, the call to mubāhala had far greater symbolic meaning than the simple delivery of his message to Muḥīṭ or even a challenge for the leadership of the Shaykhis. By summoning the "renouncers to his covenant," of whom Muḥīṭ is a representative, the Bab is allegorically announcing his mission to the people in "the most sacred place on the earth," and pledges to God to be witness and the judge between him and those who are doomed to deny him.

To escape an undesirable situation, Muḥīṭ proposed some theological problems to the Bab.[244] Though mainly insignificant or even irrelevant, his questions demonstrate the way he looked upon the Bab's claims, and how he evaluated them. On his return to Karbalā', Muḥīṭ remained unmoved by

[240]The Bab adds: "Those who heard such a call, I believe, were Ḥājj Sayyid ʿAlī Kirmānī, Ḥājj Sayyid Muḥammad Khurāsānī, Ḥājj Sulaymān Khān, and Ḥājj Muḥammad ʿAlī Māzandarānī, and there were others as well" (*ZH* 271).

[241]*al-Ṣaḥīfat bayn al-Ḥaramayn,* Browne, Or. MSS. F.7 (9), 14–16. For further details see Browne *A Descriptive Catalogue,* 58–59. The verse quoted is from Qur'ān, III, 61.

[242]*Ṣaḥīfa* 15. Emphasis on specific locations around the Kaʿba in the above passage can be explained by their symbolic significance in the Qā'im's revelation. The Qā'im stands between Rukn and Maqām. The Black Stone then testifies the truthfulness of his claim (Majlisī *Biḥār* XIII, chap. 30).

[243]*Saḥīfa* 15–16.

[244]*Nabil* 136.

the alarming tone of *Ṣaḥīfat bayn al-Ḥaramayn* which strongly advised him to purge from his soul "those signs of [false] scrutiny," since such illusions would prevent him "from grasping the knowledge of certitude."[245] In a letter to Mullā Ḥusayn Bushrū'ī, the Bab acknowledges the "accomplishment of his proof" to Muḥīṭ and expresses his doubts as to his sincerity. But he still hopes that "soon God will remove what Satan has implanted in his heart." He then instructs Mullā Ḥusayn to convey his warning to Muḥīṭ, and reminds him of the outcome of his denial.[246] But in spite of all warnings, Muḥit remained opposed to the Bab.[247]

Muḥīṭ's obdurance was doubtless a setback for the Bab, who perhaps counted on his cooperation as an important factor in the conversion of the remaining Shaykhis. But he was not the only one in the course of Ḥajj who refused to give the Bab his allegiance. Sayyid Ja'far Dārābī, better known as Kashfī, is another example. Abul-Ḥasan states: "I myself met Ḥājjī Sayyid Ja'far. He was present in Mecca, he saw with his own eyes, and heard with his own ears, but he did not become a believer."[248] Indeed, Abul-Ḥasan even claims that Kashfī was primarily attracted to Mecca because his knowledge of jafr and other hidden sciences helped him to set the time of Ẓuhūr in 1260[249] Another whom the Bab encountered in Mecca was Ḥājjī Sulaymān Khān Afshār Ṣā'īn Qal'a, called Amīr al-Umarā', son-in-law of Fatḥ 'Alī Shāh and one of the distinguished Afshār tribal chiefs.[250] Though his background was very different from most Shaykhis', Sulaymān Khān, an adherent of Rashtī and father-in-law to his daughter, had much in common with the others. His ardor to learn the time of Ẓuhūr when he visited Rashtī shortly before his death[251] was later turned into bewilderment over the delay of the emergence of the new master. By the time he visited the Bab in Mecca,[252] it appears that he had already shown some sympathy toward, if not full support of, Ḥājjī Muḥammad Karīm Khān Kirmānī.[253] After the

[245]*Ṣaḥīfa* 18.

[246]Letter to Mullā Ḥusayn, 10 Muḥarram 1261/20 Jan. 1845 from Mecca, Arabic, INBA no. 91, 11–12. Shortly after his return from Ḥajj, in a letter to Mullā Muḥammad 'Alī (probably Nahrī) the Bab recommends mubāhala to his followers as a last resort in encounters with their opponents. INBA no. 91, XXVIII, 135–36, cf. XXVI, 89.

[247]Sometimes in collaboration with Mullā Ḥasan Gauhar, Muḥiṭ tried to neutralize the Babi efforts. We are told by Shaykh Sulṭān Karbalā'ī that he also showed some inclination toward Muḥammad Karīm Khān Kirmānī, and perhaps assisted him in his earliest polemics against the Babis. Some further details on his later years appear in *Nabil* 37–38.

[248]Mīrzā Ḥabībullāh *Tārīkh* 40.

[249]Although this claim is not supported by other accounts, it is not unrealistic to assume that in the light of his interest in numerology and the science of letters, he may have anticipated some sort of Ẓuhūr in the near future.

[250]Besides *ZH* 74–77, which gives a full account of Sulaymān Khān and his Babi son, Riżā Qulī Khān, other Qajar chronicles mention his services to the Qajar government.

[251]Ibid. *Qatīl* 509 relates a similar account from a certain Sulaymān Mīrzā. *Fihrist* (II, 311–12, no. 197) refers to a treatise by in reply to Sulaymān Khān's questions.

[252]*ZH* 271.

[253]The Bab's allusion in the letter addressed to Sulaymān Khān from Medina is directed toward this very commitment to Kirmānī (INBA no. 91, 29–30, and Browne Or. MSS F.28 (9),

Mecca pilgrimage, as the nature of the Babi cause was further divulged in later years, it became increasingly apparent to the powerful chief that alignment with Kirmānī, who enjoyed respect among the Qajars, was more realistic. The conversion of his son Riżā Qulī Khān (Rashtī's son-in-law) to the Babi cause, however, was in clear defiance of his own inclinations.[254]

Kashfī and Sulaymān Khān, though from entirely different backgrounds, had in common the fact that both had sons who were later converted to the Babi movement. Both also had earlier inclinations toward ideas that anticipated some form of messianic revelation. Their rejection of the Bab indicates the attitude of the older generation who, either on theoretical or political grounds, was not prepared to recognize the Bab's radical claims. But not all those who met the Bab during his pilgrimage remained unsympathetic to him. For those who lacked Kashfī's sophistication or Sulaymān Khān's privileged status, the Bab had a special attraction.

Sayyid Jawād Muḥarrir, a low-ranking Iṣfahānī scribe who had heard of the imminent Advent of the Qā'im from Mullā Ḥusayn,[255] hurried to Shiraz to meet the Promised One. Finally catching up with him in Muscat in the house of the imām jumʿa, he found "the signs which had been related by the Imams about the Qā'im" fully identical with the features of Sayyid ʿAlī Muḥammad Shīrāzī.[256] He saw the Bab again on a few occasions in Mecca and Medina. "How could I succeed in your sublime recognition?" he asked the Bab. "How did you recognize the late Shaykh [Aḥsā'ī] and Sayyid-i Rashtī?" the Bab replied. "With intimate companionship," answered Muḥarrir. The Bab then said: "Here you should do the same."[257] This advice encouraged Muḥarrir to join a gathering of the Bab and his companions in Medina: "The companions sat all around while his excellency Quddūs was busy reading and collating the commentary on *Sūrat al-Baqara* which had been revealed from the holy pen. When he saw me he paused for a moment before his holiness [the Bab] ordered him to continue. At the end [of the meeting], as I had heard that the names of [all] true followers are registered in the Imam's book, I asked whether my name is also entered. His excellency replied: 'Yes.'"[258]

---

no. 7). The author of *Mujmal-i Badīʿ* (*NH* 401) mistook Sulaymān Khān Afshār for the well-known Babi martyr Sulaymān Khān Tabrīzī, son of Yaḥyā Khān. Browne (*NH* 31–32) repeats the same mistake.

[254]Contrary to his son's conversion, Sulaymān Kuān served as the commander of the Qajar forces in the campaigns of both Ṭabarsī and Zanjān. His role as the special envoy of the central government to Tabrīz for the execution of the Bab remains unclear. He is discussed in many Babi and non-Babi accounts: *RS* X, 445; *NT* III, 257–58; *NK* 191; and *NH* 150–62.

[255]See below, chap. 6.

[256]Sayyid Jawād Muḥarrir *Memoirs,* INBA Lib. MS no. 1028 D/a, 29–30. It is not surprising that Muḥarrir should look for "physical signs" in the appearance of the Bab. Traditions related from the Prophet and Imams about the general features of the Qā'im describe the most minor details of his appearance, e.g., Majlisī *Biḥār* XIII/6, sections 8, 17–19.

[257]Muḥarrir *Memoirs* 30.

[258]Ibid. 31.

Āqā Muḥammad Rizā Makhmalbāf, a merchant from Kashan, had a similar impression. In Mecca he observed such great "devotion and submission" in Sayyid ʿAlī Muḥammad that he felt certain that "either this person is the Qāʾim of the House of Muḥammad, or else he is one of his chiefs."[259] Āqā Sayyid-i Hindī (later known as Baṣīr), a young blind dervish of the Dāghdārīya order in India who had previously visited Rashtī and later learned about the new Bab in Bombay, was also impressed by the sayyid of Shiraz. "Though in his appearance he was blind," says the author of *Nuqṭat al-Kāf,* he recognized at once the truthfulness of his holiness and submitted to his status of Qāʾimīya with the eye of his heart. He sold the spice of his soul to the merchant of the Being and in exchange bought the elixir of love and indeed he made such good profit in this unique deal that all worldly goods could not pay for its commission."[260]

The fervor exhibited in Mecca by a few would-be Babis was hardly sufficient to convince the Bab of an impending breakthrough. In a letter to Mullā Ḥusayn he points out: "Your Lord did not testify to the faith of anyone in the month of Ḥajj except you and the one who followed the instruction in the same manner as you [Basṭāmī] and the one who accompanied me in the journey of Ḥajj [Quddūs]."[261] Although he was more convinced than ever of his divine mission, in his contacts with the public, and particularly in his interviews, he appreciated for the first time the formidable obstacles in his way. This is evident in most of his writings in this period.[262] *Ṣaḥīfat bayn al-Ḥaramayn* mirrors his deepest emotions when he encounters the pilgrims in the holy places.[263]

In spite of his warnings, the recipients of his message either ignored or renounced his call: "Those who are accusing the Remembrance of the "Di-

[259] *NK* 111. His name is entered in the margin of the text. For his account see below, chap. 8.

[260] Ibid. 256. The allegorical use of mercantile terms illustrates the association of commerce with spiritual experience in the mind of the author of *Nuqṭat al-Kāf*, who was himself a merchant.

[261] INBA no. 91, IV, 11–12. Written in early 1261/1845.

[262] The effect of the holy surroundings, at the time of his visits to the House and the Shrine of the Prophet, is clearly visible in the Bab's constant references to these places in letters, addresses, books, and treatises. In fact, the period of Ḥajj was one of the most productive in the Bab's short life. As can be reckoned from the available sources (INBA; cf. *ZH* 288–89 and Browne Or. MSS.), his writings during Ḥajj include three independent works, *Ṣaḥīfa bayn al-Ḥaramayn, Ṣaḥīfa Aʿmāl al-Sana,* and *Kītāb al-Rūḥ*; two commentaries, on *Sūrat al-Nūr* and on *Āyat al-Kursī;* two commentaries on an elegy by the Arab poet Ḥimyarī; twenty-six sermons (*khuṭab*) and numerous private letters and declarations.

[263] Pp. 8–9. Written in Muḥarram 1261/Jan. 1845 in Medina, this work consisted of an Exordium and seven chapters. The former part seems to be an answer to the questions of Muḥīṭ, whereas the latter is a direct address to a believer, probably Rashtī's student Sayyid ʿAlī Kirmānī. In answer to Muḥīṭ, the Bab deals with a wide range of subjects, from hadith (26) to occult sciences and astrology (27–41). He also elaborates on various prayers and rituals for visiting holy shrines. *Ṣaḥīfa* should be regarded as the Bab's first attempt to develop a new sharīʿa. On one occasion he commented on the necessity of ʿilm al-fiqh for the people of the Book, particularly for merchants (80–81). The style of *Ṣaḥīfa* is reminiscent of some Shiʿite books on Ḥajj.

vine Name" [of blasphemy] are among the evildoers. They are disputing my verses and finding them empty of Qur'ānic inspiration. They are accusing the 'Word of God' of falsehood. So let the word of punishment be upon them. Verily they will rest in the fire [of Hell] and they will have no guardian on the Day of Judgment."[264] Because of their negligence, he warns, "God therefore suspended the appearance of His signs" till that hour when the believers would be able to "witness the Lord." Addressing the pilgrims in Mecca, his sharp criticism conveys his disappointment: "The majority of the people are even less than animals in comprehending the words of the Qur'ān, and most of them are ignorant."[265] He then turns his attention toward the leaders of the community, more specifically the ʿulama: "Those who in their selfish illusions claim to be mandated by God, they are among liars. They have not read a word of God's Book."

His other writings convey the same anger. In his address to the people of Mecca he condemns those who declined to take his word seriously, and ranks them as "companions of fire" and idolators: "I did not see many who were believers, and I saw many who were mockers of God's verses."[266]

The above references, modeled after the Qur'ān, are the earliest demonstrations of the Bab's disillusionment with the public. These references were not made without some knowledge of the ominous developments in the ʿAtabāt. It is almost certain that the Bab was first informed of the troubles there by two ex-students of Rashtī, Sayyid ʿAlī Kirmānī and Mullā Ḥasan Khurāsānī. Sayyid ʿAlī Kirmānī, who was Rashtī's scribe and one of his close companions,[267] after meeting Mullā Jalīl Urūmī, declared his support of the Bab and repented of his past falsifications.[268] "When he decided to become one of the believers of this cause, fearing his opponents, he fled [from Karbalā'] and made the pilgrimage to Mecca, where he had the honor of accompanying the great star [the Bab]."[269]

In the early days of Muḥarram/December at the time of the rituals of visiting the shrine of Ḥusayn, the Bab writes to Sayyid ʿAlī Kirmānī: "So let it be known to you that it is not possible to visit [the shrine of Ḥusayn] unless your God's will rests upon it."[270] The same message is more openly

[264] Ibid.

[265] Ibid. 22.

[266] INBA no. 91, VIII, 25–28, tablet addressed to people of Mecca. This letter should not be mistaken for another letter to the sharīf of Mecca. (Some extracts of this are cited in *Selections from the Writings of the Bab,* trans. H. Taherzadeh [Haifa, 1976] 29–30.) The title of the former in INBA no. 91 is "Letter from Mecca to Sharīf Sulaymān." However, since the sharīf of Mecca in this period was Muḥammad Ibn ʿAbd al-Muʿīn Ibn ʿAwn (de Gaury *Rulers,* 244–48), and Sulaymān is probably a reference to the imām jumʿa of Muscat, it is likely that this is a copyist's mistake. For the tablet to the sharīf of Mecca, see *Nabil* 138–39, which confirms its delivery by Quddūs.

[267] *Qatīl* 519.

[268] Ibid.

[269] Ibid.

[270] *Ṣaḥīfa* 102.

expressed in another letter to Sayyid ʿAlī Kirmānī, probably after his return to the ʿAtabāt: "I have read your letter. So now remember that at present it is not possible for me to meet you."[271] The letter of instruction to Mullā Ḥusayn, dated 10 Muḥarram 1261/ 20 January 1845, the day of ʿĀshūrā, and addressed to Kūfa, bears the same message. (At the time the Bab was under the impression that Mullā Ḥusayn, according to the original plan, must have reached Kūfa.) The Bab indicated his change of decision and gave brief instructions to his followers:

> The Divine Word would not allow His servant [a reference to himself] to embark on His Cause. And thus for every person in the Book of your Lord there is a written destiny. . . . Therefore, depart from the land which God had destined for your soul, and then visit this house if you can afford to set your foot on his path. . . . Give the greetings of Z̲ikr-i Ismullāh to the forerunners (sābiqūn), and ask them to emigrate to the pure land of the city of safety, where they were assigned in my previous command. Give greetings to the followers. God is above the interpretation that oppressors make of the great, supreme word. When the nobles gather in the Holy Land and support this cause, advise them to wait till a new order comes from me.[272]

The above instruction was doubtless made with regard to the opposition toward Basṭāmī and others. The letter to Mullā Ḥusayn was written four days after the trial. It is likely that he was aware of Basṭāmī's arrest and imprisonment, and therefore conscious of the danger if he ever set foot in the ʿAtabāt. The news of the issued fatwā and Basṭāmī's conviction appears to have reached him later in reports dispatched by Mullā Ḥasan Khurāsānī. It is in reply to these reports that the Bab, now writing from Būshihr, instructed Khurāsānī to convey his message to "the just divines" a reference to his close followers, and instruct them to leave their homes and come to the city of Z̲ikr in order to testify to "the covenant of the Remnant of God."[273] In a later letter to Khurāsānī, he made an appeal to all believers in the ʿAtabāt: "Say! O crowd who have gathered here, call loudly for the one who is enthroned on the throne of the Great Sacred Place [Masjid al-Ḥarām], and then depart all of you according to the divine command, and enter the safe city [Shiraz], if you are among the readers of this letter."[274]

The result of the Baghdad trial unquestionably had negative effects on the followers of the Bab in Iraq. The Bab tries to encourage his doubting followers: "Do not be intimidated by the Baghdad verdict. Struggle in the path of your Lord by [means of] wisdom and firm arguments, in which there is a remedy for the denials and the denunciations of the ʿulama, if you are

[271]INBA no. 91, IX, 28–29, letter to Ḥājjī Sayyid ʿAlī Kirmānī.
[272]Ibid. IV, 13–14.
[273]Ibid. VI, 18–23, letter to Mullā Ḥasan Khurāsānī.
[274]Ibid. III, 6–10, letter to Mullā Ḥasan Khurāsānī.

conscious of the Divine cause and believe in it."[275] Henceforth the high hopes of some of those who had gathered in Karbalā' rapidly faded, or even turned to skepticism and denial. The Bab was aware of this change of attitude and tried to regain the lost support by emphasizing the truthfulness of his cause, which would soon be manifested on the Day of Judgment: "O the gathered people! How did you pass the verdict of falsehood on Our servant [himself] who first brought to you verses of proof in the manner of the Qur'ān, after accepting in your souls the cause of God? So wait for the divine Day of Judgment, and then I will judge, with the mandate of your Lord, among people."[276] Later the Bab explained his reasons for not attending the gathering of the ʿAtabāt:

> O Lord! You know of that command in which I ordered the divines [the early believers] to enter the Holy Land in order [to be prepared] for the Day of Return, when Your hidden covenant was to be revealed and they were all obedient. And You know what I heard in the Mother of the Cities [i.e. Mecca] of the opposition of the ʿulama and the denial Your servant encountered from those who were destined away from the Truth. Therefore, I gave up my goal, and did not travel to that land, hoping that the sedition (fitna) would settle and those who were obedient to You would not be humiliated, and no one would find a chance to inflict the slightest harm upon someone else. My Lord, You know what I envisaged in this decision, and You are the omniscient. My Lord, this is Your decision and this is Your command. If I failed in other duties, I have not failed in [implementing] Your words. Therefore, You arbitrate between me and them with Your justice, and forgive those who are repentant and obedient to Your tradition. . . . You know that at the time of my return [from Ḥajj] I intended what You commanded me, and You directed me toward what I understood from Your Book. I did not desire the kingdom of this world or the next. This was not my initiative but it was Your will, You Lord, the only one.[277]

The idea of *badā'*—the occurrence of circumstances that would cause a change in earlier divine ruling[278]—is no doubt hinted at in this passage and further signaled by reference to a relevant verse in the Qur'ān.[279] In fact, the Bab placed responsibility for the cancellation entirely on God's "change of

[275]Ibid.

[276]Ibid.

[277]Ibid. XXIII, 94–102 (97–98), "tablet for Mullā ʿAbd al-Khāliq Yazdī," probably written toward the end of 1261/1845.

[278]See *EI*²: BADĀ' (I. Goldziher [A. S. Tritton]).

[279]In the above passage, the phrase "and forgive those who are repentant and obedient to Your tradition" appears to be an allusion to the Qur'ān (VII, 153), one of the passages that is frequently asserted in support of the doctrine of badā'. This allusion is further confirmed by the Bab's reference to "what I understood from Your Book," which certainly means the Qur'ān. Goldziher refers to "subtleties which appear in the Shiʿite Shaykhi sect" (*RMM* XI, 1910, 435–38) regarding Badā'. On a few occasions in his writings, Ahsā'i discussed this issue; for example the treatise in reply to Sayyid ʿAlī Lāhījānī (ques. 2), and the treatise in reply to Maḥmūd Mīrzā (ques. 9), both of which appeared in *Jawāmiʿ al-Kalim*. (See also *Fihrist* II, 221, 237.)

decision." His journey to the ʿAtabāt, the most important part of his campaign, was suspended in order to prevent further hostility. The Bab realized that the chances of an overwhelming success in the ʿAtabāt, where he was faced not only with Shiʿite religious opposition but with the more important threat of secular authority, were fairly slim. Out of disillusion and despair he turned his attention to his homeland, the "city of safety," where he assumed circumstances would at least allow him to summon his followers without serious interference or organized persecution. The holy land of Kūfa and Karbalāʾ were thus exchanged for the "pure land" of Fars.

The cancellation of the gathering in the ʿAtabāt, no matter how justified by the Bab, had a strong effect on those who had anticipated a swift and even violent end to the "people of fire." Instead, in Basṭāmī's trial and in the Bab's change of decision they now witnessed the retreat of the movement, and victory for its opponents. The course of events gave an unexpected chance to critics, especially in the rival Shaykhi camps, to magnify the Babi setback. This is well illustrated in the attacks of Ḥājjī Muḥammad Karīm Khān Kirmānī, as early as Rajab 1261/July 1845. "So first came Muḥarram and then Naurūz [21 March, the Persian new year], and no revelation has come from him [the Bab]. Instead his effect vanished and news of him ceased. I do not know whether he is drowned in the sea, or burnt on land. So the disillusioned [followers] remained in shadow, discredited among the people because of their promises. They lost their ways like blind people, and praise be to God, the back of this misled people is broken."[280] Kirmānī soon realized that his wishes for the destruction of the Bab had been premature, but at the time he so cherished a disastrous outcome of the ʿAtabāt plan that he could not resist giving a fuller description:

> Then [the Bab] addressed them saying, "Soon I will rise on the day of ʿĀshūrā or day of Naurūz. I came on behalf of your Imam, the Lord of the Age, who will purify the earth with justice and equity. He will not change his word, and he does not intend to postpone his day of return." He then specified that his meeting place is in the land of Karbalāʾ, in order to persuade common and ignorant people and those who were seeking disturbance to go to that exalted shrine. Then he himself would arrive there. . . . See how God's rejection of his deception destroyed him. In fact people assembled in Karbalāʾ, but he was unable to join them because of troubles on the road to Mecca and difficulties for pilgrims in traveling via Jabal. So came Muḥarram, and then Naurūz, and he remained in Ḥijāz, and did not go to Karbalāʾ, fearing the Bedouins and the bandits. See how God, praise be to Him, disgraced him and broke his back, and thus God according to His word established truth and nullified falsehood. Henceforth his fame diminished, his effect disappeared, and news of him ceased.[281]

[280]*Izhāq al-Baṭil* 110.

[281]Ibid. 110–11. The reference in the above passage to the insecurity on the pilgrimage routes as the principal reason for the Bab's failure to reach Iraq should be treated with some

What Kirmānī highlighted in his account, though exaggerated, reflects the general setback the Babis endured in their earliest attempts. Indeed, this entire episode—the trial and death of Basṭāmī and the postponement of the public proclamation—had a dual effect on the future of the movement. On the one hand, it was damaging to the potential public support the Babis hoped to attract. There was little hope for a mass conversion outside Iran, even in the seemingly favorable environment of the ʿAtabāt. The episode also made it clear that the prospect of any toleration by the clerical establishment was nonexistent. The crisis of confidence that ensued the postponement of the Ẓuhūr thus proved to be a harsh test for the new prophet and his adherents.

During Ḥajj the Bab expected to see in earnest the symbolic realization of the messianic prophecies and the visible confirmation of his inspirations. The surroundings of Mecca and the rituals of Ḥajj aroused in him, as in many other Muslim visionaries, a spirit of exultation. The experience of Ḥajj, feeling in presence of Muḥammad, raised his aspirations, if not for a mass conversion, at least for recognition by a select few. When even that recognition was not forthcoming, he resorted to the challenge of mubāhala as a symbolic means to vanquish the forces of denial. By invoking divine intervention, the Bab was testing not his own veracity, of which at this stage he had no doubt, but God's intention. The fact that mubāhala never took place, and he was faced instead with mockery, denunciation, and a verdict of death, convinced him of change of divine will. Such an interpretation demonstrates the thrust of the Bab's fatalism but also signifies, in a paradoxical way, the emergence of a more mature, and less idealistic, understanding of the means and ends of his mission. Over the next few years, it became clear to the Bab and his chief lieutenants that even in the "city of safety" the advocacy of the new cause was not to remain unopposed by the forces of authority and orthodoxy.

Harassment and Refuge

The following eighteen months of the Bab's life were spent mostly in the isolation of his own house in Shiraz, and then, from late September 1846, in

---

reserve. It is true that around this time the main road between Ḥijāz and Iraq, which passed through Jabal Shammar, was unsafe. In 1844, owing to some internal struggle between the sharīf of Mecca and the Wahhābī Amirs, a shaykh of the ʿAbdā division of the Shammar tribe, with the help and encouragement of Sharīf Muḥammad Ibn ʿAwn, marched into al-Qasīm and defeated the forces of Faiṣal Ibn Saʿd. But this engagement, which appears to have been over by the beginning of 1845, could not have been the main obstacle in the Bab's way, since we know that pilgrims like Sayyid ʿAlī Kirmānī, Mullā Ḥasan Khurāsānī, and Sayyid Jawād Muḥarrir reached Karbalāʾ, presumably from the same route. For further information on the Jabal route see Lorimer *Gazeteer* I, part 2, App. H, 2351. For tribal disturbances in the area see de Gaury *Rulers* 247.

the refuge of Manūchihr Khān Muʿtamad al-Daula, the governor of Isfahan. Even before his arrival in Shiraz in late June 1845, the arrest and punishment of the first group of Babi activists (including his traveling companion, Quddūs, and the prominent convert Mullā Ṣādiq Muqaddas, who had openly advocated in the mosques and bazaar of Shiraz the advent of a new Bab of the Imam) had turned the ʿulama, and soon the provincial government, against the Bab.[282] En route to the "safe city" he was arrested, and upon the request of the ʿulama was put on summary trial presided over by the governor, Ḥusayn Khān Niẓām al-Daula Ājūdānbāshī. Humiliated and physically assaulted during the tribunal, he was then placed under house arrest.[283]

To appease the ʿulama and calm public excitement, he was then brought to the Friday congregation in the Vakil mosque and urged by Shaykh Abū Turāb, the imām jumʿa of Shiraz (and a friend of the Bab's uncles), to renounce claims made by or attributed to him. In conformity with his own policy of prudence, in his statement from the pulpit the Bab denied claims to the Imam's representation or deputyship, though he did not (and was not requested to) extend his denial to the claim of Qāʾimīya itself.[284] In a written statement, apparently produced under pressure, he again recanted any claims to the position of bābīya, disowned those who advocated such beliefs, and added: "If certain words flowed from my pen, they are purely instinctive and entirely against the accepted norms and thus not to be taken as proofs of any cause."[285] To the satisfaction of the relatively tolerant Shaykh Abū Turāb and perhaps the relief of his own family, the Bab's statement saved him from the death penalty sought by some mujtahids and diverted public attention from him. But for a few in the Vakil audience (mostly merchants and artisans) who in spite of the Bab's denial reinforced their allegiance to him, the rest of the population remained unmoved.[286]

During the ensuing period of confinement, the Bab's contacts with the outside world were restricted to a few intermediaries, including his uncle Sayyid ʿAlī and, for a time, Mullā Ḥusayn Bushrūʾī. Alternating phases of relief and anguish characterized the Bab's behavior in this period. Despite

[282]For the first round of Babi propagation in Shiraz and the ensuing persecutions see *Ahmad* 451–452; *Muʿīn* 67–69; *NH* 201–2; and *Nabil* 143–48. An interesting European report of the incident, the first of its kind, appeared in the London *Times*, 19 Nov. 1845 (taken from *Literary Gazette*, 15 Nov. 1845). See Balyuzi *The Bab* 77–78.

[283]For the events leading to the Shiraz trial and its aftermath see *Ahmad* 452–53; *NT* III, 42–44; *NK* 112; *Nabil* 142–43, 151–53; *RPAC* 151–55; and *Muʿīn* 69–93. The Bab himself defines the governor, Ḥusayn Khān, as "vicious and sinister," who owing to his drunkenness "was never able to pass a sound judgment" (INBA no. 64, 115 [letter to Muḥammad Shāh]).

[284]Not surprisingly, the Babi and non-Babi accounts vary in their rendering of the Bab's statement. See for example *NT* III, 44, and *Ahmad* 453 in comparison with *Nabil* 154–56 and Mīrzā Ḥabībullāh *Tārīkh* 50–54.

[285]INBA no. 91, 169–70. The content of this important and hitherto unknown statement is confirmed by no other source. Yet its style and tone—unlike the alleged recantation of 1848 (see below, chap. 9)—leaves little doubt as to its originality.

[286]*Nabil* 156–58.

his recantation, the news of his emissaries' success inside Iran and the occasional meetings in secret with converts kept him in high spirits and made him hopeful of ultimate release. The conversion of two men—Sayyid Yaḥyā Dārābī (later Vaḥīd), son of intuitionist Jaʿfar Kashfī, and Mullā Muḥammad ʿAlī Ḥujjat al-Islām (later Ḥujjat), the militant Akhbārī leader of Zanjān—was particularly gratifying. Both were of non-Shaykhi persuasion and held strong popular sway over their local communities. They were the earliest converts of any significance outside the Shaykhi sphere.[287]

By mid-1846 the growing concentration of converts in Shiraz—mostly followers from the ʿAtabāt who responded to the Bab's earlier invitation—began to disrupt his otherwise serene and uneventful life of meditation and writing. A serious power struggle between Mullā Ḥusayn and a group of more radical converts, headed by Mullā Jawād Valīyānī, came to a head as the Bab sided with his First Believer in favor of a policy of gradual and inconspicuous proselytizing. The opposing party, disappointed by the Bab's reluctance to uphold his earlier promises of open Insurrection, defected from the Babi ranks. In part motivated by personal ambitions, they were bitter about the prominence of Mullā Ḥusayn, now designated Bāb al-Bāb (the Gate of the Gate) and the de facto leader of the movement.[288]

The crisis reflected a deeper dilemma for the Bab himself; a traumatic choice between confining his inspirational utterances to himself and a small group of adepts or conveying his mission to the public at large, and thereby risking grave consequences. This inner conflict brought him to the brink of self-doubt. The course of events, however, soon made him more confident than ever of his inspiration and resolute about the validity of his mission.

The machinations of his opponents (mostly the Babi defectors), who accused him and his followers of duplicity, heresy, and subversion, soon brought him back into the glare of publicity. Under the pressure of the clergy, government agents raided the Bab's house and placed him under arrest in the residence of the chief magistrate, in an attempt to sever his contact with his disciples. Soon, however, in the chaos that followed an outbreak of cholera in the city, the Bab, who had already aroused the magistrate's sympathy, managed to escape and immediately travel to Isfahan. The existence of a growing Babi cell in that city, first organized by

[287]On the circumstances of Vaḥīd's conversions see *KD* I, 52–57; *Ahmad* 465–67; *Nabil* 173–78; *ZH* 462–64 (citing Sayyid Jawād Karbalāʾī). Also Muḥammad Shafīʿ Rauḥānī Nayrīzī *Lamaʿāt al-Anwār, Sharḥ-i Vaqāyiʿ-i Nayrīz-i Shūrāngīz* (Tehran, 130 Badīʿ/1974) 41–54. On Ḥujjat's conversion see "Personal Reminiscences of the Babi Insurrection at Zanjan in 1850, written in Persia by Āqā ʿAbd'l-Aḥad-i-Zanjānī," E. G. Browne trans., *JRAS* 1892, 259–332, and *Nabil* 178–79. See also above, chap. 2.

[288]The writings of the Bab in this period contain ample references to the machinations of the Babi defectors as well as his grievances, particularly over his followers' divulgence of his identity. Cursory references to mischiefmakers, evildoers, deceivers, and devil's companions are directed at Valīyānī and his party. INBA no. 91, 170–80, 180–82, 192–94, and no. 98, 61–85 are a few examples. For the circumstances of defection see *Nabil* 160–65.

Mullā Ḥusayn, and Manūchihr Khān's favorable response to his petition (as well as to earlier Babi propagation) were both instrumental in this decision.[289]

At the governors instructions, the Bab was graciously received and hosted by Sayyid Muḥammad Imām Jumʿa Khātūnābādī. In both men he found a momentary refuge from persecution and, for the first and only time, some recognition from prominent state and religious representatives. The governor's motives for supporting the Bab were complex. A highly capable and sagacious, though severe, eunuch of Georgian origin, he had made his way up from the harem of the previous shah to the governorship of a huge region. Constantly challenged by his deadly enemy Ḥājjī Mīrzā Āqāsī, Manūchihr Khān must have seen the advantages of an alliance with a charismatic and increasingly popular religious reformist who had the potential, as he saw it, not only to deprive the mujtahids of their hegemony over the Iṣfahānī public, but to help deter, if not unseat, the premier in Tehran. He was not devoid of sympathy and sincerity, however. A keen convener of religious debates and believer in ecumenical dialogue, he saw in the Bab a persecuted holy man whose claims went beyond the segregating barriers of Islamic sharīʿa; an answer to the troubled mind of a Muslim convert not fully disengaged from his Christian background. At his request the Bab composed a long treatise on the question of Muḥammad's special prophethood (*nubuwwa khāṣṣa*), a familiar theme in Muslim-Christian debates.[290]

Having the visible support of the governor and the implicit backing of the imām jumʿa, the Bab's popularity soared, particularly after an informal gathering of the ʿulama in the house of the imām jumʿa, where in the presence of the governor the Bab displayed his speed at producing instantaneous verses. This gathering was soon followed by another, this time in the government house. Manūchihr Khān, responding to the ʿulama's open criticism from the pulpit, denunciations, and petitions to Tehran, arranged a debate in order to deflate their claims of sedition and apostasy leveled against the Bab. Those mujtahids who accepted the invitation, mostly sons of eminent mujtahids succeeding their fathers, questioned the Bab on a variety of issues, ranging from theosophy and logic to jurisprudence and astronomy. The Bab stopped short of admitting openly his claim of gateship, but insisted on the

[289] *Muʿīn* 97. For Mullā Ḥusayn in Isfahan and early Babis of that city see below, chaps. 6 and 8.

[290] For Manūchihr Khān's background, among other Qajar sources see numerous references in *RS* X and *NT* II and III as well as Aḥmad Mīrzā ʿAżud al-Daula *Tārīkh-i ʿAżudī*, 2nd ed. (Tehran, 1328/1949) 23–24 and other entries; and Riżā Qūlī Mīrzā *Safar Nāmih* A. Farmānfarmā'īān Qājār ed. (Tehran, 1346/1967), 9–170. Of the European accounts see for example A. H. Layard *Early Adventures in Persia etc.* (London, 1894) 114–17; H. A. Stern *Dawning of Light in the East* (London, 1854) 149–61. Among Babi accounts see *NK* 116; *Muʿīn* 102–7; *NH* 208–16; *ZH* 90–94. Also *Ahmad* 455 for his interest in religious debates. The text of the above-mentioned treatise and other works of the Bab of the Isfahan period appears in INBA no. 40.

unceasing human need for inspirational access to the knowledge of the Imam. The gathering ended with no clear victory on either side.[291]

Alarmed by the Babs' threat and cautioned by their counterparts in Shiraz, a majority of the mujtahids of Isfahan who had boycotted the governor's assembly found an eager listener in the person of Āqāsī. The premier assured the ʿulama of his support, cursed the insane heretic, persuaded the imām jumʿa to disown him, and requested the governor to send the Bab to the capital. Facing the mujtahids' collective denunciatory fatwā and their infamous capacity to incite violence, and concerned with Āqāsī's eagerness to paint him as a rebel, the governor reluctantly gave in, if only on the surface. The imam jumʿa's verdict of insanity, the best he could do to subvert the mujtahids' call for the Bab's death, left the governor alone in his support.[292]

To all appearances complying with Āqāsī's order, government troops, headed by a confidant of Manūchihr Khān, accompanied the Bab out of the city in the direction of Tehran, only to smuggle him back in disguise to be lodged in a remote part of the governor's private residence. There he stayed in hiding for the remaining three months of Manūchihr Khān's life. Still waiting for a favorable political climate to topple Āqāsī, the governor promised the Bab that he would soon expound his cause, present him to Muḥammad Shāh, who would spread his religion to the lands beyond, and even arrange for his marriage with a sister of the shah. Wary of such promises, the anguished prophet was nevertheless grateful to the governor for providing him a refuge and a hope for ultimate triumph. Soon after he was discovered in the government house, the Bab was removed from his hiding place and escorted to Tehran under full security, this time in earnest.

Manūchihr Khān's motives aside, the successive episodes of Shiraz and Isfahan illustrated above all the potency of the ʿulama's opposition. Even the support of a governor unique in his own time for autonomy and control of the clergy could not guarantee the free advocacy of an otherwise popular movement, even when combined with the backing of an influential imām jumʿa. The case of Isfahan was more or less true wherever the agents of the state showed the slightest leniency to the new movement. Whatever the Bab's and his followers' expectations, the failure of Manūchihr Khan also ruled out the possibility of coming to terms with the state; one of the two chief aims of the Babi manifesto.

Yet not all chance was lost for a rapprochement with the shah. At least his attitude toward the Bab still remained tolerant, if not accommodating. In a decree issued in reply to his petition for an audience, Muḥammad Shāh addresses "his excellency . . . of the purest descent, the model for the friends [of God], Āqā Sayyid ʿAlī Muḥammad may God, the Almighty, protect

[291]For debates of Isfahan and other events see *NK* 116–18; *NT* III, 44–47; *KD* 73–105 (citing the Bab's correspondence); *Nabil* 207–8; *ZH* 93–94. Recollections of Āqā Sayyid ʿAbd al-Raḥīm Iṣfahānī (INBA Lib. MS. no. 1028D) provides some new information.

[292]Text of the premier's letter to the ʿulama of Isfahan dated Muḥarram 1263/Jan. 1847

him." Assuring him of his royal blessing that "envelops the people of Iran in general and that excellency, who is from the glorious family of the sādāt and the learned people, in particular," he nonetheless states that the Bab's request for an audience cannot be granted, "since these days the royal cavalcade is on the verge of departure and it is not possible to receive that excellency in the proper manner. Thus he should leave for Mākū and there remain in relaxation for a while and pray for the victorious state . . . until the time when the royal company returns to the capital. Thence we would summon that excellency and receive him at length and set up a proper arrangement for his affairs. Of course of this matter he should not feel offended and at all time relay to us his wishes and do not forget in his blessed prayers the sacred soul of the monarch."[293]

Realizing the Bab's value as a deterrent for keeping the troublesome mujtahids in check, Āqāsī was nonetheless reluctant to permit an audience with the shah, lest the mystically oriented monarch be impressed. He was also duly reminded by another rival, Naṣrūllāh Ardabīlī, the Ṣadr al-Mamālik (chief clerical administrator of the empire), of the grave consequences of meddling with the ʿulamā's affairs on so sensitive a ground. Hence, waiting in vain for a long-promised audience with the shah, the Bab spent several months in a camp outside Tehran before being sent in exile to Mākū. Muḥammad Shāh lived just long enough to demonstrate the supremacy of his premier's intentions over his own comforting promises.

---

appears in Iʿtiżād al-Salṭana *Mutanabbīʾīn (Fitna-yi Bāb)* 121–22. For the Imām jumʿa's fatwā see *Nabil* 209 and *ZH* 95.

[293]*Samandar* 101–2. The decree is dated Rabīʿ al-Thānī 1263/April 1847.

6

Letters of Light, Letters of Fire: The Babi ʿUlama and Their Adversaries

Prior to his departure from Shiraz, in late Jumādā al-Thānī 1260/July 1844, Mullā Ḥusayn Bushrūʾī had publicly declared that "manifestation of the Proof of God is close at hand" and by his appearance "all these regulations and customs which are in vogue among you will be abolished, and he will bring a new book and tradition."[1] The identity of the Promised One puzzled many. Mīrzā Aḥmad Shīrāzī, who was present at the time of Mullā Ḥusayn's departure, objected: "You have misguided and perplexed the people. You pretended that the True One has appeared and that these regulations will be abandoned. Now you are going, and neither has any True One appeared, nor has any sign of him been seen. The people will remain in doubt and astonishment."[2] Mullā Ḥusayn retorted that he was not "commissioned by the lawgiver to do more than this. . . . He sent me to give the warning, as an act of grace to the people, and to inform them that the appearance of the True One draws near, so that when the manifestation actually happens, they may not oppose it and perish. Whatever I was not ordered to state will be made known by the one named Mullā Ṣādiq, who will come two months after my departure."[3]

The above account is a rare specimen of early Babi propaganda. The main theme emphasized by Mullā Ḥusayn, as early as 1260/1844, was that the "lawgiver" with a new book would replace existing sharīʿa with a new one. His task was to warn people of the gravity of the Ẓuhūr and to remind them of the severe consequences of denial. This conveniently vague but effective message was meant to raise people's expectations. Mullā Ḥusayn, acting with the Bab's approval, had left the task of proclamation in Shiraz to Muqaddas.[4] After the meeting, Mīrzā Aḥmad asked Sayyid ʿAlī Muḥammad

[1] *Ahmad* 499–50.
[2] Ibid. 450.
[3] Ibid.
[4] For his account see below.

about his opinion of Mullā Ḥusayn's words. The Bab replied: "Mullā Ḥusayn is an honest and truthful man, and he is above making unfounded statements. Undoubtedly these words of his have a foundation."[5]

Over the next four years, the burden of broadening the Babi sphere and organizing a network of converts and sympathizers rested on the shoulders of Mullā Ḥusayn and a handful of other Babi activists. Organization and systematic recruitment always remained a problem for the Babis. The formidable hostility of the ʿulama, and later the state, further hindered the formation of a new community that scattered over a broad geographical area and displayed considerable social diversity.

But from within these haphazard efforts, there emerged a distinct sociocultural pattern of conversion. The Babi message proved to be more appealing primarily to the ʿulama of Shaykhi or other unorthodox persuasions and in turn to their constituency in towns and villages throughout Iran. The movement also received some significant backing among merchants, traders, and artisans. Other sectarian elements—Sufis and wandering dervishes, members of urban intelligentsia, and lower- to middle-rank state officials—were also attracted. The social composition of the early Babi community and their motives for conversion are complex and cannot be seen in isolation from the forces that interacted with the new movement: the opposition of the ʿulama, the policy adopted by the central and local governments, and prevailing socioeconomic conditions.

The Shaykhi Converts

In Isfahan, during the first stage of his mission, Mullā Ḥusayn succeeded in converting a number of favorable Shaykhi elements. As in Shiraz, his public preachings drew attention from prominent ʿulama and in due course led to their mild condemnation. En route to Tehran, Mullā Ḥusayn stopped in Kashan, where he attracted a number of Shaykhi sympathizers and called upon a celebrated mujtahid. He then proceeded to Qum, where according to Nabīl Zarandī "he found the people utterly unprepared to heed his call,"[6] perhaps due to the absence of any Shaykhi connection there. Such lack of support does not seem surprising in a city that was becoming a stronghold of the orthodoxy.[7]

In late Rajab 1260/August 1844 he reached Tehran. His stay in the capital resulted in a number of conversions among the ʿulama and some among state officials, but he also faced criticism from the Shaykhi camp.

[5] *Ahmad* 450.
[6] *Nabil* 101.
[7] However, the celebrated mujtahid of Qum, Mīrzā Abul-Qāsim Qumī, appears to have had a favorable attitude to Aḥsāʾī. *Dalīl al-Mutaḥayyirīn* 32. Some of the Qumī ʿulama embraced the new cause within the next few years. *Nabil* 101.

Despite this opposition, he was able to fulfill one of the major tasks of his mission, the delivery of the *Sūrat al-Malik* to Muḥammad Shāh and Ḥājjī Mīrzā Āqāsī. However, it looks as though Mullā Ḥusayn's activities in the capital were not as open as they had been in Isfahan and later in Mashhad.

Mullā Ḥusayn must have reached Khurasan some time in late Shaʿbān 1260/September 1844. En route he passed on the message to a number of "trusted" people who seem to have had connections with him because of previous Shaykhi links. In late 1844 he was residing in Mashhad. According to his earlier arrangement with the Bab, he sent a letter to Shiraz. In this letter, Nabīl Zarandī states, "he enclosed a list of the names of those who had responded to his call, and of whose steadfastness and sincerity he was assured."[8] It seems that, as had been planned, the Bab was anxious to know the public response to his call before he set out for Ḥijāz.[9]

Mullā Ḥusayn's efforts were generally successful among three major groups: the ʿulama and the ṭullāb, local merchants and local state officials. Unconcerned with such distinctions, he probably approached anyone whom he found responsive to his teachings, yet the converts among the clerical class in this early stage shared a degree of uniformity in their outlook as well as in their social status. His efforts in Isfahan, for instance, resulted in early recognition by Mullā Ṣādiq Muqaddas and Mullā Muḥammad Taqī Harātī, both from middle-rank clergy. Their entry into the Babi circle doubtless lent weight and reputation to the new doctrine.

Muqaddas, son of a humble mulla from Khurasan, was born and bred in Mashhad,[10] where he undertook his preliminary studies with Sayyid Muḥammad Qaṣīr Rażavī, a local mujtahid who also taught Mullā Ḥusayn.[11] For a while he became the prayer leader presumably in one of the Mashhad's mosques.[12] His title *Muqaddas* (holy) denotes exceptional devotion and perhaps ascetic practices. "From the early years of his career," it is reported, "he was well known among the people as the essence of purity and piety, and therefore was known as *Muqaddas*."[13] After Mashhad he moved

[8] *Nabil* 126.

[9] Whether such a letter ever reached the Bab before his departure is a matter open to dispute. The Bab, according to his own account, embarked from Būshihr for Jidda on 19 Ramaḍān 1260/2 Oct. 1844. Therefore, under no circumstances can *Nabil*'s date (126) for the arrival of Mullā Ḥusayn's letter to the Bab on 27 Ramaḍān 1260/10 Oct. 1844 be justified.

[10] *Samandar* 163. Sources on Muqaddas (later known by the Bahā'ī title Ismullāh al-Aṣdaq) are confined to his own accounts related to Bābī-Bahā'ī historiographers. Kāẓim Qazvīnī, who himself visited Mullā Ṣādiq toward the end of his life in ʿAkkā, gives a full account (*Samandar* 162–71). *Fu'ādī* (86–99) uses the notes of Mullā Ṣādiq's son, known as Ibn Aṣdaq, while the oral account of the same person is apparently the basis of the *SAMB* account (254–55). *Nabil* (100–101) and *NH* (40–42) both heard the account of his conversion directly from Muqaddas.

[11] *Qatīl* 521.

[12] *Samandar* 163.

[13] Ibid.

to Karbalā[14] and over the years became one of Rashtī's senior students.[15] He finally received his ijāza in Rabīʿ al-Awwal 1259/April 1843, a few months before his teacher's death.[16] Rashtī calls him "my trustworthy brother" and praises him as "an accomplished scholar" who is "superior amongst his peers." Rashtī then maintains: "I seek God's guidance and by His name, authorize him [to issue] fatwā and therefore to relate [from me] whatever this humble servant has composed whether books, compiled works, treatises, or replies to religious problems and whatever by God's will, may appear in future."[17]

Such authorization had some significance on Muqaddas' later recognition of the Bab. As an authentic bearer of the teachings of Aḥsā'ī and Rashtī, he could approve of the Bab's claims—an approval that was essential to the Shaykhi recognition of the movement. The Babi poet Ẕabīḥ Kāshānī particularly refers in his *Maṡnavī* to this accomplishment:

> He was a scholar and a mujtahid in every field,
> No mystic ever appeared as luminous as he,
> Not only was he accomplished in the path of the Shaykh [Aḥsā'ī]
> But he was also in love with the Lord.[18]

When Mullā Ḥusayn met Muqaddas in Isfahan the latter seems to have already enjoyed some acceptance in the city.[19] A Tabrīzī merchant who was visiting Isfahan at the time observed that his popularity among the inhabitants was so great that four thousand people followed him in the Friday prayer.[20]

Muqaddas is often portrayed as a fine example of an ardent seeker who, guided by his visions, finally finds his way to the Bab. Yet his previous knowledge of Sayyid ʿAlī Muḥammad must have also been of assistance to him.[21] Like Mullā Ḥusayn, he was also perplexed over the future of the Shaykhism, and no doubt his loyalty to the internal grouping in the school was influential in his conversion. The trilateral oath of fraternity among Muqaddas, Mullā Ḥusayn, and Mullā Ḥasan Gauhar, which implied a

[14]Ibid. Also *SAMB* 191, 198.

[15]*Samandar* 163.

[16]The facsimile of the original ijāza in Arabic appears in *ZH* 145 (supp.).

[17]*ZH* 145 (supp.).

[18]Ḥājjī Muḥammad Ismāʿil Ẕabīḥ Kāshānī (Fānī) *Maṡnavī*, MS no. 787, Wadham Collection, Oxford, folio 82/b.

[19]*Samandar* 163, and *Fu'ādī* 87–88. Both sources confirm that he departed from Karbalā' after the death of Rashtī. *Nabīl*'s claim (100) that Muqaddas had during the last five years been residing in Isfahan seems improbable.

[20]*Muʿīn* 67, quoting Āqā Faraj Tabrīzī. He received the bulk of this support from Shaykhi sympathizers but probably the extent of this popularity has been exaggerated.

[21]The circumstances of his conversion are recorded in Mīrzā Ḥabībullāh *Tārīkh* 34–35 and *Samandar* 163–64.

desire for unanimity in the choice of a spiritual leader upon the death of Rashtī, must not be underestimated.[22]

Immediately after realizing the identity of the Bab, Muqaddas decided to set out for Shiraz. It is reported that he traveled the distance between the two cities on foot,[23] garbed as a humble villager.[24] Just before his departure, Āqā Faraj Tabrīzī, who recognized him in the Isfahan bazaar, recalls:

> After greeting each other, I kissed his hand, and humbly asked: "Why are you dressed in this costume?" He replied: "I am leaving for Shiraz." "For what purpose?" I inquired. He said: "A new call has arisen. Someone has appeared, claiming a great authority. I am going to find out the truth of his claim." I then said, "Why are you troubling yourself? Why do you not despatch a reliable believer to inquire into the matter and bring you the result?" He replied, "This is a matter of principles of religion, and not a question of taqlīd [emulation], in which I can act on other's words." I suggested, "Then please wait until I can prepare transport and a servant and provide some means for your journey." He said, "All these are possible, but I would prefer to tread the path of the quest on foot." He then said farewell and went away.[25]

The way Muqaddas was trying to fulfil his "individual duty"[26] calls to mind the Shiʿite Traditions regarding the believer's duty to support the Mahdi's cause: "And when you see [the Mahdi], give him your word of allegiance, even if it is necessary to make your way in the snow on hands and feet, since he is God's deputy."[27] In Shiraz, as a result of his interview with the Bab, he overcame his final doubts.[28] The point that had puzzled him, like many other early believers, was that, far from possessing the "nominal accomplishments" and "official qualities"[29] of a high-ranking divine, the prophet of Shiraz lacked the conventional madrasa training. Yet at the same time, this very factor worked in his favor: "The solid, firm verses . . . revealed by the young uneducated merchant" could only be regarded as "an infallible proof for his rightfulness."[30]

Another example of the middle-rank mujtahids of Isfahan whose previous Shaykhi tendencies led them to welcome the Bab was Mullā Muḥammad Taqī Harātī (Hiravī). His educational training, similar to that of Mullā

[22]Mīrzā Ḥabībullāh *Tārīkh* 34.

[23]*Samandar* 164.

[24]*Muʿīn* 66.

[25]Ibid.

[26]Distinguishable from collective duty (*farḍ kifāya),* the fulfillment of which by a sufficient number of individuals excuses other individuals from fulfilling it. (J. Schacht *An Introduction to Islamic Law* [Oxford, 1964] 120–21).

[27]Tradition attributed to the Prophet by Ibn Māja in Majlisī *Biḥār* XIII, chap. 1, section 4 (trans. p. 65).

[28]*Samandar* 164; cf. *Muʿīn* 66–67.

[29]*NH,* 40–42.

[30]Ibid.; cf. Mīrzā Ḥabībullāh *Tarīkh*, 36. *Samandar* (164), however, believes that he reached Shiraz after the Bab's departure for Ḥijāz.

Ḥusayn and Muqaddas, no doubt facilitated his initiation.[31] A native of Herat, he emigrated to Isfahan in his early youth[32] and studied under such teachers as Shaftī, Shaykh Muḥammad Taqī Iṣfahānī and Muḥammad Ibrāhim Karbāsī.[33] But later, in the ʿAtabāt, the scope of his studies was not limited to the traditional study of fiqh and uṣūl al-fiqh.[34] Harātī's presence in both Uṣūlī and Shaykhi circles, and particularly his studies under Rashtī,[35] helped him to develop a more sophisticated taste than most of his contemporaries. His works, mainly in the form of commentaries, cover a variety of subjects, ranging from jurisprudence and theology to mathematics and rijāl.[36] He also recorded, elaborated, and argued the works and lectures of Shaftī and Rashtī.[37] On his return to Isfahan, he taught the *Qawānīn al-Uṣūl* of Mīrzā-yi Qumī.[38] He was also the chief secretary of the powerful Mīr Muḥammad Khātūnābādī, the imām jumʿa of Isfahan.[39] Later he enjoyed "full authority" in his legal rulings.[40]

Earlier in his career, Harātī seems to have been particularly keen on the question of Ẓuhūr. Qatīl maintains that Harātī was anxious to learn about the significance of the year 1261, and the time of the manifestation.[41] The qualities attributed to Sayyid ʿAlī Muḥammad and specimens of his works, no doubt influenced Harātī's view of the Shīrāzī merchant. Convinced of the Bab's claims, "he preached publicly from the pulpit the advent of the special deputy of the Twelfth Imam."[42] Though he had strong ties with the Shaykhis, Harātī never ceased to be a jurist in the traditional sense. He was the first important figure to embrace the movement from outside the close circle of confirmed Shaykhis. Further, his support strengthened the newly established Babi group in Isfahan, and may have influenced the Bab's decision to move to Isfahan.[43]

In this and following visits, according to Mīrzā Aḥmad, Mullā Ḥusayn "won over a large number of people in Isfahan."[44] Among them were some

[31] *Qatīl* 522.
[32] *TAS* II/1, 212–15 (213). He was born in 1217/1802.
[33] Ibid.
[34] Ibid.
[35] Ibid.
[36] A list of his works appears in *TAS* II/1, 213–15. His *Nihāyat al-Āmāl* (written in 1279/1863) contains his autobiography. Another later work of Harātī, *Tanbīh al-Ghāfilīn,* is a refutation of the Babis. After his death, most of his books came into the possession of Mīrzā Ḥasan Shīrāzī. For a list of his works see *MA* III, 625–31.
[37] *TAS* II/1, 213–14.
[38] *ZH* 96.
[39] Ibid.
[40] *TAS* II/1, 213.
[41] *Qatīl* 514.
[42] *NT* III, 234, which is the source for *Mutanabbiʾīn* 34, *SAMB* 255, and *RPAC* 158.
[43] In a letter which is probably addressed to Mullā Ḥusayn (circa 1261–1262/1845–1846), the Bab sends his regards to Harātī, to whom he refers with the highest veneration, while instructing Mullā Ḥusayn to spell out Harātī's doubts and perplexities (INBA no. 91, XLI, 196).
[44] *Ahmad* 451.

from Ardistān, who seem to have become aware of the new message through Muqaddas. Mullā ʿAlī Akbar Ardistānī, a student of Muqaddas, followed his teacher to Shiraz.[45] Other Ardistānīs who were resident in Isfahan also became conscious of the Bab. An old man, Āqā Muḥammad Ḥusayn, was among the people who set out for Shiraz to visit the Bab.[46] Two of the Ardistānīs, Mullā ʿAlī Akbar and Āqā Muḥammad Ḥusayn, were later involved in the events in Shiraz in 1261–1263/1845–1846. Mīrzā Ḥaydar ʿAlī, a small landowner, met Mullā Ḥusayn and accepted the new daʿwa.[47] Subsequently, together with some other believers, he founded a large Babi community in Ardistān, typical of many semirural communities formed in the early period.[48]

Mullā Muḥammad Rizā Pāqalʿaʾī, a native of Isfahan, visited Mullā Ḥusayn, perhaps through the Nahrī family,[49] and four years later fought and died in Ṭabarsī.[50] Another Iṣfahānī, Sayyid Jawād Muḥarrir (whom we met earlier in Ḥijāz), initially became attracted to the new message very probably through Muqaddas.[51] In his own account of his early conversion, Muḥarrir relates that he heard from Āqā Khān Munajjim Naṣrābādī that in the year 1260, the Qāʾim will appear. "At the same time, I heard that a young man from Shiraz claimed to be the Qāʾim."[52] Other low-ranking mullas and seminarians joined the Isfahan group.[53] Together with a few merchants and some members of various guilds and professions, they formed the basis of the Babi community in Isfahan,[54] a typical early Babi cell.

The mild clerical opposition that first appeared at the time of Mullā Ḥusayn's arrival soon developed into an open confrontation when the Babi message was clearly pronounced from the pulpits of the Isfahan mosques. As it appears from Nabīl Zarandī's account,[55] followers of Sayyid Muḥammad Bāqir Shaftī, who probably knew Mullā Ḥusayn from his previous visit, were responsible.[56] Accusing Mullā Ḥusayn of upholding a heretical doctrine with "great vehemence and vigor," they warned that "the day is

[45]*ZH* 103.

[46]Ibid. 104 (supp.).

[47]Ibid. 103.

[48]*KD* I, 182–83. The Ardistānīs participation in Ṭabarsī is described in a number of accounts. Sayyid Ḥusayn Mahjūr Zavārihʾī (*Tārīkh-i Mīmīya,* (Browne Or. MSS no. F.28(9) I and II, 18 and INBA Lib. MS p. 18) counts seven of them. Mīrzā Ḥaydar ʿAlī was one of the rare survivors of the fighting (Ẕabīḥ *Masnavī* 6/b).

[49]*Nabil* 100. According to *Nabil* (422), "a distinguished sayyid and a highly esteemed divine" in Isfahan.

[50]Ibid. 422.

[51]*Memoirs,* INBA Lib. MS. no. 1028D (probably compiled by Mīrzā Asadullāh Fāżil Māzandarānī) contains (29–32) a biography of Sayyid Jawād and his acquaintance with Muqaddas.

[52]Ibid. 29. For an account of the visits he paid to the Bab see above, chap. 4.

[53]The identity of at least seven of them is known to us. See Mīrzā Luṭf ʿAlī Shīrāzī (INBA Lib. MS and Browne Or. MSS F.28(9) III); *Tārīkh-i Mīmīya*; and the list in *Nabil* 414–29.

[54]For other members, see below, chap. 8.

[55]*Nabil* 97.

[56]Ibid. 97–98.

fast appearing when the whole of Isfahan will have embraced his cause," and called for immediate action by the eminent mujtahids.[57] Nabīl Zarandī, our main source, does not provide further information on the identity of "the disciples of Sayyid Muḥammad Bāqir [Shaftī],"[58] but without the weight of the high authorities behind them, they lacked the strength to carry through a ban on Mullā Ḥusayn's activities.

The publication of the Babi doctrine in Isfahan coincided with a vacuum in the religious life of the city. Only three months before, Shaftī had died after a long illness.[59] His influential friend and colleague, Muḥammad Ibrāhīm Karbāsī (Kalbāsī), was on his deathbed.[60] Shortly before his death, Shaftī had summoned his eldest son, Sayyid Asadullāh, from Iraq.[61] The succession of Sayyid Asadullāh was unchallenged. "At the request of the disciples, and those who benefited from him [Shaftī]," writes Hidāyat, "his honorable son, . . . who was in the ʿAtabāt acquiring religious knowledge and performing the required deeds, succeeded to the chair of his revered father."[62] Sayyid Asadullāh, on reaching full authority and public acceptance,[63] was indebted more than anything else to his father's wealth and influence; a good example of hereditary position among the ʿulama families. When he succeeded his father, he was in his early thirties.[63]

Sayyid Asadullāh proved to be a moderate leader, especially at a time of political and urban turmoil, who even to some extent abandoned the opposition the secular power of which his father had been a well-known advocate.[65] The much-quoted remark that he was "superior to his father in piety and moral virtues"[66] perhaps refers to his avoidance of certain areas, such as property and commercial enterprises, that had brought his father economic power.[67] Most of his time was divided between the production of theological works, including one on the question of the concealment of the Imam,[68] and public endowment projects.[69]

Sayyid Asadullāh was well aware of his father's encounter with Mullā

[57]Ibid.

[58]Ibid. 97.

[59]*TAS* (II/1, 194) gives the correct date; 2nd Rabīʿ al-Awwal 1260/22 March 1844. *QU* (167–68) provides an interesting account of the last years of Rashtī's life.

[60]*Nabil* 98. Karbāsī died in 8 Jumādā al-Ūlā 1261/15 May 1845 (*TAS* II/1, 14).

[61]*RJ* 127.

[62]*RS* X, 286.

[63]*TAS* II/1, 124–25 and *RJ* 126.

[64]Born in Isfahan in 1227/1812 (*TAS* II/1, 124).

[65]His intermediary role between the rebel leaders and the government in the events in Isfahan 1266–1267/1850–1851 appears in a few accounts. Among them are *NT* (III, 308–17); Chirāgh ʿAlī Khān Zanginih Kalhur *Vaqāyiʿ-i Iṣfahān* supp. of *Vaḥīd* (Tehran, 1346 Sh./1967); and *RJ* (459–66).

[66]*RJ* 126. According to one source, in spite of the ʿulama's hostility toward Sufis, he showed tolerance toward the Niʿmatullāhī order in Isfahan. Mulla ʿAbd al-Karīm Jazī Iṣfahanī *Ṭadhkirat al-Qubūr (Rijāl-i Iṣfāhān)* ed. Muṣliḥ al-Dīn Mahdavī, 2d ed. (Isfahan, 1328 Sh./1949) 148 (n.).

[67]*QU* 143.

[68]*Al-Dharīʿa* XVI, 75. A list of his works appears in *TAS* II/1, 125.

[69]*Al-Maʾāthir wa ʾl-Athār* 139 and *TAS* II/1, 125–26.

Ḥusayn and was briefed by his father's entourage.[70] He was thus reluctant to take part in a controversy that might draw him unnecessarily into the Shaykhi-Uṣūlī conflict.

The Babi opposition also failed to gain Karbāsī's cooperation. The cautious mujtahid only promised that, if he recovered from his illness, he would "investigate the matter himself" and "ascertain the truth."[71] Karbāsī, who had for years avoided participation in the frequent power struggles in the city, was not prepared to risk his reputation as an impartial authority.[72] A mujtahid who, according to *Qiṣaṣ al-ʿUlamā᾽*, gave alms to a beggar only after calling witnesses to testify to his poverty could hardly be expected to pass a fatwā of condemnation on a person with whom he shared a certain sympathy, even if he did not, as Nabīl Zarandī claims, admire his faculties.[73]

It appears that word of the controversy reached the court of Manūchihr Khān Muʿtamad al-Daula, the powerful governor of the province.[74] He in turn "refused to interfere" in a matter that "fell extensively within the jurisdiction of the ʿulama."[75] According to one source, the governor even "acknowledged that the Bab is a pious man and maintained that it could be that he is the deputy of the Hidden Imam."[76] The policy adopted by the governor in the past five years, which had to some extent subordinated the religious establishment dictated impartiality in a matter that was primarily religious. Considering the long history of urban disturbances in the city, it seems that the governor only warned the intriguers "to abstain from mischief and to cease disturbing the peace and tranquility."[77] It is unlikely that Muʿtamad al-Daula, however gifted he may have been, regarded the Babi movement at this stage as potentially threatening to the mujtahids or the central government.[78]

The failure to gain active support perhaps indicates that the time was still

[70]*Nabil* 97–98.

[71]Ibid.

[72]During his long friendship with Shaftī, they had come to an implicit agreement that Karbāsī should leave all judicial decisions to his powerful colleague, and confine himself to academic matters. This alliance is illustrated in a number of anecdotes. See *QU* 119, 140–44, 168; *TAS* II/1, 14; and Jazī *Tadhkirat al-Qubūr* 158.

[73]Though not a Shaykhi, Karbāsī's respect for his late teacher Aḥsā᾽ī occasionally extended to his followers.

[74]For his details see above, chap. 5.

[75]*Nabil* 98.

[76]*NT III*, 234.

[77]*Nabil* 98.

[78]Claims made by the author of *Miftāḥ-i Bāb al-Abwāb* ([Cairo, 1321/1903] 143–45) seem to have no bearing on reality. Muḥammad Mahdī Zaʿīm al-Daula believes that Manūchihr Khān Muʿtamad al-Daula, who was no more than the agent of Christian powers in the Islamic lands, had no aim but to destroy the solidarity of Islam. His claim that Manūchihr Khān "showed excessive kindness and hospitality" toward the disciples of the Bab, "secured them from the threats of their opponents, provided sufficient pensions for them, and persuaded them to publicize the appearance of the Bab," seems to be no more than an exaggeration of *Nāsikh al-Tawārīkh*'s brief account.

not at hand to wage a war against the Babi elements. The full weight of their teachings had not yet been felt in religious circles, and the movement was not seen as a real threat. The result was that the small Babi group managed to broaden its teachings.

Throughout his journey to Kashan and Tehran, Mullā Ḥusayn experienced the disapproval of some other mujtahids, illustrated by his visit to Mullā Muḥammad Narāqī in Kashan. Narāqī (known also as Ḥujjat al-Islām), son of Mullā Aḥmad, was brought up in a well-established ʿulama family. Like Sayyid Asadullāh Shaftī, Naraqī belonged to a generation of mujtahids who, more than anything, owed their positions to their celebrated fathers. Family connections, inherited wealth, and influence provided him with sufficient means to sustain a firm grip over the religious affairs of Kashan. Narāqī received his ijāza from his father who was known for his contribution in jurisprudence as well as less conventional subjects.[79] Further, he was the son-in-law of the chief mujtahid of Qum, Mīrzā-yi Qumī.[80] His family, originally from the village of Narāq, near Kashan, moved to the city in the 1770s.[81] The Narāqīs prospered under the Qajars, being the trustees of Sulṭānī madrasa, which was built by Fatḥ ʿAlī Shāh and the trusteeship of its endowments bestowed indefinitely upon them.[82] Narāqī enjoyed good relations with the local and central government.[83] These amicable relations as well as his scholarly works,[84] prompted Sipihr, a fellow citizen, to call him "today's most superior scholar in Iran both in knowledge and practice."[85]

When Mullā Ḥusayn encountered Narāqī, the sharp difference between the well-established mujtahid and the millenarian preacher was represented by a divergence of opinion over the question of the Imam's Advent. Beneath the theological discrepancy, however, ran a wider gap between the social standing of the two men, their past backgrounds and their future goals. When Mullā Ḥusayn presented copies of *Qayyūm al-Asmā*ʾ and other Babi works to Narāqī, the scrupulous mujtahid promptly pointed out grammatical violations throughout the text.[86] In reply, Sipihr reports Mullā Ḥusayn quoted the Bab with a symbolic remark that was no doubt totally foreign to the rational framework of an orthodox scholar like Narāqī: "Up to now the

[79]*MA* II, 555–56. For Mullā Aḥmad Narāqī: *QU* 129–31; *RA* IV, 183–86; *TAS* II/1, 116–17. Also see Algar *Religion and State* 57 and Arjomand *Shadow of God* 232.

[80]*MA* II, 556.

[81]ʿAbd al-Raḥīm Kalāntar Zarrābī (Suhayl Kāshānī) *Mirʾāt al-Qāsān (Tārīkh-i Kāshān)* ed. Ī. Afshār (Tehran, 1341 Sh./1962) 280–86 (280). Also on the Narāqīs see Ḥasan Narāqī *Tārīkh-i Ijtimāʿī-yi Kāshān* (Tehran, 1345 Sh./1966) 285ff.

[82]Kalāntar Zarrābī *Tārīkh-i Kāshān* 282–83; cf. 420–24.

[83]*QU* 131 on his relations with Muḥammad Shāh and *RS* X, 602–3 on his relations with Nāṣir al-Dīn Shāh.

[84]A list of his works appears in *RA* IV, 183–86.

[85]*NT* III, 234.

[86]Ibid. 234–35. The source of *NT*'s information on the meeting between the two probably was Mullā Muḥammad himself.

naḥw [*ʿilm-i naḥw:* grammar, and especially syntax], due to a sin once committed, was enchained and incarcerated. Now I have mediated for its sin, and set it free from its chains and bonds. Therefore it is excusable if [people] utilize an accusative instead of a nominative, or a genitive instead of an accusative."[87] While Sipihr's familiar biases may have tinted his account, it echos the Bab's (and Mullā Ḥusayn's) disgust with the rules and regulations that occupied a great part of the madrasa education.

Narāqī further criticized the Bab by stating that "it is an erroneous task for Persians to present Arabic compositions as proofs for their claims,"[88] an interesting objection from a man who himself produced most of his works in Arabic.[89] Narāqī argues that "in order to prove a claim beyond the boundary of our principles, one must produce a clear justification. With these absurd deceptions and futile nonsense verses it is impossible to arrive at a realistic conclusion."[90] Nothing positive came out of the meeting, which was repeatedly disrupted by the mujtahid's outraged cries of disapproval. But "since the Bab's call did not go beyond the state of deputyship, Mullā Muḥammad preferred not to go further in his condemnation."[91]

Narāqī was the first prominent mujtahid of Iran to repudiate the Bab. Like Shaykh Muḥammad Ḥasan Najafī, he represented a tradition that could in no way accommodate even individual niyāba, let alone tolerate the Bab's heretical claims of revelation and prophethood—claims controversial enough to agitate the "protectors of the sharīʿa." In a milieu where the slightest nonconformity ran the risk of being stamped as heresy and mujtahids were often busy issuing takfīrs against each other, chances of a prominent Uṣūlī accepting a messianic call were nonexistent. An experienced cleric like Mullā Ḥusayn, who was brought up in the same environment, could have no illusions. But like Basṭāmī, he too was motivated by a spirit of conviction and dissent to deliver the "final warning" to the religious leaders, thus drawing the line between the "people of the fire" and "people of Paradise."

The "straight line" of the *Furqān*, the Babi measure for distinction between believers and denouncers, divided the society along doctrinal lines, but by virtue of its claim it also made an inevitable though involuntary social distinction. While Narāqī, a man of rank and authority, was bound to denounce "the blasphemous lunatic," clerics of a more humble standing, even in Narāqī's own surrounding and family, were receptive to the new

[87] Ibid. Also the same account about Babis' interpretation of the Bab's grammatical errors appears in Jahāngīr Mīrzā *Tārīkh-i Nau* ed. ʿA. Iqbāl (Tehran, 1327/1948) 297–98.

[88] Ibid.

[89] Including *al-Marāṣid* on uṣūl (*al-Dharīʿa* XX, 300), *Anwār al-Tanshīd* (Tehran, 1284/1867) on Islamic dogma and *Mashāriq al-Aḥkām* on fiqh (*al-Dharīʿa* XXI, 32). Narāqī was a poet of some talent and compiled a *masnavī* with mystical tendencies (ed. M. Narāqī [Tehran, 1340 Sh./1961].

[90] *NT* III, 235.

[91] Ibid.

daʿwa. Ḥājjī Mīr ʿAbd-al-Bāqī Kāshānī, the leader of prayers in the same Ṣultānī madrasa,[92] who was a fellow student of Mullā Ḥusayn under Rashtī[93] and also a friend of the celebrated Babi Ḥājjī Mīrzā Jānī,[94] showed some interest, but according to Nabīl Zarandī felt "unable to sacrifice rank and leadership for the message which his friend brought him."[95] His skepticism toward the movement apparently did not lead him to open recognition, even after visiting the Bab in Kashan, in 1263/1847.[96] However, other sources believe that he fully recognized the Bab.[97] As the leader of the Shaykhi community in the city,[98] ʿAbd al-Bāqī, who was also qualified with an ijāza from Shaftī,[99] was himself a respected mujtahid and the chief representative of a family of ʿulama in Kashan.[100] As the imam of the main madrasa, he might have been a challenge to Narāqī, who by the shah's decree was the sole controller of the royal endowments, consisting of a number of shops in the bazaar, irrigation water, and some agricultural land.[101]

Some junior members of the Narāqī family, who were held in less public esteem in the town and its surroundings, joined the movement. His cousin, Mullā Jaʿfar Narāqī (son of Mullā Mahdī known as Āqā Buzurg);[102] Mullā Hāshim, the youngest son of Mullā Aḥmad;[103] and later two sons of another brother resident in Narāq, called Mīrzā Maḥmūd and Ḥājjī Mīrzā Kamāl al-Dīn; all became Babis.[104] There is some disagreement over the conversion of Mullā Jaʿfar, who is the author of a number of works.[105] According to *Ẓuhūr al-Ḥaqq* he first accepted the call through Mullā Ḥusayn,[106] while Nabīl Zarandī asserts that during his visit to the Bab in Kashan, "despite his consummate eloquence," Mullā Jaʿfar was compelled to acknowledge outwardly "the merits of the cause of his adversary [the Bab], though at heart he refused to believe in its truth."[107]

92 Żarrābī *Tārīkh-i Kāshān* 301.
93 *Nabil* 101.
94 See below, chap. 8.
95 *Nabil* 101.
96 According to Nabīl Zarandī, after the departure of the Bab, ʿAbd al-Bāqī renounced society and led a life of "unrelieved seclusion" (*Nabil* 221).
97 Muḥammad Nāṭiq Iṣfahānī *Tārīkh-i Amrī-yi Kāshān,* INBA Lib. MS. no. 20160, 3; cf. *NH* 214.
98 *Nabil* 101.
99 *TAS* II/2, 698. His authorization in which his ijtihād is clearly ratified, dated 1260/1844, a few months before Shaftī's death. According to Tihrānī, it resembles a public will by Shaftī.
100 Żarrābī *Tārīkh-i Kāshān* 301–2.
101 Ibid. 423–24; cf. 283.
102 *ZH* 395–96; cf. Żarrābī *Tārīkh-i Kāshān* 286.
103 Nāṭiq *Tārīkh-yi Amrī-i Kāshān* 3; cf. Żarrābī *Tārīkh-i Kāshān* 284.
104 *Samandar* 260 and *ZH* 395–96; cf. Żarrābī *Tārīkh-i Kāshān* 284.
105 *TAS* II/1, 246–47 and *al-Dharīʿa* VI, 258.
106 *ZH* 395–96.
107 *Nabil* 221. Nabīl Zarandī's disapproval of "the haughty and imperious" Mullā Jaʿfar and emphasis on his dubious recognition should be seen in the light of Jaʿfar's later Azalī tendencies. *Tadhkirat al-Ghāfilīn* (Browne Or. MSS no. F.63(9), 80–81 and *MSBR* 227–28) written by an

In Tehran, Mullā Ḥusayn stayed in the Mīrzā Ṣāliḥ (Pā Minār) madrasa, a gathering place for Shaykhis. Here he met the firm rejection of the chief lecturer, who seems to have had some previous knowledge of Mullā Ḥusayn. Ḥājjī Mīrzā Muḥammad Khurāsānī, "the leader of the Shaykhi community of Tihrān," strongly criticized him for provoking a schism in the Shaykhi camp at a time when there was an urgent need to deliver Shaykhism "from the obscurity into which it was sunk."[108] He warned Mullā Ḥusayn that his "subversive doctrines" would eventually endanger the existence of "the remnants of the Shaykhis in the city," and expressed his regret that after Rashtī's death he did not "strive to promote the best interests of the Shaykhi community."[109] Khurāsānī's worries about the "obscurity" of the Shaykhi cause and the declining state of their community is a good indication of the anxieties the Shaykhis felt in the face of continuous pressure from their opponents. Besides, Mullā Ḥusayn had already begun to attract his students,[110] and it is not unlikely that Khurāsānī was afraid of losing his entire constituency.

Mullā Ḥusayn's response to Khurāsānī appears to have been mild, even placting. He assures him that he has no intention of prolonging his stay in Tehran or indeed that he aims to "abase or suppress the teachings of the Shaykh and Sayyid."[111] He appears to have been under some pressure not only from the Shaykhi leader but also from the government. As Gobineau puts it: "He did not make himself visible in the public" but instead contented himself with "confidential interviews with people who came to visit him."[112] In spite of this secrecy, he was still able to circulate some Babi literature. He duplicated copies of *Qayyūm al-Asmā'* and distributed them among eighteen ʿulama and officials in the capital, including a certain Mīrzā Maḥmūd, the chief mujtahid of Tehran.[113] In private he also managed to attract some low-ranking mullās.

Mullā Muḥammad Muʿallim, one of Khurāsānī's favored students and a native of the Nūr district in Mazandaran, who lived next door to Mullā Ḥusayn in the Mīrzā Ṣāliḥ madrasa, became interested in the new daʿwa despite his teacher's condemnation. He called upon Mullā Ḥusayn in secret, and after some discussion expressed his approval. As his title shows, he was engaged in private tutoring in the houses of notables and government offi-

---

anonymous native of Narāq with the secret sign "1265" in the year 1284/1867 (two years prior to the death of Mullā Jaʿfar in a Tehran dungeon) is a refutation of Bahā'ullāh and advocation of Ṣubḥ-i Azal. It is perhaps composed by Mullā Jaʿfar. (Munzavī *Fihrist-i Nusakh-i Khaṭṭī-i Fārsī* [Tehran, 1346 Sh./1967] VI, 1737, no. 17210.)

108 *Nabil* 102–3; cf. *ZH* 63.

109 *Nabil* 102–3.

110 Ibid. 104.

111 Ibid. 103.

112 *RPAC* 160.

113 *Muʿīn* 71. Later Mīrzā Maḥmud Mujtahid also received some of the writings of the Bab through Shaykh ʿAlī ʿAẓīm (*ZH* 163). M.A. Malik Khusravī (*Tārīkh-i Shuhadā-yi Amr* [Tehran, 130 Badīʿ/1974] III [*Vaqāyiʿ-i Ṭihrān*] 79) believes that he was sympathetic toward the Babis.

cials.[114] After his conversion, in the same year Mullā Mahdī Kanī and his brother Mullā Bāqir who were both private tutors, were initiated.[115] Mullā Mahdī, in addition, acted as leader of prayer of one of the madrasas in the city.[116] He maintained good relations with some members of the court and government officials in Tehran.[117]

During the time of his residence in the capital, Mullā Ḥusayn also attempted to deliver the Bab's message to Muḥammad Shāh and Ḥājjī Mīrzā Āqāsī. What Sipihr briefly paraphrases as the content of "the book of the Bab" delivered to the shah and Āqāsī roughly corresponds to *Sūrat al-Malik:* "If you bear on your shoulders the weight of my allegiance and make your subordination toward me your undertaking, I will glorify your kingdom and place the foreign states under your decree."[118] To this invitation came a swift and simple answer. "The authorities of the state," reports Sipihr, "sent him a warning that if he wants to save his skin he should stop spreading such utter nonsense and make himself scarce from the city."[119] Mullā Ḥusayn's propaganda among what Sipihr call a "few ordinary fellows whose status was no higher than riffraffs" must have been effective to move the often lax and tolerant Āqāsī to issue such a warning.

The Babis of Khurasan and Other Circles

It was in his homeland, Khurasan, that Mullā Ḥusayn was most successful. In the first four years of the movement, together with a handful of his close school associates, he laid the foundation of one of the largest and most active Babi communities in Iran. On his first visit in 1260/1844 to Mashhad, in collaboration with an early convert, Mullā Muḥammad Bāqir Qā'inī, Mullā Ḥusayn created the first center for the Babi activities, known as Bābīya. A small house belonging to Qā'inī in the region of Bālā-Khīyābān, it became a center for Mullā Ḥusayn's teachings, a frequent gathering place, the abode of the Babi disciples, and the focal point for all activities in Khurasan. It was from here that in 1847–1848 the first organized recruitments were made for the march to Mazandaran.[120]

Between 1260/1844 and 1264/1848 the main concentration of the

[114] *Nabil* 104, 434, recording an account of Mīrzā Mūsā Nūrī. Also *NK* 194.

[115] *KD* I, 148–51 (148); *ZH* 213–14; *Nabil* 424.

[116] *ZH* 213.

[117] For Mullā Mahdī Kanī, *Nabil* (397–99) relies on an account of Mīrzā Musā. A more complete version appears in *KD* I, 148–51.

[118] *NT* III, 235.

[119] Ibid.

[120] *Nabil* 126–27; *Fu'ādī* 48–49. In the summer of 1264/1848, Mullā Ḥusayn, on his return from Azarbaijan and Mazandaran, was able to buy in the neighborhood of Mullā Muḥammad Bāqir's house "a tract of land on which he began to erect the house which he had been commanded to build, and to which he gave the name of Bābīya, a name that it bears to the present day" (*Nabil* 267).

Khurāsānī Babis was in three areas. In central Khurasan in the area known as Quhistān, on the edge of the highlands that surround the Khurasan desert, the triangle between Turbat-i Ḥaydarīya, Bushrūyih, and Qā'in contained one of the largest concentrations of Babis in Iran. On the northwestern side of the borderlands of Mazandaran, particularly on the northern route to Khurasan in Basṭām, Mayāmay, and Bīyārjmand, there were also sizable Babi communities. And third, there were a number of converts in cities such as Mashhad, Sabzivār, and Nīshābūr. The Babi community in Khurasan also represents a cross-section of society in terms of occupations and economic activities. A large group of the ʿulama with rural backgrounds, together with small landowners, local merchants, and manufacturers and a few of the local state officials, formed its backbone.

The distinction between the urban and rural backgrounds of Mullā Ḥusayn's early followers is not always clear. Although his own personal impact was immediately felt in Mashhad, it is important to note that the groups who received his message most enthusiastically came from rural regions of central and northwestern Khurasan. It was the middle- and lower-ranking ʿulama and ṭullāb, teaching and studying in the provincial capital, who most readily offered their support. These groups in turn were to propagate the new beliefs in their own home towns and villages. In Bushrūyih, Mullā Ḥusayn's home town, more than sixty individuals embraced the Babi creed between 1260/1844 and 1264/1848. Records also exist of the number and the identity of other early Babis in central Khurasan.[121]

However, it must be remembered that available figures represent only a section of a larger community in the area. They are based on the names of those active Babis who are known to us because of participation in certain events, death in upheavals, or persecution. A substantial portion of those who are identified are the local mullas of the small towns and villages who at some stage had the support of their local communities. It is not unlikely that they represented a larger Babi population in the area. Setting aside the cases of the learned ʿulama, it is difficult to make a clear distinction between converts and sympathizers amongst the ordinary people. The reference in *Tārīkh-i Amrī-yi Khurāsān* to the two thousand inhabitants of Būshruyih who at one stage attended Mullā Ḥusayn's preachings, set prayers with him, and were attracted to his message provides one example of this public

[121]In fact it is possible to count more than fifty-seven of them: eight in Turbat-i Ḥaydarīya; three in Azghand; three in ʿAbdullāhābād; seven in Mahnih; ten in Ḥiṣār and Nāmiq; five in Fayżābād; two in Dūghābād; three in Turshīz; nine in Qā'in (seven of them originally from Herat); two from Bajistān; two from Ṭabas; and one each from Tūn, Kākhk and Gunābād. In the northwestern region also, thirty-two can be identified in Mayāmay, five from Bīyārjmand, and a few in other places. Compared to the recorded names in other parts of Khurasan, mostly urban centers such as Mashhad (twelve), Sabzivār (seven), Nīshābūr (three), and a few in other towns, it is evident that the greater part of the Babis were concentrated in the rural towns and villages of central Khurasan.

backing. Another is the support given to Mullā Muḥammad Bāqir Qā'inī, in Mashhad; Mullā Zayn al-ʿĀbidīn, the mujtahid of Mayāmay; and Mullā Aḥmad, the mujtahid of Ḥiṣār and Nāmiq, who were converted together with all their students and followers.[122]

The foremost group among the early believers, both in position and number, were those who came from low-ranking mullas, newly authorized clerics, and a few established ʿulama, mostly in Mashhad. No doubt strong ties among the Shaykhi students, who sometimes attended the lectures of one teacher or several for years and shared a similar training, also contributed to this wide acceptance. Shaykh Aḥmad Ahsā'ī's long residence in Yazd, then a prosperous trade center and hence a center for Khurāsānī students, attracted the first serious attention towards Shaykhism. According to his son, at the time of Aḥsā'ī's stay in Yazd (1808–1813), "the cause of his reverence was disseminated in the towns, and publicized in the provinces. All ʿulama and scholars expressed their submission, and sent their problems to him. In reply he wrote treatises in which he revealed the mysteries suitable to their capacity, and publicized moral virtues as much as people could tolerate, till the fame of his knowledge and his virtues reached everywhere."[123]

On his way from Mashhad to Yazd, in 1236/1820–1821, Aḥsā'ī visited small cities like Ṭabas and Turbat-i Ḥaydarīya, where he was warmly received by the inhabitants, including the renowned chief of the Qarā'īs, Muḥammad Khān, son of Isḥāq Khān.[124] This journey laid the foundation for later conversions. Many of the clerics and seminarians who later joined the ranks of the Babis appear to have been first attracted to Shaykhism in the schools of Yazd and Mashhad. The intellectual climate in Mashhad in the early decades of the nineteenth century, in comparison with such religious centers as Isfahan and ʿAtabāt, was less dominated by the new generation of the Uṣūlīs and hence better allowed the spread of other tendencies. The attraction of would-be Babis like Mullā ʿAbd al-Khāliq Yazdī to Aḥsāʿī's circle in Yazd was due to this very fact.[125]

The diffusion of popular claims, in most cases bearing some controversial and often undeveloped message, also conflicted with the established religion. In September 1844, during his short abode in Mashhad, Dr. Wolff, who because of his own millenarian beliefs paid some attention to the religious affairs of the country, noticed the appearance of a new schism in the city:

> It is remarkable that dissenters in doctrine are now prevailing largely in the Muhammedan religion. The controversy which agitates now the Christian

[122]*Fu'ādī* 276–82.
[123]*Sharḥ-i Aḥvāl Shaykh Aḥmad Aḥsā'ī* 28–29.
[124]Ibid. 37.
[125]Ibid. 37–38.

Church, with regard to the usefulness of ceremonies and tradition, agitates now also the Muhammedan community. A Sayed [Sayyid] at Mashhad began to teach that the Koran was quite enough, and pilgrimages unnecessary. This, in the great city of Imaum Resa [Imām Riżā] was extraordinary doctrine. . . . A strong cry of heresy was raised against the Sayed, but Mirza Askeree [Mīrza-yi ʿAskarī] protected him. A fierce schism now prevails among the Sheahs [Shiʿites] at Mashed.[126]

This passage, if not a vague reference to the Babis, who at the time had just started their activities, demonstrates the existence of nonconformist tendencies in the religious milieu of the time. Wolff, who stresses the "diminishing power of fanaticism"[127] throughout Iran, seems to have noticed the vacuum that in his view ought to have been appreciated by the Christian missionaries. "I was frequently asked for copies of the Bible; and in the cities of Semnan [Simnān], Damghan [Dāmghān], Nishapoor [Nīshābūr], and Mashed [Mashhad], I was invited to open discussions about religion with the chief Mullahs. . . . Writings published against Muhammedanism by the late missionary, Mr. Pfander, are read at Mashed and Nishapoor with eagerness."[128]

In view of his eccentric zeal, Wolff's remarks on religious controversies in the province are not entirely reliable. Yet it is fair to assume that a considerable amount of religious tension among rival factions paved the way for antiorthodox claims not only to be heard by the public, but also to receive the blessing of senior mujtahids like ʿAskarī.

Mullā ʿAbd al-Khāliq Yazdī, a leading Shaykhi of his time, was also counted among "the senior ʿulama" of Khurasan.[129] A former disciple of Aḥsāʾī, he studied under him especially during his residence in Yazd,[130] and was sometimes his host in that city.[131] His father, according to one source, was a converted Jew originally from Yazd,[132] and he himself seems to have emigrated to the district of Turbat Ḥaydarīya, where his family settled in the village of Fayżābād, in the Muḥavvalāt region.[133] He completed his studies in the ʿAtabāt, particularly under the celebrated teacher Sharīf al-ʿUlamāʾ in fiqh and uṣūl,[134] and eventually received a number of authorizations.[135]

[126] *A Mission to Bokhara* 201.

[127] Ibid. 88.

[128] Ibid. 201.

[129] *TAS* II/2, 723.

[130] *Nabil* 7.

[131] *Muʿīn* 42.

[132] *NK* 203, 211. His conversion, either forcibly or voluntarily, appears to be the result of persecution in the early nineteenth century (Ḥ. Lavī *Tārīkh-i Yahūd-i Īrān* 3 vols. [Tehran, 1339 Sh./1960] III, 507–86). Also W. J. Fischel "The Jews of Persia, 1795–1940" *Jewish Social Studies* 12 (1950) 120–24.

[133] See Lavī *Tārīkh-i Yahūd* (III, 522, 592, 634) for the Jews in Turbat-i Ḥaydarīya.

[134] M. H. Iʿtimād al-Salṭana *Maṭlaʿ al-Shams* 3 vols. (Tehran, 1300–1303/1882–1885) II, 399.

[135] *TAS* II/2, 723. The text of his authorization appears at the end of his *Muʿīn al-Mujtahidīn*.

After spending some time in different centers like Shiraz and Yazd,[136] ʿAbd al-Khāliq Yazdī finally settled in Mashhad, where he held regular preaching and teaching sessions in the shrine of Imām Riżā.[137] He was praised by some for his eloquent oratory and his knowledge, and his six works covered such subjects as the sufferings of the Imams, uṣūl, and occult sciences.[138] After Aḥsāʾī's death, according to Nabīl Zarandī, he competed with and even challenged Rashtī, but in due course accepted his authority.[139] He nonetheless remained one of the chief defenders of Shaykhism in Iran. On one occasion, when Mullā Muḥammad Jaʿfar Astarābādī (known as Sharīʿatmadār), a notorious enemy of the Shaykhis, arrived at Mashhad, Yazdī openly challenged him in a public dispute.[140] Word of this controversy even reached Muḥammad Shāh, who on the way back from the Herat campaign (1254/1838) personally intervened in the matter, and subsequently obliged Sharīʿatmadār to return to Tehran.[141] Probably it was in connection with the same incident that Yazdī was confined in his house and forbidden to preach.[142]

The conversion of Yazdī, one of the earliest in Mashhad, was a great success for Mullā Ḥusayn.[143] He was a well-known divine in his own sphere, and his support gave greater weight to the new movement. *Nuqṭat al-kāf* confirms that Yazdī "presented to his excellency [the Bab] notification of his conversion . . . with the highest degree of gratefulness."[144] In an Arabic letter he pays homage to the Bab as "the most exalted Remembrance of God" among Arabs and Persians:

> I do not know with what tongue I should thank God for the honor of having been in your service for a long time, and with what speech I should apologize for my ignorance of your real status, and I feel very sorry. . . . I do not know with what words I should thank God for your writing to me, your humble obedient servant. Thus you made me hopeful, and I am hopeful, since I see myself a servant of God attendant upon the Bab. How wonderful that according to the promises of God's tongue, the paradise of justice is definitely established. Therefore my lord, I beg to be honored by being taken into the service of my lord and my master. Thus I will be gathered among his pure companions and followers, for the sake of the greater Ẕikr whom God designated as a luminous sun to us.[145]

[136] *Maṭlaʿ al-Shams* III, 523.
[137] *Maṭlaʿ al-Shams*; cf. *NK* 101.
[138] *TAS* II/2, 723.
[139] *Nabil* 11.
[140] Astarābādī as a result of his provocations had twice been phyically attacked by the Shaykhis. *TAS* II/1, 254–55, and the mentioned sources.
[141] *TAS* II/1, 254–55.
[142] *NK* 101.
[143] *NT* III, 235.
[144] *NK* 203.
[145] INBA no. 98, 109–10 (also cited in *ZH* 172).

The above passage illustrates that even the independent Shaykhis regarded the Bab's claim as the fulfillment of messianic expectations far beyond the claims of Aḥsā'ī and Rashtī.

The importance to the Bab of Yazdī's recognition is evident in his correspondence. In early 1262/1846 he informs him of the dispatch of Mullā Ḥusayn for the second time to Khurasan. "Thus I dispatched by my own authority to the 'Fourth Mashhad,' the dearest of all people, the first of the disciples to you and to all people. Therefore they may distinguish between good and evil, and therefore not one of them can claim that he was not informed of God's signs."[146] In a letter to Muḥammad Shāh a year later, he designates Yazdī and Sayyid Yaḥyā Vaḥīd Dārābī as his representatives, of whom inquiry could be made about the truth of his cause.[147]

Toward 1264/1848, Yazdī was openly propagating Babi views from the pulpit. Despite the governor's pressure he adamantly refused to revoke his beliefs, and proposed a debate with the ʿulama of the city. As a result he was again "barred from Friday prayers, and was ordered [by the governor] to stay indoors, and consider his seclusion as a condition for his safety."[148] His residence in Tehran during 1848–1849 perhaps resulted from the same dispute, which finally led to his enforced detention in the capital.[149]

The disastrous defeat of the Babi uprising a year later, however, was a serious blow to his faith.[150] The Bab's open claim for Qā'imīya, which was publicized at the same time, was even more shocking. During the final days of Ṭabarsī, Yazdī had sent a letter to his son in which he strongly urged him to desert the fighting and come out of the fortress. Shaykh ʿAlī firmly refused. Since Yazdī had "abandoned the truth," he said, his own obedience was no longer compulsory; and indeed he no longer considered him his father.[151] At about the same time in Tehran, the old mujtahid received a letter from the Bab sent to him through Vaḥīd Dārābī. When he came to the sentence "I am the righteous Qā'im whose appearance you were promised," he threw the letter aside and cried: "Alas, my son perished in vain."[152] He himself died three years later.[153]

Another example of a Babi conversion among the high-ranking ʿulama

[146]Ibid. no. 91, 94–102. *Mashhad al-Rābiʿ* in the Bab's writings is a reference to Mashhad. It ranked fourth in significance after Najaf, Karbalā', and Kāẓimayn.

[147]Letter to Muḥammad Shāh, INBA no. 64, 103–50 (123). This letter is also partly cited in *SAMB* 367–76 [373].

[148]*NT* III, 236.

[149]*ZH* 173. (Bahā'ullāh's account cited in Nabīl.) This is one of the passages used by the author of *ZH* which did not appear in the English edition, *Nabil.* Mullā Muḥammad ʿAlī Zanjānī and many other dissident ʿulama at the same time were detained in the capital. Khānlar Mīrzā probably refers to him when he accuses the Babis of being provocators and "corrupters of the earth" (*mufsidīn fī al-arḍ.*) Mīrzā Luṭf-ʿAlī Shīrāzī *Tārīkh,* INBA Lib. MS 15.

[150]*Nabil* 423; *NK* 203.

[151]Mīrzā Luṭf-ʿAlī *Tārīkh* 15.

[152]*ZH* 173–74, Bahā'ullāh's account cited in Nabīl.

[153]Iʿtimād al-Salṭana *Maṭlaʿ al-Shams* II, 399.

was that of Mīrzā (Sayyid) Aḥmad Azghandī. He was a Shaykhi mujtahid from Azghand, a village in the hinterland of Turbat Ḥaydarīya.[154] His sphere of activities extended from Mashhad to Yazd. Nabīl Zarandī, who ranks him among the most learned ʿulama of the province,[155] speaks of the "voluminous compilation" of twelve thousand Traditions that Azghandī provided to justify the Bab's manifestation.[156] In 1264/1848, in a letter to him, the Bab, perhaps for the first time, foresaw the Mazandaran upheaval.[157] Yet Azghandī himself did not participate in the campaign. Further, his reaction to Ḥājjī Muḥammad Karīm Khān Kirmānī, who enjoyed a strong backing in the city of Yazd, was one of caution and reconciliation.[158] However, this cautious approach did not protect him even in his own base, Turbat Ḥaydarīya. In the course of the persecution that followed the execution of the Bab in 1266/1850, he was arrested in Azghand and was moved to Mashhad, where he was detained for some time.[159]

If Mullā Aḥmad Azghandī represented a more moderate stance, Mullā Muḥammad Bāqir Qā'inī[160] (sometimes known as Harātī), a Shaykhi from Mashhad with some local influence, was an outstanding example of Babi radicalism.[161] It was perhaps due to past acquaintance with Mullā Ḥusayn that he was brought to the movement.[162] As already indicated, he was the cofounder of the Bābīya and a devoted preacher of the Babi cause from the pulpit.[163] His financial support covered the expenses of the Bābīya, and after 1263/1847 possibly extended to the purchase of arms in Mashhad.[164] Qā'inī's conversion was followed by that of many other relatives and followers, including his wife, his son, and his brother.[165] According to one source, as a result of his open preaching "as many as four hundred followers gave their support to the cause."[166] A large number of Babis who prayed

[154]According to *NK* (139) "one of the companions" of Aḥsā'ī.

[155]*Nabil* 125.

[156]Ibid. 184–85. (Citing Muqaddas, who quotes an unnamed Khurāsānī friend.) Azghandī's work was one of the earliest Babi apologia produced, perhaps in reply to Kirmānī's *Izhāq al-Bāṭil*. According to *Nabil* (185) the sole copy of it was destroyed by one of the followers of Kirmānī, during Azghandī's abode in Yazd.

[157]This has often been quoted to demonstrate the Bab's approval of the Ṭabarsī resistance (*NK* 139; also *Fu'ādī* 76 and *KD* I, 133). No trace of this has yet been found among the Bab's works.

[158]*Nabil* 185.

[159]*Fu'ādī* 76.

[160]His father, who was originally from Herat, had settled in Qā'in. His nephew Mullā Muḥammad Qā'inī (known as Nabīl Qā'inī), oddly enough, did not give any more details on his uncle's life in his *Tārīkh-i Badīʿ-i Bayānī.*

[161]*Fu'ādī* 49 and *ZH* 160.

[162]Mahjūr Zavārihī *Tārīkh-i Mīmīya* (Browne Or. MSS 3 and INBA 2).

[163]*Nabil* 125–26.

[164]*Fu'ādī* 48–50. Interesting accounts of the Babi armament in Mashhad appear in *Fu'ādī* 34–35 and *Tārīkh Mīmīya* (Browne Or. MSS. 5–10 and INBA 4–10).

[165]*Fu'ādī* 48–50. Mīrzā Luṭf ʿAlī Shīrāzī *Tārīkh* (Browne Or. MSS F.28(9) III, 61, and INBA 62).

[166]*ZH* 160.

with Qā'inī in the Bābīya were to form the backbone of the forces that started the Mazandaran campaign in 1264/1848.[167]

As a radical leader, Qā'inī combined two complementary abilities: he was able to mobilize people from the pulpit and to lead followers in battle. Nearly all sources agree that, "apart from his learning, he was a man of many arts and resources, . . . and that it was he who had planned most of the strategic movements" of the Babis in Ṭabarsī.[168] His vital role prior to the Māzandarān uprising underscores not only his knowledge of warfare, but his place in the development of the movement toward an armed resistance. During the phase of unrest in Khurasan, just before Mashhad rebellion of Ramaḍān 1264/August–September 1848, Qā'inī was engaged in the military training of the Babis.[169] Consequently, brief clashes occurred between the Babi armed parties and pro-Qajar factions in the city. There is some evidence that fighting between the urban crowd and government forces had been sparked by these early incidents. However, the Babi involvement ended in the hasty departure of Qāʿinī together with Mullā Ḥusayn and his followers for Mazandaran, in Shaʿbān 1264/August 1848.[170] During the Ṭabarsī episode, Qā'inī was second in command, and after the death of Mullā Ḥusayn became the military commander of the fortress. Surviving accounts of Ṭabarsī frequently refer to his skillful, often spontaneous plans for its fortification, his innovations in warfare, and his efforts to maintain discipline among the Babi corps. His violent death in the city of Āmul put an end to a career of preaching and warfare.[171]

Of other Babi mullas of Khurasan, two stand out: Shaykh ʿAlī Turshīzī, better known as ʿAẓīm, and Mullā Muḥammad Dūghābādī (Furūghī). Together with Mullā Aḥmad Ḥiṣārī, the Babi leader of the Ḥiṣār and Nāmiq regions, and Mullā Shaykh ʿAlī Fayżābādī, ʿAbd al-Khāliq's son, they shared Mullā Ḥusayn's semirural background and similar primary training.

Shaykh ʿAlī ʿAẓīm came from Turshīz, a small desert town west of Turbat Ḥaydarīya.[172] "One of the outstanding students of Sayyid Kāẓim [Rashtī]"[173] and an active member of the Khurasan circle, he rose to leadership after 1264/1848.[174] After being involved in a series of unsuccessful

[167] *Tārīkh-i Mīmīya.*

[168] *NH* 103.

[169] *Tārīkh-i Mīmīya.*

[170] On the gathering of Babis in Mashhad in 1264/1848, among other sources see *Tārīkh-i Mīmīya* (INBA 2–10 and Browne Or. MSS. 2–10) and *Nabil* 287–91.

[171] *NK* 203–4; *Tārīkh-i Mīmīya* (Browne Or. MSS 108 and INBA 110); *NH* 103.

[172] Kayhān *Jughrāfīyā* 201.

[173] Mahdī Qulī Mīrzā Iʿtiżād al-Salṭana *Mutanabbī'īn* ed. and ann. A. Navā'ī as *Fitna-yi Bāb*, 2d ed. (Tehran, 1350 Sh./1971) 79.

[174] A few sources such as *Mutanabbī'īn, Nabil, NK,* and *SAMB* provide valuable materials for a fuller biography of this important Babi figure. In a series of articles written by Muḥammad Muḥīṭ Ṭabāṭabā'ī on the sources for Babi-Bahā'ī history, the author devotes one article to a brief account of ʿAẓīm based on limited materials. Though in appearance it seems impartial and accurate, this article is no more than another repetition of the familiar biases (*Māhnāmih-yi Gauhar* VI, 178–83).

operations in Azarbaijan, with the ultimate purpose of releasing the Bab from his incarceration in Chihrīq,[175] ʿAẓīm planned an uprising in 1265/1849, to remove the premier Mīrzā Taqī Khān Amīr Kabīr and Mīrzā Abul-Qāsim, the imām jumʿa of Tehran.[176] While still in its primary stage, this plot was foiled by the secret agents of Amīr Kabīr.[177] In the leadership crisis that followed the execution of the Bab and the death of the most important Babi figures, ʿAẓīm assumed the deputyship of the Bab, which in effect led to his command over the militant faction.[178] In 1268/1852, he was the chief organizer behind the unsuccessful attempt to assassinate Nāṣir al-Dīn Shāh, which resulted in the massacre of a large group of remaining Babi activists in Tehran. After the execution of all the alleged conspirators, under pressure from the government, the imām jumʿa issued a fatwā approving ʿAẓīm's execution. Mīrzā ʿAlī Khān Ḥājib al-Daula and his executioners jointly slew him.[179]

Mullā Muḥammad Furūghī, another early convert from central Khurasan, came from Dūghābād, a hamlet in the district of Muḥavvalāt. Like Azghandī, he settled in Turbat Ḥaydarīya.[180] He was a longtime classmate and friend of Mullā Ḥusayn.[181] Nabīl Zarandī declares that among the early believers in Khurasan, his "learning was unsurpassed except" by that of Mīrzā Aḥmad Azghandī.[182] He was one of the rare survivors of Ṭabarsī (remnants of the sword: *baqīyat al-sayf)* who miraculously escaped death in the final massacre in the military camp.[183] A witness to many important incidents, and acquainted with leading figures in the early period, he is one of Nabīl Zarandī's most important sources.[184] Later, in the controversy between Bahā'ullāh and Mīrzā Yaḥyā Nūrī, Ṣubḥ-i Azal, he supported the former, and remained a devoted Bahā'ī. He died in 1295/1878.[185]

Two other major Babi communities flourished in rural Khurasan: one in Hiṣar and Nāmiq and another in Mayāmay. Mullā Aḥmad Muʿallim Hiṣārī, a student of Rashtī and for a while a tutor to his son, first met Sayyid ʿAlī Muḥammad in Karbalā' in 1258/1842 and reportedly participated in the Kūfa retreat. He returned briefly to his home village, Ḥisār, in the vicinity of Turbat Ḥaydarīya after being informed by Mullā Ḥusayn's dispatch of the

[175]*Nabil* 301–8.
[176]*Ahmad* 469 and Iʿtiżād al-Salṭana *Mutanabbiʾīn* 95–102.
[177]*NK* 259–60 and *Mutanabbiʾīn* 79, 97, 103.
[178]*Mutanabbiʾīn* 79.
[179]*Nabil* 637; cf. *Mutanabbiʾīn* 106.
[180]*Fu'ādī* 78.
[181]*Nabil* 331–34. See also above, chap. 4.
[182]*Nabil* 125. Like many of his Shaykhi peers, he was interested in numerology.
[183]*ZH* 155–57 n. (Account of Ustād Muḥammad Rizā Dūghābādī.) Also *Fu'ādī* 78–79.
[184]He seems to be *Nabil*'s main source for the early history of the movement, especially in Khurasan (580.) He is one of the few Babis who survived up to the late 1870s, when Nabīl Zarandī compiled his narrative.
[185]*Fu'ādī* 79–80, cf. *ZH* 157.

new daʿwa.[186] Between 1260/1844 and 1262/1846 in Karbalāʾ, Mullā Aḥmad was involved in a major controversy concerning the leadership of the newly formed Babi group. In an apparent dispute with Qurrat al-ʿAyn, then the most prominent Babi in Karbalāʾ, Mullā Aḥmad questioned her teachings, and her position in the early Babi hierarchy. The Bab's full support for Qurrat al-ʿAyn convinced Mullā Aḥmad of the futility of his challenge but did not result in his defection from Babi ranks.[187] Later he returned to Mashhad and joined Mullā Ḥusayn's circle. In 1263/1847 he traveled to Azarbaijan and visited the Bab in Mākū, where he was instructed to take with him to Khurasan a copy of the Bab's *Bayān*. His preachings in Ḥiṣār and the neighboring Nāmiq resulted in the conversion of nearly one hundred villagers. He also compiled several treatises in defense of the new creed, and being a calligrapher produced and distributed numerous copies of the Bab's writings.[188]

Mullā Aḥmad soon met a hostile response from other mullas. Babism only added a new dimension to the existing clan rivalries and over the years led to persecution and bloodshed. In spite of Mullā Aḥmad's perseverance, the increasing Muslim opposition forced the Babis to isolation. The case of Mullā Aḥmad is particularly interesting since it demonstrates the difficult choice for a Babi activist who neither died in the early upheavals nor abandoned his earlier enthusiasm. He and other Babis in his village remained committed converts but after the failure of Ṭabarsī chose passive resistance as the only realistic alternative to assimilation. But the adoption of Bahaʾullāh's teachings of peace and nonviolence, only led to fresh harassment by the local mullas, occasionally supported by local officials and mujtahids in the city. By the time of Mullā Aḥmad's death, in 1303/1885, after years of hiding and exile, the prevailing opposition was more than ever determined to reduce the Babi-Bahāʾīs to a helpless minority.[189]

In the rural town of Mayāmay (north of Muhavvalāt on the caravan route to Mazandaran), the old Mullā Zayn al-ʿĀbidīn, an ex-student of Aḥsāʾī, enjoyed wide popularity. His son, Mullā Muḥammad, was a supporter of Mullā Ḥusayn and according to Qatīl was one of the early believers in Shiraz.[190] On his return to Mayāmay he must have propagated the new creed, for in late summer 1264/1848, when Mullā Ḥusayn on his march to Mazandaran stopped in Mayāmay and preached in the main mosque, Zayn al-ʿĀbidīn, Mullā Muḥammad, and a group of thirty local mullas and students joined him.[191] The Mayāmay Babis constituted the largest single

[186]*Fuʾādī* 276–77.
[187]See below, chap. 7.
[188]*Fuʾādī* 278, 281.
[189]Ibid. 285–96.
[190]*Qatīl* 520.
[191]Zavārihī *Tārīkh Mīmīya*; cf. *Nabil* 326.

group among the Khurāsānīs in Ṭabarsī, of whom all but one were killed. Not surprisingly, nothing survived of the Mayāmay community.

How fruitful were the efforts of Mullā Ḥusayn? No doubt he was more successful than Baṣṭāmi and the Bab himself in delivering the Babi message to selected elements. His endeavors in central and eastern Iran in the first three years led to the formation of Babi nuclei in city and countryside based almost entirely on the existing Shaykhi network. Previous adherence to Shaykhism was an essential factor, but beneath the doctrinal affinity lay a deeper social homogeneity. Regional solidarity, educational training, and family bonds may further explain the converts' near unanimous receptiveness to Mullā Ḥusayn, their fellow citizen and schoolmate. Beyond these, one can only speculate about the existence of a common sectarian background. Like Mullā Ḥusayn, most of the Khurasan converts came from Quhistān, the same peripheral region in central-southern Khurasan that was for long the home of Persian Nizārī-Ismāʿīlī communities. It is not unlikely that, coming from villages in the region, they all shared a sectarian trait that gave them resilience and solidarity. When transformed to Shaykhi esoterism, this symbiosis found a new channel to express the latent aspirations that had long survived in concealment. Even though these rustic aspirations were clad in and mellowed by Shaykhi thought, the spirit of religious dissent survived, particularly in Khurasan, where the mainstream religion was slow to penetrate.

Complementary to Shaykhi orientation, another factor that encouraged group solidarity was the inferior place the would-be converts were given in the still-evolving religious hierarchy. The ascendancy of Uṣūlīs made climbing up the religious ladder a formidable, if not altogether impossible, task for Shaykhi outcasts. This was particularly hard for Mullā Ḥusayn and his counterparts, who saw themselves as bearers of esoteric knowledge and propagators of the true way, superior to the monolithic jurists in knowledge and devotion. Even clerics like Yazdī and Harātī who chose a middle course and tried to bridge between the Shaykhi path and the Uṣūlī legalism, had difficulty gaining recognition, and not infrequently were challenged by Uṣūlī hardliners. The fact that the Shaykhi ʿulama were able to make an impact on the public in both the city and the countryside did not guarantee their eventual recognition. In most cases, after a phase of initial success, they were faced with stiff clerical opposition, ready to label them as heretics.

In such circumstances, adherence to the tenets of Shaykhism appeared as an ideological deadlock. The doctrine of the Perfect Shiʿa, as they perceived it, made the Advent of the Promised One a necessity. Study under Rashtī and compliance with his prudent approach only helped to raise their expectations for eventual prevalence of the esoteric truth over exoteric reality, while exposure to the Uṣūlī-dominant ʿAtabāt made them realize the formidableness of the endeavor. Loyalty to Shaykhi quietism meant gradual assimilation into the majority creed. Adherence to the Bab was a way out of this deadlock, since it offered the bewildered Shaykhis not only the fulfillment of their aspirations but direction and purpose, a way distinct from assimilation and conformity. The Bab embodied qualities that they believed to be absent among the members of the clerical establishment. A merchant rather than a cleric was their ideal, safely distant from what they considered the malignant influence of madrasa training.

The dissension that had already been expressed against the domination of the mujtahids now appeared more explicitly under the banner of Babism. Mullā's Ḥusayn's preachings clarified the Bab's claims only to a limited extent, allowing the new followers to indulge in a wide variety of assumptions. After 1264/1848 some of the converted ʿulama found themselves faced with a claim far more ambitious than they had originally perceived, and equally hazardous. As Harātī and Yazdī, largely because of their association with formal scholarship and high-ranking ʿulama, became disillusioned with the Bab, abandoned the movement, and later turned against it, others from the lower ranks fought and died in Babi uprisings.

Mullā Ḥusayn's mission characterized other undertakings in Iran to broaden the Babi appeal. Mullā Yūsuf Ardabīlī, an energetic preacher and a Letter of the Living, who in his visits to various provinces never stayed in any place more than a week,[192] brought about conversions first in Azarbaijan and then in Yazd, Kirman, and Qazvin. He mostly preached in towns and villages that were possibly exposed to Ahl-i Ḥaqq teachings. There were mass conversions in the communities of Mīlān, Uskū, Salmās, and Saysān.[193] In Mīlān and Uskū, in the vicinity of Tabriz, two brothers—Ḥājjī Muḥammad Taqī, a physician, and Ḥājjī Aḥmad, a well-to-do merchant based in Tabriz—were at the center of a large Babi group converted by Ardabīlī.[194] During his imprisonment in Azarbaijan, the Bab appointed Muḥammad Taqī, called Fatīq (sharp), as his treasurer. Operating out of Tabriz, Muḥammad Taqī financed the expenses of the Bab's emissaries, including Mullā Bāqir Tabrīzī.[195] After the the Bab's execution in 1266/1850, he and other Babis of Mīlān were instrumental in rescuing the Bab's slain body from the moat surrounding Tabriz and moving it to the silk workshop of another Mīlānī Babi.[196]

In Saysān, another hamlet east of Tabriz, every villager converted to the

[192] *Nabil* 424.

[193] See above, chap. 2, for earlier messianic expectations in Azarbaijan.

[194] The accounts of the Babis of Mīlān appear in *Muʿīn* 194–96; Mīlānī *Āẕarbaijān* 32–35; Uskū'ī *Āẕarbaijān* 1–2; and *ZH* 41–44. Uskū'ī reports that Ardabīlī was already active in Mīlān region in early 1260/1844. Around 1263/1847 when he returned to Mīlān, he openly declared the new Ẓuhūr from the pulpit of Mīlān mosque and gathered a large audience from villages in the vicinity. Implementing a Babi prohibition, he instructed the converts to give up smoking and throw the silver-headed waterpipes into the mosque basin.

[195] *ZH* 41; *Muʿīn* 194–95.

[196] *Nabil* 517–19; Mīlānī *Āẕarbaijān* 45.

new creed. A village teacher, Mullā Jabbār, and a local government agent, Najaf-Qulī, were particularly ardent.[197] Saysān had already been exposed to the messianic admonitions of Ḥājjī Asadullāh, a small landowner and ascetic.[198] In Salmās and Kuhnih Shahr, three village preachers, and their congregations, were converted during the Bab's incarceration in Chihrīq (1264–1266/1848–1850).[199] In Marāghih, Mullā Ḥusayn Dakhīl, an Āẕarī elegist and an old schoolmate of Mullā Ḥusayn,[200] was informed of the new Ẓuhūr by the early Babi disciple Mullā Aḥmad Abdāl Marāghihī, who was also instrumental in the conversion of many individuals in Azarbaijan, including artillery officer ʿAbd al-ʿAlī Khān, a native of the same town.[201]

In the provincial capital of Tabriz, however, the largest commercial center in the north, the activities of the Babi emissaries were hampered by a strong body of conservative Shaykhi ʿulama. Since the later years of ʿAbbās Mīrzā in Azarbaijan, Shaykhism enjoyed a popularity still unchecked by the Uṣūlīs. The chief Shaykhi clerics in the city—Mullā Muḥammad Mamaqānī (d. 1269/1853), a student of Aḥsā'ī and Rashtī;[202] Mīrzā Muḥammad Shafīʿ Tabrīzī Ṣadr al-ʿUlamā' (later Thiqat al-Islām, d. 1301/1883), a member of an old family of notables and a student of Rashtī;[203] the influential Shaykh al-Islām family, most notably Mīrzā ʿAlī Aṣghar (d. 1278/1861) and his nephew Mīrzā Abul-Qāsim;[204] and Shaykh Murtażā Harandī ʿAlam al-Hudā, a wealthy mujtahid[205]—commanded a religious leadership over Tabriz that was rivaled only by the authority of the Uṣūlī imām jumʿa of Tabriz, Mīrzā Aḥmad Mujtahid.[206] After the death of Rashtī and the ensuing fragmentation of the Shaykhi community, Mamaqānī, and later Muḥammad Shafīʿ Tabrīzī, laid claim to the leadership of the Shaykhis.[207] Support of their claims, however, was confined largely to their own clerical and lay following in the province. The leaders of this Shaykhi faction tried to preserve Shaykhism within the limits of a sectarian entity with only minor doctrinal differences from Uṣūlism.[208] Not unlike Kirmānī and Gauhar, Mamaqānī, the Shaykh al-Islams, and another leading Shaykhi, Mullā Maḥmūd Niẓām al-ʿUlamā', later tutor to Crown Prince Nāṣir al-Dīn Mīrzā in

[197]*Muʿīn* 22–26; *ZH* 44–47.
[198]See above, chap. 2.
[199]*ZH* 67–69.
[200]For Dakhīl see *ZH* 54; Mīlānī *Āẕarbaijān* 35, Uskū'ī *Āẕarbaijān* 2; *Muʿīn* 232.
[201]*Muʿīn* 291; *ZH* 60–62.
[202]For a biography of Mullā Muḥammad Mamaqānī see *ZH* 9–10; Nādir Mīrzā *Tabrīz* 116; *Muʿīn* 190.
[203]Nādir Mīrzā *Tabrīz* 246–48.
[204]For Shaykh al-Islām of Tabriz see Nādir Mīrza *Tabrīz* 224–25; *ZH* 10–14; *Muʿīn* 215–23; *TAS* II/1, 57. For the miracle in the shrine of Ṣāḥib al-Amr see Ādamīyat *Amīr Kabīr* 422–25.
[205]*Muʿīn* 196; *QU* 142.
[206]Nādir Mīrzā *Tabrīz* 117; *Muʿīn* 299–300; *TAS* II/1, 102–3.
[207]*ZH* 9.
[208]*Muʿīn* 299.

Tabriz (d. 1271/1854),[209] were determined to halt the spread of the anti-establishment message preached by the Babi activists. Yet the increasing rivalry between the Shaykhis and the Uṣūlīs handicapped effective measures against Babi infiltration. Even before the arrival of the Bab in Azarbaijan, a number of Shaykhis secretly joined the Babi ranks. Sayyid Ibrāhim Tabrīzī, a contestant to Mamaqānī who was converted by Ardabīlī, entered into secret correspondence with the Bab and received the title Khalīl (friend).[210] Shaykh Muḥammad Taqī Hashtrūdī, the author of *Abwāb al-Hudā,* was a wandering Shaykhi mulla who preferred to keep his faith hidden in the pages of his highly valuable historical account.[211] But it was only later, during the Bab's imprisonment in Azarbaijan (1263–1266/1847–1850), that the captive prophet's widespread popularity led to further defection from the Shaykhi ranks.

In Yazd, even though from the time of Aḥsā'ī a section of the community had remained sympathetic toward Shaykhism, various attempts made by Muqaddas, Mullā Muḥammad Z̲ākir Yazdī (a Letter of the Living), and Ardabīlī to win over the public met with hostile reactions. Successive Babi missions failed to attract the allegiance of the Shaykhis, primarily because of the influence of Ḥājjī Muḥammad Karīm Khān Kirmānī and his supporters.[212] Even the implicit support given to the Babi missionaries by the non-Shaykhi mujtahid of Yazd, Sayyid Ḥusayn Azghandī, did not protect them from the intimidations and assaults of the mob.[213] The limited sympathy expressed toward the Babis in the early years, was aimed more than anything at weakening of the rival ʿulama factions by using the Babi issue—a motive comparable to the support of imām jumʿa of Isfahan or Shiʿite ʿulama of the ʿAtabāt in the trial of Basṭāmī. These ephemeral supports notwithstanding, anti-Babi feeling predominated in Yazd. It ultimately forced Mullā Muḥammad Z̲ākir to switch sides to Kirmanī's camp, abandoning his Babi commitment.[214] It was only in 1266/1850, prior to the Nayrīz uprising, that the public preachings of Vaḥīd Dārābī in Yazd attracted a large audience and caused some excitement.[215]

The Shaykhi Opposition in Kirman

Of all the opposition to the Bab in the early years, the most outspoken voice came from Kirman, where successive Babi activists tried in vain to

[209] *ZH* 9–10.
[210] *Muʿīn* 272; *Samandar* 218, 263.
[211] *ZH* 73–74; *Muʿīn* 257–59.
[212] *Nabil* 184–89.
[213] Ibid.
[214] *ZH* 458.
[215] The events of 1266/1850 in Yazd are recorded in various accounts as a prologue to Nayrīz upheaval. Good summaries appear in *SAMB* (388–90); *Nabil* (466–74); *KD* (I, 202–17) and Jahāngīr Mīrzā *Tārīkh-i Nau* (343).

persuade Ḥājjī Muḥammad Karīm Khān Kirmānī (1225–1288/1810–1871), the most prominent of the Shaykhi leaders, to join their ranks. Firmly entrenched in his home province, Kirmānī enjoyed the dual advantage of being a senior member of a powerful landowning family of khans with strong links to the ruling Qajars, as well as the spiritual leader of a sizable Shaykhi following. Since the time of his father, Ibrāhim Khān Ẓahīr al-Daula, the long-time governor of Kirman and an admirer of Aḥsā'ī,[216] a section of the population, who presumably under the Zand patronage professed adherence to Akhbārism, seem to have shifted allegiance to the Shaykhi leaders.[217] Facing the two rival camps, the Uṣūlīs and the Niʿmatullāhīs, the Shaykhi faction welcomed a strong leadership that could provide them with relative security and orientation. Kirmānī was an astute, well-versed and well-connected leader who by virtue of his wealth and rank could guarantee protection, even though his frequent clashes with the Uṣūlī ʿulama and quarrels with the provincial governors were the chief causes of bloody turmoils in a city torn by sectarian divisions.[218]

The first Babi emissary, Quddūs, arrived in Kirman in mid-1845.[219] But even prior to his arrival it appears that Kirmānī had been informed by his allies in the ʿAtabāt of the rise of the still-anonymous Bab, and possibly had access to some of his writings. His first anti-Babi polemic, *Izhāq al-Bāṭil* was an anxious yet uncompromising refutation, completed in Rajab 1261/July 1845.[220] Quddūs conveyed a "red sheet" from the Bab in which the new prophet invited Kirmānī to "obey the order of his Lord" and "renew covenant with the Remnant of God" by paying allegiance to the Ẕikr.[221] Empha-

[216]Ibrāhīm Khān Ẓahīr al-Daula (d. 1240/1824), a cousin of Fatḥ ʿAlī Shāh, ruled over Kirman almost as a semiautonomous governor for more than two decades. For his twenty-two sons he left behind a large estate consisting of numerous villages and town properties scattered throughout the province. See Yaḥyā Aḥmadī Kirmānī *Farmāndihān-i Kirmān* ed. Bāstānī Pārīzī, 3d ed. (Tehran, 1354 Sh./1975) 50–55; Vazīrī *Kirmān* 590–93. For his relations with Aḥsā'ī see Niʿmatullāh Rażavī Sharīf, ed. *Tadhkirat al-Awlīyā'* 2d ed. (Kirman, 1387/1967) 55–58.

[217]Muḥammad Hāshim Kirmānī "Tārīkh-i Mazāhib-i Kirmān," *Majallih-yi Mardumshināsī* I (1335 Sh./1956) 133.

[218]The growing tension between the rival Shaykhis and Bālāsarīs in Kirman, exacerbated by the Ismāʿīlī revolt of 1843–1844, reached its peak during the expulsion of the provincial governor and the widespread disturbances of 1848–1849. While Muḥammad Karīm Khān Kirmānī was in voluntary exile in Yazd, the Shaykhi faction in Kirman gave its tacit support to the antigovernment rebel forces organized by the Shaykhi minister Mīrzā Ismāʿīl and led by two brothers of Kirmānī. The pro-government forces in the city (and another rebellious brother of Karīm Khān), however, tried to secure the backing of the Bālāsarī ʿulama and the city quarters loyal to them. The popular riots ended in Balāsārī victory and the inconclusive restoration of the provincial government. The divided sons of Ẓahīr al-Daula were weakened and the Mīrzā Ismāʿīl was murdered by the mob. See *NT* III, 173–78. For later clashes see Chahārdihī *Shaykhīgarī* 243–65 and Vazīrī *Kirmān* 668–72.

[219]Ḥājjī Muḥammad Karīm Khān Kirmānī *Iqādh al-Ghāfil va Ibṭāl al-Bāṭil dar radd-i Bāb-i Khusrān-ma'āb* (Bombay, 1313/1896, 11, written in 1283/1866 by the order of Nāṣir al-Dīn Shāh). Also *Nabil* 180.

[220]During the compilation of the above work, it appears that Kirmānī was under the impression that after the failure of the ʿAtabāt plan the Babi affair had come to an end, since he does not refer to any future Babi activities.

[221]The text of the Bab's letter appears in Kirmānī *al-Shihāb al-Thāqib fī Rajm al-Nawāṣib*

sizing the unmatchable quality of his revealed word, which equaled the "early verses of the Book of God," the Bab declared: "Today, by the order of the great living Imam, the Remnant of God, it is imperative upon the people of the earth in the east and the west to depart from their homes and immigrate to the city of the Ẕikr."[222] He invited Kirmānī to "raise this cause at once," and "Depart instantly together with those who obey you in this cause with a strong force and with the necessary equipment."[223]

Not surprisingly, the meeting between Kirmānī and Quddūs ended in the khān's strong denunciation of the Bab. In the Bab's letter he found twenty grammatical errors, not to mention doctrinal deviations. "I wrote a book in reply to that letter and clarified its errors, and sent off Muḥammad ʿAlī [Quddūs] humiliated and defeated."[224] The Babi emissary found shelter and support in other quarters, however. The imām jumʿa of the city, Ḥājjī Sayyid Jawād Shīrāzī, a distant paternal cousin of the Bab and Kirmānī's arch rival, willingly played host to the Babi preacher. Quddus' visit to this theosophically oriented imām jumʿa may not have been without the Bab's introduction.[225] In all likelihood, the imām jumʿa saw the Babi propaganda as a weapon against his rival. Subsequently, Sayyid Jawād defied the request of the governor of Kirman, Fażl ʿAlī Khān Qarabāghī[226]—who presumably was incited by Kirmānī—for Quddūs' immediate removal, and threatened him counteraction.[227]

Being aware of the boost that the conversion of the Shaykhi community in Kirman could have given to the nascent movement, the Babis were prepared to make another attempt, this time not by inviting Kirmānī but by challenging him. Shortly after the departure of Quddūs, the second Babi emissary, Mullā Ṣādiq Muqaddas, arrived in Kirman with more writings from the Bab.[228] As Kirmānī recalled, there were "a few sūras in the style of the Qurʾān, a few prayers similar to *Ṣaḥīfat al-Sajjādīya* and sermons in the style of *Nahj al-Balāgha*."[229] The acknowledged seniority of Muqaddas among Rashtī's students seems to have given him enough credibility to prompt the governor, Fażl ʿAlī Khān—who was perhaps also pressured by the imām jumʿa—to convene a tribunal for the examination of the new claims. Confi-

(Kirman, n.d.) 25–27. This work is Karīm Khān's second anti-Babi polemic written in Yazd in 1265/1849.

[222]Ibid. 26.

[223]Ibid.

[224]*Īqādh* II. The book in question is presumably the same above-mentioned *Shihāb*.

[225]See above, chap. 3, for his account. He married a daughter of Ẓahīr al-Daula (Aḥmad ʿAlī Vazīrī *Jughrāfīyā-yi Kirmān* ed. Bāstānī Pārīzī [Tehran, 1355 Sh./1976] 49–50.

[226]For his account see Bāmdād *Rijāl* III 108–10. There is some discrepancy concerning his second term of office as governor of Kirman (see Aḥmadī *Farmāndihān* 87).

[227]*Nabil* 180.

[228]Ibid. 187; *Samandar* 167.

[229]*Īqādh* II. Muqaddas also brought a tauqīʿ for another opponent of Kirmānī, the Uṣūlī mujtahid of the city, Ḥājjī Mullā Aḥmad Kirmānī (d. 1295/1878.) For his account see Aḥmadī *Farmāndihān* 125–26 and Vazīrī *Jughrāfīya* 44–46. This mujtahid postponed his response pending the decision of the ʿAtabāt ʿulamā *(ZH* 398).

dent of his Shaykhi support, Kirmānī willingly participated, but the debate soon deteriorated into a stormy exchange during which Muqaddas accused Kirmānī of abandoning Shaykhi ideals.[230] Fearing physical harm to Muqaddas, Fażl ʿAlī Khān called off the gathering and directed the Babi activist to his own quarters where he resided for the next two months as the governor's guest, freely spreading word of the new Ẓuhūr.[231]

Despite Kirmānī's strong condemnation, Muqaddas made some headway. Of Kirmānī's better-known Shaykhi followers, two defected to the Babi side: Mullā Kāẓim, son of a mason and a student of Kirmānī[232] and Mullā Jaʿfar Kirmānī, a teacher of some stature.[233] Yet even with the tacit support of the provincial governor and the rival ʿulama, Quddūs, Muqaddas, and afterward Ardabīlī[234] could not withstand the long-established authority of Kirmānī. For the next three decades, he was able to prevent any serious defection among the Kirmānī Shaykhis by means of argument and patronage.

Kirmānī's vigorous condemnation of the Bab was not altogether unrelated to the nature of his own claims.[235] His authority over the Kirman community was acknowledged by Rashtī, who had every reason to want to see his influential and talented student in charge of a large community in an important provincial center. Kirmānī's pupilage under Rashtī in the early 1830s does not seem to have exceeded more than three years, but was enough to guarantee his loyalty to Shaykhi principals.[236] By the early 1840s, like many other Shaykhi adherents, Kirmānī was impatient with the bleak state of affairs. In his correspondence with Rashtī he underlined the need for drastic action, which probably meant some kind of messianic proclamation. "Now people are not any more content with words, they want something else," he wrote.[237] Rashtī repeatedly assured him that the

230*ZH* 151; *SAMB* 228–29 (presumably citing Ibn Aṣdaq notes). In *Īqādh* Kirmānī maintains that at his request the proceedings of the debate were recorded in a risāla. No trace of such a work has yet been found.

231*ZH* 398; *Samandar* 176.

232Advocating the veracity of the Bab from the pulpit, he was badly punished by Kirmānī's brother and died shortly after (*ZH* 399–400).

233Mullā Muḥammad Jaʿfar managed to survive Kirmānī's wrath by practicing taqīya. For his account and an interesting correspondence with the Bab see *ZH* pp. 401–5. He is the father of the celebrated dissident Shaykh Aḥmad Rūḥī. Of Kirmānī's followers who later converted to Babism there were two Iṣfahanīs: Ḥājjī Mīrzā Maḥmūd, a merchant *(Tadhkirat al-Awlīyā*ʾ 101) and Ḥājjī Mīrzā Ḥaydar ʿAlī, the celebrated Bahāʾī writer and preacher who is the author of *Bahjat al-Ṣudūr* (Bombay, 1331/1912.) This work contains interesting passages on Kirmānī.

234*Nabil* 187.

235For some observations on Kirmānī's thoughts and their significance in the Shiʿite context see M. Bayat *Mysticism and Dissent* (Syracuse, 1982) 59–86. The author provides a summary of his writings and acknowledges the dramatic shift toward the dominant orthodoxy in later stages of Kirmānī's life, but fails to emphasize that even his early anticlerical views were responses to the Babi challenge.

236*Tadhkirat al-Awlīyā*ʾ 72–75; cf. *Fihrist* 57. His intermittent stays in Karbalāʾ and his study under Rashtī were during the early 1830s.

237Cited in Rashtī's reply (*Tadhkirat al-Awlīyā*ʾ 83–85).

time was not yet ripe for action. "God, praise be to Him, revealed and solidified this great support which is the Fourth Pillar and the final supplement to the foundations [of the religion], by our means . . . and this [Fourth] Pillar also requires forbearance and good conduct."[238] Warning Kirmānī of the danger of exceeding the limits of the people's capacity, he divides the gradual process of "people's reunion with the Great Help" (presumably a reference to the Hidden Imam)[239] into six stages. Each stage in its own rights is the true name of the Great Help, the first being the status of the "companions of the sharīʿa and the people of the disputation."[240] Rashtī stresses that "people are still residing in the first stage and [some] in the second stage"—that of the holy men (nujabāʾ), the bearers of the gnosis and esoteric secrets. "How can they tolerate the third stage? . . . People are still in need of the knowledge, the gnosis, the esoteric secrets, and the light. . . . The time still has not arrived for other things."[241]

It goes without saying that Kirmānī considered himself Rashtī's sole spiritual heir. Even before receiving the news of his death, he declared that in a revelatory dream he saw the "thousand gates of knowledge" being opened to him.[242] This was a tacit indication of his self-proclaimed elevation to the state of the Fourth Pillar, which later was confirmed by numerous allusions in his early writings. His *Irshād al-ʿAwāmm,* written at the height of his career, makes repeated references to his unique qualities as the sole interpretor of esoteric knowledge both for the adept and for the laity.[243]

The highly controversial claims of the prophet of Shiraz, far beyond what Aḥsāʾī or Rashtī ever perceived, made Kirmānī more cautious of his own claim. In due course, the Bab's challenge determined the limits within which Kirmānī tried to maintain a safe proximity to the mainstream of orthodox Shiʿism. At the same time, he could not afford to ignore those Shaykhi aspirations which in an alarming way had found expression in Babism. It is no coincidence that in the years prior to the Babi defeat, Kirmānī adopted a tactful rendering of themes that were central to the Babi thought. Most significantly, he employed the Shaykhi epistemological theory of cognition and the relative capacity of the public, elaborated by Rashtī, to legitimize the necessity for his own status as the Fourth Pillar; a concept comparable to the Bab's theory of progressive revelation. In contrast to the Bab's initiation of a new prophetic cycle, however, Kirmānī chose to remain loyal to Rashtī's stage-by-stage process for reaching "the Great Helper."[244] In due

[238]Ibid. 80–81.

[239]An esoteric reference with theosophic connotations that appears in the works of Rashtī as an epithet for the Twelfth Imam.

[240]Letter cited in *Tadhkirat al-Awlīyāʾ* 83.

[241]Ibid. 84–85.

[242]Ibid. 100–101.

[243]Bayat *Mysticism and Dissent* 75–77.

[244]The treatment of Shaykhi epistemology with emphasis on relativity of knowledge and the role of the nuqabāʾ and nujabāʾ are most apparent in some of his early works, including *Irshād*

course, circumstances obliged the Kirmānī, even more than his teacher, to retreat into a conservative position that ultimately nullified, at least in public, the very essence of the Fourth Pillar.[245] This shift of position was not unrelated to Kirmānī's political stand. As long as radical Shaykhism could serve as an ideology aiding his quest for greater independence from both the central government and the religious establishment, he might have allowed it to remain a part of his doctrine. But when Shaykhi messianism turned into Babism, and Babism in turn challanged the prevailing social order, Kirmānī felt the need to draw closer to his Qajar allies and abandon his earlier stand.

But if for reasons of ideological conviction and personal privilege the road to revolutionary claims was closed to Kirmānī, he could still try to prevent the Shaykhi drift to radical messianism by attacking the Bab on his own ground. Almost from the start, prior to any other religious leader, he sensed the Babi threat, and was quick to repel it. Between 1261/1845 and 1268/1852, at the peak of Babi activities, he successfully mobilized an anti-Babi front. His numerous polemics in refutation of the Bab, first on his own initiative and later under royal instruction,[246] his petitions to the shah and the government authorities, his letters to the ʿulama, and his preaching from the pulpit witnessed his single-minded devotion to checking the new heresy. Such measures seemed even more urgent because they would clear Kirmānī of charges leveled against him of spurious beliefs, antigovernment leanings, and even revolt.[247] To remove any suspicion, Kirmānī increasingly resounded his pro-Qajar loyalties. His pro-establishment attitude—in spite of his theoretical schemes for an ideal government, and his quarrels with the local government of Kirman—is evident in his praiseful references to the Qajar sovereign after 1850. Under attack for unorthodox claims from the Uṣūlī quarter, Kirmānī gradually readjusted the doctrine of the Fourth Pillar

al-ʿAwāmm 4th ed. (Kirmān, 1325/1907) compiled between 1263/1847 and 1267/1851 (particularly vol. 4, part 1); *Fawāʾid Sabʿa* (Kirman, 1354/1935), written in 1262/1846; and *Fiṭrat al-Salīma* 2d ed. (Kirman, 1378/1958), written between 1268/1852 and 1277/1860.

[245]See for instance his revised treatment of the status of the Fourth Pillar in his risāla titled *Rukn-i Rābiʿ* (Kirman, 1368/1948), written in 1282/1865 in reply to an enquiry by Sipahsālār Aʿẓam.

[246]A prolific writer with encyclopedic interests—ranging from ḥikmat, theology, fiqh, uṣūl, and grammar to mathematics, physics, alchemy, and medicine and to literary techniques, the occult, land survey and masonry—between 1249/1883 and 1288/1871 Kirmānī produced no fewer than 277 books and treatises of different lengths of which some were published in his lifetime. (For the list of his works see *Tadhkirat al-Awlīyāʾ* 121–40 and *Fihrist* II, 360–487.) He wrote at least four independent anti-Babi polemics: *Izhāq al-Bāṭil* (1261/1845); *Tīr-i Shihāb* (1262/1846); *Shihāb al-Thāqib* (1265/1849); and *Īqādh al-Ghāfil* (1283/1866, by the order of Nāṣir al-Dīn Shāh) and frequently referred to the Babis in his other works. See MacEoin "From Shaykhism to Babism" Ph.D. diss., Cambridge University, 1979 (197–99) for a concise analysis of his Babi polemics.

[247]In the early 1850s, suspicious of Kirmānī's political ambitions and his scheme for establishing a "spiritual monarchy," Nāṣir al-Dīn Shāh summoned the khan, together with eighteen members of his family, to Tehran, where he stayed for some time. After being cleared of charges of inciting sectarian violence in Kirman, he was allowed to return. See Chahārdihī *Shaykhīgarī* 243–45.

to a point where it was indistinguishable from the Uṣūlī doctrine of collective deputyship. By 1269/1852, only six years after the completion of *Irshād al-ʿAwāmm,* he was so far submitted to the Uṣūlī position that he could declare: "Today I do not recognize a specific gate [*bāb-i makhṣūṣ*] between the Imam and the people. This is not my faith and I would consider the claimant [to such a position] a liar and slanderer. The authority at the time of Occultation are the ʿulama and I have not seen in the Traditions of the Imams nor have I heard any of the ʿulama [of the past] report that during the Occultation a bāb would ever appear."[248] Such a declaration denied, at least in public, the theoretical ground for individual mandate from the Imam and by extension rejected the claims of Aḥsāʾī, Rashtī, and Kirmānī himself, let alone those of the Bab.

His criticism of the Bab was essentially twofold. In his earlier refutations, *Izhāq al-Bāṭil* and *al-Shihāb al-Thāqib,* the thrust of his criticism rested upon the two issues of the Bab's apostatic claims and his stylistic errors. He never ceased to contrast the ultimate perfection of the Muḥammadan revelation and the unmatchable quality of the Qurʾān with "erroneous verses" of the Bab's "false scripture," which he insisted was no more than a poor imitation of the Holy Book. Scrutinizing every grammatical irregularity in the Bab's Arabic writings, he accuses the "merchant lad of Shiraz" of ignorance, falsification, insanity, and deception.[249] Producing ample evidence from the Qurʾān, the prophetic Traditions, and the Shiʿite akhbār, he endorsed the finality of the Islamic revelation and condemned the Bab in strongest terms for causing division and conflict in Shiʿite ranks.[250]

The second major issue upon which Kirmānī attacked the Bab was the question of the holy war (jihād), a criticism particularly appealing to the Qajar monarch. He employed the conventional Shiʿite argument to reject the legality of declaring jihād during the Occultation of the Twelfth Imam. Relying heavily on the Shiʿite evidence, his pro-establishment views clearly characterize practical considerations as well as his theological stand. In *Sī Faṣl,* compiled in 1269/1853 shortly after the Babis' final defeat, he states that during the Occultation of the Imam "whoever begins an uprising [khurūj] and attributes the permission for it to the Imam, he is [among] the idols and the false deities. Today if jihād was necessary, the Imam himself would have made his appearance."[251] He gives more pragmatic reasons for the futility of such an undertaking: "By God! if the people of the east and the west come together and fight with the state, all of them will perish, for God has not destined the demise of these states before the Advent of the

[248] *Sī faṣl* (Kirman, 1368/1948) 36–37.

[249] For an overcritical scrutiny of the Bab's Arabic style see *Shihāb* 27–42. A summary outline of his doctrinal objections to the Bab's earlier claims appears in *Shihāb* (42–57). In *Īqādh* (19–25), Kirmānī's chief objective is to attack the Bab on the basis of his teachings in the *Bayān.*

[250] *Shihāb* 50.

[251] P. 37. Idols and false deities are allusions to Qurʾān IV, 54.

Imam and except for the unbeliever, the godless, the sinful, the power hungry, and the fool no one would oppose the state."[252]

Such flattering homage to the invincibility of the temporal power evidently went beyond the passive cooperation of the mainstream ʿulama with the state. In the aftermath of the Babi uprising Kirmānī criticized the ʿulama for their incompetence to cope with the Babi threat: "When that cursed one [the Bab] rebelled and cast doubts in Islam, all these mullas were proved incapable of refuting him by systematic argumentation, for they did not know anything but uṣūl and fiqh. For a while he wandered among Muslims and no one could challenge him by methodological means, and when some people refuted him, it was only by employing the argument of "we do not submit" and by calling him heathen and accursed. Not even one individual could write two pages in refutation of that wicked one."[253]

Kirmānī took special pride in reporting that the production and widespread publication of his numerous anti-Babi refutations in Azarbaijan, Iraq, Ḥijāz, Khurasan, and India, his petitions to the mullas and "the trustees of the victorious state," and his sermons in Kirman, Yazd, and Khurasan were vital in eradicating the Babi menace.[254] Although he extends the credit of vanquishing the Babis to the "sword of the king, the refuge of Islam," he reserves for himself the honor of "reverting the people of Iran to Islam" and reducing the Bab by "reason and proof."[255] In performing this duty, Kirmānī undoubtedly stood in the forefront of an anti-Babi force that included many other leading Shaykhis.

Beyond the immediate concerns with Babi threat and possible loss of leadership, one can attribute the prominence of Shaykhi ʿulama in the anti-Babi campaign to their efforts to exploit the issue for the purpose of gaining proximity to the state at the time when they were under fire from the Uṣūlī jurists. At a deeper level, the Shaykhi conservative attitude may correspond to the profound duality inherent in the nature of esoteric thought. At a crucial juncture when the potential of esoteric dissent, swollen by myths of revolt and renewal, was unleashed in a millenarian action, the forces of quietism also deployed the means of acquiescence and prudence to advocate conformity.

At the expense of upholding the ideals of the Shaykhi dissent and by diverting its momentum into a sectarian pacifism capable of a precarious survival in isolation, Kirmānī and other leading Shaykhis struck a fatal blow to the Babi revolution. In the earlier stages, despite all his expressed hostility toward the Babis, he was still able to trace an implicit motive for the rise of Babism in the oppression of the state. He attributed the appearance of the movement to "the deception of those who saw that people were desperately

[252] Ibid. 39.
[253] Ibid. 34.
[254] Ibid.
[255] Ibid. 36.

short of freedom because of the intensity of oppression and lack of moderation, and therefore were willing to overthrow the state and start a revolution."[256] Two decades later, even that criticism disappeared. When "the King of kings, the mighty lord of the necks, the shadow of God upon earth, and the manifestation of God's glory in both worlds," Nāṣir al-Dīn Shāh, instructed the "sinful Karīm" to compile yet another refutation of "the fallaciously strayed and errantly perplexed" Babis, he had good reason to thank "the protector of the Muḥammadan sharīʿa" without whose endeavor, the people, who are no more than "silly idiot cows," would have flocked about that "doom-laden" Bab."[257]

In the void that appeared after the death of a number of important mujtahids in the 1840s, the younger generation of the Uṣūlīs were for a time at a loss in dealing with the emerging Babi dissent. In spite of their hereditary privileges through eminent clerical families, they were still unable to consolidate their positions as the sole religious leaders in various cities. In recovering their ground, however, these mujtahids were aided by conservative Shaykhi ʿulama like Kirmānī and Mamaqānī, who similar to Gauhar in the ʿAtabāt helped to orchestrate a united stand against the new heresy. Though at first Uṣūlīs did not see the danger of the Babis, as some of the Shaykhis did, and though their initial reaction was hesitant and halfhearted, when the movement broadened its popular base they too reacted with unanimity. Their anxieties increased when they saw the movement's appeal to the public and particularly to certain factions of the government. The imām jumʿas of various cities, on the other hand, acted with greater circumspection. After a period of relegation to secondary rank, they had now found the chance to reassert their authority by giving implicit support to the Babis, but only to an extent that would not harm their reputation.

However, the overall backing given by the state to the ʿulama, and the obedience of the public toward them, greatly assisted the mujtahids in isolating the Babi elements, thus diminishing the chances of mass conversion in major cities. The events of the first four years above all made it clear that in spite of efforts by the Babis to open a dialogue, the high-ranking ʿulama were never in a position to sympathize with the message of the movement, nor did they tolerate its growth. They were astute enough to see that the basis on which the Babi movement was founded conflicted with their own authority over the community. By isolating the Babis in the cities and applying pressure and persecution, the ʿulama forced the Babis to take a more militant stance, manifested in the armed resistances of Ṭabarsī, Nayrīz, and Zanjān.

[256] *Izhāq al-Bāṭil* 110.
[257] *Īqādh al-Ghāfil* 2–5.

7

Qurrat al-ʿAyn: The Remover of the Veil

Not long after the captivity of Mullā ʿAlī Basṭāmī, the small group of Babi sympathizers in Iraq found a new leader in the person of Qurrat al-ʿAyn. Between 1260/1844 and 1263/1847, she built up a sizable body of support among those who were demoralized by earlier setbacks. Though largely the result of an independent quest, Qurrat al-ʿAyn's conversion and her rise to leadership aptly characterized the messianic ethos around which the entire Babi movement was formed. She was a woman of great talent, with the outlook of a mystic and aspirations of a revolutionary. The part she played in shaping the movement is comparable only to the roles of Mullā Ḥusayn Bushrūʾī and Mullā Muḥammad ʿAlī Bāfurūshī Quddūs. Her career illustrates the way the new Babi alternative gave scope to the otherwise suppressed aspirations of those whose experiences, both intellectual and emotional, brought them to near rejection of society's sanctified norms.

For Qurrat al-ʿAyn, a woman of vigor and vitality, the road between the secluded enclosure of the Baraghānī house in Qazvin and her unveiled appearance at the Badasht gathering of 1264/1848 was a long one, crossing many barriers of social restriction and religious taboo.

Background and Family

Fāṭima Zarrīn Tāj Baraghānī, surnamed Umm Salma—called Qurrat al-ʿAyn (the solace of the eye) by Rashtī and Ṭāhira (the pure) by the Bab[1]—was born in Qazvin in 1231/1814 to a well-known family of ʿulama.[2] Her

[1] Also titled Zakīya, according to *Nabil* 628. *NT* (III, 220) is inaccurate on her titles.

[2] In spite of a relatively large number of short biographies and other secondary sources, there is a lack of a scholarly account of Qurrat al-Ayn's life, or an analysis of her ideas and her significance. Nearly all the histories of the Babi movement contain scattered references to her, sometimes a whole section. Shaykh Sulṭān Karbalāʾī's *Maktūb,* written in 1263/1847 (*ZH*

father, Mullā Muḥammad Ṣāliḥ, and his two brothers were originally from the village of Baraghān, in the Sāvujbulāgh district east of Qazvin, and came to Qazvin in the first decade of the nineteenth century. Later, the two elder brothers moved to Qum, Isfahan, and then the ʿAtabāt, where they studied under well-known Uṣūlī teachers and acquired their authorization.[3] On their return to Qazvin, despite their humble background and earlier poverty, both Muḥammad Taqī and Muḥammad Ṣāliḥ were soon acclaimed as first-rank mujtahids, accumulated large fortunes, and were able to establish religious control over certain quarters in the city. In the early decades of the century Qazvin was a thriving trade center between north and south. The Baraghānī brothers were beneficiaries of this commercial success as well as being frequent recipients of royal favor.

Fāṭima's father, remembered chiefly for his scholarly works in Qur'ānic exegesis and jurisprudence as well as his elegies on the tragedies of Karbalā'[4] was also known for his zeal for the execution of legal punishments. As Tunkābunī, who was his student, related: "He was rigid and firm in enjoining the good and prohibiting the evil,"[5] which probably meant active opposition to consumption of wine and other irreligious acts. In his later life, however, he seems to have been more devoted to scholarship than to par-

245–59) and *NK* are by far the earliest, though by no means the most comprehensive. *NT* (III) and *RS* (X) suffer from their usual bigotry and inaccuracy, though they still contain valuable points. *Kazem Beg* (VII, 473–76) and *RPAC* (167–69, 293–94, and other references) are heavily based on *NT* but give a few new facts and even more myths and fictions that were in circulation as early as the 1860s. Later Babi-Bahā'ī sources *Samandar, Baghdādī, Nabil, NH,* and *Tadhkirat al- Wafā'* [291–330] provide accounts that remained unrecorded up to a few decades later. *Qazvīnī* and *Qatīl,* however, are surprisingly silent. *Kashf al-Ghiṭā'* (92–111), *Muʿīn, KD,* and *ZH* add few details to earlier accounts. *SAMB,* which seems to be based on oral reports (sometimes very similar to *Samandar*), is the fullest in a European language, though far from complete. Some new details were also supplied by Browne in his notes to *TN.* The few short works and poetry that were published by an anonymous Babi-Azalī for the centennial of her death, with the title *Qurrat al-ʿAyn* (Tehran, 128 Badīʿ/1972), is largely a collection of earlier accounts. M. L. Root's *Tahirih, the Pure* (Karachi, 1938; 2d ed., Los Angeles, 1981) is a short popular narrative. D. MacEoin ("From Shaykhism to Babism," especially chap. 6, 194–96) provides a succinct account of her role in connection with the evolution of the Shaykhi community in the ʿAtabāt. M. Momen *Religions* provides some samples of lesser-known European accounts. ʿAlī al-Wardī's *Lamaḥāt Ijtimāʿīya min Tārīkh al-ʿIrāq al-Ḥadīth* ([Baghdad, 1971] II, 152–90) is the most comprehensive account in Arabic of Qurrat al-ʿAyn's life. It contains fresh details on the Iraq period, chiefly based on two as-yet-unknown manuscripts: one by ʿAbbūd Ṣāliḥī, a descendant of Mullā Muḥammad Ṣāliḥ Baraghānī, entitled *Qurrat al-ʿAyn, ʿalā Haqīqatihā wa Wāqiʿihā;* and the other by Mullā Aḥmad Ḥiṣārī Khurāsanī, *ʿAqā'id al-Shaykhīya.* As late as 1974 new information emerged in M. A. Malik Khusravī's *Tārīkh-i Shuhadā-yi Amr* (3 vols. [Tehran, 130 Badīʿ/1974] III). Occasionally the Bab's writings or the writings of Qurrat al-ʿAyn contain brief references to historical events. Some European accounts such as J. E. Polak *Persien, das Land und seine Bewohner, etc.* 2 vols. (Leipzig, 1865) and other works make brief references to her. Qurrat al-ʿAyn's life was a source of inspiration for European writers, particularly for those who sought in her a heroine of women's emancipation. Isabella Grinevskaya's Russian play *Bab, dramatichiskaya Poema* (St. Petersburg, 1903) is one example.

[3] *QU* 19, 91; *TAS* II/1, 226–28, 660–61.

[4] For the list of his works see *TAS* II/2, 660–61. Also *al-Dharīʿa* XVI, 71.

[5] *QU* 91.

ticipation in public affairs. His brother Mullā Muḥammad Taqī, a more typical Uṣūlī jurist,[6] owed his fame not merely to his scholarship but to his ambition to overcome his rivals in Qazvin and later to his denunciation of Aḥsāʾī and his successor. The youngest brother Mullā ʿAlī, on the other hand, became a devout follower of Rashtī. He was a prolific writer with mystical leanings, and his works are the best testimonies of the development of a non-Sufi mysticism within the Shaykhi school.[7]

Fāṭima and her younger sister, Marżīya, were brought up in a strictly religious yet affluent environment. In her early youth, because of her talent ("a prodigy of knowledge") and her father's tolerant view toward her education, Fāṭima managed to further her studies beyond the elementary level, a novelty for a woman of her time. Under her father and her uncles she completed her elementary studies in theology, jurisprudence, and literary sciences. She reportedly surpassed many of her father's students.[8] Sipihr wonders how a woman of her beauty could also be "highly accomplished in Arabic literature, in memorizing the ḥadīth, and in esoteric interpretations of Qurʾānic verses."[9] Her father, we are told, lamented: "If she were a boy she would have illuminated my house and come to be my successor."[10]

In spite of her promising literary and poetic talents,[11] she could not escape the family pressure that at the age of fourteen obliged her to marry, perhaps against her will, her cousin Mullā Muḥammad Baraghānī, son of Mullā Muḥammad Taqī and later imām jumʿa of Qazvin.[12] Soon after, in 1244/1828, she and her husband left Qazvin for the ʿAtabāt, where Mullā Muḥammad was to continue his studies under the celebrated Uṣūlī Mullā Muḥammad Bāqir Qazvīnī. For close to thirteen years the couple resided in Karbalāʾ. Though Fāṭima gave birth to two sons, Ibrāhīm and Ismāʿīl,[13] it appears that almost from the start the marriage was not free from domestic quarrels. She became acquainted with Shaykhi teachings through her maternal cousin Mullā Jawād Valīyānī, who gave her samples of Aḥsāʾī's works.[14] She may have also attended Rashtī's circle, against her husband's

[6]Gobineau's reference (*RPAC* 167) to Mullā Muḥammad Taqī as "traditioniste fameux dans toute la Perse" could be interpreted as a comment on his skill in Traditions (akhbār) but not as a follower of Akhbārī school, as all the evidence proves otherwise. He studied under the celebrated Uṣūlī Sayyid ʿAlī Ṭabāṭabāʾī (*QU* 19). For his biography see *QU* 19–44, *TAS* I/1, 226–28 and *MA* V, 1707–16, and notes.

[7]For his works both in prose and verse see Munzavī *Fihrist* II, 951, 1341, 1389, 1396; *al-Dharīʿa* XI, 317. His biography appears in *MA* V, 1707–16 and *RA* I, 153.

[8]*SAMB* 273.

[9]*NT* III, 219.

[10]*Tadhkirat al-Wafā*ʾ 291; cf. *NK* 142.

[11]*Tadhkirat al-Wafā*ʾ 291–92; Muʿīn al-Salṭana *Tarīkh-i Amr* appendix "Sharḥ-i Ḥāl-i Ṭāhira, Qurrat al-ʿAyn." INBA, MS B, 2.

[12]Wardī *Lamaḥāt* II, 153 (citing ʿAbbūd Ṣalihī's *Qurrat al-ʿAyn*).

[13]Both sons later became mujtahids and Ismāʿīl succeeded his father as imām jumʿa. For their accounts see *TAS* I/23, 164. A third son, Isḥāq, was born in 1841 in Qazvin (Wardī *Lamaḥāt* II, 153).

[14]*Tadhkirat al-Wafā*ʾ 292.

objections. In Qazvin, she must have heard her elder uncle's antagonistic denunciation of Shaykhism and her other uncle's veneration of Rashtī.

The years of Karbalā' were crucial for broadening Fātima's intellectual horizon. But her inclination toward Shaykhism inevitably gave an ideological dimension to the couple's private differences.[15] On their return to Qazvin in 1257/1841, although she still hesitated to express her views in public, her elder uncle, her husband, and her father all rebuked her in private for showing devotion to Shaykhism and dissuaded her from any further pursuit of her studies.[16] However, she seems to have had some support from her younger uncle, Mullā ʿAlī, and later her brother-in-law, Mullā Muḥammad ʿAlī Qazvīnī (son of Mullā ʿAbd al-Wahhāb Qazvīnī and a later Letter of the Living). Through them Fātima secretly corresponded with Rashtī and sent him a treatise she had composed in vindication of some Shaykhi tenets. In reply, Rashtī praised her and addressed her as "the delight of my eye and the soul of my heart."[17] No doubt Rashtī was impressed by the young woman's talent, and he must have also been pleased that in addition to Mullā ʿAlī he had found another ally among the Baraghānīs. Mullā Muḥammad, Fāṭima's husband, whose loyalty to his father was unwavering, must have found it taxing to compete with an independent-minded woman whose intellectual interests went beyond the standards of her time. Though she never received her authorization because "it was not customary to give ijāza of ijtihād to women,"[18] Fāṭima's scholastic accomplishment seems to have qualified her as a mujtahid. There is evidence that at least Rashtī, if not her own father, Mullā Ṣāliḥ, saw her as fit for the honor.[19]

As her marriage deteriorated, Qurrat al-ʿAyn decided to leave her husband and children and return to the ʿAtabāt. Her father apparently could not discourage her from separation. His second daughter, Marżīya, had married the son of Mullā ʿAbd al-Wahhāb, the prominent Shaykhi in Qazvin,[20] and Mullā Ṣālih himself did not seem to approve of his elder brother's public condemnation of the Shaykhis. Shortly afterward, with the advice and assistance of her uncle Mullā ʿAlī, Fātima decided to join the Shaykhi circle in Karbalā'.[21]

Together with Marżīya, she set out for the ʿAtabāt toward the end of

[15]Wardī *Lamaḥāt* 153–54.

[16]*Tadhkirat al-Wafā'* 292; Muʿīn al-Salṭana 2.

[17]*Nabil* 83; cf. Ālūsī (see below, this chapter). The sentence *yā qurrat al-ʿaynī wa ruḥ al-fu'ādī* is originally from *qurrat aʿyun* (heavenly recompense for the true believers, Qurʿān XXXII, 17, and XXV, 74). *Qurrat al-ʿayn* is a common Arabic term of endearment sometimes given by the religious teachers to their favorite students.

[18]*Samandar* 345.

[19]For other examples of women mujtahids in the nineteenth century see McEion "From Shaykhism to Babism" 194. For Shaykhi views on women see Joseph A. Gobineau *Trois ans en Asie* II, 49.

[20]See below, this chapter.

[21]*Samandar* 344.

1259/1843.[22] Her later collaboration with Mullā Ḥusayn and his friends, as well as her own remarks, confirm that she was watchful for some form of messianic revelation.[23] It is not clear whether she left Qazvin after Rashtī's death or whether indeed she was aware of it. In her risāla in reply to Mullā Jawād Valīyānī she states that "at the beginning of his excellency's [the Bab's] cause I was in Qazvin, but as soon as I heard of this cause, even before reading the holy commentary [*Qayyūm al-Asmā*ʾ] or *Ṣaḥīfat al-Makhzūnīya*, I recognized it."[24] This statement only makes sense if we assume that she heard of the Bab before 1260 in Qazvin, possibly through her brother-in-law, Mullā Muḥammad ʿAlī Qazvīnī.

Conversion and Leadership

When Qurrat al-ʿAyn arrived in Karbalāʾ in the last days of 1259/1844, shortly after Rashtī's death,[25] she found herself embroiled in the controversy that divided the Shaykhi students. Reports regarding her participation in the Kūfa retreat cannot be wholly dismissed,[26] but what is certain is that from the start she supported Mullā Ḥusayn. She was apparently informed of the proclamation of the Bab through a letter delivered to her by Mullā Muḥammad ʿAlī Qazvīnī, in reply to her earlier petition she had presented to the then unknown Bab when Mullā Ḥusayn was departing from the ʿAtabāt.[27] *Nuqṭat al-Kāf* stresses that after receiving the writings of the Bab, "she reached the state of intuitive certitude";[28] perhaps an allusion to the fact that Qurrat al-ʿAyn was never able to meet the Bab in person. The Bab's "immediate response to her declaration of faith" was "an exalted ordinance revealed to her honor."[29]

In Karbalāʾ, Qurrat al-ʿAyn resided in the house of Rashtī and became acquainted not only with his widow and the other women of the household but also with his former students and followers.[30] By allying herself with the more radical elements, she was able to organize a chorus of support with ultimate loyalty to the Bab. In creating this united front, she was faced with the challenge of three groups that between 1844 and 1847 constantly hindered her efforts: the conservative Shaykhis, headed by Gauhar and aided

[22]Possibly also accompanied by Mullā Muḥammad ʿAlī Qazvīnī, her brother-in-law (*ZH* 313).

[23]*Tadhkirat al-Wafā*ʾ (295) reports a "veracious dream" in which Qurrat al-ʿAyn visited the Bab prior to his claims. This is another example of the way accounts of intuitive dreams were utilized to register anticipation for messianic Ẓuhūr or even allude to the claimant's identity.

[24]*ZH* appendix I, 499–500.

[25]*Tadhkirat al-Wafā*ʾ (294) dates her arrival ten days after the death of Rashtī.

[26]*Muʿīn* 46, without specifying his source.

[27]*Samandar* 346, cf. 78; *KD* 61–62.

[28]*NK* 140.

[29]Muʿīn al-Salṭana 3.

[30]Shaykh Sulṭān Karbalāʾī *Maktūb* (*ZH* 246); *Samandar* 346.

by defectors from Babi ranks; the conservative Babis, headed by Mullā Aḥmad Ḥiṣārī, who despised her anti-Sharīʿa radicalism; and the Islamic orthodox establishments, both Shiʿite and Sunni, who were happy to see the growing animosity among the Shaykhis but were increasingly wary of Qurrat al-ʿAyn's potential as a charismatic leader.[31]

Between Muḥarram 1260/January 1844 and Shaʿbān 1262/August 1846, while in Karbalā',[32] Qurrat al-ʿAyn was able to broaden her popular following. By complying with the policy of prudence that prevailed over the activities of the Babi sympathizers, particularly after the captivity of Basṭāmī, she partially avoided intrigues and open hostility. Yet even from the start she did not hesitate to air views contradictory to the interpretations of Rashtī's senior students. Holding regular gatherings in Rashtī's house, she spoke to large audiences from behind a curtain.[33] In the inner quarters she also held classes for women. Her personality, theological knowledge, and mastery of Arabic impressed Arabs and Persians alike. Shaykhi ʿulama of some rank and seniority, such as Shaykh Muḥammad Shibl (father of Muḥammad Muṣṭafā al-Baghdādī), saw in her, if not signs of intuitive inspiration, at least a determined leadership. The Qurratīya, as her followers came to be known in Iraq, were successful in transmitting her message to the Shiʿite public beyond Karbalā', thus causing excitement in the ʿAtabāt and anxiety for the Shaykhi and Uṣūlī leaders alike.[34]

In Shaʿbān 1262/August 1846, Qurrat al-ʿAyn and her followers temporarily moved to nearby Kāẓimayn, presumably as a result of pressure from Gauhar's quarter, which obliged her to seek refuge with the Kāẓimayn Babi ʿulama.[35] There she stayed for the next six months as their guest, continuing her public sermons with greater vigor and freedom.[36] An eyewitness confirms that "a large number of people attended her teaching circles and prayed behind her. As she spoke, they listened with great astonishment in their hearts and were moved by her speeches."[37]

The thrust of Qurrat al-ʿAyn's debate was based on Shaykhi ideas, but with a distinct messianic overtone. In many respects she went beyond the limits that hold Shaykhism within the boundaries of Islamic theology. Some sources report that she even assumed the title of "the Point of the Divine Knowledge," which implies that she may have envisaged some revelatory

[31]See below, this chapter, for details.

[32]Wardī *Lamahāt* II, 156–57.

[33]*NK* 140; *KD* I, 61.

[34]Wardī *Lamaḥāt* 155–56.

[35]Moreover, the death of Rashtī's widow, who was a supporter of Qurrat al-ʿAyn at the beginning of 1262/1846, gave new excuses to Mullā Aḥmad Ḥiṣārī to press for the removal of Qurrat al-ʿAyn and the return of *Dīvān* to his control. *Nabīl* 270; cf. Karbalā'ī *Maktūb* (*ZH* 252), which implies that Mullā Aḥmad was in collaboration with the "scum of the people" and "the riff-raffs."

[36]Ibid.

[37]Ibid., citing an oral account from a resident of Kāẓimayn.

status for herself.[38] The fact that she had her own views contradictory to the Islamic law and legal injunctions, combined with the fact that she adopted certain ascetic practices like devotional prayers[39] and eschewing meat and cooked food,[40] underscores her independent religious stance. Clearly, her commitment to the Bab provided her with a framework for the propagation of many of her preconceived views. At the earlier stages it is difficult to say how far her commitment to Babism was purely a consequence of messianic expectations. Only from 1262/1846 is it certain that she was fully aware of the ideas of the Bab as they were reflected in his writings.

The surviving samples of Qurrat al-ʿAyn's works from this early period testify to her skill in making use of the Qur'ān and ḥadīth for arguing the theme of progressive revelations.[41] In a treatise written in 1262/1846 in reply to her cousin Jawād Valīyanī (who first became a follower of the Bab but later, following the events of 1845–1846 defected to the anti-Babi camp) she discussed the legitimacy of the new Ẓuhūr. The position of Sayyid ʿAlī Muḥammad the Bab in relation to that of Aḥsā'ī and Rashtī was a crucial question that preoccupied many of the Shaykhi converts. She argues that the Grand Divine Proof, the title by which she refers to the Bab, is the ultimate fulfillment of Shaykhi thought. Those who had not grasped the essence of Shaykhism to the extent that Rashtī expected are naturally foreign to the continuous process of unfolding revelation:[42] "This is not to say that the two gates [*bābayn*: i.e., Aḥsā'ī and Rashtī] were in darkness and that their words were imperfect. All in all today in the face of the universe [the position] of those two revered souls has not been recognized except by this point of the point in the circle of the being [the Bab]."[43]

She states that Rashtī himself regarded his position as being above the

[38]*ZH* 314; cf. *RPAC* 167.

[39]*Tadhkirat al-Wafā'* 295.

[40]*KD* I, 61.

[41]Of the tracts, treatises, letters, poems, and prayers that she wrote, the majority either remain unidentified or have perished. Of her published works, besides her 1261/1845 *Risāla* in Persian in reply to Mullā Jawād Valīyanī (*ZH* appendix I, 484–501), *ZH* produces six other works in prose: a letter to Mullā Ḥusayn (in Arabic, 334–38); two public addresses to Babis and the general public written circa 1263/1847 (338–65); a letter addressed to Ālūsī (356–59); a tract in defense of the Bab (359–62); and two letters addressed to the Babis of Isfahan (362–66). The centennial volume *Qurrat al-ʿAyn* (36–52) produced six new Persian prayers and letters. *Kashf al-Ghiṭā'* (appendix II, 1–21) added another long Arabic treatise and *KD* (I, 323–27) cited part of another apologia. Browne provided the text and translation of a letter addressed to Shaykh ʿAlī ʿAẓīm (*NH* appendix IV, 434–41) and added useful notes. Of her poetry some samples were also printed in various sources. There is some degree of uncertainty on the authenticity of some of the pieces, arising from the fact that some of her poems are similar in style to those of Ḥātif Iṣfahānī and Ṣuḥbat Lārī. *ZH* produces seven poems (366–69) and the centennial volume adds eight more (25–35). Browne in *MSBR* gives the text and translation of three better-known poems and Ẕukā'ī Bayżā'ī in *Taẕkira-yi Shuʿarā-yi Qarn-i Avval-i Bahā'ī* (3 vols. [Tehran, 1965–1970] III, 107–32) gives an analysis of her style and produces some new poems. Two manuscripts in INBA Library contain some further tracts and poetry.

[42]*Risāla* (*ZH* 488).

[43]Ibid.

Four Gates of the period of Lesser Occultation, a sign that after him the process will continue to result in a revelation of a greater magnitude. There is no evidence "from the word of God or that of the guardians of the faith" or "the gates to the Infallibles" (i.e., Aḥsā'ī and Rashtī) that prevents the occurrence of such complimentary revelations.[44] To acknowledge this unfolding process, she points out, it is necessary to bear in mind that "the divine norm" basically differs from "the human norm" and indeed from the habits of the past, and therefore "the norms for testing the truthfulness of the proof of God are not apparent to the people."[45] To recognize the proof, only an inner awareness of the divine norm would lead the seeker to the right path. This, she insisted, is the essence or "the secret of the secrets" in the new revelation.[46]

To experience this "secret of the secrets," she suggests the teachings of Aḥsā'ī and Rashtī should be used as keys for unraveling the complexities of the revelatory process. Here she distinguishes two complementary concepts and prescribes *mujāhada* (spiritual endeavor) as opposed to *mujādala* (rational argumentation) as the essential approach to the truth.[47] This implies that, contrary to her rejection of the contemporary Sufis, in some respects she is influenced by their intuitive methods. The truthfulness of the Bab, as indeed that of the prophets of the past, is conceivable only "by insight of the inner heart and [search] in the true essence of one's existence."[48]

But in Qurrat al-ʿAyn's view, this intuitive approach is inseparable from the proof of wisdom (*dalīl-i ḥikmat*).[49] Such rational proof, according to her, is complementary to spiritual endeavor for acknowledgment of the fact that "in every age there is a necessity for a bearer and interpretor who would supervise all matters."[50] Passionately, Qurrat al-ʿAyn argues that she herself came to recognize the Bab when in a moment of intuitive insight she grasped the unceasing necessity for divine revelation:

> With an insight free from intruders, I observed God's power and omnipotence [and realized] that this great cause most definitely needs a locus of manifestation for after God made His Fourth Pillar and His encompassing sign and His manifested locality known to people, and [thus] brought them close to His presence and showered them from His high exalted Heaven with His [spiritual] nourishment, then by proof of wisdom it is incumbent upon Him, whose status is high, not to leave the people to themselves as it is necessary for His grace to increase, His benevolence to broaden and His blessing to mature since [in the past] His norm always rested upon this. And day after day the cycle of universe

[44]Ibid. 493.
[45]Ibid. 486–87.
[46]Ibid. 488.
[47]Ibid. 490–91.
[48]Ibid. 491.
[49]Ibid.
[50]Ibid.

is in progress *(kaur dar taraqqīst)* and "there is no suspension in his emanation." Praise to God and our prayer and gratitude [to Him] that the cause is everlasting.[51]

The theme of spiritual evolution in this passage conveys an unmistakable historical dynamism that is absent even from the nonorthodox currents of the time. The rule of benevolence makes continuous divine emanation an unsuspending responsibility. This is reminiscent of the Muʿtazilite theology of the past, but it also tends to go a step beyond Sufi and even Ismāʿīlī thoughts, as it implies that "the unfolding destiny" of mankind necessitates an evolutionary perfection in successive revelations. It is as if Qurrat al-ʿAyn has elaborated this view on her own initiative and as a result of a personal inquiry that employed both "the intuitive endeavor" and the "proof of the wisdom."

This was a significant step forward in the Shaykhi-Babi thinking that employed ḥikma (in the sense of rational endeavor) in conjunction with intuition to explain a continuous spiritual progress of mankind, and hence to conclude that "the unceasing emanation of God" would inevitably evolve into a new prophecy. The logical outcome was the notion of spiritual progress that the Bab, and Babi writers like Qurrat al-ʿAyn, adapted in support of their liminal relation with Islam. Here the maxim "The cycle is in progress," viewing the forward movement of man in the rotation of celestial spheres as a historical process, expresses one of the most essential breakthroughs in the Babi thought. Distinguishing between the past and the present, Qurrat al-ʿAyn alludes to a sense of betterment in the course of time. Such a view was essentially irreconcilable with the doctrine of prophethood in orthodox Islam. Human progression was thus her prime concern in seeking a new revelation in the Bab. At the basis of the Bab's theory of successive resurrections[52] lay a vision of the future that could only materialize if a break occurred with the past religious legacy. Perhaps this very desire to break with the past should be taken as the origin of a widening difference between the orthodox Shiʿite and the Babi world views.

Qurrat al-ʿAyn's actions complemented her theoretical position. On the one hand, she questioned and in many instances rejected the soundness of the practices of past generations in the matter of legal injunctions *(furūʿ)*; on the other, by emphasizing the imminent advent of a new prophetic cycle she sharpened the distinction between believers and denouncers. In what amounted to a symbolic protest, she enjoined her followers not to buy food from the market, because people who denounced the Bab were infidels and therefore eating their food was unlawful—no doubt a defensive response to

[51]Ibid. 494.
[52]*Bayān* VI/2, 30–32.

the pressure on the Babis, who were now rejected as unbelievers.[53] She justified her new prohibition on the basis of the Bab's assertion that since in the state of "initial truth" of the Fourteen Infallibles she stands as the manifestation of Fāṭima, the daughter of the Prophet, her sight is purifying. She ordered the Babis to bring all the food to her, so that by her purifying sight she could make it suitable for use. The eyesight of the clan of God, of which the daughter of the Prophet is one, is symbolic of their will, upon which rests the prohibition or confirmation of religious commands. *Nuqṭat al-Kāf* notes: "This was the first breach of the religious code . . . among those people."[54]

But not all the "infringements of the religious injunctions" were limited to the Babis' relations with their adversaries. Perhaps her most daring act was her appearance, unveiled, at a gathering of her followers. The gesture was utterly unacceptable, even to some of the Babis in the ʿAtabāt.[55] Still more blasphemous was her belief that the Islamic compulsory obligations, including the daily prayers, should be lifted altogether, because interregnum prior to the advent of the next dispensation had begun. The use of the Islamic concept of *faṭra* (an interval between two successive messengers) in a new historical context connotes Qurrat al-ʿAyn's interpretation of her own age not simply as a period of slackening the rules of sharīʿa but as an age of willing transition toward the final break. Similar to the unitarians (Ḥunafāʾ) of the pre-Islamic times, she viewed her own mission, and those of the other early Babis, as a precursory vigilance. Thus the infringement of the legal and devotional boundaries was a necessary distancing from the customary norms of the community in order to grasp the signs of the new Ẓuhūr. Such messianic certitude was to be achieved not by devotional acts and religious duties but by spiritual endeavor combined with the proof of wisdom.

Publication of such a controversial doctrine at a time when every infringement of the religious norms met with strongest opposition was hazardous, especially for a woman. As the first Persian woman in modern times who advocated unveiling on her own initiative and as a result of an intellectual quest, Qurrat al-ʿAyn was bound to be concerned with the inferior role assigned to women in the society of the time. Her challenge to men on a ground traditionally closed to women must have had a strong appeal to the small circle of women that formed around her,[56] who appear to have achieved a nascent feminist consciousness defined by Qurrat al-ʿAyn's personality and inspired by her words and deeds. Coming from different social backgrounds, they were all later distinguished for their Babi commitment. Khurshīd Bagum, called Shams al-Ḍuḥā, wife of Mīrzā Muḥammad ʿAlī

[53] *NK* 140–41.

[54] Ibid. 140.

[55] *Baghdādī* 109. The author specifies that Qurrat al-Ayn "appeared unveiled in the gatherings of believers, but in the gatherings of nonbelievers she spoke from behind a curtain."

[56] Wardī *Lamaḥāt* II, 162; cf. *Samandar* (81), who calls them "women companions."

Nahrī,[57] and Qurrat al-ʿAyn's sister, Marżīya, were both deeply influenced by her. Also known to us are Mullā Ḥusayn's mother, a poetess; Bībī Kūchak, later called Warqat al-Firdaus, Mullā Ḥusayn's sister and wife of another Babi, Shaykh Abū Turāb Ishtihārdī;[58] Rashtī's wife, who was originally from Shiraz,[59] and Qurrat al-ʿAyn's maid, Kāfiya.[60] In the later years in Qazvin, daughters of Ḥājjī Asadullāh Farhādī, Khātūn Jān, Shīrīn, and Ṣāḥiba also became her faithful followers. It was Khātūn Jān who assisted Qurrat al-ʿAyn in her escape from Qazvin.[61] On her return from the ʿAtabāt in 1263/1847 Qurrat al-ʿAyn also attracted the wives of local notables in Kirmānshāh and Hamadan, two in particular: Zubayda Khānum, better known as Firishtih, the daughter of Fatḥ ʿAlī Shāh and mother of the vālī of Kurdistan, Muḥammad Ḥusayn Khān Ḥisām al-Mulk Qaraguzlū, who was a poetess with the pen name Jahān;[62] and the wife of Maḥmūd Khān Nāṣir al-Mulk.[63] Qurrat al-ʿAyn's influence is also seen in another Babi poetess, Shams Jahān, the daughter of Muḥammad Riżā Mīrzā and granddaughter of Fatḥ ʿAlī Shāh, with the pen name Fitna. In her lyric *masnavī* Fitna gave an account of her first acquaintance with Qurrat al-ʿAyn when she was imprisoned in the house of Maḥmud Khān Kalāntar, the chief of police of Tehran, between 1266/1850 and 1268/1852.[64]

Even before her return to Karbalāʾ in February 1847, Qurrat al-ʿAyn's casting off of her facial veil in the presence of men aroused strong misgivings inside the Babi community.[65] In the first of Muḥarram of 1262/30 December 1845, the annual month of mourning for the Shiʿite martyrs, she instructed the Babis to joyfully celebrate the anniversary of the Bab's birthday in Rashtīs house. Ignoring the custom of wearing black during Muḥarram, she herself dressed in color and appeared at the feast without wearing a veil.[66] This open disregard for the Shiʿite mourning rites, even though per-

[57]For her details see below, chap. 8.

[58]*Fuʾādī* 23; cf. *Tadhkirat al-Wafāʾ* 297.

[59]*Nabil* 270–71.

[60]*Samandar* 358. Also known as Qānita (*NK* 141).

[61]See below, chap. 8. Other Babi women of Qazvin with special adherence to Qurrat al-ʿAyn included the literate sister of Karbalāʾī Luṭf ʿAlī Ḥallāj (carder), the wife of Mullā Valīullāh Qazvīnī, and the mother of Ibn Abhar (*Samandar* 370). The same source maintains that even before 1260/1844, Qurrat al-ʿAyn was well known in women's circles of Qazvin and that the women relatives of traders, merchants, and notables referred to her as the "daughter of *āqā*" and *khānum* (lady) (*Samandar* 73, 345).

[62]*KD* I, 117; cf. ʿA. Ishrāq Khāvarī *Tārīkh-i Amrī-yi Hamadān,* INBA MS, 2–4 and *Kashf al-Ghiṭāʾ* 105. Her details and some samples of her poetry appear in Aḥmad Mīrzā *Tārīkh-i ʿAżudī*, 14–16.

[63]*KD* I, 117.

[64]Zukāʾī Bayżāʾī (167–202) gives an account of her life and some parts of her *masnavī*. The women of the household of Āqā Khān were also impressed by Qurrat al-ʿAyn when she resided briefly in Nūrī's house in Tehran in 1264/1848 (Muʿīn al-Ṣalṭana 10; J. E. Polak *Persien* I, 242). For impression on Shahrbānū, a woman in Dizvā in Nūr region, see Malik Khusravī *Shuhadāyi Amr* III, 205.

[65]Wardī *Lamaḥāt* II, 157.

[66]*Samandar* 78, 346–47.

formed at a gathering of the Babis, enraged some Babi ʿulama, such as Mullā Aḥmad Ḥiṣārī and Sayyid ʿAlī Bushr Kāẓimaynī, who still tended to see the Bab and his daʿwa as the continuation of Shiʿite traditions. The manner in which Qurrat al-ʿAyn implicated the Bab's mission as being a manifestation independent from Islam and thus criticized the traditional-minded Babis for their failure either to appreciate "the state of inner heart" or to grasp the participatory role of the early believers, the Sābiqīn, doubtless troubled many who joined the movement with very different expectations.

Already in 1262/1846, Jawād Valīyānī returned from Shiraz to Qazvin utterly disenchanted with the Bab and his voluntary isolation. Staging a vigorous anti-Babi campaign, Valīyānī questioned the Bab's referral of worldly affairs to Mullā Ḥusayn and attacked the exclusive status the former bestowed upon the Sābiqīn. In her letters from Karbalā' Qurrat al-ʿAyn tried in vain to vindicate reasons for deputations in a Shaykhi context and to clarify the hierarchical structure of the early believers envisaged by the Bab. Valīyānī soon defected to Kirmānī's side,[67] yet many of the questions he raised troubled other loyal Babis such as Mullā Aḥmad Muʿalim Ḥiṣārī, who could not easily come to terms with the fast-changing message of the movement.

Ḥiṣārī, a tutor of Rashtī's son Aḥmad,[68] was the representative of the conservative Babis of the ʿAtabāt. For ideological and personal reasons, contrary to Qurrat al-ʿAyn, he advocated conformity and prudence. In collaboration with Mullā Ḥusayn, and with the tacit support of Muḥīṭ and Gauhar, he was able for a while to exercise some control over the Dīwān and the household of Rashtī.[69] Some twenty-three students, mostly his own relatives, constituted the core of his support and attended his teaching circle in the Rashtī's house.[70] His risāla *ʿAqā'id al-Shaykhīya*[71] is harshly critical of Qurrat al-ʿAyn and her supporters, accusing, among others, Mullā Muḥammad Bāqir Tabrīzī, one of the sābiqīn and a Letter of the Living, of deliberate misrepresentation of "cognition of the Imam" in order to elevate Qurrat al-ʿAyn to deputyship or even gateship, on a level with Mullā Ḥusayn.[72] He chastised "the daughter of evil" (*bint-i ṭāliḥ;* a pun for *bint-i ṣāliḥ*) not only for disregard of taqīya, recommended by the Bab, but for propagating the end of Islamic era, the abrogation of sharīʿa, and misrepresentation of the Ẕikr as an independent revelation. To vindicate his views, Mullā Aḥmad, amid a growing hostility, sent letters of inquiry to leading Babis and to the Bab himself in Isfahan.[73]

[67]*ZH* 337–38. See below, this chapter, for his earlier conversion in Qazvin. See also MacEoin "From Shaykhism to Babism" 199–200.

[68]For Ḥiṣārī's later career see above, chap. 6.

[69]Karbalā'ī *Maktūb* (*ZH* 245, 253, 256).

[70]Ibid. 246.

[71]Partially cited in Wardī *Lamaḥāt* II, 159–63.

[72]Karbalā'ī *Maktūb* 246–47; cf. *Lamaḥāt* II, 160 citing Hiṣārī *ʿAqā'id.*

[73]*Lamaḥāt* citing Ḥiṣārī *ʿAqā'id* 161; cf. Karbalā'ī *Maktūb* in *ZH* 256–57.

Qurrat al-ʿAyn and her supporters were equally uncompromising. Shaykh Sulṭān Karbalāʾī, one of Qurrat al-ʿAyn's closest companions, accuses Mullā Aḥmad of hypocrisy, unjustified compromise, personal ambition, collaboration with Shaykhi and Uṣūlī adversaries, conspiracy against Qurrat al-ʿAyn, and slander.[74] It was Mullā Aḥmad's shameless allegations, Karbalāʾī declares, that poisoned the minds of Kāẓimayn Babis and turned them against Qurrat al-ʿAyn.[75]

Indeed, Sayyid ʿAlī Bushr and other Babis of Kāẓimayn, already enraged by Qurrat al-ʿAyn's behavior, were appropriately encouraged by Mullā Aḥmad to write to the Bab asking his opinion of her conduct, her status, and her advocacy of termination of Islamic sharīʿa. Baghdādī reports that her critics insisted: "[The Bab] has not abrogated the old sharīʿa and did not renew any command but increased [observation] of the religious injunctions and emphasized [the necessity] of prayers and fasting and prohibited smoking and now this woman Qurrat al-ʿAyn has exceeded the limit and abrogated the sharīʿa that we inherited from our fathers and grandfathers without the mandate of his holiness the Exalted One [i.e., the Bab]."[76]

The Bab defended Qurrat al-ʿAyn and her positions publicly and unequivocally, entitling her *Ṭāhira* (the Pure) to emphasize his disapproval of the charges of immorality. He not only approved of Qurrat al-ʿAyn and her leadership over the Babis of the ʿAtabāt but significantly acknowledged the progressive tendency in the movement, even at the expense of losing some of the more traditionalist followers.[77] The Bab emphasizes: "Concerning what you have inquired about that mirror which has purified its soul in order to reflect the word by which all matters are solved; she is a righteous, learned, active, and pure woman; and do not dispute al-Ṭāhira in her command for she is aware of the circumstances of the cause and there is nothing for you but submission to her since it is not destined for you to realize the truth of her status."[78] Perhaps for the first time, the Bab openly approved the ideas and actions of his most outspoken and radical disciple. The fact that the matter was referred to the judgment of the Bab underscores his significance as the movement's core and supreme authority.

When his reply was read to a gathering of seventy Babis in Kāẓimayn, a number of followers, seeing it as an open breach of the Islamic code, declined to accept his command and left the Babi ranks.[79] Later, in a commen-

[74]Karbalāʾī *Maktūb* in *ZH* 245–59.

[75]*Lamaḥāt* citing Ḥiṣārī *ʿAqāʾid* 161; cf. Karbalāʾī *Maktūb* in *ZH* 257.

[76] *Baghdādī* 109–10.

[77]The Bab's reply came from Mākū in mid-1263/1847, when Qurrat al-ʿAyn was perhaps already out of the ʿAtabāt.

[78] *Baghdādī* 110. For an even stronger endorsement of Qurrat al-ʿAyn's status by the Bab see passages from a letter cited in *ZH* (331–34), where she is praised as "the proof for all" (*ḥujja alā al-kull)*, whose instructions are binding for all believers.

[79]*Baghdādī* 109–10. Of the Kāẓimaynī defectors, the author names five.

tary on *Sūrat al-Ḥamd* that is probably addressed to Bushr and his faction, the Bab confirmed his approval of Ṭāhira, at the same time urging the defectors to set themselves free of these "nonessential matters."[80]

The Bab also answered Mullā Aḥmad's inquiries. He tried not to alienate the zealous Babi for his criticism of Qurrat al-ʿAyn, yet he remained unreservedly praiseful of "the pure leaf." Approving even her claim of "being a proof of God," the Bab states: "Let none of those who are my followers repudiate her, for she speaks not save with evidence that have shown forth from the people of sinlessness [the Imams] and tokens that have radiated from the people of truth."[81] Even such strong endorsement of Qurrat al-ʿAyn did not dissuade Mullā Aḥmad from further criticism. Nor did her conciliatory gestures and offers of cooperation bridge the widening ideological gap between the two.[82]

Apparently it was during this period that Qurrat al-ʿAyn, who seems not to have been apprehensive of the recurrence of anti-Babi feeling, first invited the Uṣūlī mujtahids to an open debate and, when none responded to her challenge, called upon them to stand with her for mubāhala.[83] Naturally the mujtahids were not prepared to risk an encounter that in the eyes of the public would lend credibility to a heretic. An angry mob, outraged by her open vilification of sharīʿa and incited by the Shaykhi elements, attacked Rashtī's house and arrested her. She was detained in the house of Ḥājjī Mahdī Kamūna.[84] To prevent any further disturbance the Ottoman governor of the city interfered, making her release contingent on a ruling from Baghdad.[85] Defending herself, she explained that she advanced no claim save that of learning. "Assemble the doctors both Sunnī and Shiʿite, that we may confer and dispute, so the truth and falsity of either side, and the wisdom of both parties may be made apparent to all persons of discernment."[86]

While in temporary detention, she summoned Mullā Aḥmad for the last time. To him she clearly stated her intention to move to Baghdad, where she would "lift the taqīya and prove the veracity of the Ẕikr."[87] After some three days she was released, apparently on condition that she leave Karbalā' immediately.[88] The departure of Qurrat al-ʿAyn and her followers was a

[80]INBA no. 69, 127.

[81]*ZH* 333; trans. D. MacEoin "From Shaykhism to Babism" 207. For other passages and further discussion on the controversy see 206–7.

[82]*Lamaḥāt* citing Ḥiṣārī *ʿAqāid* 161–62.

[83]Samandar 347; *KD* I, 62.

[84]*Lamaḥāt* citing Ḥiṣārī *ʿAqā'id* 162. It is not inconceivable that Mullā Aḥmad also had a hand in the incident.

[85]*NK* 141; cf. *Tadhkirat al-Wafā'* 296–97.

[86]*NH* 272.

[87]*Lamaḥāt* citing Ḥiṣārī *ʿAqā'id* 162–63; cf. *NK* 141.

[88]Al-Baghdādī maintains that "she was sent to Baghdad by the order of vālī," who probably had decided on this as a result of Shaykh Muḥammad Shibl's intervention (*Baghdādī* 108).

victory for the Shaykhis, Babi conservatives, and Uṣūlīs alike, successfully frustrating the Babis' last chances for mass conversion in the Shiʿite centers of learning.

The news of Qurrat al-ʿAyn and the rumors about her "immoral" acts must have soon reached Qazvin and caused great anxiety for the Baraghānīs. In the face of "all the ado, incitement, and malicious defamation," Qurrat al-ʿAyn, in a letter to her father, defended herself: "I plead with you! This humblest of people is your daughter. You know her, and she has been brought up and educated under your supervision. If she had, or has, a worldly love, that could not have remained a secret to you. If you want to inquire into her affairs, God who holds the scale and is the remover of the veils would testify for her."[89] She reminds him that last year her "declaration of the word of God" received no response except "accusations of disbelief and paganism [*shirk.*]." Whoever ignores the "glorious cause of the great living Imam," she warns, will see all his deeds end in sorrow and will no more be saved than the Khārijites who rejected ʿAlī. She criticizes the literalists' trivial preoccupation with the appearance of the Bab's words and urges upon her father to heed their spirit instead. She ends on a note of sympathy and concern: "Dear father! So many times when I visit the holy shrine of the Imam, may peace be upon him, in the flood of my tears I pity you and pray for you that perhaps you may be saved."[90] Other letters reecho the same urgency and admonition: "If you fail to recognize the cause, there will be no benefit for you in all your acts of devotion."[91]

It is not known how Mullā Ṣāliḥ received his daughter's letters, but they could have been instrumental in convincing the Baraghānīs to dispatch a special envoy, Mullā Muḥammad Ḥammāmī, to Iraq to bring back the rebellious Qurrat al-ʿAyn.[92]

Residing in the house of Shaykh Muḥammad Shibl in Baghdad, Qurrat al-ʿAyn again renewed her activities. The public was curious to learn about the woman who was proclaiming the advent of a new revelation.[93] Her rising fame in Baghdad faced the vālī, Najīb Pāshā, once more with the Babi menace and the risk of factional unrest if she continued preaching. Mullā Ḥasan Gauhar, who apparently carried some weight with Najīb Pāshā, helped arouse his concern.[94] But this time, contrary to Basṭāmī's case, in-

[89]*ZH* op. 314, facsimile of Qurrat al-ʿAyn's letters to her father. For reasons unknown, Māzandarānī, ignoring repeated references in the letters to Qurrat al-ʿAyn's father, identifies her uncle Mullā Muḥammad Taqī as the addressee.

[90]Ibid.

[91]Ibid.

[92]Wardī *Lamaḥāt* II, 171; cf. *SAMB* 274–76.

[93]Shibl Baghdādī also provided three other quarters: one for Qurrat al-ʿAyn's women companions, one for men, and the third for her teaching (Wardī *Lamaḥāt* II, 168 citing Ṣāliḥī *Qurrat al-ʿAyn*).

[94]Wardī *Lamaḥāt* II, 168–69.

stead of calling for a tribunal Najīb simply summoned Qurrat al-ʿAyn and questioned her about her beliefs. The details of this interrogation are not known, nor are the names of those present, but it appears that Najīb, and possibly his aides, could find no convincing evidence of her heretical or even non-Islamic beliefs.[95] Perhaps it was for the purpose of further investigation by the chief muftī that he then ordered her transfer to the house of Shaykh Maḥmūd Ālūsī, the leading man in Basṭāmī's trial, in the meantime referring her case to the Sublime Porte.[96] The pasha's milder response to the renewal of Babi activities may have resulted from the fact that in the case of Basṭāmī, the only definite result of the trial was the tacit victory of the Shiʿites, who wisely caused Basṭāmī's banishment from the ʿAtabāt. To put a woman on trial was unprecedented, and particularly ill advised when neither the evidence nor the laws of apostasy, as applied to women, showed any prospect of a definite verdict.[97] If there was a trial, Qurrat al-ʿAyn's oratory might work in her favor and publicize her views even further.

Ground for these speculations can be found in a passage attributed to Ālūsī, who seems, in passing a verdict on Qurrat al-ʿAyn, to reserve his praise for her:

> She was one of those who followed the Bab after the death of Rashtī, but later even disagreed with Rashtī in many matters such as on the question of the religious duties [*takālīf*]. Some people alleged that Qurrat al-ʿAyn believes in the total abolition of all the duties but I do not see any truth in this though she stayed in my house about two months and so many discussions took place between me and her in which there was no taqīya or apprehension. Verily, I saw in her such a degree of merit and accomplishment as I rarely saw in men. She was a wise and decent woman who was unique in virtue and chastity. I have referred to my discussions with her on another occasion; if one became aware of them, one would realize that there is no doubt about her knowledge. It became obvious to me that Bābīya [Babis] and Qurratīya [Qurratis] are the same. They believe that the time for five times obligatory prayers is over and that revelation is unsuspended and therefore the Perfect [Man] will have [further] revelations. However, these revelations are not canonical but are for explanations of what has been previously laid down. This is similar to the ideas of the Sufis. . . . Some of [the Babis] are vigilant at nights with prayers and devotion. They are [all] opposed to the Ithnā ʿAsharīs and they denounce them and avoid them.[98]

[95] *Samandar* 347–48.

[96] *Baghdādī* 109; cf. *NH* 272.

[97] According to both Ḥanafī and Shiʿite law, a woman must be imprisoned until she again adopts Islam. See *Shorter EI*: MURTADD.

[98] Cited in *KD* (I, 64) and partly in *Kashf al-Ghiṭāʾ* (94–96), both without clear reference to the title of Ālūsī's work. However, it is possible that this quotation is taken from Ālūsī's incomplete and unpublished work *Nahj al-Salāma ilā Mabāḥith al-Imāma*, his last work written in 1270/1854 (MS no. B 4/678 in Library of *Awqāf ʿĀmma*, Baghdad), in which according to *Ālūsī Mufassiran* (125) he discussed Shaykhīya, Rashtīya, Bābīya, and Qurratīya with impartiality. For a slightly different version of Ālūsī's comment cited in Maḥmūd Shukrī al-Ālūsī *Mukhtaṣar al-Tuḥfat al-Ithnā ʿAsharīya* (Cairo, 1373/1953) see Wardī *Lamaḥāt* II, 169–70.

The Sunni scholar's tone implies that during Qurrat al-ʿAyn's stay in his house there was an exchange of views. (Perhaps it was this sympathetic dialogue that prompted the Bab, some months later, to write to Ālūsī calling upon him to recognize his mission.[99]) Apparently while Qurrat al-ʿAyn was in the house a gathering was held there, attended by the Sunni ʿulama. The details of such an assembly are not known.[100]

A number of observations can be made on the above passage. Most striking is that, even in the presence of the muftī who had condemned her coreligionist Mullā ʿAlī Basṭāmī to death, Qurrat al-ʿAyn unhesitatingly declared her allegiance to the Bab. Equally noteworthy is the fact that her compelling propagation of her views caused one of the most revered Sunni scholars of the time to admire her intelligence and make some unbiased assessment of her beliefs. Third, Ālūsī's remarks contain an apparent contradiction, for although the Sunni mufti did not detect that Qurrat al-ʿAyn abrogated all duties, he reports her rejection of the obligatory daily prayers. This suggests that Qurrat al-ʿAyn still regarded the Bab's claim, as Ālūsī puts it, a "noncanonical revelation" complementary to the previous Islamic revelation. This the muftī identifies as similar to the Sufi doctrine of the Perfect Man.

Two months later orders came from Istanbul for Qurrat al-ʿAyn's deportation. The contents of the Porte's instruction are not known, but Ālūsī gives some insight into the situation that finally persuaded the pasha to arrange for her banishment and that of her followers: "And thus appeared in that time [early 1260s/1844] a group of Shiʿite extremists [ghulāt] calling themselves Bābīya. . . . All those who possess wisdom would testify to their blasphemous beliefs. A group of them would have remained in Iraq if it had not been for the endeavors of Najīb the vālī, about whose zeal and religiosity there is a consensus. He humiliated them, may God support him, and disturbed their assembly and became furious at them, may God be content with him, and upset their activities, may God repay him with his benevolence."[101] The muftī's remarks sound contradictory to his praise for Qurrat al-ʿAyn if one does not consider his apprehension of the Babi threat, for the removal of which he praises Najīb Pāshā so effusively. The second passage was written in circa 1265–1266/1849–1850, when the Babi uprisings in Iran made it appropriate for Ālūsī to make public his resentment at the resurgence of Shiʿite extremism lest it spill over to Iraq, whereas the first passage regarding Qurrat al-ʿAyn was probably written in 1270/1861–

[99]Part of this tablet cited in Jadīd al-Islām *Minhāj al-Ṭālibīn* (342–46). A direct quotation in *Kashf al-Ghiṭā*ʾ (96, taken from a servant in Ālūsī's house) reports Ālūsī as saying, "O Qurrat al-ʿAyn! I swear by God that I share in thy belief. I am apprehensive, however, of the swords of the family of Uthmān," should be regarded as mere exaggeration. At most, it may point out Ālūsī's sympathetic approach to her views.

[100]Only *Samandar* (348–49) reports of a certain Ḥakīm Masīḥ, a Persian Babi of Jewish descent, who saw Qurrat al-ʿAyn in Baghdad conversing with the Sunni ʿulama.

[101]*Rūḥ al-Maʿānī* VII/22, 39. Other references can also be found in this work to Ālūsī's discussions with Qurrat al-ʿAyn.

1862, two years after the final defeat of the movement and Qurrat al-ʿAyn's execution.

Ḥājjī Mullā Muḥammad Ḥammāmī, the envoy dispatched by Baraghānīs, met Qurrat al-ʿAyn in the house of Ālūsī, and discussed with him the release of the "chaste women" whom he argued had been "overwhelmed with satanic temptations." He reported to her uncle Mullā Muḥammad Taqī, that Ālūsī agreed to intercede with the vālī for Qurrat al-ʿAyn's release. He also stated that Qurrat al-ʿAyn was particularly angry at Gauhar, presumably for his mischievous calumny. Moreover, he observes: "The entire nobility and the ʿulama of Baghdad greatly respect her and confer on her highest praises. Whatever has been relayed to you and rumored [about her] is slander and fabrication."[102]

En Route to Qazvin

Sometime in Rabīʿ al-Thānī 1263/March 1847, accompanied by an Ottoman officer, Qurrat al-ʿAyn was sent to Khānaqīn on the Persian border. With her traveled about thirty of her followers. As Ālūsī rightly observed, her deportation was the end of the effective presence of the Babis in the ʿAtabāt for the next five years, before the arrival of Bahāʾullāh and his party, who were exiled to Iraq toward the middle of 1269/1853. Her journey from Baghdad to Qazvin took about three months, in the course of which she passed through Karand, Kirmānshāh, and Hamadan before reaching Qazvin toward the middle of 1263/1847. All along the way, accompanied by her Persian and Arab disciples, led by Mullā Ibrāhīm Maḥallātī, Mullā Ṣāliḥ Karīmāvī, and Shaykh Sulṭān Karbalāʾī, she publicly advocated the new Ẓuhūr[103] and in numerous gatherings entered into discussions with mujtahids, Sufis, and notables. In spite of her disappointments in the ʿAtabāt, she seems to have been in high spirits throughout and did not flinch from the violent reactions that she and her followers frequently encountered during the journey.

In Karand, a large Kurdish village west of Kirmānshāh, and later in Ṣaḥna, halfway to Hamadan, Qurrat al-ʿAyn received a warm welcome from the Ahl-i Ḥaqq population, who reportedly even gave her their allegiance.[104] The enthusiasm shown by the villagers and their chiefs is a clear indication of the potential support in rural sectarian communities of western Iran, communities that were often harassed and persecuted[105] but main-

[102]Wardī *Lamaḥāt* II, 172, citing Ṣāliḥī *Qurrat al-ʿAyn* 45–47. See also *Samandar* 349 and *SAMB* 274–76 for references to Ḥammāmī and his recollections.

[103]The news of a number of her Arab and Persian mullas who accompanied her as far as Hamadan, and some to Qazvin, are given in *Baghdādī* (111) and *Nabil* (273).

[104]*Baghdādī* 111, 116. As a result of Qurrat al-ʿAyn's preaching, some of the inhabitants remained Babis for some time.

[105]The militant mood of the people of Karand can be seen in their successive clashes with

tained their messianic spirit untouched by the religion of the large cities. The fact that Qurrat al-ʿAyn declined the offer of the people of Ṣaḥna to participate in the march—all twelve thousand of them[106]—signals her unwillingness to organize the popular backing into anything beyond preliminary conversion. At this stage, the main issue was the "conveyance of the word."

Upon arrival in Kirmānshāh, Qurrat al-ʿAyn set up a center of public preaching, where her disciples recited the Bab's commentary on *Sūrat al-Kauthar* and she answered queries and challenged the ʿulama to public debate.[107] In the early part of her forty-day stay, she conversed with the governor of the province, Muḥibb ʿAlī Khān Mākū'ī,[108] his wife, and some notables. Her activities seem to have created enough excitement among the population, predominantly Kurdish with a strong Ahl-i Ḥaqq presence, to alarm the ʿulama and oblige the chief Uṣūlī mujtahid Shaykh ʿAbdullāh Kirmānshāhī (one of Bihbahānī clan, great-grandson of Āqā Muḥammad Bāqir and grandson of Muḥammad ʿAlī, the famous Ṣūfī Kush[109]), to plead with the governor for expulsion of the troublesome heretic and her more than thirty Arab and Persian disciples. The governor willingly transmitted to the mujtahid the two options Qurrat al-ʿAyn proposed: to debate or to stand for mubāhala.[110] Obliged to choose between the undesirable and the irrational, Shaykh ʿAbdullāh wrote for assistance to Qurrat al-ʿAyn's father and uncles. With ʿAbdullāh's advice, the dispatched party from Qazvin, in collaboration with the chief officer of the local garrison, a rival of Muḥibb ʿAlī, bypassed the governor and ordered the troops to storm the dwellings of Qurrat al-ʿAyn and her retinue by night. The Babis were battered, their belongings were looted, and some twenty-five of the Arab followers were detained while she and her close companions were forced out of the city.[111] By the governor's intervention the next day, the detainees were released and their belongings recovered, but Qurrat al-ʿAyn, humiliated by the harrowing treatment, declined to return to the city.

Despite family pressure demanding her hasty return to Qazvin, Qurrat al-ʿAyn was determined to carry her public declaration to Hamadan. At her request, and presumably through the good offices of the influential women

---

government forces. On one occasion in the early 1840s, the governor of Kirmānshāh, Ḥājjī Shakī Khān, because of his "misconduct, immorality, excessive killing, numerous rapes," as well as "difference in religion," was killed in Karand along with two hundred of his troops (*RS* X, 316).

[106]*Baghdādī* 116.

[107]Ibid. 111–13.

[108]Muḥibb ʿAlī must have been already informed of Qurrat al-ʿAyn through the Persian agent in Baghdad. For his account see above, chap. 5.

[109]*TAS* II/2, 774.

[110]*Baghdādī* 113. According to this source, in 1263/1847 Qurrat al-ʿAyn declared the purpose of her mission to be the conveyance of "the glad tiding of the advent of the promised Qā'im, the compassionate lord."

[111]Ibid. 114–15.

of Qaraguzlū nobility,[112] the governor, Khānlar Mīrzā Iḥtishām al-Daula, a brother of the shah and an effective member of the princely ruling elite[113] convened a gathering of local divines and scholars representative of all tendencies[114] in his quarters.[115] The invited parties chose Ḥājjī Mīrzā ʿAlī Naqī Hamadānī, better known as Jannat ʿAlī Shāh, son of Mullā Rižā Hamadānī and head of the Kauṯar ʿAlī Shāhī suborder,[116] as their spokesman. Speaking from behind a curtain, Qurrat al-ʿAyn set three rules for disputation: reliance on prophecies; abstinence from smoking—a strict Babi prohibition; and most significantly, adopting decent language and avoiding abuse and execration.[117] She unequivocally reiterated the basic themes of the early Babi doctrine: everlasting divine guidance, the progressive cycle of revelation, need for a new creed to meet the challenge of a changing age, and the legitimacy of the Bab as the sole recipient of divine inspiration.

Ḥājjī Mīrzā ʿAlī Naqī can hardly have missed Qurrat al-ʿAyn's underlying mystical themes, yet her messinic dynamism must have appeared too far-fetched. Reports on his response range from sheer dismissal to, more plausibly, tacit conviction.[118] Whatever his reaction, it must have been difficult for him, as a mystic of some repute, to challenge her main argument concerning the necessity of divine revelation. The omnipresence of the Perfect Man, the pivotal tenet of Sufism,[119] was turned upside down by words of an eloquent preacher to relay messianic consequences far beyond what any contemporary Sufi, even the celebrated Nūr ʿAlī Shāh, the spiritual guide of ʿAlī Naqī's father, had dared to entertain, even in the privacy of his own mystical experience.[120] But if ʿAlī Naqī hesitated to quarrel with Qurrat al-ʿAyn, others did not—a mujtahid named Mullā Ḥusayn[121] struck up a violent argument with her. The governor angrily reproached the intruder and dispersed the meeting.

Later, when Mullā Ibrāhīm Maḥallātī presented a risāla by Qurrat al-ʿAyn to the chief mujtahid of the city, the raʾīs al-ʿulamāʾ,[122] he was

[112]The above-mentioned Zubayda Khānum and the wife of Rustam Khān Qaraguzlū.

[113]Bāmdād *Rijāl* I, 473–76.

[114]Like many Persian cities, Hamadan was divided along sectarian lines. Though Uṣūlīs were in ascendancy, the city was still regarded as one of the last footholds of declining Akhbārīs (*RPAC* 30), of whom a good number turned to Shaykhism (*KD* 117). The Sufis, most significantly Niʿmatullāhīs and Khāksārs, were also represented.

[115]Ishrāq Khāvarī *Tārīkh-i Amrī-yi Hamadān* 4; cf. *KD* I, 117–18.

[116]For his account, among other sources see M. Darakhshān *Buzurgān va Sukhansarāyān-i Hamadān* 2 vols. (Tehran, 1341 Sh./1962) II, 80–81 and cited sources.

[117]Ishrāq Khāvarī *Hamadān* 4.

[118]Ibid. 1–4; cf. Gulpāyigānī *Kashf al-Ghiṭāʾ* citing Mullā Riża Hamadānī, son of ʿAlī Naqī.

[119]For Niʿmatullahīs, like many other later Shiʿite orders, the *quṭb al-aqṭāb* (pole of the poles) deputizes the Mahdi.

[120]See above, chap. 2.

[121]Possibly Sayyid Ḥusayn Rażavī Hamadanī, son of ʿAbd al-Ṣamad (*TAS* I/2, 596).

[122]Possibly Sayyid ʿAbd al-Ṣamad Rażavī Hamadānī, who according to Ṭihrānī (*TAS* II/2, 738) was the religious judge of Hamadan (*TAS* I/2, 596).

showered with abuse, severely battered, and then thrown out.[123] Perhaps fearing an attack by the mujtahid's supporters, Qurrat al-ʿAyn took refuge in the house of a sympathetic Jewish rabbi, Ḥākhām Ilyāhū, whose son, Ilʿāzār, had already been attracted by her passionate preaching.[124] The next day she moved to the Qaraguzlū-owned village of Shavarīn, on the outskirts of Hamadan, and from there accompanied her relatives to Qazvin. Only a few of her adherents, mostly Persian, followed her. The rest were ordered by Qurrat Al-ʿAyn to return to the ʿAtabāt.[125]

As in other cities, the mujtahids of Kirmānshāh and Hamadan emerged as the chief adversaries of the Babis. Once they sensed government hesitation, they had no reservations about resorting to intimidation and violence. Curiosity aside, the local authorities' main motive for allowing religious debates was to remind the ʿulama that if need be they could be challenged on their own grounds; a prospect that the ʿulama found particularly repellent. The chief mujtahids of both Kirmānshāh and Hamadan rejected invitations to debates. The people of the cities were curious bystanders, leaving the lūṭīs, the ṭullāb, and occasionally the troops to implement the will of the mujtahid. For Qurrat al-ʿAyn, still a believer in dialogue and debate, these were days of mixed feelings—short-lived hopes and growing frustration. A year later (1264/1848), in Tehran, she was sufficiently disappointed with the prospects of "accomplishing the proof" and "delivering the word" to advise Sayyid Yaḥyā Vaḥīd Dārābī to abandon the old policy and demonstrate his commitment by action instead.[126] This recommendation was in anticipation of the Bab's open declaration of Qā'imīya. It aptly grasped the changing mood within the Babi community in the wake of the Badasht conference and armed resistance in Ṭabarsī. In a famous ode, she had already expressed

[123] *Baghdādī* 117.

[124] Ishrāq Khāvarī *Hamadān* 3, citing a historical tract by Yuḥanā Ḥāfiẓī. Except for Ḥakīm Masiḥ, a Persian Jewish physician who saw Qurrat al-ʿAyn at a gathering of the ʿulama in Baghdad and later became a Babi-Bahā'ī (*Samandar* 348), the above-mentioned Ilʿāzār (Lālizār) is the earliest-known Jewish convert. Another Jewish physician, Ḥakīm Īlīyā, was an eyewitness to the Hamadan debate. His son Ḥakīm Raḥīm (Raḥamīm) apparently became a Bahā'ī. It is difficult to believe that the above-mentioned Il'āzār is the same Mullā Lālizār Hamadānī who helped Gobineau in his translations of Kant into Persian (*RPAC* 101) and possibly the Bab's Arabic *Bayān* into French (Momen, *Religions* 18–19). Gobineau makes no reference to Qurrat al-ʿAyn's visit to Hamadan. For other early Jewish converts in Khurasan see below, chap. 8. Qurrat al-ʿAyn's appeal to non-Muslim minorities—Jewish or Ahl-i Ḥaqq—once again illustrates the way the early Babis considered the new revelation not simply as a Shiʿite or Muslim affair.

[125] Except for accompanying women, *Baghdādī* counts twelve of her chief adherents who followed Qurrat al-ʿAyn to Qazvin. The remaining twenty-odd adherents returned to the ʿAtabāt. *NK* maintains that Qurrat al-ʿAyn's ultimate destination in her journey was Tehran, where she intended "to caution" Muḥammad Shāh, presumably of the consequences of the Bab's incarceration in Mākū. Under family pressure, she canceled her plan.

[126] *Tadhkirat al-Wafā'* 306.

an urge to hear the "tale of woe" to which, she declared, she would give her passionate assent:

> The effulgence of thy face flashed forth and rays of thy visage arose on high;
> Then speak the word, "Am I not your Lord?" and "Thou art, thou art!" we will all reply.
> Thy trumpet-call "Am I not?" to greet how loud the drums of affliction beat!
> At the gates of my heart there tramp the feet and camp the hosts of calamity.[127]

Captivity, Revolt, and Death

The arrival of Qurrat al-ʿAyn in Qazvin, accompanied by her brothers,[128] after three years of residence in Iraq, again exposed her to family tensions and doctrinal conflicts, which had sharpened since her departure. She had left as a Shaykhi devotee and returned as a Babi leader. During the two troubled months of her stay in the city (Shaʿbān-Ramaḍān 1263/July–September 1847) she was drawn into a series of events that led ultimately to the assassination of her uncle Mullā Muḥammad Taqī by a militant Babi and her subsequent flight from Qazvin—events that had their roots not only in the quarrels within the Baraghānī family, but also in the ongoing factional disputes in Qazvin.

The divisions within the family seemed inevitable now that both sons of Mullā ʿAbd al-Wahhāb Qazvīnī, Mullā Hādī and Mullā Muḥammad ʿAlī, Marżīya's husband, had become devotees of the Bab. Mullā ʿAbd al-Wahhāb himself remained safely distant but nevertheless sympathetic to the Bab.[129] The vacuum that was created in Qazvin after his death in 1263/1847,[130] further weakened the Shaykhi constituency. Mullā ʿAlī Baraghānī, Qurrat al-ʿAyn's Shaykhi uncle, "confessed submission" to the Bab and testified to "the veracity of the Great Remembrance," but publicly remained noncommital.[131] Being a mystic and a scholar, his clerical influence in the

[127] *MSBR* 349–51, trans. by E. G. Browne. "Am I not your Lord" is from Qur'ān VII, 171. *Samandar* (349; cf. *Nabil* 81–82) dates this poem to the time prior to the Bab's open declaration of Qā'imīya. *TH* (III, 318) ascribes it to Ṣuḥbat Lārī, a contemporary of Qurrat al-ʿAyn (d. 1251/1835 in Shiraz), who is said to have been acquainted with the Bab's family (Ḥ. Nuqabā'ī *Bishārāt-i Kutub-i Āsimānī* [n.p., n.d.] 268–70). However, the mystical tone of the poem does not appear to be far from Qurrat al-ʿAyn's outlook.

[128] *Baghdādī* 117. One of them presumably is the same ʿAbd al-Wahhāb, whom Nicolas (*SAMB* 273) considers Qurrat al-ʿAyn's brother.

[129] *ZH* 304; cf. *Qazvīnī* 495.

[130] *RS* X, 345. At the age of eighty-three, in Najaf.

[131] *ZH* (309–10) cites a testimony of recognition by Mullā ʿAlī in which the author, in the cryptic language common to Shaykhis, acknowledges the Ẕikr and counts himself among his subordinates. In the end he wishes a hasty "relief" *(faraj)* for the "weak" who are anticipating the events of 1260. Both *QU* (19) and *Samandar* (344) refer to his Shaykhi and then Babi

city seems to have been overshadowed by that of his elder brothers. Qurrat al-ʿAyn's father, deeply affectionate toward his daughter, was hopelessly trying to close the widening breach in the family by maintaining a middle course, while her elder uncle, Muḥammad Taqī, now in his eighties, aided by his son Mullā Muḥammad (Qurrat al-ʿAyn's deserted husband), were publicly denouncing the Shaykhi creed, its initiators, and its recent offshoot: the Babi heresy. The relation between the two elder brothers was further complicated over the issue of Qurrat al-ʿAyn's divorce. She strongly resisted Mullā Muḥammad's demands that she return to his living quarters (presumably to maintain a closer watch over her activities). She told her father, tormented by the submission of his articulate daughter to a "Shīrāzī lad," that she considered her marriage unilaterally dissolved, for the practice of the Prophet dictates that the bond of marriage with unbelievers, among whom she counted her husband, must be broken without divorce.[132]

Their polarity of convictions found an even greater resonance in the ongoing disputes in Qazvin. Over the past decades Qazvin had experienced a trilateral clerical rivalry, with Muḥammad Taqī Baraghānī and Muḥammad Taqī Qazvīnī Imām Jumʿa as the chief actors and ʿAbd al-Wahhāb as the eventual loser, resulting in a gradual decline of the Shaykhi constituency. Theoretical debates among the mujtahids served as a pretext for a more material conflict, however, which owed much to the city divisions and possibly the Ḥaydarī-Niʿmatī hostility (known in Qazvin as *lūṭī bāzār).*[133]

Mullā ʿAbd al-Wahhāb (1180–1263/1766–1847), from Dār al-Shafāʾ neighborhood in the Darb-i Kūshk quarter, was a respected, well-established mujtahid who studied under the important ʿulama of the first generation. But ʿAbd al-Wahhāb's religious control over Qazvin seems to have been threatened by Muḥammad Taqī Baraghānī, who gradually broadened his sphere from the quarters of Dīmaj and Qumlāq in the west of the city toward the center, where the city's two major mosques, the Jāmiʿ mosque and the Shāh mosque were located.[134] Control of the central mosques and advancement toward the office of imām jumʿa were Muḥammad Taqī's objectives. The office provided a larger public audience and greater attention from the government; and even more important, the mosques held extensive endowments, both in land and property, which were almost solely under the control of the trustees.[135]

In the years after his return from the ʿAtabāt, Muḥammad Taqī Baraghānī

---

beliefs, which are also confirmed by his own letter to the Bab cited in INBA no. 98, XXIII, 110–11. The Bab himself mentions him as one of his followers in *al-Ṣaḥīfa al-Rābiʿa fi Sharḥ Duʿāʾihi fi Zamān al-Ghayba,* INBA no. 60, XIII, 150–54.

[132] *NK* 142; cf. *Nabil* 273–76.

[133] Malcolm *History of Persia* II, 6. For Qazvin's quarters in the nineteenth century as it is specified in *Majmūʿa-yi Nāṣirī* see Muḥammad Gulrīz *Mīnū Dar yā Bāb al-Janna, Qazvīn* (Tehran 1337 Sh./1958) 391–404, 759–60.

[134] Gulrīz *Bāb al-Janna* 393–94.

[135] For endowments of the Jāmiʿ mosque see *Bāb al-Janna* 514–21.

was well received by ʿAbd al-Wahhāb, who even helped him to establish himself in the city.[136] But this did not hinder his drive for power. The anecdotes related by Tunkābunī indicate that in his legal and religious judgments his private interests frequently held sway over his judicial impartiality.[137] By presiding over substantial monetary disputes, of which he received a large percentage for expenses and legal charges; by collecting alms, expropriating the revenues of the unmanaged endowments, taking possession of the crown lands or directly participating in commercial activities, Muḥammad Taqī soon amassed a large fortune. In less than two decades the erstwhile ṭalaba, who in his youth knew such poverty that frequently he could not even afford to eat decently for several days, became one of the richest ʿulama of Iran. The mosque and madrasa of Ṣāliḥīya in the Qumlāq quarter, one of the largest mosques in Iran, and the mosque of the neighboring Dīmaj quarter, built in the 1250s and 1260s (1830s-1840s) at the Baraghānīs' (Muḥammad Taqī and Muḥammad Sāliḥ) expense, were signs of their prosperity.[138]

Muḥammad Taqī was determined to outstrip any rivals in gaining a superior religious leadership, even at the cost of denying the ijtihād of his own brother.[139] At one stage, contrary to Uṣūlī doctrine, he ruled for the prohibition of the Friday prayer. However, when the opportunity arose he overruled his own fatwā and in the absence of another rival, Sayyid Muḥammad Taqī Qazvīnī, conducted the Friday prayers of the city.[140] Gaining the office of imām jumʿa and the trusteeship of the Jāmiʿ mosque, over which he was in dispute with Qazvīnī, was doubtless to control the mosque's extensive endowments, a portion of which included shops and houses located in the Qumlāq quarter, where the Baraghānīs were already in control.[141] In the early 1850s after the death of all important mujtahids of Qazvin, the office of imām jumʿa was finally transferred to Mullā Muḥammad, son of Muḥammd Taqī Baraghānī.

Muḥammad Taqī's opposition to Shaykh Aḥmad Aḥsāʾī in due course gave rise to recurrent condemnation of Shaykhis by the mujtahids of the ʿAtabāt and Iran.[142] One reason for his hostility is particularly relevant to the internal conflict in Qazvin. In the mid-1820s, Muḥammad Taqī Baraghānī, who regarded himself as the chief mujtahid, and the most knowledgeable, of the ʿulama of Qazvin, invited Aḥsāʾī to stay in his house, but Shaykh Aḥmad preferred to reside in the house of ʿAbd al-Wahhāb.[143] The

[136]*QU* 22.
[137]Ibid. 22–23.
[138]*Bāb al-Janna* 91, 557, 574–77.
[139]*QU* 34.
[140]Ibid. 29. The Uṣūlīs generally considered it lawful to perform Friday prayers in the absence of the Imam.
[141]*Bāb al-Janna* 516.
[142]See above, chap. 1.

rejection was more humiliating than a simple breach of social etiquette. As in Yazd and Isfahan, in Qazvin the arrival of an eminent scholar in the house of a local mujtahid was regarded as a status symbol and added to his public esteem. Receiving support from Aḥsāʾī was a compliment that cannot be underestimated. On another occasion Sayyid Muḥammad Ṭabāṭabāʾī, better known as Mujāhid, a mujtahid of great repute from Najaf, elected to stay in ʿAbd al-Wahhāb's house.[144] As Tunkābunī reported, the mujtahids of Iran were generally supportive of ʿAbd al-Wahhāb. In a lengthy legal dispute that involved both mujtahids, Muḥammad Taqī, contrary to all his colleagues in Iran and the ʿAtabat who upheld ʿAbd al-Wahhab's rulings, adamantly insisted on his own controversial verdict.[145] Moreover, ʿAbd al-Wahhāb's relation with the Qajar rulers was more congenial than Muḥammad Taqī's. Fatḥ ʿAlī Shāh in particular revered ʿAbd al-Wahhāb as one of senior mujtahids of Iran, perhaps in the hope of balancing the power of Mīrzā-yi Qumī and Shaftī. In contrast, Muḥammad Taqī's earlier rapport with Fatḥ ʿAlī Shāh soon turned into rancor. During Muḥammad Shāh's reign, the chief minister, Āqāsī, had ample reasons to be annoyed with Muḥammad Taqī's anti-Sufi provocations. As part of his clerical policy of reducing the mujtahids' influence, had it not been for the shah's personal intervention Āqāsī would have banished the Baraghānīs from Iran, or at least collected the long-overdue taxes on Muḥammad Taqī's extensive agricultural holdings.[146]

It was not therefore unpredictable that Mullā Muḥammad Taqī Baraghānī try to boost his popularity, recover his lost favor with the Qajars, and ameliorate his isolation in the clerical community by adopting a controversial stand against the Shaykhi leader. The initiation of the anti-Shaykhi takfīr served as a pretext for recovering ground against pro-Shaykhi ʿAbd al-Wahhāb. By extension, such condemnation guaranteed financial awards, an incentive that lured many Uṣūlīs, both in the ʿAtabāt and in Iran, to his camp. In an important letter to Mullā ʿAbd al-Wahhāb, Aḥsāʾī refers to Muḥammad Taqī's fear of losing his economic and religious privileges: "The devil incited him [Mullā Muḥammad Taqī] to declare that what I say is blasphemy, and I am blasphemous and Ākhūnd Mullā ʿAbd al-Wahhāb is blasphemous, and others in his faction helped him. Thus came persecution and hardship, and he who was the leader among them, may great misery be upon him, was anxious for the specie coming from Iran and India."[147] In the condemnation of the Shaykhis, the leadership of Muḥammad Taqī and

[143] *Fihrist* I, 155–56, and *Shaykhīgarī va Bābīgarī* 36–37, citing ʿA.ʿA. Kayvān Qazvīnī *ʿIrfān Nāmih* (Tehran, 1348/1929).

[144] *QU* 24.

[145] Ibid. 22–23.

[146] Ibid. 27–28.

[147] Text of the letter cited in *Fihrist* I, 157. See also II, 242, no. 56.

many other mujtahids was at stake, and with it their control over endowments, religious courts, alms, madrasas, and seminarians.

Even before the arrival of Qurrat al-ʿAyn, the introduction of the new Babi element had already brought Shaykhi-Uṣūlī tension to a new pitch. Mullā Jaʿfar Qazvīnī relates that when the writings of the Bab first reached Qazvin, Mullā Jawād Valīyānī (then still a supporter of the Bab) was exhilarated by the news, exclaiming: "Now the time has arrived for us to take our revenge on Baraghānī." The next day, he ascended the pulpit and proclaimed the Advent of the Bab, calling for the support of believers. After forty days, in company with a large group of followers, he set out for the ʿAtabāt.[148] Mullā ʿAlī Baraghānī, Abd al-Wahhāb Qazvīnī's two sons, Muḥammad ʿAlī and Muḥammad Hādī, and others joined the Babi ranks. Among them there were three from Rudbār region: Mullā Taqī, Mullā Jaʿfar (the author of an important narrative), and Mullā ʿAbd al-Ḥusayn Qazvīnī. Shaykh Muḥammad Nabīl Qazvīnī, a student of Rashtī who after his studies preferred to continue his father's trade, was another important early Babi.[149] Conversions in Qazvin were chiefly due to the efforts of Mullā Jalīl Urūmī but also Mullā Yūsuf Ardabīlī, and Qurrat al-ʿAyn.[150]

These conversions were bound to provoke a reaction from Muḥammad Taqī's quarter. The physical punishment of ʿAbd al-Jalīl by order of the powerful mujtahid began a new phase of hostility in Qazvin. The small but active band of Babis, who were now recruiting among merchants, traders, and artisans, in the city was determined to retaliate.[151] Residing in her father's inner quarter, Qurrat al-ʿAyn, was meanwhile pressured by her family to disown her Babi followers. Her repeated pleas with the remaining ʿAtabāt adherents to leave Qazvin and join other Babis in Tehran and Khurasan, were reluctantly obeyed.[152]

The heightening of tension seems to have been related to rumors of Qurrat al-ʿAyn's alleged unchastity and immoral conduct. The stories originated in Qurrat al-ʿAyn's strong views on the need for abrogation of Islamic law particularly on the issue of unveiling in public. Most sources agree that before the Badasht conference, she never unveiled publicly, and some even doubt that she did so on that occasion.[153] Her conversations with men were often conducted from behind a screen.[154] In gatherings of the Babi adepts in Karbalā', however, as indicated earlier, she felt secure in casting off her

148 *Qazvīnī* 473–74.
149 For his account see *Samandar* 15–54.
150 For the early Babis of Qazvin see *Samandar* 54–370; *ZH* 301–91; and *Qazvīnī* 447–52, 473–88, 494–98.
151 See below, chap. 8.
152 *Baghdādī* 118–19.
153 Muʿīn al-Salṭana 5–6.
154 *Baghdādī* 109; Wardī *Lamaḥāt* 156.

facial veil.[155] Such an act, or even hints of its desirability, was considered an anathema of the gravest nature. As we were told by a contemporary observer, facial unveiling in the presence of any male except members of the immediate family, even for the purpose of medical examination, was regarded as no less sinful than prostitution.[156]

Even if Qurrat al-ʿAyn had never unveiled in public, her controversial views on the Islamic sharīʿa and the very presence of the large body of male companions who followed her from Karbalāʾ to Qazvin were enough to arouse suspicion.[157] The allegations of Qurrat al-ʿAyn's unchastity and sexual liberty were widespread enough to reach the court chronicler, Sipihr, who rendered a wildly fictitious account of the "moonfaced" Qurrat al-ʿAyn and her relations with the "wandering Babis" long deprived of their homes and wives. Sipihr takes a prurient pleasure in reporting that Qurrat al-ʿAyn not only believed in unveiling but endorsed the marriage of one wife to nine husbands.[158] The Qajar chronicler goes on:

> She would decorate her assembly room like a bridal chamber and her body like a peacock of Paradise. Then she summoned the followers of the Bab and appeared unveiled in front of them. First she ascended a throne and like a pious preacher reminded them of Heaven and Hell and quoted amply from the Qurʾān and the Traditions. She would then tell them: "Whoever touches me, the intensity of Hell's fire would not affect him." The audience would then rise and come to her throne and kiss those lips of hers which put to shame the ruby of Rammān, and rub their faces against her breasts, which chagrinned the pomegranates of the garden.[159]

The pictoral details are figments of Sipihr's wild imagination. The sexual tone, however, is typical of the way Qurrat al-ʿAyn's wish to unveil was perceived.

Such allegations obviously were damaging to the Baraghānīs' reputation. Qurrat al-ʿAyn's above mentioned allusions to "slanderous defamation" and her denial of entertaining "worldly love" presumably refer to the accusations that horrified her relatives. Nevertheless her father does not seem to have believed the rumors, and indeed he may not have remained unmoved by his daughter's sincerity and fortitude. Even after the assassination of Mullā Muḥammad Taqī later that year, Mullā Ṣāliḥ was confident enough

[155]See above, this chapter. Also *KD* I, 110.

[156]Polak *Persien* I, 157.

[157]The defamation campaign of Mullā Aḥmad Ḥiṣārī and his allies in Karbalāʾ and his correspondence with the Shaykhis and non-Shaykhis of Iran and Iraq in defiance of Qurrat al-ʿAyn must have affected her reputation. See Wardī *Lamaḥāt* (II, 160–62, citing Mullā Aḥmad's *ʿAqāʾid*) and Shaykh Sulṭan Karbalāʾī *Maktūb* (*ZH* 245–59).

[158]*NT* III, 219.

[159]Ibid. 200. In his discussions with Gobineau, Sipihr again repeated, this time in a sarcastic tone, the allegations concerning the followers of Qurrat al-ʿAyn, who he believed were simply her lustful lovers (*RPAC* 180).

of his daughter's innocence to deny categorically the accusations of immorality brought against her by the imām jumʿa of Qazvin in a gathering of prominent ʿulama of the city. In response the sarcastic imām jumʿa mockingly read a verse: "No glory remains on that house / From which the hens crow like the cocks." Mullā Ṣāliḥ remained silent, tears running down his cheeks to his beard.[160] Bitter reproaches of this kind eventually forced him to emigrate from Qazvin and retire in the ʿAtabāt, where he died in 1283/1866.[161]

Mullā Muḥammad Taqī seems to have been even more humiliated by the infamous rumors. This was another reason for him to react ever more harshly and intensify his attacks on those who he believed had brought ill repute to his house.[162] His criticisms and harassments however, were to cost him his life. In Ramaḍān 1263/August–September 1847, the Babi sympathizer Mīrzā ʿAbdullāh Shīrāzī struck a deadly blow to Muḥammad Taqī's throat during the dawn prayers, in his own mosque. The assassin, a Shīrāzī baker (later camoflaged under a new name, Mīrzā Ṣāliḥ), was outraged by Muḥammad Taqī's open enmity toward the Shaykhis. In reply to Mīrzā ʿAbdullāh's personal query concerning Aḥsā'ī, the mujtahid had declared: "Him as well as his followers I regard as the very embodiment of error."[163] This reply is given by most sources as the chief motivation for the assassination, but it is not unlikely that Mīrzā ʿAbdullāh was assisted in the act by Babi accomplices. Āqā Muḥammad Hādī Farhādī, a militant merchant from Qazvin who was already involved in an earlier incident, cannot be ruled out.[164] However, all the evidence suggests that if there was a premeditated scheme, it was without Qurrat al-ʿAyn's knowledge. In spite of her later endorsement of militant action in Badasht, it is highly unlikely that she would have sanctioned any act of violence against a member of her own family.

The assassination of Mullā Muḥammad Taqī cost the Babis dearly. This was the earliest symptom of a militant mood prevailing over an active minority frustrated by the growing hostility, for which the ʿulama were held responsible. The shift from "the conveyance of the word" to active defiance, symbolized in the assassination of a high-ranking mujtahid, set the Babis on an irreversible path that eventually led them to the holy war of Ṭabarsī. It was the Babi rank and file who preceded the leadership in this transformation, and gradually forced it to the point of no return.

Immediately after the murder of Muḥammad Taqī, most well-known Babis of Qazvin, then one of the largest groups in Iran, were rounded up. A

[160] *Samandar* 75.
[161] *TAS* II/2 661.
[162] *Nabil* 276; cf. *Samandar* 354–56.
[163] *Nabil* 276.
[164] *Muʿīn* (244–46) names two accomplices: Āqā Muḥammad Hādī Farhādī and Sayyid Ḥusayn Qazvīnī, a Shaykhi. *QU* (57) also speaks of few individuals. All other sources insist on Mīrzā ʿAbdullāh's personal initiative.

wave of anti-Babi persecution followed. Mullā Muḥammad, who considered the killing a Babi conspiracy led by Qurrat al-ʿAyn, organized the joint forces of the ṭullāb, most notoriously Mullā Muḥsin the Babi Killer (Bābī Kush), and the governor's agents to raid the houses of the suspected Babis and to otherwise harass them.[165] Qurrat al-ʿAyn herself, together with her maid Kāfiya and another woman, was arrested and interrogated in the government house.[166] The severe punishment of the accused apparently persuaded the assassin, Mīrzā ʿAbdullāh, to surrender. The evidence he provided to support his confession was not convincing enough for Mullā Muḥammad to release the detainees.[167] By insisting on the punishment of all alleged accomplices, the vengeful mujtahid hoped to eliminate the menace of the Shaykhi-Babi heresy once and for all.

In Tehran, where the accused were sent for further investigation, after much bargaining with the shah, Āqāsī, and the minister's rival, Naṣrullāh Ṣadr al-Mamālik Ardabīlī,[168] Mullā Muḥammad secured the death penalty for Shaykh Ṣāliḥ Karīmī, an Arab follower of Qurrat al-ʿAyn, in revenge for the murder of his father. He was executed in Sabzih Maydān square.[169] Ḥājjī Asadullāh, the elder of the Farhādī family, also perished in detention.[170] Warning Ṣadr al-Mamālik that any clemency toward the Babis would "unloose a flood of calumny against those who are the chief repositories of the teaching and principles of our faith" and "embolden the enemies of Islam" to shatter the structure of clerical power, Mullā Muḥammad persuaded the monarch to leave the rest of the Babi detainees in his charge.[171] Upon their return to Qazvin, contrary to earlier promises, two of the Babi activists—Mullā Ibrāhīm Maḥallātī, a learned convert from the ʿAtabāt who apparently had challenged Mullā Muḥammad Taqī on an earlier occasion, and Mullā Ṭāhir Shīrāzī, another follower of Qurrat al-ʿAyn—were put to a long and cruel death in front of his house.[172] In spite of the government's pronounced unwillingness to permit the outbreak of violence, thereby involuntarily playing into the mujtahids' hands, those earliest ex-

[165]Vivid accounts of the persecutions appear in *Samandar* (21–30 [under the biography of Mīrzā Muḥammad Qazvīnī], 73–76, 91–100, 354–56). After his murder, Mullā Muḥammad Taqī came to be known in Shiʿite literature as the "Third Martyr" (*Shahīd Thālith*), named after the two medieval Shiʿite martyrs from the ʿulama class.

[166]*Samandar* 357–58; cf. Muʿīn al-Salṭana 8–9.

[167]*Samandar* 358–59; *Nabīl* 277–78.

[168]For his biography see Bāmdād *Rijāl* IV, 336–37.

[169]*NK* 143–44; *Nabīl* 277–80; *Baghdādī* 120. According to *NK* (143), Mullā Maḥmūd, the tolerant mujtahid of Tehran, refused to ratify the death sentence. For Shaykh Ṣāliḥ see *ZH* 261. According to an enigmatic reference in *Nabil* (271), Qurrat al-ʿAyn was "so profuse in her praise of Shaykh Ṣāliḥ that a few suspected him of being equal in rank to Quddūs."

[170]*Nabil* 281–82. For the Farhādīs see below, chap. 8.

[171]*Nabil* 281.

[172]*Samandar* (111–13) cites a gruesome eyewitness account of the executions in Qazvin: After a severe beating with sticks, Shaykh Ṭāhir, half burned, was dragged along and stoned to death by the mob. Mullā Ibrāhīm was first struck on the head with a hatchet by a passing carpenter, then stoned and burned.

ecutions marked the ominous start of an agonizing era of Babi killing that reached a climax in the executions of 1268/1852 and continued thereafter. The Qazvin executions, typical of many in later years, were carried out by the mob, incited by religious leaders. Either to accumulate rewards for the hereafter or to discharge their deep hatred for advocates of nonconformity and dissent, the participating crowd performed an act that was sanctified by mujtahids and increasingly tolerated by the state.

The adventurous Mīrzā ʿAbdullāh, however, survived and was bribed out of Tehran detention, only to be slain two years later in Ṭabarsī.[173] Qurrat al-ʿAyn, only barely cleared of the charges against her, was ordered by Mullā Muḥammad to be confined in his inner quarters. Shortly after, a perilous escape to Tehran set her free not only from the horrors of her birthplace, to which she never returned, but also of her father's house, where she was fearful of being poisoned by Mullā Muḥammad's female agents.[174] In Tehran, under the protection of Mīrza Ḥusayn ʿAlī Nūrī, Bahā'ullāh, the influential Babi in the capital, she spent several months in hiding in and out of the city.[175] Toward the middle of 1264/1848, following the general call for the Babis to assemble in Khurasan, she left Tehran and attended the Badasht gathering, where she played a major role in determining the movement's future.[176]

The assembly of Badasht was the culmination of Qurrat al-ʿAyn's Babi career. Convinced of her own mission and free from family ties, she was more than ever determined to press home to the Babi audience her vision of religious independence and political revolt. The gathering also registered a new momentum in the history of the movement. The rising tides of persecution, highlighted by the Bab's captivity and the growing isolation imposed on the Babis by their opponents, gave rise to a new spirit of defiance. The Bab's call on his followers to gather in Khurasan, presumably in anticipation of the long-awaited Insurrection, was an implicit acknowledgment of this spirit.[177]

The conference was held between late Rajab and mid-Shaʿbān 1264/ June–July 1848 in the hamlet of Badasht, east of Basṭām, on the Khurasan-Mazandaran road. The eighty-one participants, mostly Babis of Khurasan,

[173]He took refuge in the house of the Babi notable Riżā Khān Sardār (*Nabil* 287) and later in the house of Bahā'ullāh (*Samandar* 366). He is presumably the same Mīrzā ʿAbdullāh who saved Qurrat al-ʿAyn in the incident of Niyālā in 1264/1848 (*Nabil* 299). *NK* (143, 189) confirms his death in Ṭabarsī. For his justification of the assassination see *Samandar* (359, 361).

[174]*Samandar* 362. For further details on her escape see below, chap. 8.

[175]Ibid. 364–66; *Nabīl* 286–87; Malik Khusravī *Shuhadā-yi Amr* 190–91.

[176]The assembly of Badasht, though covered by most Babi sources, remains shrouded in ambiguity. *Nabil* (292–300) and *NK* (145–54) are both remarkable for their efforts to explain the radical conduct of Qurrat al-ʿAyn. *NH* (281–83); *RPAC* (180–84); *SAMB* (277–87); *KD* (127–31) among others add little to our knowledge. Their attempts to put the events in a logical sequence are not always successful. *ZH* (109–12) provides some new data.

[177]See below, chap. 9.

Mazandaran, and Qazvin, camped for three weeks in orchards on the hamlet's outskirts. The growing unrest in Mashhad had driven Quddūs and his companions out of the city, forcing the wandering Babi group to hold its meeting en route at a location chosen purely by chance, where Qurrat al-ʿAyn and other Babis traveling to Khurasan met other Babis returning from that province. Mullā Ḥusayn's absence from Badasht became increasingly significant in the course of the debates.[178]

If the choice of the location was spontaneous, the issues that made such a gathering urgent had for long troubled the eager participants. This was the first time that a mostly prominent group of the Babis could review—and as it turned out heatedly debate—a range of questions essential to the identity and the future strategy of the movement. Chief in the unwritten Babi agenda was the plight of the Bab, now incarcerated in a remote castle in Azarbaijan. There was an unchallenged consensus as to the binding duty of the Babis to rescue their spiritual leader. But any effort in this direction required an answer to a more pressing question concerning the Babis' future course of action. Moderation and prudence in the face of mounting hostility, radical Babis argued, could lead only to further suffering. Yet the final Insurrection against the forces of oppression would materialize only if the Qāʾim made his advent unequivocally apparent. This in turn raised questions as to the Bab's precise claim, and, even more crucial, the nature of his mission. Was the Bābīya merely an effort to rejuvenate Islam's inner truth? Or did it go beyond to establish a revelatory cycle altogether independent of Islam?[179]

Questions of such magnitude were bound to uncover strong differences of opinion within an embryonic body of converts whose loyalty to the founder of the movement was not yet translated into a consensus on the identity of his proposed creed. Moreover, the ideological polarization evident in Badasht could not have remained untouched by the equally agonizing problem of the movement's leadership and hierarchical order. The Bab had lately promoted Mullā Ḥusayn to the rank of gateship and authorized him to lead the Babi forces into concerted action. But such delegation of power did not relieve the need for a charismatic leader while the prophet of Shiraz was absent from his flock. Both Qurrat al-ʿAyn and Quddūs were obvious candidates, and both were keen to register their self-avowed leadership.

It was only to be expected that Qurrat al-ʿAyn, who had already challenged the Babi conservatives of the ʿAtabāt, would emerge as the chief representative of the radical tendency. Her antiorthodox positions became ever more clear when, in a symbolic act of defiance, she removed her veil in the middle of her speech to the Badasht gathering; an act that turned some

[178]For the events in Mashhad preceding Badasht see *Nabil* (288–92) and *Tārīkh-i Mīmīya* (Browne Or. MSS. F.28(9), 1–10). Mullā Ḥusayn's reasons for staying behind are not entirely clear. Undeterred by the threats of the chief of the police, it is possible that he was still hoping to raise Babi recruits among the people of the city.

[179]*RPAC* 183–84 and *SAMB* 277–81.

away from the movement forever and caused agony and despair to others. One Iṣfahānī zealot cut his own throat. Unrepenting, Qurrat al-ʿAyn proclaimed to the gathering: "Our days are the days of interregnum. Today all religious obligations are abrogated and such acts as prayer, fasting, and salutation [to the House of the Prophet] are futile. When the Bab conquers the seven kingdoms and unites different religions, he will bring a new sharīʿa and entrust his Qur'ān to the community. Whatever new obligations he ordains would then be compulsory to the people of the earth. Thus burden not yourselves with the worthless."[180] The abrogation of Islamic sharīʿa, Qurrat al-ʿAyn argued, was to be complemented with an active endeavor to remove the forces of disbelief and corruption. "I am the word that the Qā'im will utter," she claimed, "the word that shall put to flight the chiefs and nobles of the earth."[181]

With little hesitation in airing her views, Qurrat al-ʿAyn was able to win over some of the more liberated participants, but at the expense of isolating others. Accusing her of "indiscreetly rejecting the time-honored traditions of the past"—charges already branded on her in the 'Atabāt—a majority of the bewildered Babis turned to Quddūs.[182] The rise to prominence of the Bab's young disciple was no accident. Earlier, in Mashhad, Mullā Ḥusayn had displayed exceptional reverence for Quddūs, presumably with the Bab's prior consent, and in effect treated him as a spiritual lieutenant to the captive prophet. Taking sides with the sharīʿa-minded, Quddūs criticized Qurrat al-ʿAyn's radicalism, even denouncing her as "the author of heresy" and chastising her supporters as "victims of error."[183] This rejection of her doctrinal innovations reflected the misgivings of a number of prominent Babis present (including Muḥammad Hādī and Muḥammad ʿAlī Nahrī, whose wife, Shams al-Ḍuḥā, had already fallen under Qurrat al-ʿAyn's spell).

The doctrinal controversy, now transformed into a power struggle, was not relieved by Qurrat al-ʿAyn's open challenge to her critics. Referring to Quddūs as "a pupil" whom the Bab sent to her to "edify and instruct,"[184] she rebuked him not only for having failed to raise the banners of Babi revolt in Mashhad but for his pietistic intransigence. On one occasion, she interrupted his prayers, sword in hand, declaring: "Wrap up this spectacle, the time for prayer and liturgy is over. Now is the time to prepare for the battlefields of sacrifice and dedication."[185] Later, defending herself against

[180]*NT* III, 239. Further on, Sipihr attributes to Qurrat al-ʿAyn recommendations of sexual promiscuity and communistic beliefs—ancient charges common to most Islamic antiheretical literature. His allegations when Gobineau questioned him in 1865 remain unabated (*RPAC* 180).

[181]*Nabil* 296.

[182]Ibid. 293.

[183]Ibid. 297.

[184]Ibid.

[185]*ZH* 325.

charges of blasphemy and the threat of punishment, she reminded her outraged opponents, perhaps sarcastically, that as believers in Islamic sharīʿa they must bring her, a woman heretic, back to the true path of religion only by the word, not the sword. It was therefore incumbent on them to prove her errors with arguments.

In the course of a debate requested by Qurrat al-ʿAyn, however, it was she who managed to convince her chief rival, Quddūs. Reiterating with passionate eloquence her antinomian stance, she tried to show the doctrinal weaknesses of the opposing party. Subsequently, in a daring act that perhaps challenged Quddūs' meekness in the face of hostilities instigated by the Babis' archenemy, Saʿīd al-ʿUlamāʾ (the mujtahid of Bārfurūsh), she perhaps tried to show symbolically that her radical commitments surpassed her male critics'. Dressed in men's clothing, unveiled and mounted, she waved her bare sword and cried: "Down with Saʿīd al-ʿUlamāʾ and his followers!" The Babis responded: "Death to them all!" She repeated: "Down with this villain of all the villains!" They replied: "Sudden death to all of them!"[186] No more effectively could she acquire the Babi mandate, thus outmaneuvering Quddūs and silencing her critics. Other symbolic gestures by her supporters—discarding prayer rugs and breaking the prayer seals (equating them to idols)—were to further convey to the Babis the termination of the era of pietistic devotion and longing for otherworldly recompense.

To his followers' dismay, Quddūs himself began to lean toward Qurrat al-ʿAyn's positions, an apparent curious shift not fully explicable by the enigmatic tone of the sources. The existence of a preconceived plan between the two leaders to introduce to the traditionally minded Babis the innovations of the new religion is too farfetched.[187] The differences were real. What could have tilted the balance in Qurrat al-ʿAyn's favor, however, was Quddūs' gradual disillusionment with acquiescence and suffering, which had inundated his earlier writings. The experience of Ḥajj, the persecutions of Shiraz, Kirman, Bārfurūsh, and most recently Mashhad, where once again he was forced to retreat, must have already eroded his conciliatory stance. Qurrat al-ʿAyn's challenge only brought home the inevitability of armed struggle and its corollary, the unequivocal pronouncement of the independent Babi faith.

The role of Mīrzā Ḥusayn ʿAlī Nūrī, Bahāʾullāh, who after 1847 emerged as representative of a nascent tendency within the movement, should not be overlooked.[188] He tried, with some success, to bring about an uneasy understanding between the two conflicting factions. The earliest signs of an emerging third approach within Babism—that of a break with the past but

[186]Ibid. 325–26. Quoting an eyewitness account.
[187]One example of such treatment is *SAMB* (280–83).
[188]For Bahāʾullāh see below, chap. 8.

nonviolent moderation in its implementation—can be seen in his very mediatory initiative.

The most obvious outcome of the Badasht debate was perhaps the prevalence of Qurrat al-ʿAyn's views. They were undoubtedly decisive to the future of the movement. The Bab's claim to Qāʾimīya and the open pronouncement of a new prophetic cycle, as expressed in the *Bayān* and during the Tabriz tribunal, only reasserted her advocacy of religious renewal.[189] The Babi resistance in Ṭabarsī and other places proved the inevitability of confrontation. The gathering also brought to the surface the conflict between the traditional revivalists and the innovative revolutionaries; a conflict deeply rooted in the sociocultural diversity of the Babi structure.

No overall course of Babi policy was achieved beyond the acknowledgment of an urgent need for collective action. As a first pragmatic step in this direction, one can surmise, a march to Mazandaran was undertaken under the joint leadership of Qurrat al-ʿAyn and Quddūs, in order to establish a Babi foothold in his home town, Bārfurūsh. This venture however, ended in total disaster when the Babis were raided by a band of villagers in the nearby Nīyālā. The local mulla who led the aggressive crowd was apparently outraged by the sight of the unveiled Qurrat al-ʿAyn sitting inside a huda next to Quddūs and chanting poems out loud, together with her companions. The assailants must have seen the Babi party as no more than a group of libertine infidels worthy of death. Even for the Babis, who witnessed with amazement, perhaps horror, the unrestrained conversation between a daring woman and her male traveling companion, perhaps even her unspoken affection for him, it was hard not to perceive the prevailing climate of emancipation as "abuse of liberty" and excesses from "bonds of moderation."[190] Reportedly, after hearing the news of Badasht, Mullā Ḥusayn vowed that if he had been present he would have punished the transgressors with sword.

The incident of Nīyalā, the first fatal clash between the Babis and a frenzied crowd, ended in several deaths and the dispersion of the confused Babi party in different directions. Quddūs escaped in diguise to Bārfurūsh, while Qurrat al-ʿAyn, accompanied by Bahāʾullāh, headed for his home region, Nūr. It remained for Mullā Ḥusayn and his companions to complete the march to Mazandaran.

After Badasht, between the end of 1264/1848 and the beginning of 1266/1850, Qurrat al-ʿAyn wandered in Mazandaran. For a brief period during Ramaḍān 1264/September 1848 she was in Bārfurūsh in the house of pro-Babi Mullā Muḥammad Ḥamza Sharīʿatmadār, and even preached to his congregation.[191] Later, presumably before the arrival of the Babi

[189] See below, chap. 9.
[190] *Nabil* 298.
[191] *ZH* 326–27.

party, she went into hiding in the Nūr region, slipping from village to village. For about a year she took refuge in a farmhouse on the outskirts of the village of Vāz, south of Āmul, where she was the guest of Āqā Naṣrullāh Gīlārdī.[192] She was hoping ultimately to join the Babis in Ṭabarsī,[193] but her hiding place was discovered by government secret agents and she was arrested on charges of collaboration in the assassination of her uncle. Reportedly, she had already been listed by the government of Mīrzā Taqī Khān Amīr Kabīr as a wanted Babi rebel.[194] She was brought to Tehran in Rabiʿ al-Awwal 1266/January 1850, and after an interview with Amīr Kabīr[195] and a brief audience with the young monarch, Nāṣir al-Dīn Shāh,[196] was sentenced to imprisonment in the upper chamber of the house of Tehran's chief of police, Maḥmūd Khān Kalāntar, for the rest of her short life.

Even in detention in Kalāntar's house, Qurrat al-ʿAyn did not relinquish contacts with the Babis of Tehran, and continued to win new converts among the women of the capital.[197] Writing in Qazvīnī dialect on grocery wrapping paper, using a pen made out of broom twigs and ink made of juice from green herbs, she used go-betweens to send out secret messages.[198] In late 1268/1852, after the unsuccessful attempt of the Babis on the life of the shah, her fate was eventually decided. She was first interrogated for several days by two senior mujtahids, Mullā ʿAlī Kanī and Mullā Muḥammad Andarmānī.[199] What presumably could not have been decided on the ground of religious prohibition of the execution of female heretics was eventually settled when in Dhū al-Qaʿda 1268/September 1852 the mujtahids, apparently complying with government's wishes, passed a death sentence.[200] Remaining unrepentant throughout her interrogation, she refused their offer of clemency in exchange for recantation. Shortly after, she was brought in the middle of the night to Bāgh Īlkhānī, where she was

[192]While in Nūr she gave her signet ring to a woman to be eventually sent to Quddūs in Ṭabarsī. The verse on the signet ring read, "Lord of Ṭāhira, remember her" (*rabb al-Ṭāhira adrikhā*) (*ZH* 327).

[193]Malik Khusravī *Shuhadā-yi Amr* 204–5.

[194]Ibid. 206. His host, Āqā Naṣrullāh, was killed on the spot by government agents.

[195]*Samandar* 368.

[196]It has been reported that Nāṣir al-Dīn Shāh, after seeing Qurrat al-ʿAyn, had said, "I like her look, leave her, and let her be" (*TN* 313, reported by Mīrzā Yaḥyā Ṣubḥ Azal to E. G. Browne).

[197]*Tadhkirat al-Wafā*ʾ 309. Of those who met her in the custody of Kalāntar, the poetess Shams-i Jahān, daughter of Muḥammad ʿAlī Mīrzā, recorded her interview in her *maṣnavī* cited in Bayżāʾī *Shuʿarā-yi Bahāʾī* III, 179–80; cf. *KD* I, 309–11.

[198]*Samandar* 84, 368; *ZH* 328.

[199]*SAMB* 449.

[200]Mīrzā Āqā Khān Nūrī, the chief minister and the co-architect of the massacre of the Babis in Tehran, was himself on shaky ground. His wife, his sister, and the other women of his harem were accused of being Qurrat al-ʿAyn's sympathizers (Muʿīn al-Salṭana 10; cf. Polak *Persien* I, 353, and Malik Khusravī *Shuhadā-yi Amr* III, 191). It is not therefore unlikely that Nūrī himself, being anxious to clear himself of any charges, pressured the mujtahids to come up with Qurrat al-ʿAyn's death sentence.

strangled in secret by a drunken bodyguard. Her body was dumped in a shallow well at the back of the garden.[201]

Qurrat al-ʿAyn's ideas and actions were decisive in the course of the movement toward independence and the conscious break that occurred with the dominant norms of Islam. In this respect she ranks equal to the Bab himself, at times even more determined than him and other leading Babis to register her rejection of the prevailing order. Having come from a clerical background, she revolted against traditions keenly revered by members of her own family. Exceptionally interesting is the way the messianic legacy, chiefly through the Shaykhi school, led to a full transformation of her Shiʿite outlook. She is perhaps the embodiment of what she calls a soul "enamoured with torment" (*shīftih-yi balāʾ*).[202] Such an outlook only made sense in a messianic setting where "proof of wisdom" and "intuitive endeavor" are to culminate in a historical cognition. Although one may partly agree with Browne that Babi thought was essentially Shiʿite in its weltanschauung and that Babi history was a reenactment of the idealized Shiʿite past,[203] at the core of this preoccupation with suffering and martyrdom lay the seed of a dynamic future; a drive aptly encapsulated in the Babi maxim, "The time cycle is in progression." Qurrat al-ʿAyn's abandonment of the Islamic sharīʿa was the logical outcome of such an assumption. For her, cognition was a human responsibility that must be materialized in action. Abrogating prayers, whatever the theological justification, symbolized a divorce from the old notion of salvation through devotion. Instead, action was to be interpreted as "the conveyance of the word" and ultimately the establishment of the new Babi dispensation. Once the increasing pressure proved to Qurrat al-ʿAyn, as to the other Babis, that action by the sword was unavoidable, martyrdom became the ultimate realization of the faith.

Qurrat al-ʿAyn has sometimes been portrayed by posterity as a champion of women's rights. In her writings, however, she makes no direct reference to the position of women in her society. It is unlikely that she was ever aware of a suffragist movement or other trends in contemporary Europe. Indeed, her entire world view differed fundamentally from the Western notion of women's emancipation as it first appeared in Iran after the Constitutional Revolution. Her outlook and motivations were primarily religious and remained so. But inevitably, being a Babi leader of high caliber with unconventional ideals, Qurrat al-ʿAyn experienced dual disadvantages and deprivations, not only as an "outspoken heretic" but as a "rebellious

[201]Accounts of Qurrat al-ʿAyn's last days and her execution appear in *Nabil* (621–28) and *SAMB* (446–52), both recording the recollections of Kalāntar's wife. The *Times* of 13 Oct. 1852 also refers to the execution of the "Fair Prophetess of Kazoeen [Qazvin]" (see Momen *Religions* 132). Polak (*Persien* I, 353) claims to have been present at the event. Lady Sheil calls slaying Qurrat al-ʿAyn a "cruel and useless deed" (*Glimpses* 281).

[202]From a *ghazal* cited in the centennial volume *Qurrat al-ʿAyn* 25.

[203]*The Literary History of Persia* IV, 197.

woman." Both religious institutions and social norms sanctified women's subordination with stringent and jealously observed rules, infringements of which were severely punished. For Qurrat al-ʿAyn not to be conscious of her disadvantages, and even more not to react to them, would have been impossible. Frustrations in her family life and persecutions in her Babi career both served as impetuses for inspirations that she transposed into a religious paradigm; what she terms "the state of primal truth." By assuming the symbolic role of Fāṭima, she envisaged a feminine model—a "primal truth," as she called it—that substantially differed from the role assigned to Faṭima in the Islamic, more particularly Shiʿite, tradition as the daughter of the Prophet, the wife of ʿAlī, and the mother of Ḥasan and Ḥusayn; the role that guaranteed her sanctitude by lineage, marriage, and motherly love. Qurrat al-ʿAyn's Fāṭima was one of independent will and action. The leadership she assumed in the ʿAtabāt and later in Badasht was the realization of this paradigm.

All the way back to Rābiʿa al-ʿAdawīya, the ninth-century Baṣran to whom Qurrat al-ʿAyn probably looked as another role model, the heterodox movements were often a breeding ground for women of vision and talent. This association should not be interpreted merely as an outlet for discharging frustration with the socioreligious order however. Qurrat al-ʿAyn's religious convictions were almost inseparable from her feminine consciousness. The only solution she saw, for women and men alike, was a break with the past, and as the first step, a deliberate infringement of religious norms. To find her in the forefront of Babi radicalism and an advocate of progressive revelation is only logical. Her initiation into the Letters of the Living, on the other hand, was an acknowledgment of her equal place with men in the first unit of the ideal Babi order of All-Beings.

8

The Shaping of the Community: Merchants, Artisans, and Others

In 1262/1846, Ḥājjī ʿAbd al-Karīm Bāghbānbāshī, a Qazvīnī merchant of some substance, read to a gathering of Shaykhis a letter from his son, Muḥammad Mahdī, in Isfahan. In this letter, to which he had attached a booklet containing extracts from the writings of the Bab, Muḥammad Mahdī informed his father of the loss of merchandise during a journey to Bombay: "Five thousand tūmāns' worth of silk that belonged to us, to my uncle, and to others, was totally sunk in the sea. Divers and rescue workers tried to salvage it, but with no success. However, God granted us an unexhaustible treasure of which not a particle will be lost if we consume till the Final Day. Here I send it to you to benefit and let others benefit without fearing of its exhaustion."[1] Mullā Jaʿfar Qazvīnī, who was present, relates that after reading the letter the weeping ʿAbd al-Karīm complained, "How on earth can this booklet provide money for the expenses of my family?"[2]

Muḥammad Mahdī's letter sums up the moral attitude of many Babi converts of younger generation who, sometimes contrary to the wishes of their fathers, found in the new movement a message of salvation and moral renewal. For Muḥammad Mahdī material loss in business became unimportant compared to his spiritual gains when he visited the Bab in Isfahan. Yet the new venture in which he had invested his faith and his means proved to be no less hazardous than the perils of the sea. Four years later he fought and died in the fortress of Ṭabarsī, together with other Babi mullas, merchants, artisans, and peasants who, like himself, looked upon the merchant of Shiraz and his mulla lieutenants as sacred models of moral perfection.[3]

[1] *Qazvīnī* 473–74.
[2] Ibid. 474.
[3] Ibid. 494; *Samandar* 158–59.

The Changing Economy

In the early years of the movement, parallel to the conversion of the Shaykhi ʿulama, some progress was also made in converting members of the merchant class (tujjār). The conversion of the tujjār, predominantly from the lower ranks but also including some big merchants, and following them the conversions of members of the guilds *(aṣnāf)*—shopkeepers, wholesalers, and artisans—created the second largest group of believers after the ʿulama in the early Babi community. The Bab's emissaries also gained ground among other urban and rural groups: civil servants and local functionaries, court renegades and ex-officials on the fringe of the state establishment, Sufis and wandering dervishes in the cities, and small landowners, seminomadic chiefs, and peasants, in villages and small agricultural towns. The nationwide network that was thus created in a short span of time, often on the pattern of the existing Shaykhi network, witnessed to the effectiveness of the Babi message to remold groups with heterogenous origins and persuasions into a dynamic community with a common loyalty and sense of purpose. At no other juncture in modern Persian history, at least since the suppression of the Nuqṭavīs in the early seventeenth century, had a religious movement of protest achieved such a degree of popularity and social mobilization. After the failure of the Babi attempt, it took another half-century before a mass mobilization of any significance could unite people under the joint aegis of the ʿulama, the merchants, and the lay intellectuals.

In the conversion of merchants and the affiliated guilds at least two factors may be traced. First is the intercommunal bonds between this group and the ʿulama. The mutual links between the madrasa and the bazaar, a familiar feature of Persian urban life, were reasserted in a new context. Unlike their non-Babi counterparts, the Babi merchants did not look to the Babi ʿulama merely for protection and guidance, but rather tended to see themselves as equal partners in a joint undertaking. Secondly, for converts with similar professional backgrounds and similar ascetic and mystical preoccupations, Sayyid ʿAlī Muḥammad Shīrāzī presented a role model to whom they could look for moral inspiration, and with whose message they could identify themselves.

A number of questions arise concerning the motives of the merchants and guilds, and the nature of their involvement. To what extent did economic activities or occupational connections contribute to the shaping of the new affiliation? Bearing in mind the economic climate of the time, it is vital to see in the new movement a reflection of the growing aspirations, or the dissatisfaction, of the business community. To what extent did awareness of economic stagnation serve as an impetus for the renewal of messianic interests? Equally important are the aspirations of the converts and the way conversion affected the material well-being and social status of the new believers.

Addressing these questions tests the validity of those interpretations that stress the role of the merchants and artisans, often merely as a mechanical response to the prevailing economic condition, almost to the exclusion of all other elements. To assume that the professional identity of these groups, and consequently the fluctuations in their economic fortune, were the only mobilizing forces behind their participation in the movement would be an oversimplification. Yet there is enough evidence to suggest that the parallel between the rise of the movement and changes in the economic conditions of the time was no coincidence.

The majority of tujjār converts had been brought up in families that were traditionally engaged in commerce. Either by means of inheritance or collaboration with senior members of the family, the new generation enjoyed the respect and social standing that usually accompanied a reasonable amount of capital in the form of the family business. Toward the end of the 1830s and in the early 1840s, when most of these younger tujjār, including the Bab himself, became active, the economy was in the throes of major change, particularly in sections of urban industry and trade.

In the early nineteenth century, a rapid increase in the volume of foreign trade, followed by a degree of internal security under the Qajars, brought about a commercial revival. The opening of new trade routes and a rise in the consumption of the home markets made it possible for the merchants to reemerge as an influential group. Thanks to their professional bonds, internal and international contacts with colleagues at home and abroad, financial credit and relative immunity from government intervention, they seem to have prospered throughout the first third of the century.[4] By the mid-1830s, however, although commerce was still expanding, Persian merchants found themselves surrounded with unexpected difficulties, chiefly due to an increasing European presence. During this period the full impact of Western commercial domination, in terms of industrial superiority as well as political presence, made itself felt for the first time. Communities of local traders, craftsmen, and those engaged in small-scale urban industries began to suffer the effect of foreign competition. The rapid rise in the volume of European imports made Iran not only less self-sufficient, but susceptible to fluctuation in international trade.[5]

Trade in the south, which up to then had flourished through ports of the

[4]Limited research has been carried out so far on the position of merchants in early Qajar Iran. Two examples are: G. Hambly "An Introduction to the Economic Organisation of Early Qājār Iran" *Iran* 2 (1964) 69–81 and A. K. S. Lambton "The Case of Ḥājjī ʿAbd al-Karīm: A Study on The Role of the Merchants in Mid-nineteenth Century Persia" in *Iran and Islam, in Memory of the Late Vladimir Minorsky* ed. C. E. Bosworth (Edinburgh, 1971) 331–60. See also W. M. Floor "The Merchants (*tujjār*) in Qajar Iran" *Zeitschrift der Deutschen morgenländischen Gesellschaft* 129 (1976) 101–35 and *Cities and Trade* xxxv-xl and cited sources.

[5]A. K. S. Lambton "Persian Trade under the Early Qājārs" in *Islam and the Trade of Asia* ed. D. S. Richards (Oxford, 1970) 215–44. See also G. G. Gilbar "The Persian Economy in the mid-19th Century" *Die Welt des Islams* 19 (1979) no. 1–4, 196–211.

Persian Gulf, had begun to stagnate by the end of the 1830s, mainly because of the competition of the northwestern route. The decline of the southern trade, owing also to the insecurity prevailing in the region, piracy in the Gulf, remoteness from the markets of central and northern Iran, and the incompatibility of the prices of imports, jeopardized the business of many southern tujjār, forcing them to seek other exporting alternatives.[6] By the 1840s the southern trade began to suffer a serious setback. The import of cotton fabrics in particular, which in the early 1830s amounted to about two-thirds of the volume of Persian Gulf trade, was reduced to one-seventh of the total by the late 1840s.[7]

The competition of the trade centers of the north was not the only reason for this decline. Southern merchants were also faced with trade restrictions and high tariffs imposed by the British in India, particularly with regard to the import of opium, tobacco, and wool. Reporting on the plight of Persian merchants, the British consul in Tehran, Keith Edward Abbott, emphasizes: "If some of the few exportable productions which Persia possesses continue to be prohibited as returns for what she takes from India, there is no doubt that increased difficulties will attend the future prosecution of the trade; indeed they are already beginning to be experienced without any other cause being assignable than the gradual exhaustion of the country under the partial state of commercial restriction abroad, and the continual drain upon her of the precious metals."[8]

The volume of the Baṣra-Baghdad trade with cities in western and central Iran underwent similar crises. In addition to the frequent Ottoman attempts to redirect commercial vessels to the Ottoman port of Baṣra rather than Persian Muḥammara, the insecurity on the western frontiers and the additional custom duty levied by the Baghdad government on exports to Iran[9] made it difficult for Persian merchants to operate successfully on this route.[10] Writing in 1843, Edward Burgess states that the Baghdad route is more competitive than any other trade route to Persia, yet due to a variety of obstacles such as the "disturbed state of the Arab tribes," which made the

[6]On the trade of southern Iran in this period sees Lambton's "Persian Trade" 235, 239; J. B. Kelly *Britain and the Persian Gulf (1795–1880)* (Oxford, 1968) 260–89, 343–53; Lorimer *Gazetteer* I/2, 1956–1959, 1976–1981; Issawi *Economic History* 85–91; and R. T. Olson "Persian Gulf Trade and the Agricultural Economy of Southern Iran in the Nineteenth Century" in *Modern Iran: The Dialectics of Continuity and Change* ed. M. E. Bonine and N. R. Keddie (Albany, 1981) 173–90.

[7]*Cities and Trade* 86–89 (on Būshihr and Shiraz), 79–85 (on Yazd, Kirmān, and Bandar ʿAbbās), and the relative appendixes provide an account of the southern trade in the late 1840s. For a comparison with the 1860s see L. Pelly, "Remarks on the Tribes, Trade and Resources around the Shoreline of the Persian Gulf" in *Transactions of the Bombay Geographical Society*, 17 (1864).

[8]"Report on Commerce" *Cities and Trade* 89.

[9]F.O. 195/237, no. 22, 15 May 1844, Rawlinson to Canning.

[10]An account of the trade of Baghdad and Muḥammara in the late 1840s appears in Abbott's "Report on Commerce" *Cities and Trade* 89–93.

river navigation "dangerous and uncertain" and disturbed frontiers between Iraq and Iran, it is very doubtful whether this trade can survive.[11] The long-drawn-out dispute between the Persian and Ottoman governments frequently disrupted the normal flow of trade. The Ottoman authorities lost no opportunity to exert a "forcible interruption in the commerce of Muḥammara,"[12] which served as a better alternative to Baṣra for long-distance merchants.

One evidence of these difficulties is revealed in the correspondence of Manūchihr Khān Muʿtamad al-Daula, the governor of Isfahan, Luristān, and Khūzistān. In March 1845 he reports to Tehran that as a result of the recent Ottoman attack on Muḥammara, some 200,000 tūmāns' worth of merchandise belonging to Persian merchants established in Iraq and Kirmānshāh was damaged and lost.[13] Shortly afterwards, Manūchihr Khān strongly objects to the measure taken by the Ottoman fleet in preventing the entry of commercial vessels to the port of Muḥammara and forcibly redirecting them to Baṣra.[14]

In Baghdad itself, the discriminatory treatment of the Persian tujjār by Ottoman authorities put an extra burden on those who were already suffering from the insecurity on both sides of the border. The negligence of the Persian representative in Baghdad, plus the shortcomings of the central government to raise the matter with the Ottomans, made the Persian tujjār even more susceptible. Rawlinson, the British consul in Baghdad, reports: "A strong feeling of dissatisfaction has long prevailed among the numerous and wealthy Persian community of Baghdad at the conduct of their national representative at this court. They allege, apparently with reason, that he is devoid of the local weight or influence necessary for the due vindication of the interest committed to his charge."[15]

The trade of northern and northwestern Iran, however, enjoyed greater prosperity. Thanks to the flourishing Russian trade through the ports of the Caspian, especially Bārfurūsh, Persian merchants as far inside as Kashan and Isfahan could export their products to Caucasus and beyond. But conclusion of the treaty of Turkamanchāy (1828) gave great commercial advantages to Iran's northern neighbor. As an outcome of Russian infiltration into Persian markets, by the late 1830s an increase had occurred in the volume of Russian imports.[16] More significantly, the reopening of the Tabriz-Tre-

[11]*Letters from Persia* 53.

[12]F.O. 60/114, no. 61, 28 May 1845, Sheil to Canning, enclosed in Sheil to Aberdeen, 3 June 1845.

[13]Manūchihr Khān Muʿtamad al-Daula, in reply to the inquiry of Comte de Meden (the Russian envoy) about the events in Muḥammara. French translation enclosed in F.O. 60/113, no. 25, 18 March 1845, Sheil to Aberdeen.

[14]F.O. 60/114, no. 61, supp. 3 June 1845, Manūchihr Khān to his agent in Tehran, translation.

[15]F.O. 195/237, no. 25, 29 May 1844 and 248/114, no. 28, 12 June 1844, Rawlinson to Sheil.

[16]In the period under consideration, some details appear in: Lambton "Persian Trade" 226–

bizond route in the mid-1830s made the volume of the European imports grow to a higher level.[17] Irregularities in the price of imported goods,[18] and the arrival of European entrepreneurs as well as colonies of Greeks and Armenians in Tabriz acting as agents and factors to the European manufacturers, however, threatened Persian traders, who feared a complete takeover by their privileged foreign rivals. A series of Persian bankruptcies in the early 1840s and futile protests by the Persian merchants were the outcomes of this unfair competition.[19]

Other economic problems contributed to the crisis as well. The constant drain of precious metals and the resultant scarcity of money, the rapid fall in the value of the tūmān contrasted by a rise in prices and a ravaging inflation, the gradual accumulation of a vast deficit in Iran's balance of payments, a decrease in the international demand for certain Persian export products, the exaction of new limitations on Persian exports by neighboring countries, and the implementation of the Anglo-Persian commercial treaty of 1841, which provided extra commercial advantages for British subjects and their protégés, all had deleterious effects on Iran's fragile domestic economy.

The amount of pressure exerted upon the economy, particularly in the sector of local manufacturers and local merchants involved in the distribution and export of their products, is most visible in the vulnerable textile industry. In the early 1830s, owing to the increased consumption of European goods, production of all sorts of Persian cloths declined in the domestic weaving centers. A considerable number of cotton-weaving workshops in Isfahan, Kashan, and other industrial cities, which had prospered in the earlier part of the century, were completely wiped out. A Russian regulation prohibiting the entry of silk piece goods into the Caucasus also contributed to the decline of silk weaving and other workshops dependent on their exports.[20]

By the mid-1840s, local manufacturers and distributors felt the full effect

---

28, 240–41; M. L. Entner *Russo-Persian Commercial Relations, 1828–1914* University of Florida Monographs, no. 28 (1965) chaps. 1 and 2, 1–38; F.O. Confidential Papers no. 136 (Persia): "Report by Consul Abbott of his journey to the coast of the Caspian Sea, 1847, 1848" in *Cities and Trade* 11–14 (on Bārfurūsh), 19–21, 39–40 (on Astarābād); and various other reports by Abbott including F.O. 60/117 on trade of Tehran and Tabriz. Also Issawi *Economic History* 142–46 and MacKenzie *Safarnāmih* 80–102, 185–95.

[17]C. Issawi, "The Tabriz-Trabzon Trade, 1830–1900: Rise and Decline of a Route" *International Journal of Middle East Studies* (1970), 18–27. Also *Economic History* 92–103.

[18]Lambton "Persian Trade," 241.

[19]F.O. 60/107, "Translation of the Petition from the merchants of Tabreez to the Prime Minister of Persia presented at Tehran in November 1844" enclosed in no. 16, 25 November 1844, Sheil to Aberdeen. Also F. O. 60/107, no. 13, 1 July 1844, Bonham to Sheil; and F.O. 60/117, no. 3, 31 March 1845, Abbott to Aberdeen. For the discussion on this subject see W. M. Floor "Bankruptcy in Qajar Iran" *Zeitschrift der Deutschen Morgenländischen Gesellschaft* 127 (1977) 61–76.

[20]On the Russian commercial and customs policy in the Caucasus and the effects of the frequent closing of the border between the 1820s and 1880s see Entner *Russo-Persian Commercial Relations* 21–25.

of this decline. The merchants of Kashan and Isfahan, who like their colleagues in Shiraz, Yazd, or Tabriz had been alarmed by the prospect of bankruptcy and loss of business, could do little more than express their discontent in the form of petitions and delegations to the state authorities, who were either unsympathetic or incapable of any effective measures. Abbott's March 1845 dispatch is one of many accounts documenting the unsuccessful attempts of Persian merchants and manufacturers to resist foreign competition. Reporting on Muḥammad Shāh's apparent lack of interest in a previous petition forwarded by the manufacturers of Kashan "praying for protection to their commerce which . . . [was] suffering in consequence of the introduction of European merchandise," the British consul continues:

> Deputations from the traders and manufacturers both of Kashan and Isfahan have however just arrived and though it is said their principal object is to complain of some Regulations of the Russian Government by which the entry into the Caucasian Provinces of silk piece goods having gold embroidery or figuring, the manufacture of the above named towns, is prohibited, I understand they have also the intention of making observations on the injury which European trade has occasioned them. They say that in Fath ʿAly Shah's reign there were in Isfahan alone 12,000 looms in use in the manufacture of the above mentioned goods, but that in consequence of the increased consumption of European manufactures and the change in the fashions at Court, only a very few now remain of that number, and that these as well as the manufacturers of Kashan are threatened with ruin by the refusal of the Russian government to admit the goods within its frontier. They represented this before to His Majesty when at Isfahan and they were promised that the matter should be made the subject of a communication to the Russian Minister but the restriction still continues.

Abbott also expresses concern at the grievances of the Tabriz delegate over the issue of Greek competition: "He can find no one to listen to him. The Prime Minister's aversion to business of any kind is too well known to leave him anything to hope for from that quarter, and the other Ministers will do nothing without a sufficient bribe. I should fear the present deputations had little chance of succeeding in the avowed object of their journey."[21]

From the 1830s onwards, most of the European observers noticed the sharp decline in the textile industry. Eugene Flandin, passing through Kashan in 1841, maintains: "If a few industries have still survived, the majority of them are unfortunately inactive only waiting to vanish altogether."[22] He

[21]F.O. 60/117, no. 3, 31 March 1845, Abbott to Aberdeen, Tehran. The Persian government, however, raised the matter with the Russian authorities, though not with much immediate success (F.O. 60/116, no. 127, 14 November 1845, Sheil to Aberdeen, Tehran, including translation of Ḥājee Meerza Aghasi's letter to Comte Meden).

[22]E. Flandin and P. Coste *Voyage en Perse de M.M. Eugène Flandin, peintre, et Pascal Coste, architecte, 1840–41* 2 vols. (Paris, 1851) I, 267–68.

states that the devastating effects of European competition were not solely the outcome of the incompatible prices or the low cost of British products, but also the deliberate trade policy of the British government.[23] Changes in fashion, particularly among the women of the royal household, and Muḥammad Shāh's austere life-style and avoidance of silk and embroidered clothes in the style of his grandfather Fatḥ ʿAlī Shāh, also affected the production of luxurious piece cloths.[24] With the production of cotton fabrics hampered by foreign competition, the religious prohibition in Shiʿite fiqh on the use of pure silk dresses prevented manufacturers from turning to silk weaving as on alternative product for the home market.[25]

Ruination of domestic manufacturers, decline in the export of textile products, and diversion of trade from south to northwest were particularly felt in central and southern Iran, though merchants in the north did not remain untouched. Commercial communities in Kashan, Isfahan, Shiraz, and Yazd, as well as those in Tabriz and Qazvin, came under heavy pressure to adapt themselves to the prevailing conditions. The troubled years of the 1840s thus witnessed a transition in the Persian economy, with lasting effects. Many import merchants of larger capital and resiliency managed to stay in business either by acting as wholesale agents and factories of European manufacturers or by gradually diverting to new exporting fields, most noticeably cash crops: tobacco, cotton, silk (before the 1860s), and opium. Export merchants, domestic distributors, and middle- and lower-rank manufacturers faced a harder choice. Tied to domestic products for which there was little demand, they could not easily be absorbed into the tight imports market. Some went bankrupt or withdrew from trade; others were reduced to mere petty traders and shopkeepers.

The Babi Merchants

Perhaps more than its immediate impact on the material well-being of the merchants, the message of this rapid, inexorable process of change was one of far-reaching decline. Without the logic of modern mind, which makes a distinction between the sacred and the profane, for the Persian merchant of the period this growing awareness of material decline could only emerge within a religious frame of reference. The boundaries between material and spiritual were not, and perhaps could not have been, clearly drawn, and their correlation was subtle and complex. For a merchant of some sophis-

[23]Ibid.

[24]See Comte de Sercey *Une Ambassade extraordinaire: La Perse en 1839–40* (Paris, 1928) 226–27.

[25]It was some time later, during the first years of the reign of Nāṣir al-Dīn Shāh, that Mīrzā Taqī Khān Amīr Kabīr encouraged the manufacturers of Kashan to overcome the religious restriction by introducing new mixed silk-cotton fabrics known as *qadak* and *qaṭnī*. Sheil *Glimpses of Life and Manners in Persia* (Note H., p. 378).

tication who was acquainted with something beyond the parochial world of jurists and theologians, such an awareness was likely to bring about a crisis of values far broader than mere economic concerns. The sense of moral complacency and religious superiority so apparent in members of the clerical class could more easily crumble for a merchant when the bare realities of his professional life forced him to recognize his material inferiority. For the older generation the set practices of religious devotion, professional fortitude, and godliness, for which they were known and of which they were proud, could still guarantee a reward, if not in this world at least in the hereafter. For the younger generation, however, facing the harsh realities of a changing world led to moral predicaments of different nature.

Exposure to the world of scholastic learning had already transformed some younger individuals of unusual vigor to crossbreeds of mullas and merchants. Those who were inclined to Shaykhism and like tendencies found it ever more gratifying to engage themselves, in conjunction with their business, in theological and mystical endeavors for which the esoteric discourses of Shaykhis and Sufis were the departure points. The outlook of these merchants, like that of the Bab himself, was no doubt profoundly pietistic, but it was not bound by the rationale of devotion for salvation. Nor was it petrified in the arid wilderness of science of uṣūl or entangled in the tedious web of applied fiqh (furūʿ). Shiʿite as their world view and frame of mind might have been, they were able to carve for themselves an intellectual niche in the labyrinth of religious learning where they could erect an edifice of religiosity and messianic faith. These merchants on the fringe of the learned domain questioned the time-honored norms of the conventional mind and vigorously searched for new definition for the fundamentals of the faith. For them, as for their Babi clerical counterparts, acts of devotion or mystical experiences could only be meaningful if they carried a tangible message of comprehensive redemption. Such eschatological preoccupations, the reverse of the jurists' depersonalization of the Shiʿite faith, became impregnated with expectations for a messianic figure who in character and aspiration would personify their moral ideals. Concern with resurrection was thus an attempt to bring about a new moral order that can translate the otherworldly promises to worldly realities.

Such aspirations are evident, albeit under a guise of unworldliness, in the careers of young Babi merchants. In Isfahan, Kashan, Tabriz, Yazd, and Shiraz, the same concurrence between material concern and messianic expectations can be observed. Sayyid Muḥammad ʿAlī and Sayyid Muḥammad Hādī Nahrī Ṭabāṭabāʾī, two brothers from a well-established Shaykhi family of Isfahan who were known for their religiosity and social status, provide good examples. Their attention was first drawn to the new claimant, the Bab, when they were in the ʿAtabāt in 1260/1844. The Nahrīs' association with the Shaykhi community of the ʿAtabāt started with their father, Sayyid Mahdī, who emigrated from India to Najaf and later became a devoted adherent of Shaykh Aḥmad Aḥsā'ī.[26] He gained a reputation as a religious benefactor by founding a number of charitable endowments, such as a caravanserai and public bath in Najaf, and constructing a channel to supply drinking water.[27] He invested the family fortune in land and property and acquired a number of shops in the area. Upon the Wahhābī invasion of southern Iraq, he returned to Isfahan, where he married a relative of Sayyid Muḥammad Bāqir Shaftī.[28]

His son Sayyid Muḥammad ʿAlī, brought up in a devoted Shaykhi environment, joined the ranks of the ʿulama. He finished his primary studies in Isfahan, and later joined Sayyid Kāẓim Rashtī's circle in Karbalā'. His brother, Sayyid Hādī, though a Shaykhi, developed close relations with Shaftī and later married his niece, Khurshīd Baygum.[29] Later, Hādī also moved to Karbalā', where he and his wife both attended Rashtī's lectures.[30]

Like their father, the Nahrī brothers represented an intermediary link between the ʿulama and the tujjār. Parallel to their enthusiasm for religious studies, Muḥammad ʿAlī and Hādī, as members of the Persian mercantile community of Iraq, were also conducting trade from their office in Baghdad.[31] Their brother in Isfahan, Sayyid Ibrāhīm, who was also involved in trade, probably acted in partnership with them.[32] The fortune they accumulated during the next few decades came not only from trade, but mainly from their investments in land, agriculture, and property.[33] The pattern of collaboration between Sayyid Ibrāhīm and some of the religious figures in Isfahan suggests that the Nahrīs acted for a time as agents and bankers to such mujtahids as Muḥammad Ḥusayn Imām Jumʿa and Shaftī, who were always on excellent terms with them.[34]

Conversion to the new movement, however, brought about some dramatic changes in the life of the family. The two brothers had met Sayyid ʿAlī Muḥammad Shīrāzī during his pilgrimage in 1258/1842, and like many others, were impressed.[35] By the time the Bab announced his mission in Shiraz, Hādī and Muḥammad ʿAlī, who had probably heard of the new

[26]Sayyid Mahdī's father, Ḥājjī Sayyid Muḥammad Ṭabāṭabā'ī of Zavārih, emigrated to India at the end of the eighteenth century and married into a wealthy Shiʿite family (ʿAbd al-Ḥamīd Ishrāq Khāvarī *Nūrayn-i Nayyirayn* [Tehran, 123 Badīʿ/1967] 11–12 and *ZH* 96). See A. Rafīʿī Mihrābādī *Ātashkadih-yi Ardistān* (Tehran 1336 Sh./1957) for an account of the Ṭabāṭabā'ī sayyids of Zavārih (I, 166–206).

[27]His surname, Nahrī, is derived from the word *nahr* (channel, stream) because of his useful endowment.

[28]Ishrāq *Nūrayn* 13–14. Both Sayyid Mahdī's wife and Shaftī's wife were Shaykhi.

[29]Later known as Shams al-Ḍuḥā'. She was a devoted Babi and a companion of Qurrat al-ʿAyn, who accompanied her on her journey from Baghdad to Qazvin. Both ʿAbd al-Bahā' *Tadhkirat al-Wafā'* (268–90) and Ishrāq *Nūrayn* (41–52) give her biography.

[30]Sayyid Ibrāhīm remained in Isfahan, presumably to look after the family business (*ZH* 98).

[31]*KD* 410.

[32]Ibid. 413.

[33]Ibid. 413 and Ishrāq Khāvarī 28.

[34]*KD* 413 and *Nabil* 208.

[35]Ishrāq *Nūrayn* 15–16, 31.

claims through Basṭāmī, were among the first to give their allegiance. When they arrived in Shiraz, the Bab had already left for Ḥijāz.[36] On their return to Isfahan, they met Mullā Ḥusayn, whom they knew from the ʿAtabāt and to whom they declared their faith.[37] Later, in 1261/1845, they made another journey to Shiraz to pay a visit to the Bab.[38] Afterward, Muḥammad ʿAlī returned to Karbalāʾ. Hādī, however, remained in Isfahan. As Shaykhi dignitaries, the Nahrīs were able to encourage others to give their support to the movement. Yet their brother, Sayyid Ibrāhīm, showed no great enthusiasm at this time.[39]

The family's economic condition was also affected by the new movement. After their conversion, the Baghdad trade was gradually liquidated, probably as a result of the economic stagnation in southern Iran and in particular the Baghdad trade. At the same time, the Nahrīs were gradually pulling out of business, devoting their time, money, and effort to the progress of the movement.

The Nahrīs' preoccupation with messianic prophecies is evident in a number of inquiries that they made to Rashtī prior to 1260.[40] In their correspondence with the Bab, they later asked about certain remarks in the first part of *Qayyūm al-Asmāʾ* regarding "the signs and the evidences" of the "pure religion."[41] Further, their inquiries on the esoteric meaning of prayers, intercession, and the angels of the grave witness their search for a more realistic interpretation of religious beliefs and practices. They also asked the Bab's view about those who prior to the Advent of the Qāʾim preached his impending Ẓuhūr, a clear effort to link the Bab with Aḥsāʾī and Rashtī. Quoting a Tradition attributed to ʿAlī, they asked the meaning of badāʾ (change in God's intention, an issue of pivotal importance to Shaykhi theology)[42] in order to explain perhaps the incompatability of the new revelation with the promises of the Shiʿite tradition. In reply, the Bab cited a verse from the Qurʾān: "God blots out and he establishes whatever He will; and with Him is the Essence of the Book."[43] To justify badāʾ in the case of his earlier

[36]Ibid. 16, 31–32, 42–43 (citing from an autobiographical risāla by Sayyid Muḥammad ʿAlī). Also *ZH* 97 and *KD* 410.

[37]Ishrāq *Nūrayn* 31–32; cf. *Nabil* 100.

[38]Ishrāq *Nūrayn* 16, 32; cf. *ZH* 97.

[39]*KD* 411. In a letter that is partly cited in Ishrāq *Nūrayn* (28–30), Qurrat al-ʿAyn, writing in 1262/1846 to Sayyid Muḥammad ʿAlī, advised him to return from the ʿAtabāt to Isfahan and try to convince his elder brother of the truth of the Ẓuhūr. This attention to Sayyid Ibrāhīm is perhaps owing to his relations with the prominent ʿulama in the city. Later in 1263/1847 when the Bab was residing in Isfahan, the three brothers arranged for a feast in his honor at which Sayyid Muḥammad Imām Jumʿa, his brother Sayyid Ḥusayn, Muḥammad Taqī Harātī, Muḥammad Rižā Pāqalʿaʾī, and others were present (ibid. 18–20, 28; cf. *Nabil* 208–9).

[40]*Qatīl* 516.

[41]Letter in reply to the questions of Mullā Maḥmūd, Sayyid Muḥammad ʿAlī Nahrī, and other believers, INBA no. 91, XXXIII, 154–61 (156).

[42]Ibid. 157.

[43]Qurʾān XIII 39.

cancellation of the ʿAtabāt declaration, the Bab in effect goes against the deterministic bent of the Shiʿite prophecies. Such adjustment to the realities of the world, its perils and possibilities, must have been particularly appealing to his mercantile audience accustomed to change.[44] The Nahrīs further inquired about the meaning of the word *ḥujja* (proof) in the visitation prayer of the Seventh Imam, and the esoteric meaning of related Qurʿānic verses. Acknowledging the seven evolutionary stages of divine emanation, the Bab emphasizes that God reiterated badā' in all seven Imams in the same way that He renewed His badā' in the case of the new ḥujja, the Bab. But in his case, he points out in his usual invocatory style, it is reason that determines human salvation: "My Lord! You know that I do not like any one to face your countenance except with the proof of reason. This is the status of man and by this the people of *Bayān* are distinguished from perplexed people."[45]

In the course of the next few years, the Nahrīs were instrumental in the conversion of a number of believers from among merchants. Their pietistic approach to the Bab's message is best reflected in their opposition to Qurrat al-ʿAyn's unveiling in the Badasht gathering. Yet it appears that Shams al-Ḍuḥā', Hādī's wife, held more liberated views. Her association with Qurrat al-ʿAyn, and possibly her unveiling, may have aroused her husband's misgivings about the Babi heroine. Immediately after Badasht, Hādī was killed during a night attack in Niyālā. Muḥammad ʿAlī returned to Isfahan. After the events of Ṭabarsī and the execution of the Bab, he remained largely inactive, though he remained firmly committed to his Babi and later Bahā'ī beliefs.[46]

Ḥājjī Muḥammad Riżā Jawāhirī, a young merchant in his twenties, was also converted when the news of the appearance of the Bab first spread to Isfahan. Like many other mystical experiences of early Babis, Muḥammad Riżā's recognition was preceded by a dream in which he had visited the Imam of the Age at the time of his pilgrimage to the shrine of Ḥusayn. This dream, as he himself related, inspired him to pursue the Imam in the world of reality. Like the Nahrīs, he also conducted trade through the Baghdad route, and enjoyed inherited wealth. After his conversion, his new commit-

[44]INBA no. 91, 158.

[45]Ibid. Also the Bab's letter in reply to questions asked by Mīrzā Muḥammad Hādī and Sayyid Muḥammad ʿAlī Nahrī, INBA no. 91, XXXI, 152–53.

[46]Two of Sayyid Ibrāhīm's sons, Sayyid Ḥasan and Sayyid Ḥusayn Ṭabāṭabā'ī, faithful followers of Bahā'ullāh, continued with the family trade in Isfahan, where they ranked among the well-known merchants in the 1860s and 1870s. They continued their collaboration with the imām jumʿa, which brought substantial benefits for both parties. However, the excessive debts of the imām jumʿa to his creditors and partners finally persuaded him to join the powerful mujtahid of the city, Muḥammad Bāqir Najafī Iṣfāhānī (Āqā Najafī), in issuing a condemnation of the Ṭabāṭabā'īs' heretical beliefs and demanding their death. The fatwā was finally confirmed by the governor, Ẓill al-Sulṭān, and the two brothers met their death in 1296/1879 (Ishrāq *Nūrayn* 52 ff); Wills *Land of the Lion and Sun* 153–56.

ments not only cost him financial loss and finally bankruptcy, but the hostility and antagonism of his relatives. He was arrested for a brief period in 1266/1850 and jailed in Tehran prison before an Armenian merchant paid for his freedom. Two years later he was arrested and executed in Tehran together with a few other Babi merchants.[47]

There were Babi converts in other commercial centers. One of the most celebrated was Ḥājjī Mīrzā Jānī (sometimes called Parpā), a young merchant from Kashan who is mostly known for his authorship of the important historical account, *Nuqṭat al-Kāf.*[48] He was first attracted to the Bab when, in 1844, he met Mullā Ḥusayn in Kashan. Mīrzā Jānī's earlier enthusiasm originated in the admiration he felt for the eminent Shaykhi leaders, rather than in a systematic study of the Shaykhi doctrine. "Although because I had not studied the principals of the sciences [of religion]," he writes, "I was not formally affiliated to this highly elevated order [Shaykhism], yet in my inner self I adored the excellencies the two illustrious bābs [Aḥsā'ī and Rashtī], and therefore was attached to their sympathizers."[49] His preoccupation with Ẓuhūr is not inseparable from his sectarian sympathies: "I visited the holy shrines of Karbalā' and Najaf shortly after the death of Ḥājjī Sayyid Kāẓim [Rashtī], and learned from his disciples that during the last two or three years of his life he had spoken in lecture-room and pulpit of little else but the approaching advent of the promised Proof, the signs of his appearance and their signification, and the attributes by which he would be distinguished, declaring that he would be a youth of the clan of Hāshim, untaught in the learning of men."[50]

At the time of the Shaykhis' retreat in Kūfa,[51] Mīrzā Jānī must have been present in the ʿAtabāt.[52] Considering his commercial links with Baghdad, it is not unlikely that he was in contact with the Shaykhi community there, and therefore was aware of the developments within the circle.

Mīrzā Jānī's younger brother, Ḥājjī Mīrzā Muḥammad Ismāʿīl Kāshānī, known as Ẕabīḥ, also acknowledged Aḥsā'ī and Rashtī.[53] In his *Maṡnavī,*[54] Ẕabīḥ stresses the spiritual insight that enabled the Shaykhi leaders to unveil

[47]*ZH* 101–3; cf. *NK* xv, 111–12.
[48]For further details on the above account and its authenticity, see bibliography.
[49]*NK* 102.
[50]*NH* 30.
[51]See above, chap. 4.
[52]*NH* 30–33, 39 and Browne's introduction, xiv-li.
[53]This title, apparently bestowed on him by the Bab, alludes to the tale of Ibrāhīm's offer for the sacrifice of his son Ismāʿīl in Qur'ānic stories. He also sometimes refers to himself by his other pen names Fānī and ʿĀrif. Later, the title of Anīs was conferred upon him by Bahā'ullāh in the tablet of *Ra'īs.* (Mīrzā Abul-Fażl Gulpāyigānī *Risāla-yi Iskandarīya,* in reply to A. Toumansky [Cairo, 1318/1900], also partly cited in *Zapiski* of the Oriental Section of the Russian Imperial Archaeological Society (1893–1894) 33–45 and translated by E. G. Browne in *NH* xxxiv-xlii [xii]. Reference to Anīs appears in Bahā'ullāh *Majmūʿa-yi Alwaḥ-i Mūbāraka* [Cairo 1338/1920], "Lauḥ-i Ra'īs" [Arabic] 90.
[54]For details of the *Maṡnavī* see bibliography.

the truth of the forthcoming Ẓuhūr. The author's anticlerical feelings are evident:

> The ʿulama of the time are the false lights.
> They are obstacles to the appearance of the sun, for this reason, the sun of universe ordered: "Unveil the curtain from his face."
> The emergence of the Shaykh [Shaykh Aḥmad] and Kāẓim [Sayyid Kāẓim] disclosed all the hidden veils.
> They lifted the false curtain from the face of the truth, therefore the ʿulama became their enemies, and prevented people from understanding.[55]

Nuqṭat al-Kāf and the *Masnavī* of Ẕabīḥ show certain similarities that in turn suggest their authors' common intellectual background. *Masnavī*'s clear mystical influence is evident not only in the style of the poetry and the extensive usage of Sufi vocabulary but in its treatment of the Bab's (and later Bahāʾullāh's) spiritual status. The same influence is evident in the introduction of *Nuqṭat al-Kāf,* which gives a Shiʿite-Sufi justification of the Bab's revelation.[56]

The origins of this mystical interest must be traced back to Shaykhism. Yet a Sufi connection, particularly through the study of classical texts and possible contact with dervishes, cannot be ruled out. Mīrzā Jānī sometimes refers to dervishes who accompanied him on his journeys in Iran and Iraq, both for the purpose of trade and later for visiting the Babis in other cities.[57] Indeed, the pantheistic tone and narrative style of both *Nuqṭat al-Kāf* and *Masnavī,* as well as Mīrzā Jānī's interpretation of the signs of Ẓuhūr, betrays mystic influence.[58] This influence must have been reaffirmed by the writings of the Bab and later by the pantheistic ideas current in Babi circles.[59] In the early phases of the Bahāʾī thought, Ẕabīḥ too must have shared the mystical bent of its founder.[60] It is hard to imagine that such a tendency could have been developed without a previous knowledge of Sufi terminology and content, however. Ẕabīḥ's *Masnavī* seems largely inspired by the *Masnavī* of Jalāl al-Dīn Rūmī. It is divided into seven books (compared with five of Rūmī's) and in many parts has clear signs of the allegorical stories and parables of the above work. The style of *Nuqṭat al-Kāf,* however, is in

[55]*Masnavī* 68 a.
[56]*NK* 1–98 (particularly 86–98).
[57]*Fuʾādī* 54.
[58]For Sufi messianism see above, chap. 2.
[59]*NK* 252–63 gives a good example of the prevailing Babi views after the execution of the Bab. The authenticity of the above section in *NK* is questioned by H. M. Balyuzi (*Edward Granville Browne and the Bahāʾī Faith* [London 1970] 42–48), yet it could still be regarded as a sample of the current tendencies.
[60]In his *Masnavī,* Ẕabīḥ refers to his visits to Bahāʾullāh on several occasions. He met him first in Baghdad in 1265/1849–1850 (39 b), and in 1270–1271/1853–1854 (41 a-b). In 1285/1868, he met Bahāʾullāh in the port of Gallipoli and accompanied him to his new exile at ʿAkkā (Acre) (46b-54a). He gives a vivid picture of Bahāʾullāh and the evolution of his ideas.

some parts reminiscent of such Sufi biographical works as Farīd al-Dīn ʿAṭṭār's *Tadhkirat al-Awlīyā'*.

This mystical tendency laid the foundation for the reshaping of eschatological expectations. The sense of awe and respect for Shaykhi leaders gradually turned into a sense of anticipation for the Promised One. For Z̲abīḥ as for his brothers, the Advent of the Imam was primarily defined in terms of the Shiʿite expectation, but it also benefited from the concept of the Perfect Man. In a passage of the *Mas̲navī* that is reminiscent of the Shaykhi visitation dreams, Z̲abīḥ describes a vision of the Lord of the Age. After a long and laborious vigilance, Z̲abīḥ became aware of the material existence of the Imam, whom he is able to visit later in reality in the character of the Bab:

> Twenty years ago, in the state of *khalsa,*[61] I saw that perfect countenance.
> From then onwards, in order to come to his presence, I sought for Ṣāḥib al-Zamān [the Lord of the Age]
> Because I was aware that the lord of the universe is alive, therefore I sought for his visit. . . .
> Whether it was a vision or a dream, I cannot say what state I was in,
> I only know that I saw him, twenty years prior to his Advent.[62]

In 1263/1847, when the Bab was passing through Kashan on his way from Isfahan to Tehran, Z̲abīḥ expresses his own eagerness for visiting the Bab in the form of another anticipatory dream:

> Before "the lord of the people" sets out for Kashan, every day and night, I prayed to God for the honor of his sight.
> One night, I had a serene dream, that his excellency, who resembles the sun, shone in Kashan.
> Next morning I said to my brother, that soon the sublime sun will rise.
> He said, there is no news of him in the whole world.
> I briefly replied: "He will come today."
> It so happened that his excellency arrived the same day, shining like the sun.[63]

It was the Bab's visit to Kashan that brought to the surface the devotion of the Kāshānī brothers.[64] They arranged several meetings between the Bab and some sympathizers among the Shaykhi ʿulama and tujjār. The Kāshānī Babis also offered their assistance to the Bab to be rescued from the government escort that was taking him to the capital. Z̲abīḥ, in conformity with the other believers, declared that they were ready to provide the necessary

[61]*Khalsa* is a state between sleep and wakefulness in which the soul witnesses the occurrence of certain matters in advance. Tahānawī *Kashshāf* 597.

[62]*Mas̲navī* 2 b-3 a.

[63]Ibid. 2 b.

[64]In addition to other well-known sources, such as *Nabil* 217–22 and *NH* 213–16, the account of the Bab's abode in Kashan is also described in *Mas̲navī* 3/a-4/b and Nāṭiq Iṣfahānī *Tārīkh-i Amrī-yi Kāshān* 1–4.

means for his escape, "and we will attend and accompany you wherever it be; for we will thankfully and gladly give up our lives, our wealth, our wives, and our children for your sake."[65] The Bab's response to this offer was his usual unwillingness to take any violent action lest such action would ruin his dim chances of coming to terms with the government: "We need the help and support of none but God, and His will only do we regard."[66]

The Bab's reluctance did not turn the Kāshānī brothers away. Over the next few years, their growing adherence to the movement lessened their popularity in Kashan and harmed their good name as honest and forthright merchants:

> About ʿĀrif [Z̲abīḥ] and Ḥājjī [Mīrza Jānī] people believed that "these youths are the most pious people of the time.
> Both brothers are generous and openhanded, not even for one moment did they ignore the name of God. . . .
> Both are crusaders [*mujāhid*] for the truth, they never search in the world for anything but the truth."
> Then the ignorant ones said, "It is a pity that these two, in spite of all their invocations and prayers, abandoned their faith and became infidels.
> They became Babi and shunned the truth.
> They deserted their forefathers' religion, and became alienated with their own souls."[67]

Despite mounting criticism and open hostility, especially after 1265/1849, both brothers remained "the slaves of [the Bab's] threshold."[68] Z̲abīḥ refers to his brother as "a lost-hearted Ḥājjī, who was ready to sacrifice his life"[69]—an aspiration that soon turned into reality. After the unsuccessful attempt on the life of Nāṣir al-Dīn Shāh in 1268/1852, together with many other Babis, he was arrested in the shrine of Shāh ʿAbd al-ʿAẓīm near Tehran, where he probably compiled his historical account. Soon, however, the sanctuary was invaded, and he was taken by government agents to the Anbār dungeon, to be killed shortly after by Āqā Mahdī Malik al-Tujjār and other merchants of Tehran—a highly uncharacteristic brutality to be commited toward a fellow merchant.[70] Z̲abīḥ remembers his brother's death in the following words:

> That lover of the truth, the adorer of the *Rabb-i Aʿlā* [the Bab]
> He dedicated his possession and his life in the path of his Lord. . . .

[65] *NH* 216. A similar account appears in *Mas̲navī* 2/b.
[66] *NH* 216.
[67] *Mas̲navī* 152 a.
[68] Ibid. 2/b.
[69] Ibid.
[70] An account of the execution of Ḥājjī Mīrzā Jānī appears in among other sources *Vaqāyiʿ-i Ittifāqīya* no. 82 (10 Dhū al-Qaʿda 1268/26 Sept. 1852); also cited in *Shuhadā-yi Amr* III, 271.

He was finally taken to the dungeon of oppression, and then they strangled him with a piece of rope.
No man the like of that devoted man ever came to this world.
His death burnt the heart of sorrowful Z̲abīḥ.
A mystic like him the world never witnessed, he finally was martyred in the path of truth.
His name would remain in the book of lovers, his soul would ascend to Heaven.[71]

The Shaykhi merchants of Isfahan and Kashan were not the only converts in the tujjār ranks. In Qazvin the Farhādīs were among the first who supported the new cause, as early as 1261/1845.[72] Prior to 1260, two brothers of Āz̲arbāijānī origin, Ḥājjī Allāh Virdī Farhādī and Ḥājjī Asadullāh Farhādī, who had been engaged in the internal trade between the Caspian ports and Yazd, had established themselves in Qazvin.[73] The fortune they accumulated in the silk trade brought them affluence and was one reason for their social distinction. Their religious affiliation, on the other hand, made them chief defenders of non-orthodox cause.[74] Whether it was due to their previous acquaintance with Aḥsa'ī or their association with ʿAbd al-Wahhāb Qazvīnī,[75] the Farhādīs became devoted Shaykhis and on Aḥsā'ī's last visit to Qazvin, around 1235/1819, played host to him.[76] In the tense struggle for religious control of Qazvin, the Farhādīs were in ʿAbd al-Wahhāb's camp, and thus in opposition to Mullā Muḥammad Tāqī Baraghānī.

What other elements beside personal affection for Shaykhi leaders attracted merchants like the Farhādīs to Shaykhism? Above all, the Shaykhis were critical of the vigorous participation of prominent mujtahids in economic life. By the 1840s, the economic power of high-ranking Uṣūlī ʿulama, either by direct investment or by other means such as expropriation of endowments or exorbitant commissions from commercial contracts, had reached such a point that merchants, especially those who lacked reliable ties to mujtahids or could not afford their high fees for protection and legal backing, sought an alternative clerical body in Shaykhism. On a few occasions, for instance, Mullā Muḥammad Taqī Baraghānī's controversial verdicts on

[71]*Mas̲navī* 29/a. On the Kāshānī brothers Gulpāyigānī *Kashf al-Ghiṭā'* 42–45 and *NK* 113, 120–24, 259, 175–76 and 198. Besides references in *Mas̲navī*, both *Samandar* (222–23) and *NH* provide further information on Z̲abīḥ.

[72]Information on the Farhādīs in *Samandar, ZH,* and *KD* are based on the recollections of Āqā Muḥammad Jawād Farhādī. *Qazvīnī* and *Nabil* provide further details. Accounts on Qurrat al-ʿAyn also have references to the Farhādīs.

[73]*ZH* 372 and *Samandar* 91.

[74]*Nabil* 165. Allāh Virdī was known in Qazvin for his holy dreams.

[75]For ʿAbd al-Wahhāb see above, chap. 7. Also *QU* 22–24, 35; *TAS* II/2, 809–12. Ṭihrānī points out that Tunkābunī's doubts on ʿAbd al-Wahhāb's qualifications for ijtihād are entirely baseless. Also see *MA* V, 1736–40 and notes for the collection of his authorizations.

[76]*KD* 95.

transactions and contracts annoyed merchants of Qazvin, who protested against his shady practices.[77]

Moreover, it is possible that Shaykhism was more lenient toward certain forms of interest taking—a practice that was later legalized by the Bab. But primarily, it was on moral and intellectual grounds that Shaykhi mullas were deemed superior. The conduct of some Uṣūlī mujtahids, on the other hand, was deplored not only because of their assumed corruption and profligacy but because they were viewed as narrow-minded and intellectually sterile. They were frequently criticized for their rigidity and lack of interest in matters beyond trivial details of fiqh.

The polarization of the Qazvin community into two camps inevitably drew the Farhādīs further into a confrontation. In the elder generation opposition to the Uṣūlī jurists was expressed in terms of moral and financial support for the Shaykhi leaders—in the younger generation it turned into a more militant approach. It is not a coincidence that animosity between the two sides intensified at a time when the decline in the southern trade, particularly the fall in demand in the Indian market for Persian silk and ensuing restrictions, made the tujjār more dependent on their agricultural and urban holdings in Qazvin, a source of revenue that possibly caused friction with Muḥammad Taqī Baraghānī.

After the death of Allāh Virdī Farhādī in 1844, his four sons, who had married the four daughters of their uncle, Ḥājjī Asadullāh, continued the family business in collaboration with him.[78] The news of the proclamation of the Bab came through Ḥājjī Mīrzā Maḥmūd, a merchant from Shiraz. He visited Qazvin after his pilgrimage of Ḥajj, during which he traveled with the Bab in the same boat.[79] Enthusiasm for learning the identity of the Lord of the Age encouraged Ḥājjī Asadullāh to dispatch Mullā Jawād Valīyānī to Shiraz.[80] Afterward, when ʿAbd al-Jalīl Urūmī, a Letter of the Living, came to Qazvin, the Farhādīs became fully converted to the Bab.[81] In the course of the next few years, they were in the center of Babi activities and played host to many Babi missionaries. In moments of need, they also gave them financial help.[82]

The second of the four brothers, Āqā Muḥammad Hādī Farhādī, gradually emerged as one of the leaders of the Qazvin Babis.[83] This was in part due to the changing religious climate in Qazvin. Mullā ʿAbd al-Wahhāb, who was then in his seventies, remained undecided over the Bab's claims. Despite his sons' attempts to convince him, he never publicly endorsed the

[77]*QU* 24, 32–33.
[78]*Samandar* 91–96, 229–31.
[79]*ZH* 372, citing Āqā Muḥammad Jawād's notes.
[80]Ibid., citing the same source. For Valīyānī see above, chap. 6.
[81]Ibid., citing the same source.
[82]*Samandar* 353.
[83]The eldest of the four, Muḥammad Rafīʿ, who was a resident of Yazd, was not a Babi. The other two were Muḥammad Mahdī and Muḥammad Jawād.

Bab.[84] The task of the protection and security of the Babis thus inevitably transferred to persons who had the courage and the means of defying the opposing ʿulama. In the face of mounting hostility in 1263–1264/1847–1848, the Farhādīs used all they had at their disposal, including their money and their connections with the artisans and the lūṭīs, to defend themselves and their fellow Babis. Shortly after the return of Qurrat al-ʿAyn and her companions to Qazvin, the departure under duress of Mullā ʿAbd al-Wahhāb for the ʿAtabāt left the stage clear for Muḥammad Taqī to attack the Babis from the pulpit, denouncing them as infidels and religiously unclean.[85] Violent clashes and physical attacks on the Babis followed the verbal onslaught.[86] When ʿAbd al-Jalīl Urūmī, who was preaching in Qazvin under the protection of the Farhādīs, was attacked by the mob and dragged to the madrasa of Mullā Muḥammad Taqī to be bastinadoed in his presence, Muḥammad Hādī, his brother Muḥammad Jawād, and their supporters climbed over the walls of the madrasa and rescued him. [87] Earlier, in 1263/1847, when the Bab was passing through Mīyānih on his way from Tehran to Azarbaijan, Āqā Muḥammad Hādī and a group of his followers offered to rescue him. But as on other occasions, the offer was turned down.[88]

In the next two years, as the Bab in his isolation in the fortress of Mākū and Chihrīq was more and more cut off from his adherents, the Babis turned more toward a militant and uncompromising struggle. Āqā Muḥammad Hādī, preparing for the jihād, set up a workshop in the basement of his house to produce swords, and distributed them among the followers.[89] When Vaḥīd Dārābī, who appears to have been experienced in warfare, arrived in Qazvin that year, Āqā Muḥammad Hādī even arranged for training sessions in his house.[90]

The assassination of Mullā Muḥammad Taqī in the middle of 1263/1847 brought the conflict to its peak. As we have seen, Muḥammad Hādī may have assisted the assassin. Consequently, the Farhādīs came under strong suspicion and were accused of being the chief instigators and accomplices in the crime. Riots broke out in the city and the house of the Farhādīs was twice sacked by the mob. Ḥājjī Asadullāh and one of his nephews, Muḥammad Mahdī, were arrested and detained in the government house, together with seventy other Babis.[91] Later, at the insistence of Muḥammad

[84] *Qazvīnī* 494–95.

[85] Mullā ʿAbd al-Wahhāb died in Muḥarram 1264/Dec.–Jan. 1847–1848 in the ʿAtabāt (*MA* V, 1736).

[86] *Samandar* 351–52 and *QU* 56–57.

[87] *Samandar* 352; cf. *ZH* 347–48, citing Muḥammad Jawād Farhādī.

[88] *KD* I, 95–96 and *ZH* 374. According to *Nabil* (235) and *Samandar* (97–99), an earlier meeting took place in Sīyāh Dihān (a village southwest of Qazvin) between the Bab and some of the Qazvīnī and Zanjānī followers. Mullā Jaʿfar Qazvīnī and others met the Bab at other stages in the villages around Qazvin (*Qazvīnī* 479–80).

[89] *ZH* 374, citing Muḥammad Jawād.

[90] Ibid.

[91] *Samandar* 92 and *ZH* 375.

Baraghānī, husband of Qurrat al-ʿAyn, who now succeeded his father, Ḥājjī Asadullāh and other Babis were sent to Tehran where he soon died in prison.[92]

Muḥammad Hādī avoided certain arrest and persecution by escaping to Tehran in disguise, but daringly returned to Qazvin in the disguise of a Yazdī caravaneer to rescue his younger brother from government detention.[93] The rescue of Qurrat al-ʿAyn was more difficult. She was under strict surveillance in her father's house, guarded by trusted women of the household and a group of lūṭīs at the gate.[94] Muḥammad Hādī, in collaboration with Bahā'ullāh, drew up a plan for her rescue. Āqā Muḥammad Hādī's wife, Khātūn Jān, disguised as a laundress, smuggled a message to Qurrat al-ʿAyn. Āqā Ḥasan Najjār, a carpenter and Valī and Qulī, both lūṭīs, helped Muḥammad Hādī to free Qurrat al-ʿAyn by night, and the party rode all the way from Qazvin to Tehran without the Baraghānīs being able to stop them.[95]

The escape of Qurrat al-ʿAyn was a blow to Mullā Muḥammad and the rest of the Baraghānīs. For the third time ṭullāb and lūṭīs sacked the house of the Farhādīs. Fearing for their lives, Khātūn Jān and her three sisters, all admirers of Qurrat al-ʿAyn, took refuge in the ruined tomb of Imāmzādih Aḥmad outside the city for four months.[96] Muḥammad Hādī accompanied Quarrat al-ʿAyn on her journey to Badasht, but no further trace of him is found. He was probably killed in the Nīyālā incident.[97]

The other Babis of Qazvin were also persecuted. Their houses and properties were confiscated as a surety for payment of larger ransoms and they themselves were either imprisoned or forced into exile.[98] But in spite of the harrowing experiences of 1848, the spirit of dissent persisted, even intensified. In a narrative written some years later, Ḥājjī Muḥammad Naṣīr Qazvīnī, a domestic trader and one of Ṭabarsī's "Remnants of the Sword," after describing the Babis' sufferings in Ṭabarsī, concludes with a militant note undiminished by the emerging Bahā'ī moderation: "The opponents [of the Babis] who are still around would soon come out of their garb of Pharaonism and instead wear the cloak of poverty and misery so that this pure land would be purged of these abominables and the tree of morality which is planted would bear fruit."[99] In the years ahead, his diehard Babi activism frequently exposed him to persecution and arrest on charges of conspiracy against the state.[100] Shaykh Kāẓim Samandar, Naṣīr's partner in

[92]*Samandar* 230.
[93]*ZH* 375.
[94]*Samandar* 362 and *ZH* 376.
[95]*Samandar* 363–66.
[96]*ZH* 378–79 and *Samandar* 369.
[97]*Samandar* 93 and *ZH* 337.
[98]*Qazvīnī* 486–88; *Samandar* 21.
[99]Narrative of Ḥājjī Muḥammad Naṣīr Qazvīnī, appendix to *Tārīkh-i Samandar* 517–18. Only a portion of this account is now extant.
[100]Ibid. 518–20 and *Samandar* 215.

business, states that "because of successive persecutions his commercial affairs were completely disturbed."[101] In 1300/1882–1883 he was again arrested in Rasht and died in jail.[102]

Shaykh Muḥammad Qazvīnī (later known as Nabīl Akbar), father of Kāẓim Samandar, another domestic merchant and a colleague, may not have matched Naṣīr in radicalism but shared his aspirations. His father, Āqā Rasūl, a devout Shaykhi residing in Karbalā', was among those who met the Bab in 1258/1842.[103] Shaykh Muḥammad, like the Nahrī brothers, studied under Rashtī and named his son Kaẓim after him. Returning to small-scale trade after his conversion,[104] his house was a center of Babi gatherings. In the aftermath of Mullā Muḥammad Taqī's assassination, though he escaped persecution in his home town, he was later arrested in Tabriz, where he had temporarily sojourned, and was severely bastinadoed by order of Mullā Aḥmad Mujtahid. Subsequently, he was bailed out by merchants sympathetic to his plight and, fearing the same fate in Qazvin, was helped to set up an office in the Tabriz bazaar.[105] About the same time, when he visited the Bab, presumably in Chihrīq, Sayyid ʿAlī Muḥammad bemoaned the injury and indignity inflicted upon his follower and fellow merchant. "It was not you who was punished, it was me," he said.[106]

In Khurasan, some members of the local merchant community also joined the movement. Ḥājjī ʿAbd al-Majīd Nīshābūrī perhaps is the most remarkable example. He was a dealer in turquoise and high-quality shawls,[107] and his father enjoyed prestige as the owner of the best-known turquoise mine in Nīshāpūr.[108] Though nothing is known about any past connections, his name appears among the first converted through Mullā Ḥusayn, when he was passing through Nīshābūr in 1846.[109] Not fully convinced of the validity of the Bab's claims, he embarked on a personal quest. After visiting the Bab,[110] he returned to Mashhad, where he continued his trade in luxury goods.

On the eve of the Ṭabarsī episode, ʿAbd al-Majīd accompanied Mullā Ḥusayn on his march to Mazandaran, and not only paid most of the expenses with valuable shawls and Nīshābūr turquoise, but also participated actively in the fighting of Ṭabarsī, although he was in his mid-fifties.[111]

[101] *Samandar* 215.
[102] Ibid. 216.
[103] Ibid. 17–18.
[104] Shaykh Muḥammad, like most other merchants of Qazvin, was chiefly engaged in the distribution of raw silk (ibid. 24).
[105] Ibid. 24–30.
[106] Ibid. 30.
[107] *Fu'ādī* 55 and *ZH* 162.
[108] *Nabil* 125.
[109] *Fu'ādī* 55.
[110] *ZH* 162.
[111] Most of the Ṭabarsī accounts, including *Tārīkh-i Mīmīya,* narrative of Mīrzā Luṭf ʿAlī, and *Nabil*, refer to his role as the treasurer of Ṭabarsī.

After the fall of Ṭabarsī, he was captured and brought to the city of Bārfurūsh together with Quddūs and the others. The prince commander, Mahdī Qulī Mīrzā, realized that ʿAbd al-Majīd, being a prosperous man, was too valuable to be slaughtered by the crowd, and saved his life.[112] Subsequently he escaped from the Tehran jail, after paying a ransom of a hundred tūmāns.[113] Returning to Mashhad, Ḥājjī ʿAbd al-Majīd remained a devout Babi and later Bahāʾī. Some twenty-eight years after Ṭabarsī, in 1294/1877, he met his death, in his mid-eighties. Aqā Muḥammad Bāqir Najafī Iṣfahānī (better known as Aqā Najafī),[114] the notorious enemy of the Babi-Bahāʾīs, who had temporarily moved from Isfahan to Mashhad, put his seal of approval on the fatwā concerning his blasphemy, and after much controversy, the unrepentant ʿAbd al-Majīd was executed.[115]

Āqā ʿAlī Riżā Tājir Shīrāzī, a less conspicuous but more typical example of the Babi merchants of Khurasan, stood as an intermediary link between bazaar and madrasa. A merchant from Shiraz who had long settled in Mashhad, he was at one stage a ṭalaba in the madrasa of Mīrzā Jaʿfar, where he swore an oath of fraternity with his classmate Mullā Muḥammad ʿAlī Bārfurūshī (Quddūs).[116] His recognition of the Bab was apparently due to this earlier friendship.[117] It also appears that he and Quddūs belonged to a group of which Mullā Ḥusayn was also a member.[118] At the time of his departure from Mashhad Quddūs reportedly withdrew his oath since he believed that it would be impossible for Āqā ʿAlī Riżā to fulfill the strict terms of the pledge.[119] Nonetheless, his erstwhile membership in the Khurasan circle made ʿAlī Riżā respond to Mullā Ḥusayn's call for jihād and subsequently offer financial aid to the Khurāsānī followers. During the turmoil of 1848 in Mashhad, ʿAlī Riżā, while preparing himself to join the

[112]Zavārihī *Tārīkh-i Mīmīya* 109.

[113]*Samandar* 175 and Malik Khusravī *Tārīkh-i Shuhadā-yi Amr* II, 75.

[114]Shaykh Muḥammad Bāqir Iṣfāhānī (son of Shaykh Muḥammad Taqī), better known as Āqā Najafī, was the inheritor of his father's clerical fame and the founder of the Najafīs' financial power (*TAS* I/1, 198–99, 247–48 and II/1, 215–17). The wealth and the influence of the Najafīs and their dispute with the governor of Isfahan Ẓill al-Sulṭān over legal and economic domination in the city made them outstanding in the clerical history of the nineteenth century. Their anti-Babi-Bahāʾī stand, which is apparent in Ṭabāṭabāʾī affairs (see above), caused them to receive opprobrious treatment in Bahāʾī sources.

[115]*Fuʾādī* (56–65) contains a full account of the events that finally led to the execution of Ḥājjī ʿAbd al-Majīd. Ḥājjī ʿAbd al-Majīd's son Mīrzā Buzurg, later titled Badīʿ, was for some time in doubt about his father's Babi-Bāhāʾī faith. Later, he was converted and while on a mission to the court of Nāṣir al-Dīn Shāh to deliver Bahāʾullāh's tablet of the shah of Iran, he died under torture and became one of hero martyrs of Bāhāʾī history. This was six years before the execution of Ḥājjī ʿAbd al-Majīd.

[116]Ibid. 74.

[117]Ibid. This was a common practice among ṭullāb. It served not only practical purposes such as sharing meals and rooms, but often indicated a common orientation or primary training. After completion of studies, sometimes these links served as basis for alliance between the mujtahids; for example, the oath between Mullā Muḥammad Bāqir Shaftī and Ḥājjī Ibrāhīm Karbāsī (*QU* 140).

[118]*ZH* 174. Fāżil Māzandarānī seems to draw his information from a certain ʿAbd al-Muʾmin, who is perhaps identified Āqā Sayyid Muʾmin, cited in *Muʿīn* 62–63.

[119]*Fuʾādī* 74.

Babi marchers on their way to Mazandaran, was arrested by Sām Khān, the Mashhad chief of police, who flogged him on the pretext of blasphemy and extorted a large sum from him.[120] Later in his life, perhaps because of financial troubles, he abandoned his trade and became a local grain merchant.[121]

Ḥājjī ʿAbdul Jawād Yazdī, a relative of Mullā ʿAbd al-Khāliq Yazdī and presumably one of his close adherents,[122] joined the Bābīya in its early days, perhaps through Yazdī's influence.[123] Established in Mashhad as a reliable broker, he was basically a commission-agent for the merchants in the city. His son-in-law, himself a Babi, acted as the representative of the uncles of the Bab in Yazd.[124] Their connection with the Bab's uncles in Shiraz and Būshihr sheds light on the channels through which merchants like ʿAbd al-Jawād and Āqā ʿAlī Riżā Shīrāzī may have first heard of the Bab. The trade organized by merchants on the Shiraz-Mashhad route, with representatives in Ṭabas, Yazd, and Būshihr, provided a Shaykhi network often linked to Shaykhi ʿulama, throughout the country.

In Shiraz and Būshihr, the conversion of the merchants, even from Shaykhi persuasion, seems to have been hindered by the harassment the Bab underwent after 1845. Though a number of merchants, often connected to the Bab's uncles, were attracted in the early stages, only a handful joined the Babi ranks. One example was Mīrzā Aḥmad Shīrāzī Īshīk Āqāsī, a descendant of a merchant family and later the author of a general history that contains some new details on the Bab and the beginning of the movement. Mīrzā Aḥmad's curiosity is apparent throughout the pages of his narrative. As the claims and objectives of the movement unfolded, however, he became disillusioned with the Bab, and critical of his disciples. He apparently was not alone in this change of attitude. Babi sources refer to the presence of other sympathetic merchants in the early debates of Mullā Ḥusayn and Muqaddas in Shiraz.[125] But only the names of a few who remained loyal to the Bab are known: Mīrzā Abul-Ḥasan Shīrāzī, who met the Bab in the Ḥajj, Āqā Muḥammad Karīm Shīrāzī, and Ḥājjī Mīrzā Muḥammad.

For the Afnāns, the maternal side of the Bab's family, the claims of the young Sayyid ʿAlī Muḥammad posed an agonizing dilemma. His eldest and the youngest uncles, Ḥājjī Sayyid Muḥammad and Ḥājjī Sayyid Ḥasan ʿAlī, a resident of Yazd, categorically refused to recognize his claims and chas-

[120]Ibid. Sām Sām Khān Urus, the commander-in-chief of the regiment of Bahādurān, was the biglarbagī of Mashhad (*RS* X, 329, 416–20). He was the first official in Mashhad to become aware of Mullā Ḥusayn's activities in the city, and to report to the governor Ḥamza Mīrzā *(RS* X, 422). See also Lady Sheil *Life and Manners* 141.

[121]*ʿallāf*, possibly a vendor of fodder (*Fuʾādī* 74).

[122]*Fuʾādī* 104–5. Among the relatives of Mullā ʿAbd al-Khāliq there were other Babis—Āqā Muḥammad Ḥasan Muzahhib (book illuminator), his nephew, and Mīrzā Muḥammad Ḥusayn Iʿtiżād al-Aṭibbāʾ, his son-in-law, who was a physician.

[123]Ibid.

[124]Ibid.

[125]*NH* 36; *Nabil* 65.

tised him for his heretical utterances.[126] Ḥājjī Mīrzā Sayyid ʿAlī, closest of the Bab's three maternal uncles, however, was a devout follower from the start. In contrast to most other members of his family, who showed apprehension and embarrassment on the publication of the new claims, he missed no opportunity to support his nephew. In 1216/1845, after the Bab's return from Ḥajj, in an important letter from Būshihr to his brother in Shiraz, Sayyid ʿAlī declared his full conviction.[127] A few months later, during the first round of the anti-Babi persecution, when the Bab was taken into custody by the governor of Fars, Ḥusayn Khān Ājūdānbāshī, Sayyid ʿAlī guaranteed bail and acted as his nephew's sponsor.[128] Even after the Bab's departure from Shiraz he did not lose contact with him. In 1265/1849 he visited the Bab for the last time, in the fortress of Chihrīq. A few months later he was arrested in Tehran, together with a number of other Babis, by order of Mīrzā Taqī Khān Amīr Kabīr. Admitting his commitment to the Bab and refusing to retract, he and six other Babis, known as the Seven Martyrs, were found guilty of conspiracy and corruption of belief, and put to death in the Sabzih Maydān market. "Eminent merchants of Shiraz and Tehran," including Malik al-Tujjār himself, interceded to save his life, offering ransom, but "he refused to heed their counsel and faced . . . the persecution to which he was subjected."[129]

The Babi Artisans

The main contribution of the Babi tujjār in the movement was perhaps their role as intermediaries in attracting members of various guilds (*aṣnāf*), small manufacturers and artisans, to the Babi ranks. Although no mass conversion ever took place (except in the case of Zanjān, later, which culminated in the uprising of 1849–1850), many individuals were drawn to the new faith through local contacts and association with the Babi tujjār and ʿulama.[130]

The trade routes of central and western Iran give one indication of the

[126]See above, chap. 3 on the Afnāns.

[127]The letter is partly cited in Fayẓī *Khāndān-i Afnān* 25–31. The author believes that these letters were written by the elder brother, Ḥājjī Mīrzā Sayyid Muḥammad, but the contents of the letter, the fact that the other brothers showed no sympathy toward the new claim, and the presence of Ḥājjī Sayyid ʿAlī in Būshihr at the time prove that the writer is none but Sayyid ʿAlī.

[128]*Nabil* 151; cf. Mīrzā Ḥabībullāh *Tārīkh* 45–46 and *NK* 113.

[129]*Nabil* 442–64 (447). The full incident is recorded in various sources, including *NK* 215–22. Also see Momen *Religions* 100–105.

[130]Gobineau, with regard to the mutual relation between the artisans and merchants, points out: "It is clear that these organized cooperations are backed on the one hand by the merchants for whom they work and on the other by the *mullahs* who, their prestige requiring that they be surrounded by the masses, are glad to take up the interests of apprentices, craftsmen *(artisans)*, and even master craftsmen" (*Trois ans en Asie,* translation cited in Issawi *Economic History of Iran* 37).

way Babism spread among local merchants and their associated groups. Ḥājjī Mīrzā Jānī's pilgrimage to Iraq in 1843–1844 doubled as a journey connected to his trade. Zabīḥ was also present in Baghdad on a few occasions between 1849 and 1854, presumably for the same purpose.[131] Sometime prior to 1264/1848 we find Ḥājjī Mīrzā Jānī in Bārfurūsh "for the purpose of trade."[132]

A group of young local merchants and manufacturers who assembled around Ḥājjī Mīrzā Jānī and Zabīḥ in Kashan typifies Babi communities around the country. In addition to the younger brothers, Mīrzā Aḥmad and Āqā Muḥammad ʿAlī,[133] Mīrzā Mahdī Kāmrānībāf,[134] Ḥājjī Sayyid Maḥmūd,[135] Mīrzā Āqā Tājir Kāshānī,[136] and Ḥājjī Mīrzā Muḥammad Rizā Makhmalbāf Kāshānī[137] were all manufacturers and local merchants who were in professional contact with them. Muḥammad Rizā Makhmalbāf, for example, owned a number of velvet-weaving workshops, and operated a trade with India, Istanbul, and Baghdad,[138] the same pattern of trade as Mīrzā Jānī and Zabīḥ, who both seem to have been engaged in the export of silk products to Baghdad and the Caucasus.

In Isfahan, the conversion of members of various professions was due chiefly to the efforts of the Babi mullas, but Nahrīs were also instrumental. Among the Babis of Isfahan, Jaʿfar Gandum Pākkun (sifter of wheat), Aḥmad Ṣaffār (tin-plater), Ḥusayn Misgar (coppersmith),[139] and ʿAlī Muḥammad Sarrāj (leather worker)[140] all bore the title of *mullā*. In other cases, such as Kāẓim Bannā (mason) in Kirman,[141] Mahdī Kūrihpaz (kiln worker), Muḥammad Mūsā Namadmāl (felt-maker) and Jaʿfar Muzahhib (book gilder), all in Nayrīz,[142] the same title is used for the Babi artisans. One may assume that while engaged in various professions, the title mullā was added to their names as an acknowledgment of their literacy or possibly religious training, a fact that may indicate the success of the Babi recruitment among literate guild members.

A special place in the early success of the movement in Isfahan is at-

[131] *Masnavī* 39/b, 41/a.

[132] *NK* 175–76.

[133] *Kashf al-Ghiṭāʾ* (45) and *KD* (I, 90–92) believe that there was a fourth brother but this is not confirmed by Nāṭiq (*Tārīkh-i Amrī-yi Kashan* 4), which seems to be more reliable. On Mīrzā Aḥmad and his fate see *TN* 332, 371; *NH* 391 (n.) Balyuzi *E. G. Browne and the Bahāʾī Faith* 64 and Aḥmad Ruḥī Kirmānī (?) *Hasht Bihisht* 282.

[134] *Tārīkh-ī Amrī-yi Kashan* 4–5 and *Nabil* 221. Mīrzā Mahdī was executed in Tehran in 1268/1852 (*Vaqāyiʿ-i Ittifāqīyyih* no. 82 and Recollections of Āqā Ḥusayn Āshchī cited in *Tārīkh-i Shuhadā-yi Amr* III, 310–12).

[135] *Tārīkh-i Amrī-yi Kashan* 3.

[136] *Samandar* 227.

[137] *Muʿīn* 75.

[138] Ibid.

[139] *Nabil*, list of the participants in Ṭabarsī, p. 421, nos. 115, 116.

[140] *ZH* 105.

[141] Ibid. 398.

[142] *SAMB* 402 n. citing an anonymous Babi account.

tributed to Jaʿfar Gandum Pākkun. Nabīl Zarandī believes that he was the first person to become a Babi in Isfahan,[143] due to "a close association with Mullā Ḥusayn."[144] He later fully recognized the Bab at the latter's arrival in Isfahan in 1262/1846.[145] Emphasis on the early acceptance of Gandum Pākkun is perhaps attributable to his low status. Indeed, the Babi sources regard the conversion and wholehearted devotion of Gandum Pākkun, which ended in his death in the fortress of Ṭabarsī,[146] as an example of the attention paid by the poor and underprivileged to the new message. The Bab himself points up the significance of this conversion by portraying Mullā Jaʿfar as a humble man who grasped the reality of his cause: "Look at the Land of Ṣād [Isfahan] which in appearance is the greatest of lands where in each corner of its schools numerous students are found under the name of knowledge and ijtihād, yet, at the time of refining Gandum Pākkun will put on the garb of primacy. This is the secret of the word of the People of the House regarding the time of Manifestation when they say: 'The lowest of the people shall become the most exalted and the most exalted shall become the lowest.'"[147]

Further spread of the Babi word among craftsmen, local traders, and other humble people was often the result of personal and intercommunal contacts. Āqā ʿAlī Akbar Najjār (carpenter) and Āqā Muḥammad Ḥanāsāb (henna miller), for instance, first learned of the new Bab and his claims through Mullā Ḥusayn. Āqā Sayyid ʿAbd al-Raḥīm, who was one of Muḥammad Bāqir Shaftī's bailiffs in the village of Sīyāfshād, in turn heard of the movement through ʿAlī Akbar Najjār.[148] On a trip to Isfahan, while in the city to complain about a recent robbery in the village, he accidentally met his close friend ʿAlī Akbar and noticed in his possession a tablet written in red ink, probably a copy of *Qayyūm al-Asmāʾ*. ʿAlī Akbar Najjār revealed that he had received the tablet from a "learned man" who had recently arrived from Shiraz, and directed his friend to the quarter of Darb-i Kūshk, where during his first visit to Mullā Ḥusayn, ʿAbd al-Rahīm professed his conversion. His belief was strengthened after he had paid a visit to the Bab in Isfahan in 1263/1847 and received a tablet from him in which he was addressed with a grand title.[149]

By 1848–1850 the number of artisans, craftsmen, and skilled workers who had joined the Babi ranks formed a sizable part of the movement's

[143]*Nabil* 99.
[144]Ibid.
[145]Both *KD* I, 71 and *Muʿīn* 98 refer to a dream that led Mullā Jaʿfar to recognize the Bab in Isfahan.
[146]*NK* 202 and *Nabil* 99.
[147]*Bayān* VIII/14 296. Neither Nabīl Zarandī's quotation of the above remark (99) nor Nicolas's French translation (A. L. M. Nicolas *Le Béyan persan* [Paris, 1914] IV, 113) is accurate.
[148]INBA Lib. MS. no. 1028 D, *Miscellaneous notes* 32–33.
[149]Ibid. and *ZH* 101.

urban population. There is no comprehensive record of the number, the identity, and the occupation of the Babis to enable us to make any accurate assessment, but even judging by the names of those who participated in Babi resistances in Ṭabarsī, Nayrīz, and Zanjān, it is evident that a sizable body of guild members with variety of occupations were present. Among the 360 participants in Ṭabarsī, for instance, there were forty-one Iṣfahānīs, of whom the occupation of thirty-two were specified. Besides eight mullas and seminarians there were twenty-four members of various guilds and professions: eleven masons; five workers in the hand-weaving industry (one handloom weaver, two knotters, two cloth-stampers); four other skilled workers (a coppersmith, a tin-plater, a leather worker, and a sifter of wheat); and four shopkeepers and traders (two apothecaries, a butcher, and a cloth dealer). Of forty-one Iṣfahānīs, forty were killed in Ṭabarsī and one "Remnant of the Sword" was later executed in Tehran.[150]

If, due to its wide geographical distribution, the occupational pattern of the participants of Ṭabarsī can be taken as representative of the Babi community throughout the country around 1264/1848, it is evident that the participation of the guilds in the movement is second only to that of the ʿulama. As a whole, of 222 participants whose occupations are known, 60 percent were middle- and lower-rank mullas, 26 percent were from guilds, about 8 percent were small landowners, and the remaining 6 percent were merchants, lower- and middle-rank government officials, and other professionals. Of 138 participants whose occupations are unknown, we can assume that a large proportion were either artisans or else peasants who, because of their humble occupations (or because of the inadequacy of the sources), remained unspecified.

The urban nature of the Zanjān uprising is evidenced by the large number of "the poor, the traders of the bazaar, the sādāt, and the students."[151] Among them were three ironsmiths (Ḥājjī Kāẓim, Mashhadī ʿAbbās, and Ustād Mihr ʿAlī, who together improvised two makeshift cannons for the Babi defense), two hatters (Ustād Sā'il, the chronicler of the Zanjān events, and Ustād Khalīl), an apothecary, a shoemaker, a carpenter, a dyer, a clothier, a tobbaconist, a gardener, and a maker of gunpowder. Also among the Babi defenders in Zanjān were two gunners, a courier, a wandering dervish, a reformed thief, and a few lūṭīs.[152]

In the urban resistances of 1267/1851 in Isfahan and 1268/1852 in Tehran, members of the guilds, under the direction of the ʿulama and the merchants, again played an effective role. Ṣādiq Tabrīzī, a confectioner, and

[150]See table of geographical distribution and occupations of the participants of Ṭabarsī.

[151]Mīrzā Ḥusayn Zanjānī *Tārīkh,* INBA Lib. MS. no. 3037, folio 10.

[152]The above list, only a sample of the participants in Zanjān, was compiled from several narratives: Mīrzā Ḥusayn *Tārīkh;* Āqā ʿAbd al-Aḥad Zanjānī "Personal Reminscences," trans. by E. G. Browne *JRAS* 29 (1897) and 761–827; and narrative of Hāshim Fatḥī Muqaddam Khalkhālī, INBA Lib. MS no. 3037.

Geographical distribution and occupations of the participants of Ṭabarsī

Provinces	Mullas	Guilds	Small landowners	Merchants	Gov't. officials	Other	Unknown	Total	%
Khurasan	55	10	—	1	2	—	43	111	30
Mazandaran	27	7	14	—	1	1	36	86	23
Isfahan	8	24	—	1	—	—	8	41	11
Sangsar & Shahmīrzād	10	6	1	—	—	—	15	33	9
Qazvin	5	2	—	2	—	—	7	15	4
Fars	5	—	—	—	—	1	5	11	3
Ardistan	1	1	2	—	—	—	7	11	3
Azarbaijan	6	1	—	1	—	—	2	10	2.7
Zanjān	1	—	—	1	—	—	8	10	2.7
Yazd & Kirman	1	4	—	—	—	—	4	9	2.5
Tehran	2	—	—	—	1	1	1	5	1.3
Other places	13	3	—	—	—	—	2	18	5
Total	134	58	17	6	4	3	138	360	100
% of 222 known occupations	60	26	7.6	1.6	1.8	1.3			

Note: This table is based on information supplied by four major sources: Narrative of Mīrzā Luṭf ʿAlī Shīrāzī; *Tārīkh-i Mīmīya; Nabil;* and Narrative of Āqā Mīr Abū-Ṭālib Shahmīrzādī.

Mullā Fatḥullāh Qumī, an engraver, who was the son of a bookbinder, were two of the three main participants who made an attempt on the life of Nāṣir al-Dīn Shāh and later were executed together with many other Babi merchants, small landowners, and lower-rank state officials who were assembled from all over the country in Tehran.[153]

In addition, some of the new converts to Islam (*jadīd al-Islām*), Jews of Turbat-i Ḥaydarīya, for instance, who were involved in local trade, became curious about the Bab. The Jewish converts of Turbat, originally from Yazd, had suffered persecution and forced conversion of 1839–1840 in Khurasan and were often adhering to a crypto-Judaic faith.[154] In 1850, at the time of Mullā Aḥmad Azghandī's arrest and banishment, six of these Jews, who were on friendly terms with him, sympathized with the Babis, though their full conversion took place a few years later.[155] The motives behind this interest, shared by Jews of Hamadan during Qurrat al-ʿAyn's visit, are to be found in the manner in which a deprived minority expressed itself in the face of persecution, forced conversions, and strict control. Increasingly in later decades of the century, the members of the Jewish community sought messianic salvation in the promises of the Bab and later Bahāʿullāh. They were seeking consolation in a movement which could restore to them, not security, prosperity, or their lost faith, but a sense of ecumenical solidarity, courage in the face of hostile forces, and hope for ultimate relief.

The merchants and artisans who were attracted to the Bab constituted only a tiny minority of that class but their conversion was symptomatic of a dual crisis, both economic and moral. Not surprisingly, the Babi movement spread rapidly along major trade routes of Iran and received support in almost all commercial centers. The opening of the Persian market to foreign trade had already changed the traditional commercial network. Conversion to the Babi faith demonstrated the potentials of a new generation of merchants to embrace an ideology responsive to their widening intellectual horizons. Their pietistic ethos and mystic preoccupations served as an impetus to bring out the merchants' aspiration upon a messianic stage on which the chief actor was one of their own. For many of these merchants, already exposed to the esoteric discourses, the only conceivable vision for moral-material reconstruction was that of a messianic renewal. Rather than encouraging the merchants to take action against material disadvantages and reversals, the changes in the economic climate only made them keener in their moral crusade. Attraction to esoteric and millennial ideals came with a

[153]For quantitative analysis of the background, occupations, and distribution of the early Babis see M. Momen "The Social Basis of the Bābī Upheavals in Iran (1848–53): A Preliminary Analysis" *International Journal of Middle East Studies* 15 (May 1983) 157–83.

[154]*Fu'ādī* 183–85; cf. Lavī *Tārīkh-i Yahūd-i Irān* III, 634. See also Wolff *Mission* (103, 199–200); W. J. Fischel "The Jews of Persia 1795–1940" in *Jewish Social Studies* 12 (1950) 119–60 (124 and sources in footnote 18); *RS* X, 248.

[155]*Fu'ādī* 76, 185–86.

sense of criticism of the moral decline, if not resentment and contempt for material life. This did not mean, however, that they were turning away from the respected norms of the merchant class. Rather, their conversion to a movement with a radical puritanistic message, at least as they saw it, was to reaffirm their loyalty to the values characteristic of their class. During the first phase of the movement, the presence of the merchants in the Babi ranks hardly managed to divert the course of the movement toward further moderation. On the contrary, the Babi merchants willingly pursued the apocalyptic millennium of the Babi mullas at the expense of their own. Only later, after 1852, did the exclusion of the militant activism from the Babi agenda allow the remnant of the Babi merchants to seek in the Bahā'ī faith moral values congruent to their own mercantile world view.

Converts from the Government Ranks

The efforts of the Babi activists among the nonclerical population were not limited to the merchants and their associated groups. Civil servants (*ahl-i dīvān*) of the lower ranks and individuals on the fringe of the Qajar government, both in the capital and in the provinces, also responded to the Bab's message. In Tehran, the early Babi nucleus included young sons of court functionaries, provincial ministers, and army chiefs, as well as low-ranking officials in the central administration. In the provinces, especially in Khurasan and Azarbaijan, there were Babis belonging to the local bureaucratic families. In general the converts did not represent any one faction within the Qajar administration, nor did their adherence to the Bab stem from overt political ambitions. In a few cases, conversion even resulted in voluntary relinquishment of a governmental post; in even fewer cases, it was a consequence of involuntary exclusion from the state establishment. Previous Shaykhi adherence was often a factor in conversions, though there were other religious affiliations as well.

Among the early followers in Tehran who were in some way associated with the government, Mīrzā Ḥusayn ʿAlī Nūrī (d. 1309/1892), known as Bahā' and later Bahā'ullāh, was probably the first who responded favorably to the new claims.[156] During Mullā Ḥusayn's abode in Tehran, Nabīl tells us, Mullā Muḥammad Muʿallim Nūrī, a private tutor to the children of the

[156]The extensive primary sources on the life and thoughts of Bahā'ullāh, including his own works, deserve a separate treatment. Worth mentioning among the existing studies are: H. M. Balyuzi *Bahā'ullāh, the King of Glory* (Oxford, 1980); three entries under BAHĀ'ALLĀH in *EI*[1] by E. G. Browne, in *EI*[2] by A. Bausani, and in *EIr* by J. Cole; Momen *Religions* 177–306. M. A. Malik Khusravī *Iqlīm-i Nūr* (Tehran, 118 Badīʿ/1962) contains new material on Bahā'ullāh's family background and early life. Beside Babi-Bahā'ī primary accounts, including *Nabil,* which covers Bahā'ullāh's life in some detail, three other accounts are of special importance: Sayyid Mahdī Dahajī, Browne Or. MSS no. F.57(9); Mīrzā Jawād Qazvīnī, Browne Or. MSS no. F.26, trans. E. G. Browne in *MSBR* 3–112; and ʿIzzīya Khānum *Tanbīh al-Nā'imīn* Browne Or. MSS no. F.60(8) and F.61(9).

Nūrī household, handed Mīrzā Ḥusayn ʿAlī a written message from the Babi missionary to which he responded with enthusiasm.[157] However, it is after 1847 that he becomes openly active in the Tehran Babi circle.[158] Other members of Mīrzā Ḥusayn ʿAlī's large family, including Mīrzā Yaḥyā (later known as Ṣubḥ-i Azal), Mīrzā Musā and four other brothers, an uncle, and a nephew, also joined the movement.[159]

Mīrzā Ḥusayn ʿAlī (Bahā'ullāh) was born in Tehran to a family of Māzandarānī landowners, in 1233/1817.[160] His father and grandfather, judging by the size of their households and their estate, were established rural notables in the district of Mīyānrūd in the Nūr region.[161] His father, Mīrzā ʿAbbās Nūrī (also known as Mīrzā Buzurg), a distinguished master calligrapher of the early Qajar era,[162] had moved to the capital sometime in the early 1810s. Owing to the Qajars' patronage of artists as well as their special predilection for employing Māzandarānī officials (and because of his cocitizenship with Mīrzā Asadullāh Nūrī, father of Mīrzā Āqā Khān Nūrī), Mīrzā ʿAbbās joined the central army office as a junior secretary and accountant.[163] He was gradually promoted to private secretary, then minister (i.e., the chief administrator: *vazīr*) to the chief of the imperial guard, Imām Virdī Mīrzā, Fatḥ ʿAlī Shāh's twelfth son and the head of the Qajar tribe (*īlkhānī*).[164] He also received royal approbation for his excellent calligraphic work.

In the events immediately after the death of Fatḥ ʿAlī Shāh, in spite of Imām Virdī's collaboration with one of the pretenders to the throne, Mīrzā ʿAbbās seems to have escaped the consequences of his affiliation with the prince, though only temporarily. Because of his past amicable relations with Mīrzā Abul-Qāsim Qā'im Maqām Farāhānī, he was even promoted to the post of vazīr of Burūjird and Luristān.[165] Less than a year later, however, in a widespread purge of the old administration under the newly appointed premier, Āqāsī, Mīrzā ʿAbbās lost not only his office and his tenure but a great portion of his fortune.[166] His brief, ill-fated marriage to Żīyā' al-Salṭana, the celebrated daughter of Fatḥ ʿAlī Shāh, contributed to his downfall.[167] Whatever purpose this marriage was initially intended to serve, its

[157] *Nabil* 104–8. Mullā Ḥusayn distributed copies of the Bab's *Qayyūm al-Asmā'* among other notables in the capital (*Muʿīn* 71).

[158] *TN* 58–62; M. J. Qazvīnī "Epitome" (*MSBR* 3–4); *KD* I, 257–70; and *NK* 200, 239–40.

[159] *Nabil* 109–19; *TN* 373–74; *Samandar* 161.

[160] Shaykh Muḥammad Nabīl Zarandī "Chronological Poem" Browne, *JRAS* (1899) B. II, 985.

[161] *Iqlīm Nūr* 2–16, 86–97.

[162] See in *EIr*: ʿABBĀS (P. P. Soucek) for his calligraphical works and administrative career.

[163] Bamdād *Rijāl* VI, 126–29.

[164] *Iqlīm Nūr* 113–14; Bamdād *Rijāl* VI, 127.

[165] For his relations with Qā'im Maqām see the latter's *Munsha'āt* ed. J. Qā'im Maqāmī (Tehran, 1337/1958) 37, 116, 117, 126, and 181.

[166] Bamdād *Rijāl* VI, 128; *Iqlīm Nūr* 118–26; *Nabil* 109.

[167] *Iqlīm Nūr* 205–8, 122.

outcome was ominous for Mīrzā ʿAbbās and his family. Between 1835 and 1839, mainly under the pretext of resisting the reimbursement of Żīyāʾ al-Salṭana's huge marriage portion *(mahr)*, apparently after being forced to divorce the princess, Mīrzā ʿAbbās was disgraced, put under house arrest, and bastinadoed by the prime minister's agents and collaborators.[168] The family's houses were confiscated and Mīrzā ʿAbbās's wives and thirteen children were separated. In 1839, Mīrzā ʿAbbās died in isolation and despair.[169]

His father's unhappy fate and sudden ruination appears to have generated in Bahāʾullāh a distaste for temporal power. His own later experiences further confirmed his denunciation of "worldly ambitions," even when in late 1840s and early 1850s he stood a chance to secure a government post. In spite of a brief rapprochement with Āqāsī[170] and later with Āqā Khān Nūrī, the ministers' suspicion and lack of interest kept him away from administrative positions. The affairs concerning the ownership of the village of Qūch Ḥiṣār, a private property in the southern outskirts of Tehran belonging to Mīrzā ʿAbbās to which Āqāsī laid a claim, renewed animosity between Bahāʾullāh and the chief minister.[171] During the premiership of Mīrzā Taqī Khān Amīr Kabīr (1848–1851), Bahāʾullāh's disclosed Babi leanings met with the premier's disapproval, and in summer of 1851 he went briefly into voluntary exile in the ʿAtabāt.[172] On his return to Tehran, a few months later after the downfall of Amīr Kabīr, Bahāʾullāh's hopes of reaching an understanding with the new premier Mīrzā Āqā Khān Nūrī (a distant relative) were shattered when, in the wake of the 1852 Babi assassination attempt against Nāṣir al-Dīn, he was imprisoned on suspicion of involvement in the plot. Though Mīrzā Āqā Khān was effective in saving him from execution, his ensuing exile to Baghdad severed his remaining links with the Tehran political establishment.[173]

The events of 1848–1852 and Bahāʾullāh's unsuccessful efforts to maintain a middle ground between his fellow Babi coreligionists and the state no doubt confirmed his original ambivalence toward political power. In 1868, when he was imprisoned in ʿAkkā, on the tablet of Raʾīs addressed to the Ottoman grand vazir, Bahāʾullāh related a childhood memory when a scene of puppetry unfolded to him the elusive nature of temporal power. At the end of the show, the puppeteer told the astonished boy that all the displayed pomp and circumstance of Sulṭān Salīm's court, including the sultan, his chiefs, and his ministers, were inside a chest. "From that day," Bahāʾullāh

[168]Ibid. 121–22; cf. Bahāʾullāh *Lawḥ Mubārak Khiṭāb bi Shaykh Muḥammad Taqī* (Tehran, n.d.) 199 trans. Shoghi Effendi *Epistle to the Son of the Wolf* (Wilmette, Ill., 1941).

[169]*Iqlīm Nūr* 122–23; Bāmdād *Rijāl* IV, 128.

[170]*Nabil* 120.

[171]*Nabil* 120–21; cf. *Iqlīm Nūr* 182–85.

[172]*Nabil* 32, 587, 593–94.

[173]For Bahāʾullāh's involvement in the events of 1852 and its aftermath see *Nabil* 595–602; Momen *Religions* 128–46.

recalls, "all the [material] instruments of this world in the eye of this slave [himself] resembled that performance, and had no significance whatsoever [for me], even as much as a grain of mustard. The people of insight can see with the eye of certainty beyond the pomp of possessors of material power its decline. Like those puppets, soon the superficial instruments [of power], the apparent treasures, the worldly ornaments, the military ranks, the luxurious clothes, and their arrogant possessors will proceed toward the grave chest. In the eyes of the people of insight, all those conflicts, struggles, and arrogance resemble children's toys."[174]

This attitude permeates the writings of Bahā'ullāh, demonstrating a mystical trait not unrelated to his earlier exposure to Sufism of his own time. His acquaintance with Sufi dignitaries in Muḥammad Shāh's court and his attraction to wandering dervishes may suggest a vigorous interest in Sufism. In his youth, reportedly, "he was keen to speak about saints and mystics. . . . In any feast or gathering, if someone criticized the sayings of the mystics or brought forward a problem about the words of the saints, he would reply to the criticism or resolve the problem without any hesitation."[175] Some of his later works composed in the Sufi tradition, as well as his later retirement in the refuge of Khālidī-Naqshbandī convents in Kurdistan (1854–1856), reveal a mystical outlook pivotal to his later messianic claims and his sociomoral reforms.[176] Yet, it seems that his earlier preoccupation with mysticism did not prevent him from regarding the claims of his contemporary Sufis with skepticism.[177] Bahā'ullāh's mystical bent was in harmony with the growing popularity of Shiʿite-Sufi orders, particularly Niʿmatullāhīs, among the notables of Muḥammad Shāh's time. But for Bahā'ullāh, as for some Sufis who joined the movement, mysticism provided a channel through which the notions of human perfection and moral renewal could be contemplated, and tenets of orthodox Islam could be reevaluated, and at times rejected.

An essential feature of Sufi thought—the doctrine of the Perfect Man, the need for a living spiritual guide together with the methods of purification and self-denial—were synonymous with Shaykhism. In spite of Aḥsā'ī's denunciation of Sufism, many of its features were adopted into his theosophy. The point of confluence between the apparently diverse streams of Shaykhism and Sufism was the yearning for moral perfection. Bahā'ullah's

[174]"Lawḥ-ī Raʿīs" in *Majmūʿa Alwāḥi Mubāraka* (Cairo, 1920) 107–11.

[175]*KD* I, 264.

[176]Among his works with evident mystical leanings are *Haft Wādī, Chahār Wādī va Jawāhir al-Āthār* (Tehran, 129 Badīʿ/1972) trans. ʿAlī Qulī Nabīl al-Daula as *The Seven Valleys and the Four Valleys* (Wilmette, Ill., 1945, rev. ed. 1952) and "Kalamāt Maknūna" *Majmūʿa-yi Alwāḥ-i Mubāraka* (Cairo, 1338/1920) trans. Shoghi Effendi as *The Hidden Words* (Wilmette, Ill., 1939). See also J. Cole "Bahā'ullāh and the Naqshbandī Sufis in Iraq, 1854–1856" in *From Iran East and West* ed. J. Cole and M. Momen (Los Angeles, 1984) 1–28 and A. Taherzadeh *The Revelation of Bahā'ullāh* 2 vols. (Oxford, 1974–1976) I, 45–149.

[177]Abul-Fażl Gulpāyigānī "Risāla Iskandarīya" *Sī risāla* (Cairo, 1318/1900).

vision of such perfection, however, was as different from that of Babi mullas and merchants as his social background and his causes of grievance. Yet the appeal of the nascent Babism was broad enough to allow a convergence of views; a consensus upon which converts from all walks of life could share a common goal. Bahā'ullāh's later rediversion of the course of militant Babism after 1852 (and more noticeably after 1864) toward moderation was in sharp contrast to the policies of the radical wing of the movement, headed, at least nominally, by his own brother, Mīrzā Yaḥyā Nūrī Ṣubḥ-i Azal. The politically pacifist current founded by Bahā'ullāh, which eventually evolved into the Bahā'ī religion, was no doubt affected by his frustration with the disastrous outcome of the Babi experience. Unlike many of his coreligionists, who were preoccupied with the Shiʿite vision of a utopian political order under the aegis of the Imam of the Age, Bahā'ullāh focused his efforts on disentangling moral ideals from political claims; a Sufi legacy that he stretched to new frontiers in order to resolve an eternal problem of Islamic faith. By forging a new source of loyalty on a largely moral basis, Bahā'ullāh envisaged a suprareligious ecumen free from the political claims of the Islamic community (*umma*). The later Bahā'ī-Azalī division, which plunged the Babi community into a bitter sectarian conflict, was above all a division over policy and outlook, though the dispute over succession, legitimacy, and leadership played its role as well. Unlike the Azalī faction, still largely reminiscent of the early years, Bahā'ullāh urged a compromise with the state, perhaps as early as Badasht days of 1848. In later years, in bitter disillusion with their political defeat, the majority of the Babis turned to him for a leadership free of political ambitions but not devoid of a sociomoral program.

Bahā'ullāh was not typical of the Babi converts with administrative or courtly backgrounds. Most other believers of this category showed a greater degree of militancy and zeal, which though directed primarily against the religious establishment were not free from antistate sentiments. One of the most active, and probably the closest to court circles, was Mīrzā Riżā Qulī Turkamān, son of the Turkoman chief Muḥammad Khān Mīr Ākhur, head of the royal stable under Muḥammad Shāh (Muḥammad Khān, later known as Sipahsālār Aʿẓam, the prime minister under Nāṣir al-Dīn Shāh, was his brother-in-law.)[178] Like Bahā'ullāh, Riżā Qulī Khān became acquainted with the Babis through Mullā Ḥusayn's contacts in Tehran, Mullā Muḥammad Muʿallim Nūrī and the Kanī brothers. A man of wealth and influence, Riżā Qulī did not hesitate to publicize his Babi beliefs, nor to spend large sums—four to five thousand tūmāns—to promote the Babi cause.[179] His house in Tehran was the gathering place for some Babis, a refuge for the others. In 1263/1847, in the village of Khānluq on the outskirts of Tehran,

[178]For his account see Bāmdād *Rijāl* III, 228–32.
[179]*NK* 194.

his offer to rescue the Bab from government detention was turned down. A year later, an unsheathed sword on his shoulder, he was in Bārfurūsh defending Quddūs against growing physical threats from his opponents.[180] He then joined Mullā Ḥusayn in Mashhad, during the earliest Babi clashes in that city. After Badasht, he returned to Tehran, where he joined the Qajar contingency forces and left for Ṭabarsī, presumably in the hope of mediating between the Babis and the prince governor, Mahdī Qūlī Mīrzā. When negotiations failed, he defected to the Babi side and fought against government troops before surrendering himself at the end of the fightings. Eventually, by the order of Mahdī Qūlī Mīrzā, he was torn to pieces.[181]

In close contact with Riżā Qulī Khān and Bahā'ullāh was another convert from Nūr: Mīrzā Sulaymān Qulī, son of Shāṭirbāshī, chief of the royal footmen. His recitation skills earned him the title *Khaṭīb al-Raḥmān* (the orator of the merciful). His missionary activities took him throughout Iran before being captured and executed; at the insistence of his brother,[182] in the massacre of 1268/1852 in Tehran.

Another well-known member of the Tehran Babi group to perish in the 1852 massacre was Sulaymān Khān Tabrīzī, the son of Yaḥyā Khān, an army chief and previously commander of the royal stewards of the crown prince ʿAbbās Mīrzā.[183] An adherent to Shaykhism, presumably from the Shaykhi quarter of Amīr Khīz in Tabrīz, Sulaymān Khān spent some time in Karbalā', where he frequented Rashtī's lectures.[184] In a second journey to the ʿAtabāt, through his acquaintance with Mullā Mahdī Khu'ī and other Āẕarbāijānī activists, he joined the Babis. In Tehran, in collaboration with Bahā'ullāh, he tried in vain to reverse the death sentence imposed on the Bab.[185] In the same year, Sulaymān Khān's brother Farrukh Khān, who was sent to Zanjān to crush the Babi uprising, was killed by followers of Mullā Muḥammad ʿAlī Ḥujjat Zanjānī.[186] Mīrzā Taqī Khān Amīr Kabīr, knowing of Sulaymān Khān's Babi leanings, tolerated him. He was ordered by the prime minister to change his white Arabian dress and wear a civilian hat instead of a turban; presumably to underline his disapproval of Sulaymān's involvement with the radical mullas.[187] After 1266/1850, the house of Sulaymān Khān became the center of the Babi clandestine activities led by Shaykh ʿAlī ʿAẓīm.[188] Following the unsuccessful attempt on Nāṣir al-Dīn and the ensuing Babi killing of 1852, Sulaymān Khān was captured and put

[180]Ibid. 195.
[181]Zavārih-ī *Mīmīya;* cf. *NK* 196.
[182]Malik Khusravī *Shuhadā-yi Amr* III, 264–65, citing ʿAbdulbahā'.
[183]For Yaḥyā Khān's services to the Qajars during the Russo-Persian wars see *RS* IX, 670–71. During the Sālār revolt of 1847–1849 he was given the charge of transferring the captive Sālār to Tehran (*RS* X, 381–84).
[184]*ZH* 23.
[185]Ibid. 24.
[186]Mīrzā Ḥusayn Zanjānī *Tārīkh* folio 19 a-b; cf. *NT* III, 295.
[187]*ZH* 24.
[188]*Vaqāyiʿ Ittifāqīya,* no. 82; cf. Malik Khusravī *Shuhadā-yi Amr* 227.

to death. His cruel and painful death earned him a special place in the chronicles of the Babi martyrs.[189]

Other members of Tehran group with bureaucratic backgrounds included Mīrzā Ḥasan Tafrishī Mustaufī (accountant), Mīrzā Muḥammad, the deputy chief of the Chāpār Khānih (the postal service), Mīrzā Masīḥ Nūrī, a nephew of Mīrzā Āqā Khān Nūrī, and three low-rank scribes who were executed in 1852 in Tehran.[190] It is not unlikely that at some stage before 1852 the Tehran Babis had attracted other sympathizers among state officials.

In provincial level, governmental functionaries with local tribal or urban bases were attracted to the Babis. A remarkable example was Riżā Qulī Khān, son of Sulaymān Khān Afshār Ṣā'īn Qalʿa and son-in-law of Sayyid Kāẓim Rashtī.[191] He was an Afshār chief with the rank of *sartīp* (bregadier) in the Azarbaijan army. In spite of his father's zealous adherence to Muḥammad Karīm Khān Kirmānī, Riżā Qulī showed sympathy and respect to the Bab during his mission of transferring him from Mākū to Chihrīq in 1264/1848.[192] His Babi leanings added fuel to what appears to have been an old dispute with his father. The breach between the two widened following the key role played by Sulaymān Khān in crushing the Babi resistance in Ṭabarsī and shortly after, in the execution of the Bab.[193] Some years later, Sulaymān Khān's complaints to the provincial government concerning his son's heretical beliefs—accusing him of even cutting off the ear of a muezzin at the height of his anti-Islamic rage—ended in Riżā Qulī's detention and probably loss of his family estate in Ṣā'īn Qalʿa. Residing in Tehran during later Nāṣirī period, he was reportedly poisoned by his own son for reasons of religious enmity.[194] Other Babi converts of Azarbaijan included Mīrzā Luṭf ʿAlī Salmāsī (possibly from Ahl-i Ḥaqq), a steward in Muḥammad Shāh's court. Following his conversion by Vaḥīd he was instructed to deliver Bab's addresses to the monarch and his minister. As a result he was dismissed from service and took residence in Salmās, where he played host to the Bab in 1266/1850.[195]

A small group of low-ranking local officials among the early converts in Khurasan also deserves some attention. During his first mission to Khurasan, when passing through Sabzivār, Mullā Ḥusayn paid a brief visit to a number of local *mustaufīs* (government accountants), who had perhaps had Shaykhi sympathy. Later, two brothers, Mīrzā ʿAlī Riżā Mustaufī and

[189]The account of Sulaymān Khān's brutal execution is recorded by many sources including *Vaqāyiʿ Ittifāqīya*, no. 82; *NT* IV, 42; *ZH* 26 (n.). For European accounts see *TN* 330–31 and Momen *Religions* 128–46.

[190]*ZH* 216–17.

[191]For Sulaymān Khān see above, chap. 5.

[192]*Muʿīn* 169–72. See below, chap. 9.

[193]For his involvement in Ṭabarsī see *NT* III, 244.

[194]*Muʿīn* 173–76.

[195]*ZH* 66.

Mīrzā Muḥammad Riżā (later Mu'taman al-Salṭana), and some of their relatives became supporters of the Bab.[196] Their affiliation to the movement largely remained secret, but they donated funds to the Mazandaran march,[197] and in the following years provided comfort for the Babis at times of persecution and trouble.[198] Toward the 1290s/1870s, both brothers were promoted: Mīrzā ʿAlī Riżā became a revenue accountant "in the royal presence",[199] and Mu'taman al-Salṭana, the chief accountant of Khurasan.[200] Nāṣir al-Dīn Shāh, highly suspicious of Mu'taman al-Salṭana's Babi sentiments, ordered his transfer to the city of Kashan, where he was in virtual exile. Later, the shah summoned him to the capital, where he reportedly was forced to marry the shah's sister, then to drink "poisonous coffee" (1310/1892–1893).[201]

Mīrzā Muḥammad Taqī Juvaynī, another early Babi convert, was a humble scribe and accountant from the village of Juvayn. He encountered Mullā Ḥusayn on one of his visits to Sabzivār. Juvaynī's active participation began during the Ṭabarsī upheaval, when he held the responsibility for receipts and expenditure of the common funds[202] and on a few occasions acted as the representative of the Babi party in negotiations with the local chiefs and state officials.[203] His most dramatic act, which could be seen as a final declaration of war against the government, was the slaying of Khusrau Khān Qādīkalā'ī, a tribal brigand in the service of the local government, as a reprisal for his deceitful behavior toward the confused Babi column. In the final surrender of the Babi fighters, Mīrzā Muḥammad Taqī was captured and put to death. His head was spiked on a spear and carried around the city of Bārfurūsh.[204]

The Babi Community: An Assessment

The activities of the Babi disciples influenced a spectrum of individuals with diverse affiliations and stretching over a broad geographical span throughout Iran and Iraq. In this nationwide appeal, the largest and the most prominent body of believers were from the religious class, often from

[196]*Fu'ādī* 30, 67.

[197]Ibid. 67.

[198]Ibid. 67–72. *Tārīkh-i Amrī-yi Khurāsān* uses many local sources, including oral accounts from the members of the Mustaufī and Mustashār Daftar families (30, 73).

[199]Muḥammad Ḥasan Khān Iʿtimād al-Salṭana *Mir'āt al-Buldān-i Nāṣirī* (Tehran 1296/1878) III, supp. 12.

[200]Iʿtimād al-Salṭana *al-Ma'āthir wa'l-Āthār* supp. 29, 55; *Tārīkh-i Muntaẓam-i Nāṣirī* III, supp. 23.

[201]*Fu'ādī* 70–72. See also Sheil *Glimpses of Life and Manners* 92.

[202]*NT* III, 236. *Nabil* (417) refers to his "literary accomplishment."

[203]*Tārīkh-i Mīmīya* 22 (negotiations with the governor of Mazandaran Khānlar Mīrzā), 34–35 (with ʿAbbās Qulī Khān Lārījānī).

[204]*Nabil* 417.

lower and middle echelons and always with nonorthodox leanings. Merchants and the members of the guilds made up the second largest group. Together with urban mullas and state officials, the merchants formed the intellectual elite of the Babis, with the seminarians, the guilds, and the peasantry as its rank and file. The counterparts of the Babi ʿulama in the countryside, the village mullas, also had some success in converting their small constituencies. A few landowners of higher status and economic caliber and chiefs of settled nomadic clans also joined, especially in Mazandaran and Fars. Notwithstanding the Sufis' apathy toward Babism, a few Niʿmatullāhīs, theosophists *(ḥikamī)*, and wandering dervishes were also in the Babi ranks. The state officials, not a large group, gained some prominence, for they were able for a time to provide limited protection for their coreligionists.

The Babis' geographical distribution can be divided into six regions. Khurasan probably contained the largest number of Babi believers, some from the provincial capital Mashhad and smaller cities such as Sabzivār, Nīshābūr and Qāʾin but mostly from rural regions of central-southern Khurasan. Mazandaran contained the second-largest number, with some concentration in Bārfurūsh, and with exceptionally large numbers in rural regions of Nūr, ʿAlīābād, Bahnamīr, Sangsar, and Shahmīrzād and smaller numbers in Sārī, ʿArab-Khayl, Savād-Kūh, Āmul, and the surrounding villages. The third region included communities in central and western provinces roughly corresponding to provinces of Isfahan, ʿIrāq ʿAjam, and beyond. A sizable group existed in Isfahan, a large community in Ardistān, and a noticeable group in Kashan and the surrounding villages: Narāq, slightly later in Qamṣar, Jaushiqān, Vādiqān, and Naṭanz. The larger bodies of converts in Tehran, Qazvin, and Zanjān (by 1850 probably the largest single Babi community in Iran) were mostly of urban origin, with some rural connections. While the first two included some notables, the latter was predominantly constituted of lower classes. Other Babis were scattered in small groups in Kirind, Ṣaḥna (both of Ahl-i Ḥaqq), Hamadan, Kirmānshāh, Qum, and Ishtihārd. The fourth region was Iraq, with concentration among the Shaykhis of Karbalāʾ and a few others in Kāẓimayn and Baghdad. The fifth region, Fars and Yazd, consisted of both urban and rural Babis. In Shiraz they were mostly artisans and lower-rank merchants. Nayrīz, a base for Sayyid Yaḥyā Dārābī (Vaḥīd) and the scene of later conflict during 1849–1852, housed a semirural community under the joint leadership of the landed notables and religious leaders. Other communities in Iṣṭahbānāt, including Hindījān and Mihrījird, another in Sarvistān, and individuals in villages and towns throughout southeastern districts, were mostly converted through Vaḥīd. The Babis of Yazd and the environs, including mullas, merchants, a physician, and members of guilds as well as peasants and small landowners, were also among his followers. Azarbaijan, the sixth region, witnessed noticeable examples of mass conversion in the rural areas as well as individual conversions in the cities. Smaller Babi groups were also scattered in Kirman, Astarābād, possibly Luristān, Kurdistan, and even the Shiʿite kingdom of Lucknow in India.

The entire population of the Babis in the late 1840s can hardly have exceeded the rough estimate of a hundred thousand indicated by various observers.[205] The Babi minority constituted some 1.6 percent of Iran's total population of a maximum six million in the same period. Quantitatively, the ratio does not present a breakthrough. But of the total population, about three million were nomads, and of the remaining half perhaps only 10 percent, or six hundred thousand, were urban. The rest were villagers. As far as can be ascertained, there were no nomadic Babis. Moreover, the ratio of the urban to rural Babis was probably no less than one to three. Thus, the Babis perhaps constituted over 4 percent of the urban population and some 3 percent of the village population.

By the token of its message, Babism was bound to remain a minority movement even during its short history as a dynamic social force. But its broad diffusion and intensive proselytism made its bold message audible throughout the country out of proportion to its size. Regional nuances no doubt influenced both the pattern of Babi conversion and the reception of its message. One definitely influential factor was the preexistence of numerous heterodox communities, both open and semisecret, on the highly diverse map of religious adherence. Above all these were Shaykhi nuclei and communities of various size. If not converts defecting from mainstream religion, the Shaykhi adherents were often individuals or groups with heterodox history who resisted assimilation by choosing Shaykhism as a replacement for the older affiliation. Of all the alternatives to majority Shiʿism in the mid-nineteenth century Shaykhism probably had the largest adherence, widest distribution, and greatest visibility, superseding both Sufi orders and the declining Akhbārīs. Such extensive grass-roots support was the most effective factor in the success of the Babi recruitment.

The Babis were able to recruit from other nonconformist minorities, however. Though often overlooked, the conversions from the Ahl-i Ḥaqq and associated "extremists" to the Babi movement were perhaps second only to the Shaykhis. Both as individuals and occasionally as a community, they showed greater receptivity, since their messianic expectations and their outlook, especially on the doctrine of prophethood, could be accommodated by the Babi Ẓuhūr. By the nineteenth century Ahl-i Ḥaqq had become largely a peasant religion with a syncretic belief system that had survived openly only in Kurdish, Persianized Kurdish, and Āẕārī communities of western and northwestern Iran. But in all probability the geographical distribution of the Ahl-i Ḥaqq included many scattered localities in central, northern, and even

[205] See P. Smith "A Note on Babi and Bahā'i Numbers in Iran" *Iranian Studies* 17 (Spring-Summer 1984) 295–301 and cited sources.

eastern Iran. The same is true with Ismāʿīlī village communities in central and southern Khurasan. Their receptivity to Shaykhism and then Babism came at a time when the Ismāʿīlī revival since the late eighteenth century, first through the Niʿmatullāhī medium and then under Shāh Khalīlullāh and Āqā Khān, had already kindled the messianic hopes of ʿAṭā'ullāhī tribe in southern Khurasan and Kirman.

Mass conversion among followers of Mullā Muḥammad ʿAlī Zanjānī (Ḥujjat), himself a militant Akhbārī, is another indication of the Babi appeal to nonconformist minorities. The socioreligious background of Zanjān Babis still remains a mystery, but certain peculiarities in their mass behavior betray the likelihood of religious extremism far distinct from the learned Akhbāriṣm of the madrasa tradition.

While to contribute the rapid expansion of Babism solely to the preexistence of heterodoxies would be a gross simplification, it must be stressed that even in the mid-nineteenth century, Persian society was far less monolithic, less religiously homogeneous, than often acknowledged. The network of heterodoxies—whether those that reemerged in post-Safavid era in the Sufi guise or those that survived in their original form—was still not conquered by the Twelver Shiʿism of the Uṣūlī ʿulama. More often than not, the plethora of invisible heterodoxies found a common ground in a single current that could shield them against the pressure of the majority religion. The upsurge of Babism was thus a point of confluence for diverse trends that shared as much common messianic aspirations as repulsion of the religious establishment and hatred for the oppressive temporal power. The potential of the movement was immense, even unique, as it was able to fuse the popular messianism of the countryside with the socially complex and intellectually elaborate nonconformism of the cities. The catalysts of this process were sectarian conflicts, material decline, and naked oppression. In such circumstances the special appeal of the Babi movement was to individuals and groups on the fringes of society who were troubled, more in heart than in mind, by the increasingly visible manifestations of disorder and decay. In its formative stages, the movement was fluid enough to project grievances of groups as diverse as mullas and women. What cemented these groups into one and gave them a focus and a symbol of sanctity was the Bab, and under him a circle of semiprophetic figures to whom the Babis could attach new bonds of loyalty beyond their professional and regional affiliations. The symbolic presence of the Bab, and the message he advocated in conjunction with the evolving aspiration of his followers, at least for a time, maintained the momentum and guaranteed the solidarity of the movement.

9

The Final Break

In Jumadā al-Ūlā 1263/late May 1847, en route to his exile to the mountains of western Azarbaijan, the Bab arrived in Tabriz after several months of seclusion in Isfahan and later waiting in vain on the outskirts of the capital for an audience with the shah. His incarceration in the remote border town of Mākū, which had a predominantly non-Shiʿite population, came as a shock to the sayyid of Shiraz. After some hesitation, and for the third time since his captivity, he had rejected an offer of rescue, made by the Babis of Zanjān.[1] Fearing that such an act might cast him as a rebel, the Bab preferred direct petition to the state authorities. From Sīyāh Dihān, outside Zanjān, he wrote the shah the first of several letters urging him to reconsider his decision:

> If I am a believer, and that I am, may God and his friends be witness . . . such treatment is not fair, and if I am an infidel, and that I swear to the sacred divine essence and the high status of the Prophet of the House of Innocence I am not—and be it known that under the shadow of that imperial bounty in every [part of this] land there are many infidels—still such verdict is unjust. . . . I have not the slightest doubt of my own innocence and if you look at the work revealed from the secret of the divine Providence, your suspicions will be removed. However, if you still believe that I deserve death I swear to the sacred divine essence that I am eager to die more than an infant is eager for his mother's breast. In the name of God and by God I am waiting for that verdict and I am resigned to God's judgment.[2]

[1]The incident incited a riot in the city and intensified the factional strife, and shortly after led to the expulsion of the governor of Zanjān, ʿAlī Ashraf Khān Mākū'ī. For the Bab's passage through Zanjān see *NK* 125–26; *Nabil* 236, 531–33, and *ZH* 75. For the Zanjān riot of 1847 see *NT* III, 130–31.

[2]For the full text see Fayżī *Nuqṭa-yi Ūlā* 220–21.

Imprisonment and Protest

Resignation and willingness to die are a predominant theme in the Bab's writings of the Azarbaijan period, paralleling his utmost reluctance to accept exile and imprisonment. His complaints rang with the indignation of a wronged ascetic dishonored by the king's heedless treatment. In another letter to the shah, from Mākū, he makes his objection bitterly plain: "When I learned of your command, I wrote to the administrator of the kingdom: 'By God! Kill me and send my head wherever you please because for me to live and be sentenced to the place of the criminals is not honorable.' No reply was ever received since I am certain his excellency the Ḥajji [i.e., Ḥājjī Mīrzā Āqāsī] has not fully brought the matter to your attention."[3]

As the Bab suspected, the "administrator of the kingdom" had no ear for the grievances of a Shīrāzī sayyid whom he considered nothing more than an insane imposter. Exile in Mākū, where he hoped to keep his potentially valuable captive in isolation, was the best alternative to Āqāsī's initial plan to keep the Bab under house arrest in Tehran. The Mākū'ī officials constituted a critical component of Āqāsī's regime, and his lifelong association with the family of ʿAlī Khān Sardār, the chief of Mākū, was an extra incentive.[4]

Disappointed at receiving no positive answer from Tehran, the Bab turned to the shah's brother, Bahman Mīrzā, the governor general of Azarbaijan. But again his repeated petitions fell on deaf ears. From Mīyānih, some hundred miles east of Tabriz, the Bab dispatched Muḥammad Bag Chāpārchī,[5] the chief of the guards in charge of his transfer to Azarbaijan, with a message urging the prince to permit him to remain in Tabriz. In exchange, the Bab hinted, he would extend his blessings to the governor.[6] Bahman Mīrzā, whose alleged political ambitions had already made him the latest target of Āqāsī's antagonism toward potential successors of the dying Muḥammad Shāh, was clearly in a predicament.[7] Any leniency toward the Bab would be taken by his watchful opponents, both in Tabriz and in Tehran, as a sign of betrayal of the shah. Yet the prospect of the Babi support in the ongoing power struggle could not be altogether dismissed. During the Bab's forty-day stay in Tabriz, the prince seems to have toyed

[3]INBA no. 64, 103–26 (118).

[4]See *EIr*: ĀQĀSĪ and the cited sources.

[5]A Nuṣayrī (Ahl-i Ḥaqq) from Azarbaijan, Muḥammad Bag was Āqāsī's trusted courier. Deeply impressed by the Bab, he eventually converted in Mākū. For his account see *ZH* 16, 39–40, and *NK* 130.

[6]*Muʿīn* 136.

[7]An educated prince and a patron of literature and scholarship, Bahman Mīrzā was a member of the anti-Āqāsī coalition that toward the end of Muḥammad Shāh's reign unsuccessfully tried to remove the premier. For his account see E. B. Eastwick *Journal of a Diplomate's Three Years' Residence in Persia* 2 vols. (London, 1864).

with the idea, at the same time testing the reaction of the Tabriz clergy. But the ʿulama of the city, both Shaykhis and Uṣūlīs, perhaps fearing a repetition of the Isfahan events, made their displeasure clear by refusing to grant interviews to the Bab.[8]

In early July the Bab was finally sent to Mākū. On foot, he made "the journey of oppression" to a remote frontier fortress, where he remained incarcerated for the next nine months.[9] But life in Mākū proved to be less stringent than either premier or the Bab expected. Soon after his arrival, a stream of the Babi and non-Babi visitors began to reach Mākū. In spite of some early restrictions imposed by ʿAlī Khān Sardār, the visitors were allowed to communicate with the Bab, often through his aide and secretary, Sayyid Ḥusayn Yazdī (and his brother, Sayyid Ḥasan Yazdī) and even at times to visit him inside the fortress. With occasional censoring, he was allowed to maintain his correspondence with his disciples and relatives.

Solitary life in the awesome fortress, located beneath a huge hanging cliff and looking across a vast, lonesome plain, generated mixed feelings in the Bab.[10] In a letter to Muḥammad Shāh the Bab describes his solitude: "[I] swear by the Great Lord [i.e., Muḥammad] that if you knew in what place I dwell, you would be the first to pity me. Admist the mountain there is a fortress and there by your majesty's favor I dwell. Its inhabitants are limited to two guards and four dogs."[11] In this unfamiliar, melancholic surrounding, grief and joy came to the Bab at rapid intervals. Moments of "intense grief" reached their height during the customary recitation of the tragedies of Karbalāʾ. Frequently, readings from the Shiʿite book of elegies, *Muḥriq al-Qulūb,* or recitations by the Babi elegist Dakhīl Marāghih'ī stirred his deepest emotions.[12] The same sense of grief is reflected in his private correspondence with members of his family in Shiraz.

Greater consciousness in his writings in this period of his own emotional impulses, together with a noticeably improved clarity and assertiveness of style, demonstrate the Bab's intellectual maturation. The Mākū period proved to be one of the most prolific phases of his short life. Besides numerous letters and sermons, he compiled parts of the Persian *Bayān*, his most

[8]For an account of the Bab's first abode in Tabriz see *Muʿīn* 137–49. Among visitors to the Tabriz citadel (*Arg*, also known as Shanb-i Ghāzān) where the Bab was detained was a certain Jawād Khān Ātash Bagī, who commented that the ʿulama were fearful of the Bab because "he made redundant their parasitic tutelage."

[9]*NK* 129.

[10]The Bab himself acknowledged the relative ease by which he could make contact with the outside by referring to Mākū as the "open mountain" (*jibal-i bāsiṭ; bāsiṭ* being numerically equivalent to Mākū). This may also be an allusion to a state of mind. The state of openness (*basṭ*), as in Sufi terminology, contrasts the state of contraction or depression (*qabż*).

[11]INBA no. 64, 116–17.

[12]*Nabil* 252. Later in Chihrīq, as the local Babi rawża khwān Mullā ʿAlī Kuhnih Shahrī relates, every Thursday night the Bab listened to his rawża khwānī. "He remained on his feet from the beginning to the end with his eyes closed while the flow of tears would cover his face and drip on his cloak" (*Muʿīn* 131). See also *Bayān* VI/5, 197 for recommendations concerning the prohibition of enduring grief upon others.

systematic and textually coherent work, and wrote an apologia, *Dalāʾil-i Sabʿa* (the Seven Proofs), in defense of his claims. It was in Mākū, too, that for the first time the nascent theme of a new prophetic dispensation took consistent shape.

Preoccupation with his fateful destiny and unavoidable suffering at the hands of his oppressors brought the Bab closer to the point of rebellion. Homesickness, confinement, and the looming prospect of death brought to the surface a far more daring and resolute Bab unrestrained by prudence and self-protectiveness. The Bab was convinced of God's irreversible plans; his frustration with the negative response to his call generated two apparently contrasting impulses of resignation and protest. Writing in late 1263/1847 from the "land of grief," he expressed his disillusionment clearly: "Let us not bother with people's opinion. Although their cries of 'Hurry up! Hurry up!' [i.e., pleas for the Advent of the Mahdi] have filled the earth, they are not sincere. We have tested them. Now nothing for us is more expedient than leaving them to themselves to read their prayers of *ʿAhd-nāmih* and Repentance [*Nudba*] but remain ignorant of the real lord."[13]

It was in Mākū that the Bab voiced his first unequivocal protests against government in plainly messianic terms. Such protests were not unrelated to the apparent shift in his doctrinal position. His inner conviction of his divine mission now emerged with greater clarity in a claim to the Qāʾimīya itself.

The most open expression of doctrinal independence, and consequent break from Islam, appears in the sermon of *Qāʾimīya*, where the Bab plainly declares both his mission as the fulfillment of the prophecies for the Return of the Mahdi and, more important, the abrogation of the Islamic sharīʿa. Addressed to Mullā ʿAlī Turshīzī ʿAẓīm, then the foremost among the believers in Azarbaijan, the sermon calls upon him as the messenger between the people and the Qāʾim "who by God's benevolence has now manifested himself." It then declares:

> I am that divine fire which God kindles on the Day of Qiyāma. By which all will be resurrected and revived, then either they shun away from it or enter the Paradise through it. Say! those who enter the gate (*bāb*) with reverence, by the Lord of the Heavens and the Earth, the Lord of both worlds, God will add to the number of their fire [*nāruhum: nār* numerically equals 251] the number of

[13]INBA no. 40, 221, letter to an unspecified member of his family in Shiraz. In his correspondence with his wife, Khadīja, the Bab nevertheless extended his usual reassurances and his affection. In a letter presumably from Tabriz, he consoles his "dearest soul" for the unfortunate turn of events that caused their separation. He also sends her a piece of velvet and a bottle of perfume (INBA no. 59, 166–69). In another letter from Mākū he informs his family that he has sent a booklet containing "prayers for the people of the house" and asks for five scarves and ten handkerchiefs (INBA no. 58, 160–62). He also orders for his personal use a volume of his own prayers to be written on "*tirma* paper with golden illumination and in best calligraphy" (INBA no. 91, 179).

> the bāb [i.e., the value of 5] and thus will place upon them the light [*nūr:* 256]; then they will know that he is the Qā'im in whose Day they all expected and to all he was promised. For fifty thousand years we awaited the Day of Qiyāma until All-Beings [Kullu-Shay'] would purify and nothing remain but the face (*vajh*) of your Lord (*rabb*), the Lord of glory and might.[14]

The Bab thus identifies himself as the Qā'im and, more significant, considers the Advent of the Qā'im concomitant with the Day of the Qiyāma, when the distinction between the light and the fire is the criterion for salvation. The privilege of the recognition of the Qā'im was attributed to the fourteen early followers (*vajh:* 14), whom the Bab considered as the Return of the Fourteen Innocents, and after them other believers whom he equated with resurrected prophets and saints of the past: "Say! God sent down before in "the Mother of the Book" that He created Muḥammad so as he wished; now too he will create what he wishes since His word is: 'Be! and it was.' Henceforth whoever expects the Advent of the Mahdi or the Return of Muḥammad or any of the believers, he is devoid of knowledge; today God made me return and returned whoever believes in me; this is His Day when all creation is renewed."[15]

The clear assumption of Mahdihood and declaration of Qiyāma were the Bab's most straightforward statements so far. Although even in his first utterances in *Qayyūm al-Asmā'* he had implicitly claimed the status of Qā'imīya,[16] it was after 1263/1847 in Mākū that he finally relinquished his practice of dissimulation. But contrary to the conventional notion of the Mahdi rendered by the Shiʿite orthodoxy, such a declaration did not strive for the consolidation of the Islamic sharīʿa and the reaffirmation of the Muḥammadan order.[17] Quite on the contrary, the "new creation" on the Day of Resurrection required the replacement of the past dispensation with a new order: "We thus initiate this creation and we fulfil it as it was promised to you and we are among the possessors of power. Henceforth whoever [among you] benefits from whatever you benefited before of duties which [were] bestowed upon you, those which were sent down to you in the Qur'ān, they are not any more permitted for him. I thus abrogated whatever [duties] you had been performing. I thereby brought forth the final dispensation (*nash'at al-ākhira*) and eliminated all that people believed and acted upon . . . and whoever performs the commands of the past after the proof of God has reached him, his acts will not be accepted."[18]

The sermon of *Qā'imīya* seems to have been composed concurrently with the *Bayān*, and in many ways encapsulates the chief argument of that book.

[14]*ZH* 164. See above, chap. 4, for the Bab's numerological deciphering of the famous verse (Qur'ān XXVII, 88) alluded to in the above quotation.

[15]Ibid.

[16]See above, chap. 4.

[17]See above, introduction, for further discussion.

[18]*ZH* 165.

The Advent of the Mahdi not only generated a resurrectionary rebirth, thus abrogating the validity of the past revelation, but replaced it with a new cycle of prophetic revelation. The Bab warns that "the yearnings of the fifty thousand years is now fulfilled" and urges the believers "to give their assistance, within their capacity, to the religion of God." He calls upon his followers not to appear in places where they used to set their prayers [the mosques] but instead to "come to the presence of the Lord and assist the one who restores you to your primal existence." Though the past sharīʿa has been nullified, the Bab insists, he has "not exceeded, even by a word, the Primal Book," and calls upon God to witness that whatever he has abolished or initiated was with His blessing.[19]

The unequivocal claim to Mahdihood and the break with the sharīʿa came through with a sense of confidence and authority. But unlike his earlier declaration, the works of the Azarbaijan period convey deep feelings of anger and embitterment, expecially toward the government. In a letter to the shah, for example, the Bab openly alludes to the impending ordeal (fitna) of the Final Day and warns him with a verse from the Qurʾān: "So when the time for the first of these [ordeals in the earth] came, We sent against you servants of Ours, men of great might who ravaged [your] country, and it was a promise performed."[20] He quotes a commentary on the above verse by Ḥasan al-ʿAskarī, the Eleventh Imam: "And these people, God will delegate them before the rise of the Qāʾim, peace be upon him, as it is promised." These men, the Bab asserts, are his followers, who would redress the injustices of the past by taking revenge upon the present oppressors: "[I] swear by the sole Truth that God has not conferred upon me the apparent signs and symbols [of His authority] but that His command be obeyed by all. And His servants [the Babis] have done so in order to take the vengeance of the Lord of the Martyrs [Ḥusayn] may peace be upon him. And in me all the ordeals which were mentioned in the Traditions are now fulfilled."[21]

Similarly, in *Dalāʾil-i Sabʿa* the Bab quotes from *Miṣbāh al-Kabīr* of Shaykh Ṭūsī a salutary prayer in praise of the Hidden Imam in order to emphasize the tormenting circumstances of his Advent. After citing the verse "O God! relieve him from the will of the oppressors and rescue him from the hands of the tyrants," he comments: "Think and understand that that [promised] day is today. See who is now residing in the mountains of

[19]Ibid. On receipt of the sermon ʿAẓīm distributed copies of it with an accompanying letter to all the leading Babis of Iran, including Mullā Ḥusayn Bushrūʾī, Sayyid Yaḥyā Dārabī, and the Bab's uncle Sayyid ʿAlī Shīrāzī. In two of these letters cited in *ZH* (166–69), ʿAẓīm calls upon the Babis of Tehran, Kashan, Isfahan, Shiraz, Yazd, and Būshihr to publicize the contents of the sermon but be aware of the fitna that will follow. The Bab's declaration must have had a considerable impact upon the Babis' understanding of the new faith.

[20]XVII, 5.

[21]INBA no. 64, 110–11. Further on, the Bab quotes four other ḥadīth related from the Shiʿite Imams (including Mufaḍḍal's) on the promised fitna (111–13).

Mākū!" He quotes another passage of the same prayer: "God! Renew through him [the Hidden Imam] what is alive in Your religion and revive with him what has been changed in Your Book. . . O God! enlight by his light all the darkness and crush by his rod all the innovations and destroy by his glory all deceptions and break by him all the tyrants and extinguish by his sword all the fires and eliminate by his justice all the oppressors and enforce his command over all commands and humble by his might all the mighty."[22]

The desire to revenge the martyrdom of Ḥusayn and redress the wrongs of Karbalā' had a symbolic meaning for the Bab. Above all the Advent of the Qā'im would restore the religious authority to its real possessor and make all others, including the ruler, obey, though his advent would not necessarily abolish the temporal rule.

Even if the actual text of the Bab's dispatches had never reached the shah, such an open anticipation for an apocalyptic ordeal could not remain unnoticed by the state authorities. Nor, it appears, did the growing number of Babi visitors to Mākū remain secret to the more vigilant observers in the capital. Prince Dolgorukov, the Russian minister in Tehran, had already requested the Persian government to remove the Bab from Mākū to another location. In late 1847 he reports from Tehran: "A Sayyid, known in this country under the name of 'The Bab,' who was exiled from Isfahan due to a rebellion which he caused there, and who last year, on my demand, was removed from the vicinity of our frontiers, to which he was exiled by the Persian Government, has recently circulated a small compilation in which he foretells an impending invasion by the Turkomans as a result of which the shah would have to leave his capital."[23]

Dolgorukov was no doubt wrong to assume that the Bab had already been removed from Mākū in 1847. Indeed, some months passed before Āqāsī decided to comply with the prince's request. Dolgorukov's concern was probably due to the recent events in Azarbaijan and the downfall of Bahman Mīrzā, who after being charged of treason by Āqāsī, defected to Russia to reside in Tiflis.[24] In the absence of a friendly governor in Azarbaijan, the Russian envoy viewed the Bab's presence so close to the Russian border as hazardous to security. Under Russian rule, the dissatisfied Shi'ite population of the conquered Caucasus had already welcomed at least two other messianic preachers.[25]

The Russian minister's remark concerning the Turkoman threat, if accu-

[22]Pp. 67–68.

[23]Dolgorukov to Nesselrode no. 6, 4 Feb. 1848 OS (16 Feb. NS): Dossier No. 177, Tehran 1848, pp. 49–50, cited in M. S. Ivanov *Babidskie vosstaniya v Irane* (1848–1852) (Moscow, 1939) 141–43. Translated by F. Kazemzadeh "Excerpts from Dispatches Written during 1848–52 by Prince Dolgorukov, Russian Minister to Persia" *World Order* (Fall 1966) 17–24.

[24]*NT* III, 118–23.

[25]See above, chap. 2.

rate, must have been based on an unknown work of the Bab. One can only speculate on the Bab's motives for making such a statement. It no doubt referred to the growing unrest among the Turkoman chiefs of the north-eastern frontier who, in collaboration with the governor general of Khurasan, Allāhyār Khān Āṣaf al-Daula, and his son, Ḥasan Khān Sālār, had already begun what came to be the Khurasan revolt of 1848–1851.[26]

In Rabīʿal-Thānī 1264/late March 1848, Mullā Ḥusayn arrived in Mākū. He came from Mashhad, presumably after he received the sermon of *Qāʾimīya*, to seek the Bab's instructions and his consent to a collective Babi action, possibly an armed resistance, with the help of the Babis from all over Iran. Nabīl Zarandī insists that Mullā Ḥusayn's hurried departure from Mashhad was to avoid Sālār, who in order "to extend the scope of the rebellion, had determined to approach him and obtain his support."[27] However, it is not inconceivable that the purpose of Mullā Ḥusayn's journey was to report to the Bab the prospect of collaboration with Sālār. Mullā Ḥusayn's negotiation with Sālār in June 1847 and his brief detention in the government camp outside Mashhad the following August on the suspicion of collaboration with the rebels—which ultimately resulted in the Babi march to Mazandaran—gives some weight to this theory.

It is likely that the Bab's call for the gathering of the Babis in Khurasan was a result of this visit. Such an initiative may have been part of a greater scheme to hoist the banners of Insurrection and ultimately to try to rescue the Bab. It is hard to believe that Mullā Ḥusayn's efforts in the following months to bring together the Babi forces in Khurasan were unrelated to the Bab's allusions to the impending occurrence of the fitna. The Bab's predictions must have encouraged his disciple to capitalize on the existing support for the movement while the precarious political climate still promised success.

The discussion in Mākū may also have touched on the issue of delegating the actual responsibility for Babi mobilization to Mullā Ḥusayn, and with it the position of bābīya, which now replaced his previous title Bāb al-Bāb (the Gate of the Gate). Even the latter assumption of the titles Qāʾim-i Khurāsānī by Mullā Ḥusayn and Qāʾim-i Gīlānī by Quddūs, on the eve of Ṭabarsī, may have been an acknowledgement of their shared leadership. Mullā Ḥusayn's visit with Quddūs on his way back from Mākū and the veneration which he displayed toward the latter may also have been part of the same scheme.

Whatever the circumstances, it is certain that the Bab's call: "Proceed toward the land of Khāʾ [i.e., Khurasan]" in March–April 1848, while Mullā Ḥusayn was still in Mākū, was interpreted by most Babis as the first step toward a collective action; possibly as the prelude to the final fitna. The

[26]Āṣif al-Daula and his son were the tactical allies of Bahman Mīrzā and deadly enemies of Āqāsī. Soon after Āṣif al-Daula was exiled to the ʿAtabāt, a temporary victory for Āqāsī that nevertheless did not root out the sources of revolt in Khurasan.

[27]*Nabil* 254–55.

rapid deterioration of the shah's health and the general dissatisfaction of the populace with Āqāsī's regime probably made them conclude that the time was ripe for action. The Bab's own frustration with the prospects of a peaceful release from captivity and the growing harassment of the Babis may have also contributed to their shift toward militancy.

The change of mood must have caught Āqāsī's attention; by now he had become increasingly wary of Babi activities. The choice of Mākū proved to be an error after all. Only five miles from the Ottoman border and less than fifty from the Russian province Nakhichevan, Mākū was an easily accessible caravan station of the newly revived Trebizond-Tabriz route.[28] Moreover, the predominantly non-Shiʿite inhabitants, with a presence of Ahl-i Ḥaqq, were ripe for the Babi propagation. The premier's repeated instructions to ʿAlī Khān to restrict access to the fortress had no enduring effect, for the khan himself seemed to have fallen under the spell of the Shīrāzī prophet.[29]

Whether because of the pressure of the Russian minister or Āqāsī's own apprehension, on 4 Jumadā al-Ūlā 1264/10 April 1848 the Bab was finally escorted from Mākū to a new prison in the remote castle of Chihrīq, where except for a short interval in Tabriz he spent the rest of his life. The premier's immediate aim was to keep his increasingly troublesome captive in the safe detention of a trustful Kurdish chief. Located on the frontier of Persian Kurdistan, some five miles southwest of Salmās and almost adjacent to the disputed Ottoman border, the village of Chihrīq was inhabited by a mixed population of Sunnis (including Naqshbandīs), Yazīdīs, the Ahl-i Ḥaqq and a small community of Nestorian Christians.[30] The governor of the fortress and chief khan of the region, Yaḥyā Khān Shakākī, was the brother of Muḥammad Shāh's favorite wife and an ally of Āqāsī.[31]

The early months of captivity in Chihrīq were as rigorous as any faithful frontier khan could make them in order to please his political patron. The "grievous mountain" (*jabal-i shadīd*), as the Bab named it,[32] was far less welcoming than Mākū. Visitors, except for a few, had to content themselves with distant glimpses of the Bab from the rooftops of surrounding houses. After the fall of Āqāsī in late 1848, Yaḥyā Khān adopted even stricter measures.[33] Servants and aides were searched and correspondence was for-

[28]For an account of Mākū by H. Picot see Adamec *Historical Gazetteer* I, 428–29.

[29]*Nabil* 244–45; *Muʿīn* 167.

[30]*Muʿīn* 171, 176; *Nabil* 302.

[31]In the later part of his premiership, Aqāsī apparently set his hopes, farfetched though they were, on the succession of Yaḥya Khān's nephew, ʿAbbās Mīrzā Mulk Ārā. See *RS* X, 250–54, and H. Saʿādat Nūrī *Zindigī-yi Ḥājj Mīrzā Āqāsī* (Tehran, 1356 Sh./1977) 308–12.

[32]*TN* 276. Numerically *shadīd* is equivalent to Chihrīq.

[33]Shortly after Yaḥyā Khān was summoned to Tabriz and imprisoned, presumably on the charge of being an accomplice of Āqāsī. He was a follower of the Naqshbandī order. See ʿAbbās Mīrzā Mulk Ārā *Sharḥ-i Ḥāl* (Tehran, 1325 Sh./1946) 17.

bidden. The Babis employed ingenious methods, however, for maintaining contact with the Bab.[34] The role of Sayyid Ḥusayn Yazdī, the Bab's aide and secretary, was particularly crucial.[35]

During his first months in Chihrīq, the Bab addressed two letters to the shah and his chief minister, the first of a series of Arabic letters known as the "sermons of wrath" (*khuṭab-i qahrīya*). They were written in a solemn tone and with almost no reservation in expressing the writer's outrage and frustration. The Bab strongly rebuked the shah for giving in to the temptations of "the Satan" (perhaps an allusion to Āqāsī) in condemning him, "an innocent descendant of the Prophet," to exile in the "remote prison" among unbelievers who denied the holy Shiʿite Imams. He warns the shah that the divine gift of kingship will soon be taken away from him if he persists in his arrogant conduct, and that he will be punished for his sins in the fire of the impending Day. "For four years I have seen from you and your people [lit., your army] nothing but intense oppression and arrogance. It is as though you suspected that I entertain the mundane possession of the worldly trifles. Nay, by God, for those who seek His compassion, the worldly kingdom and whatever there is in it is less than the eye of a corpse. I take refuge in God from those who take partner for Him; my intention is to take revenge, as it is destined in the Book of God, from those who slew the true martyred Imam [Ḥusayn]; their descendants too will join them in the sufferings of Hell."[36]

Nowhere before have the Bab's two themes of revenge and martyrdom come so close to each other. The paradigm of Karbalāʾ and the sacrifice of Ḥusayn in the path of the true religion are now linked with the promised task of the Qāʾim, who is destined to re-enact the tragedy of the martyred Imam. Though he specifically denies any ambition for worldly power, the Bab does not rule out punishment of the ruler for his failure to heed the new creed.[37] Nor does the disowning of worldly ambitions prevent the Bab from

[34]See *NH* (n. L, 273–74; recollections of Ṣubḥ-i Azal) for an account of such methods.

[35]Kazem Beg's assertion (VII, 376 and n.) concerning Yazdī's "sinister" role may be no more than a figment of the author's imagination. Before his execution in 1850, the Bab instructed his secretary to denounce him in public and escape death in order to convey "the jewel of the divine knowledge and wisdom" to its future bearer (*ZH* 460). See also *NK* (212) and a letter by Dakhīl Marāghih'ī (cited in Fayżī *Nuqṭa-yi Ūlā* 280) for a reference to Yazdī during Chihrīq. For his interview with the Russian consul (presumably Anitchkov) in Tabriz in 1850 see *NH* appendix II, 395–96 and *NK* 267; cf. Dorn *Bulletin* VII, 248 (also cited in Momen *Religions* 48).

[36]*ZH* 84.

[37]References to the shah's suspicion of the Bab's worldly interests in the above passage, as in the Bab's earlier letters to the shah, may also suggest an assumption by the Bab that the monarch held him in prison in the hope of recovering from him the legacy of the now-deceased Manūchihr Khān Muʿtamad al-Daula. Indeed, it is not wholly unlikely that Muḥammad Shāh, perhaps under the influence of Āqāsī, entertained such an idea. This suspicion initially arose from the fact that in 1847 in Isfahan, Manūchihr Khān, who probably saw his days were numbered, tried to purify his enormous wealth, largely acquired through extortion, through

challenging the shah to make his final decision: "If you are not afraid of the triumph of the truth and the abolition of the falsehood, why then are you not summoning the ʿulama of the land and not calling me forth to put them in their place, similar to those who were previously bewildered, and they are among the deniers. This is my challenge to you and to them. . . . If however you intend to shed my blood then why do you hesitate since you are mighty and powerful? For me this is blessing and mercy from my God and for you and those who act like you this is toil and suffering from Him."[38]

Though it is doubtful whether this letter ever reached Muḥammad Shāh, the call for the summoning of the ʿulama indicates the Bab's desire to face their challenge as he had already done in Isfahan. Moreover, he now viewed the shah as united with the ʿulama and essentially against himself.

The letter to Āqāsī is even more scornful and uncompromising. The Bab regards the chief minister's machinations as the real cause for his own misfortune and views his claims to "gnostic knowledge" and "guidance," an open allusion to the premier's mystical sway over the shah, as less than "Pharaoh's paganism." Reminding Āqāsī of a verse in the Qurʾān, "To you your religion, and to me my religion," he concludes: "If you are an infidel so be then what you are. If you do not help the truth why then are you humiliating it, and if you do not obey it, why then [do] you confine it?"[39] The Truth, the Bab asserts, is the light that God "embedded in the back of Adam and commanded the Angels to worship." Now the Truth has appeared in him, and the followers of the new cause are the Angels of the time. The rebellious Satan, however, is Āqāsī himself, whose apostasy is attested by God and by His friends. Alluding to the premier's waning popularity even among the non-Shiʿites of Mākū and Chihrīq, he states: "Such dishonor is enough for you that even the infidels mock you and curse you." The Bab compares his unjust confinement to that of Joseph and Musā Kāẓim, the Seventh Imam, and states: "I did not come to this second prison but that your disbelief and your enmity toward the son of the Messenger of God become manifest in the realms of the Heavens and the Earth. You threaten me with death and intimidate me with what is the motto of the unitarians and the maxim of the adepts. God's curse be upon you if you can [kill me] and not do so."[40]

---

the ritualistic (and lawful) practice of donating it to a saintly figure, in this case the Bab, who would then duly return it to its original owner. In his previous letter to the shah (prior to the open declaration of Qā'imīya) the Bab acknowledges that he had accepted the donation and then returned it to Manūchihr Khān. "I also accepted his repentance," writes the Bab, "and permitted him to take his possessions. . . . Now I do not desire to have a trifle of that. All his wealth belongs to the Proof. Whatever that Holiness would see fit, he would ordain" (INBA no. 64, 121–22). Noticeably, the Bab regards the legacy of the deceased governor as the Mahdi's property. Though he disowns any claims for himself, he clearly implies the overriding authority of the Imam over the monarch on not only spiritual but temporal matters.

[38] *ZH* 84–85.

[39] Ibid. 86.

[40] Ibid. 88. The Bab also blames the premier for his "despicable conduct" in managing the

The Bab's open repudiation of the shah and Āqāsī is symbolic of his growing impatience with the state authorities, whom he now holds, together with the ʿulama, accountable for opposition to his cause. But his criticism of the state is still primarily motivated by religious concerns rather than temporal ambitions. The myth of martyrdom and the predestined divine plan, as the Bab saw it, prevented him from entertaining any immediate desire for political power. He remains a prophet who, in spite of his sharp criticism of the temporal ruler, is essentially loyal to the de facto separation of the religious and political spheres, a position that is further developed in the *Bayān* into a de jure distinction.[41]

The Bab's imprisonment in Azarbaijan attracted a small but active group of Babi followers in that province. Their propagation in the towns and villages of western Azarbaijan, from Mākū to Khuy, Marāghih, Kuhnih Shahr (Salmās), and Urūmīya, was the chief factor in drawing public attention to the Bab. Foremost among them was Shaykh ʿAlī ʿAẓīm, who from the early days at Mākū emerged as the Bab's chief agent and the leader of the Babis of the region. Sayyid Ibrāhīm Madā'inī, a Shaykhi teacher in Tabriz, was the Bab's confidant and his cheif contact in that city. Another disciple of the Mākū period was Asadullāh Khu'ī, who bore the Babi epithet *Dayyān* (the judge). He was a learned mulla with a bureaucratic family background and a rare syncretic education. His knowledge of Hebrew and Syriac (in addition to Arabic, Persian, and Turkish), possibly the result of his contacts with Assyrian and Jewish communities in northwestern Iran, must have been instrumental in earning him the Bab's praise for writing the best apologia in defense of the Babi faith, presumably utilizing the Old and New Testaments. He was addressed by the Bab as "the unique person and the singular manifestation of the divine name Dayyān."[42]

Mullā Bāqir Tabrīzī, a Letter of the Living, and Mullā Ādī Gūzal, called *Sayyāḥ* (the traveler), a convert from Marāghih, acted as emissaries between the Bab and believers of other provinces.[43] A number of low-ranking mullas and rawża khwāns from the neighboring towns and villages were also active.

---

affairs of the state—more specifically for sending a robe of honor to the Sunni ʿālim (presumably the Naqshbandī leader Shaykh Ṭāhā) and granting an ignorant boy the highest offices of the state. The latter perhaps is a reference to the notorious Allāh Qulī Khān, the premier's stepson, who was promoted by Āqāsī to the office of Īlkhānī of the Qajar tribe. See *EIr:* ĀLLĀH-QULI KHAN Īlkhānī (A. Amanat).

[41]Two other examples of the *qahrīya* sermons appear in *Muʿīn* 151–60 and Fayżi *Nuqṭa-yi Ūlā* 304–6, both apparently written after the trial of Tabriz (see below).

[42]After 1850 he was one of many claimants to the position of He Whom God Shall Manifest (*man Yuẓhiruhu'llāh*), and his followers, the Dayyānī Babis, survived for some time in Azarbaijan and Gīlān. In 1853 he was killed in Baghdad, presumably by the rival Babi factions. For his account see *ZH* III, 64, and *Nabil* 303–5.

[43]On Sayyāḥ's missions see *Muʿīn* 186; *Nabil* 431–33; and *ZH* 59. He was a student of the messianic preacher Mullā ʿAlī Akbar Marāghih'ī.

Chief among them was the Azarī elegist Dakhīl Marāghih'ī.[44] Others included Mullā ʿAlī of Kuhnih Shahr, a certain Mullā Ḥusayn of Urūmīya, Mullā ʿAlī Vāʿiẓ Zand, and others from Khuy and Salmās.[45]

Among the visitors of Chihrīq was the Bab's uncle Sayyid ʿAlī, who in late 1849 met his nephew for the last time before being executed in Tehran less than a year later. The prudent Babi chronicler Muḥammad Taqī Hashtrūdī also met the Bab in Chihrīq.[46] Mīrzā Luṭf ʿAlī Salmāsī, the shah's former steward, now banished to his own estate near Chihrīq, twice hosted the Bab on his way to Tabriz.[47] Mulla ʿAbd al-Karīm (Aḥmad) Qazvīnī Kātib (the scribe) was the Bab's chief link to the Babis of Tehran and the bearer of the Bab's *Dalāʾil-i Sabʿa* to a number of Qajar princes and state officials.[48] Repenting his earlier defection from the Babi ranks in 1261/1845, he became the Bab's close companion in Isfahan. On his last visit to Chirhrīq in 1266/1850, shortly before the Bab's execution, he was entrusted with certain "tablets" to be delivered to Mīrzā Ḥusayn ʿAlī Nūrī (Bahā'ullāh) and his brother, Mīrzā Yaḥyā Nūrī Ṣubḥ-i Azal. The tablets were later interpreted by both the Bahā'īs and the Azalīs as proof of the Bab's delegation of the leadership to the rival Nūrī brothers. ʿAbd al-Karīm was instrumental in bringing to the Bab's attention the necessity of appointing a successor, a task deemed ever more urgent as it became clear that his days were numbered.[49]

The Babi movement attracted a growing crowd around Chihrīq. Under the leadership of ʿAẓīm and Dayyān, Babis of neighboring cities were able to establish a popular base. In mid-1848 the American Presbyterian missionary stationed in Urūmīya, Dr. Austin Wright, observed that the Bab's followers "became more and more numerous."[50]

The arrival of an adventurous wandering dervish demonstrated the extent to which the fame of the Bab brought new disciples to Chihrīq. The "Indian Believer," as the Bab called him, soon attracted public attention in Salmās. Declaring himself a manifestation of God, and even the Qā'im, the dervish stirred up "an unprecedented commotion" in the region. "His fame reached all corners and waves of visitors came to pay their homage."[51] The Bab, himself in a state of spiritual trance, seemed to condone the dervish's extraordinary utterances as though they were a resonance of his own. He even

[44]For his account see above, chap. 4.

[45]See *Muʿīn* 176, 231, 240, 254 for an eyewitness account of Chihrīq given by Dakhīl and Mullā ʿAlī. Also Dakhīl's letter in Fayżī *Nuqṭa-yi Ūlā* opp. 280.

[46]*Mu ʿīn* 255–58.

[47]The main reason for his exile was reportedly his pro-Babi propagations in the court in early 1847, while the Bab was outside Tehran (*Muʿīn* 175, 223).

[48]*Samandar* 156; *Muʿīn* 237–40. He was a student of the Uṣūlī teacher Mullā ʿAbd al-Karīm Īrvānī and later Sayyid Kāẓim Rashtī, who advised him to engage in his family trade.

[49]*ZH* 370.

[50]"Bab und seine Secte in Persien" *Zeitschrift der Deutschen Morgenlädischen Gesellschaft* (Leipzig, 1851) V, 384–85. For his account see *TN* 19 (n.) and Momen *Religions* 73.

[51]*NK* 213.

conferred upon him the title *Qahrullāh* (wrath of God); perhaps a reflection of the Bab's growing militancy. The dervish's excesses, however, did not please the Babi leader ʿAẓīm, who persuaded him to leave Chihrīq. The prince governor of Khuy, probably already alarmed by the Babi presence in Salmās, also took no risks with the dervish, fearing the recurrence of religioethnic clashes with the neighboring Dīlmān (Dīlmaqān). The dervish and two of his Babi accomplices were captured and brought to Khuy, where they were severely punished. A certain Ṣāliḥ ʿArab died under bastinado. The dervish himself, who in the presence of the prince had spoken of "the vengeful sword," was battered and humiliated before being banished to Turkish territory.[52]

The Khuy incident was a warning to the Babis. The ʿulama of the province, particularly the Shaykhis, now began to send petitions to Tehran urging the government to take action. Āqāsī, who was already dismayed by the activities of Dayyān, the son of an ally of his, saw an opportunity both to stigmatize the Babis and to demonstrate to the ʿulama the extent of their dependence on the government.

The Tribunal of Tabriz

Some three months after his arrival in Chihrīq, the Bab was summoned to Tabriz in order to stand a trial by the ʿulama. By Āqāsī's order, Riżā Khān Afshār, a would-be convert, escorted him to Tabriz. Fearing further disturbances in Khuy, he was brought to the provincial capital via Urūmīya, where he received a courteous welcome by the prince governor, Malik Qāsim Mīrzā. A cultivated uncle of the shah (twenty-fourth son of Fatḥ ʿAlī Shāh) and previously an ally of Manūchihr Khān Muʿtamad al-Daula, the prince was on bad terms with Āqāsī and subsequently with the shah.[53] Only three months earlier he had been approached by ʿAẓīm, who apparently tried to seek his mediation for the release of the Bab and a place of refuge under his protection. Urūmīya at this time was less attuned to the general religiosity of other Persian cities and hence was less susceptible to, or supportive of, the ʿulama. Malik Qāsim's friendly though noncommittal policy

[52]*Muʿīn* (226–30) distinguishes between the Indian believer, whom he portrays as a devout Babi, and the dervish who was involved in the incident in Khuy. The latter is identified as Darvish Saʿīd Iṣfahānī with the Sufi title Masʿūd ʿAlī Shāh. No other source confirms this otherwise plausible distinction (see *NK* 212–14 and *Nabil* 305–6). Although outlandish exclamations were not uncommon among wandering dervishes, particularly Khāksār and Jalālī, it is hard to believe that an Indian would engage in so serious an affair.

[53]He was out of favor with the shah owing to his alleged involvement in an anti-Āqāsī plot in 1845. Knowing French and English, which he learned from the American missionaries, the prince was open to Western ideas. He also looked favorably on American missionary work among the Nestorians of western Iran. See J. Perkins *A Residence of Eight Years in Persia, among the Nestorian Christians* (Andover, Mass. 1843) and W. Stuart *Journal of a Residence in Northern Persia* (London, 1835). Also Momen *Religions* 511 and Bamdad *Rijāl* IV, 138–39.

toward the minorities made the city a fertile ground for the Babi message.[54] The public enthusiasm during the Bab's short stay reached a momentum. In one incident people rushed to a public bathhouse to collect the water used by the Bab for ablution.[55] On the Bab's growing support in province Austin Wright states: "On the way to Tabriz, the Bab was taken to Urumiyih, where the Governor treated him with special consideration and many people received permission to visit him. On one occasion, a crowd were with him, and as the Governor afterwards remarked, they were all mysteriously moved and burst into tears."[56] In previous months the Bab's followers throughout the country had become involved in "fierce quarrels with the so-called orthodox party." The matter became so serious that "the Government gave orders that the founder of the sect should be brought to Tabriz and given bastinado" while his disciples "should be arrested wherever they were found and punished with fines and beatings."[57]

"The fierce quarrels" noted by Wright probably refer to the events of Qazvin and the assassination of Muḥammad Taqī Baraghānī in the middle of 1263/1847.[58] This as well as the clashes in Mashhad and Bārfurūsh in early 1848 were seen by the ʿulama of Tabriz, and to some extent the government in Tehran, as ominous signs of the imminent insurgency already promised by the Bab. Incidents in Salmās and Khuy and the warm reception in Urūmīya only confirmed these fears. Already the ʿulama of Tabriz, both Uṣūlī and Shaykhi, who saw themselves as the obvious targets of the Babis' anti-ʿulama drive, had begun to take precautionary measures. The imām jumʿa of Tabriz, Mīrzā Aḥmad, fearing a possible Babi attack, reinforced the walls around his house, while his Shaykhi counterpart, Mullā Muḥammad Mamaqānī, hired a band of Mamaqānī vigilantes to escort him to and from his mosque.[59] Mullā Muḥammad Taqī Mamaqānī, son of Mullā Muḥammad, relates that when the news of the Bab's enthusiastic welcome in Urūmīya reached Tabriz, "the ordinary people of Tabriz, too . . . began to entertain illusions about him. They were waiting for his arrival and for the gathering of the ʿulama so that if in that gathering he triumphed or if the verdict of that gathering turned out to be in his favor, then the learned and the lay, the stranger and the native, and even the government troops would pay their allegiance to him without hesitation and consider obedience to whatever he commands an obligation. In short, so strange a spirit fell upon the city that the possessors of wisdom would wonder."[60] The ʿulama's

[54]In late 1850 Dakhīl Marāghih'ī informed ʿAẓīm that in Urūmīya, as had been relayed to him by a colleague, "Islam is weakened." However, he warned that ʿAẓīm's arrival might lead to fresh turmoil (Fayżī *Nuqṭa-yi Ūlā* opp. 280).

[55]*Nabil* 311.

[56]"Bab und seine Secte" 384–85, also cited in Momen *Religions* 73. Also *TN* 200.

[57]"Bab und seine Secte" 384–85.

[58]See above, chap. 7.

[59]*Muʿīn* 244.

[60]Risāla of Mamaqānī cited in part in Mudarrisī *Shaykhīgarī* 311.

alarm, apparent in the above passage, was not unwarranted. The potential support for the new prophet demonstrated the public impatience with the clerical establishment. Torn by sectarian schism, the ʿulama of Tabriz, like their counterparts in other cities, now appealed to the state for protection. Their ability to arouse instant anti-Babi sentiments should not be underestimated, yet challenge of the new Bab was potent enough to be taken seriously.

In Shaʿbān 1264/early July 1848, amidst an uneasy climate of popular expectation, the Bab arrived in Tabriz. In anticipation of the trial, he had cautioned his follower Sayyid Ibrāhīm Madāʾinī, called Khalīl (Abraham's Qurʾānic title), that "the fire of Nimrod will shortly be kindled in Tabriz."[61] He alluded to the tormenting trial, out of which he expected himself and his followers to emerge triumphantly.

Since February 1848 the government of Azarbaijan had been assigned to the seventeen-year-old crown prince, Nāṣir al-Dīn Mīrzā. He was accompanied in this post by his maternal uncle Amīr Aṣlān Khān Quvānlū and aided by the chief steward, Fażl ʿAlī Khān ʿAlīābādī. Tabriz then ranked as the second most important religious center after Isfahan, in terms of both the number of the mujtahids and their influence over the public. The Shaykhis were particularly prominent. In most cases their loyalty to the tenets of Shaykhism was nominal and their practice of ijtihād was not far different from their Uṣūlī counterparts' except on legal details. Indeed, what encouraged them to persist on their Shaykhi identity was the transformed sectarian divisions they inherited from earlier times. Mullā Maḥmūd Niẓām al-ʿUlamāʾ, the crown prince's chief tutor, was himself a Shaykhi and an informal representative of the Shaykhis in the court.

Staging an inquisitorial gathering was the best Āqāsī could conceive in order to exploit the complaints of the clergy for his own advantage. In staging the trial of Tabriz, Āqāsī hoped to achieve two objectives. By exposing the Bab to the hostile Shaykhis, who had already called for his execution, the premier was sending a signal to the Babis and warning them of the fatal consequences of any militant action. He was also using the occasion to remind the troublesome ʿulama of Tabriz of their ultimate dependency on his good will.

Aware of Āqāsī's intention and concerned with Babi retaliation, the majority of the ʿulama in the city followed the example of their counterparts in Isfahan and refused to participate in the tribunal. Muḥammad Taqī Mamaqānī recalls that in spite of government's invitation "to all trusted ʿulama of the city to be present in the disputation gathering, none of the ʿulama complied with the order and all made excuses of different sorts. This issue further aroused unfounded suspicions of the people."[62] The chief Uṣūlī

[61] *Nabil* 306.
[62] Risāla cited in *Shaykhīgarī* 315.

mujtahid of Tabriz, Mīrzā Aḥmad, in spite of the government's week-long insistence, replied to the crown prince: "From the declarations of numerous trustworthy persons and the perusal of documents, [it appears that] this person [i.e., the Bab] is devoid of religion, and that his infidelity is clearer than the sun and more obvious than yesterday. After such evidence of witnesses there is no obligation on your humble servant to renew the discussion."[63] The mujtahid skillfully evaded passing a sentence on the Bab, however, perhaps fearing that his verdict might be used by his adversaries to turn the public against him. He may have preferred to stand by and watch his Shaykhi rivals being threatened by the Babis. Furthermore, it was an open secret that the government, whatever the verdict of the ʿulama might be, would not feel it expedient to carry out a death sentence on the Bab.

Perhaps it was with this consideration in mind that the most influential Shaykhi mujtahids of Tabriz, Mīrzā ʿAlī Aṣghar Shaykh al-Islām and his nephew Shaykh Abul-Qāsim, who were likely to insist on the death sentence, were excluded from the gathering. The chief clerical participants were Mullā Muḥammad Mamaqānī, Mullā Murtażā Harandī (better known as ʿAlam al-Hudā), a wealthy mujtahid, and Niẓām al-ʿUlamāʾ himself, all of Shaykhi persuasion.[64] The government was represented by Nāṣir al-Dīn Mīrzā, his uncle, his chief steward, and a host of other officials and courtiers.[65]

The chief purpose of the trial was to discredit and humiliate the Bab in the eyes of the public. It was clear from the start that the Bab's growing popularity would preclude any serious punitive measures. At best, the participating ʿulama could only hope for a collective condemnation. The agenda for the gathering seems to have been decided in advance, to dispute with the Bab "with the arguments, proofs and laws of the perspicuous religion" and arrive at a verdict that would demonstate to the public the heretical nature of his claims.[66] To expose the Bab's theological disabilities, the ʿulama resorted to the conventional techniques of disputation, which inevitably put the opposing party on the defence. As well as can be ascertained from the conflicting accounts, the trial followed this line of argumentation.[67]

[63]Official report of the Bab's examination, *MSBR* 249 (English translation by Browne 252).

[64]There are contradictory accounts as to the identity of the participating ʿulama. *RS* (X, 423) includes Mīrzā ʿAlī Aṣghar. *Nabil* (314) and *Muʿīn* (196) add Mīrzā Abul-Qāsim, but none are confirmed by the official report. Zaʿīm al-Daula *Miftāḥ* (185) identifies five other mujtahids, including two other tutors of the shah as well as Zaʿīm al-Daula's own grandfather. This is not confirmed by Muḥammad Taqī Mamaqānī (*Shaykhīgarī* 315) and others. Hashtrūdī (in *Muʿīn* 201) and *TN* (19–20) are obviously mistaken in including Mīrzā Aḥmad.

[65]For the list of the participants see the official report, *MSBR* 249 (trans. 253). *Miftāḥ*'s list (186) appears to be inaccurate. Among others it gives the name of Muḥammad Khān Zanginih, who had died in 1257/1841. A conspicuous absentee from the trial was Mīrzā Tāqī Khān Amīr Kabīr, then the army secretary (Vazīr Niẓām) of Azarbaijan. Only three months later he was promoted to the office of *Amīr Niẓām*, and then premiership.

[66]Official report, *MSBR* 249 (trans. 252).

[67]At least eight independent accounts of the proceedings have survived. Of the three Babi accounts, Hashtrūdī's *Abwāb al-Hudā* (cited in *Muʿīn* 201–7) and *NK* (135–38), which is the

In reply to the preliminary questions of the chief interrogator, Niẓām al-ʿUlamāʾ, the Bab admitted the sole authorship of his works then in public circulation. He declared that his position of "specific gateship" (*bābīyat-i khāṣṣa*) resembled that of ʿAlī in relation to Muḥammad.[68] He recited the famous hadith "I am the city of knowledge and ʿAlī is its gate," then stated: "It is incumbent on you to obey me, by virtue of [the verse] 'Enter the gate with reverence!'[69] But I did not utter these words. He uttered them who uttered them."[70] Asked "Who then is the speaker?" he replied: "He who shone forth on Mount Sinai." He then read the famous verse: "[If to say] 'I am the Truth' be seemly in a Tree, why should it not be seemly on the part of some favored man?" and continued, "There is no selfness in between. These are God's words. I am but the Tree [the Burning Bush] on Sinai. At that time [the divine word] was created in it, now it has been created in me."[71] When pressed on the nature of his extraordinary claim, the Bab angrily responded: "I am that person whom you have been expecting for more than a millennium. . . . I am the Lord of the Command (*Ṣāḥib al-Amr*)" whose return was yearned for from "the dawn of Islam."

The Bab's unequivocal claim to Mahdihood took the audience by surprise and prompted the outraged mujtahids to begin an aggressive argumentation. Mamaqānī in particular rebuked the Bab in strong terms, and compared the humble origin of the son of a Shīrāzī clothier with the holy ancestry of the Twelfth Imam, who "was born in Sāmirra in the year 256 [869] and will return from Mecca with sword."[72] The ʿulama then asked the Bab to demonstrate, as signs of his veracity, the "heirlooms of the [past]

---

source for *NH,* summarize the interrogation. Hashtrūdī claims to have been present at the gathering. *Nabil* (314–22) also provides some new details. Most important of the non-Babi accounts is the report produced by Browne in *MSBR* (248–55). Though neither signed nor dated, this official report was prepared for the shah and addressed to him. Some inconsistencies in the text suggest modifications, probably to emphasize loyalty to the shah or to augment the role of the crown prince and the provincial officials, but there is little doubt as to its overall authenticity. H. Dreyfus, who first supplied this document to Browne, failed to mention its source. *RS* (X 423–30), which is based on a report supplied by Niẓām al-ʿUlamāʾ, is the longest, though certainly not the most accurate, of the accounts (see *TN,* n. M, 277–90 for an abridged translation, with additional material from *QU*). *NT* (III, 126–30) is another, shorter version with some differences from *RS.* The less-well-known account by Mulla Muḥammad Taqī Mamaqānī, which claims to be most accurate in recording the proceedings (see Mudarrisī *Shaykhīgarī* 308–14 for excerpts but with unfortunate omissions by the editor), is based mostly on the recollections of his father, and recorded some years later for Nāṣir al-Dīn Shāh. It rejects the elaborations of *RS* and *NT* and provides new details. Despite its obvious bias, this account has some resemblance to the Babi sources in stressing the Bab's unequivocal assertion of his claims. Zaʿīm al-Daula *Miftāḥ* (184–97) is based on the recollections of the author's father and his grandfather but also benefits from *RS* and *NT.* Its many obvious errors make it a less reliable source.

[68]Hence alluding to the Bāṭinī designation of ʿAlī as the nāṭiq of the Muḥammadan cycle. See above, introduction.

[69]Qur'ān IV, 153.

[70]Official report, *MSBR* 250 (trans. 253).

[71]Ibid.

[72]Ibid.; cf. Mamaqānī's risāla cited in *Shaykhīgarī* 312.

prophets: David's coat-of-mail, rod of Moses, Solomon's ring and the white hand [of Moses]" as well as the support of "the leaders of men and the Jinn and their forty thousand followers," which are "all promised in the hadith." The Bab answered: "I am not permitted to bring such things."

"You had no business to come without permission!" exclaimed Mamaqānī. He then challenged the Bab to perform a Mosaic miracle by turning a walking stick into a serpent. Other requests for miracles followed. "My proof is my verses," answered the Bab. He followed by extemporizing a passage in Arabic, which was soon interrupted by the ʿulama correcting his faulty grammar.

Thereafter the examination degenerated into a mujtahids' contest of incrimination, sarcasm, and self-aggrandizement as the Bab was put through a series of inquisitorial tests with the obvious aim of ridiculing him. From the simple conjugation of Arabic verbs to subtle points of syntax, Qur'ānic exegesis, the hadith, and jurisprudence (including some ludicrous problems of sexual purification), as well as geography, astronomy, and medicine, questions were showered on the indignant Bab. To some he responded with a plain declaration of ignorance. Others he ignored. He tried unsuccessfully to divert the discussion to the nature of his mission, repeating what he had already declared in sermons addressed to the shah: "I am that very light which shone forth on Sinai, for it hath come down in tradition that that light was the light of one of the Shiʿites."[73] Further attacks obliged him to remain silent as the questions' banality and the inquisitors' sardonic tone became more apparent. Nāṣir al-Dīn—who began by offering the Bab the seat of honor and promising that in the case of the Bab's victory he would relinquish his throne in his favor—ended by sarcastically demanding a miracle that could cure the chonric ailment of his tutor.

The trial brought no decisive victory to either side. The participating ʿulama were either unable to issue a harsh verdict on the claims or the fate of the Bab, or were discouraged by the government. As such, they had to improvise some justification for their indecision. They were clearly under pressure, the government pressing them to pass a lenient judgment while some overzealous ʿulamas were calling for the death penalty. As none of the accounts of the Tabriz trial mentions any allegations of the Bab's disturbed mind, we can conclude that the possibility of insanity was suggested only afterward, probably by Niẓām al-ʿUlamā', to preempt a drastic verdict imposed by mujtahids who feared the Bab would appear to the public as the victorious party in the trial.[74] It is also likely that the government, in order to appease the opposing mujtahids and as a face-saving measure, spread rumors that the Bab had recanted.

[73]*MSBR* 251 (trans. 255).

[74]A verdict of insanity had been passed once before by the imām jumʿa of Isfahan, Sayyid Muḥammad Khātūnābādī, in 1263/1847, with the same intention of saving the Bab from a death sentence passed by the mujtahids in that city (see *Nabil* 209).

The main pressure on the government was exerted from the quarter of ʿAlī Aṣghar Shaykh al-Islām, who though not present in the trial emerged as the champion of the anti-Babi campaign. To counter the newly raised question of insanity, Shaykh al-Islām and his nephew Abul-Qāsim issued, as last resort, a conditional death sentence pending on confirmation of the Bab's sanity. Addressed to Sayyid ʿAlī Muḥammad Shīrāzī and sealed by the two mujtahids, their fatwā established the Bab's apostasy on the ground of the charges admitted by him in the "royal gathering" and in the presence of a number of the ʿulama. It then declared: "The repentance of an incorrigible apostate is not accepted, and the only thing which has caused the postponement of thy execution is a doubt as to thy sanity of mind. Should this doubt be removed, the sentence of an incorrigible apostate would without hesitation be executed upon thee."[75] The mujtahids' fatwā plainly rejected the applicability of repentance, presumably on the ground that the Bab had overturned his earlier recantation in Shiraz in 1261/1845. The possibility of insanity, however, could not be easily ignored.

Under pressure from Shaykh al-Islām, the provincial authorities instructed the crown prince's physician, Dr. William Cormick, together with two Persian physicians, to examine the Bab and determine "whether he was of sane mind or merely a madman."[76] Some years later, Dr. Cormick recorded his recollections of his visit to the Bab in the Tabriz citadel: "He only once deigned to answer me on my saying that I was not a Musulman and was willing to know something about his religion, as I might perhaps be inclined to adopt it. He regarded me very intently on my saying this, and replied that he had no doubt of all Europeans coming over to his religion. Our report to the Shah at that time was of a nature to spare his life."[77]

The physicians' medical opinion saved the Bab from execution. But Mīrzā ʿAlī Aṣghar, who probably saw this as a countermaneuver by the government to neutralize his verdict, insisted that the Bab should at least be subjected to corporal punishment. After some resistance, the government yielded to the mujtahid and agreed reluctantly to bastinado the Bab. Hidāyat states that when the orders were sent for his punishment, "the government *farrāshes* (servants in charge of punitive duties), because of their great sympathy [toward the Bab], refrained from administering the punishment."[78] Thereupon the angry mujtahid summoned the Bab to his own residence and ordered a clerical aide[79] to administer twenty lashes to the Bab's feet.[80]

The official report of the tribunal then informs the shah that as the result

[75]A facsimile of the fatwā and its translation appear in *MSBR* 259.

[76]*MSBR* 261.

[77]Ibid.

[78]*RS* X, 428; cf. Hashtrūdī (cited in *Muʿīn* 212).

[79]A certain Mullā Ṣādiq, nicknamed Shimr (killer of Ḥusayn); a derogatory designation denoting callousness.

[80]The injury endured from this punishment was not restricted to his feet. "A great wound

of this "examplary chastisement . . . [the Bab] apologized, recanted, and repented of and asked pardon for his errors, giving a sealed undertaking that henceforth he would not commit such faults. Now he is in prison and bonds awaiting the decision of His Most Sacred Royal and Imperial Majesty, may the souls of the worlds be his sacrifice!"[81] Though other progovernment sources report the Bab's recantation, there is little convincing evidence as to their validity. One may suspect that the above assertion is no more than a face-saving step by the Tabriz authorities to please the monarch and embarrass the Bab. The text of the recantation (*tauba-nāmih*) published by Browne also merits the utmost reservation.[82] Undated and unsigned, the document hardly qualifies as the "sealed undertaking" in the official report. Moreover, its plain language and wording are highly distinct from the Bab's peculiar style. We can assume that if at all authentic, the recantation was prepared by the authorities but for reasons unknown—perhaps due to the Bab's refusal—remained unsigned.

Indeed the Bab had every reason not to waver. Public enthusiasm in Tabriz and the ʿulama's indecision in the trial must have convinced him of his immunity, at least so long as the government was able to harness the hardline mujtahids. Earlier, during the traumatic events in Shiraz of 1845, he had submitted a recantation of his claims to the status of gateship.[83] By 1848, however, he had reached that level of resoluteness not to observe prudence even when there was a serious possibility of physical punishment.

The open declaration of Qā'imīya in the Tabriz trial, a major shift from the earlier policy of dissimulation, should not be seen as a spontaneous response. On the eve of the Tabriz gathering, the Bab had already informed ʿAẓīm of his intention.[84] Such a daring act in the presence of religious and temporal authorities was no doubt a considerable boost to the morale of his followers in the months to come. Yet the Bab evidently failed to capitalize on his popular support during the Tabriz episode by challenging the ʿulama in more decisive terms. His displeasure, confusion, and outrage at the way he was incriminated and ridiculed, evident from the proceedings, may have affected his performance. Yet it should be noted that the Bab was not contemplating an overall strategy, at least not in conventional terms; nor did his followers expect him to do so. The fact that he proclaimed his

---

and swelling" on the Bab's face was severe enough to require a second visit by Cormick (*MSBR* 261).

[81]Ibid. 255.

[82]Ibid. 256–58. This document, which was sent to Browne by French Bahā'ī Hippolyte Dreyfus, was apparently later traced in the Majlis Library in Tehran (see Ādamīyat *Amīr Kabīr* 441). Since its publication in 1918, it became part and parcel of all anti-Babi-Bahā'ī polemics and an effective weapon in the growing arsenal of fictitious documentation.

[83]See above, chap. 5.

[84]ʿAẓīm's bewilderment (*Nabil* 313) must have been rooted in his apprehension concerning the ill effects of such deceleration rather than the Bab's claim per se, since he was himself the recipient of the Qā'imīya sermon.

assumed status in plain terms, rather than his ability to answer the complex and largely irrelevant inquistorial tests posed by the ʿulama, was enough to secure their continuous devotion. Suffering and imprisonment only helped to augment the Bab's public image as an innocent sayyid of holy descent who was captured and wronged by an unpopular government and tormented by its clerical allies.

The trial of Tabriz symbolized the ongoing encounter between two opposing interpretations of religion. Whatever the outcome, here was a messianic claimant who sought to restore the long-overshadowed authority of the Imam by challenging the legitimacy of the mujtahids who claimed the Imam's collective deputyship in their own right. The confrontation between the "prophet" and the "priests" brought to the surface the deep tension ingrained within the body of Shiʿism. The gulf of difference between the two world views could not have been bridged by a theological disputation. The irreconcilability of the two positions was clear at the outset and neither side seems to have had any illusions. What the Tabriz trial denoted, however, was the struggle for winning over the public.

The victory of the ʿulama was partial at best. Popular sympathy for the Bab forced them to be more cautious and less candid in their judgment. They succeeded in humiliating the Bab and tarnishing his image as an invulnerable saint, but they failed to destroy him altogether. The ominous prospect of losing their constituency was particularly acute for the Shaykhi mujtahids. Despite a façade of confidence and control, the Shaykhi leaders were perturbed by the Babi propaganda and its effect of weakening their popular support vis-à-vis their enemies, the Uṣūlīs.[85]

The government's reluctance to leave the matter in the mujtahids' hands stemmed primarily from a genuine fear of popular agitation. The state of affairs in the capital, and in Azarbaijan, was too critical to risk additional trouble. Only during the premiership of Amīr Kabīr, when a new policy of centralization was vigorously pursued, was the implicit tolerance of the Babis gradually abandoned.

The late summer of 1264/1848 was a turning point in the history of the Babi movement. The examination of Tabriz coincided with two other developments in the Babi community: the conference of Badasht in July and Mullā Ḥusayn's march from Mashhad at the head of a Babi contingent (19 Shaʿbān 1264/22 July 1848). Like the Bab's declaration in the Tabriz trial, both these events were symbolic of a new dynamism within the movement. It consciously aimed at two objectives—a doctrinal break from Islam, and the organizing of the Babi resistance. While the gathering at Badasht was declaring the abrogation of Islamic sharīʿa and the independence of the Babi dispensation, Mullā Ḥusayn and his companions set out from Khurasan

[85]The growing hostility between the Shaykhis and the Uṣūlīs in Tabriz soon after the trial of Tabriz resulted in a major confrontation between the rival city factions.

with the ultimate intention of rescuing the Bab. How much the coincidence between these events was orchestrated by the Babi leadership and how much it was the spontaneous outcome of diverse circumstances is difficult to ascertain. What is clear is that the new spirit of defiance was reciprocal. No doubt it was both influenced by the Bab and in turn was influential on him.

Less than two months after the Tabriz examination and the Bab's return to Chihrīq, the long-expected death of Muḥammad Shāh and the accession of Nāṣir al-Dīn Mīrzā to the throne in September 1848 brought Mīrzā Taqī Khān Amīr Kabīr to power as premier. Shortly after, the clashes in Bārfurūsh between the Babi party and their adversaries eventually led to the insurgency of Ṭabarsī (October 1848–May 1849). The long-awaited fitna of which the Bab had cautioned his opponents had finally, though unexpectedly, arrived.

Martyrdom

The next two years in Chihrīq passed uneventfully. Though after the start of the Babi insurrection the government imposed stricter security, the Bab was not totally isolated. In spite of the disheartening news of the Babi fighting, in the early months of his return to Chihrīq he was still confident of the triumph of his religion, which, as he saw it, could only be achieved by sacrifice and martyrdom. In late 1849, in one of his last surviving letters the Bab urged the ʿulama of Tabriz "to remove the veil of bigotry and ignorance" and recognize the reality of his mission: "From the beginning of this manifestation up to now, day by day this cause has been in progress and under no circumstances there was or ever will be a halt in its expansion. . . . Whatever objection will be made to the legitimacy of this cause, that objection would aptly apply to the mission of the Prophet. Thus it is incumbent upon you to either accept this cause or to default your own religion and reject the authority of the Qur'ān."[86] In unusually lucid language, the Bab calls upon the 'ulama to recognize the recurring nature of the prophetic revelation:

> There is no doubt that he [the Bab himself] is the Expected One, the sun of the truth, since no one else is, or will be, capable of [revealing] the divine signs. In every revelation he appears under a different name. Earlier he was Muḥammad, the Messenger of God; now on the Day of Qiyāma he has appeared in the guise of this manifestation. . . . Whatever has been said in the Qur'ān about seeing God's countenance (*liqā'ullāh*), it meant encounter with the Truth. Because of his honorable relation with God, [his countenance] has been referred to as

[86]*Muʿīn* 263.

> God's countenance. . . . He is the one who is expected to renew the duties and the traditions.[87]

Here the Bab has spoken of the renewal of the sharīʿa in a way unprecedented in his public addresses. Simultaneously, he has defined the encounter with God on the Day of Resurrection as tantamount to the recognition of His manifestation. The coincidence of the two themes is not accidental. The Advent of the chiliastic Mahdi of the Shiʿite prophecies on the Final Day required the termination of the sharīʿa and the encounter with God on the plain of the Gathering. The recurrence of this theme, as it was envisaged in the scenario of the Qiyāma, symbolized the culmination of the Bāṭinī legacy.

The disastrous end to the Ṭabarsī insurgency and the fall of some of his most prominent disciples had a profound effect in the Bab's morale, however. When the news of the execution of Quddūs reached Chihrīq, "for nineteen days his holiness the Zikr wept and refrained from food."[88] After Ṭabarsī, he became increasingly tormented by the painful reality of frequent persecutions and bloodshed. He never learned of the execution of his uncle Sayyid ʿAlī in early 1850, since, we are told, he had prohibited "the mention of grief" in his presence.[89]

By the middle of the year 1850, the Babi resistance in Zanjān was rapidly crumbling. In other places too the Bab's followers were increasingly subjected to harassment. The uncompromising policy of the new premier, Amīr Kabīr, was far less accommodating than Āqāsī's stratagem. It aimed at eradication of a heresy whose members, isolated and demoralized, were held responsible for the country's general state of turmoil. The suppression of the Babi insurgencies in Ṭabarsī and Nayrīz boosted the government's morale and in turn prepared the ground for the execution of the Bab.

But even as late as Rajab 1266/June 1850, a few days before his fateful departure for Tabriz, the Bab still attracted new followings, especially in the regions neighboring Chihrīq. The Russian agent, Mochinin, who was touring the province, saw the Bab in Chihrīq standing in the upper chamber of the castle "teaching his doctrine" to the crowd. The concourse of people was so great that the court could not contain them all; the majority remained in the road and listened, engrossed, to the new Qur'ān.[90]

A few days after Mochinin's visit, the Bab was transferred to Tabriz. A detachment of Afshār horsemen came from Ṣā'īn Qalʿa to escort the Bab.

[87]Ibid. 264. Shortly after, in response to this letter, Mīrzā Abul-Qāsim Shaykh al-Islām composed a parodical polemic called *Qalʿ al-Bāb* (eradication of the Bab). *Muʿīn* (268–69) cites the exordium but omits the rest because of its abusive language.

[88]*NK* 208.

[89]Ibid. 222.

[90]*Kazem Beg* VII, 371, translation in Momen *Religions* 75.

The Babi preacher of Salmās, Mullā ʿAlī, recalled later that throughout the Bab's stay in Salmās, "he predicted the imminence of his martyrdom."[91] There was even some attempt by the local population to rescue him. A party of local Babis hid their weapons under the prayer mat in the mosque in the expectation of clashes with the escorting troops. Only with great difficulty did Mullā ʿAlī convince them of the futility of their action.[92]

By the time the Bab reached Tabriz, on 19 June 1850, Amīr Kabīr had already come to the conclusion that his execution was the only way to prevent future Babi insurgencies. The religious intensity of the Babi resistance in Ṭabarsī and Nayrīz, as well as the ongoing uprising in Zanjān, convinced him as to the symbolic place the Bab reserved in the mind of his followers. By eliminating the Shīrāzī imposter he hoped to demonstrate to the Babis, and their sympathizers, the futility of any future defiance of the overriding power of the state. Failure to do so, he argued, would send the wrong signal to the remnants of the Babi forces and to the population at large.

The minister's decision met some resistance in the capital. The young Nāṣir al-Dīn, whose previous encounter in the gathering of Tabriz must have influenced his assessment of the Bab's personality, criticized the deposed minister, Āqāsī, for not allowing the Bab to reside in the capital and freely engage in disputation so that people would realize the hollowness of his claims and "the derangement of his mind."[93] He appeared to have implied, out of fear rather than compassion, a more conciliatory course of action to prevent further bloodshed. The powerful minister Mīrzā Āqā Khān Nūrī, second in command after Amīr Kabīr, had also argued in favor of such a policy, though for different reasons.[94] His fierce competition first with Āqāsī and then with Amīr Kabīr had already directed his attention to the Babis, whom he saw as useful pawns in the power struggle with his political rival.[95] His humanitarian concerns, therefore, were highly tainted by his personal ambitions, as his conduct during his premiership made clear.

Amīr Kabīr's answer to these reservations was undaunted. He argued that in allowing the Babis to thrive, "the interests of the state" would be in jeopardy, and he could "in no wise tolerate these periodic upheavals."[96] Neither the shah nor Nūrī could have essentially opposed this position. After 1848, the need for containment of the movement was strongly felt in

[91] *Muʿīn* 289.
[92] Ibid.
[93] *NT* III, 302.
[94] *Nabil* 502–4.
[95] Besides his "acquaintance" with his distant Nūrī relatives, Mīrzā Ḥusayn ʿAlī Bahāullāh and his family, some years earlier when he was exiled to Kashan, in 1263/1847 he became aquainted with the Babi activist Ḥājjī Mīrzā Jānī. Nūrī tried to strike a deal with the Babis but he did not seem to have found in them a determined support (see *Nabil* 522–23). Soon after, in 1848, he found collaboration with the queen mother, Jahān Khānum, and the backing of the British envoy in Tehran more helpful for the fulfillment of his political ambitions.
[96] *Nabil* 509; cf *NT* III, 303.

government circles, and the prevailing circumstances in Nayrīz and Zanjān left little room for tolerance.

Amīr Kabīr had to act quickly in order to benefit from the weakening Babi morale following defeat in Nayrīz. Two days after the Bab's arrival in Tabriz, the government troops succeeded, and then only by stratagem, in suppressing the first Nayrīz uprising. The unfolding of an alleged Babi plot for the assassination of the premier in February of the same year and the subsequent execution of seven Babis in Tehran emboldened the prime minister in the implementation of further Draconian measures. His hand was already red with Babi blood and his heart was set on their total eradication, especially after he met an unexpectedly stiff resistance in Zanjān. Since mid-May 1850 the Zanjān uprising had reached dangerous proportions. The fact that the government troops, in spite of several reinforcements, were incapable of quelling the insurgency may explain the timing of the Bab's execution.

The approval of the ʿulama of Tabriz was of crucial importance to Amīr Kabīr, who needed to legitimize his decision by their legal ratification. The ʿulama were reluctant to extend their blessing to a man who in a short time gained the reputation of being both anticlerical and a skillful maneuverer. Amīr Kabīr's anticlerical policies had already alienated many mujtahids, especially in Tabriz. The challenge of his government came at a time when the morale of the Tabrīzī mujtahids was at its lowest ebb. In the face of the difficulties created by the premier and the threat of the ongoing Babi insurgencies, both the Shaykhis and the Uṣūlīs searched desperately for a means to boost their image. In the words of Watson: "The priests of Tabreez, about this time, resolved to show the world who believed in miracles that such manifestations of a direct interference with the ordinary course of nature were not exhibited solely through the medium of the person of the Bab."[97]

Less than a month before the arrival of the Bab, the alleged miracle of the shrine of Ṣāḥib al-Amr (Lord of the Command) was the Shaykhis' answer to the dual threats of Sayyid ʿAlī Muḥammad and Amīr Kabīr. The popularity of the trustees of the shrine, Mīrzā ʿAlī Aṣghar Shaykh al-Islām and his nephew Mīrzā Abul-Qāsim, who staged the miracle of the holy cow, knew a temporary upsurge. The refuge in the sanctuary of a stray cow from the slaughterhouse was portrayed as a sign of the Imam's favor. The inviolable sanctity of the shrine was reaffirmed and the promises for relaxation of the taxes, under the pretext of the Imam's impending appearance, kept the people of the Shaykhi quarters on their side. The subsequent riots in the city and clashes with the government during the Bab's stay resulted in the exile of the Shaykh al-Islāms to the capital in early June 1850.[98] About the same

[97]Watson *History of Persia* 393.

[98]For the shrine of Ṣāḥib al-Amr see above, chap. 2. A series of reports by the British envoy

time, Amīr Kabīr also engaged in a serious quarrel with Mullā Muḥammad Bāqir Imām Jumʿa (son of Mīrzā Aḥmad, who had died in the previous year[99]) on the issue of violating the sanctity of the holy shrines. His open defiance to the government's order and later refusal to accept exile in the capital created more excitement in Tabriz.[100]

There were other reasons for mujtahids to withhold the reissuance of the Bab's death warrant. Their fear of Babi retaliation could not be underestimated at a time when five thousand Babis were still fighting a long and bloody war against the government troops in so close a location as Zanjān. If the government had taken it on itself to wipe out the Babis, there was no need for the ʿulama to be in the forefront of the campaign. Factional rivalries made it even more difficult for each side to take the initial step.

With the Tabriz ʿulama reluctant to associate themselves with the government's action, the state authorities saw little alternative but to stage a mock trial with the obvious aim of confirming the condemnation of the Bab. The ʿulama had already voiced their refusal to participate in another inquisitorial gathering. Even Ḥamza Mīrzā, the prince governor of Azarbaijan, who ordered that the Bab be brought to a small gathering of the state officials, was unwilling to risk his reputation (and his lucrative governorship) on an obviously unpopular task. He must have felt indignant at being saddled with the responsibility of putting to death a sayyid in a faction-ridden city for the sake of adding credit to the career of an ambitious minister whose reform measures had already reduced the privileges of the Qajar elite. Conversation with the Bab did not remove the prince's ambivalence, even though he sneered at the utterances of the Shīrāzī prophet.[101]

Faced with Ḥamza Mīrzā's reservations, Amīr Kabīr instructed his brother and confidant, Mīrzā Ḥasan Khān, now Vazīr Niẓām (the secretary of the army) of Azarbaijan, to carry out the reconfirmed orders from the capital for the Bab's execution.[102] By bypassing the governor and placing the mat-

Sheil and the British consul in Tabriz (F.O. 60/152, Sheil to Palmerston: no. 65, 4 June 1850; no. 69, 17 June 1850; no. 71, 18 June 1850) records some new details on the role of the Shaykh al-Islams, their magnification of a simple incident into an undisputed miracle, their plea to the British consul for help in the face of opposition from Amīr Kabīr, and the reasons for their exile. The arrest and banishment of the mujtahids by the government's special envoy, Sulaymān Khān Afshār, led to fresh protests. See also Watson *History of Persia* 393–94.

[99] *TAS* II/1, 97.

[100] Watson *History of Persia* 393–94; Nādir Mīrza *Tabrīz* 119. See also Ādamīyat *Amīr Kabīr* 424–27.

[101] For accounts of this gathering see *NT* III, 303–4, and *KD* I, 234–39. The latter source, which presumably relies on Ḥamza Mīrzā's own recollection, insists that the prince was truly impressed with the Bab's ability to reveal verses. Others present at the gathering were Mīrzā ʿAlī Khān Anṣārī (son of Mīrzā Masʿūd), who conducted the inquisition, and the previously mentioned Shaykhi dignitory Sulaymān Khān Afshār. For Ḥamza Mīrzā Ḥishmat al-Daula see Bāmdād *Rijāl* I, 462–68.

[102] *Muʿīn* (303–4, based on Hashtrūdī's *Abwāb al-Hudā*) refers to a threatening message sent by Vazīr Nizām to the ʿulama of Tabriz warning them of his brother's wrath should they refuse to comply with his wishes. Mīrzā Ḥasan Khān was his brother's trusted agent in Azarbaijan.

ter directly into the hands of the army, Amīr Kabīr hoped to force through his order and secure the majtahids' consent. After some hard negotiation, Vazīr Niẓām—aided by Amīr Kabīr's special envoy and troubleshooter, Sulaymān Khān Afshār (the Shaykhi follower of Kirmānī and already the anti-Babi champion of Ṭabarsī)—succeeded in inducing the leaders of both clerical factions to ratify the death penalty. It is not unlikely that in exchange he promised them an end to government interference in their affairs.

Three weeks after his arrival in Tabriz the Bab was taken to the houses of three chief mujtahids for the issuance of the final fatwā. There was little uncertainty as to the nature of the recommended penalty. He was apparently brought first to the house of Mullā Muḥammad Bāqir Imām Jumʿa and then to that of Mullā Murtażā Harandī, ʿAlam al-Hudāʾ. Both mujtahids either avoided lengthy interrogation or refused to admit him to their presence. Both, however, appear to have reluctantly produced their fatwās for execution. The Bab was then brought to Mamaqānī's house.[103]

Mamaqānī, the most prominent of the three, seemed willing to save the Bab provided that he renounce his "ambitious claims." As the leader of the Shaykhis he preferred not to add weight to the government's initiative at the time of high tension by committing himself to a dangerous verdict.[104] Mamaqānī's son, Muḥammad Taqī, in an eyewitness account of this last encounter, recalls that his father seated the Bab opposite himself and "extended to him all the sagely advises and tender counsels with greatest compassion and care." But "on the granite the rain drops had no effect."[105] The Bab's persistence in his divinely inspired claim once more made the mujtahid dispute the validity of his proofs. Neither the writings of the Bab nor the recognition of the Babi ʿulama, the mujtahid reasoned, were sufficient testimony to rightousness. Muḥammad Taqī recalls:

> Then my father said: "The confirmation of the others is not a proof for us. Furthermore, the claims that you make to the Imamate, the divine inspiration and so on can not be verified but by miracles or the confirmation of an Innocent [i.e., one of the Imams]. If you have them, demonstrate them, otherwise you have no proof for us." "No," said he, "the proof is what I told you." [My father]

With full control over the Azarbaijan army, the two brothers treated Ḥamza Mīrzā like a nonentity. The grievances of the people of Tabriz were directed mostly against Mīrzā Ḥasan, with good reason (F.O. 60/152, no. 65, 4 June 1850, Sheil to Palmerston). For his despotic and highly capricious conduct see J. P. Ferrier (cited in Momen *Religions* 504–5), which utterly contradicts those accounts which portray him as a benevolent agent of reform. See Ādamīyat *Amīr Kabīr* (index) and Bāmdād *Rijāl* I, 352–53.

[103]There is confusion as to the identity of the signatories of the fatwā and the order in which they gave their verdicts. See *Nabil* 509–10; cf. *NT* III, 304. The latter source omits ʿAlam al-Hudā and instead names Sayyid ʿAlī Zunūzī, which is an obvious error. *ZH* (9) also includes an Uṣūlī, Ḥajjī Mullā Sharīf Shirvānī. *Muʿīn* (300–301) mistakenly believes that a second gathering of the ʿulama was convened and could not reach a concrete result.

[104]*Muʿīn* 305.

[105]*Shaykhīgarī* 315.

> then asked: "Do you still insist on the same claims that you made in our presence in the royal gathering of being the Lord of the Command and having opened the gate of revelation and being capable of producing similar to the Qur'ān? Do you still persist in such claims?" He replied: "Yes." My father then said: "Renounce these claims, it is not proper to put yourself and other people so vainly into ruination." He replied: "No and never."[106]

The Bab's unequivocal confirmation of his claims was made with full awareness of its fatal repercussions. Mamaqānī's persuasions, on the other hand, demonstrate the mujtahid's last-minute effort to find a way out of the government-imposed obligation without losing face. When the government agents wanted to remove the Bab, writes Muḥammad Taqī:

> The Bab asked my father: "Now, do you intend to issue the fatwā of my death?" My father replied: "There is no need for my fatwā, these heretical claims that you make are themselves standing as your fatwā." He said: "I am asking for your opinion." [My father] answered: "Now that you insist, yes. So long as you remain adamant on these refuted claims and these corrupt beliefs which are reasons for your apostasy, according to the glorious sharīʿa your death is imperative. But since I recognize the repentance of the inherent apostate, if you express repentance, I would save you from death."[107]

The fatwās of Mamaqānī and Imām Jumʿa condemned the Bab to death on the ground of apostasy. Confirming his sanity, both mujtahids declared that the ultimate ambition of the Bab was "to possess the throne" and "take over the state and the monarchy."[108] There is little doubt that the political charges were dictated by the government in order to dramatize the Bab's case and to justify the death sentence. Though not explicitly stated, such allegations established the necessary link to the Babi uprisings and therefore removed possible doubt in the minds of the people concerning the Bab's innocence. It is ironic how readily the ʿulama were persuaded to comply with the government's wishes. Whereas in 1848 they ratified the Bab's insanity, by 1850 they were implicating secular charges of treason and insurgency.

The question remains, however, why that segment of the public sympathetic to the Bab failed to take any action to prevent the execution, particularly at the time when the ʿulama were at odds with the government. The answer may well be found in Amīr Kabīr's policy of intimidation. His suppression of popular revolts, in Tabriz and elsewhere, and the punitive measures enforced by Vazīr Niẓām must have especially terrorized the Tab-

[106]Ibid. 316–17.

[107]Ibid. 317. The author of *Miftāḥ* (233–35), on the authority of his grandfather, Mullā Muḥammad Jaʿfar, and his father, Mullā Muḥammad Taqī, both of whom he claims to have been present on the occasion, gives a summary version of the above testimony with some variations.

[108]*Muʿīn* 304–5, on the authority of Hashtrūdī. Another version is given in *KD* I, 241.

rīzī public. Even the Bab's devout followers were demoralized by the disastrous defeats, massacres of their coreligionists, and the crumbling Babi resistance. Amīr Kabīr's orders had already specified the arrest and execution of those who declared loyalty to the Bab.

The Bab himself from the time of his arrival in Tabriz repeatedly recommended passivity and prudence to his followers. All the way from Chihrīq, the small Babi company remained at a safe distance from the Bab for fear of being arrested as accomplices.[109] On the final day of his life he even instructed his secretary to publicly denounce him and save his own life.[110] Sayyid Ḥusayn Yazdī complied, as did most other accompanying Babis, who stayed out of trouble and were saved.

One exception was a young Babi mulla in the Tabriz jail. Mīrzā Muḥammad ʿAlī Zunūzī, called *Anīs* (the intimate companion) by the Bab, had been arrested some time before in a confrontation with the ʿulama of Tabriz while disseminating Babi literature. The stepson of a well-known mujtahid, Sayyid ʿAlī Zunūzī, and the brother of an affluent merchant, he had been converted during the Bab's earlier stay in Tabriz. Muḥammad ʿAlī openly admitted devotion to the Babi creed and was brought together with the Bab for the final verdict. In spite of several emotional appeals by his relatives and Mamaqānī's persuasion, he refused to retract. He wrote to his brother: "You warned me that this affair has no future; [I wonder] what affair has. I am content with this turn of events and indeed cannot be thankful enough for this blessing. At most it will be death in the path of God and this is most blissful. The God's ordinance would prevail upon his creatures. Prudence will not alter destiny. . . . For all the end is death."[111]

Muḥammad ʿAlī mirrored the Bab's desire for martyrdom. On the night prior to the execution, Muḥammad ʿAlī volunteered to act as the Bab's executioner rather than permit infidels to carry out the sentence the next day. The Bab had assured him that next day he would be his companion in witnessing "what God has decreed."[112]

"That night," recalled Yazdī, "the face of the Bab was aglow with joy, a joy such as had never shone from his countenance. . . . The sorrows that had weighed so heavily upon him seemed to have completely vanished."[113] Society, the ʿulama, and the government had deprived the Bab of his free-

[109]*Muʿīn* 291; cf. 309.

[110]*NK* 247; *Nabil* 508; *NT* III, 304.

[111]*KD* I, 240. *ZH* (31–37) cites the proceedings of an interrogatory exchange in Tabriz between Muḥammad ʿAlī and a Shaykhi mulla. In all probability the defendant is a Babi other than Zunūzī and the document may belong to a later date. Both the style and the argument testify to this. It nevertheless provides an insight into the early Babi mentality and its perception of the Bab's claims.

[112]*Nabil* 507. See also Anitchkov's report (cited in Momen *Religions* 77), which refers to Muḥammad ʿAlī's "singular firmness of character."

[113]Ibid. For other accounts of the Bab's final night see *NK* 246–47 and *KD* I, 240–45. The latter source on the authority of Sayyid Ḥusayn Yazdī cites some passages of Arabic poetry as well as prayers composed by the Bab in Mākū.

dom and of the accomplishment of his ideals, but they did not deny him the satisfaction of personal sacrifice. The obstacles that he and his followers had encountered from the outset and the disillusionment of defeat could only be vanquished through suffering and martyrdom, for which the paradigms of the Shiʿite past had already laid the path. In unconditional surrender to "the divine will," which he was now convinced had determined on his death, the Bab, like his followers in Ṭabarsī and other places, found comfort and confidence.

On the same day that the fatwās were issued, 28 Shaʿbān 1266/9 July 1850,[114] Vizīr Niẓām's head steward (Farrāshbāshī) conducted the Bab around the city quarters and through the bazaar before being brought to the barracks square for public execution. The purpose was to demonstrate to the public the government's full control. The Bab's execution was perhaps one of the first to be carried out in public by the firing squad. On the appearance of the Bab "there was a tremendous commotion" in the crowd gathered around the barracks. In anticipation of public turmoil, the government had deprived the Bab of all symbols of holy lineage and dignity. His green turban, his green sash, and his cloak were removed and he was barefoot. On his arrival in the barracks he was approached by a group of the city inhabitants led by Mullā Muḥammad Taqī Tabrīzī, who in a last-minute appeal urged him to repent, but to no avail.[115]

The manner in which the public execution was conducted reflected the government's anxieties. The army barracks was the safest location for containing possible disturbance and execution by a large firing squad prevented the placement of blame on one or few persons. Of the three regiments present, Farrāshbāshī was apparently instructed to employ the Bahādurān regiment.[116] The Bahādurān, headed by Sām Khān, himself a Russian renegade, was recruited predominantly out of the remnants of Russian deserters who had defected to Iran during the second Russo-Persian war and was reinforced by native Assyrian recruits. The choice of the Bahādurān was prudent since it was suspected that Muslim regiments might not volunteer to take the responsibility for the killing of a descendant of the Prophet. Sām Khān seems to have had some apprehension about carrying out the orders, but succumbed to Farrāshbāshī's pressure.[117]

[114]There is an irreconcilable inconsistency concerning the date of the execution. Bahā'ī sources (*Nabil* 517 and *KD* I, 245) give the above date while *NT* III, 305 and the British consul in Tabriz (F.O. 248/142, no. 68, 24 July 1850, R. Stevens to Sheil) give 27 Shaʿbān 1266/8 July 1850. July 9 is preferred for two reasons: Sipihr (*NT*) mistakenly believes that the 27th falls on a Monday, and therefore his recollections could be erronenous; and Stevens was absent from Tabriz at the time of the execution and could have recorded the date incorrectly.

[115]Zaʿīm al-Daula *Miftāḥ* 238, on the authority of the author's father.

[116]Ibid. Zaʿīm al-Daula asserts that after the refusal of Āqā Jān Bag Khamsa, the chief of the Nāṣirī regiment, the Bahādurān was chosen. There is a faint confirmation of this in *NK* 249.

[117]Better known as Samsām Khān Urus, he was a convert to Islam (*Muʿīn* 306). As the chief of Bahādurān he participated in all major campaigns of Muḥammad Shāh's period (*RS* X, 210, 329, 416–22). In 1848 in Mashdad, during the Sālār revolt, his intelligence concerning

The Bab and Mīrzā Muḥammad ʿAlī were suspended side by side on a rope attached to one of the pillars surrounding the barracks' quadrangle, and the firing squad discharged three volleys of bullets. When the smoke cleared away, there was no trace of the Bab. The voices of the bewildered multitude who had gathered on the surrounding rooftops rang out: "The Sayyid-i Bab has gone from our sight!"[118] Amid great confusion the excited bystanders rushed into the square. Sām Khān ordered his troops to form a triangle and force the crowd out.[119] The seemingly miraculous disappearance of the Bab had resulted from a missing shot, which severed the rope and caused the two condemned to land safely on the ground. Possibly the unwilling troops missed their target deliberately.[120] A frenzied search of the barracks soon ended when the Bab was found unharmed in one of the adjacent rooms. He was forced out, battered, and dragged back to the execution spot. This time the shots were accurate. The crowd dispersed and the bodies of the Bab and his companion were fastened to a ladder and dragged through the streets of Tabriz before being thrown into a ditch outside the city walls.[121]

Sipihr was apparently the first to speculate, with the benefit of hindsight, on the possible course of events had the Bab acted differently in his execution scene: "[His] escape [to one of the rooms in the barracks] was a demonstration of the might of the [Islamic] sharīʿa since at that time when the bullets hit the rope and he was set free, if he exposed his bosom and cried out: 'O, ye the soldiers and the people, didst thou not see my miracle that of a thousand bullets not even one hit me but instead untied my bonds,' then no one would have fired a shot at him any more and surely the men and women in the barracks would have assembled around him and a riot would have broken out. It was God's will that the truth should be distinguished from falsehood and doubt and uncertainty be removed from among the people."[122]

Mullā Ḥasayn's activities led Ḥamza Mīrzā to arrest him. According to *RS* (X, 420) Sām Khān died in Mashhad in March or April 1848, but this is certainly an error.

[118] *Nabil* 513.

[119] Zaʿīm al-Daula *Miftāḥ* 240.

[120] Although *NT* (305) states that Muḥammad ʿAlī Zunūzī was killed in the first attempt, it would have been practically impossible for the troops to distinguish between him and the Bab.

[121] There is much confusion in the sources as to the identity of the regiment that finally shot the Bab and his disciple. All non-Babi sources state that it was the Bahādurān, while Bahā'ī accounts (e.g. *Nabil* 514) insist that it was Āqā Jān Bag of the Nāṣirī regiment who, after Sām Khān's refusal to make a second attempt and the subsequent withdrawal of the Bahādurān, volunteered to carry out the execution. It is difficult to determine which version is correct. After the failure of the first attempt—a miracle in the eyes of the public—it would have been less likely that a Muslim regiment would agree to put a sayyid to death. On the other hand, it can be argued that Sām Khān might have decided to withdraw, if not for reasons of personal doubt, at least because he sensed the reluctance of his men. However, when a Muslim army sergeant, Ghūj ʿAlī Sulṭān, hit the Bab in the face and dragged him back to the execution scene, the Muslim troops could have also found it fit to carry out the orders.

[122] *NT* III, 305.

Such speculation has preoccupied many later writers—some to sneer at the Bab's folly, others to bemoan his fateful error. There was a little real chance, however, for the realization of this scenario. The intensity of the moment of execution and the panic of the condemned would rule out such a farsighted reaction. Moreover, the Bab's desire for martyrdom was too deep-rooted to be checked by natural instinct for self-protection. Even if he had acted "heroically," as Sipihr prescribed, it is doubtful that his fate would have altered. The few words that he apparently uttered before his execution were understood by those few who knew Persian "while the rest heard but the sound of his voice."[123]

The execution of the Bab deprived the movement of its charismatic leader and accelerated its collapse. Firm action of the government, far more effective than the adversity of the ʿulama, helped to reduce the Babis to a despised heresy. The new prophet's human vulnerability turned the ephemeral sympathy of the miracle-seeking public into indifference and soon into hostility. A few days after the Bab's death, in the month of Ramaẓān, when the Babi elegist Dakhīl Marāghih'ī recited his customary rawża in the Jāmiʿ mosque, he blamed the people of Tabriz for not preventing the execution. "Do you think that God will forgive you for killing the forgiver of your sins?" he asked the audience. "You slew the light of the Prophet's eye and broke your fast with his blood."[124] After he left, the audience, outraged by his angry remarks, began a search for his arrest. Dakhīl escaped the city and went into hiding. The tide of public opinion had already began to turn against the Babis.

[123]*TN* 44.

[124]*ZH* 58, citing from a biography of Dakhīl written by his grandson.

Epilogue

The execution of the Bab was a turning point in the short history of the Babi movement. The psychological impact of that event on the young Babi community was immense. Six months later, the Zanjān uprising was put down with an unrelenting severity perhaps unsurpassed by any other military action in the course of the nineteenth century. Confrontations with the government and the death of many prominent disciples left the Babis demoralized, leaderless, and vulnerable. The crisis of leadership that followed led to several claims to the position of He whom God shall Manifest (*man Yuẓhiruhullāh*) already promised in the *Bayān*, but none attracted an overwhelming following. The remaining Babi activists, confused, vengeful, and drastically radicalized by the events of the preceding years, withdrew into clandestine circles and adopted a new strategy of urban struggle.

The unsuccessful attempt to assassinate Nāṣir al-Dīn Shāh in Shawwāl 1268/August 1852 was the final death blow to the moribund Babi resistance. The assassination attempt reflected the depth of Babi frustration with six years of persecution and defeat. In spite of the ingenuity of Shaykh ʿAlī ʿAẓīm, its chief instigator, this symbolic act of reprisal was poorly planned. As in previous cases of Babi resistance, the price was too dear. Many of the remaining Babi activists, including ʿAẓīm, Mīrzā Jānī, Sayyid Ḥusayn Yazdī, Sulaymān Khān Tabrīzī, Ḥājjī Qāsim Nayrīzī, and Mīrzā ʿAbd al-Karīm Qazvīnī, were arrested and put to death in an indiscriminate frenzy of Babi killing. Qurrat al-ʿAyn met the same fate. Mīrzā Ḥusayn ʿAlī Bahāʾullāh and a few other Babis, however, narrowly escaped death and were banished to Ottoman Iraq. The Babi community never recovered from the heavy blows it suffered during the short but bloody years of Amīr Kabīr. Ironically, Amīr Kabīr himself, even before the events of 1852, fell victim to the calculative callousness of the same Qajar autocracy that he had tried so tirelessly to reform and save from collapse.

The confrontation between Amīr Kabīr and the Babis was between two visions of modernity: that of a reformist, secular, and authoritarian, envisaged by the dedicated premier, and that of an all-embracing religious renewal, proposed by the Bab. Both currents were in revolt against the prevailing religious establishment as well as the existing political order. The Babis were advocating a grass-roots revolution to reform religious doctrine and remedy the ills of the clerical class and those of the community as a whole. Amīr Kabīr, on the other hand, in typical reformist vein sought to eliminate all expressions of religious dissent while trying unsuccessfully to subordinate the clerical class to the authority of the state.

Collision between the two forces was inevitable. This was not because the Bab, if not the Babis, refused to reconcile with the state, provided that it would tolerate them and recognize the validity of their cause. It was because the European-inspired secularism of Amīr Kabīr (partly modeled on the perception of Tanẓīmāt reforms) was antithetical to serious reconsideration of religious tenets; especially if such reconsideration lent itself to a heresy that could disturb the precious, dearly acquired, security and order. By denying the Babis a chance to survive as a viable alternative, the Qajar state reaffirmed the unrivaled status of the clergy as the sole arbiter of religious norms. Once Amīr Kabīr succeeded in afflicting mortal blows on the Babi resistance, thus fulfilling one of the chief functions he was called to perform, the reactionary Qajar elite and the associated groups saw fit to rid themselves of him. When both the Babis and Amīr Kabīr were eliminated, the precarious but enduring equilibrium between state and clergy was restored.

The extent to which the teachings of the Bab and his disciples offered an alternative to the religion of the time can be demonstrated by the following factors. Foremost was the fact that Babism responded to the changing socio-moral climate by consciously incorporating the notion of recurring renewal into the body of religious doctrine; something that the orthodox Shiʿite establishment (and the later Islamic reformers of all persuasions) tended to reject or ignore. In introducing the theme of progressive revelation, the Bab benefited from the dynamics of the Bāṭinī theory of cyclical manifestations. Hence the religion of the Bayān employed the old symbols of Shiʿism in order to offer a fresh answer to an equally old tension within that religion.

The earlier currents of the Bāṭinī thought, with very few exceptions, rarely exceeded the claim to the individual deputyship of the Hidden Imam. Only in Shaykhism, preoccupation with the Imam's this-worldly whereabouts subjected his existence to a historical process that ultimately was to culminate in his Advent. The Bab sought the solution to the dichotomy of the Shiʿite Imamate: the simultaneous presence and absence of the Imam, in the outward declaration of Mahdihood and its logical corollary, the Qiyāma. This revolutionary step set the Babis on the road to a complete break from Islam and the creation of a new religious dispensation. The mind that conceived this break, and set about to achieve it, though primarily religious, shared the modernity of a secular mind as it traced the stagnation of the community not in the irreversible fate of its members but in their failure to see the incompatibility of their past religious values with the realities of a new era. Before the introduction of Western ideologies would definitively revise the ideals of reform, this was the only answer generated in nineteenth-century Shiʿite Iran which coped with the threat of an alien and materially superior culture without resorting to rejectionism or falling prey to complacency.

The claim to the Qāʾimīya posed a direct challenge to the authority of Uṣūlī mujtahids, whose self-assigned function in the absence of the Imam was to guide the community. The collective deputyship on behalf of the Imam equipped them with a potent doctrinal weapon that could be employed whenever necessary to challenge the legitimacy of the temporal rulers. In practice, however, they mostly remained the government's tactical allies in maintaining a religio-political sway over the populace. The Babi theory, on the other hand, recognized, at least in principle, the de jure legitimacy of the temporal rulers as the protectors of the true religion. The Bab envisaged himself as a prophet, not a ruler; his misgivings about the state were directed at the conduct of the government rather than its legitimacy. The religious discipline of the Bayān, however, was considered comprehensive. The rulers of the Bayān era were to comply with the teachings of the new religion and after that with the teachings of future manifestations. Most Babis shared the observance of this duality of religious and political spheres.

Recognizing the legitimacy of the temporal state, however, did not mean acceptance of the rulers' oppressive conduct. At the heart of the Babi ethos was a spirit of rebellion against social injustice and moral mischief, for which the Babis held both the ruler and the ʿulama responsible. The Babis were unanimous in their condemnation. The methods they prescribed, however, differed widely.

The most obvious indication of their diversity in outlook was the dichotomy between the moderates, represented by the Bab and many of his more affluent followers of mercantile and bureaucratic backgrounds, and the militants, represented by Quddūs and Qurrat al-ʿAyn and including mullas of lower ranks, the artisans, and the peasantry. The uneasy merger between two social tendencies rarely found an open expression. The moderates, dissatisfied with their lack of access to the sources of power but not fundamentally opposed to the system, sought social, moral, and economic reform within the existing framework. The militants, however, saw the Babi movement as a revolutionary drive to purge society of its repressive norms and institutions. As the moderate approach, with its conciliatory attitude toward the ʿulama and the state, failed to fulfill its objectives, the radical tendency, which prevailed over the course of the Babi action after 1848, rallied the Bab and his followers and finally determined the fate of the movement. The inclination toward militancy was precipitated by increasing persecution and harassment.

The Babis' belief in the commencement of the Qiyāma turned the very concept of salvation upside down. It was the recognition of the new manifestation that for them determined the reward and punishment of the Final Day. To be included in the "letters of light" was to realize that Resurrection had begun with the Bab's abrogation of the previous sharīʿa, and with it the good works that promised the believer eternal blessings in the other world. The reward and punishment of the hereafter, though not rejected, were perceived to be the outcome of the believer's initiative in this world, making man responsible for his earthly conduct. Paradise was an allegory for inclusion in the community of light; for those who recognized and assisted the manifestation of God upon earth and would ultimately sacrifice themselves for his sake. Hell, on the other hand, was seen as a symbolic state for those who remained in the fire of their denial. The means of redemption on the Day of Reckoning hence was placed in the human hands. In the ongoing battle between the forces of light and fire, man was given the choice of seeking his own salvation.

The three themes of progressive revelation, conditional recognition of temporal authority, and this-worldliness of human salvation were in contrast to the Islamic precepts of the finality of Islam, the totality of the prophetic authority, and the other-worldliness of the Qiyāma. As such, the Babi religion sought to address the historic issues that preoccupied the Islamic, and more particularly the Shiʿite, consciousness. It was an attempt to render a religious answer to the moral and material stagnation of the community by proposing a continuous regeneration of religious essence, while preserving the historical relevance of the prophethood. Moreover, by perceiving the new manifestation as a spiritual mission, it tended to remove the age-old tension in Islam concerning the question of temporal rule. By interpreting the Resurrection as a recurring state of rebirth in which man by his own choice will be fashioned anew in this world, Babism subordinated eschatological redemption into a historical process of everlasting change.

Babi thought could not remain untouched by the sheer force of Shiʿite messianic legacy, however. Just as its innovations were a spontaneous response to the realities of the time, they were also indigenous to the ethos of the Persian Shiʿite past. The claim to Mahdihood and the doctrine of the recurring Qiyāma were bound to awaken the paradigms of martyrdom and self-sacrifice which were so closely interwoven with the Advent of the Qāʾim and the return of the past prophets, Imams, and saints. Most prominent in the minds of the Bab and his followers were the memory of Ḥusayn and the tragedy of Karbalāʾ, as they saw themselves the actors of the same battle now reenacted on the scene of the Qiyāma. The inner paradigms of Shiʿism had almost from the outset determined the course of the drama—its antagonists and protagonists, and its tragic end. The heroic Imam and his helpers, the returned prophets and the Imams, were to be opposed and ultimately slain by the Dajjāl and his allies.

Babi thought never liberated itself from the precomposed drama of the Qiyāma, the components of which could easily find symbolic equivalents in reality. Every act of compassion and congeniality struck a familiar cord in the collective memory of the believers; every wrongdoing, betrayal, and enmity had its prototype. The preoccupation of the Babis with the past was a symbolic one almost to the point of being mythological. This was not a nostalgic resort to the pristine and highly idealized Islam of the Prophet's time and that of the forefathers. Neither did it seek to reassert the old values of the Islamic sharīʿa. The "pure religion" of the Babis, though distantly related, was remote from the Traditionism of the Akhbārīs and even further removed from the revivalism of the Sunni neo-Ḥanbalites and their modern Shiʿite counterparts.

The preoccupation with past paradigms, symbolic as it was, had permeated every aspect of the Babi thought and action to the extent of molding it to the shape of a religious system with its own scripture, laws, and rituals. Most distinctive was the Babi sharīʿa. Unlike most heterodoxies of premodern times, Babism from the start intended to replace the old cycle not only by rejuvenating the inner truth (bāṭin), but also by reconstructing a new exterior (ẓāhir). Whereas the divine essence of religion—of all religions—remained identical, the Bab argued, the nonessential aspects were subject to constant change. The new sharīʿa therefore was to supplant that of Islam.

In reality, the Babi sharīʿa lacked the consistency, comprehensiveness, and independence to address the pressing issues of its time. It was largely modeled out of the practices, rituals, prohibitions, and injunctions of the existing sharīʿa. Despite the Bab's progressive doctrinal orientation and his desire to overcome the shortcomings of the existing sharīʿa, the bulk of the practical teachings of the *Bayān* was an amalgamation of popular religion and the imitation of the Shiʿite fiqh, though it also reflected the Bab's innovative views. Not infrequently, the Babi moral and legal code was even stricter than the existing sharīʿa. The injunctions concerning the expulsion of nonbelievers from the realm of Bayān and confiscation of their property; the burning of books that would not promote the cause of the new revelation; the prohibition of the study of those conventional sciences which could potentially bar the student from grasping the divine truth, may be seen as examples of the *Bayān*'s social intolerance and intellectual rigidity. However, both expulsion of the infidels and rejection of the conventional sciences reflected the nature of the Babi resentments. The growing threat of the foreign powers, both military and economic, could not have remained unnoticed by the Bab and the mercantile body of his supporters. The Bab's Shaykhi-Babi followers, on the other hand, had every reason to endorse his misgivings about the madrasa curriculum.

Far more detrimental to the implementation of a pragmatic Babi belief system was the built-in theological notion of the ever-occurring revelations. The idea of perpetual Ẓuhūr, conceived by the Bab and enshrined in the chiliastic notion of the He Whom God Shall Manifest, essentially militated against the institutionalization of the Babi religion. The Babi theology was erected on the precept of the prophetic continuity and the sense of vigilance for future divine revelations. This was especially enhanced in the latter period of the movement in conjunction with the Bab's own claim to Mahdihood and beyond. The believers were urged by the Bab to constantly keep vigil for future revelations, to evaluate every claimant with utmost impartiality, and even to tolerate claimants whose veracity was not apparent, lest the believers in this cycle should remain behind the veil of ignorance and denial like the people of previous cycles.

The possibility of the Babi sharīʿa's being nullified and replaced by a future manifestation, particularly since the time of his advent was signaled in the *Bayān* in the cryptic code of *mustaghāth* (he who shall be called upon for help), was an open invitation for messianic innovation. Similar to the earlier nonorthodox currents, the Babi formulation of the doctrine of progressive revelation and the sense of urgency attached to it was an inherent doctrinal twist with mixed blessings for the future of the Babi religion. While it permitted the continuity of leadership in the shape of future manifestations, as was the case in ensuing decades of the Babi history, the very presence of a charismatic element, especially when sanctified by Babi scripture, prevented the routinization of the theological and legal orders for which the Babis had striven.

The failure of the Babis to bring their message to a larger audience cannot be wholly subscribed to the inadequacies of the Babi sharīʿa. Far more instrumental were the forces that undermined the success of the movement both from within and without. The inherent message of the movement—"The cycle is in progression"—was potent enough to allow the ultimate liberation of Babi thought from the yoke of scriptural rigidity had it not been for the obstacles that barred its natural evolution from the outset—above all, the lack of determined planning and leadership that could guide the community toward well-defined goals. The tragic determinism inherent in the Babi mind, most evident in the fatalistic attitude of the Bab himself, left limited room for realistic assessment of their methods and their resources. The Babi theodicy guaranteed their ultimate triumph even if its realization meant the sacrifice of the Bab and the annihilation of the entire community. The Shiʿite legacy of tragic heroism could not have found a more apt presentation in the world of reality.

Like the Akhbārīs, the Niʿmatullāhīs, and the Shaykhis, the Babis were opposed, isolated, and eventually suppressed, even more violently than the others, by a combination of clerical denunciation and the government's punitive action. The Babis' failure to inspire a lasting support by the masses, even in the strongholds of Shaykhism, came about above all because the ʿulama, both Uṣūlī and conservative Shaykhi, continued their control of their traditional domains—the mosque, the madrasa, the religious courts, and the pious endowments. The Babis succeeded in penetrating the madrasa and to some limited extent the mosque, thus momentarily threatening the ʿulama's sway over its two most effective means of professional support and mass control. They failed, however, to fully neutralize the sanctifying power of the mujtahids, to build a parallel network to the clergy, and to gain a support similar to what the doctrine of ijtihād could rally behind the ʿulama when they were up against a stigmatized heresy. By emphasizing the values of personal inquiry for all and by repudiating the precept of emulation (taqlīd), Babi religion remained handicapped in comparison to Uṣūlī Shiʿism in being able to engender a sense of loyalty. Even if, in spite of their repeated fatwās of condemnation, the ʿulama failed to eliminate the Babis, they were nonetheless able to deprive them of free access to the masses. The voice of the Bab and the Babis remained a voice of persecuted dissent. It could not benefit from the weight of traditions and the sanctity of the established norms available to their adversaries.

What both Uṣūlī and conservative Shaykhi mujtahids lacked, the government eventually made available, for reasons of political expediency. The Qajar state, both provincial and central, was anxious to maintain the status quo so as to preserve the customary privileges associated with its temporal rule while allowing the other interested parties, most notably the mujtahids, to keep their own spheres of control. Any force that could disturb this precarious coexistence was viewed with utmost suspicion. Under Āqāsī, the state partially tolerated the Babis and ignored the ʿulama's call for their elimination as long as the Babis restricted their criticism to the higher echelons of the clerical class. But when the ʿulama managed to isolate the Babis by turning the public against them, thus forcing them into militancy and active resistance, the government had little choice but to intervene on their side. Even if Amīr Kabīr's policy tended to chastise the more independent ʿulama in the hope of greater centralization and secular reforms, his drastic action against the Babis could not have been more beneficial to the ʿulama community as a whole.

In the decade following the political collapse of the Babi movement, the ʿulama remained largely in harmony with, if not subservient to, the Qajar state. They could not have been more grateful to the Qajar state for ridding them of both the Babis and Amīr Kabīr. The new generation of mujtahids preferred the safe enclosure of the madrasas to the hazards of the bazaar, and clerical intervention came to a temporary halt. The rise to prominence of figures like Shaykh Murtażā Anṣārī, the great Uṣūlī scholar in the late 1850s and early 1860s, demonstrated a strong desire within the clerical community for political acquiescence and scholarly persuasion.

Perhaps the most significant impact of the Babi experience on the ʿulama was their greater awareness of the institutional inadequacies of the Uṣūlī theory. The Bab's claim to bābīya and then Mahdihood encouraged the mujtahids to find more consistent answers to the problems of leadership and institutional hierarchy. It is not accidental that in the aftermath of the Babi episode, Anṣārī, and after him the mujtahids of the late nineteenth century, attempted a clearer formulation of the requisites of ijtihād. The conceptual evolution from the diffuse status of collective deputyship of the Imam, claimed by the mujtahids, to the status of individual leadership (riyāsat) of the clerical community, and ultimately the emergence of the office of *marjaʿīyat-i taqlīd-i tāmm* (the ultimate source of emulation), was not divorced from the challenges posed by the Bab and his claims to specific deputyship and Imamate itself. Emphasis on the qualities of knowledge, virtue, and justice, as articulated by Anṣārī and others, was to address the shortcomings for which the mujtahids were blamed by their Babi critics. Moreover, the fear of another internal revolt in the lower clerical ranks, similar to that of the Babi mullas, was probably influential in the later conception of a more elaborate hierarchical scheme.

In the cities, and to a lesser extent the countryside, the Babi minority recruited from all social groups. It represented a broad geographical distribution covering all major provinces and present in most urban centers. Yet it remained essentially an urban-based movement lacking the nomadic support that ideally could have prevented its military defeat. The participating groups belonged predominantly to the lower and middle classes. Some were from major trade centers, others from small cities, and still others from villages. The Babi ideology served as the mortar for cementing these groups together and gave them a new sense of identity and purpose that was largely absent in the society at large.

The highly visible presence of low-rank mullas, the merchants, and the bureaucrats as well as a woman in the leadership of the movement is no coincidence. The Shaykhi mullas resented the high-ranking mujtahids' monopoly of clerical offices, their material excesses, and their intellectual stagnation; the merchants were impatient with the government's inefficiency, the decline of the economy, and the moral decadence of the holders of the highest political and religious offices. Women, represented by Qurrat al-ʿAyn and the small group around her, were arguably the most oppressed of all social groups. Such small representation is all the more important given the nature of the socioreligious order that demanded women's subservience to the opposite gender, deprived them from public life, and denied them, even more than other groups, expression of their grievances.

Despite their widely diverse aspirations and resentments, and thus diverse expectations for joining the movement, the Babi converts found in the new religion a mystical union and a spirit of defiance against the privileged elite. The convergence of these aspirations into one messianic current under the leadership of a merchant with messianic claims was symptomatic of a desire to replace the old norms with a more equitable order. This was perhaps the only way that the messianic ethos of Shiʿism could regenerate a pristine sense of national identity representative of emerging social groups that could loosely be defined as a middle class. The dismal failure of the state to retain the loyalty of its subjects as the chief prerequisite for the survival of a homogeneous nation-state, combined with the failure of the ʿulama to provide satisfactory doctrinal answers to the needs of a changing society, for a brief but critical moment of time made the Babis a serious alternative.

The Babi phenomenon sprang up at a time when Persian society was on the verge of a crucial transition. Tormented by its age-old dilemmas, the Persian mind was beginning to be exposed to a materially superior civilization. The emergence of the Babi doctrine thus was perhaps the last chance for a indigenous reform movement before that society became truly affected by the consequences of the Western predominance, first in material and then in ideological spheres. Notwithstanding its weaknesses, the Babi doctrine attempted to address, rather than ignore, the issues that lay at the foundation of the Persian consciousness. The Babi solution was the product of an esoteric legacy, one that sought redemptive regeneration in a break with the past without being essentially alien to the spirit of that past.

Unlike later currents of modernity and religious reform active in the second half of the nineteenth century, the Babi mind was not consciously affected by Western ethos. Nor was its doctrinal exposition fashioned out of the current Western positivist models of progress and humanism. Unlike later Islamic reformers, who shrank from any alteration of sacred and eternal religious dogmas, the Bab strove to resolve the predicaments of Islamic eschatology by returning to the basic issues of prophethood, resurrection, and the hereafter. Daring and dangerous as it was, Babi thought sought to culminate what the heterodoxies of previous centuries had potentially tended to achieve.

The long, laborious road to salvation, as it was perceived by the Shiʿite Bāṭinīs, reached a new momentum when the inner secrets of the "pure religion" were divulged in the Qiyāma only to pave the way for a new cycle of Babi epiphany. The challenge of Bāṭinī thought was in its effort to crystallize in the figure of the Perfect Man the attributes of an inaccessible and incomprehensible God. Babi thought went a long way to fulfill this aspiration. The pantheistic exclamations of the *Bayān*, while still bearing marks of mystical determinism, bore in its inception the prototype of a new Perfect Man who sought not only to encompass the divine attributes, but to share it with the community of believers, in Babi terms the All-Beings. Out of the confusing labyrinth of Babi mystical theology there could have emerged a revolutionary answer to the long-standing dichotomy of divine and human existence, a division essential to all monotheistic religions.

The exposure of the messianic paradigms to new historical circumstances thus prompted a phenomenon which though other-worldly in its ethos was peculiarly this-worldly in its objectives. The tension arising from this duality survived in the Babi movement even after the termination of its initial phase. Both the Bahā'ī and the Bābī-Azalī currents bore in their own ways its stamp. The Bahā'ī religion came to represent revisionist tendencies within the movement that sought to achieve further religious innovation by means of moral aptitude and adoption of modern social reforms. The Azalī-Babi current, on the other hand, tended to represent the non-adaptive tendency in the movement, which remained loyal to the tenets of the Babi sharīʿa and thus was more inclined, at least in theory, to political activism.

Behind the sad and bitter sectarian conflict that marred the history of the Babi community in later decades and divided it along Bahā'ī -Azalī lines lay a fundamental difference in outlook. Though it was the dispute over the succession of the Bab that turned the supporters of the Nurī half-brothers Mīrzā Ḥusayn ʿAlī Bahā'ullāh and Mīrzā Yaḥyā Ṣubḥ-i Azal against each other, and though it was the aggravation of this dispute in the small exile community of Baghdad and then Edirne that led to the eventual break between the two rival creeds in the late 1860s, the ongoing quarrel laid bare the same ideological divisions implicit in the first phase of the movement.

In the aftermath of the Babi persecutions of 1852 and the exile to Iraq, Bahā'ullāh gradually transformed the messianic militancy of the Bābīs into a pacifist, largely nonpolitical current. Moreover, he utilized the Babi theory of perpetual revelations to justify the necessity for a new and, as he saw it, more comprehensive epiphany. The Bab's mission was thus considered by the Bahā'īs as a heraldic intermission before the "total divine manifestation." Bahā'ullāh's advocacy of peaceful proselytism, fortitude, and non-political activism especially appealed to the demoralized Babis because they promised them hope and moral security at a time of political defeat and confusion in leadership. This was particularly, though not exclusively, attractive to those sections of the urban Babi community that sought in the Babi message a nonrevolutionary liberation from the yoke of the old values and traditions. The Bahā'ī current most effectively regained the loyalty of the Babis, to whom it offered ethical values attuned with temporal success and a theology reasonably rationalized to relieve the community from excessive preoccupation with ritual and religious prohibitions. The social message of the new faith spilled over the bounds of Babi religion and implied in its universalism a greater reconciliation with the needs of the modern secular world. Increasingly in the closing decades of the nineteenth century, Bahā'ī social doctrine tended to distance itself from its own Shiʿite origin and move in the direction of modern morality and ethics. The Babi legacy was no doubt crucial in the way the Bahā'īs were able to adopt this essentially non-Islamic outlook.

By the beginning of the twentieth century the Bahā'ī current was crystallized in a new religious mold with its own moral framework and social message. It remained faithful to the Babi creed only to the extent of selective reaffirmation of its sharīʿa. Under the leadership of ʿAbd al-Bahāʾ and then Shoghi Effendi, greater institutionalization of the Bahāʾī religion turned memories of the Babi past into a heroic story of martyrdom and self-sacrifice that could supply the Bahāʾī mind with new paradigms and give a sense of continuity with the past. It consistently tended to mellow the Babi defiance and militancy, however, in order to highlight the Bahāʾī pacifism and political nonintervention.

Less receptive to doctrinal innovation than the Bahāʾīs, the Azalī minority tended to preserve the spirit of Babism, but more as a religious creed than as a social discipline. In the old tradition of the Islamic heterodox sects, it maintained secrecy and prudence to the point of conformity. In a less-organized fashion, however, it survived within a network of family loyalties and with occasional outbursts of clandestine antigovernment activism. The Azalī family background of two of the renowned dissident reformists of the late nineteenth century, Mīrzā Āqā Khān Kirmānī and Shaykh Aḥmad Rūḥī Kirmānī (both sons-in-law of Ṣubḥ-i Azal), may not be altogether unrelated to their early ideological convictions. Their later modernist critiques of religion and society, however, were influenced more by nineteenth-century European trends than by Babi thought.

By the turn of the twentieth century, the Azalī-Babism briefly re-emerged as a noticeable trend before and during the Constitutional Revolution. A number of key advocates of constitutional reforms, both preachers and lay intellectuals, reportedly adhered in secret to the Babi-Azalī creed. So far as can be ascertained, their attachment to Babism was more a nostalgic reverence for the memory of the Bab and the early Babis than adherence to the teachings of that religion.

Whichever turn the two diverse currents of the Babi thought took in the latter decades, their impact upon society hardly exceeded the limits of a small minority. The Bahāʾīs in particular were frequent targets of intolerance and persecution. After 1852, scenes of "Babi killing" in the cities and villages of Iran were commonplace. Incited by a vengeful clergy, the hysterical mob often found satisfaction in looting, killing, and forced conversion of the Babis and later the Bahāʾīs. The ultimate reward for the killing of a heretic, so the ʿulama assured the believers, was the same as for any act of devotion. The petty quarrels between the state authorities and the ʿulama more often than not turned the Babi-Bahāʾīs into easy scapegoats. Unable to protect themselves and unwilling to protest, the victims saw martyrdom as the only alternative to recantation and conformity. The government, out of expediency rather than conviction, was often obliged to comply with the mujtahids' wishes. For the latter, the persecution of the Babi heretics could serve some worldly purposes. Participation in the anti-Babi campaigns of hatred and cruelty often had the miraculous effect of reversing the mujtahids' social and even economic fortunes and restoring their fading popularity.

The elimination of the Babi movement as an alternative current to the Shiʿite orthodoxy was a turning point in the religious history of modern Iran. Ironically, the eradication of the movement by the forces of a modernizing state had the reverse effect of securing the survival of a conservative religious establishment that was essentially antireformist. In the long run, such drastic removal of the antiorthodox factor guaranteed further solidifcation of the clerical institution with definite obscurantist orientation.

Whatever its weaknesses, in theory and practice, the Babi movement was an effort to find a timely answer to the most fundamental problem of Shiʿism, and in a broader sense that of Islam. The Return of the Imam was the only Shiʿite solution to the two dilemmas of sacred authority and religious renewal. This Babi alternative was duly rejected but the predicaments of Shiʿism persisted, albeit in the collective subconscious of Persian society. Neither exposure to Western secularization nor the transformation of Shiʿite political thought in the twentieth century seems to have diminished the dimensions of these problems or made them altogether irrelevant. Yet both developments had a far-reaching impact on the way contemporary Iranian society is now experiencing the imposition of a tragically anachronistic solution to problems as old as Shiʿism itself.

Glossary

Ahl-i Ḥaqq Lit. the People of the Truth. The followers of a semiclandestine rustic religion often categorized among the ghulāt and with gnostic beliefs not dissimilar to Ismāʿīlīya. *ʿAlīullāhī* is used in a pejorative sense in reference to a believer in Ahl-i Ḥaqq.

akhbār (sing. *khabar*) Lit. message, report. The Traditions (words and deeds) of the Prophet and of the Shiʿite Imams as transmitted by chains of narrators. In post-Safavid Shiʿism, *akhbār* often denoted the body of Traditions reported by a single transmitter or by a less than "sound" chain of transmitters and thus are vaguely distinguished from the ḥadīth. In the technical sense, *khabar* is the message of the ḥadīth.

Akhbārīya The Shiʿite school of jurisprudence and ḥadīth, which rejects deductive methodology in the study of law and requires unmitigated adherence to the limited meaning of the akhbār as well as recognition of their authenticity, often regardless of the "soundness" of their chain of transmitters.

ākhūnd From the Persian *khudāvandgār* (the lord). General title for the Persian clergy. In the nineteenth century often as an honorific designating the scholarship of a member of the Shiʿite ʿulama class.

āl The people, family, clan, or house of. (Not to be confused with the definite article *al-* .)

āqā Lit. lord, master. In the Qajar period used to designate the people in the positions of authority, particularly in the religious class but also notables and high-ranking officials. Occasionally *āghā*.

aṣnāf (sing. *ṣinf*) Guilds and guild organizations.

ʿAtabāt Lit. the thresholds. The Shiʿite holy shrines in Iraq and the cities of their location: Karbalāʾ, Najaf, Kāẓimayn, and Sāmarrā.

bāb Lit. gate, threshold. In Shiʿism the human mediator between the Hidden Imam and his followers. More specifically, the means of communication with the Hidden Imam. The four Deputies of the Twelfth Imam are thus termed *Abwāb* (pl. of *bāb*). In the Babi context, the title first assumed by Sayyid ʿAlī Muḥammad Shīrāzī in 1844. The "exclusive mediator" (*bāb-i khāṣṣ*) of the Imam is used in distinction from occasional Shiʿite references to the collective body of the high-ranking ʿulama as the general mediators (*abwāb-i ʿāmm*) of the Imam.

bābīya (Persian *bābīyat*) The status of the bāb. *Bābīya* is also used in reference to the Babi movement and community.

badāʾ Lit. new occurrence. In Shiʿism, signifies new circumstances that bring about a change in an earlier divine will. This doctrine serves to explain the delay in the appearance of the Mahdi.

bāṭin Lit. inner, inward. The inner meaning behind the literal text of the scripture and the ḥadīth. *Bāṭinīya* thus refers to all Shiʿite and Shiʿite-Sufi currents (most notably the Ismāʿīlīya) that seek and stress an esoteric interpretation for the religion.

Bayān Lit. eloquent explanation. The title of two of the Bab's most important works. *Al-Bayān* is one of the attributes of the Qurʾān. Also of the Babi religion.

bidʿa Lit. innovation. A belief or practice for which there is no precedent in the time of the Prophet or the Imams. The prohibited innovation generally considered as unacceptable but distinguished from heresy.

Dajjāl Lit. deceiver. The Antichrist of the Islamic eschatology. Endowed with miraculous powers, he will arrive before the End of Time and for a limited period will let impurity and tyranny rule the world before being defeated by the Mahdi.

dhikr (Persian *z̲ikr*) Lit. remembrance. One of the attributes of the Qurʾān and its deliverer, Muḥammad. In the Babi context, Z̲ikr refers to the Bab's revelatory claim, with stress on his ability to deliver the word of God.

faqīh (pl. *fuqahāʾ*) A jurist specializing in the science of fiqh. In the nineteenth century, it implies specialization in applied religious law (furūʿ).

farangī A European.

fatra Lit. interregnum, interval. A period of transition separating two successive prophetic revelations. More specifically, the period of slackening of the religious law between the end of one cycle and the start of another.

fatwā A ruling on a point of religious law by one of the ʿulama. In the Ottoman Empire, only by the mufti.

fiqh Lit. comprehension. The knowledge of the religion with emphasis on jurisprudence and the exercise of independent but informed judgment.

fitna Lit. temptation, sedition, trial of the faith. Any revolt with religious, and specifically messianic, aspirations. In Shiʿism, *al-Fitna al-Ākhir al-Zamān* (the Uprising at the End of Time) will occur with the appearance of the Mahdi. In the Babi context, a reference, both by the Babis and their opponents, to the Babi insurgence.

Furqān Lit. discriminator. A term of messianic connotation by which the Qurʾān defines itself as the criterion for deliverance. In the Babi context, it refers both to the Qurʾān and to the Bab's body of writings, particularly *Qayyūm al-Asmāʾ*.

ghayba Lit. occulation. In Twelver Shiʿism, the Occultation of the Twelfth Imam, Muḥammad ibn Ḥasan Askarī, with the understanding that he would return as the Qāʾim and the Mahdi. The Complete Occultation (*al-Ghayba al-Kubrā*) presumably occurred in 941. The Babi doctrine honors Ghayba but rejects the possibility of the physical return of Muḥammad ibn Ḥasan in person.

ghulūw Lit. exaggeration. Extremism of any kind in matters of religious belief.

Specifically, a reference to a wide variety of heterodox and heretical currents that hold excessive reverence for ʿAlī or other Shiʿite Imams.

ḥadīth The words and deeds of the Prophet Muḥammad, and in Shiʿism of the Imams, as they are reported by the transmitters.

Ḥajj Pilgrimage to Mecca undertaken according to prescribed ritual during the month of Dhū al-Ḥijja.

Ḥājjī One who has completed the Ḥajj.

ḥikma (Persian *ḥikmat*) Lit. wisdom; Islamic philosophy. In Shiʿite context often stands for *ḥikmat-i ilāhī* or theosophy of the Ṣadrā'ian school.

ḥujja (Persian *ḥujjat*) Lit. proof. In Shiʿism, the attribute *Ḥujjatullāh* (the Proof of God) is used for the Imams, and particularly for the Hidden Imam, who is the proof of the continuation of the divine presence on earth.

Ḥurūf-i Ḥayy (sing. *Ḥarf-i Ḥayy*) The Letters of the Living. The first group of Babi believers, who in 1847 were designated by the Bab as the first unit of the Babi community.

ijāza Lit. authorization, permission. Certificate permitting a student either to report the ḥadīth on the authority of his teacher and/or to exercise *ijtihād*.

ijtihād Lit. endeavor. The process of arriving at independent legal judgments in specific matters of religious law by employing the sources of the law and by using the "principles of jurisprudence" (*uṣūl al-fiqh*).

Imām Lit. the one who stands in front. In Twelver Shiʿism, one of the twelve recognized hereditary successors of Muḥammad, beginning with ʿAlī and continued in his House. After the tenth century, both *Imām-i Zamān* (the Imam of the Age) and *Imām-i Ghā'ib* (the Hidden Imam) refer to the Twelfth Imam.

imām(-i) jumʿa Leader of the Friday communal prayer appointed by the government in each city. Often a hereditary position in nineteenth-century Iran, with broader responsibilities.

Ithnā ʿAsharīya Lit. the Twelvers. That branch of the Imami Shiʿism that believes in twelve Imams, beginning with ʿAlī and ending with Muḥammad ibn Ḥasan.

jihād Lit. striving. The holy war undertaken against the infidels to defend, or to expand, Islam. In Babism synonymous with *khurūj*.

Khurūj Lit. departure. An act of rebellion against authorities. In Shiʿite messianic context, *Khurūj* denotes the final Insurrection of the Mahdi against the forces of disbelief and the enemies of his house.

Kullu-Shay' Lit. everything, All-Beings, as in the Qur'ān. In the Bab's numerological system it equals 19 units (*vāḥid*.)

lūṭī A member of a city brigandage, with distinct customs, outfit, vocabulary, and code of conduct.

Maʿād Lit. a place of return. Denotes the return of the dead to the point of origin after Resurrection (*Qiyāma*); in a broader sense, the hereafter.

madrasa In the nineteenth century, a religious college where Islamic sciences were taught. Often financed by charitable endowments and supervised by the ʿulama.

Mahdī Lit. guided one. The Islamic messianic savior who would destroy disbelief and oppression. In Twelver Shiʿism, he is identified as the Hidden Twelfth Imam, who would appear at the End of Time.

mīrzā (from *amīr-zādih:* prince). In the nineteenth century, if placed before proper name, Mīrzā indicates religious or bureaucratic training. If placed after, it indicates that the bearer is a prince.

mubāhala Mutual execration by means of sincere praying to God for the annihilation of the other party. An ancient religious test.

muftī One whose opinion is sought on a point of religious law. In the Ottoman Empire, a judicial office appointed by the government.

mujtahid One who has studied sufficiently to attain the level of competence in matters of religious law necessary to exercise *ijtihād.*

mullā (from *mawlā)* Lit. lord, master. Usual Persian term for a person from the ʿulama class. In the nineteenth century it denoted no hierarchical gradation.

nāʾib Lit. deputy. In Shiʿism *nāʾib al-Imām* is the representative of the Imam. *Nāʾib al-khāṣṣ* is thus the exclusive representative of the Imam. Orthodox Twelvers recognize this status only for the first four Gates (*abwāb*) to the Twelfth Imam. *Nāʾib al-ʿāmm* is the general representative of the Hidden Imam. Mainstream Shiʿism recognizes this status for the collective body of the ʿulama.

nār Lit. fire, inferno. In the Babi doctrine, the state of human ignorance as well as the social sphere to which belong all the opponents of the new faith.

nāṭiq Lit. enunciator. In heterodox Shiʿism, the prophet who in each of the seven prophetic cycles reveals the divine message. He is supplemented in his mission by a silent one *(ṣāmit.)*

niyāba Deputyship. The status claimed by the *nāʾib al-Imām.*

nūr Lit. light. In the Babi doctrine, the state of human enlightenment and the sphere to which all the believers of the new faith belong.

pāshā An honorific in the Ottoman Empire as well as the title of the governor of an administrative unit. It is synonymous to *vālī* in the Arab provinces of the empire.

Qāʾim Lit. riser. In Shiʿism, *al-Qāʾim* and *Qāʾim Āl Muḥammad* (the Riser of the House of Muḥammad) is a title of the Imam (after the tenth century of the Twelfth Imam), denoting his uprising at the time of his appearance to redress wrongs.

Qiyāma (Persian *Qiyāmat*). At the end of Time, the Qiyāma of bodies follows the annihilation of all creatures and precedes the Day of Judgment. In Babi doctrine, it is the termination of a prophetic cycle and the start of a new one.

rajʿa Lit. return. In a general sense it is synonymous with *maʿād.* In Twelver Shiʿism, *Rajʿa* means the Return of the Hidden Imam, who is the Mahdi, with a given number of his supporters to the material world immediately before the Resurrection.

rawża Lit. garden, from the title of a book of mourning *Rawḍat al-Shuhadāʾ* (Garden of the Martyrs). Recitation of the sufferings of the Imams, particularly of Imam Ḥusayn and his companions in the battle of Karbalāʾ. *Rawża-Khwānī* is the gathering for such recital; *rawża-khwān* is the professional reciter of the sufferings.

rijāl Lit. men, notables. *ʿIlm al-rijāl* is the study of the biographies of the transmitters of the ḥadīth and religious scholars in general.

risāla A treatise.

riyāsa Lit. leadership. In Shiʿism, the religious leadership of the community, specifically of the ʿulama community, by one or several high-ranking mujtahids.

Ṣāḥib al-Zamān The Lord of the Age. One of the titles of the Imams, specifically of the Twelfth Imam, emphasizing his sole sovereignty at his time of appearance.

sayyid (pl. *sādāt*) Lit. master. In the Shiʿite world, designates a descendant of the House of Muḥammad. A sayyid, distinguished by the color of green in his outfit, is entitled to special privileges.

sharīʿa The canonical law of Islam as defined by orthodox authorities. In a broader sense, any religious orthodoxy or body of teachings brought by a divine messenger.

shaykh Lit. an elder. Designation sometimes used for high-ranking ʿulama.

shaykh al-Islām In Iran the official title given to the members of the ʿulama appointed to preside over religious courts. By the nineteenth century, a hereditary title.

sūra A chapter of the Qurʾān.

takfīr The formal denunciation, usually by the ʿulama, of an individual on the charge of heresy and disbelief.

ṭalaba (pl. *ṭullāb*) A religious student of a madrasa.

taqīya The prudential dissimulation of true religious beliefs in circumstances where there is fear of being killed or captured, or of being insulted. It is sanctioned by the Shiʿite sharīʿa.

taqlīd Lit. emulation. The process of following the practices and pronouncements of a mujtahid in matters relating to religious law without independent investigation. Opposite of *ijtihād*.

tujjār (sing. *tājir*) The merchant class. In the nineteenth century, often merchants of substance who were engaged in long-distance trade.

tūmān Lit. ten thousand. Persian main unit of currency in the nineteenth century, equivalent to 20 shāhīs or 10,000 Persian dīnārs.

ʿulamāʾ (sing. *ʿālim*) Lit. learned men. A body of religious scholars, specifically, the religious establishment. *ʿĀlim* is rarely used in the nineteenth century as a denominator, but can be said for any learned man (fem. *ʿālima*), but the ʿulamā are restricted to the scholars of religious law.

uṣūl al-fiqh Lit. roots of jurisprudence. The science of the principles of jurisprudence and the methodological means of arriving at legal standards, as opposed to *furūʿ* (branches) of fiqh, which is the actual body of law.

Uṣūlīya The school of jurisprudence that emphasizes the study of uṣūl al-fiqh. In the nineteenth century, it is almost synonymous with the mujtahids.

vāḥid (Arabic *wāḥid*) Lit. numeral 1. In the Babi context, the unit of communal organization consisted of nineteen persons. Each chapter of the Persian *Bayān* is a vāḥid and itself is divided into nineteen sections.

wilāya (Persian *vilāyat*) In the strict legal sense, guardianship. In nonorthodox Shiʿism, vicegerency of the Hidden Imam while he is in Occultation. Sometimes synonymous with *walaya,* which is often defined as love and devotion toward ʿAlī and his house.

ẓāhir Lit. exterior. In heterodox Shiʿism, exterior of religion as conveyed by the literal meaning of the scripture.

ẕikr See *dhikr*.

ẓuhūr Lit. emergence, appearance. In Shiʿite messianic terminology, the Advent of the Imam of the Age and the events associated with his Return. In a broader sense, any prophetic revelation.

Note on the Sources

The historiography of the Babi movement is surrounded by controversy. Most of the general accounts were recorded after the end of the first phase in 1268/1852, and are riddled with misinterpretations, contradictions, and inaccuracies. The intensity of the events during the first decade, and the persecution they endured, prevented the Babis from keeping consistent records except for a few important occasions. The necessity for recording the earlier events inspired some early Babis to write general narratives, which were either completely destroyed or reached later generations only in fragments or, more often, in a distorted form. A relatively poor standard of historiography, added to the inherent hostility of the non-Babi chroniclers, also caused gross exaggerations and irrecoverable gaps. Furthermore, the events of the earlier period were often skewed by later writers with the specific purpose of substantiating or invalidating a given claim or point of view. Beyond the obvious distortions and misuses of the hostile non-Babi writers, a more important example of this diverse interpretation is that which occurred as a result of the Baha'ī-Azalī controversy between 1860 and 1890, which in many ways affected the tone and the content of the historical works produced in this period and after.

Yet in spite of these obstacles the early Babi narratives, and even in some instances their traces in secondary accounts, often possess a freshness and sincerity that are lacking in most other historical writings of the time. In most cases the Babi writers were ordinary people who recorded their observations about other ordinary men and women in a most natural form, differing widely from the superficial elaboration of the chroniclers or the reserved tone of secondary accounts.

In general, sources of the early period can be divided into five categories: (1) Persian and Arabic primary sources; (2) European primary sources; (3) Persian and Arabic accounts that should be counted as primary in content and secondary in rendering; (4) Persian and Arabic secondary sources; (5) secondary European accounts.

Persian and Arabic primary sources are the general accounts produced over a period of more than thirty years after the execution of the Bab. There are occasional references to an "old history" (*tārīkh-i qadīm*) that covered the events of the early years and is supposed to have been written by one of the early believers of the Bab, most likely Ḥājjī Mīrzā Jānī Kāshānī sometime prior to his execution in 1268/1852. Browne's edition of *Nuqṭat al-Kāf* appears to be the nearest to this yet-untraced old history. But there is no definitive proof that *Nuqṭat al-Kāf* is the original version of the old history. Controversy surrounds the authenticity of some of its passages, and the possibility exists of later distortions. Since it was first published in 1910, the text of *Nuqṭat al-Kāf* and Browne's introduction (written with the unacknowledged assistance of Muḥammad Qazvīnī) inspired some Bahā'ī writers, such as Mīrzā Abul-Fażl Gulpāyigānī in *Kashf al-Ghiṭā'*, to try to resolve some of the complexities of the text and to criticize some of Browne's views. Yet neither Browne's speculations nor Gulpāyigānī's efforts came to any definite answer. Suggestions by such later scholars as Balyuzi (*Edward Granville Browne and the Bahā'ī Faith*), Muḥīṭ Ṭabāṭabā'ī, Denis MacEoin, and others led to a better understanding of problems, rather than solving them. What is certain, however, is that *Nuqṭat al-Kāf*, itself a combination of two separate theological and historical parts, was produced sometime in the early 1850s by one or a few writers, among whom Ḥājjī Mīrzā Jānī was the original author. They had either witnessed the early events or reported them from other eyewitnesses. While it is possible that some of the passages, the events 1266–1267/1850–1851 for example, were added later, as far as the events of the earlier years are concerned, *Nuqṭat al-Kāf* is largely in agreement with other sources of the period.

Decades of suppression and persecution suffered by the Babis caused a sense of disillusionment that in turn led to the temporary neglect of Babi historical recording, both oral and written. Toward the 1880s, however, the revival of the Babi circles in Iran generated a need for the compilation of the new general narratives, more in Bahā'ī than in Azalī circles. These narratives were of a different tone and style and their emphasis on historical events was to satisfy the new ideological orientation of the Babi community. The revised version of the old history, entitled *Tārīkh-i Jadīd* (the New History)—by Mīrzā Ḥusayn Hamadānī under the patronage of Mānakjī Hataryārī, the Indian Zoroastrian representative in Tehran, and with the preliminary supervision of Mīrzā Abul-Fażl Gulpāyigānī—was the first in a series of attempts to produce new general histories. Browne's assessment of *Tārīkh-i Jadīd* in his introduction to the English translation of this work (as in his introduction to *Nuqṭat al-Kāf*) demonstrates, in content and style, the omissions and additions as well as the different religious and political (or rather apolitical) orientations of the author in comparison to *Nuqṭat al-Kāf*. However, some of Browne's harsh criticisms of what he regarded as Bahā'ī distortions and deviations in *Tārīkh-i Jadīd* can be questioned, when it is considered that the additional information in *Tārīkh-i Jadīd* might have come from a copy of Ḥājjī Mīrzā Jānī's old history different from that of Browne's *Nuqṭat al-Kāf*. So long as no earlier manuscript is found than Gobineau's copy in the Bibliothèque Nationale, a final verdict cannot be passed. Meanwhile, *Nuqṭat al-Kāf* remains one of the most valuable narratives available. It is probable that the author of *Tārīkh-i Jadīd* did not consider himself bound to write a history identical to the old version, and naturally, in many ways, he considered his own rationalized, sometimes naïve, viewpoint superior. Browne often exaggerates the importance of some ideas and attitudes that he believed, almost entirely on the basis of *Nuqṭat al-Kāf,* to be those of all the early Babis. Moreover, when he wrote his introduction to *Nuqṭat al-Kāf,* in the aftermath of the Constitutional Revolution, he was actively involved in amplifying the ideas and activities of those whom he appears to have believed (though he never openly expresses it) were the legitimate Azalī descendants of the early Babis. Thus perhaps beyond the boundaries of historiography, he sometimes saw himself as an advocate of a cause of which he thought the Azalīs, and not the Bahā'īs, were the true representatives.

Accusations, counteraccusations, and speculations in this controversy sometimes pass the limits of historical enquiry to become purely a mental exercise, a kind of detective investigation, or ammunition for religious refutations and polemics. The important thing is that *Tārīkh-i Jadīd* was not a successful attempt to compile a general narrative. And as Browne rightly argues, it missed, or rather intended to miss, the militant spirit of the early Babi period. The shift of emphasis and alterations which were carried out in the more recent versions of this history, of which *Tārīkh-i Badīʿ-i Bayānī* is one example, did not help to disentangle the earlier confusions. *Tārīkh-i Jadīd,* too, contains some reliable information that is verified by other early sources.

Various other attempts were made to assemble a written history of the early Babi movement. *Maqāla-yi Shakhṣī Sayyāḥ* (A Traveler's Narrative), by ʿAbd al-Bahā', written shortly before 1890, is a relatively brief account from the viewpoint of an onlooker, a *sayyāḥ* (traveler). It was loosely based on the available information in both the Babi and non-Babi oral and written sources and adds only a little fresh information to the knowledge of the early period. Perhaps more significantly, from the viewpoint of style and approach, it was an effort to write an account that could justify the Bahā'ī stand while avoiding the highly committed language of other Bahā'ī polemics. Browne's edition and translation of this work, entitled *A Traveller's Narrative,* appeared a year after the Bombay edition of 1890.

Another attempt at writing a general history of the early years was that of the early convert Shaykh Muḥammad Nabīl Zarandī, known as Nabīl Aʿẓam, by far the most complete of the general narratives. Written in its final version between 1305/1888 and 1308/1890, Nabīl Zarandī's narrative was based not only on his own personal observations but on the oral and written memoirs of many early Babis, to whose authority he refers throughout. He also benefited from the assistance of Mīrzā Mūsā Nūrī, brother of Bahā'ullāh. Nabīl Zarandī's work covered the history of the movement up to the time of completion. An articulate writer, he was able to compile his history in a systematic and chronological order. Yet his narrative suffers from some serious handicaps. His personal religious sentiments and his subdued fatalism (typical of the change of attitude in many Babi-Bahā'īs of the first generation), frequently made him tone down, or in some cases intentionally ignore, the revolutionary nature of the movement and the early Babis' militancy, particularly by adopting a melodramatic language that he has no hesitation in putting into the mouths of his characters. His style and approach seldom caused any deliberate distortion of fact, yet his strong commitment to Bahā'ullāh, like many other early Bahā'īs, reached the extremes of admiration and praise, and made him see in the earlier events a mysterious cause for the later mission of Bahā'ullāh. The gap of about forty years between the actual events and their recording no doubt caused some inaccuracies as well as inconsistency in the sequence and details of the events, for which the author tried to compensate by adding an element of the marvelous and the mysterious. Moreover, the original Persian manuscript preserved in the Bahā'ī archive in Haifa regrettably is not available, and the English translation by Shoghi Effendi, which covers only the first part up to 1268/1852, may be an abridgement. In spite of these deficiencies, however, *Nabil* remains a relatively reliable source that in most cases corroborates the facts supplied by earlier accounts. A careful reading of *Nabil* can reveal many hidden traits.

The second group of Persian and Arabic primary sources comprises the non-Babi general accounts, basically recorded in the years immediately following the end of the first phase. The best known of these are the two official chronicles of the mid-nineteenth century, Sipihr's *Nāsikh al-Tawārīkh (Tarīkh-i Qājārīya)* and Hidāyat's *Rauḍat al-Ṣafā*, which both pay considerable attention to the rise of the movement. Both chroniclers are biased, cynical, and frequently inaccurate. Their accounts are charged with enough exaggeration and accusations to discredit the movement and please the authorities. Yet both contain some interesting details and remarks, which in some instances reflect the attitude of the state authorities and in others their authors' secret admiration. *Nāsikh al-Tawārīkh* is particularly interesting, since Sipihr seems to have gathered some of his information on the early years from sources close to the Babis. His detailed account of the events of Ṭabarsī (and particularly the details on the fortification and defence of the fortress), on the other hand, seems to have been provided by some of the army chiefs and officials present at the event. Hidāyat's detailed account of the proceedings of the trial of the Bab in Tabriz was supplied by the chief examiner and by others present at the gathering. Other chronicles—Khurmūjī's *Ḥaqā'iq al-Akhbār* or later Iʿtimād al-Salṭana's *Munṭaẓam-i Nāṣirī* (volume III, Tehran, 1300/1882)—either give brief references or reiterate the above accounts. One exception is *Mutanabbi'īn* by Iʿtiżād al-Salṭana, which relies for the earlier events on *Nāsikh al-Tawārīkh* but adds valuable information on the events of 1267–1268/1851–1852, in which he was indirectly involved.

Somewhat different from these official chronicles is the history of Aḥmad ibn Abul-Ḥasan Sharīf Shīrāzī Īshīk Āqāsī, which according to the author was initially intended to rectify the discrepancies and distortions of the chronicles. His final draft, completed in 1286/1869, is based partly on his notes collected in earlier years. His early interest in the movement as a member of a Shīrāzī merchant family who was in contact with the family of the Bab makes his account an important source. He is generally an impartial and informed writer. Part of this work relating to the Babi movement is translated into English by Bahadur, who published another section, on Mīrzā Taqī Khān Amīr Kabīr, in the original Persian. The complete manuscript, which is in private hands, remains to be published.

The third group of primary sources in Arabic and Persian are the narratives that were written on three major Babi uprisings between 1264/1848 and 1267/1851. These accounts are more reliable than the general histories, being written by ordinary people who had themselves participated in these events. Mīrzā Luṭf ʿAlī Shīrāzī's narrative of Ṭabarsī was written as day-to-day chronicles during the course of the upheavals, whereas *Tārīkh-i Mīmīya,* by Mahjūr Zavārih'ī, and the narrative of Āqā Mīr Abū-Ṭālib Shahmīrzādī on Ṭabarsī were written a few years later; others, like "The Personal Reminiscences of the Babi Insurrection at Zanjān in 1850," by Āqā ʿAbd al-Aḥad Zanjānī, or another account on Zanjān by Mīrzā Ḥusayn Zanjānī, were written a few decades later and thus did not escape occasional errors in chronology and other details. The tone of all these narratives is clear and straightforward, and they give us perhaps the most telling insights into the ordinary Babis. Except for Āqā ʿAbd al-Aḥad's "Personal Reminiscences" and Ḥājjī Naṣīr Qazvīnī's account of Ṭabarsī, these narratives have remained unpublished.

The fourth group of the primary sources contains works that can be classified as memoirs and personal narratives. Though they were often written decades later and thus suffer the defects of fading memory, they contain a great deal of valuable information particularly important for the study of the early period. These are personal experiences of conversions, and many include the narrator's account of his acquaintance with early disciples or the events he witnessed. The *Masnavī* of Ḥājjī Mīrzā Muḥammad Ismāʿīl Ẕabīḥ Kāshānī contains, among other things, the author's own reminiscences of the early days up to the time of Bahā'ullāh's exile to ʿAkkā. This work, which was probably compiled in the 1880s toward the end of Z̲abīḥ's life, remained largely unknown and is only briefly referred to by Fāżil (*Z̲uhūr al-Ḥaqq*) and Bayżā'ī (*Taz̲kirih*). Z̲abīḥ's account of the first few years is selective, but it is an important source for understanding the merchants' viewpoint. Both Nabīl Zarandī and Hamadānī, the author of *Tārīkh-i Jadīd,* cite Ismāʿīl Z̲abīḥ as one of their sources, yet it is not clear whether they also consulted his *Masnavī.* Browne and others sometimes confuse him with Z̲abīḥ Qannād, Z̲abīḥ Zavārih'ī, and Ḥājjī Muḥammad Riżā Kāshānī. Throughout his *Masnavī* Z̲abīḥ refers to his brother, but makes no note of *Nuqṭat al-Kāf* or indeed of any other work by Ḥājjī Mīrzā Jānī. The first few pages of a rare manuscript of this work in the Mīnāsīān Collection, Wadham College Library, Oxford, are missing, and the whole work is not free of spelling mistakes. It is not clear whether this is the original copy.

Among the manuscripts preserved in the Iran National Bahā'ī Archive, the memoirs of Sayyid Jawād Muḥarrir and Āqā Sayyid ʿAbd al-Raḥīm Iṣfahānī, which both appear to be part of a greater collection of narratives on the local Babi-Bahā'ī history of Isfahan, also contain new information. Among the manuscripts in Browne's collection, the accounts of Mullā Rajab ʿAlī Qahīr, Sayyid Mahdī Dahajī, and Mirza Muḥammad Jawād Qazvīnī (translated by Browne in *Materials for the Study of the Babi Religion [MSBR]*) basically deal with the events of the period after the 1850s, but nevertheless they contain scattered references to the early events.

Among the published sources, the personal account of Mullā Jaʿfar Qazvīnī of the early years of the movement in Qazvin is of great value. Himself a middle-rank Shaykhi mulla before becoming a Babi in the first year of the movement, he gives an uninhibited account of the sectarian conflicts in Qazvin in the early 1840s, as well as some fresh information on the lives of Aḥsā'ī and Rashtī, the introduction of the Babi movement in Qazvin, its effects on the ʿulama, and the first waves of persecution in the city. Between descriptions of the events he adds lengthy accounts of his own dreams and intuitive experiences, illustrative of the Shaykhi-Babi mentality.

Another published account of this kind is that of Āqā Muḥammad Muṣṭafā al-Baghdādī, which was compiled at the request of Abul-Fażl Gulpāyigānī. He was an Arab Babi and later Bahā'ī (still in his early youth, when his father, Shaykh Muḥammad Shibl al-Baghdādī, became one of the early Babi converts in Iraq and a follower of Qurrat al-ʿAyn). In his narrative, which is compiled mainly from his own and his father's recollections, he describes the mission of Basṭāmī to the ʿAtabāt and gives some valuable information about Qurrat al-ʿAyn and her supporters.

Finally, the general account written by Mīrzā Yaḥyā Nūrī, Ṣubḥ-i Azal, *Mujmal-i Badīʿ dar Vaqāyiʿ Z̲uhūr-i Manīʿ* (The unique compendium on the events of the mighty manifestation), should be mentioned. This is a short account written in reply to several inquiries by Browne. It contains some new details on the first eight years of the movement and should be treated as a brief recollection intended to express the Azalī point of view.

These four groups of works written with the intention of recording historical events form only a part of the total corpus of primary sources. The fifth group, made up of early Babi works that are mainly theological, all contain scattered historical information. The most important are the writings of the Bab himself—independent works, commentaries on Qur'ānic verse and sūras as well as on Shiʿite Traditions, addresses, sermons, prayers, private letters, public statements, and testimonies. They contain frequent references to the Bab's intimate emotions and reactions to people and events. These are important for a better understanding of the Bab and for going beyond the conventional image presented in the chronicles and general accounts. When expressing his intuitive experiences, his claimed mission, and his impressions, he is honest and sincere, though not always intelligible or unambiguous. He often makes his point by adopting an allegorical language or through allusions and metaphors.

Three successive phases can be distinguished in the Bab's writings. In his very early works, from 1260/1844 to 1261/1845, such as *Qayyūm al-Asmāʾ, Khaṣāʾil-i Sabʿa,* and even *Ṣaḥīfat bayn al-Ḥaramayn,* he presents his claims with clarity and straightforwardness. In his works between 1261/1845 and 1263/1847, however, such as *Ṣaḥīfa-yi ʿAdlīya, Dalāʾil-i Sabʿa,* and a number of statements he was forced to write in Shiraz, he is often cautious and prudent, but not totally repentant. In the works after 1263/1847, such as the Persian and Arabic *Bayān, Tauqīʿ al-Qāʾimīya,* and *al-Khuṭba al-Qahrīya,* he fully abandons taqīya and openly declares his real claims.

The Bab's complex style and his allusive and inconsequential remarks sometimes make it difficult for the reader to follow his line of argument. Preoccupation with numerology, cryptic references to persons, places, and dates, and his peculiar and in some respects unprecedented terminology make the study of his works a formidable task. Yet in his own way, he is sometimes meticulous on dates and chronology, which he believed are important to be recorded for posterity. Most of the writings of the Bab are still unpublished and those which are published are not edited in a scholarly fashion. Manuscript copies of some of his better-known works are preserved in private and public collections, including Browne's collection, the Bahā'ī Archives, and elsewhere. Lesser-known works of the Bab, including tracts, treatises, and other miscellaneous works, are scarce and difficult to trace. A manuscript copy of thirty-two letters of the Bab also exists in Browne's collection. The most outstanding of all his lesser-known works are in private hands. The INBA series (nos. 40, 64, 67, 82, 91, and 98) contain some of his early letters, addresses, sermons, and prayers and are of special value for the early period.

Some of the writings of the Bab's disciples are worth mentioning from theological and historical points of view—notably a short tract (*ZH* 136–39) and a risāla by Mullā Ḥusayn Bushrū'ī, some works of Mullā Muḥammad ʿAlī Bārfurūshī (Quddūs), including some Persian apologia (*ZH* 407–18, 426–30), and a collection of his works titled *Abḥār* (or *Āthār*) *al-Quddūsīya.* Of greater historical significance, however, are the apologia written in the first three years to vindicate the claims of the movement in the wave of the growing criticism from Shaykhi opponents. An Arabic risāla in reply to Ḥājjī Muḥammad Karīm Khān Kirmānī (probably in response to his first refutation, *Izhāq al-Bāṭil*), which was compiled toward the end of 1262/1846 by an unknown Babi who calls himself al-Qatīl ibn al-Karbalā'ī, is of exceptional value. Apart from some of the early works of the Bab, this risāla is perhaps the most important document for the study of the early years. Although Fāżil Māzandarānī published the text of this work as an appendix to his *Ẓuhūr al-Ḥaqq,* he did not appear to have realized its historical significance. At first glance, the unclear identity of the author raises doubts of its athenticity. Māzandarānī's usual vagueness on the origin of his materials certainly does not help to resolve this ambiguity. Yet for a work with such highly sensitive and controversial claims to appear under a pseudonym is not unusual—if indeed al-Qatīl was a pseudonym, and not the real name of a Babi writer who like many others has remained in obscurity.

The risāla's information, style, and argument remove the slightest doubt as to its authenticity and the date of its compilation. This is the best example of the Shaykhi-Babi stand in the transitory period of 1844 to 1848 in the ʿAtabāt. Qatīl claims to have been a student of Rashtī for ten years, a claim supported by the text's detailed information on Sayyid Kāẓim and his students, of whom many were Qatīl's personal friends. A considerable amount of previously unknown data—of the religious milieu in the ʿAtabāt; Rashtī's messianic ideas and claims; the tensions and conflicts within the Shaykhi circle, particularly after the death of Rashti; the intentions of Mullā Ḥusayn and his supporters, their social background and their training; the proclamation at Shiraz and the formation of the first Babi group; the return of the Babi disciples, the first declaration of the movement in the ʿAtabāt, and the responses from within and outside the Shaykhi community—as well as the accurate dating of many events that otherwise would have remained unknown, leave no doubt that Qatīl himself was closely involved with the early Babi activities. From a theological point of view, his strong attacks on Kirmānī reveal the depth of conflict between the two divided factions. The noticeable absence of any direct reference to Qurrat al-ʿAyn, who by the end of 1262/1846 was largely regarded as the leader of the majority of the Babis in the ʿAtabāt, suggest that Qatīl may have been no other than Qurrat al-ʿAyn herself. Such a theory is further substantiated by many references in the text to Qurrat al-ʿAyn's close supporters.

A risāla in Persian by Qurrat al-ʿAyn and a maktūb by Shaykh Sulṭān

Karbalā'ī, written in the same period and in the same milieu, follow a similar line of argument but contain relatively less historical information. Qurrat al-ʿAyn's risāla, discussed at some length in chapter 7, and some other examples of her works are valuable for tracing the development of new trends of Babi thought. In some instances the style and the information of Karbalā'ī's maktūb resemble those of Qatīl's risāla. Their common view is no doubt partly explained by the fact that they were criticized from the same quarter. Refutations produced by Shaykhis, above all Kirmānī, as well as the hostile propaganda of the defected Babis and other critics of Qurrat al-ʿAyn, motivated some to search for theological proofs and historical evidence. The long list of refutations written by Kirmānī started with his *Izhāq al-Bāṭil* (Rajab 1261/September 1845; probably the earliest non-Babi source on the early activities of the Babis) and continued with *Tīr-i Shihāb* (1262/1846), *Shihāb al-Thāqib* (1265/1849), and *Īqādh al-Ghāfilīn* (1283/1866–1867). Regardless of his theological objections, examined in chapter 6, in some of these refutations, as in his other works, he gives important indications of the activities of Babis that had caused him such anxiety.

On developments within the Shaykhi school, the works of Sayyid Kāẓim Rashtī himself provide some clues. Most of his works, both published and unpublished, are devoted to answering theological queries and replying to criticism. One good example of his works is *Dalīl al-Mutaḥayyirīn*. This apologia, intended to vindicate the Shaykhi position and difference with Bālāsarīs, not only discusses the religious issues in dispute but often describes the historical origins of the intercommunal conflict.

The opposite view in the Shaykhi-Bālāsarī dispute is expressed, among other sources, in two of the important religious biographical dictionaries of the period. In a relatively long section in *Qiṣaṣ al-ʿUlamā'*, Tunkābunī treats Shaykhis in partial and rather sarcastic language, while in *Rauḍāt al-Jannāt* Khwānsārī speaks of Aḥsā'ī with respect. Some fresh details on the background of the Bab and the mission of Basṭāmī can also be obtained from *Qiṣaṣ al-ʿUlamā'*, but in general the author borrowed most of his information from *Nāsikh al-Tawārīkh*. The real significance of Tunkābunī's work, however, lies in the information it supplies on the social and political behavior of the ʿulama, somewhat unusual for this type of religious biography. The anecdotes and details of everyday life of the ʿulama, initially supplied to enhance their image, paint an informal picture that is highly revealing of the madrasa life in his time. He is criticized by some of exaggerating and by others of underestimating the reality, and his standard of scholarship certainly leaves much to be desired, yet it is through these very details that the sociomoral characteristics of the ʿulama and their position in society can be assessed. Biographical works like *Ṭarā'iq al-Ḥaqa'iq*, *Ṭabaqāt Aʿlām al-Shīʿa*, *Aḥsan al-Wadīʿa*, and *Makārim al-Āthār* and bibliographies like *al-Dharīʿa* and Ibrāhīmī's *Fihrist* are also of value for obtaining information on the background of many of the personalities involved.

The European primary sources are important for the study of Babi history not always for what they say but often for what they leave unsaid. Their position at least enabled them to observe the movement from a different angle, relatively detached from both the accusations and bigotry of the non-Babi sources and the emotional and highly committed stance of the Babi-Bahā'ī writers.

Of these the first group comprises the diplomatic dispatches and reports by the British and Russian envoys in Iran and Iraq written during the course of the first eight years of the movement or immediately after. After 1264/1848, as the Babis gained strength and eventually came to a confrontation with the government, the European envoys in Tehran and their consuls and agents in other cities felt it necessary to report on "the new schism in Mohammedanism" and its political threats to the country. Earlier, Rawlinson, then consul-general in Baghdad, dispatched reports on the trial of Mullā ʿAlī Basṭāmī. Yet they are few, and not free of the usual inaccuracies of other diplomatic accounts. They suggest Rawlinson's unfamiliarity with the Shiʿite religious environment, which in his case, being himself a scholar, is surprising.

Similarly, the reports dispatched by Prince Dolgorukov, the Russian minister in Tehran, and those of Colonel Justin Sheil, the British envoy (in 1839–1847 and again in 1849–1853) and his chargé d'affaires, Lieutenant Colonel Francis Farrant (1847–1849) suffer from the same weaknesses. They are scanty, misinformed, and badly presented. In some instances the causes of these inaccuracies may be traced back to the agents and servants of the missions, who were the envoy's main informants on matters concerning popular events. But in spite of their deficiencies, when studied in comparison with other sources they can be useful, particularly on the Babi resistances in Ṭabarsī, Nayrīz, Yazd, and Zanjān or other major events, such as the assassination attempt of 1268/1852 and its aftermath. Dolgorukov's twenty-five dispatches (between 1848 and 1852, published as an appendix to Ivanov's *Babidskie vosstaniya v Irane* (Babi uprisings in Iran), provide a somewhat more systematic observation of the movement's development.

These reports should also be examined from the point of view of the envoys' intervention, both Russian and British, in the central government's policies and especially when their interests were endangered. One example is Dolgorukov's request in 1263/1847 for the removal of the Bab from the castle of Mākū near the Russian frontier. Besides Dolgorukov's reports, some extracts of British and Russian reports were also published by Nicolas ("Le Dossier russo-anglais de Seyyèd Ali Mohammed dit le Bâb") and more recently by Baluyzi (*The Bab*) and Ādamīyat (*Amīr Kabīr va Īrān*). A more comprehensive collection of Western accounts, however, appears in Momen's *Bābī and Bahāʾī Religions*. The diplomatic dispatches in this period also provide additional information on matters connected to the religious, economic, and political climate of the time.

The second group of European primary sources is made up of early travel accounts, memoirs, and other published materials, which either give eyewitness records of specific events or more frequently provide fragmentary (and often highly confused) accounts. Some, like Polak, Vambery, and Binning, have a few pages on the Babis, which in spite of their inaccuracy are still useful for their details. The brief record of the American missionaries in Azarbaijan (such as Wright) or those of itinerant missionaries (such as Stern) also have occasional references, particularly to the events after 1264/1848. Most of these early sources are surveyed in Browne's *Traveller's Narrative* (note A, section III) and *MSBR* (section III). More of them appear in Momen's *Bābī and Bahā'ī Religions*.

The account of Lady Sheil, despite a certain confusion on the facts and misinterpretation of Babi ideas, remains a valuable one. Some of her errors are identical to those of Colonel Sheil; particularly the special report of 21 June 1850 (F.O. 69/152, no. 72). This report claims to be based on two accounts given by "a disciple of the Bab" and by "a chief priest" in Yazd, which Sheil claims are correct and can be trusted. Actually, however, they reflect more the rumors and fantasies in circulation than the facts. In this respect, both the European published accounts and the diplomatic reports are revealing. They often demonstrate the impact of the movement on the public imagination and the fears and anxieties in government and diplomatic circles. Frequent identification of Babi doctrine with socialism and communism is typical among the travelogues of the period. No doubt such a tendency, at least in a primitive form, did exist among certain sections of the Babis, particularly during Ṭabarsī, but it is hard to believe that any of the diplomats and travelers were aware of it. Their accounts, clearly tainted by their attempt to equate Babism with the ongoing socialist currents in Europe, betray traces of popular distortion.

Watson's account in *A History of Persia* is relatively free of exaggeration. Yet the author, for a time resident in Iran, missed his opportunity to produce a more original account of the Babis. He relied instead for most of his narrative on *Nāsikh al-Tawārīkh,* as well as on the British and possibly Russian diplomatic reports. His book reflects the weakness of both sources.

If the information of diplomats and travelers was scant and fragmentary, two important accounts—by Joseph Arthur de Gobineau and Alexandr Kazem-Beg, which appeared in 1865 and 1866 respectively—to some degree compensate for these weaknesses. Gobineau's *Religions et philosophies dans l'Asie centrale* is a significant primary source, not so much because of its historical narrative but for the author's astute observations. A political philosopher of some weight and a founder of what developed into the modern theory of racism, during the time he spent as the French envoy in Iran (1855–1858 and again in 1861–1863), Gobineau devoted his attention to studying the intellectual and emotional characteristics of the "Oriental people." In his *Religions,* as in *Trois ans en Asie,* he is quite unequivocal in assigning to the Europeans the task of "civilizing" the Orientals, since in his view "the political and material interests" of the West were dependent on its relations with these nations. While his attitude toward the people of the East is somewhat more advanced, and more refined, than the crude arrogance of some Europeans, whom he sometimes deplores in his writings, such an attitude ultimately did not affect his interpretation of the Asians (by which term he often meant Persians). Yet perhaps more than many of his contemporaries, he was able to make an intelligent, if not always impartial, assessment of the intellectual and religious merits of Persian culture. In the long introduction that forms the first part of his work he tries to define the main cultural axis of Persian society. He regards the Asians' excessive preoccupation with metaphysics and the hereafter as one of the main distinctions between their way of thought and the modern Western mind. Persian culture, he believes, is the meeting point of diverse ancient trends and the outcome of a long process of intellectual diffusion. The key to understanding the Persian interest in esoterics, the practice of taqīya, and the fatalism prevalent in Shiʿism in his view should be found in the irreconcilable gap between appearance and reality in the Persian world view. Perhaps for the first time in Western scholarship, Gobineau (somewhat disregarding the historical realities) interprets Shiʿism as a manifestation of Persian national identity. Moreover, he regards Sufism as the natural response of the free-thinkers to the domination of rational orthodoxy. Such broad generalizations, while they may seem outdated and even unfounded, demonstrate the author's efforts to fit the rise of the Babi movement into an intellectual context that was largely unknown to his contemporaries.

In the second part of his work, Gobineau's narrative is heavily based on the account of *Nāsikh al-Tawārīkh,* of which Sipihr provided a summary for his use. But Gobineau had other sources at his disposal. Some direct indications in the text as well as the nature of the additional materials suggest that he obtained his information from Babi sources, yet the internal evidence suggests that he did not use *Nuqṭat al-Kāf* (a manuscript of which came to his possession later) or any other Babi historical account. For the third part of his work, in which he deals with the doctrine of the Bab, he relied on the Bab's works, and particularly a version of the Arabic *Bayān,* of which he gives a full but not always accurate translation under the title "Ketab-e-Hukkam (Le Livre des préceptes)" in the appendix.

Gobineau regards the emergence of the Babi movement as a response to the ʿulama's misuse of power, their negligence, and the general corruption in the religious and civilian institutions. His picture of the Bab sometimes suffers from his idealistic presuppositions, and to substantiate his views he relies excessively on speculation and circumstantial evidence. He repeats most of *Nāsikh al-Tawārīkh*'s errors and adds some of his own, but he is able to grasp both the movement's potential and its limitations.

Gobineau was not a scrupulous historian or a first-class scholar, but he possessed a sharp and inquisitive mind, thanks to which some of his ideas on the Babi movement remain useful and even stimulating. He is the first source who refers to the Letters of the Living. He distinguishes between the Bab and his followers in respect to their attitudes and their policies, and holds the latter responsible for confrontation with the government. He is inattentive toward the social and economic background of the movement and perhaps even his image of the ʿulama and their position is not close to reality, yet he rightly attributes the collapse of the movement to the alliance between the ʿulama and the government. He emphasizes the role of Amīr Kabīr as a representative of a centralized bureaucratic power and indirectly makes him responsible for suppressing the natural course of popular protest against an oppressive state. In his analysis of Babi theory and doctrine he overlooks the significance of Shaykhism as the breeding ground for Babi theory, yet he is still able to point out those aspects which distinguish Babi thought from other contemporary trends.

The Russian Orientalist Alexandr Kazem-Beg, who also relies heavily on *Nāsikh al-Tawārīkh,* tries as well to see the movement in an analytical light. But although he holds his own with Gobineau in committing factual errors and making bold interpretations, he lacks the French scholar's originality and clearness of mind. His representation of the Babi history deserves credit because of the additional information he injected into his account, mostly from Russian sources. He occasionally refers to a Babi narrative of Ṭabarsī, in Māzandarānī dialect, by a certain unknown Shaykh al-ʿAjam. This is the manuscript obtained by Dorn during his sojourn in the province in 1860 and later described by him in the *Bulletin de l'Académie Imperiale de St. Petersbourg.* Kazem-Beg believes that it is "full of inexactitudes" and "of no historical value," but doubtless it might reveal new details on Ṭabarsī. It remained unknown even to Russian scholars such as Ivanov, who inexplicably has failed to make use of it. Moreover, Kazem-Beg uses the memoirs and notes of two previous students—Sevruguin, "who for twenty years resided in Tehran," and Mochinin, a Russian agent who at the time of the Bab's imprisonment in Chihrīq in 1850 saw the Bab addressing the public. Yet the same sources, especially Sevruguin's notes, seems to be the cause of some of the exaggerations in the text. In distinguishing between the peaceful nature of the Bab's teachings and the militant tendencies of some of his followers, Kazem-Beg is largely justified and indeed some of his speculations may be supported by other sources, but no doubt his gross assertion about the alleged "mischievous" and "deceitful" Babi disciples, such as Sayyid Ḥusayn Yazdī, should be treated with utmost caution. They reflect Kazem-Beg's own twisted outlook, portraying the Bab as an inactive instrument powerless in the hands of his followers.

The third group of sources consists of general accounts, narratives, local histories, and memoirs that were written much later, some in the early decades of twentieth century, often by men who recorded the recollections of the last survivors of the early Babi period. While not always accurate and consistent, they contain a considerable amount of new historical detail and previously unrecorded complementary data. The general outlook of Bahā'ī writers such as Shaykh Kāẓim Samandar Qazvīnī, Ḥājjī Muḥammad Muʿīn al-Salṭana, and Mīrzā Abul-Fażl Gulpāyigānī renders their accounts milder in tone and less controversial in content. From the viewpoint of historical value they are reasonably reliable though on occasion, when dealing with sensitive issues, they tend to observe self-censorship. Muʿīn al-Salṭana's general history, which was finally completed circa 1340/1921–1922, contains some fresh information on Azarbaijan. He frequently quotes from *Abwāb al-Hudā* of Mullā Muḥammad Taqī Hashtrūdī—a valuable narrative, now unobtainable, by an early Shaykhi-Babi who witnessed many events and knew many of the early disciples. Confusions and obvious errors, however, make one particularly cautious about details which are outside the sphere of Muʿīn al-Salṭana's personal experience or given without specifying his source. This is an unpublished account, which was originally intended to cover the events up to the author's time but in fact stops with Ṭabarsī. One of the two copies in INBA (MS A) is a revision by the author himself.

Samandar Qazvīnī's *Tārīkh* is also a relatively long account, written in two parts. The first part, compiled in 1303/1855–1886, was in six chapters dealing with the history of his own family, the Babis of Qazvin, and his memoirs. The second part, compiled in 1332–1333/1913–1914, is mainly arranged under biographical headings of more than seventy early Babis and Bahā'īs, but also contains new information both on the early period of the movement and on the Bahā'ī-Azalī controversy. Born in 1268/1852 and son of a celebrated Babi, Shaykh Muḥammad Qazvīnī, Nabīl Akbar, he was a merchant of some significance in Qazvin. In many instances his account reflects his mercantile outlook. He based his narrative chiefly on his own childhood memories, eyewitness experience, interviews with some of the surviving Babis of the early period, and the scattered information he gathered in Qazvin. He is reasonably accurate on the Babis of Qazvin, introduces a number of new characters, and describes new events that are barely referred to in other sources, if at all.

Abul-Fażl Gulpāyigānī's *Tārīkh-i Ẓuhūr* is a brief introductory account that was compiled in the style of *Maqāla-yi Shakhṣī Sayyāḥ* sometime in the early twentieth century. In the first two parts of this work, which cover the history of the Babi and the Bahā'ī religions up to 1892, the year of Bahā'ullāh's death, the author clearly distinguishes between the two religions, though he is careful to establish an intellectual link as well as a historical continuity between the two. This is an important distinction that the Bahā'ī writers had to make in order to defend themselves against the Azalīs' accusations of deviation and revisionism. But unlike the impassioned tone of *Hasht Bishisht,* in reply to which it appears this account was written, the writer's tone is moderate.

More important for the study of the early period is Gulpāyigānī's *Kashf al-Ghiṭāʾ*, which was completed after his death by his nephew, Sayyid Mahdī Gulpāyigānī. This is a Bahāʾī apologia that initially aimed at resolving the problem of *Nuqṭat al-Kāf* and exposing its distortions. Although the authors are successful in exposing some discrepancies, in general, rather than resolving the assumed distortions, they created more problems and introduced new errors. *Kashf al-Ghiṭāʾ*, particularly in the section written by Abul-Faẓl Gulpāyigānī, casts doubt on the originality of those passages in *Nuqṭat al-Kāf* which enhance Ṣubḥ-i Azal's position. Yet the entire work is so charged with zeal that it can hardly defend its argument with objectivity. Part of its criticism is directed toward Browne's introduction, which the authors argue exceeds the limits of scholarly investigation by accusing the Bahāʾī writers of forgery and distortion with no viable evidence. Gulpāyigānī believes, perhaps with some justification, that Browne's criticism of the Bahāʾīs is based more upon Azalī influence than on historical fact.

Some of Gulpāyigānī's treatises, such as *Risāla-yi Iskandarīya,* have occasional interesting points. Aḥmad Suhrāb's work on the life of the Bab, *al-Risālat al-Tisʿa ʿAshrīyata,* a collection of nineteen talks delivered in Haifa around 1918–1919, is also useful. *Tadhkirat al-Wafāʾ*, by ʿAbd al-Bahāʾ, a collection of seventy-one biographies compiled in 1915 on the lives of the early Babi-Bahāʾīs, is perhaps the first example of Bahāʾī hagiography. This work is concerned mainly with those Babis who after 1268/1852 emigrated to Baghdad and then followed Bahāʾullāh in his exile to Edirne (Adrianople) and ʿAkkā (Acre), but it also gives many references to earlier events.

A series of narratives of the local history of the Bahāʾī communities throughout Iran, often based on the accounts and memoirs of the older generation, is also recorded in this period. Among them the narratives of Mīrzā Ḥabībullāh Afnān Aʿlāʾī on Shiraz is of special value, as it throws new light not only on the early life of the Bab but on the other Babis of Fars. Fuʾādī's history of the Babi-Bahāʾī community of Khurasan, compiled in 1931, relies on both local written and oral accounts and is of great value for the study of the Babis in that province. The author, himself originally from Bushrūyih and educated in Ashkhabad, attempted to produce his history in a more systematic way. Consisting of ten chapters under different regions, it gives detailed accounts of the history of most towns and villages of Khurasan.

Two accounts of the local history of Azarbaijan are written by Mīrzā Ḥaydar ʿAlī Uskūʾī and Muḥammad Ḥusayn Mīlānī. Uskūʾī's memoir of the Babis and Bahāʾīs of Uskū, Milān, and other parts, compiled in 1343/1924–1925, is relatively short. Milānī, writing shortly afterward, provides a more comprehensive account. The first part deals with the Babi-Bahāʾī missions to Azarbaijan, the important converts, the martyrs of Azarbaijan, and finally the main historical events of the community. The second part contains additional notes on Uskūʾī's account. Other local accounts by Nāṭiq Iṣfahānī on Kashan (1309 Sh./1930), Zaraqānī on Tehran, and Ishrāq Khāvarī on Hamadan and others on Yazd and its vicinity, Rasht, and Isfahan are important because they expand the sphere of Babi history beyond the central themes and enable us to know more about the lesser-known Babis and events.

Two other works by non-Babi writers fall into this category. Zaʿīm al-Daula's *Miftāḥ Bāb al-Abwāb* is an Arabic work published in 1903 as an abridged version of a longer, unpublished account called *Bāb al-Abwāb*. Zaʿīm al-Daula was the editor of the Persian weekly *Ḥikmat,* published in Cairo at the turn of the twentieth century. Part of this work was again based on *Nāsikh al-Tawārīkh* but he also used other, less known or quite unknown sources. He was the son of Mullā Muḥammad Taqī and grandson of Mullā Jaʿfar Tabrīzī. Both his grandfather and his father were among the ʿulama present at the Bab's trial in Tabriz, and as he himself confirms, part of his information is drawn from his grandfather's narrative of his interrogations of the Bab, carried out presumably in 1264/1848 or 1266/1850. He also refers to the narrative of Ḥājjī Mīrzā Jānī (without specifying a title), which he maintains make no indication of the succession of Ṣubḥ-i Azal or Bahā'ullāh. Though he may have inserted this remark as a counter to Browne's views in his introduction to *The Tārīkh-i Jadīd,* of which he was certainly aware, this is still a piece of interesting evidence on the problem of *Nuqṭat al-Kāf.* Zaʿīm al-Daula met Bahā'ullāh, ʿAbd al-Bahā', and some well-known Bahā'īs of his time, including Nabīl Zarandī in Haifa. He also met with Ṣubḥ-i Azal, in Famagusta. Throughout the 181 pages dealing with the early history of the Babi movement, he is reasonably impartial, though he occasionally makes gross mistakes. In some respects, his views have been influenced by the teaching of Sayyid Jamāl al-Dīn Asadābādī (al-Afghānī) and Shaykh Muḥammad ʿAbduh, of whom he speaks with great respect. Occasionally such influences led him to pass unjustified judgments on the Babis.

Hasht Bihisht, a relatively long Azalī work, produced circa 1890, was allegedly cowritten by Shaykh Aḥmad Rūḥī Kirmānī and Āqā Khān Kirmānī. It is designed to vindicate the Babi-Azalī position, which toward the end of the nineteenth century was seriously overshadowed by the spread of Bahā'ī teachings. The goal of the authors is to reintroduce Babi theology in a style and language comprehensible to late-nineteenth-century Persian intelligentsia, yet in interpreting Babi theory and practice they are predisposed to ideas popular at the time in Persian intellectual circles outside Iran. The brief and somewhat confused account of early Babi history in chapter 8 of this work demonstrates the relatively weak standard of Azalī historiography. Yet it still contains some interesting points. The writers' ugly and offensive language in the latter part of this chapter, which is marred by accusations and abuse against the Bahā'īs, further illustrates the depth of Bahā'ī-Azalī hostility at the end of the past century.

Some Persian and Arabic secondary sources also contain a great deal of less accessible primary material. *Ẓuhūr al-Ḥaqq,* by Fāżil Māzandarānī, is a nine-volume work on the Babi-Bahā'ī history during its first century, of which only volume 3 (published circa 1944) and parts 1 and 2 of volume 8 (published 1975–1976) are available. Volume 3, a biographical dictionary arranged alphabetically under names of provinces, refers to more than 660 Babis and other important characters of the first eight years of the movement. It is based not only on the better-known chronicles and general accounts (including the Persian text of Nabīl Zarandī's narrative) but also on local histories, memoirs, and the writings of the Bab and early Babis. Less than half of this work is a full or partial citation of fresh materials, most of which cannot be found in any other source. It is this access to the lesser-known sources that makes *Ẓuhūr al-Ḥaqq* an important work for the study of the early period. Yet in some ways Fāżil Māzandarānī is a less-than-meticulous historian, bound within the limits of traditional historiography. He makes errors on dates and personalities, and almost never discloses the origins of his material.

Another attempt to compile a general history is a two-volume work by ʿAbd al-Ḥusayn Āyatī (Āvārih), *al-Kawākib al-Durrīya,* published in 1923–1924. The first volume deals with Babi-Bahā'ī history up to the end of the Bah'ullāh's time; the second comes to the end of ʿAbd al-Bahā's period. *Kawākib* contains less fresh material and new detail than *Ẓuhūr al-Ḥaqq,* and more inaccuracies. Malik Khusravī's *Tārīkh-i Shuhadā-yi Amr* and *Iqlīm-i Nūr,* Fayżī's *Khāndān-i Afnān* and *Ḥażrat-i Nuqṭa-yi Ūlā,* Ishrāq Khāvarī's *Nūrayn-i Nayyirayn,* and other Bahā'ī works are useful for the study of particular aspects of early Babi history. In these more recent works, the authors suffer from the same inhibitions of earlier Bahā'ī historiography.

The non-Bahā'ī secondary sources, for the greater part, consist of a wide range of refutations or polemics designed to discredit Babi history rather than add anything to our knowledge. The authors, often from the clergy or associated groups, are hostile, their use of the sources is biased, and their facts are often distorted. Even compared to the earlier refutations of a more traditional kind, their standard is surprisingly low. A good example of traditional refutations is Ḥusayn-Qulī Jadīd al-Islām's *Minhāj al-Ṭālibin,* published in 1320/1920–1923. In spite of its belligerent tone, it still contains some new material, including some lesser-known specimens of the Bab's writings.

A small group of writers tried to give a more scholarly character to their narratives. Ḥasanī (*al-Bābīyūn wa al-Bahā'īyūn*) and Mudarrisī Chahārdihī (*Shaykhīgarī va Bābīgarī*) give a reasonably balanced version of the events. The latter adds some valuable new information to both Shaykhi and Babi history. Kasravī's *Bahā'īgarī* is a short polemic of little historical value. In his criticism of the Bab and the Babis, he hardly takes into account the historical circumstances under which the movement first appeared and his pontifical judgments no doubt are influenced by his own vision of *Pākdīnī.*

A more problematic treatment of Babi history is found in Ādamīyat's *Amīr Kabīr va Īrān.* Though in his introduction the author promises to pursue an "analytical method free from bigotry" and claims that his "historical analysis" is "realistic" and "rational," he is by no means prepared to apply these much-vaunted values to his own work. Besides his obvious errors in historical fact, which demonstrate his insufficient knowledge and careless methodology, throughout his chapter on the Bab ("Dāstān-i Bāb") he uses highly polemical and abusive language in describing the beliefs and activities of the Babis. Referring to the Bab's ideas as "a sackful of straw" that has no bearing on "the world of knowledge and thought," calling the Babi fighters in Zanjān "miserable idiots" and other Babis "charlatans," "murderers," "executioners," and "villains," he indeed gives a disturbing picture of that so-called progressive school of modern Persian historiography of which he is a pioneer.

The earliest and perhaps most significant secondary works in European languages are those of E. G. Browne and A. L. M. Nicolas. Though he never attempted to compile a history of the Babi movement, Browne's contribution in translating, editing, identifying, and publishing the Babi, Bahā'ī, and Azalī sources is of importance in preparing the way for a more comprehensive understanding of Babi history. He was the first scholar who seriously undertook the study of the Babis, and he dedicated a great deal of time and effort to introducing it to others. As he indicates, one of his first attractions toward Iran—and indeed toward the "mysterious East," by which he was fascinated after reading Gobineau's work—was his interest in the Babis. Contrary to the prevailing Orientalism of his time, he writes with great sympathy and understanding toward Persians in general and Babis in particular. Most of his writings, including *A Year amongst the Persians* and the introductions to his translations of Babi works, bear witness to this attitude. In his four books and three long articles on Babis, he often rendered an accurate translation and a careful edition. Moreover, he added a store of useful notes and comments on sources, the history, and the ideology of the movement. His criticism of the Bahā'īs and the Azalī-Bahā'ī controversy, which perhaps occupies more than its fair share in his introductions to both *The New History* and *Nuqṭat al-Kāf,* is moderated to a more balanced view in *MSBR* and *A Literary History of Persia* (volume 4). He seldom attempts to interpret the Babi history in an analytical way and indeed never claims to be a historian in the more modern sense, yet some of his general comments, particularly in his later works, are noteworthy.

Nicolas, a French diplomat who served as consul-general for thirty-five years in various cities of Iran and spent most of his life there, shares Browne's sympathy and understanding, but in some respects lacks his scholarly standards. In the course of his long acquaintance with Babi history he published a number of translations, which start with the Bab's *Dalā'il-i Sabʿa (Le Livre des sept preuves de la mission du Bâb)* and continue with translations of the Arabic *Bayān* (1905) and the Persian *Bayān* (1911–1914). His most important work, however, is his *Seyyèd Ali Mohammed dit le Bâb* (1905), a general history of the first phase of the movement up to 1854. Besides general chronicles and better-known accounts, Nicolas also used a number of lesser-known written and oral sources. He provides a summary list of them, but often fails to specify them in the text. While his sometimes disorganized presentation reduces the value of his work, in many parts, including his accounts of the upheavals of Zanjān and Nayrīz, the execution of Qurrat al-ʿAyn, and the events of 1268/1852, it remains an irreplaceable source. His use of the Bab's writings is also important, as he had access to some of his private correspondence. But here again, his references are unclear and his translations are not always accurate.

Selected Bibliography

I. Persian and Arabic Unpublished Sources

ʿAbd al-Raḥīm Iṣfahānī, Āqā Sayyid [Ismullāh]. Memoirs. INBA Library, MS no. 1028D/6. (In a collection of narratives and memoirs by the Babis of Isfahan.)

Afnān Aʿlā'ī, Abul-Qāsim ibn Ḥabībullāh. Unpublished notes on the history of the Afnān family.

Afnān Aʿlā'ī, Mīrzā Ḥabībullāh ibn Mīrzā Āqā. *Tārīkh-i Amrī-yi Shīrāz.* INBA Library, MS. no. 1027D.

Aḥsā'ī, Shaykh Aḥmad ibn Zayn al-Dīn. *Ḥayāt al-Nafs.* Mīnāsīān Collection, Wadham College Library, Oxford, MS no. 282. Persian trans. Sayyid Kāẓim Rashtī, 2d ed., Kirman, n.d.

The Bab, Sayyid ʿAlī Muḥammad Shīrāzī. Collections of various Arabic and Persian works including commentaries (*tafāsīr*) on the verses and *sūras* of the Qur'ān; treatises (*rasā'il*) on theology, traditions, and other subjects; prayers (*adʿīya*); sermons (*khuṭab*); ordinances (*tawāqīʿ*); and private letters. INBA, private photostat publication, vols. 14, 40, 58, 60, 64, 67, 69, 82, 91, and 98.

——. Collection of commercial accounts, invoices, and bills in *siyāq* script dated between 1250/1834 and 1260/1840. INBA Library, file 32.

——. Collection of 32 letters in Arabic. Browne Or. MSS no. F.21(9).

——. *Qayyūm al-Asmā'*: commentary on *Sūrat Yūsuf* known as *Aḥsan al-Qiṣaṣ.* Browne Or. MSS no. F.11(9). (Also INBA no. 4 and INBA Library, MS. no. 3034C.)

——. *Ṣaḥīfa-yi ʿAdlīya.* INBA, no. 82, XII, 134–205.

——. *Ṣaḥīfat bayn al-Ḥaramayn.* Browne Or. MSS no. F(9). (Also INBA Library MS.)

Bushrū'ī, Mullā Ḥusayn. *al-Akhbār allatī Jamaʿahā Sayyid al-Aṣḥāb . . . Maulānā Bāb al-Bāb fī Arż-i Qāf*, INBA Library, MS no. 3032C and INBA no. 80, II, 198–211.

Dahajī, Sayyid Mahdī. *Risāla.* Browne Or. MSS no. F.57(9).

Fāżil Māzandarānī, Mīrzā Asadullāh. Miscellaneous notes. INBA Library, MS no. 1028D.

Fu'ādī Bushrū'ī, Ḥasan. *Manāẓir-i Tārīkhī-yi Nahżat-i Amr-i Bahā'ī dar Khurāsān*, being the first part of *Tārīkh-i Amrī-yi Khurāsān*. INBA Library.

Gani Collection [of Persian private and official letters and documents], Sterling Memorial Library, Yale University, Series I.

Gulpāyigānī, Mīrzā Abul-Fażl. *Tārīkh-i Ẓuhūr-i Dīyānat-i Ḥażrat-i Bāb va Ḥażrat-i Bahā'ullāh*. INBA no. 9.

Hamadānī, Mīrzā Ḥusayn. *Tārīkh-i Jadīd* [also known as *Tārīkh-i Mānakjī*]. INBA Library. Another copy in British Library Or. 2942. (See E. G. Browne for trans.)

Iran, Vizārat-i Umūr-i Khārija (Ministry of Foreign Affairs), Markaz-i Asnād, *Aṣl-i Mukātibāt* [the original documents], files 18, 23.

Ishrāq Khāvarī, ʿAbd al-Ḥamīd. *Tārīkh-i Amrī-yi Hamadān*. INBA Library.

Luṭf ʿAlī Shīrāzī, Mīrzā. *Tārīkh* [a chronicle of Ṭabarsī]. Browne Or. MSS no. F.28(9) 3 and INBA Library.

Mahjūr-i Zavārih'ī, Sayyid Ḥusayn. *Tārīkh-i Mīmīya* [also known as *Vaqāyiʿ Mīmīya*]. Browne Or. MSS no. F.28(9) 1 and 2 and INBA Library.

Mīlānī, Mīrzā Muḥammad Ḥusayn. *Tārīkh-i Amrī-yi Āẕarbāijān*. INBA Library, MS no. 3030B.

Muḥarir Iṣfahānī, Sayyid Jawād. Memoirs. INBA Library, MS no. 1028D/1.

Muʿīn al-Salṭana Tabrīzī, Ḥājjī Muḥammad ibn ʿAbd al-Bāqī. *Tārīkh-i Amr[-i Bahā'ī]*. INBA Library, MSS A and B.

Nabīl Qā'inī, Mullā Muḥammad (Nabīl Akbar). *Tārīkh-i Badīʿ Bayānī*. INBA Library, MS no. 3033.

Nāṭiq-i Iṣfahānī, Muḥammad. *Tārīkh-i Amrī-yi Kāshān*. INBA Library, MS no. 2016D.

Qahīr, Mullā Rajab ʿAlī. Historical account. Browne Or. MSS F.24(9).

Quddūs, Mullā Muḥammad ʿAlī Bārfurūshī. *Abḥār al-Quddūsīya* [also known as *Āthār al-Quddūsīya*], British Library Or. MS 5110.

Rashtī, Sayyid Kāẓim. *Risāla* [Arabic, in reply to four questions]. Mīnāsīān Collection, Wadham College Library, Oxford, MS no. 382.

——. Collection of two treatises. INBA no. 4: I. *Risāla-yi Fārsī dar Uṣūl-i ʿAqā'id*. 1–216; II. *Risāla* [in reply to Muḥammad Riżā Mīrzā's enquiry on *Maʿād*] 216–63.

Rustam al-Ḥukamā', Muḥammad Ḥāshim (Āṣaf). *Naṣīḥat Nāmih va Fihrist-i Munsha'āt va Rasā'il*. University of California Los Angeles, Research Library, MS no. 1270.

——. *Tadhkirat al-Mulūk*. Original MS. [dated 1255/1839]. School of Oriental and African Studies Library, London, Pers. MS 3511/EW.

Shahmīrzādī, Āqā Mīr Abū-Ṭālib. Historical narrative of Ṭabarsī. INBA Library, MS no. 3032.

Uskū'ī, Mīrzā Ḥaydar ʿAlī. *Tārīkh-i Amrī-yi Āẕarbāijān*. INBA Library, MS no. 3030A.

Ẕabīḥ Kāshānī, Ḥājjī Mīrzā Muḥammad Ismāʿīl (Fānī). *Masnavī*. Mīnāsīān Collection, Wadham College Library, Oxford, MS no. 787.

Zanjānī, Āqā Mīrzā Ḥusayn. *Tārīkh-i Vaqāyiʿ Zanjān*. INBA Library, MS no. 3037. Parts I and II. (together with two other narratives by ʿAbd al-Wahhāb Zāhid al-Zamān [III] and Hāshim Fatḥī Muqaddam Khalkhālī [IV].)

Zaraqānī, Mīrzā Maḥmūd. *Vaqāyiʿ-i Ṭihrān*. INBA Library, MS no. 3047.

II. European Unpublished Sources

Great Britain, Foreign Office. Volumes of diplomatic and consular correspondence and other reports preserved in the Public Record Office, London. F.O. 60 series, vols. 104, 105, 107, 108, 113, 114, 116, 117, and 152. F.O. 248 series, vols. 113 and 114.

III. Published Works in Persian and Arabic

ʿAbd al-Bahāʾ, ʿAbbās. *Maqāla-yi Shakhṣī Sayyāḥ ki dar Tafṣīl-i Qażīya-yi Bāb Nivishtih Shudih*. 1st ed. Bombay, 1890. (See E. G. Browne, *A Traveller's Narrative*.)

———. *Tadhkirat al-Wafāʾ fī Tarjamat Ḥayāt Qudamāʾ al-Aḥibbāʾ*. Haifa, 1342/1924.

Ādamīyat, F. *Amīr Kabīr va Īrān*. 3d ed. Tehran, 1348 Sh./1969.

Ādamīyat, Muḥammad Ḥusayn Ruknzādih. *Dānishmandān va Sukhansarāyān-i Fārs*. 4 vols. Tehran, 1337–1340 Sh./1958–1961.

Afnān, Muḥammad. "Marāḥil-i Daʿwat-i Ḥażrat-i Nuqṭa-yi Ūlā" *Muṭāliʿa-yi Maʿārif-i Bahāʾī* X. Tehran, 132 Badīʿ/1976.

Aḥsāʾī, Shaykh ʿAbdullāh ibn Aḥmad. *Risāla-yi Sharḥ-i Aḥvāl-i Shaykh Aḥmad ibn Zayn al-Dīn Aḥsāʾī*. (Persian trans. Muḥammad Ṭāhir Kirmānī. 2d ed. Kirman, 1387/1967.)

Aḥsāʾī, Shaykh Aḥmad ibn Zayn al-Dīn. *Jawāmiʿ al-Kalim*. 2 vols. Tabriz, 1237–1267/1856–1859.

———. *Sharḥ al-Ziyāra al-Jāmiʿa al-Kabīra*. 2 vols. Tabriz, 1276/1859 (4th ed. Kirman, 1355 Sh./1976).

Ālūsī, Shaykh Shihāb al-Dīn Maḥmūd (Abu al-Thanāʾ). *Rūḥ al-Maʿānī fī Tafsīr al-Qurʾān al-ʿAẓīm waʾl-Sabʿ al-Mathānī*. Bulāq, 1301–1310/1883–1892.

Anonymous. *Bi Yād-i Ṣadumīn Sāl-i Shahādat-i Nābigha-yi Daurān Qurrat al-ʿAyn* [a centennial volume]. [Tehran?], 1368/1949.

Āvārih, ʿAbd al-Ḥusayn Āyatī Taftī. *al-Kawākib al-Durrīya fī Maʾāthir al-Bahāʾīya*. 2 vols. Cairo, 1342/1923–1924.

Āyatī, Muḥammad Ḥasan. *Bahāristān dar Tārīkh va Tarājim-i Rijāl-i Qāʾināt va Quhistān*. Tehran, 1327 Sh./1948.

ʿAżud al-Daula, Aḥmad Mīrzā. *Tārīkh-i ʿAżudī*. Ed. ʿA. Navāʾī. Tehran, 1355 Sh./1976.

al-ʿAzzāwī, ʿAbbās. *Dhikra Abī al-Thanāʾ al-Ālūsī*. Baghdad, 1377/1958.

———. *Tārīkh al-ʿIrāq bayna Iḥtilālayn*. 8 vols. Baghdad, 1353–1376/1935–1956.

The Bab, Sayyid ʿAlī Muḥammad Shīrāzī. *Bayān* (Arabic) [including Lawḥ-i Ḥaykal al-Dīn and Tafsīr]. Tehran, n.d.

———. *Dalāʾil-i Sabʿa*. Tehran, n.d.

———. *Kitāb-i Bayān-i Fārsī*. Tehran, n.d.

———. *Muntakhabāt-i Āyāt az Āsār-i Ḥażrat-i Nuqṭa-yi Ūlā*. Tehran, 134 Badīʿ/1978.

———. *Qismatī az Alwāḥ-i Khaṭṭ-i Nuqṭa-yi Ūlā va Āqā Sayyid Ḥusayn Kātib*. [Tehran?], n.d.

Al-Baghdādī, Āqā Muḥammad Muṣṭafā ibn Shaykh Muḥammad Shibl. *Risāla*. With A. Suhrāb *al-Risāla*. Cairo, 1338/1919.

Bahā'ullāh, Mīrzā Ḥusayn ʿAlī Nūrī. *Majmūʿa-yi Alwāḥ-i Mubāraka*. Cairo, 1338/1920.
Baḥrānī, Shaykh Yūsuf. *Lu'lu'at al-Baḥrayn*. Tehran, 1269/1853.
Bāmdād, Mahdī. *Sharḥ-i Ḥāl-i Rijāl Īrān dar Qarn-i 12, 13, 14 Ḥijrī*. 6 vols. Tehran, 1347–1353 Sh./1968–1974.
Bayżā'ī, Niʿmatullāh Ẕukā'ī. *Taẕkira-yi Shuʿarā-yi Qarn-i Awwal-i Bahā'ī*. 3 vols. Tehran, 121–126 Badīʿ/1965–1970.
Browne, Edward G., ed. *Nuqṭatu'l-Kāf [Nuqṭat al-Kāf] Compiled by Ḥājjī Mīrzā Jānī of Kāshān*. London and Leiden, 1910.
Burqaʿī, Abul-Fażl. *Ḥaqīqat al-ʿIrfān*. Tehran, n.d.
Dakhīl Marāghih'ī, Mullā Ḥusayn. *Dīvān-i Marāṡī*. Tabriz, n.d.
Davānī, ʿAlī. *Vaḥīd-i Bihbahānī*. Qum, 1378/1958.
Dunbulī, ʿAbd al-Razzāq (Maftūn). *Tajribat al-Aḥrār wa Taslīyat al-Abrār*. Ed. H. Qāżī Ṭabāṭabā'ī. 2 vols. Tabriz, 1350Sh./1971.
Fānī, Muḥsin [Mullā Mū'bad]. *Dabistān al-Maẕāhib*. Luknow, 1298/1881.
Fasā'ī, Ḥājjī Mīrzā Ḥasan. *Fārs Nāmih-yi Nāṣirī*. 2 vols. (in one). Tehran, 1312–1313/1894–1895.
Fayżī, Muḥammad ʿAlī. *Ḥażrat-i Nuqṭa-yi Ūlā*. Tehran, 132 Badīʿ/1973.
——. *Khāndān-i Afnān, Sidra-yi Raḥmān*. Tehran, 127 Badīʿ/1971.
Fāżil Māzandarānī, Mīrzā Asadullāh. *Kitāb-i Ẓuhūr al-Ḥaqq* III. Tehran, n.d. [1323 Sh./1944?].
Gulpāyigānī, Mīrzā Abul-Fażl. *Rasā'il va Raqā'im*. Ed. R. Mihrābkhānī. Tehran, 134 Badīʿ/1978.
—— and Sayyid Mahdī Gulpāyigānī. *Kashf al-Ghiṭā' ʿan Ḥiyal al-Aʿdā'*. Tashkand, n.d. [1919?].
Gulrīz, Muḥammad. *Mīnū-Dar yā Bāb al-Janna, Qazvīn*. Tehran, 1337 Sh./1958.
al-Ḥasanī, ʿAbd al-Razzāq. *al-Bābīyūn wa'l-Bahā'īyūn fī Ḥāḍirihim wa Māḍīhim*. Sidon, 1376/1957.
Hidāyat, Rižā-Qulī Khān. *Rauḍat al-Ṣafā'-yi Nāṣirī*. 3d ed., VIII–X. Tehran, 1338–1339 Sh./1959–1960.
——. *Riyāḍ al-ʿĀrifīn; Tadhkirat al-Muḥaqqiqīn*. Tehran, 1316 Sh./1927.
Ibrāhīmī Kirmānī, Abul-Qāsim ibn Zayn al-ʿĀbidīn (Sarkār Āqā). *Fihrist-i Kutub-i Shaykh-i Ajall-i Auḥad Marḥūm-i Shaykh Aḥmad Aḥsā'ī va Sā'ir-i Mashāyikh-i ʿIẓām*. 2 vols. (in one). 3d ed. Kirman, n.d.
Iqbāl, ʿAbbās. *Khāndān-i Naubakhtī*. Tehran, 1311 Sh./1922.
——. *Mīrzā Taqī Khān Amīr Kabīr*. Ed. Ī. Afshār. Tehran, 1340 Sh./1961.
Iran, Vizārat-i Umūr-i Khārija. *Fihrist-i Bakhshī az Asnād va ʿAhdnāmihā va Safarnāmihā va Rasālihā-yi Daurih-yi Qājārīya*. Tehran, 1345 Sh./1975.
Ishrāq Khāvarī, ʿAbd al-Ḥamīd. *Nūrayn-i Nayyirayn*. Tehran, 123 Badīʿ/1967.
——. *Taqvīm-i Tārīkh-i Amr*. Tehran, 126 Badīʿ/1970.
Iʿtimād al-Salṭana, Muḥammad Ḥasan Khān [Ṣanīʿ al-Daula]. *al-Ma'āthir wa'l-Āthār*. Tehran, 1306–1888.
—— *Maṭlaʿ al-Shams*. 3 vols. Tehran, 1300–1303/1882–1885.
Iʿtiżād al-Salṭana, ʿAlī-Qulī Mīrzā. *Mutanabbi'īn*. Ed. and ann. ʿA. Navā'ī as *Fitna-yi Bāb*, 2d ed. Tehran, 1350 Sh./1971.
Jadīd al-Islām, Ḥājjī Ḥusayn-Qulī. *Minhāj al-Ṭālibīn fī al-Radd ʿalā al-Firqa al-Hālika al-Bābīya*. Bombay, 1320/1902.
Jahāngīr Mīrzā Qājār. *Tārīkh-i Nau*. Ed. ʿA. Iqbāl. Tehran, 1327 Sh./1948.

Jazī Iṣfahānī, ʿAbd al-Karīm. *Rijāl-i Iṣfahān yā Tadhkirat al-Qubūr.* Ed. M. Mahdavī. 2d ed. [Isfahan?], 1328 Sh./1949.

Kalāntar Żarrābī, ʿAbd al-Raḥīm [Suhayl Kāshānī]. *Mir'āt al-Qāsān (Tārīkh-i Kāshān).* Ed. Ī. Afshār. Tehran, 1341 Sh./1962.

Kāshānī, Ḥājjī Mīrzā Jānī [Parpā]. See E. G. Browne *Nuqṭatu'l-Kāf.*

Kayhān, Masʿūd Khān. *Jughrāfīyā-yi Mufaṣṣal-i Īrān.* 3 vols., Tehran, 1310–1311 Sh./1921–1922.

Khūrmujī, Muḥammad Jaʿfar. *Ḥaqā'iq al-Akhbār-i Nāṣirī.* 2d ed. Ed. Ḥ. Khadīv Jam, Tehran, 1344 Sh./1965.

Khwānsārī, Muḥammad Bāqir. *Rauḍāt al-Jannāt fī Aḥwāl al-ʿUlamā' wa al-Sādāt.* Tehran, 1307/1889.

Kirmānī, Shaykh Aḥmad Rūḥī and Mīrzā Āqā Khān Kirmānī [?]. *Hasht Bihisht.* Tehran, n.d.

Kirmānī, Ḥājjī Muḥammad Karīm Khān. *Īqādh al-Ghāfilīn wa Ibṭāl al-Bāṭilīn dar Radd-i Bāb-i Khusrān Ma'āb.* Tehran, n.d.

____. *Irshād al-ʿAwāmm.* 1st ed. 4 vols. Bombay, 1268/1852 (5th ed. Kirman, 1353–1355 Sh./1974–1976).

____. *Izhāq al-Bāṭil.* Kirman, 1392–1972.

____. *Risāla fī al-Radd ʿalā al-Bāb al-Murtāb.* Kirman, 1383/1963.

____. *Risāla-yi Sī faṣl.* Kirman, 1368/1948.

____. *al-Shihāb al-Thāqib fī Rajm al-Nawāṣib.* Kirman, n.d.

____. *Tīr-i Shihāb dar Radd-i Bāb-i Khusrān Ma'āb* (Kirman,1387/1967).

Kirmānī, Shaykh Yaḥyā Aḥmadī. *Farmāndihān-i Kirmān.* Ed. M. I. Bāstānī Pārīzī. Tehran 1344 Sh./1965. 2d ed. Tehran, 1354 Sh./1975.

Kīyā, Ṣādiq. *Nuqtavīyān yā Pisīkhānīyān (Īrān Kudih)* XIII. 1320 Sh./1941.

Lāhījī, ʿAbd al-Razzāq. *Gauhar-i Murād.* Tehran, 1377/1957.

Lavī, Ḥabīb. *Tārīkh-i Yahūd-i Īrān.* 3 vols. Tehran, 1339 Sh./1960.

Maḥallātī, Āqā Khān [Ḥasan ʿAlī Shāh]. *ʿIbrat Afzā.* Bombay, 1287/1870.

Mahdavī, Muṣliḥ al-Dīn. *Dānīshmandān va Buzurgān-i Iṣfahān.* Isfahan, 1348 Sh./1969.

Majlisī, Muḥammd Bāqir ibn Muḥammad Taqī. *Biḥār al-Anwār.* 25 vols., 1st ed. Tehran, 1303–1315/1385–1897 (vol. XIII, *Fī aḥwāl al-Ḥujjat al-Munṭaẓara,* trans. into Persian by Muḥammad Ḥasan Urūmī. Tehran, 1397/1976.)

____. *Ḥaqq al-Yaqīn.* Tehran, n.d.

Malik Khusravī, Muḥammad ʿAlī. *Iqlīm-i Nūr.* Tehran, 118 Badīʿ/1962.

____. *Tārīkh-i Shuhadā-yi Amr.* 3 vols. Tehran, 130 Badīʿ/1972.

Muʿallim Ḥabībābādī, Muḥammad ʿAlī. *Makārim al-Āthār dar Aḥvāl-i Rijāl-i Daurih-yi Qājār.* 5 vols. Isfahan, 1377–1396/1958–1976.

Mudarris Tabrīzī Khayābānī, Muḥammad ʿAlī. *Rayḥānat al-Adab.* Tehran and Tabriz, 1326–1333 Sh./1947–1954. 2d rev. ed. Tehran, 1335 Sh./1957.

Mudarrisī Chahārdihī, Murtażā. *Shaykhīgarī va Bābīgarī az Naẓar-i Falsafa, Tārīkh, Ijtimāʿ.* 2d ed. Tehran, 1351 Sh./1972.

____. *Tārikh-ī Ravābiṭ-i Īrān va ʿIrāq.* Tehran, 1351 Sh./1972.

Mudarrisī Chahārdihī, Nūr al-Dīn. *Khāksār va Ahl-i Ḥaqq.* Tehran, 1358 Sh./1979.

Mūsawī al-Iṣfahānī al-Kāẓimī, Muḥammad Mahdī. *Aḥsan al-Wadīʿa fī Tarājim Ashhar Mashāhīr Mujtahidī al-Shīʿa.* 2 vols. Baghdad, n.d.

Muẓaffar ʿAlī Shāh, Mīrzā Muḥammad Taqī Kirmānī. *Dīvān-i Mushtāqīya.* Tehran, 1347 Sh./1968.

Nādir Mīrzā. *Tārīkh va Jughrāfī-yi Dār al-Salṭana-yi Tabrīz.* Tehran, 1323/1905.

Naṣīr Qazvīnī, Ḥājjī Muḥammad. Historical account [of Ṭabarsī] published in *Tārīkh-i Samandar va Mulḥaqqāt.* Ed. ʿA. ʿAlāʾī. Tehran, 131 Badīʿ/1975. Pp. 500–520.

Nāṭiq, Humā. *Az Māst ki bar Māst.* Tehran, 1345 Sh./1966.

——. *Muṣībat-i Vabā va Balā-yi Ḥukūmat.* Tehran, 1358 Sh./1979.

Navāʾī, ʿAbd al-Ḥusayn. *Fitna-yi Bāb.* See Iʿtiżād al-Salṭana.

Nūr ʿAlī Shāh, Muḥammad ʿAlī Iṣfahānī. *Dīvān-i Nūr ʿAlī Shāh Iṣfahānī.* Ed. J. Nūrbakhsh. Tehran, 1349 Sh./1970.

——. *Majmūʿa-ī az Āsār-i Nūr ʿAlī Shāh.* Ed. J. Nūrbakhsh. Tehran, 1350 Sh./1971.

——. *Masnavī-yi Jannāt al-Wiṣāl.* [Completed by Raunaq ʿAlī Shāh Kirmānī and Niẓām ʿAlī Shāh Kirmānī.] Ed. J. Nūrbakhsh. Tehran, 1348 Sh./1969.

Nūrī, Mīrzā Ḥusayn Ṭabarsī. *al-Najm al-Thāqib dar Aḥwāl-i Imām-i Ghāʾib.* Tehran, n.d.

al-Qatīl al-Karbalāʾī. *Risāla.* Published in Fāżil Māzandarānī *Ẓuhūr al-Ḥaqq* III, appendix 2, 502–32.

Qazvīnī, Mullā Jaʿfar. Historical account Published in *Tārīkh-i Samandar va Mulḥaqqāt.* Ed. ʿA. ʿAlāʾī. Tehran, 131 Badīʿ/1975. Pp. 446–500.

Rashtī, Sayyid Kāẓim. *Dalīl al-Mutaḥayyirīn.* 2d ed. Kirman, n.d. (Persian trans. by Muḥammad Riżā. Tehran, n.d.)

——. *Lawāmiʿ al-Ḥusaynīya.* Tabriz, 1271/1854.

Raunaq ʿAlī Shāh, Mīrzā Muḥammad Ḥusayn Kirmānī. *Masnavī-yi Gharāʾib.* Ed. J. Nūrbakhsh. Tehran, 1352 Sh./1973.

Rustam al-Ḥukamāʾ, Muḥammad Hāshim [Āṣaf]. *Rustam al-Tawārīkh.* Ed. M. Mushīrī. Tehran, 1348 Sh./1969.

Saʿādat Nūrī, Ḥusayn. *Zindigī-yi Ḥājjī Mīrzā Āqāsī.* Tehran, 1356 Sh./1977.

Samandar Qazvīnī, Shaykh Kāẓim ibn Shaykh Muḥammad. *Tārīkh-i Samandar.* Published in *Tārīkh-i Samandar va Mulhaqqāt.* Ed. ʿA. ʿAlāʾī. Tehran, 131 Badīʿ/1975.

Sāsānī, Khān Malik. *Sīyāsatgarān-i Daurih-yi Qājār.* 2 vols. Tehran, 1346 Sh./1967.

Shīrāzī, Muḥammad Maʿṣūm Nāʾib al-Ṣadr [Maʿṣūm ʿAlī Shāh]. *Ṭarāʾiq al-Ḥaqāʾiq.* 2d ed. Ed. M. J. Maḥjūb. 3 vols. Tehran, 1345 Sh./1966.

Shīrvānī, Zayn al-ʿĀbidīn [Mast ʿAlī Shāh]. *Bustān al-Sīyāḥa.* Tehran, 1315/1897.

Sipihr, Mīrzā Muḥammad Taqī [Lisān al-Mulk]. *Nāsikh al-Tawārīkh (Tārīkh-i Qājārīya).* Ed. M. B. Bihbūdī. 4 vols. Tehran, 1385/1965.

Suhrāb, Aḥmad Afandī. *al-Risālat al-Tisʿa ʿAshrīyata fī Tārīkh Ḥaḍrat al-Aʿlā.* Cairo, 1338/1919.

al-Tahānawī, Muḥammad ʿAlī. *Kashshāf Iṣṭilāḥāt al-Funūn waʾl-ʿUlūm (A Dictionary of the Technical Terms Used in the Sciences of the Musulmans).* Ed. A. Sprenger et al. 2 vols. Calcutta, 1854–1862.

Ṭihrānī, Āghā Buzurg [Muḥammad Muḥsin]. *al-Dharīʿa ilā Taṣānīf al-Shīʿa.* 25 vols. Najaf and Tehran, 1355–1398/1936–1977.

——. *Ṭabaāt Aʿlām al-Shīʿa:* I (in 3 parts): *Nuqabāʾ al-Bashar fī al-Qarn al-Rābiʿa ʿAshar.* II. (in 2 parts). *al-Kirām al-Barara fī al-Qarn al-Thālith baʿd al-ʿAshara.* Najaf, 1373–1388/1954–1968.

al-Ṭuʿma, Salmān Hādī. *Turāth Karbalāʾ.* Najaf, 1385/1964.

Tunkābunī, Mīrzā Muḥammad ibn Sulaymān. *Qiṣaṣ al-ʿUlamāʾ.* Tehran, 1304/1886. 2d ed. Tehran, n.d.

Ṭusī, Shaykh abī-Jaʿfar Muḥammad ibn al-Ḥasan. *Kitāb al-Ghayba.* Najaf, 1385/1965.

Vazīrī Kirmānī, Aḥmad ʿAlī Khān. *Tārīkh-i Kirmān (Sālārīya).* Ed. M. Bāstānī Pārīzī. Tehran, 1340 Sh./1961.

Al-Wardī, ʿAlī. *Lamaḥāt Ijtimāʿīya min Tārīkh al-ʿIrāq al-Ḥadīth.* 3 vols. Baghdad, 1971.

Zaʿīm al-Daula, Mīrzā Muḥammad Mahdī ibn Muḥammad Taqī. *Miftāḥ Bāb al-Abwāb au Tārīkh al-Bābīya.* Cairo, 1342/1903.

Zanjānī, Ibrāhīm Mūsavī. *Tārīkh-i Zanjān: ʿUlamāʾ va Dānishmandān.* Tehran, n.d.

IV. Published Works in European Languages

Adamec, L. W., ed. *Historical Gazetteer of Iran.* I: *Tehran and North-Western Iran.* Graz, 1976.

Algar, H. *Religion and State in Iran, 1785–1906: The Role of the Ulama in the Qajar Period.* Berkeley and Los Angeles, 1969.

———. "The Revolt of Āghā Khān Mahallātī and the Transference of the Ismāʿīlī Imamate to India." *Studia Islamica* 29 (1969) 55–81.

———. "Shiʿism and Iran in the Eighteenth Century." *Studies in Eighteenth Century Islamic History.* Ed. T. Neff and R. Owen. Carbondale, Ill., 1977, 288–302, 400–403.

Amanat, A., ed. *Cities and Trade: Consul Abbott on the Economy and Society of Iran, 1847–1866.* London, 1983.

Andreas, F. C. *Die Babis in Persien, ihre Geschichte und Lehre.* Leipzig, 1896.

Arberry, A. J. *The Koran Interpreted.* London, 1964.

Arjomand, S. A. *The Shadow of God and the Hidden Imam.* Chicago, 1984.

Balyuzi, H. M. *The Bāb.* Oxford, 1964.

———. *Edward Granville Browne and the Bahāʾī Faith.* London, 1970.

Bausani, A. *L'Iran e la sua tradizione millenaria.* Rome, 1971.

Bayat, M. *Mysticism and Dissent: Socioreligious Thought in Qajar Iran.* Syracuse, N.Y., 1982.

Berger, P. L. "Motif messianique et processus social dans le Baháisme." *Archive de Sociologie des Religions* IV (1957) 93–107.

Binning, R. B. M. *A Journal of Two Years' Travel in Persia, etc.* 2 vols. London, 1857.

Browne, Edward G. "The Bābīs of Persia: I. Sketch of Their History and Personal Experience amongst Them. II. Their Literature and Doctrines." *JRAS* 21 (1889) 485–526, 881–1009.

———. "Catalogue and Description of 27 Bābī Manuscripts." *JRAS* 24 (1892) 433–99, 637–710.

———. *A Literary History of Persia.* 4 vols. Cambridge and London, 1902–1924.

———. *Materials for the Study of the Bābī Religion.* Cambridge, 1918.

———. "Some Remarks on the Bābī Texts Edited by Baron V. Rosen." *JRAS* 24 (1892) 259–322.

———. *A Year amongst the Persians.* London, 1893 (reprinted 1926).

———, ed. and trans. *The Tārīkh-i-Jadīd or New History of Mīrzā ʿAlī Muḥammad the Bāb.* Cambridge, 1893. (See also Hamadānī, Mīrzā Ḥusayn.)

———, ed. and trans. *A Traveller's Narrative Written to Illustrate the Episode of the Bāb.* 2 vols. I: Persian text; II: English translation and notes. Cambridge, 1891. (See also ʿAbd al-Bahāʾ, *Maqāla.*)
———, trans. "Personal Reminiscences of the Bābī Insurrection at Zanjān in 1850, Written in Persian by Āqā ʿAbdu'l-Ahad-i-Zanjānī." *JRAS* 29 (1897) 761–827. (Original MS in Browne Or MSS F.25[9], 6.)
——— and R. A. Nicholson. *A Descriptive Catalogue of the Oriental MSS. Belonging to the Late E. G. Browne.* Cambridge, 1932.
Burgess, C., and E. Burgess. *Letters from Persia, 1828–1855.* Ed. B. Schwartz. New York, 1942.
Busse, H., trans. *History of Persia under Qājār Rule: Translated from Persian of Ḥasan-e Fasāʾī's Fārsnāma-ye Nāṣiri.* New York and London, 1972. (See also Fasāʾī.)
Corbin, H. *Cyclical Time and Ismaili Gnosis.* London, Boston, etc., 1983.
———. *L'École shaykhie en théologie shīʿite* (Extrait de *L'Annaire de l'École Pratique des Hautes Études, Section des Science Religieuses 1960–1961).* Tehran, 1967.
———. "Étude sur l'Imam Caché et la renovation de l'homme en théologie shʿite." *Eranhos-Jahrbuch* XXVIII. Zürich, 1960.
———. *En Islam iranien: Aspects spirituels et philosophiques.* 4 vols. Paris, 1971–1972.
———. *Terre céleste et corps de résurrection.* Paris, 1960. (English trans. N. Pearson, *Spiritual Body and Celestial Earth.* Princeton, 1977.)
Dolgorukov, Prince D. "Excerpts from Dispatches Written during 1848–1852." (Trans. [from French into Russian] M. S. Ivanov in *Babidskie vosstaniya v Irane [1848–1852],* 143–59. Trans. [into English] F. Kazemzadeh in *World Order* [Fall 1966] 17–24. For Persian trans. M. Mudarrīsī Chahārdihī, *Shaykhīgarī*]).
Effendi, Shoghi *God Passes By.* Wilmette, Ill., 1944.
Entner, M. L. *Russo-Persian Commercial Relations, 1828–1914.* University of Florida Monographs, No. 28, Gainesville, Fla., 1965.
Ferrier, J. P. *Caravan Journey and Wanderings in Persia, etc.* London, 1857.
Flandin, E., and P. Coste. *Voyage en Perse de M. M. Eugène Flandin, peintre, et Pascal Coste, architecte, 1840–41.* 2 vols. Paris, 1851.
Fraser, J. B. *A Winter Journey from Constantinople to Tehran.* 2 vols. London, 1838.
Gibb, H. A. R., and J. H. Kramers. *Shorter Encyclopaedia of Islam.* Leiden, 1953.
Gobineau, Comte Joseph A. de. *Religions et philosophies dans l'Asie centrale.* Paris, 1865 (2d ed. 1900).
———. *Trois ans en Asie.* Paris, 1859 (2d ed. 1923).
Gramlich, R. *Die Schiitischen Derwischorden Persiens.* 2 vols. Wiesbaden, 1975–1976.
Gulpayganī, Mīrzā-Abul-Fażl. *The Bahai Proofs: Hujaj'ul Behäyyeh. Also a Short Sketch of the History of Lives of the Leaders of This Religion.* Trans. Ishtael-ebn-Kalantar. Chicago, 1914.
Huart, M. C. *La Religion de Bab, réformateur persan de XIXᵉ siècle.* Paris, 1889.
Issawi, C. ed., *The Economic History of Iran, 1800–1914.* Chicago, 1971.
Ivanov, M. S. *Babidskie vosstaniya v Irane (1848–1852).* Moscow, 1939.
Ivanow, W. *Ismaili Literature: A Bibliographical Survey.* Tehran, 1963.
Kazem-Beg, Mirza Alexandr. "Bab et les Babis, ou Le Soulèvement politique et

religieux en Perse, de 1845 à 1853" *Journal Asiatique* 7 (1866) 329–84, 457–522; 8 (1866) 196–252, 357–400, 473–507.

Keddie, N. R. "Religion and Irreligion in Early Iranian Nationalism." *Comparative Studies in Society and History* 4 (1962) 265–95.

Kelly, J. B. *Britain and the Persian Gulf (1795–1800)*. Oxford, 1968.

Khan Bahadur, Agha Mirza Muhammad. "Some New Notes on Babiism." *Journal of the Royal Asiatic Society* n.v. (July 1927) 443–69.

Lambton, A. K. S. "Persian Trade under the Early Qājārs." *Islam and Trade of Asia*. Ed. D. S. Richards. Oxford, 1970.

———. "Some New Trends in Islamic Political Thought in Late 18th and Early 19th Century Persia." *Studia Islamica* 39 (1974) 95–128.

Longrigg, S. T. *Four Centuries of Modern Iraq*. Oxford, 1925.

Lorimer, J. G. *Gazetteer of the Persian Gulf, Oman and Central Arabia*. 2 vols. Calcutta, 1915.

MacEoin, D. M. "From Shaykhism to Babism: A Study in Charismatic Renewal in Shīʿī Islam." Ph.D. diss., Cambridge University, 1979.

Madelung, W. "Ibn Abī Ǧumhur al-Aḥsāʾī's Synthesis of Kalām, Philosophy and Sufism." *Acts du 8me Congrès de l'Union Européenne des Arabisants et Islamisants*. Aix-en-Provence, 1978. Pp. 147–56.

Malcolm, J. *The History of Persia*. 2 vols. London, 1815.

Migeod, H. G. "Die Lūtīs, ein Ferment des städtischen Lebens in Persien." *Journal of the Economic and Social History of the Orient* 2 (1959) 82–91.

Miller, W. M. *The Baha'i Faith: Its History and Teachings*. South Pasadena, Calif., 1974.

Minorsky, V. "Iran: Opposition, Martyrdom and Revolt." In *Unity and Variety in Muslim Civilization*. Ed. G. von Grunbaum. Chicago, 1955. Pp. 183–206.

———. "Review of M. S. Ivanov *The Babi Risings in Iran 1848–1852*." *Bulletin of the School of Oriental and African Studies* (1947) 878–80.

———. "The Sect of Ahl-i Ḥaḳḳ." *Iranica (Twenty Articles)*. Tehran, 1964.

Momen, M. *The Bābī and Bahāʾī Religions, 1844–1944, Some Contemporary Western Accounts*. Oxford, 1981.

———. *Shīʿī Islam*. New Haven and London, 1985.

———. "The Social Basis of the Bābī Upheavals in Iran (1848–53)." *IJMES* 14 (1983) 157–83.

———. "The Trial of Mullā ʿAlī Bastāmī: A Combined Sunni-Shīʿī *Fatwā* against the Bāb." *Iran* 20 (1982) 113–43.

Nabil Zarandi, Shaykh Muhammad. *The Dawn-Breakers: Nabil's Narrative of the Early Days of the Bahāʾī Revelation*. Trans. and ed. Shoghi Effendi. Wilmette, Ill., 1932.

Nicolas, A. L. M. "Les Béhais et le Bâb." *Journal Asiatique* 222 (1933) 257–63.

———. "Le Dossier russo-anglais de Seyyed Ali Mohammmad dit le Bâb." *Revue du Monde Musulman*. 14 (1911) 357–63.

———. *Essai sur le Chéïkhisme*. 4 vols. I. *Cheikh Ahmad Lahçahi*. Paris, 1910. II. *Seyyed Kazem Rechti*. Paris, 1911. III. *La Doctrine* (extract from *Revue du Monde Musulman)*. Paris, 1911. IV. *La Science de Dieu*. Paris, 1911.

———. *Le Livre des sept preuves de la mission du Bâb*. Paris, 1902.

———. "Quelques documents relatifes au Babisme." *Journal Asiatique* 204 (1933) 107–42.

——. *Seyyèd Ali Mohammad dit le Bâb*. Paris, 1905.
——, trans. *Le Béyan arabe: Le Livre sacré de Bâbysme*. Paris, 1905.
——, trans. *Le Béyan persan*. 4 vols. Paris, 1911–1914.
Polak, J. E. *Persien, das Land und seine Bewohner, etc.* 2 vols. Leipzig, 1865.
Poonawala, I. S. *Biobibliography of Ismāʿīlī Literature*. Malibu, Calif., 1977.
Pourjavady, N. "Ismāʿīlīs and Niʿmatallāhīs." *Studia Islamica* 41 (1975) 113–35.
——. *Kings of Love: The Poetry and History of the Niʿmatullāhī Sufi Order*. Tehran, 1978.
——, and P. L. Wilson. "The Descendants of Shāh Niʿmatullāhī Walī." *Islamic Culture*. Hyderabad, January 1974.
Robson, J., trans. *Mishkāt al-Maṣābiḥ of Abu Muḥammad al-Baghāwī, Ibn al-Farrā.'* 2 vols. 2d ed. Lahore, 1975.
Roemer, H. *Die Bābī-Behā'ī, die jüngste Mohammedanische Sekte*. Potsdam, 1912.
Sachedina, A. *Islamic Messianism: The Idea of the Mahdi in Twelver Shiʿism*. Albany, N.Y., 1981.
Ṣadr al-Dīn Shīrāzī (Mullā Ṣadrā) *The Wisdom of the Throne, Being the Translation of "Ḥikmat al-ʿArshīya.'* Trans. J. Morris. Princeton, 1981.
Scarcia, G. "Intorno alle Contraversie tra Aḫbārī e Uṣūlī presso gli Imamiti di Persia." *Rivista degli studi orientali* 33 (1958) 211–50.
Sheil, M. *Glimpses of Life and Manners in Persia*. London, 1856.
Southgate, H. *Narrative of a Tour through Armenia, Kurdistan, Persia and Mesopotamia*. 2 vols. New York, 1840.
Stern, H. A. *Dawning of Light in the East*. London, 1854.
Tabātabā'ī, H. M. *An Introduction to the Shīʿī Law*. London, 1984.
Tag, Abd el-Rahman. *Le Babisme et l'Islam: Recherches sur les origines du Babisme et ses rapports avec l'Islam*. Paris, 1942.
Taherzadeh, H., trans. *Selections from the Writings of the Bâb*. Haifa, 1976.
Trimingham, J. S. *The Sufi Orders in Islam*. Oxford, 1971.
Vajda, G. "Le Problème de la vision de Dieu (*ru'ya*) d'après quelques auteurs shiʿites duodecimains." *Le Shīʿism imāmaite*. Colloque de Strasbourg (6–9 mai 1968). Paris, 1970. Pp. 31–54.
Watson, R. G. *A History of Persia from the Beginning of the Nineteenth Century to the Year 1858*. London, 1866.
Wensinck, A. J., et al. *Concordance et indices de la tradition musulmane*. 7 vols. Leiden, 1936–1969.
Wolff, J. *Narrative of a Mission to Bokhara*. London, 1847.
Wright, A. H. "Bâb und seine Secte in Persien." *Zeitschrift der deutschen Morgenlandischen Gesellschaft* V. Leipzig, 1831. Pp. 384–385.

Index

Library of Congress Cataloging-in-Publication Data

Amanat, Abbas.
Resurrection and renewal.

Bibliography: p.
Includes index.
1. Babism—History. 2. Iran—Religion—19th century. 3. Shīʿah—Iran—History.
I. Title.
BP340.A45 1988 297′.88 88-47716
ISBN 0-8014-2098-9